The Nature of Price Theory

The Nature of
Price Theory

H. H. LIEBHAFSKY, Jur.D., Ph.D.

Professor of Economics
The University of Texas

1963

THE DORSEY PRESS, INC.

Homewood, Illinois

First Printing, January, 1963
Second Printing, August, 1963

Library of Congress Catalog Card No. 63–8445

PRINTED IN THE UNITED STATES OF AMERICA

To Nancy and Lesley

Preface

This book has been designed primarily for use in an undergraduate or first year graduate course in price theory and as a reference for readers with limited mathematical training. It assumes that the reader can add, subtract, multiply, and divide, but that he does not know calculus and that he remembers very little of his earlier mathematical training.

Basic concepts are explained in four different ways throughout the book: (1) in words, (2) by means of simple algebraic equations, (3) by use of numerical equivalents inserted into the simple algebraic formulations, and (4) by means of graphical illustrations based on these numerical equivalents. Moreover, all algebraic operations are fully explained.

The treatment of economic concepts is highly integrated. For example, the basic production function and the numerical equivalents assumed in the explanation of the theory of production in Chapter 6 are the basis for the cost curves in Chapter 7 and are employed also in the explanation of the theory of the firm in Part IV, as well as in the discussions of the marginal productivity theory and the factor market in Part V. The diagrams in these various parts of the book are similarly interrelated.

Chapter 3 contains an explanation of basic quantitative concepts employed in price theory and is a kind of "handbook" to which the reader may make reference at various points throughout his further study of economic concepts in later chapters. In it I have stated basic quantitative relationships and ideas without providing proofs of any of them, although references to proofs in other works are provided for those who desire them. In this chapter, for example, the reader is introduced to the idea of contour diagrams, which become indifference curves in Chapter 5 and isoquants in Chapter 6. Similarly, in this chapter, he is introduced for the first time to the marginal concept and to the average-marginal relationship.

A glance at the table of contents will show that the first sixteen chapters contain a comprehensive coverage of the standard material, beginning with the nature of price theory and continuing through static welfare economics. Chapter 17 contains an arithmetical explanation of linear programming and emphasizes an *economic interpretation* of the various magnitudes which are manipulated in solving linear programming problems. This chapter can be used in two ways: the explanation of the complete description method, which is covered first, can be employed alone; or, the former can be employed together with the arithmetical and graphical explanation of the more useful, but more difficult, simplex method. Not only does the instructor have this kind of a choice with respect to the use of this chapter, but those who do not wish to cover linear programming in a price theory course can omit the chapter without loss, since none of the rest of the book depends upon it. Chapter 18 contains a summary and evaluation of Schumpeter's theory of economic development as a dynamic extension of the general model of price theory and briefly but frankly presents views (both pro and con) of some representative economists about the extent to which the general model of price theory can be usefully employed in dealing with the problem of economic development. This chapter can be assigned as outside reading or it can be made the basis of one or two hours of class discussion at the end of the course. The four appendices on demand theory include, among other things, an arithmetical illustration of most of Slutsky's basic equations (not merely of the "Fundamental Equation of Value Theory") and a critical evaluation of Professor J. R. Hicks's methods of measuring "income" and "substitution" effects. These appendices are intended primarily for use in a graduate course and for reference.

I have opened the discussion of most new topics with a brief look at the history of the concepts to be considered, and, where possible, I have concluded each major subdivision with a brief survey of important statistical work in the area, making use of studies of the National Bureau of Economic Research, Reports of the Joint Economic Committee, and similar publications for this purpose.

My debts to colleagues and critics are many. Dean E. T. Weiler of Purdue University gave me much encouragement as well as helpful suggestions. Professor William B. Palmer of the University of Michigan and Professor Peter O. Steiner of the University of Wisconsin provided helpful critical reviews of an earlier draft of the first half of the manuscript. Professor Murray E. Polakoff of the University of Rochester cheerfully read and freely offered useful advice and constructive criticism concerning the chapter on interest theory. Professor E. E. Liebhafsky of North Carolina State College critically evaluated the chapter on wage theory and offered constant encouragement throughout the period in which I was writing this book. Professor Valdemar Carlson of Antioch College provided useful comments on portions of the manuscript.

Practically all of my colleagues at the University of Texas read one or more chapters in various draft stages and made many useful suggestions. Included in this group are Professors Warren E. Adams, Clarence E. Ayres, Wendell C. Gordon, E. E. Hale, Benjamin Higgins, David S. Huang, Stephen L. McDonald, Daniel C. Morgan, Walter C. Neale, and Carey C. Thompson. Final responsibility for the book is, of course, my own, since I did not always take the advice I requested.

A group of bright and enthusiastic young people served as my assistants at various times during the preparation of the manuscript. James W. Christian, Carolyn Hooper, Mary Huston, Raymond Robak, and Clifford E. Wheeler worked long and hard hours, as did my daughter, Lesley. I owe special thanks to Professor Carey Thompson and to Mrs. Bonnie Whittier, who extended themselves in a hundred ways to make possible the completion of the manuscript on schedule.

But my greatest debt is to my wife, Nancy, who not only drew all of the original graphs to scale (and who served me in the capacity of Professor Viner's draftsman on a few occasions) but who also finally read the entire manuscript and improved it immeasurably. Literally, without her help this book would not have been written.

H. H. LIEBHAFSKY

December, 1962
Austin, Texas

ACKNOWLEDGMENTS OF PERMISSIONS TO QUOTE

Acknowledgments are due to the following journals for permission to make use of earlier publications by the author: *The American Journal of Economics and Sociology; The Canadian Journal of Economics and Political Science;* and *The Quarterly Journal of Economics.*

Acknowledgments are due to the following authors and publishing companies for permission to quote: Kenneth J. Arrow, *Social Choice and Individual Values* (1951), John Wiley & Sons, Inc., New York; Clarence E. Ayres, *The Industrial Economy* (1952), Houghton Mifflin Co., Boston; P. T. Bauer, *Economic Analysis and Policy in Underdeveloped Countries* (1957), Duke University Press, Durham; J. B. Clark, *The Distribution of Wealth* (reprinted 1938), The Macmillan Co., New York; J. M. Clark, *Competition as a Dynamic Process* (1961), The Brookings Institute, Washington, D.C.; Donald E. Cullen, *Minimum Wage Laws* (1961), New York State School of Industrial and Labor Relations, Cornell University, Ithaca; Robert A. Dahl and Charles E. Lindblom, *Politics, Economics and Welfare* (1953), Harper & Bros., New York; Paul A. Douglas, *The Theory of Wages* (1934), The Macmillan Co., New York; Solomon Fabricant, *Basic Facts on Productivity Change* (1958), National Bureau of Economic Research, New York; Milton Friedman, *Essays in Positive Economics,* Copyright 1953 The University of Chicago, University of Chicago Press, Chicago; Benjamin Higgins, *Economic Development* (1959), W. W. Norton & Co., Inc., New York; W. A. Johr and H. W. Singer, *The Role of the Economist as Official Advisor* (1955), George Allen and Unwin, Ltd., London; Alfred Marshall, *Principles of Economics,* 8th ed. (1920; 1938 reprint), Macmillan & Co., Ltd., London; The Macmillan Co., Ltd., Canada; and The Macmillan Co., New York; Chester A. Morgan, *Labor Economics* (1961), The Dorsey Press, Inc., Homewood, Ill.; David Ricardo, *The Principles of Political Economy and Taxation,* Everyman's Library No. 590 (1943), E. P. Dutton & Co., Inc., New York; and J. M. Dent & Sons, Ltd., London; J. A. Schumpeter, *The Theory of Economic Development* (1951), Harvard Economic Studies XLVI, translated Redvers Opie, Harvard University Press, Cambridge; J. A. Schumpeter, *Capitalism, Socialism and Democracy* (3rd ed., 1950), Harper & Bros., New York; Henry Schultz, *The Theory and Measurement of Demand,* Social Science Studies XXXVI, Copyright 1938 The University of Chicago, University of Chicago Press, Chicago.

Acknowledgments are also due to the following authors and journals for permission to quote or paraphrase: Joe S. Bain, "Economies of Scale, Concentration, and Condition of Entry into Twenty Manufacturing Industries," *American Economic Review,* Vol. XLIV (March, 1954); Richard A. Easterlin, "The Baby Boom in Perspective," *American Economic Review,* Vol. LI (December, 1961); Robert F. Lanzillotti, "Pricing Objectives in Large Companies," *American Economic Review,* Vol. XLVIII (December, 1958); Harold Levinson, "Postwar Movement of Prices and Wages in Manufacturing Industries," Study Paper No. 21, Joint Economic Committee, U.S. Congress (January, 1960); Walter C. Neale, "Economic Accounting and Family Farming in India," *Economic Development and Cultural Change,* Vol. II (April, 1959), Copyright 1959 The University of Chicago.

Table of Contents

xi

PART IV.   THE PRODUCT MARKET

PART V.   THE FACTOR MARKET

PART VII.   LINEAR PROGRAMMING

PART VIII.   BEYOND STATIC PRICE THEORY

APPENDICES.   ADVANCED DEMAND THEORY

INDEX

LIST OF FIGURES

PART I

INTRODUCTION AND
BASIC CONCEPTS

1

Introduction

What This Book Is About

This book undertakes to explain the basic concepts and relationships of price theory and to provide the student with a knowledge of the language of price theory. Acquisition by the student of such knowledge is a first step in the process of evaluating the usefulness of these concepts and relationships as research tools to be employed in solving particular problems in a given case. And a complete understanding of them is an essential part of the equipment of the student who seeks to develop explanations of particular economic activities and events or to evaluate policy pronouncements of price theorists. However, such an understanding cannot be acquired by one who does not also understand the basic assumptions and method of analysis employed in price theory. For this reason, an examination of these becomes our first task.

Accordingly, this introductory chapter seeks to explain the method of price theory, to state the basic assumption about human behavior made by most price theorists, and to examine the question of why a knowledge of price theory is important to an economist. It is further concerned with a brief, elementary consideration of the meaning and significance of the concepts of "economic efficiency" and of "economic welfare" and of the meaning of the term "prediction" in the context of price theory. (A detailed technical study of "welfare" is the subject of Chapter 16.) Finally, the concluding paragraphs of this chapter provide the student with an overall view of the plan and scope of this book.

A. THE METHOD AND BASIC BEHAVIOR ASSUMPTION OF PRICE THEORY

Price Theory as a Kit of Tools

The late Professor Joseph Schumpeter once defined economic theory as the "technology" of economics.[1] Technology is a toolmaking and

---

[1] Joseph A. Schumpeter, *A History of Economic Analysis* (London: George Allen & Unwin, Ltd., 1954), pp. 6–20.

tool-behavior function. And so price theory, as a particular branch of economic theory, is, among other things, concerned generally with the making and manipulation of definitions (tools). Recognition of this fact at the outset can do much to clarify the nature of the subject matter of price theory and of the operations which are employed in it.

The definitions and the methods by which they are manipulated are, in fact, often referred to as the "kit of tools" of the economist. Indeed, price theory is both a language and a system of logic; and this book, it may be repeated, proposes nothing more elaborate than to give the student access to these "tools" and to the process of "toolmaking" so that he may determine for himself the extent to which, in a given case, they may be useful in solving the problem at hand and the extent to which they are not.

The Abstract Nature of Price Theory: Model Building

A definition is a limited meaning assigned to a word or a symbol. And since price theory is concerned with the making and manipulation of definitions as tools of analysis, it is necessarily abstract. In general, price theorists seek to provide explanations of economic activities and events by assigning limited meanings to words or symbols and then, by postulating relationships concerning economic behavior among these meanings, to draw from such definitions and relationships all of their implications. These implications may provide subjects for empirical verification, since they are inherent in the original statements. Of course, no more can be withdrawn from the original statements than was originally said, but discovery of hidden meanings and of tacit assumptions and the realization of the full consequences of a statement may require that it be repeated in several different ways and include the use of mathematics and graphs. At the same time, it should not be inferred from this precise method of presentation that all, nor indeed very many, of the original quantitative concepts and relationships employed are capable of precise quantification, nor that they have been verified as a result of controlled experimentation.

On the other hand, to the extent that the definitions used and the relations described are consistent with reality, understanding may be furthered, and research tools may be invented. And so, as Professor Fritz Machlup has remarked, it is no objection to an economic model, defined as an abstraction from reality, that it is unrealistic, "so long as it is based on realistic assumptions."[2] In other words, a model or theory must

---

[2] Fritz Machlup, *The Economics of Sellers' Competition* (Baltimore: The Johns Hopkins Press, 1952), pp. 7–8.

try to center attention upon realistic relationships among *strategic variables* if it is to provide a useful basis for explaining or classifying data. That is, a model must extract from a mass of data those relationships which are significant and concentrate attention upon them if it is to be useful.

In short, price theory employs a method of reasoning about economic data which deals in abstractions and not with the facts in any *specific* case. For this reason, the conclusions which appear in any piece of *general* analysis have no application to any *specific* factual cases except possibly by coincidence. Specific content must be injected into the general concepts before they can be applied to particular cases. Accordingly, these general conclusions do not often provide a *direct* basis for public policy in *specific* cases. Moreover, an analysis may be what is called *operationally meaningful* without being *operationally feasible.*[3]

Operationally Meaningful and Operationally Feasible Hypotheses

An *operationally meaningful* hypothesis is one which completes, expands, or extends existing hypotheses or establishes a new hypothesis so that it becomes an accepted part of the "tool kit." An *operationally feasible* hypothesis is one which relates to an attempt to solve a specific existential, as distinct from a hypothetical, problem. Often the theorems and hypotheses of contemporary price theory are "operationally meaningful" but not "operationally feasible."

The test of whether or not a hypothesis is operationally meaningful lies in the ability of the theorist who proposes it to specify the "ideal conditions under which it could be tested" even though in fact it cannot be tested. Thus an operationally meaningful hypothesis is one involving an "iffy" question and an "iffy" answer; and although it may complete, expand, or extend an existing hypothesis, it cannot generally be utilized directly as a basis for public policy without a considerable risk of error.[4]

The test of an operationally feasible hypothesis, on the other hand, is whether or not it can in fact be tested; that is, whether or not in fact it can serve as a basis for action. Of course, the two categories need not be mutually exclusive, but in practice they often are, for a hypothesis *need not be* operationally feasible to be operationally meaningful. An

---

[3] See Ralph W. Pfouts and C. E. Ferguson, "Market Classification Systems in Theory and Policy," *Southern Economic Journal,* Vol. XXVI (October, 1959), pp. 111–18.

[4] See Henry Schultz, *The Theory and Measurement of Demand* (Chicago: University of Chicago Press, 1938), pp. 10–11; and Paul A. Samuelson, *Foundations of Economic Analysis* (Cambridge: Harvard University Press, 1947), pp. 3–6.

operationally feasible hypothesis, however, *is* *always* operationally meaningful.

The distinction between operationally meaningful and operationally feasible hypotheses is similar to but not identical with the difference between mathematical economics and econometrics. The former is concerned with quantitative, but not necessarily quantifiable, formulations of economic ideas and their manipulation by means of mathematical methods and is really a form of economic theorizing. In other words, mathematical economics is essentially a system of deductive reasoning in which the "consistency" and "reasonableness" of assumptions is determined. Econometrics, on the other hand, is concerned with the quantitative and quantifiable formulation of economic situations and seeks, by means of statistical techniques, to test the relationships which are postulated. And so econometrics encompasses much of mathematical economics but is a much broader field of study.

The Generality of Price Theory

Although price theory is highly abstract, its basic ideas are quite simple. For example, the theory of consumer behavior and the theory of production each raise the same question and answer it in precisely the same way: "When does a society (or a consumer) get the most output (total utility) from the given amount of resources (money income) at its (his) disposal?" Answer: "When output (total utility) is at a maximum." The answer is, of course, an affirmative restatement of the question asked, and the analysis next concerns itself with a definition of the term "most" or the term "maximum."

Thus: "The total output (utility) will be maximized when the amount of output obtained from any given use of an *additional* unit of expenditure on inputs (unit of income) is just exactly equal to the amount of output (utility) which could be obtained by using the given unit of expenditure (unit of income) in any other way. For, otherwise, the total could be increased by transferring units of expenditure (income) from the less valuable use to a more valuable one."

The wide generality of the analysis is thus illustrated, for the analysis consists principally of a restatement of the original answer to the question (or of the original assumption of maximization), this time in terms of the *conditions* which must be met for a maximum to exist, rather than of a statement that a maximum must be attained. Whether or not the conditions exist in a *given* case is a question of fact, an empirical question. It makes no difference to the result in this process of analysis whether the conditions are stated graphically, algebraically, or in words. However, a graphical or algebraic statement is often more precise than is a statement in words alone.

In summary, then, the *method of price theory* (but not of all of economics) is deductive reasoning, a process of drawing conclusions from given premises or assumptions. It is no accident that some people have remarked that Alfred Marshall and other great neoclassical economists of the late nineteenth century invented an "economic calculus of variations" when they developed the marginal analysis which is the essence of price theory. For, like those of mathematics, the general concepts and relationships of price theory are devoid of specific substantive content, and this content must be supplied when the concepts and conclusions are applied in a specific case to a particular problem.

The Basic Assumption of Price Theory about Behavior

Economic theorists recognize that the units of action which enter into the analyses (individuals, households, firms, or a society) are actuated by many motives but point out that to take account of all of them would make impossible the formulation of general "tendencies" or "economic laws." Accordingly, the simple assumption is usually adopted that most units of action are motivated by "self-interest," by the motive of personal gain, and the general "tendencies" or "economic laws" are deduced from this assumption. Further, it is assumed that these units of action behave "rationally" to maximize that "self-interest," however these terms may be defined for the purposes at hand.

These assumptions (self-interest as the prime mover and rational behavior as the process) do not rest upon empirical studies by psychologists. Rather, they are usually justified by an appeal to the "common experience of everyone" and rest upon the analyst's belief that they are representative of "typical" experience. That is, these assumptions are obtained by a process of what has been called "intellectual experiment" or "intelligent introspection." In other words, they are open to refutation, and it is always open, to anyone who can do so, "to build a better mousetrap."

B. WHY STUDY PRICE THEORY?

Price Theory as a "Positive Science"

If the general concepts and conclusions derived from price theory cannot be directly applied to policy problems, and if price theory concerns itself mainly with abstract ideas and employs primarily the technique of deductive reasoning, is the study of price theory worthwhile? This is a legitimate question, and, indeed, intellectual honesty requires an admission at the outset that there is today much dissatisfaction among professional economists with some parts, and in some cases with the whole, of price theory in its present form. Thus, a number of economists have expressed doubt as to whether or not the static theory of the firm which appears in all elementary textbooks and in practically all price theory textbooks is today either realistic or satisfactory, whatever may have been the case when it was first developed. (We will face this issue squarely in Part IV.)

Indeed, there seems today to be a growing acceptance of a notion that economics should be reconstituted as "political economy" and that frank recognition should be given to the fact that the making of value judgments with respect to particular policy proposals by economists is probably inescapable. To a large extent, the current ferment and dissatisfaction have been the result of increased interest of many economists in the problems of economic development and balanced growth and the recognition by them that the basic behavior assumption employed in price theory has not been particularly helpful in solving such problems.

Such misgivings may thus merely be a manifestation of a tendency noted by Alfred Marshall in the *Principles*. He pointed out that despite the wide applicability and great generality of economic concepts and relationships, nevertheless, new social problems would give rise to new developments in economic theory.[5] The development of macroeconomic analysis since the Great Depression is a case in point.

On the other hand, some price theorists argue that price theory is a "positive science," and most price theory textbooks assert that a knowledge of price theory is important because (1) "price theory has welfare implications" and (2) "the theory has predictive accuracy in exploring the real world of experience." There is a very limited sense in which both statements are true, but, standing alone and unexplained, they are open to misinterpretation. This point will be amplified further below. A mere counterassertion of this nature hardly serves as a convincing reply to those who are currently dissatisfied with price theory.

Price Theory as the Language of Economists

As a matter of fact, one does not really need to rely upon the two rationalizations stated above to justify the study of price theory. For

---

[5] Alfred Marshall, *Principles of Economics* (8th ed.; London: Macmillan & Co., Ltd., 1938), p. 37.

price theory, whether or not its general conclusions can be employed in particular cases to solve particular problems, *is the basic language of economists.* Particular words have particular meanings in the context of economic analysis; and often words and phrases are substituted for complex ideas. Thus, for example, the phrase "value of the marginal product" is employed by an economist as a shorthand expression to convey to other economists a particular idea, an idea which cannot be conveyed in this simple and economical way to anyone who has not learned the same language. The same is true of the phrase "elasticity of demand." And, so, anyone who does not have a knowledge of the language of price theory is truly an "economic illiterate," whatever may be his other accomplishments. A knowledge of this language will not guarantee his ability to solve economic problems, but it may help him to be more precise in analyzing them and to avoid some errors in logic.

Thus, price theory is *not today merely a cultural subject,* any more than is the study of a modern foreign language a mere cultural pursuit (by someone who intends to work abroad in a country in which that language is the official language). On the contrary, *there is a very practical reason for acquiring a knowledge of price theory: the language and concepts of price theory permeate the whole of economics, and in all fields of economic analysis they serve the practical purpose of economy of effort and constitute a generally accepted method of organizing and classifying ideas about economic activities and magnitudes.* The principal emphasis in this book will therefore be placed upon acquisition by the reader of a knowledge of this language and of these concepts rather than upon the universal use of price theory as a method of solving welfare problems or upon the use of price theory as a method of "predicting" the behavior of economic entities in the real world, although we will also consider these two uses from time to time. In order to understand the reason for this emphasis, let us briefly consider what is meant by the two uses mentioned last and what criticisms have been made of them. (In Chapters 16 and 18, we will consider the question of "welfare" more fully.)

C. PRICE THEORY AS A BASIS FOR "WELFARE"

The Concepts of "Economic Efficiency" and "Economic Welfare"

Precisely what is meant by the statement that price theory has welfare implications? Presumably, this statement means that anyone who is an expert in the techniques of price theory will be able to make

public policy recommendations which will lead to "the good society."
And if this is the case, evidently what is required is an objective definition of the concept of "the good society." To what extent does price
theory provide us with such a definition?

Those who argue that it can and does generally define *the economic
problem* as one of allocating scarce resources among competing ends in
order to satisfy the ends as completely as possible. However, such a
definition implies that there exist "ends" which can be taken as data.
An assumption is therefore made that consumers' wants can be taken as
data and are the ends in question. Accordingly, *the* economic problem
then becomes one of *allocating the given quantity of resources available to a society at a given moment of time among the competing
culturally determined wants* (or ends) *of its members.* Consequently,
what has been culturally determined as an end is not questioned by the
analysis, and definitions of *economic efficiency* are invariably framed on
this basis. (In Chapter 16 this definition will be stated in precise
terms.)

To the extent that the economist takes the culturally determined
wants or ends as given, does he make a subjective judgment in favor of
the *status quo?* Some would say that he does; for, to paraphrase the
words of former Chief Justice Harlan Stone, "Inaction involves as
much choice as action." However, others would argue that the question
of "ends" is a political question and that an economist can effectively
advise a policy maker on how to go about attaining certain objectives
without judging the objectives themselves. On the other hand, such a
procedure would sharply limit the effectiveness as well as the activities
of economists, and, in fact, probably no economists actually limit themselves completely to such a purely technical function. To employ this
argument and *then* to make judgments with respect to ends is, of
course, a subterfuge at worst and self-delusion at best; and, to the extent
that some economists have done so, there is a legitimate ground for
criticism.

It is often argued that a state of economic efficiency has been attained whenever it is impossible to increase the welfare of any one
individual within a given society *without reducing* the welfare of any
other individual. However, it is recognized that the notion of economic
efficiency so defined is not alone a basis for public policy recommendations, since considerations of equity, which admittedly rest on subjective
grounds, are also important. For this reason such considerations (for
example, whether or not total welfare will be increased by increasing
the welfare of some at the expense of others) are often eliminated

from the problem by assuming that the distribution of income is "given." Moreover, it is not enough to assume merely that the wants of consumers are given, but it must also be assumed that "consumers should get what they want" (to use Professor Kenneth Boulding's phrase) and that these wants are independent of the other variables in the system.

By making these assumptions, the concepts and definitions of price theory can be and have been employed to build models in which that allocation of resources which would occur in a perfectly competitive economy is rationalized as being in accordance with "optimum conditions of welfare." In fact, in a perfectly competitive system there would be no advertising, and no selling costs would be incurred by firms (we will develop this point further in a later chapter); and, thus, the most obvious connection between production and wants is eliminated from this model. Too, in such a system no firm's sales would be large enough, in relation to the total market for the given output, to lead it to believe that by its own actions it could influence the price of the product which it sells. And so the firm would sell at prices fixed by market forces.

However, it is not clear that the conditions which are envisaged by this model could ever be attained without a social revolution in this country, and even then, it is not clear that production by many small firms, none of which is large enough to affect the price of its product by its own actions, is desirable in a society in which automation and large capital investments are the order of the day. The model is thus open to the charge that it lacks realism and cannot serve as a basis for public policy.

Price Theory and Public Policy

In arguing that price theory performs a welfare function, some price theorists have asserted that "presumably" the model of a perfectly competitive economy serves as the "norm" for evaluation of the performance of our economic system and, specifically, that this model "underlies the philosophy and enforcement" of our antitrust laws and of public regulation generally. Yet, in 1955 the group of scholars who constituted the Attorney General's National Committee to Study the Antitrust Laws (including such well-known economists as Professors J. M. Clark, George Stigler, and Walter S. Adams) said in their report:

. . . economic analysis can and does utilize varying sets of assumptions, excluding or including factors which are irrelevant for one kind of problem but decisive for another kind. Unless the particular set of assumptions is specified, the analysis may be irrelevant or even misleading . . . "pure" and "perfect" competition . . . are technical terms identifyng conditions of equilibrium with logical precision and completeness. *They do not purport to indicate ideal conditions.*[6]

And, as if to emphasize the point, somewhat later the *Report* continues:

> The concepts of pure and perfect competition are tools of theoretical analysis. They are not intended to and do not constitute a description of reality. As a theoretical model, these ideas give economists means for rigorously exploring the interrelationships of certain specified market forces. And, as previously stated, they define rigidly the theoretical conditions necessary to a form of long-run equilibrium in which prices would equal costs, including the minimum economically necessary supply price of capital . . . .
>
> . . . It should be emphasized that pure and perfect competition are wholly theoretical standards, in that they are not intended *as such* to be guides to public policy.
>
> . . . When taken out of context, the very precision of the theoretical standards of pure and perfect competition can be misleading. Nonetheless, these concepts, used in connection with the study of other factors outside their terms, have helped to orient economists' studies of actual situations, and have contributed, along with other influences, to the elaboration of the theory of workable competition, as an instrument for the direct study of market conditions.[7]

These excerpts speak for themselves. Faced with the concrete problem of deciding whether or not the welfare conclusions of price theory should be applied in the case of the antitrust laws, these scholars specifically rejected the ideal Instead, they devoted themselves to an attempt to select "economic concepts which are usefully relevant to antitrust problems." With respect to this action, Professor J. M. Clark, an outstanding and respected economist in his own right and the son of J. B. Clark, the most important neoclassical economist in the United States at the end of the last century, remarked that such an attempt "results in a presentation which is selective, *not only as to concepts included, but as to views held by economists on these concepts.*"[8]

Finally, at the conclusion of their study comparing the legal and economic concepts of competition, some of these scholars stressed the point that the " 'doctrine' of workable competition is only a rough and ready judgment by some economists, each for himself, that a particular industry is performing reasonably well." Moreover they asserted: "There are no objective criteria of workable competition, and such

---

[6] *Report of the Attorney General's National Committee to Study the Antitrust Laws* (Washington, D.C.: U.S. Government Printing Office, 1955), p. 316. (Italics mine.)

[7] *Ibid.,* pp. 337–38. (Italics in the original.)

[8] *Ibid.,* p. 317. (Italics mine.)

criteria as are proffered are at best intuitively reasonable modifications of the rigorous and abstract criteria of perfect competition."[9]

Our brief case study of the extent to which the welfare implications of price theory serve as a *norm* in the antitrust field thus suggests that the assertion that they do is open to considerable doubt. Yet, it is clear that this area is an extremely important one in the field of public policy.

Most often, the criticisms of the proposition that price theory has welfare implications useful for public policy purposes have consisted of arguments that the general model is "irrelevant" because it assumes away the principal problems, that its assumptions are unrealistic, and that wants are not in fact independent of production in our society. And even if they were, it is not clear that that allocation of resources which would be decreed by the competitive market is the "best" allocation from the dynamic point of view of economic growth or even from the point of view of establishing and maintaining a democratic and educated society.[10]

The proposition that wants are not independent of production has been emphasized in an argument advanced by Professor Kenneth Galbraith to the effect that if it is the process of satisfying wants which creates wants (by means of salesmanship and advertising in our own society), one can no longer assume that welfare will be greater at a higher level of output of goods and services than at a lower one and that, therefore, increased expenditures in the social sector of the economy (on schools, housing, and the like) may be more valuable than increased output of private consumption goods. To the relationship of the dependence of wants on output, Professor Galbraith has assigned the term "Dependence Effect"[11] (and in stating his argument he has made much use of the *language* of price theory!).

As a matter of fact, what Professor Galbraith has done in his analysis is to put into a broader context ideas developed in a slightly different way much earlier by Professor Edward H. Chamberlin in a classic

---

[9] *Ibid.,* p. 339.

[10] See, for example, Clarence E. Ayres, *The Industrial Economy* (Boston: Houghton Mifflin Co., 1952), pp. 1–29; Morris A. Copeland, "Institutionalism and Welfare Economics," *American Economic Review,* Vol. XLVIII (March, 1958), pp. 1–17; John S. Gambs, *Beyond Supply and Demand* (New York: Columbia University Press, 1946); Allan A. Gruchy, *Modern Economic Thought* (New York: Prentice-Hall, Inc., 1947); and E. E. Witte, "Economics and Public Policy," *American Economic Review,* Vol. XLVII (March, 1957), pp. 1–21. (The Witte and Copeland articles are Presidential Addresses delivered at annual meetings of the American Economic Association.)

[11] J. K. Galbraith, *The Affluent Society* (Boston: Houghton Mifflin Co., 1958), chap. xi.

work, *The Theory of Monopolistic Competition.*[12] In this work Chamberlin incorporated the additional variables of product differentiation (existence of a preference in the mind of the buyer for a given seller's product) and of selling expenses into the theory of the firm and also developed the concept of monopolistic competition. Indeed, some of these ideas were stated in an embryonic form earlier still by Alfred Marshall in his greatly neglected book, *Industry and Trade,*[13] and we will consider them further in Chapter 11.

It should be noted, in the context of these criticisms of price theory, that the assumption (upon which the welfare judgments rest) that wants can be taken as data represents a rationalization of free individual choice within the limits of a given culture pattern as a way of life rather than of capitalism as a political system. Price theory is *not* a rationalization of capitalism as a political system, although some price theorists and some critics of price theory sometimes speak as if it were. For, as a number of writers have shown, the same optimum conditions of welfare apply, assuming wants as data and that the distribution of income is given, both under capitalism and in a decentralized socialist economy.[14]

Although this proposition has been greatly refined in recent years, it was clearly stated by an outstanding American neoclassical economist, Professor Fred M. Taylor, in his Presidential Address before the American Economic Association as early as 1928.[15]

On the other hand, it must also be recognized that the optimum conditions of welfare which are derived from the general microeconomic models of an economy are not *absolute* conditions. They are *static relative* conditions. That is to say, they specify what are the static conditions of "economic efficiency," or of maximization of total output from given inputs, provided that consumers' wants can be taken as data and provided that the distribution of income is assumed to be unchanged. If, or to the extent that, any of these assumptions is not warranted in a given case, the conditions of "economic efficiency" cannot be taken as guides in the formulation or evaluation of public policy, or at least they must be qualified and corrected, usually by some kind

---

[12] Edward H. Chamberlin, *The Theory of Monopolistic Competition* (5th ed.; Cambridge: Harvard University Press, 1947).

[13] Alfred Marshall, *Industry and Trade* (London: Macmillan & Co., Ltd., 1919); also see my article, "A Curious Case of Neglect: Marshall's *Industry and Trade*," *Canadian Journal of Economics and Political Science,* Vol. XXI (August, 1955), pp. 339–53.

[14] See Abba P. Lerner, *The Economics of Control* (New York: The Macmillan Co., 1946); and Tibor Scitovsky, *Welfare and Competition* (Homewood, Ill.: Richard D. Irwin, Inc., 1951).

[15] Fred M. Taylor, "The Guidance of Production in a Socialist State," *American Economic Review,* Vol. XIX (March, 1929), pp. 1–8.

of value judgment, to take account of the facts which exist. (This question, too, will be further considered in Chapter 16.)

It has been noted that the conditions of economic efficiency derived from the general model are static conditions. Attempts to make the analysis dynamic do not escape the problem of value judgments. For example, in 1961, in a study prepared for The Brookings Institution, Professor J. M. Clark has argued that the "imperfectly competitive mixed economy" which exists in the United States today "is *better* than the impossible abstraction of 'perfect competition.'" Clark has taken this position on grounds that the present economy is dynamic and has argued that although the forms of competition have changed through time, the pressures of competition continue to be strong.[16] In making his study, he has flatly rejected the use of consumers' preferences as "authoritative standards of welfare" by remarking that to use such standards "is to abdicate the problem."[17]

Clark's emphasis of the dynamic nature of competition is akin to Professor Schumpeter's much earlier attempt to rationalize the free enterprise system functionally, also on instrumental or technological grounds, by incorporating dynamic elements into it. In his classic work, *The Theory of Economic Development,* which will be considered more closely in Chapter 18, Schumpeter frankly recognized that wants cannot be taken as independent "as soon as we analyze change," and his concept of economic development includes increases in the money value of the output which result from artifically created scarcities ("trustification"), as well as the notion that consumers must be taught by producers to want new things, "or things which differ in some respect or other from those which they have been in the habit of using." And so Schumpeter's dynamic system completely rejects the notion that wants can be taken as data and rests finally on the proposition that economic development consists, in part at least, of a state of affairs in which welfare is increased if consumers get what the entrepreneur teaches them to want. Obviously, the meaning of "welfare" in such a case becomes quite "fuzzy," if, indeed, it is not highly subjective.[18]

A claim that the general model of price theory performs a welfare

---

[16] J. M. Clark, *Competition as a Dynamic Process* (Washington, D.C.: The Brookings Institution, 1961), p. 490. (Italics mine.)

[17] *Ibid.,* p. 217. See also his comments on page 38 and page 71.

[18] See Joseph A. Schumpeter, *The Theory of Economic Development,* trans. Redvers Opie (Harvard Economic Studies, Vol. XLVI) (Cambridge: Harvard University Press, 1951), esp. pp. 65–66; and see also my own article, "Institutions and Technology in Economic Progress," *American Journal of Economics and Sociology,* Vol. XIX (January, 1960), pp. 139–50.

function by providing objective criteria against which the performance of an economic system can in fact be tested thus apparently amounts (as a minimum) to a tacit value judgment that one culture is as good as another or else that there is no basis for choosing among different cultures, provided only that goods are distributed in accordance with consumer preferences. Recognition that this is the case does not imply either acceptance or rejection of cultural relativism, but it does suggest that, at bottom, a basic value judgment is, nevertheless, involved. And it does require an admission that the claim that "price theory provides a basis for welfare judgments" must be revised to read that "price theory provides a basis for a *conditional* or *relative* judgment of welfare and is subject to some rather strict assumptions which may sharply limit the extent to which the welfare criteria can be applied in dealing with real world situations." Such an admission, whatever may be its significance for reasons given by others for studying price theory, does not affect the argument which has been made in this book, namely, that price theory is the basic language of economics and that, therefore, the study of price theory is functional from the point of view of the aspiring economist. Indeed, one who has not acquired this knowledge would probably not fully understand either Clark's or Schumpeter's books!

D. PRICE THEORY AS A BASIS FOR PREDICTION

The Meaning of "Prediction"

What of the second reason which is generally given for studying price theory: namely, "price theory has predictive accuracy in exploring the real world of our experience"? Does price theory enable us to predict in the sense of forecasting future events? The answer to this question depends upon the extent to which empirical verifications have been provided for the concepts and relationships employed, unless, of course, the word *prediction* is defined in a very special way to mean the process of drawing new conclusions from new or different assumptions introduced into a model dealing with a hypothetical case and *not* the forecasting of future events. To refer to the former process as "prediction," without fully explaining the special definition of the word which has been employed, invites misinterpretation at the very least.

There is at least one advocate of "positive economics" who agrees with this position. Thus, Professor P. T. Bauer has remarked:

Two important and related distinctions must be remembered in the framing and testing of economic generalizations. The first is the distinction between a functional relationship and a historical sequence of events. The law of demand is not invalid because in a boom both the prices and quantities sold of many commodities are higher than in a depression . . . . *Second, prediction, in the sense of assessment of results of specified occurrences or conditions, must be distinguished from the forecasting of future events.* Even if the prediction that the producers of a particular crop respond to a higher price by producing more is correct, this prediction does not enable us to forecast accurately next year's output (still less the harvest in the more distant future), which in the event will be affected by many factors besides changes in prices. You will appreciate that in this sense prediction and explanation are, as Marshall has reminded us, the same operation (the establishment of uniformities) in opposite directions. The confusion between these two different meanings of prediction (that is between assessment of the probable results of specified occurrences and forecasting of unknown future events) which is rife in contemporary literature, notably on underdeveloped countries, does not usually arise in academic discussion outside the social sciences.[19]

General Classificatory Models as a Basis for Prediction

Professor William J. Baumol has recently argued that "a model can only be designed around and judged in the light of a specific problem," although not necessarily a problem of public policy. Instead, Baumol argues, a model must be defined by the facts of the problem and the questions to which answers are sought.[20] This is essentially a pragmatic or instrumentalist view. A model of the general classificatory type, Baumol adds, can never have general validity.

In the same vein, Professor W. A. Johr and Dr. H. W. Singer have recently pointed out: "In contrast to the natural sciences, forecasting in economics on the basis of empirically established laws is—apart from a few exceptional cases—impossible . . . we have to work out the effects of certain constellations of measures by means of appropriate models." They add that the conclusions drawn from a model have validity in a real situation "only insofar as the investigator has done justice to *that* situation in constructing his model."[21]

Similarly, Professor Andreas Papandreou has used symbolic logic to demonstrate that models have no predictive powers and are merely ex-

[19] Peter T. Bauer, *Economic Analysis and Policy in Underdeveloped Countries* (Durham: Duke University Press; and London: Cambridge University Press, 1957), pp. 10–11. (Italics mine.)

[20] William J. Baumol, *Business Behavior, Value and Growth* (New York: The Macmillan Co., 1959), p. 2.

[21] W. A. Johr and H. W. Singer, *The Role of the Economist as Official Advisor*, trans. Jane Degras and Stephen Frowein (London: George Allen & Unwin, Ltd., 1955), p. 64. (Italics mine.)

planatory schemata; and he has added, it is time to admit that the "folklore" about economics as a science "interferes with the development of new tools" and the investigation of new and interesting problems.[22] These remarks, of course, come from men whose contributions to the field of economic theory are highly regarded, and they cannot be lightly dismissed.

Apparently, then, the statement that price theory performs a predictive function must also be qualified to read: "to the extent that the concepts and assumptions have been empirically verified, and upon the assumption that the future will be like the past, it should be possible to predict by means of the models of price theory; but, in general, the predictions which are derived from the *general* models are not 'forecasts'; rather, as is true of all deductive reasoning, they are new conclusions derived from changing existing assumptions or from introducing new ones." That is, the term *prediction* has a special meaning when it is used in this context.

Marshall also recognized, perhaps more clearly than some others, that limitations must be attached to the meaning of the word "prediction" when it is used in this context. Throughout the *Principles,* despite the fact that much of his analysis was stated in very general terms, he emphasized the fact that many variables were being held constant for the purposes of the analysis, in short, that he was assuming "other things equal."[23]

Recognition of the limited power to predict of the general model of price theory, like recognition of the limited application to real world situations of the welfare criteria derived from the model, does not invalidate the reason for studying price theory which has already been given in this book. For, even though both points are admitted, the functional reason for studying price theory stated earlier remains untouched by such criticisms.

E. THE SCOPE AND PLAN OF THIS BOOK

Accordingly, this book adopts Professor Kenneth Boulding's proposition that there does exist in the world a "tribe or subculture" of economists, a "tribe" with a special language and special skills developed especially to assist its members in exploring economic problems, however these may be defined.[24] And thus, since the principal objective of

---

[22] Andreas G. Papandreou, *Economics as a Science* (Chicago: J. B. Lippincott Co., 1958).

[23] Marshall, *Principles of Economics,* n. 2, p. 37.

[24] Kenneth Boulding, *The Skills of the Economist* (Indianapolis, Ind.: Howard Allen, Inc., 1958).

this book is to provide the student with a source from which he may learn that special language and acquire some of these skills, attention will be given in the following chapters to the historical origins of the concepts and ideas, that is, in a sense, to the etymology of that language. Most especially, references will often be made to the work of Alfred Marshall, who laid the foundations upon which much of contemporary price theory is based, to emphasize the fact that current price theory did not spring full-blown from the minds of contemporary economists.

This book consists of eight major parts and several appendices. The next chapter is an elementary one which states the relationship between macroeconomics and microeconomics and introduces the student to some basic concepts, such as perfect competition, comparative statics as a method of analysis, and the notion of equilibrium. It also describes the basic general model of price theory in broad elementary terms. Chapter 3 assumes that the student's knowledge of mathematics is limited to an understanding of how to add, subtract, multiply, and divide and explains general quantitative (but not necessarily quantifiable) concepts and relationships, also in an elementary way. The student will probably wish to refer often to the material in Chapter 3 to refresh his memory as his study of the various aspects of price theory progresses throughout the rest of the book. The present chapter and the two which follow constitute the whole of Part I.

Part II is concerned with an explanation and a comparison of the Marshallian "utility" and the contemporary "indifference" analyses of demand. Chapter 4 contains a statement of the basic Marshallian theory, and Chapter 5 contains an explanation of the contemporary theory.

Part III concerns itself with the concepts of production and costs and their determinants within the framework of price theory. The data relating to production which are assumed in Part III are employed next in Part IV, which deals with an explanation of the theory of the determination of output and product prices according to different assumptions concerning the state of competition in the short and long run. Thus Part IV contains an explanation and a critical discussion of the static theory of the firm. Part V deals with the theory of the determination of the employment of and returns to factors of production, and, so, it also contains an explanation of the "marginal productivity theory of income distribution." It, too, employs the basic data of Part IV.

Part VI contains an explanation of the so-called static "welfare equations," the equilibrium conditions of the state of "economic efficiency"; and Part VII provides a brief introduction to the basic concepts and methods of solving problems by *linear programming,* the process of selecting the "best" method of attaining given ends subject to given restraints or conditions, as an example of the way in which the language of price theory is developing. A simple maximization problem and its dual, involving two products and three inputs, are solved by the complete description method, and the simplex method is also explained. In a very real sense, Part VII treats in a slightly different way some of the problems which are dealt with in the chapters on production, on the theory of the firm, and on the determination of input values in Parts III, IV, and V, respectively.

Finally, Part VIII deals with the relationship between price theory and theories of economic development. Where it has been convenient and appropriate to do so, brief summaries and evaluations of econometric studies, which have sought to test one or another of the theories and relationships explained in the following pages, have been included at various points in this book.

SELECTED READINGS

BAUMOL, WILLIAM J. *Business Behavior, Value and Growth,* chaps. i and vi. New York: The Macmillan Co., 1959.

BOULDING, KENNETH. "Welfare Economics," *A Survey of Contemporary Economics* (ed. B. F. HALEY), Vol. II, pp. 1–38. Homewood, Ill.: Richard D. Irwin, Inc., 1952.

COOPER, G. "The Role of Econometric Models in Economic Theory," *Journal of Farm Economics,* Vol. XXX (1948), pp. 101–16.

COPELAND, MORRIS A. "Institutionalism and Welfare Economics," *American Economic Review,* Vol. XLVIII (March, 1958), pp. 1–17.

HUTCHINSON, T. W. *The Significance and Basic Postulates of Economic Theory.* London: Macmillan & Co., Ltd., 1938.

KEYNES, JOHN NEVILLE. *The Scope and Method of Political Economy.* London: Macmillan & Co., Ltd., 1917.

KLEIN, L. R. "The Use of Econometric Models as a Guide to Economic Policy," *Econometrica,* Vol. XV (April, 1947), pp. 111–51.

LANGE, OSCAR. "The Scope and Method of Economics," *Review of Economic Studies,* Vol. XIII (1945–46), pp. 12–32.

ROBBINS, LIONEL. *An Essay on the Nature and Significance of Economic Science.* 2d ed. London: Macmillan & Co., Ltd., 1936.

SAMUELSON, PAUL A. *Foundations of Economic Analysis,* pp. 1–6. Cambridge: Harvard University Press, 1947.

2 Some Basic General Concepts

Introduction

This chapter, as its title indicates, provides an explanation of some basic general concepts and a picture, broadly sketched, of a basic general model employed in price theory. This model is one of a stable, stationary economy and can be employed to explain both the "circular flows" of money and goods and the relationship between product and factor markets. The full statement and explanation of the equilibrium conditions of this model, together with numerous modifications of it, will occupy most of the chapters which follow. In the last chapter we will consider the extent to which some dynamic analyses assume that the reader is already familiar with this model and its equilibrium conditions and employ it as a starting point.

A. THE CONCEPT OF COMPETITION

Perfect Competition

The term *competition* is defined differently by different writers.[1] *Perfect competition* may be rigorously defined as a state of affairs characterized by the following conditions: (1) there are a large number of buyers and sellers, none of whom thinks that he can influence the price of a commodity through his own individual actions; (2) all sales involve perfectly homogeneous (interchangeable) commodities; (3) all buyers and sellers have perfect knowledge of the situation confronting them and of their alternatives; (4) all buyers and sellers behave rationally to maximize their own self-interests (however defined) on the basis of that knowledge; and (5) freedom of entry into the market and perfect mobility of inputs exist.

---

[1] See Fritz Machlup, *The Economics of Sellers' Competition* (Baltimore: The Johns Hopkins Press, 1952), chap. iv, esp. n. 16, p. 104, where Professor Machlup provides different meanings of the term collected from the works of numerous writers.

So defined, perfect competition exists only in the world of the model builder. In this sense it is a useful logical construction. By removing one or another of the limiting assumptions or conditions, the degree of competition assumed in the analysis can be made less than perfect. Thus, by reducing the number of buyers or of sellers (eventually rational individuals who are few in number on one side of the market must realize that by their own actions they do affect prices), the situation of *oligopoly* (a few sellers), or of *oligopsony* (a few buyers), may be created. By having them deal in nonhomogeneous commodities, the effect of differentiated products can be considered.

Workable or "Effective" Competition

The *model concept, perfect competition,* must be distinguished from the *policy prescription, workable competition.* The latter term, as has already been noted in the preceding chapter, refers to the subjective opinion of a given economist in assessing the degree of competition which he thinks is tolerable in a given case. That is, it constitutes a subjective judgment by a given economist concerning the extent to which he thinks that absence of one or another of the conditions of perfect competition will not prove *unduly* harmful to economic welfare. It has been characterized as the economist's "Rule of Reason," an apt description for a value judgment.[2]

B. A BASIC ECONOMIC MODEL

The Product and Factor Markets

Figure 2–1 depicts a model of a stationary economy. All individuals in this model are assumed to play two roles (among all their others). They are both consumers of products (outputs) and suppliers of services of factors of production (inputs). As consumers they spend their money incomes for products and thus demand them. In a free enterprise system (or under decentralized state socialism), firms purchase inputs or factor services in the factor markets and transform them into products or outputs. These are sold in the product markets. Thus firms demand inputs and supply outputs. The source of the inputs is the individuals who own them. In exchange for their inputs, the individuals receive incomes which are equal to the prices paid by the firms (their

---

[2] *Report of the Attorney General's National Committee to Study the Antitrust Laws* (Washington, D.C.: U.S. Government Printing Office, 1955), chap. vii, "Economic Indicia of Competition and Monopoly," esp. pp. 318–42.

costs) for these inputs multiplied by the quantities of these inputs supplied by the individuals.

In Figure 2–1 there are two sets of markets: (1) *product or output
markets* and (2) *factor or input markets*. In each, prices are determined according to the assumptions one makes. If one assumes perfect
competition, in the long run, the prices which consumers pay for goods
(determined by the wants of the consumers, which are taken as ultimate data) will be equal to the average costs of producing and selling

Figure 2–1

A SIMPLE MODEL

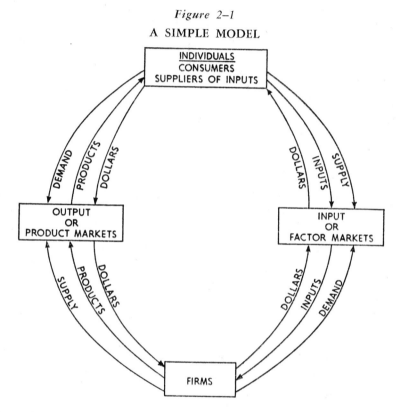

these goods. These prices, in turn, will be just equal to the costs of
producing and selling additional units of goods. If consumers' wants
are taken as data, and if prices truly reflect consumers' preferences,
then resources are being allocated in accordance with consumers' preferences; and assuming the distribution of income as given, welfare is
said to be at a maximum in this society. Whether or not welfare would
be greater under some other scheme of social organization cannot be
determined from the model.

The word *inputs* which has been employed in our analysis is broader than the term generally employed by the neoclassical economists who used the word *factors.* The factors of production, or the agents of production, according to this view, can be classified broadly as land, labor, capital, and the entrepreneur (the undertaker of the enterprise). Each of the factor services has a price: thus the payment for the service of land is rent, the payment for labor service (including the service of routine management) is wages, and the payment for the use of capital is interest. The residual—the difference between the sum of the three preceding payments and the total revenue—can, in the present context, be designated as either profits or losses, and this is the amount payable to the entrepreneur for his foresight or enterprise (profits) or his lack of them (losses). The broad classification of inputs in these terms is useful for many purposes. For others, however, the simple term "inputs" is preferable, since it recognizes that there may be various categories of labor and various kinds of capital.

The Concept of Equilibrium; Comparative Statics

An *equilibrium position* is one from which there is no tendency to move. Specification of the conditions of an equilibrium position is known as *static* analysis. *Partial equilibrium analysis,* the method of analysis generally associated with the name of Marshall, allows one variable to change slightly, while other things are held constant, so that the analyst can determine the effect on the system of this slight change. *General equilibrium analysis,* developed by Leon Walras (1874), a French mathematical economist, is not completely general (no system is) but presumably is based on all of the relevant economic data in the problem and allows other things to change equally as the given variable changes.[3] Its use will be illustrated in Chapter 4.

The system depicted in Figure 2–1 may be thought of as in a position of *stable, stationary equilibrium.* There is movement in it, but the magnitude of the national income does not change. The flow rates of money and of goods are constant through time, and prices remain stable. However, the equilibrium can be disturbed by introducing a change into it. If it is a stable system, eventually the effects of the change will be incorporated into the system and it will once more return to a position of stable equilibrium, though not necessarily at the same *level* as before.

Comparison of the data for the previous and the new positions of equilibrium constitutes a method of analysis known as *comparative*

---

[3] Leon Walras, *Elements of Pure Economics,* trans. William Jaffé (Homewood, Ill.: Richard D. Irwin, Inc., 1954).

statics. This method concerns itself with a comparison of the differences between two stable equilibrium (or "limiting") positions which result from a change in one of the variables. Thus, in the microeconomic sense, if we ask what is the effect of an increase in the demand on price, other things remaining the same, the answer may be that the price will increase. In the new position the price will be higher and the quantity exchanged greater than in the old. Such a result, if it should be true, is inherent in the definitions of supply and demand which are employed. Nothing is said in the analysis of the effects on the variables of the path of movement. Only the initial and the final positions are compared. In general, this is the basic method of analysis of price theorists.

Finally, in Figure 2–1 if the flow of money and the flow of goods increase proportionately so that the general price level remains unchanged, the system is in a *stable, moving equilibrium.* Such a system differs from one which is in a *stable, stationary equilibrium,* since, in the latter, the flow of goods and the flow of money remain unchanged year after year. Dynamic analysis, which involves changes in the variables through time, will not be much used in this book. Contemporary price theory has not progressed very far in this direction.

The Relationship between Macroeconomics and Microeconomics

In Figure 2–1 goods flow from firms to individuals, and factor services flow from individuals to firms into eternity. In the opposite direction, money flows from individuals to firms, and then back again to individuals into eternity. There are opposite circular flows of money and goods (measured as a constant dollar value of national income), as indicated by the arrows in Figure 2–1.

This model incorporates both the macroeconomic and the microeconomic approaches to economic analysis. On the one hand, it is possible to view the overall opposite flows of money and of goods and to define inflation as a situation in which the flow of dollars increases relative to the flow of goods. By making the model more complicated it is possible to break down consumers' incomes into portions saved (which slow down the flow of dollars into output markets) and portions spent, and to insert into the stream of dollars the effects of actions by central banks to increase or decrease the money supply. Similarly, it is possible to show the government as a purchaser of inputs or of products, or as a tax claimant upon the consumers' incomes. Finally, it is possible to incorporate into this model the effects of international trade on the flow of goods and on the flow of money. Most of these matters are the concern of macroeconomics, which deals with the *level* of operation of the system.

Price theory, on the other hand, concerns itself with the microeconomic aspects of the system and assumes generally that it is operating at a full employment level. What determines the prices of the inputs and of the products? How are prices and outputs affected if the degree of competition is decreased? How do rational consumers determine the quantities of products which they purchase? These are the questions posed, and thus price theory is concerned with an analysis in detail of the various determinants of, and relationships among, the parts of the system. Instead of taking an overall view of the system, we consider its parts.

But the two methods of analysis are concerned with an attempt to explain the same economic system. They merely emphasize different aspects of it, and, indeed, they are dependent upon each other. Thus, in macroeconomic analysis, the national income can be defined as the sum of the earnings of the factors of production during a given period of time, and the gross national product is defined as the sum of all final products multiplied by their final prices. These measures are employed because it is not possible to reduce all of the products to a homogeneous mass for purposes of counting them without employing the common denominator of their money value. At the same time, the money value of a unit of product to a consumer, that is to say the price he pays for it, represents the value *to him* in terms of opportunity cost (the value of the alternative given up by the expenditure on that product rather than on some other of an amount of purchasing power equal to the price of the product) of his purchase. The concept of the value to the consumer of a unit of product is a microeconomic one.

In order to measure national income in real terms (in terms of constant dollars) it is necessary to deflate the money value of the national income by an appropriate price index. Since index numbers are merely a logical extension of Marshallian demand theory (see Appendix D), both by virtue of the method of computing national income in terms of market prices of final products adjusted for depreciation and indirect taxes and by this statistical operation, the basic assumptions of Marshallian demand theory have been incorporated into our national income concept.

The reader should not, however, make the mistake of thinking that macroeconomics deals with economic aggregates while microeconomics deals with the things aggregated. Aggregation is employed in both types of analyses. In Chapter 4 we will see that the total market demand curve is merely the aggregation of individual consumers' demand curves, and in Chapter 9 we will see that the total short-run market supply is simply the aggregate of the individual firms' short-run supplies under perfect competition.

The Functions of an Economic System

The functions of an economic system are derived from its postulation. The following functions must be performed in the system depicted in Figure 2–1 by definition: (1) decisions must be made as to what products are to be produced; (2) decisions must be made as to the quantities and kinds of resources which are to be used and the proportions in which they are to be devoted to the production of particular products; (3) decisions must be made as to how the product is to be distributed; and (4) some provision must be made for the maintenance, and possibly the growth of the system. In the circular flow diagram of Figure 2–1, if the total output is consumed year after year without any provision for replacement of the capital equipment which is used in the production of products, eventually the system must expire. But if such provision is made, it can continue to operate indefinitely. Consequently, some provision for maintenance of the system is a *necessary* condition to its continued existence.

In general, microeconomic analysis seeks to establish the principles according to which these functions are or will be accomplished in the system *by making assumptions* regarding the degree of competition and regarding the rationality of the behavior of and extent of the knowledge had by producers and consumers, in the absence of governmental intervention. Thus it devotes itself primarily to an analysis of the principal determinants of prices in the product and in the factor markets. The prices in the product markets are interpreted to be reflections of the wants of the consumers and to serve as guides to producers in their allocation of resources to the production of products; and in the factor markets, prices are seen as the costs to the producers of the resources so employed.

The detailed analysis of the process by which consumers' valuations are reflected in the prices which they pay for the products is known as the theory of demand. Presumably those products on which consumers place the highest valuations will command the highest prices. Changes in such valuations will be reflected in these prices. Thus it is argued that the decisions as to what is produced are made by consumers and reflected in the prices which they are willing to pay. Goods for which there is no demand will not command a price, and producers will not, in the long run, continue to produce such goods because the prices received for the products which they produce, in turn, determine the abilities of the producers to cover their costs. The costs of the producers are, however, the prices of the services of the factors of production which are used to produce the products. And so, the factors will be employed to produce those products which are most urgently desired by the consumers, and the most "valuable" factors will command the highest prices.

' However, if consumers' valuations are not independent of the other variables in the system—and to say that they are independent is to deny that advertising expenditures and selling activities of firms exert any influence on consumers' absolute or relative valuations of goods—it can no longer be asserted categorically that the decisions as to what products are to be produced are made by consumers alone. In this situation the prices may still reflect the valuations which consumers place on the products, but these valuations can no longer be considered independent of other variables in the system. At the very least such valuations must then be considered to be the product of interactions between firms and consumers. Recognition of this fact does *not* destroy the theory of demand, but it does seriously weaken many of the welfare conclusions which are derived from many of the existing general models of the economy. ◢

Decisions as to the quantities of resources or inputs used and concerning the proportions in which they are to be devoted to the production of particular products are made by firms. These decisions can, of course, be influenced by governmental policies. However, under conditions of perfect competition, and in the absence of governmental action, since no firm thinks it can by its own actions affect the price of the product which it sells, there would be no advertising and no selling expenses. In such a situation also, firms would be guided by the prices paid for products in the product markets, and assuming they were seeking to maximize their profits and behaved rationally, they would also seek to make use of the least costly methods of production. Competition would drive the inefficient firms out of business; competition would also insure that no firms made greater than normal profits in the long run, for freedom of entry is one of the conditions of perfect competition, and, thus, new firms would enter industries in which greater than normal profits were being made, driving profits down to a "normal" level.

But even in this idealized state of affairs there are difficulties of definition. The term "profits" requires further definition. Do firms maximize their long-run or their short-run profits? Do firms maximize profits at all? Professor Baumol has recently suggested, on the basis of his experience as a consultant to several large firms, that a more reasonable hypothesis is that firms maximize sales revenue subject to a minimum profit constraint (that is, subject to a recognition by the managers that stockholders will require a minimum profit to remain "happy") because salaries of executives are more closely correlated with sales revenues than with profits.[4] (We will consider his argument in detail in Chapter 11.)

When the model is made more realistic, when it is recognized that many firms do influence the prices of products by their own actions and often make decisions on "noneconomic" grounds, and when it is recognized that firms which produce joint products (for example, the production of many products from crude oil in the petroleum industry) do not know the cost of producing individual products and thus follow a procedure of allocating expenses to particular products on the basis of revenues obtained from their sales, further questions of the usefulness of the general model as an *explanation* of reality arise. Its usefulness is thus primarily analytical and pedagogical.

The prices which firms pay for the factors of production which they employ to produce products are costs to the firms. When the prices paid for the factors are multiplied by the quantities of the factors which are used, the arithmetical products are the incomes of the given factors of production. The incomes of individuals thus depend on both the prices of the factors and the quantities of them which are owned by such individuals, and this fact provides an explanation of how the final outputs are distributed. The quantities of the factors owned by the individuals are determined by the institutional arrangements of the society in question. The prices which are paid for the factors depend on the availabilities of the factors (their supplies) and on the demands for them which arise out of their usefulness in the production of final products. The extent of competition among firms in bidding for factors and the extent of competition among suppliers of factors thus influences the prices which are paid for the use of such factors.

In general the rationalization of payments for factors of production or of the "functional distribution of income" proceeds along the following lines. Under perfect competition, in the long run, the price paid for the use of a unit of a given factor of production is exactly equal to the additional value of the product which results from the use of an additional unit of such a given factor of production. In the long run, profits

---

[4] William J. Baumol, *Business Behavior, Value and Growth* (New York: The Macmillan Co., 1959), chaps. i and vi.

in such a situation are "normal," which means that they are just sufficient to keep the "proper" amount of entrepreneurship engaged in the production of the final products. Later we will consider in detail the logical principles on which rests this theory of income distribution.

Maintenance of the system is provided by including in the cost of the final product an amount just sufficient to replace the capital equipment which is used up; thus depreciation allowances are functionally a proper inclusion in the cost of the final product.

In this analysis, too, temporary profits greater than normal can be rationalized on functional grounds by making the system dynamic. If, for one reason or another, profits in the production of one class of products or of a new class of products become greater than normal, this fact is a signal for additional entrepreneurs to enter the field and to bid resources away from their existing uses and to use them to increase the production of the given products. Thus, the supply of the wanted products is increased, while that of the relatively less desirable products is decreased. Eventually only normal profits are once more being made in all industries, and the economy finds itself in a new position of stable equilibrium, perhaps at a higher level of output than before. In this way change and growth are also explained, although perhaps somewhat superficially. This problem, too, will be considered later when we study Professor Schumpeter's theory of economic development.

The statement of the ways in which the functions of an economic system are performed cannot be separated from a factual judgment with regard to the question of whether or not consumers' valuations of products are or are not independent of the other variables in the system. To assume that they are *completely* independent (and this is the usual procedure) is to introduce an unrealistic assumption into the model, just as to assume perfect competition is unrealistic. A model which makes these unrealistic assumptions explains the ways in which the functions of the economic system would be performed *if* its assumptions were valid, but it does not explain how they are actually performed in our own system today.

Yet the model contains grains of truth. Perhaps the principal service which it performs is its emphasis of the complicated nature of the market process and its demonstration that there are in fact two sets of markets and two sets of prices to be considered. Also, the model provides a useful starting point for the study of the concepts of price theory, and this is probably its principal justification. In this book it is employed as an analytical and pedagogical device, not as a guide to policy.

The Following Chapters

Most of the remaining chapters of this book are devoted to a technical exposition of the basic concepts and relationships of price theory. As has already been noted, these consist of specific and refined treatments of various aspects and assumptions of the basic general model which has been broadly sketched in this chapter. The next chapter contains an explanation of basic quantitative concepts employed throughout the rest of the book.

SELECTED READINGS

BEACH, E. F. *Economic Models,* chap. i and pp. 199–201. New York: John Wiley & Sons, Inc., 1957.

GALBRAITH, J. K. *The Affluent Society,* chaps. i and xi. Boston: Houghton Mifflin Co., 1958.

HICKS, J. R.; HART, A. G.; AND FORD, J. W. *The Social Framework of the American Economy,* pp. 235–38. New York: Oxford University Press, Inc., 1955.

LINDBLOM, C. E. "Policy Analysis," *American Economic Review,* Vol. XLVIII (June, 1958), pp. 298–312.

PETERSON, SHOREY. "Antitrust and the Classic Model," *American Economic Review,* Vol. XLVII (March, 1957), pp. 60–78. Reprinted in *Readings in Industrial Organization and Public Policy* (eds. R. B. HEFLEBOWER AND G. W. STOCKING), pp. 316–33. Homewood, Ill.: Richard D. Irwin, Inc., 1958.

SCHUMPETER, J. S. "The Nature and Necessity of a Price System," *Economic Reconstruction,* pp. 170–76. New York: Columbia University Press, 1934. Reprinted in *Readings in Economic Analysis* (ed. RICHARD V. CLEMENCE), Vol. II, pp. 1–7. Cambridge: Addison-Wesley Press, 1950.

———. *The Theory of Economic Development.* Harvard Economic Studies, Vol. XLVI, chap. i. Cambridge: Harvard University Press, 1951.

WITTE, E. E. "Economics and Public Policy," *American Economic Review,* Vol. XLVII (March, 1957), pp. 1–21.

3 Basic Quantitative Concepts and Relationships

Introduction

This chapter explains certain basic quantitative (but not necessarily quantifiable) concepts used in economic theory. An understanding of these concepts is probably crucial to an understanding of most of economic analysis. In this chapter, and throughout this book, an attempt is made to develop these concepts in such a way as to make them intelligible to a reader who is not mathematically sophisticated. The utility framework is employed in this chapter as a background for the explanation of these concepts primarily because it can then be employed directly in the discussion of demand theory in the immediately following chapters. The ideas can just as easily be developed in terms of the economic concepts employed in the theory of production, and some writers have followed this procedure.[1]

A. SOME ELEMENTARY CONCEPTS

The Concepts of Purchasing Power and of Utility

Let us, therefore, *define total utility,* for which we will use the symbol, *u, as the total satisfaction which a consumer can derive from his given income, m.* Then, following the lead of Alfred Marshall, in Figure 3–1, assume that the total utility (u) derived from a given consumer's income (m) can be measured on the vertical or Y axis.[2] Now in fact the *total* utility of a given income cannot be determined. However, *changes* in total utility, we will see, can be and often are roughly estimated in many areas of economic analysis, even though this fact is not usually explicitly stated in price theory books.

---

[1] This approach is adopted by George Stigler in *The Theory of Price* (rev. ed.; New York: The Macmillan Co., 1952); see esp. chap. iii.

[2] Compare Alfred Marshall, *Principles of Economics* (8th ed.; London: Macmillan & Co., Ltd., 1938), Book III, pp. 95–96 and Mathematical Note II, p. 838.

Income, or m, means purchasing power (or spending power) and is itself a function of the consumer's given *money* income (*M*) and of prices (*P*) which he must pay for the commodities which he buys. The term *real income* will not be used in this book, largely because it has different meanings in the works of different writers, and, indeed, sometimes it has different meanings in the work of a given writer![3] Both total utility (*u*) and income (*m*) change when *money* income (*M*),

Figure 3–1

THE TOTAL UTILITY OF INCOME CURVE

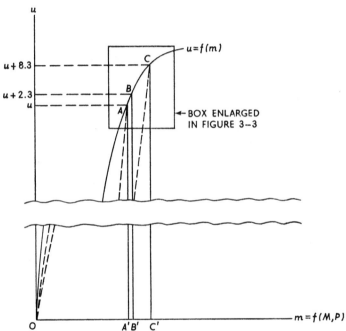

or prices (*P*), or both change. Total utility (*u*) is a function of the uses to which the income, *m,* is put, and one of these uses may be saving. *Income or purchasing power, m, is measured on the horizontal or X axis in Figure 3–1 and is defined as the number of dollars contained in given sums of money, however determined, which are taken as equivalents of the various quantities of commodities which the consumer purchases.*

---

[3] See, for example, Fritz Machlup, "Professor Hicks' *Revision of Demand Theory,*" *American Economic Review,* Vol. XLVII (March, 1957), pp. 119–35, esp. pp. 119–20. Professor Machlup has noted that Hicks uses the term *real income* to mean utility as well as collections of goods in his book, and that although Hicks eliminated the word *utility* from a good part of his book, nevertheless, he did *not* eliminate the concept. Machlup cites many examples and asks, ". . . is this more than a terminological gesture?"

If the consumer's money income increases, one moves to the right from point A' to point B' along the m or X axis in Figure 3–1. Similarly, if the prices of commodities (or one of them) decrease, one also moves to the right along the X axis. And if the consumer experiences an increase in money income at a time when prices decline, the movement is again to the right along the X axis, but further to the right than if only one of these things had happened and not the other. A movement to the right along the X axis produces a movement up the Y axis.

The Budget Equation

In order to explain how the consumer's purchasing power or income changes as a result of a price change, let us assume that the consumer is initially spending part of his given *money* income, M, on the commodity, x, and that that part of his money income *not spent* on x is devoted to all other conceivable uses of his money income, including saving. Designate all these other uses by the symbol y. Thus we have defined y as the number of dollars devoted to all uses other than purchases of x, and the price of a unit of y, or p_y, can be taken as equal to $1.00.

What we have just assumed can be set out in the form of a simple algebraic equation, called the *budget equation*, which really constitutes a kind of limitation on the analysis

$$xp_x + yp_y = M. \tag{3-1}$$

What this equation states is that the total amount spent for x, or xp_x, plus the total amount spent for y, or yp_y, is equal to the total *money* income of the consumer, M. For xp_x is the quantity of x purchased times the price of a unit of x, and so represents the total amount spent for x. Similarly, yp_y is the amount of y purchased times the price of a unit of y, and so represents the total amount spent on y, or on all uses other than x.

Let us now assume that $y = 60$, $p_y = \$1.00$, $x = 60$, and $p_x = \$1.00$. It follows, therefore, that we can write our budget equation arithmetically as

$$(60)(\$1.00) + (60)(\$1.00) = \$120 = M. \tag{3-1'}$$

The Effect of a Price Decrease: The "Cost Differences"

The consumer's total money income has thus been accounted for. Next allow the price of x to decrease by Δp_x, which is read *delta p_x*, or *change in the price of x*, which we will assume to be equal to $-\$.28$.

Then the new price of x will be defined by the formulation $(p_x + \Delta p_x)$, which is necessarily equal in our arithmetical example to $1.00 — $.28 = $.72. Thus, $\Delta p_x = -$.28 < 0$, where < 0 means *less than zero or negative.*

In Figure 3–2 this change in the price of x is depicted as the dis-

Figure 3–2

A GRAPHICAL ILLUSTRATION OF THE "COST DIFFERENCES"

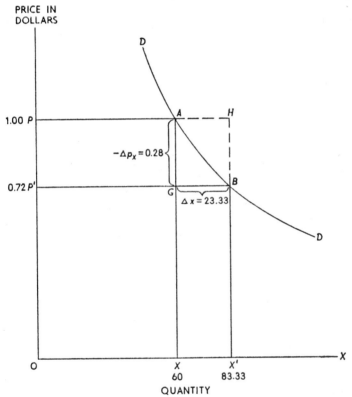

tance *AG* or *PP'*. Each unit of x purchased at the old price of x will now cost the consumer $-\Delta p_x = $.28$ less than it did before the price decrease. Thus, in order to determine the reduction in the cost of the quantity of x purchased at the original price of x, we must multiply this price reduction by the original quantity of x (or by *OX* in Figure 3–2) to produce $x\Delta p_x$, *defined as the change in cost* of the initial quantity. Since we have assumed x equals 60 units as the amount purchased at the initial price of $1.00, we have

$$x\Delta p_x = (60)(-$.28) = -$16.80 = AGP'P ,$$

Now the *negative of this change in cost,* or $-x\Delta p_x = \$16.80$, *shows that in the case of a price decrease the consumer's spending power has actually increased* by an amount equal to $-\Delta p_x = \$.28$ for each unit of x consumed. *Thus his purchasing power has increased* by $-x\Delta p_x = \Delta m = P'PAG.$ For although his *money* income (M) remains unchanged, that money income will now allow him to continue to purchase the original quantities of x and of all other goods; and, also, he has $\$16.80$ left over to spend for more x or to use in any other way he desires. The original quantity of x now costs him $-x\Delta p_x = \$16.80$ *less* than before.

· After the price change, the value of the original quantity of x to the consumer has not necessarily changed, and we will assume that it has not. Since he was willing to and did pay 60 dollars for the original 60 units of x, their value to him after the price change must still be equal to that of at least 60 dollars. Thus we are *now* measuring the *utility* of the 60 units of x as equal to *at least* that of the amount of money which was paid for them at the old price of x. Furthermore, after the price decreases, if the consumer *does not increase his consumption of* (and so expenditures on) x at all, he will no longer be devoting 60 dollars to uses other than purchases of x, but will be devoting to y the original 60 dollars plus the 16.80 additional dollars which have accrued as a result of the decrease in the price of x. Thus, if no part of the increase in spending power is spent for additional x, we will have $-x\Delta p_x = \Delta y p_y$, and the new amount spent on y will be $(y + \Delta y)p_y = \$60 + \$16.80 = \$76.80$. Consequently, we can estimate the *value* of the consumer's money income, or u, after the price change as equal to $xp_x + yp_y + (-x\Delta p_x) = xp_x + yp_y + \Delta y p_y = \$60.00 + \$60.00 + \$16.80 = \$136.80$.

Thus, we have estimated the *change* in total utility indirectly by reducing all the dissimilar items on which the consumer spends his money income to a common denominator, and we have made a welfare judgment concerning the effect of the price change.

This, in general, is the procedure employed by contemporary index number theories in their attempt to explain the welfare effect of a price change. Basically what is involved is a quantitative comparison of different levels of utility by a reduction of dissimilar items to a common denominator—a money value, units of purchasing power, or a *numeraire* (a unit of account, a measuring rod)—and an assertion that "more is better than less."

What, however, if the consumer has in fact increased his consumption of x after its price has decreased and he has spent all or part of the increased purchasing or spending power equal to $16.80 on x rather than having kept it all in the form of y?

In this case our problem becomes more difficult. We can still (and both index number theory [see Appendix D] and contemporary demand theory [see Appendix C] follow this procedure) take the value of the original 60 units of x as equal to that of the amount of money spent for them at the old price, or to $60, and we can still add to this the $60 which represent the amount originally spent on y. But how shall we now value the effect on his total utility of the change in purchasing power?

If the consumer had retained the increase in income ($-x\Delta p_x = \$16.80$) in the form of y (i.e., not spent on x), our problem would have been easy, for obviously he was then better off by exactly $16.80, or by $16.80y$ because one y costs one dollar. But if he spent the $16.80 for additional x, then it follows that if he was behaving rationally, the additional units of x thus acquired were worth more to him than was the $16.80 in the form of y (or not spent on x). Evidently the magnitude $-x\Delta p_x$ represents the *lower limit* to his gain. In every case then, the consumer's total utility will be increased by an amount which is *at least* equal to the utility of the increase in income ($-x\Delta p_x$) when the price of x declines.

Can we also determine an *upper limit* to his gain? In fact, if the consumer does spend all of the $16.80 = $P'PAG$ for additional x, he will purchase $16.80/$.72 = 23.33$ additional units of x. For he has $16.80 more spending power, and the price of a unit of x is $.72. In the case of Figure 3-2, after the price change, the consumer is at B, where he consumes OX' units of x, and in our diagram OX' exceeds OX (the original quantity of x at the original price) by exactly $\Delta x = XX' = 23.33$.

Suppose then, instead of a price decrease, that the consumer had been given a subsidy equal to $23.33 when he was at A, consuming 60 units of x and 60 units of y when the price of x was $1.00. If this had been done, he would have been able to consume *exactly the same quantities* of x and of y *at the old prices* as he does consume after the price decline. Such a subsidy is apparently the *upper limit* on his gain and is measured as follows.

First, if the consumer had been given such a subsidy, he could have reached point H in Figure 3-2, for, as we will learn in the next chapter, an increase in income without a price change results in a movement to the right of the entire demand curve. Thus, there could be another demand curve like DD running through point H.

Next, note that if the consumer buys OX units of x at the old price of OP in Figure 3–2, he will be spending an amount equal to the price, OP, times the quantity, OX, or area $OPAX$, for x; and if he buys OX' units at a price of OP', he will be spending an amount equal to $OP'BX'$ for x. How much will he spend if he buys OX' units (the new quantity) of x at the old price of OP? Clearly he will be spending an amount equal to $OPHX'$. Now $OPHX'$ exceeds area $OP'BX'$ by exactly $P'PHB$.

Thus the magnitude of a subsidy which would enable the consumer to purchase *exactly the same quantities of x and of y at the old prices as he does purchase at the new prices* must be area $P'PHB$. But this area is nothing other than the *negative* of the change in price $(-\Delta p_x)$ times the *new* quantity of x, or $(x + \Delta x)$. Thus the *upper limit* to the consumer's gain is measured by the formula $-(x + \Delta x)\Delta p_x$. The two magnitudes, $-x\Delta p_x$ and $-(x + \Delta x)\Delta p_x$, are known as *cost differences*. We will have occasion to make much further use of these concepts in Chapter 5 when we study the "indifference" analysis of demand.

Somewhere between these two magnitudes lies the true measure of his gain. We cannot on the basis of our data determine the true amount of his gain, and this is, of course, why no "true" index numbers have been invented. Conceivably, however, by making additional assumptions about his behavior pattern, we may be able to approximate the gain somewhat more closely.[4]

In the *Principles,* in explaining the effect of a price change, Alfred Marshall said that he was assuming the marginal utility of "money" constant. Now *just what is meant by the concept of "marginal utility"?* Our next task is to develop the meaning of this idea.

"Marginal Utility" and "Total Change in Total Utility"

The concept of a marginal quantity is probably the most important quantitative one in the field of economics. Yet, this quantity is peculiarly difficult to define in words because a distinction must be made between that concept which is defined as a *marginal quantity* and the concept of a *total change in a total quantity.* This distinction appears clearly in the work of neoclassical writers such as Stanley Jevons and Alfred Marshall, but most modern writers do not emphasize it. Henry Schultz consti-

---

[4] See, for example, my article, "Marshall and Slutsky on the Theory of Demand," *Canadian Journal of Economics and Political Science,* Vol. XXVII (May, 1961), pp. 176–91; or Appendix B, where I have suggested use of the arithmetic average of the cost differences as a measure of the gain for small price changes.

tuted a notable exception.[5] The distinction is important for a complete understanding of much of price theory. Formal definitions of these concepts will first be provided. They will then be explained graphically in terms of Figures 3–1 and 3–3.

Marginal utility (marginal quantity) *is defined as the rate of change of total utility* (total quantity) *as purchasing power* (independent variable) *changes. The total change in total utility is defined as the change in total utility which corresponds to a GIVEN* (not necessarily a [one] unit) *change in purchasing power.* Clearly, these are two different concepts. These two concepts will be numerically the same if the *given* change happens to be equal to unity (or one), but even in this case the meaning of the two concepts is different. These concepts will now be explained.

In terms of Figure 3–1, the *marginal utility* of income is the *rate of change* of total utility as income or purchasing power changes at a given point, say at *A*. That is, it is the instantaneous or *exact rate of change* and is often represented by the symbol du/dm when the units of measurement are infinitesimally small. In terms of geometry it may be defined as the *tangent* to the curve at the same point, *A,* in Figure 3–1. The *marginal utility of income* at *A,* is, however, *not the same thing as the total change in the total utility of income* between points *A* and *B* or *A* and *C* in Figure 3–1. The *total change in the total utility of income* between, say, *A* and *B* in Figure 3–1 *is the marginal utility of income multiplied by the total change in purchasing power* (or by Δm) between the two positions, and it is the vertical distance from u to $u + 2.3$. Thus the *total change in the total utility of income is the differential increment,* and it has the formula $(du/dm)\Delta m$. Clearly, $du/dm = (du/dm)\Delta m$ only if $\Delta m = 1$.

The student who is inexperienced in the use of mathematical formulations of ideas because the symbols and the terminology are new to him need not retract in horror from the preceding paragraphs. Mathematical symbols and graphs are, of course, only pictures of ideas, and it may comfort him to know that the author of this textbook understands and sympathizes with his plight.

What, after all, is the meaning of the tangent? It is simply the slope

[5] Marshall, *op. cit.,* Mathematical Notes I and II, pp. 838–39, uses the term "marginal *degree* of utility" to mean what today is defined as "marginal utility." Marshall uses "marginal utility" to mean "total change in total utility." Henry Schultz, *The Theory and Measurement of Demand* (Chicago: University of Chicago Press, 1938), n. 17, p. 14, suggested the same usage. J. B. Clark, *The Distribution of Wealth* (New York: The Macmillan Co., 1900), followed Jevons and used the term "final degree of utility" to refer to the concept today known as "marginal utility."

of the total utility curve in Figure 3–1 at point *A,* and the derivative, du/dm, is in reality the value of the ratio $\Delta u/\Delta m$ as Δm approaches zero, or as the distance between the two points A' and B' approaches zero, which is another way of saying it becomes infinitesimally small.

As a matter of fact, the ratio $\Delta u/\Delta m$ is the *average rate of change*

Figure 3–3

COMPARISON OF THE EXACT AND AVERAGE RATES OF CHANGE

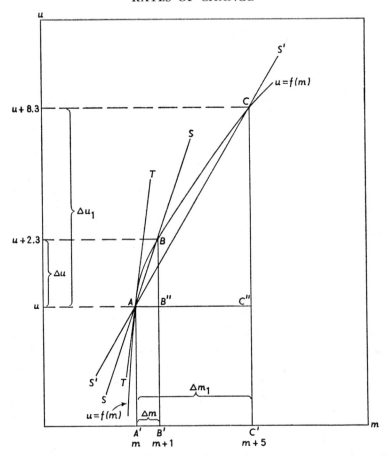

of total utility (*u*) as purchasing power (*m*) changes between any two points, say between A' and B' in Figure 3–1. This point can be made clear by reference to Figure 3–3, which contains a detailed freehand (not drawn fully to scale in the interest of graphical clarity) depiction of the boxed-in section pictured in Figure 3–1.

In Figure 3–3 we see that the line *TT* is tangent to the total utility curve at A, and that TT *touches* the curve only at point A, while the line SS is the *secant,* a line which *intersects* the curve at A and at B. Thus the slopes of TT and SS are different. Now the distance $A'B' = AB''$ is the change in m, or Δm, and represents one unit of m between the two points A' and B'; and the distance $B''B$ is the change in u, or Δu, between the two points B'' and B, which corresponds to the change in m between A' and B'.

Thus, $\Delta u/\Delta m = B''B/AB''$. The numerical values *written* in Figures 3–1 and 3–3 are comparable. Now the value of m at A is m, while the value of m at B'' is $m + 1$. And so, we have $\Delta m = (m + 1) - m = 1$. Also, since the value of u at A is u, and the value of u at B is $u + 2.3$, we have for the change in u, $\Delta u = (u + 2.3) - u = 2.3$. Thus the ratio $\Delta u/\Delta m = 2.3/1 = 2.3$. And this would be the slope of the line SS in Figure 3–3 if it were drawn exactly to scale.

Now the slope of the line TT is greater with respect to the m or X axis than is the slope of the line SS. Thus it is clear that the marginal utility of income decreases between the two points, or that the exact rate of change $(du/dm = 2.5)$ at A is somewhat greater than the average rate of change $(\Delta u/\Delta m = 2.3)$ between A and B. This is merely another way of saying that the total utility curve becomes flatter in Figure 3–3 with respect to the m or X axis as the quantity of m increases (as we move to the right on the m or X axis). This quality has an economic meaning, but we shall postpone consideration of it until later in this chapter.

For the present, note that the slope of the line SS is the average slope of the curve segment between the points A and B only. In fact, in terms of the total quantities and scale of Figure 3–1, the curve segment AB actually looks like the straight line, SS. Thus, by assuming that the units are very small, we will often be able to make use of the concept of an average rate of change, that is, to treat segments of our curves as if they were straight lines. And, in so doing, *we will be able to avoid the use of complicated mathematical operations in this book.* Use of the exact rate of change at A would require us to know the equation of the curve, and this will not generally be the case in fact. Use of the average rate of change implies merely that we know the coordinates of the two points, A and B.

Most especially in the case of the theory of demand it will be more reasonable for us to assume that we have or can obtain data for the quantities a consumer purchases at two different prices than to assume that we know or can obtain data for his entire demand curve. Price theory, after all, employs the method of comparative statics, and this method, as we already know, involves generally the comparison of two (equilibrium) positions.

Further inspection of Figure 3–3 reveals that the line $S'S'$ is a poorer approximation to the total utility curve drawn through ABC than is the line SS to the shorter curve segment, AB, for between A' and C', m changes by five units.

Let us define the *ratio* $\Delta u/\Delta m$ as the *marginal utility of income*. Thus we cannot define the *total change in total utility* in Figure 3–3 equal to $\Delta u_1 = C''C$, which is produced by the *given* change in purchasing power equal to $A'C'$ in the same way, for the *total change in total utility is a distance* on the Y axis which corresponds to a change in purchasing power equal to $A'C'$, and *not a ratio*.

Thus, in the case of Figure 3–3, the *distance* $C''C$ is equal to $(\Delta u/\Delta m)\Delta m_1 = \Delta u_1$. Now, $\Delta m_1 = A'C' = (m+5) - m = 5$, and we have already determined that $\Delta u/\Delta m$ between A and B is 2.3. Thus we have as a first approximation: $C''C = (\Delta u/\Delta m)\Delta m_1 = \Delta u_1 = (2.3)(5) = 11.5$. However, we are dealing with a very large change in the present case. Moreover, we have used the average rate of change between A and B in the above calculation, and we know that the rate is less at B than at A, and less at C than at B. In fact, by construction in Figure 3–3, we have for the distance $C''C$: $\Delta u_1 = (u + 8.3) - u = 8.3$. Accordingly, we know that between A and C, $\Delta u/\Delta m = 8.3/5 = 1.66$. This number is *the average rate of change* of total utility as income changes between the two positions, A and C. The quantity $\Delta u_1 = 8.3$ is the differential increment, the total change which corresponds to the *given* change of $5m$ between A' and C'. When we used the rate of change corresponding to the change of one m between A' and B' in our calculation, we overstated this total change considerably because the rate of change decreases as the quantity of purchasing power or of income increases.

Now since the marginal utility corresponding to the change in m between A' and C' in Figures 3–1 and 3–3 is 1.66, while that between A' and B' is 2.3, it is clear that we have not assumed that the marginal utility is constant along our curve. For the marginal utility of income is less between A and C than it is between A and B. Thus, the marginal utility of income *decreases,* for 2.3 is greater than 1.66, or symbolically, $\Delta u_{ab}/\Delta m > \Delta u_{ac}/\Delta m$.

A summary statement of the two definitions which have been given in this section will be useful: the *marginal quantity means the rate of change,* exact or average, depending on the circumstances of the analysis, of the relevant dependent variable as the independent variable changes $(\Delta u/\Delta m)$. The *total change in the dependent variable is the rate of change of the dependent variable multiplied by the total change in the independent variable*, or $\Delta u_1 = (\Delta u/\Delta m)\Delta m_1$, where Δm_1 is *not* necessarily equal to unity or *one*.

The Total Quantity

The total utility curve, $OABC$, in Figure 3–1 has the symbolic representation, $u = f(m)$. Of course $m = f(M,P)$ also. What this means is merely that the dependent variable, u, is a function of, or depends on, the independent variable, m. Now, in the case in which total utility is a function of only one variable, it should be obvious that the sum of all the changes in the dependent variable produced by all the units of the independent variable up to a certain point must equal the total quantity. The distance $C''C$ has been treated above (in Figure 3–3) as if it were made up of the sum of five quantities of utility, each 1.66 units large. In fact, however, the distance $A'B'$ is included *within* the distance $A'C'$ in Figure 3–3, and we know that $B''B = 2.3u$. Thus it follows that if the marginal utility of income decreases, the utility of the fifth unit of purchasing power in the quantity $A'C'$ must be considerably less than 2.3. Obviously they cannot all be equal to 2.3, for we have computed the average as 1.66.

In Figure 3–1, the vertical distance $C'C$ is made up similarly of the sums of all the marginal utilities of income from O to C'. The curve $OABC$ has been drawn upon the assumption that the first unit of purchasing power has a greater utility than does any succeeding unit, for it flattens out as m increases. In Figure 3–1, if the curve had been drawn as a straight line from O to C, the assumption would have been that each unit of purchasing power had equal utility, or that the marginal utility of income was *constant*.

The assumption that the marginal utility of income decreases as income increases is the theoretical basis of progressive income taxation. The argument in support of such a tax policy is that since the marginal utility of income is less at high levels of income than at low levels, sacrifices of greater amounts of purchasing power by the rich in the form of higher taxes will, nevertheless, result in proportional sacrifices of satisfaction, or of utility. In this sense the rich can afford to pay more taxes than the poor. But the argument needs to be qualified, as we will see shortly.

A similar argument has been recently invoked by Professor Galbraith in support of his position that an affluent society can afford to increase its investments in the social sector via increased public expenditures at the expense of increased production of goods, gadgets, and gimmicks.[6] In the *Principles,* in Mathematical Note II, Marshall clearly stated his belief that the marginal "degree of" utility of income decreases. However, contemporary demand theory, which relies largely on quite complicated methods of analysis to be explained in a later chapter, denies that any statements can be made about the behavior of this magnitude. In general, its authors have wished to avoid "subjectivity" and believe that utility is not measureable. Paradoxically, most of these writers have supported the idea of progressive income taxation which rests upon the same notion. The attempt to escape measurable utility is an attempt to avoid making value judgments. But now and then, in one context or another, we all assume that utility is roughly measurable and make value judgments. And so we may as well face up to that fact.

The Average Quantity: The Average-Marginal Relationship

The *average quantity, u/m,* must be sharply distinguished from the *average rate of change* of the quantity, or the marginal quantity, $\Delta u/\Delta m$. In Figure 3–1, when the consumer has OA' units of purchasing power, the *average quantity* is equal to the ratio $A'A/OA'$, and it is the slope of the line OA. The average quantity may change, and whether or not it does depends on the behavior of the marginal quantity. Thus, in Figure 3–1, the slope of the line OC is less than the slope of the line OA (with respect to the m or X axis), indicating that the average quantity also decreases in that case.

The marginal quantity has been defined as the *average* (or per unit) *rate of change* of the dependent variable as the independent variable changes. Thus, *if* the marginal utility at A in Figure 3–1 is *less* than the average utility of OA' units of m, since the addition to total utility resulting from a (one) unit increase in m between A and B will be less than the preceding average, average utility will *decrease* as m increases.

In Figure 3–4, the curves of average utility and of marginal utility are both depicted. The average quantity, u/m, decreases (the curve u/m slopes down and to the right) as we move to the right along the m axis, because the marginal quantity is *less* than the average quantity. That is, the marginal curve lies *below* the average curve. The relationship between an average quantity and the marginal quantity is thus *asymmetrical,* for it is concerned with the *direction of movement of*

---

[6] J. K. Galbraith, *The Affluent Society* (Boston: Houghton Mifflin Co., 1958), pp. 251–356.

the average quantity and the relative magnitudes of the average and the marginal quantities.

A simple example can make this relationship more clear. If a student receives a grade of 50 points on his first hour price theory examination, his total points on all examinations taken is 50, and his average grade is 50. If on his second examination he earns a grade of 70, he has added 70 points to his total, and his new total of points is now 120. The grade of 70 points on the second examination is the marginal grade, and his average after the second examination is 60—it has increased. The superficial reason why his average grade has increased is

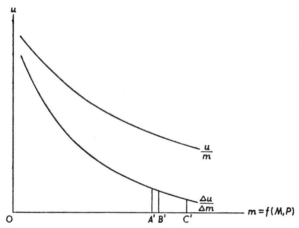

Figure 3–4

**CURVES OF THE MARGINAL AND AVERAGE
UTILITY OF INCOME**

that the addition to his total from the second examination, the marginal grade, is greater than the preceding average. In short, his total points on examinations are increasing more than proportionately.

Suppose now that on his third hour examination he earns a grade of 60. The marginal grade is now 60, and it is the same as his preceding average of 60. Thus his total is now increasing proportionately. The marginal grade and the average are equal, and the average does not change.

Finally, suppose that on his fourth hour examination he receives a grade of 40. His total points are now $50 + 70 + 60 + 40 = 220$, and his average grade is $220/4 = 55$. His average has decreased because the marginal grade after the fourth examination was *less* than the preceding average. His total points have increased less than proportionately. It is *not the direction of movement* of the marginal quantity *which controls, but the relationship between the magnitudes* of the marginal and the average quantity. Additions to the total (the marginal quantity) operate either to pull up the average, or to bring it down, or to keep it constant (unchanged). In the case of Figure 3–4 the marginal quantity is consistently less than the average, and so the average quantity decreases consistently. It happens, in Figure 3–4, that the marginal quantity is also consistently decreasing, but that is another matter.

B. MORE COMPLEX CONCEPTS

Two or More Variables

In our analysis it will often be necessary to consider functions involving two or more variables. Suppose that instead of assuming that total utility depends on, or is a function of, a single variable, purchasing power, i.e., $u = f(m)$, as we have done in the case of Figure 3–1, we had assumed that total utility depended on the quantities of all the commodities on which the given purchasing power was spent. In this case, we would have been making utility a function of a number of different variables, i.e., $u = f(x, y, \ldots n)$. However, our concepts of a marginal quantity and of the total change in the total quantity can be extended to cover such cases without great difficulty. A case involving two commodities can be depicted graphically as in Figure 3–5, but a case involving more than two commodities cannot be depicted graphically.

Consider Figure 3–5. This figure is a three-dimensional diagram showing total utility, or u, as a function of the quantities of x and of y possessed or purchased. Thus u is measured as an *elevation* in this diagram, while quantities of x and of y are measured in the *base plane, YOX*. Movements to the right from the origin along the X axis represent increases in the commodity, x. Movements to the left from the origin along the Y axis represent increases in the commodity, y.

Next consider the curve labeled $u = f(x, y = 0)$. This curve shows how u varies as x changes when y is zero. At P' on the former curve, $X_0 P'$ is the total utility obtained from OX_0 units of x and no units of y. At P'', $Y_0 P''$ is the utility obtained from OY_0 units of y and no units of x. At P_0, in the center of the diagram, the vertical distance, $X_0 Y_0 P_0$, represents the utility obtained from OY_0 units of y and OX_0 units of x. Note that P_0 is the intersection of one of the curves which shows how total utility changes as y changes when x is constant at a given level, with one of the curves which shows how total utility changes when x changes and y is constant at some given level. Thus u (the elevation) depends both on x and y.

The slopes of such curves at the points P', P'', and P_0 are, of course, the same as those of the tangents to these curves, and the meaning of any of these tangents is the same as the meaning we gave to the tangent in our discussion of Figure 3–1 earlier, that is, it is the slope of the curve at a point.

Figure 3–5

UTILITY AS A FUNCTION OF TWO VARIABLES

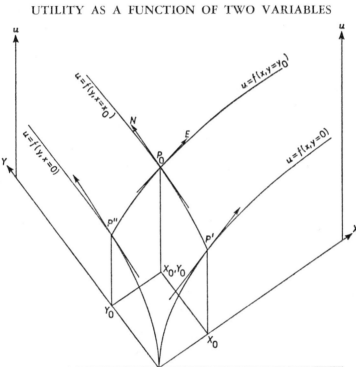

Thus at P', the tangent to the curve indicated by the arrow represents the relevant slope of the curve $u = f(x, y = 0)$, and at P_0, the arrow, P_0E, represents the relevant slope of the curve $u = f(x, y = y_0)$. We could symbolize the average slope at P_0, or the average rate of change of u as x changes, *when y is assumed constant,* by writing, $\Delta u / \Delta x_{,y\ =\ constant}$, or $\Delta u / \Delta x_{,y\ =\ k}$, to show that we were concerned with the average rate of change of u under these conditions. Thus, $y = k$ *means "y remains constant."* In general, the exact rate of

change is identified by the symbol $\partial u/\partial x$, the symbol of a partial derivative. In terms of our previous analysis, such a symbol merely represents the marginal utility of x when all other variables are assumed
constant at some given level. Similarly, the symbol $\partial u/\partial y$ represents
the marginal utility of y, or the change in u, when y alone changes at
different levels of x. Terms such as f_x and f_y or u'_x and u'_y are also

Figure 3–6

A CHANGE IN TOTAL UTILITY IN THE TWO-VARIABLE CASE

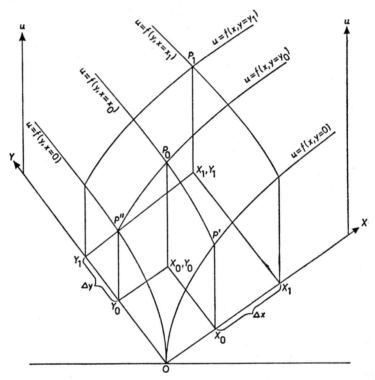

often used to designate such partial derivatives. These symbols need not
alarm the student when he encounters them in the literature. They
merely designate the exact rate of change in one variable as another
given variable changes when all other variables are held constant, or,
in the language of economics, in our case, the respective marginal
utilities of x and of y.

Now if both x and y change, the *total change* in u will be different
from what it will be if only one variable changes. In Figure 3–6, consider the effect on u of a change in y from Y_0 to Y_1 and of a simultaneous change in x from X_0 to X_1. This change involves a change in
u from P_0 to P_1. And since P_1 is at a higher elevation than P_0 in our

diagram, u has increased as a result of the increases in both x and y. *Such a change in u is approximately equal to the sum of the change in u produced by the change in x alone and the change in u produced by the change in y alone.* Symbolically we have

$$\Delta u = \frac{\partial u}{\partial x}\Delta x + \frac{\partial u}{\partial y}\Delta y = u'_{x_0}\Delta x + u'_{y_0}\Delta y . \tag{3-2}$$

This equation states the total change in u resulting from simultaneous changes in x and y. The total change in u is thus taken as approximately equal to the sum of the changes in u produced by each of the variables separately, when the other is assumed constant.[7]

An Arithmetical Illustration of a Two-Variable Case

Assume that we actually know the form of the utility function depicted in Figures 3–5 and 3–6 and that it is

$$u = f(x,y) = (ax - bx^2) + (a'y - b'y^2) .$$

Assume further that in this equation $a = 50$, $b = 1$, $a' = 30$, and $b' = 2$. Then our function would read:

$$u = (50x - x^2) + (30y - 2y^2) .$$

Also assume that $OX_0 = x_0 = 1.25$ units of x in Figures 3–5 and 3–6. In the case in which $u = f(x, y = 0)$, we would have $u = 50x - x^2 + 0$. Thus, if the consumer had $OX_0 = x_0 = 1.25$ units of x and *no* y in Figure 3–6, the total utility of his income would be equal to X_0P'. According to our function, we would have $X_0P' = 50x - x^2 + 0 = (50)(1.25) - (1.25^2) = 60.94$. Now assume $OY_0 = y_0 = 1.5$. If the consumer had $OY_0 = y_0 = 1.5$ units of y and *no* x, the total utility of his income would be equal to Y_0P''. According to our function, we would then have $Y_0P'' = 30y - 2y^2 + 0 = (30)(1.5) - (2)(1.5^2) = 40.50$. Our diagrams have not been drawn to scale according to these functions, although they have been drawn in perspective.

Next consider point X_0Y_0 in the base plane YOX in Figures 3–5 and 3–6. The utility of OX_0 of x and of OY_0 of y *together* is $X_0Y_0P_0$. Making use of our assumed utility function, we have the *total* utility of income obtained from $OX_0 = 1.25$ units of x *and* from $OY_0 = 1.5$ units of y or the *elevation*, $X_0Y_0P_0$, as

$$X_0Y_0P_0 = (50)(1.25) - (1.25^2) + (30)(1.5) - (2)(1.5^2)$$
$$= 60.94 + 40.50 = 101.44 .$$

---

[7] See R. G. D. Allen, *Mathematical Analysis for Economists* (London: Macmillan & Co., Ltd., 1950), pp. 326–30, for a derivation of the equation.

Assume now that $OX_1 = x_1 = 3.00$ and $OY_1 = y_1 = 2.75$ or that $\Delta x = x_1 - x_0 = 1.75$ and $\Delta y = y_1 - y_0 = 1.25$. We can compute the total utility obtained at P_1 from $OX_1 = 3.00$ units of x and from $OY_1 = 2.75$ units of y or the *elevation*, $X_1Y_1P_1$, as

$$X_1Y_1P_1 = (50)(3) - (3^2) + (30)(2.75) - (2)(2.75^2)$$
$$= 141.00 + 67.38 = 208.38 .$$

Note that P_1 lies at the intersection of two curves, along one of which y remains constant as x changes and along the other of which x remains constant as y changes. In our example, P_1 lies at the intersection of the two curves, $u = f(x, y_1 = 2.75)$ and $u = f(y, x_1 = 3)$. *Each curve could be plotted in two dimensions* by allowing one of the variables to assume different values, while the other was assumed constant at the given level. (See e.g. Figure 6–1.) The elevation, $X_1Y_1P_1$, can thus be determined by making use of either of these equations.

Now *the movement from P_0 to P_1 in Figure 3–6 results from increases in both x and y.* We have assumed that $OX_1 - OX_0 = \Delta x = 1.75$ and that $OY_1 - OY_0 = \Delta y = 1.25$. We have learned that the total change in total utility between P_0 and P_1 is $X_1Y_1P_1 - X_0P_0Y_0 = 208.38 - 101.44 = 106.94$. That part of the *total change* in total utility resulting from the *change* in x when y is held constant is equal to $141.00 - 60.94 = 80.06$. That part of the *total change* resulting from the *change* in y when x is held constant is equal to $67.38 - 40.50 = 26.88$. *The total change is the sum of these two changes,* or $\Delta u = 80.06 + 26.88 = 106.94 = X_1Y_1P_1 - X_0Y_0P_0$. This result can be obtained by using Equation (3–2), if we let u'_x and u'_y represent average rates of change, or

$$\Delta u = u'_x \Delta x + u'_y \Delta y = (45.748)(1.75) + (21.423)(1.25) = 106.94 . \quad (3\text{-}2')$$

Euler's Theorem

One special case deserves brief notice at this point, although we will not illustrate it arithmetically until Chapter 6. *In the special case* in which proportionate changes in x and y produce a proportionate change in u, for example, if when x and y are doubled, u is also doubled, so that in our diagram we would have $OY_1 = (2)(OY_0)$ and $OX_1 = (2)(OX_0)$ and $X_1Y_1P_1 = (2)(X_0Y_0P_0)$, the function is *linearly homogeneous* or homogeneous of the first degree.

In the case of such a linearly homogeneous function, a mathematical theorem called Euler's Theorem can be employed. It is written:

$$u = \frac{\partial u}{\partial x}x + \frac{\partial u}{\partial y}y . \quad (3\text{-}3)$$

This equation is really a statement that in such a case, total utility at any given point, say at P_0, is equal to the product of the marginal utility of x multiplied by the *number* of units of x, plus the product of the marginal utility of y multiplied by the *number* of units of y.[8] Note that this theorem is *different* from the proposition stated in Equation (3–2) above. In fact, our diagrams do not meet the condition for application of Euler's Theorem, but in Chapter 6, graphical and arithmetical illustrations of the theorem will be provided. For the mo-

Figure 3–7

A CONTOUR MAP

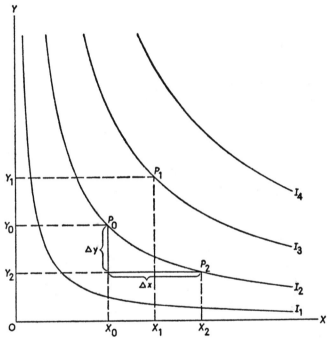

ment, let us merely note again that the proposition stated in Equation (3–2) explains *changes in output produced by changes in input,* while Euler's Theorem in Equation (3–3) refers to the *division of total output.*

Contour Lines

In Figure 3–7 is depicted a family of *contour* lines. Such lines represent combinations of x and y which produce equal elevations along the u axis in Figures 3–5 and 3–6. By making use of contour lines, we can dispense with three dimensions in our graphs and employ only

[8] *Ibid.*, pp. 315–20.

two dimensions. Thus Figure 3–7 contains the information which might appear in a three-dimensional graph but states that information in two dimensions. All points along I_2 represent points of equal elevation, and since P_0 lies on I_2, all points along I_2, such as P_2, have the same elevation as P_0 in Figures 3–5, 3–6, and 3–7. Similarly, P_1 lies on I_3, which represents a contour line showing points having higher elevations than those on I_2. We will make considerable use of families of contour lines in our subsequent explanations of the contemporary theories of demand and of production.

Consider now the meaning of such a contour line.[9] Along such a contour line the elevation is a constant by definition. This means, of course, that u is constant along such a line, and that, therefore, there is no change in u (or that $\Delta u = 0$ along the contour line) when x and y change, and there is a movement from P_0 to P_2. Consequently, the equation of such a contour line is simply a special case of our Equation (3–2), such that $\Delta u = 0$. Accordingly, we can write the equation of the contour line as

$$\Delta u = 0 = \frac{\partial u}{\partial x}\Delta x + \frac{\partial u}{\partial y}\Delta y = u'_x\Delta x + u'_y\Delta y \ . \qquad (3\text{–}4)$$

Clearly if u'_x and u'_y are both positive (which means that both are greater than zero and so have plus signs) when $\Delta u = 0$, either Δx or Δy must be negative (have a minus sign) while the other is positive. Otherwise the sum of the two terms on the right would not be equal to zero. In Figure 3–7 we see that the movement from P_0 to P_2 along I_2 in fact involves an increase in x (that is, $\Delta x > 0$) and a decrease in y (or $\Delta y < 0$). Thus, Δx is positive and Δy is negative.

Movements from One Contour Line to Another

Since the elevations of different contour lines are different, it is clear that the condition that u remains constant, or that Δu is zero, does not apply to movements from one contour line to another, such as that from P_0 to P_1 in Figure 3–7. Equation (3–2), or

$$\Delta u = u'_x\Delta x + u'_y\Delta y \ , \qquad (3\text{–}2)$$

is thus really an explanation of movements from one contour line to another, while the case in which $\Delta u = 0$, or Equation (3–4), which is concerned with movements *along* a contour line, is merely a special case of this equation.

---

[9] *Ibid.,* pp. 334–36.

The Principle of Diminishing Marginal Utility

A number of early writers, including an Englishman, Jeremy Bentham (1843), a French engineer, Dupuit (1831), and a German economist, Herman Gossen (1854), stated clearly the concept of diminishing marginal utility.[10] In general, *the principle of diminishing marginal utility can be briefly stated: The satisfaction acquired from additions to one's stock of a good diminishes,* or total utility from purchases (or consumption) of a given commodity increases at a decreasing rate as the quantity of the commodity purchased increases, and may eventually decrease absolutely.

The total quantity curve in Figure 3–1 thus assumes diminishing marginal utility of income, for it becomes flatter as purchasing power increases. Similarly, the curves exemplified by the equations $u = f(x, y = 0)$ and $u = f(y, x = 0)$ in Figure 3–5 also assume diminishing marginal utilities of x and of y, respectively, for they, too, become flatter as x or y respectively increases. These individual curves in Figure 3–5 depict the total utility which is derived *not* from the consumer's total uses of his money income, but from the consumption or purchase of different quantities of a given commodity or service when the quantities of all other goods remain constant. Such curves also reflect whatever assumptions are made about the way in which the satisfaction from *additional* units of the commodity changes. If the satisfaction from additional units of the commodity decreases, the curves look like the curves in Figure 3–5; that is, they become flatter and flatter with respect to the X or Y axis as the quantity of the commodity purchased increases.

It is also possible to draw such curves depicting the utility which is derived from the use of successive quantities of purchasing power in one particular way when prices are constant. In such a case the curves exemplified by $u = f(x, y = 0)$ would be interpreted as curves depicting the satisfaction which is obtained from *additional* units of expenditures on x when expenditures on y are held constant. In such a case also, the X axis would be interpreted as measuring units of purchasing power spent on x rather than units of x directly. A similar interpretation would apply to the family of curves represented by the equation $u = f(y, x = 0)$ and to the Y axis.

The principle of diminishing marginal utility is thought to be a reasonable assumption if one assumes that tastes do not change and

---

[10] See L. H. Haney, *History of Economic Thought* (3rd ed.; New York: The Macmillan Co., 1936).

that everything else remains unchanged as well. According to such an assumption, other things equal, the first cup of coffee which the student drinks at breakfast probably affords him greater satisfaction than he derives from the second at that sitting; the third affords him less satisfaction than the second; the fourth less than the third; and so on. Even if the second tastes better than the first, eventually there must come a point at which another cup of coffee affords little additional satisfaction. Accordingly, although the first cup may in fact afford him a greater amount of satisfaction than he would derive from spending in some other way the amount of purchasing power which is represented by the price of the cup of coffee, eventually, after the third or fourth cup at this sitting, he reaches a point at which he is "satisfied"; that is to say, a point at which the satisfaction which is to be obtained from using in some other way the amount of purchasing power he would have to surrender in order to purchase another cup of coffee exceeds that of the additional cup of coffee. Thus, other things equal, he ceases drinking coffee at this point.

Indeed, in the case of some commodities, it is possible that marginal utility first increases, then diminishes, and eventually becomes negative. And in the case of some items (garbage to the homeowner) marginal utility may even be negative, which is to say that the less he has of it, the less unhappy is the householder. Moreover, curves of the marginal utility of different commodities are different. Some things are more preferred than others; and in the case of some things, the satiation point is reached more quickly than in the case of others. Finally, to the extent that people's tastes differ, the curves of the marginal utility of the same thing for different people will be different.

The utility argument on behalf of progressive income taxation mentioned earlier thus, seemingly, needs to be qualified somewhat because it makes the assumption that the curves of the marginal utility of income of different people are alike and that individuals are merely located at different points on identical curves. One economist, however, has argued that the rational procedure in a society which seeks to maximize total satisfaction is to divide the income on an equalitarian basis on grounds that although a blind shift of income away from larger incomes to smaller incomes is just as likely to increase total satisfaction as it is to decrease total satisfaction (leaving no choice between them), nevertheless, every time a movement is made away from an equalitarian division the probable size of the total loss in satisfaction is greater than the probable size of the gain. Therefore, an equalitarian division of income is probably the one which maximizes total satisfaction. On this basis the utility case for progressive income taxation can be saved.[11] (There are, of course, also other arguments which can be made on behalf of such a tax.)

The basic concepts developed in this chapter will be employed many times in the following pages. Our first use of these concepts appears in Part II, which follows. In Part II we will examine both the Marshallian and the indifference curve explanations of demand.

SELECTED READINGS

ALLEN, R. G. D. *Mathematical Analysis for Economists,* chaps. i–iv. London: Macmillan & Co., Ltd., 1950. See also the specific page references cited in the footnotes in the text of this chapter.

BAUMOL, WILLIAM J. *Economic Theory and Operations Analysis,* chaps. ii–iv. Englewood Cliffs, N.J.: Prentice-Hall, Inc., 1961.

BEACH, E. F. *Economic Models,* pp. 40–47. New York: John Wiley & Sons, Inc., 1957.

BUSHAW, D. W., AND CLOWER, R. W. *Introduction to Mathematical Economics,* chaps. i, viii, and ix. Homewood, Ill.: Richard D. Irwin, Inc., 1957.

GALBRAITH, J. K. *The Affluent Society,* esp. chaps. x–xxv. Boston: Houghton Mifflin Co., 1958.

HENDERSON, JAMES M., AND QUANDT, RICHARD E. *Microeconomic Theory,* chap. i and pp. 262–71. New York: McGraw-Hill Book Co., Inc., 1958.

MARSHALL, ALFRED. *Principles of Economics,* Book III, chap. ii, esp. pp. 92–96 and Mathematical Notes I and II. 8th ed. London: Macmillan & Co., Ltd., 1938.

MILLER, DENNING. "Much Ado about Nothing," pp. 138–215; and "The Brightest Pebble on the Beach," pp. 513–85, *Popular Mathematics.* New York: Coward-McCann, Inc., 1942.

THOMPSON, S. P. *Calculus Made Easy,* esp. chaps. i–iii and x. New York: The Macmillan Co., 1929.

TINTNER, GERHARD. *Mathematics and Statistics for Economists,* pp. 3–16, 28–30, 69–70, and esp. 76–88, 123–25, 128–30, 145–51, and 159–63. New York: Rinehart & Co., Inc., 1953.

---

[11] The argument appears in Abba P. Lerner, *The Economics of Control* (New York: The Macmillan Co., 1946), chap. iii, esp. pp. 28–32.

ELEMENTARY DEMAND
THEORY

4 The Marshallian Theory of Demand

Introduction

Although it is, of course, possible to break into the circular flow diagram of Figure 2–1 at any point to begin our exposition of microeconomic concepts and techniques, traditionally (perhaps because wants have been taken as ultimate data) the starting point has been the theory of demand.

The theory of demand has been greatly refined since the publication of Alfred Marshall's *Principles* in 1890.[1] This chapter explains Marshall's analysis. The next one provides a statement of the same ideas in terms of contemporary indifference curve analysis.

A. BASIC CONCEPTS

The Definition of Demand

Individual consumer demand is defined as the quantities of a given commodity which a consumer will buy at all possible prices at a given moment of time. Thus the term *demand* refers to a *list* or *schedule* of possible price-quantity combinations, and it may be represented graphically by a *curve*. Figure 4–1 depicts a family of demand "curves."

The demand curve is traditionally drawn, or demand is defined, subject to certain assumptions or *parametric constants*. In the case of an individual's demand these are: (1) prices of all other goods are unchanged when the schedule is drawn up; (2) the consumer's *money* income is assumed to be unchanged; and (3) the tastes of the consumer are unchanged. Note that the two assumptions, that (1) the prices of all other goods are unchanged and (2) the consumer's *money* income is unchanged, do not amount to an assumption that his

---

[1] Alfred Marshall, *Principles of Economics* (8th ed.; London: Macmillan & Co., Ltd., 1938), Book III and Mathematical Notes I–III.

purchasing power, or *m,* is unchanged, for *m* changes by $-x\Delta p_x$, the
change in purchasing power when the price of the commodity changes.
In his analysis of the effect of a price change, Marshall employed
partial equilibrium analysis and assumed *"all other things the same"*

Figure 4–1

A FAMILY OF DEMAND "CURVES"

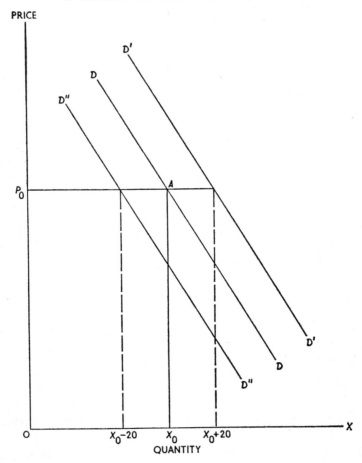

(*ceteris paribus*). The meaning of this assumption will be considered
further later in this chapter.

   Market demand is defined as the quantities of a given commodity
which all consumers will buy at all possible prices at a given moment
of time. Thus the term *market demand* really refers to a schedule or a
list which is produced by summing the demand schedules of individual
consumers. If consumer A will buy five apples when the price is 10

cents each and consumer B will buy seven apples at that price, and if these two constitute the total number of consumers in the problem, the market demand *at that price* is 12 apples, or the sum of the individual demands. The market demand curve is drawn subject to all the assumptions of the individual demand curves and, in addition, it rests on one new one: (4) the number of consumers is assumed unchanged.

A Change in Demand

Since the demand schedule or curve is drawn subject to certain assumptions (or parameters), if any one of these assumptions is changed, the entire schedule must be changed, or the demand curve must be *shifted*. Thus, *the term "a change in demand" refers to a movement of the entire curve.* If the curve shifts to the right, this means that the demand has increased, as indicated by the new position of the curve DD in Figure 4–1. After the demand has increased, the new demand curve is $D'D'$. A decrease in demand is depicted by the shift of the curve DD to the left to $D''D''$. And so (1) if the consumer's money income increases; or (2) if the prices of other goods decrease, thereby increasing the total amount of purchasing power available to the consumer without a change in the price of the given commodity; or (3) if the consumer's tastes change (if he decides he likes this good better than he did before); or (4) if the number of consumers increases, the demand curve may shift to the right to $D'D'$ in Figure 4–1. Next we will consider the case of a movement *along* the demand curve.

Definition of "Quantity Demanded" or "Amount Purchased"

The effect of the limiting assumptions subject to which the demand curve is drawn is presumably to make the *quantity demanded* or the *amount purchased* a function of the price of the given commodity alone. *Thus the term "quantity demanded" or the terms "amount purchased" or "purchases" refer to movements along a given demand curve. The curve is not shifted when the amount purchased changes.* In Figure 4–2, if the price decreases by Δp from OP to OP' while the quantity increases by Δx from OX to OX', the "amount purchased" has increased by XX'. Thus a change in the "quantity demanded" refers to a movement *along* the given demand curve.

The Concept of "Point" Price Elasticity of Demand

Price elasticity is the name given to a measure of the responsiveness of a buyer or of buyers to price changes. This measure was developed by Marshall in order to provide a method of comparing the responsive-

ness of a buyer to changes in the prices of different commodities. It is
a *relative* not an *absolute* measure, for if it were stated in an absolute
form such comparisons would not be possible. (A *relative measure* is
stated in *percent;* an *absolute measure* is stated in *units* of something.)

The *"point"* (at a point on the demand curve) *price elasticity of demand is defined as the negative of the rate of percentage change in*

Figure 4–2

A CHANGE IN THE QUANTITY DEMANDED

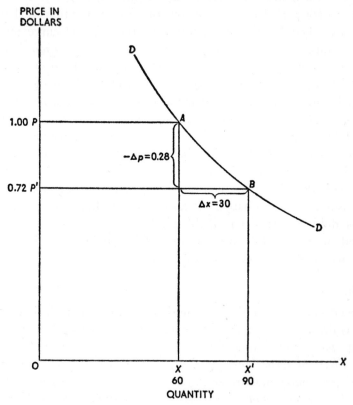

purchases divided by the rate of percentage change in price, and this
definition results in the formula

$$E_d = -\frac{p}{x}\frac{\partial x}{\partial p}.\qquad(4\text{–}1)$$

Note that since a *point* on a given demand curve is involved, the
exact rate of change, $\partial x/\partial p$, is used in the formula. The minus sign
is attached since in the case of negatively sloped demand curves, which
are thought to be the most usual kind in the real world, and which
have the characteristic $\Delta p\Delta x < 0$, the measure would otherwise be

negative. (The proposition $\Delta p \Delta x < 0$ means that Δp and Δx have opposite signs since their product is negative.)

In practice, *arc* price elasticity formulas rather than point elasticity formulas are generally employed. The former employ small finite changes in prices and quantities. How an arc price elasticity may be defined will be discussed as soon as the classification of elasticities has been explained. Arc price elasticity formulas measure elasticity over a range of, rather than at a given point on, the demand curve. Thus they measure the elasticity *between* A and B in Figure 4–2 rather than the elasticity *at* A or B.

The Classification of Elasticities

The case of *unitary price elasticity* [when the formula in Equation (4–1) produces a result of unity or (1)] *has been* conventionally *selected as a* convenient *dividing line in the classification of commodities on the basis of their price elasticity.* Commodities whose price elasticity is *greater than unity* (i.e., the formula produces a number *greater than one*) are said to have an *elastic demand.* Those whose price elasticity is *less than unity* (if the formula produces a number *smaller than one*) are said to have an *inelastic demand.* It is misleading to say as students sometimes do, "The elasticity of demand is elastic"; or "The elasticity of demand is inelastic." Such statements are more properly rephrased: "The elasticity of demand is greater than unity," or "The demand is elastic"; and "The elasticity of demand is less than unity," or "The demand is inelastic."

The relationship between this conventional classification and the behavior of total expenditures on the commodity is important, and it will be examined in detail as soon as we have defined the concept of "arc" price elasticity.

The Concept of "Arc" Elasticity of Demand

Since *arc* price elasticity formulas are concerned with measuring the elasticity *over a range* of the demand curve rather than *at a point* on it, they are concerned with finite changes in the price and quantity. One possibility (and some writers employ it) is, of course, simply to write the arc price elasticity formula as a direct counterpart of the point elasticity formula, or as

$$E_d = -\frac{p}{x}\frac{\Delta x}{\Delta p}. \tag{4-2}$$

This formula, however, is ambiguous since it is possible to use the values of p or x at either point A or B in Figure 4–2 in the formula, or any combination of these values, making a total of four possible values for the elasticity.

In order to avoid the ambiguity, some writers have suggested that the smaller p and x values be used in the formula. Others have developed special formulas designed to measure the average elasticity between the two points, such as

$$E_d = - \frac{[p + (p + \Delta p)]/2}{[x + (x + \Delta x)]/2} \frac{\Delta x}{\Delta p} = - \frac{p + (p + \Delta p)}{x + (x + \Delta x)} \frac{\Delta x}{\Delta p}. \quad (4\text{--}3)$$

Such formulas, however, do not throw very much light on the question of how total expenditures behave when prices change, and the *economic* reasons for taking such an average are not clear. An alternative formula, which does not suffer from these disadvantages can, however, be written, and the logic of this formula will now be explained. (A full explanation of the economic reasons for the formula appears in Appendix A.)

First, consider the fact that the total amount spent on the commodity in Figure 4–2, when the price is $1.00 or OP, is equal to area $OPAX$. For, as we already know from Chapter 3, this area represents the product of the price (OP) times the quantity (OX).

We have also already learned from our discussion of the budget equation in Chapter 3 that this area can be computed according to the formula px, where p represents the price of the commodity at A and x is the quantity purchased.

Similarly, the total amount spent on the commodity at B after the price change is simply area $OP'BX'$, and it can similarly be computed by multiplying the new price of the commodity ($p + \Delta p$) by the new quantity purchased ($x + \Delta x$). Thus the formula for area $OP'BX'$ is $(p + \Delta p)(x + \Delta x)$.

Further, the *difference* between these two areas—the total amount spent on the commodity in the new position at B and the total amount spent in the original position at A—must be the *total change in the total amount spent* on the commodity. Designate the *total change in the total amount spent* on x by the symbol ΔE. Then we can write:

$$\begin{aligned}
\Delta E &= (p + \Delta p)(x + \Delta x) - px \\
&= px + p\Delta x + x\Delta p + \Delta x \Delta p - px \\
&= p\Delta x + x\Delta p + \Delta x \Delta p,
\end{aligned} \quad (4\text{--}4)$$

and, by adding the terms $p\Delta x + \Delta x \Delta p$ and factoring Δx out of them, we have $p\Delta x + \Delta x \Delta p = (p + \Delta p)\Delta x$. And so,

$$\Delta E = (p + \Delta p)\Delta x + x\Delta p. \quad (4\text{--}4a)$$

Next, by subtracting ΔE and $(p + \Delta p)\Delta x$ from both sides of Equation (4–4a), we have

$$-(p + \Delta p)\Delta x = x\Delta p - \Delta E . \qquad (4\text{-}4a.1)$$

Finally, by dividing both sides of the preceding formulation by $x\Delta p$, we produce

$$E_d = -\frac{(p + \Delta p)\Delta x}{x\Delta p} = \frac{x\Delta p}{x\Delta p} - \frac{\Delta E}{x\Delta p} = 1 - \frac{\Delta E}{x\Delta p} . \qquad (4\text{-}4b)$$

Now, if the numerator of a fraction is zero, the entire fraction reduces to zero. Thus, in the case in which total expenditures on the price changing commodity do not change, since $\Delta E = 0$, the second term on the right in Equation (4–4b) reduces to zero, and the arc elasticity formula reduces to unity. Indeed, our arc elasticity formula produces the same result as would the point elasticity formula in such a case, or $E_d = 1$. The relationship between *changes* in total expenditure and elasticity can be easily understood with the help of Equation (4–4b), and this problem is our next concern.

Relationship between Total Expenditures and Elasticity

We have already seen that the total amount spent for the commodity when its price is OP in Figure 4–2 is the area $OPAX$, for OX is the quantity purchased, and OP is the price. And the total amount spent on the commodity when its price is OP' is $OP'BX'$, for the quantity purchased has increased by $XX' = \Delta x$ as a result of the price decrease. If the elasticity of demand were unity, that is to say, if $E_d = 1$, these two total amounts spent on x would be equal. In such a case $\Delta E = 0$, and the demand curve would *not* look like DD in Figure 4–2; rather it would have the appearance of the curve DD in Figure 4–3 or of a rectangular hyperbola.

A *rectangular hyperbola* is defined as a curve which has the equation $xp = a$, where a is a constant. In words, it is a curve which can be defined as the locus of a point, the product of whose distances (PA and XA) from two fixed perpendicular lines (in Figure 4–3, the X and P axes) is a positive constant, a. Consequently, if p decreases, x must increase in an offsetting way so that a, the total amount spent on x, will not change. In Figure 4–3, therefore, we would have $OPAX = OP'BX'$, for $OPAX$ is the same as the constant a in the equation. Or, making use of our continuing arithmetical example, if $px = (\$1.00)(60) = \$60$ and $(p + \Delta p)(x + \Delta x) = (\$.72)(83.33) = \$60$, $E_d = 1$. In none of the other diagrams is this the case.

In the case of unitary price elasticity, when the signs are ignored, the rate of *percentage* change in quantity is equal to the rate of *percentage* change in price, but this does not require that the *absolute* change in quantity be equal to the *absolute* change in price. In short, the elasticity is *not* measured by the relevant slope of the demand curve ($\Delta x/\Delta p$), although the relevant slope of the curve is a part of the elasticity formula. *When the price elasticity of demand is unity, total expendi-*

Figure 4–3

A RECTANGULAR HYPERBOLA AS AN ILLUSTRATION OF UNITARY PRICE ELASTICITY

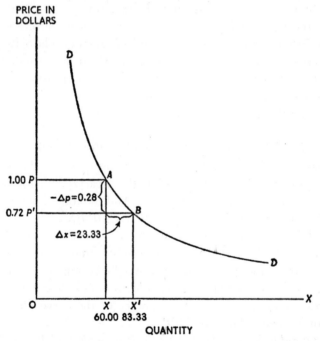

tures (*a* in the formula for a rectangular hyperbola) *on the commodity remain constant as price declines and also when it rises.* For this is the meaning of the condition stated by the formula $xp = a$. Moreover, when the elasticity of demand is unity, the demand curve *must* have a negative slope, for if p declines x must increase, or their product would not remain constant.

If the demand is inelastic, the total amount spent on the commodity decreases when price declines and increases when price rises. For in this case, when signs are ignored, the rate of percentage change in quantity is less than the rate of percentage change in price. Or, as before, if the amount spent in the old position at A were $px = (\$1.00)$ $(60) = \$60$, while the amount spent in the new position were $(p + \Delta p) (x + \Delta x) = (\$.72) (80.00) = \$57.60$, then, $E_d < 1$.

In terms of our elasticity formula,

$$E_d = 1 - \frac{\Delta E}{x \Delta p}, \qquad\qquad \text{(4-4b)}$$

and we would have the arithmetical result in this assumed case as

$$E_d = 1 - \frac{-\$2.40}{(60)(-\$.28)} = 1 - .14 = .86 . \qquad \text{(4-4b')}$$

Note that in this case we have $\Delta E = \$57.60 - \$60.00 = -\$2.40$, and, thus, total expenditures on x have decreased, or ΔE is negative. Since price has declined, Δp is negative. The result is that the fraction, which constitutes the second term on the right, is positive (for a minus value divided into a minus value yields a plus value), but it is subtracted from unity, producing $E_d = .86 < 1$.

Finally, *if the demand is elastic, the total amount spent on the commodity increases when price declines and decreases when the price rises.* In this case, when signs are ignored, the rate of percentage change in quantity is greater than the rate of percentage change in price; or, if the total amount spent on x at A were again $px = (\$1.00)$ $(60) = \$60$, while the amount spent at B were $(p + \Delta p) (x + \Delta x) = (\$.72) (90) = \$64.80$, $E_d > 1$.

Again, in terms of our elasticity formula, we would have

$$E_d = 1 - \frac{\$4.80}{(60)(-\$.28)} = 1 + .2857 = 1.2857 . \qquad \text{(4-4b'')}$$

In this case we have $\Delta E = \$64.80 - \$60.00 = \$4.80$, a positive number. Thus, if price declines and total expenditures on x increase, the elasticity is greater than unity, or $E_d = 1.29 > 1$.

The Use of the Elasticity Formula

Since we have determined in Equation (4-4b'') that the elasticity of demand in that assumed case would be 1.29, we also know that a 1 percent decrease in the price of x will increase purchases of x by 1.29 percent. Thus, if the price of x declines by $\$.28$ to $\$.72$ when the consumer is at A, the total decline in price will be $\Delta p/(p + \Delta p) = \$.28/\$.72 = 38.88$ percent. Multiplying the total percentage decline in price by the arc price elasticity of x, we have $(1.2857)(38.88) = 50$ percent, as the total percentage increase in purchases of x produced by the price decline. Thus, we finally have $(60x)(.50) = 30x$, as the total change in x resulting from the price decline. The demand is elastic because the percentage change in the quantity (50 percent) is greater than the percentage change in price (38.88 percent).

Infinitely Elastic and Perfectly Inelastic Demands Illustrated

Figure 4–4 illustrates the case of an *infinitely elastic* demand curve, a horizontal line parallel to the X axis. In such a case the consumer will take any amount of x at the current price but will purchase nothing at a

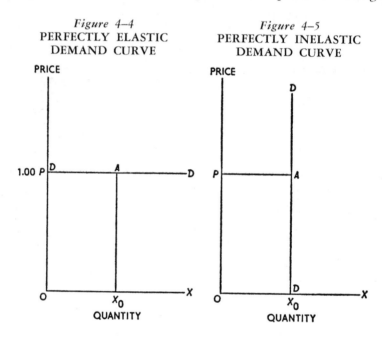

Figure 4–4
PERFECTLY ELASTIC
DEMAND CURVE

Figure 4–5
PERFECTLY INELASTIC
DEMAND CURVE

higher price than this. Presumably an infinitely elastic demand curve involves a situation in which the consumer's purchases of x at the given price are limited only by his income.

Figure 4–5 illustrates the case of a *perfectly inelastic* demand curve, a vertical line parallel to the Y axis. In such a case the consumer purchases the same quantity of x at all possible prices.

These two extremes may be considered to be limiting cases. For, if there is a decrease in the price of a good whose demand is infinitely elastic, presumably the consumer will spend all of the increased purchasing power equal to $-x\Delta p_x$ which results from the price decrease on that commodity. On the other hand, if the demand is perfectly inelastic and the price of x decreases, the consumer will not spend any of the increased purchasing power equal to $-x\Delta p_x$ on x.

Graphical Determination of Point Elasticity

When the demand curve is known, the point elasticity of demand can be determined by means of the formula, or it can be determined graphically. The graphical procedure involves drawing a tangent, AC, to the demand curve DD as shown in Figure 4–6. The ratio of the line segments BC/AB is the elasticity of demand.

The proof of this proposition was first presented by Marshall in Mathematical Note III of the *Principles*. His proof runs along the fol-

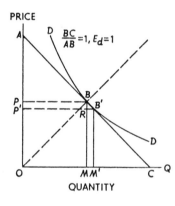

Figure 4–6

GRAPHICAL ANALYSIS
OF ELASTICITY

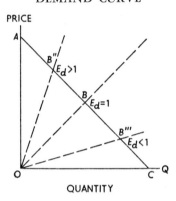

Figure 4–7

ELASTICITY ALONG
A STRAIGHT LINE
DEMAND CURVE

lowing lines. If the change in price is infinitesimal, the formula $-(p/q)(\partial q/\partial p)$ is represented in Figure 4–6 by (BM/OM) (RB'/RB), or by $(BM/OM)(MC/BM)$ because we are dealing with similar right triangles, and this is the same as $MC/OM = MC/PB$, or $BC/AB = E_d$.

It follows from the preceding argument that when $BC = AB$, the elasticity of demand is equal to unity, for then $BC/AB = 1$. In Figure 4–7, the elasticity of demand is unity at B, for $AB = BC$ by construction.

It also follows from the foregoing argument that the elasticity of demand of a straight line demand curve is *not* the same at all points along it. Thus at B in Figure 4–7, the elasticity of demand is unity, for $AB = BC$. But at B'', the elasticity of demand is greater than unity, for $B''C/AB'' > 1$. And, at B''', the elasticity of demand is less than unity, for $B'''C/AB''' < 1$.

Factors Affecting the Elasticity of Demand

Among the factors generally believed to affect the elasticity of demand are (1) availability of substitutes; (2) proportion spent on the good in relation to the buyer's total income; (3) proportion of the total cost of a more expensive good represented by the commodity in question; (4) durability of the good; and (5) habit.

If substitutes for the good are available, the demand will probably be elastic. However, if the amount spent on the good represents only a small proportion of the consumer's total expenditure, or a small part of the total cost of some more expensive commodity (thread used in a custom tailored suit), the demand will probably be inelastic. On the other hand, if a good is durable and purchases can be postponed if prices rise, the demand will probably be elastic. Goods purchased through force of habit have inelastic demands (cigarettes).

B. THE MARSHALLIAN DEMAND THEORY

The Condition of Consumer Equilibrium

Both the Marshallian and the contemporary demand theory assume that the individual consumer purchases under conditions of perfect competition insofar as the demand side of the market is concerned, although it is not necessary to assume that sellers are also selling under conditions of perfect competition. Both theories also assume that wants are data and that a rational consumer will seek to maximize the total utility which is obtainable from his *given* money income and, finally, that commodities are finely divisible.

The quantity of each commodity which the consumer purchases is determined when his total utility is maximized, and at this point he is said to be in *equilibrium*. For, if he is maximizing the total utility available from his given money income, there is no reason for him to change his position, that is, to redistribute his purchasing power differently among the different commodities (thus changing the amounts purchased).

And so the conditions of this maximum position must be specified, subject to the overriding restraint that the consumer's money income is given and is all accounted for by the uses to which it is put. The conditions of this maximum are the same whether one assumes that the utilities of marginal units of expenditures on different uses are dependent or that they are independent. If they are assumed dependent, these marginal utilities change when expenditures on a given commodity change and may change without a change in such expenditures as the amounts of expenditures on other uses change. If they are assumed independent, these marginal utilities are a function only of the expenditures on the given commodity.

Marshall states the equilibrium condition, the condition under which total utility will be maximized, as one under which the consumer will so distribute his given income or purchasing power, *m*, that it will have the same marginal utility in all the uses to which it is put. Accordingly, *a consumer with a given income* (given amount of purchasing power) *will be in equilibrium, maximizing his total utility, when the utility of the marginal unit of purchasing power devoted to any one use is just exactly equal to the utility of the marginal unit of purchasing power devoted to any other use.* For if this were not the case, it would pay him to increase his expenditures on those commodities which were relatively more important to him (where the utilities of marginal units of purchasing power were greater) and to reduce his expenditures on those uses in which the utilities of marginal units of purchasing power were less. This statement of the equilibrium condition describes the maximum, but it does not tell us how the consumer attains the equilibrium position.

A Graphical Illustration of the Equilibrium Condition

It is difficult, if not impossible, to illustrate the process by which equilibrium is attained by means of utility curves without assuming that the marginal utilities of units of purchasing power devoted to different uses are independent. For if they are dependent, it is necessary to shift the curves (or change the numbers in an arithmetical illustration) of some uses of income as expenditures on other uses change.

Consequently, *for purposes of the immediate exposition only,* let us assume that the marginal utilities of units of expenditures are independent and that the consumer has a given money income, *M*, which he devotes to two uses, *x* and *y*. As before, let *x* be a single use of his purchasing power or income, and let *y* represent all other uses, including saving, to which he can devote his given income. Thus, again, *y* represents the number of dollars devoted to all uses other than expenditure on *x*, and yp_y is the amount spent on *y*.

Next let us write the budget restraint, or the budget equation, which states, as in Chapter 3, that all of the consumer's money income must be accounted for in equilibrium:

$$xp_x + yp_y = M . \qquad (3\text{-}1)$$

This equation can be stated in terms of y by dividing both sides of it by the price of y, or by p_y, as

$$\frac{xp_x}{p_y} + \frac{yp_y}{p_y} = \frac{xp_x}{p_y} + y = \frac{M}{p_y} = xp + y = \frac{M}{p_y},$$

where $p = p_x/p_y$, in which case y becomes the *numeraire*, or the unit of account. We will use this formulation in the next chapter.

It can also be written in units of purchasing power by dividing both sides of it by $1.00, or

$$\frac{xp_x}{\$1.00} + \frac{yp_y}{\$1.00} = \frac{M}{\$1.00} = m_{x_0} + m_{y_0} = m_0.$$

Figure 4–8 contains the assumed curves of the marginal utility of units of purchasing power devoted to the uses of x and y, which are assumed

Figure 4–8

MARGINAL UTILITIES OF DIFFERENT USES OF INCOME

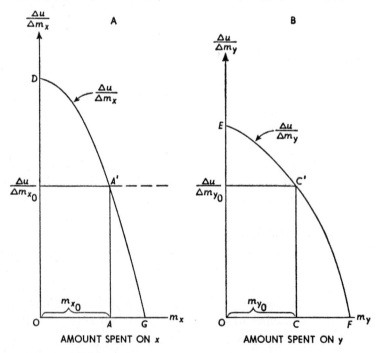

to be independent. In this diagram the amount of purchasing power devoted to x, as determined from the preceding equation, is shown equal to OA, or to m_{x_0}; and the amount of purchasing power devoted to y is shown as OC, or as m_{y_0}, in the initial equilibrium positions at A' and C', respectively. In Figure 4–8 the distance AA' represents the marginal utility of purchasing power devoted to x when the consumer has spent OA on x, and the distance CC' represents the marginal utility of purchasing power devoted to y when OC is spent on y. These two magnitudes must be equal in equilibrium when the consumer's total income is accounted for, or $AA' = CC'$.

Now note: if the consumer increased his expenditures on x, moving to the right from A in Figure 4–8, *he would add less than* $AA' = CC'$ to his total utility; and if at the same time he decreased his expenditures on y by moving to the left from C in Figure 4–8B (for this is the only way in which, with a given money income, he can increase his expenditures on x), *he would reduce his total utility by at least* $CC' = AA'$. Therefore, he cannot gain by further changing his position. He can only lose. Accordingly, *in equilibrium, the utility of the marginal unit of income must be the same in all the uses to which income is put.*

An Algebraic Statement of the Equilibrium Condition

In order to understand the equation in which the equilibrium condition is usually stated, consider this fact: the *ratio* of the marginal utility of any given commodity to its price represents the utility of that amount of the commodity which the marginal unit of income will buy. That is, if the utility of the marginal unit of a given commodity, say x, is taken as equal to 15 utils, and if the price of a unit of x is equal to 10, the utility of the marginal dollar's worth of x is equal to 15 utils/$10 = 1.5$ utils. And so, the condition that the utility of the marginal unit of income must be the same in all the uses to which income is put is usually stated in an equation which states that the *ratios of the marginal utilities of the various given commodities on which income is spent to their respective prices must be the same,* or

$$\frac{u'_{x_0}}{p_x} = \frac{u'_{y_0}}{p_y} = u'_0 . \tag{4-5}$$

In this equation u'_{x_0} is the marginal utility of x; u'_{y_0} is the marginal utility of y; and u'_0 is the marginal utility of one dollar's worth of x or y. The subscript x or y denotes the commodity; the subscript 0 denotes the original equilibrium position, and another subscript such as 1 or 2 rather than 0 would denote some quantity of x in a position other than the initial equilibrium position. Thus u'_{x_1} would denote the marginal utility of x when the consumer has x_1 rather than x_0 units of x. If the marginal utility of x decreases as the quantity of x increases, then $u'_{x_1} < u'_{x_0}$ when $x_1 > x_0$, or the marginal utility of x is less when the consumer has a larger stock of x.

Thus, for the consumer to be in equilibrium it is necessary that

(1) total income be accounted for and (2) the utility of the marginal
unit of income be the same in all uses to which income is put, or

$$xp_x + yp_y = M ,$$ (3-1)

and

$$\frac{u'_{x_0}}{p_x} = \frac{u'_{y_0}}{p_y} = u'_0 .$$ (4-5)

Marshall's "Proof" that the Demand Curve Slopes Negatively

Demand curves are generally drawn with a negative slope; that is,
in Figures 4–2 and 4–3, the demand curve has been drawn sloping
down and to the right. What this negative slope states is that at higher
prices consumers will buy less than they will buy at lower prices. That
this is the correct way to draw a demand curve which describes a real
world situation cannot be proved deductively. Therefore contemporary
economists have generally tried to defend this proposition as a realistic
one by showing that the conditions under which such a curve would
slope up and to the right are so unrealistic that they are hardly, if ever,
encountered in the real world.

Marshall's argument that the demand curve should be drawn with a
negative slope rests, however, on an assumption that the marginal
utility of the *numeraire* commodity is *constant*.[2] His argument is as
follows.

First, the equilibrium condition is known to be

$$\frac{u'_{x_0}}{p_x} = \frac{u'_{y_0}}{p_y} , \text{ with income constant.}$$ (4-5)

Now, in the case of a price decrease, the new price of x becomes less
than the old, and the equation above becomes

$$\frac{u'_{x_0}}{(p_x + \Delta p_x)} > \frac{u'_{y_0}}{p_y} , \text{ where } \Delta p_x < 0.$$ (4-6)

That is, at the new lower price, the *ratio* of the marginal utility of x to
its price *increases*. Or, the utility of an additional dollar spent on x is
now *greater* than that of an additional dollar spent on y, for one dollar
will now buy more x. Now, *if the marginal utility of y is assumed*

---

[2] My position is the same as that taken by Paul Samuelson, "Constancy of the Marginal
Utility of Income," in O. Lange, F. McIntyre, and T. O. Yntema (eds.), *Studies in Mathematical Economics and Econometrics* (Chicago: University of Chicago Press, 1942), pp.
75–91, esp. p. 91.

constant and the price of y is also constant, the ratio between them will remain unchanged. Accordingly, the *ratio* of the marginal utility of x to its price is now too high relative to that of y. However, if the marginal utility of x decreases as its quantity increases, by increasing the quantity of x purchased, the marginal utility of x will be reduced and the ratio will be reduced to its former level. In the new position the equation will read:

$$\frac{u'_{x_1}}{(p_x + \Delta p_x)} = \frac{u'_{y_0}}{p_y} , \qquad (4\text{-}7)$$

where u'_{x_1} *is less than* u'_{x_0} *because the quantity* x_1 *is greater than the quantity* x_0, *or* $u'_{x_1} < u'_{x_0}$ *when* $x_1 > x_0$.

It follows, therefore, that a decrease in price ($\Delta p < 0$) must be accompanied by an increase in purchases of x ($\Delta x > 0$) if the equilibrium is to be restored when the marginal utility of the numeraire and *money* income are both assumed constant. Thus, when the signs attached to the price and quantity changes are taken into account, $\Delta p \Delta x < 0$, or the demand curve has a negative slope. The logic is impeccable.

A Graphical Illustration of Marshall's Argument

Marshall's argument is illustrated in Figure 4–9, which depicts curves of the marginal utilities of x and of y. Note that the X axes now measure *units* of x and y and *not expenditures* on x and on y. The consumer is initially in equilibrium at A and at B in Figures 4–9A and 4–9B, respectively, consuming OA' of x and OB' of y. The marginal utility of y is a horizontal line, ZB'', in Figure 4–9B because the marginal utility of y is constant. The marginal utility of x decreases as the quantity of x increases in Figure 4–9A.

After the price of x declines ($\Delta p_x < 0$) from p_x to ($p_x + \Delta p_x$), the quantity of x increases from OA' to OA'''. At A'', the new equilibrium position of the consumer, the marginal utility of x is less than before, for $A'''A'' < A'A$, and the consumer is once more in equilibrium. When the marginal utility of the numeraire, y, is assumed constant, the elasticity of the demand for x is equal to unity, and consumption of y does not change when the price of x declines. Figure 4–9 has been drawn consistently with this proposition, for consumption of y remains constant at OB' both before and after the price change, while that of x increases by $A'A'''$.[3] Recall also that the Marshallian

---

[3] See Note A at the end of Chapter 5, or the discussion of Equation (A–13) in Appendix A, for a proof of this proposition.

Figure 4-9

MARGINAL UTILITIES OF DIFFERENT COMMODITIES

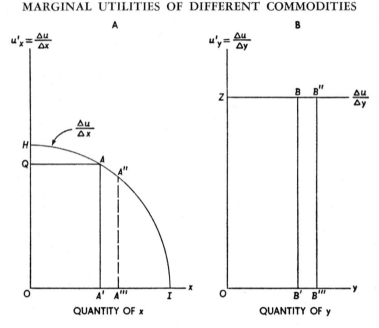

QUANTITY OF x   QUANTITY OF y

analysis is partial equilibrium analysis and rests on the assumption that "other things remain equal" (*ceteris paribus*) when the price of *x* changes. The fact that the elasticity of demand for *x* is equal to unity when the marginal utility of the numeraire is assumed constant is completely consistent with this assumption. For, if other things do not change when the price of *x* changes, then the *amount spent* on *y* will not change, and, hence, with a constant price of *y*, the *amount* of *y* purchased does not change either!

C. DEMAND AND INCOME

A Change in Income, Prices Constant: Income Demand Curves

As has already been noted, the effect of a change in income with prices constant can be shown by shifting the (price) demand curve in the relevant direction in Figure 4-1, because such (price) demand curves assume that *money* income remains constant.

An alternative method of showing the effect of changes in income with prices constant is to measure income on the X axis and the commodity on the *y* axis, as in Figure 4-10. In this diagram the *income demand curve, DD,* shows how purchases of *x* change as income

Figure 4–10

AN INCOME DEMAND CURVE

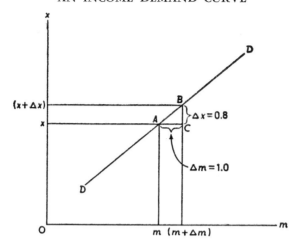

changes when prices of *all* goods (including that of *x*), tastes, and the number of consumers remain constant. Since prices of *all* goods are assumed constant, such curves really show how purchases of *x* change when *money* income changes, for income, or purchasing power, can only change if money income or prices or both change. Income demand curves are known as *Engel's Curves,* named for the German statistician who first studied them.

A decrease in prices, an increase in the number of consumers, or a better liking for *x* will shift the curve to the left in Figure 4–10. An increase in prices, a decrease in the number of consumers, or a reduction in preference for the commodity will shift the curve downward.

Income demand curves should not be confused with *income consumption curves* which are employed in indifference curve analysis and explained in the next chapter. These two curves always slope in the same direction, but the numerical values of their slopes are different.

The Rate of Change of Purchases as Income Increases, Prices Constant

Consider now the meaning of the concept, *average rate of change of purchases of x as income increases when prices are constant,* which can be designated by the symbol $\Delta x_a / \Delta m$. The subscript *a* attached to *x* in Δx_a means prices are constant at a given level, say at *A* in Figure 4–2. This rate of change defines the way in which purchases of *x* change when income increases *while prices remain constant,* and it is nothing other than the slope of the income demand curve in Figure

4–10, or $\Delta x_a/\Delta m = CB/AC$. This rate of change is a "marginal propensity to consume" the single commodity, x.

Thus, if prices are unchanged and purchases of x increase by .8 of a unit of x as income increases *with prices constant* by, say, one small unit, we would have $\Delta x_a/\Delta m = .8/1 = .8$. In the case of our examplé, $\Delta x_a/\Delta m$ is positive, so we can write $\Delta x_a/\Delta m > 0$. In such a case, the income demand curve will slope up and to the right as in Figure 4–10. However, if purchases of x decrease as income increases *with prices constant,* we would have $\Delta x_a/\Delta m < 0$, or the rate of change would be negative, and the curve would slope upward and to the left. Finally, if purchases of x do not change as income increases *when prices are constant,* that is if purchases of x remain constant as income increases, we would have $\Delta x_a/\Delta m = 0$, and the income demand curve would be a straight line parallel to the m axis. If the marginal utility of the numeraire, y, is constant, it will be true that $\Delta x_a/\Delta m = 0$. Why this is so will now be explained.

Constant Marginal Utility of the Numeraire

Consider the effect of a change in income equal to $B'B'''$ in Figure 4–9B on purchases of y when prices are assumed constant and the marginal utility of y is also assumed constant. If the increase in income is given in the form of y, since prices are unchanged and since the marginal utility of y is assumed constant and therefore unaffected by changes in x or y, all of the increased income will accumulate in the form of $y!$ There is no reason, since the equilibrium has not been disturbed and since neither the quantity of x nor its price have changed, for the consumer to change his purchases of x. Thus, the income demand curve would be a straight line parallel to the m axis, and $\Delta x_a/\Delta m = 0$ in Figure 4–10.

Thus, in Figure 4–9, if the consumer were initially in equilibrium at A and at B when he experienced such an increase in income, after the change in income, he would be in equilibrium at A and at B'', having increased his purchases of y only by $B'B'''$, the amount of the increase in income. His total utility, however, would have increased at a constant rate by an amount equal to $B'BB''B'''$, measured in y.

Even if he were given the increase in income in the form of x, the consumer would still eventually readjust his purchases so that in the final position he would be at A and at B''. For the immediate increase in income in the form of x would lower the marginal utility of x (while that of y is assumed constant) and move him to the right of A, say to A'' in Figure 4–9A. But at this point, since the marginal utility of x would now be lower than before, while the price of x were not changed, he would be in disequilibrium. The ratio of the marginal utility of x to its price would now be too low. Accordingly, he would reduce his holdings of x, raising its marginal utility, and increase his purchases of y until he regained the former equilibrium position at A in Figure 4–9A, and thus had also attained B'' in Figure 4–9B. The effect of the increase in income on purchases of x is thus zero, although total utility would again be increased by $B'BB''B'''$. Consequently, *when the marginal utility of the numeraire, y, is constant,* it is true that $\Delta x_a / \Delta m = 0$. That is, *the rate of change of purchases of x as income increases when prices are constant is zero,* while total utility increases at a constant rate equal to BB' (the marginal utility of y) per unit of y.

The Income Elasticity of Demand

The income elasticity of demand is a measure of the responsiveness of buyers to changes in income when prices remain constant. It is the absolute value of the rate of percentage change of purchases divided by the rate of percentage change of income, and this definition employs the concept, defined above, of the rate of change of purchases of the commodity, x, as income increases, *with prices constant.* It results in the formula

$$E_i = \frac{m}{x} \frac{\partial x}{\partial m} \cdot \qquad (4\text{-}8)$$

In order to determine the *arc* income elasticity, we use the formula

$$E_{i_x} = \frac{m}{x} \frac{\Delta x_a}{\Delta m} \cdot \qquad (4\text{-}9)$$

The use of the formula can be illustrated as follows. Let us assume that, when the consumer is at A in Figure 4–2, the average rate of change of purchases of x as income changes is determined to be $\Delta x_a / \Delta m = .1905$ and that his total income is equal to \$120, or to 120 units of purchasing power. Then, since he is consuming 60 units of x at A, we could compute the income elasticity at the given prices at A as

$$(120/60)(.1905) = .3810 . \qquad (4\text{-}9')$$

Thus, a 1 percent increase in the consumer's income when he is at A, *while prices remain unchanged,* will produce an increase in purchases of x equal to .3810 of 1 percent. And so, if his income increased by 1 percent or by \$1.20 (or by 1.2 units of purchasing power) at A, while prices remained unchanged, he would increase his consumption of x by $(.003810)(60) = .229$ of one unit of x. Moreover, since the price of a unit of x is $1.00, he would spend approximately $.23 for x and would devote the remainder of the increase in income, or $.97, to y. That is, $1.20 = $.23 + $.97, and all of the increase in income is thus accounted for by additional expenditures on x and on y, as it must be according to one of our basic assumptions.

D. ALL OTHER THINGS NOT EQUAL

The Cross Elasticity of Demand

The cross elasticity of demand is a measure of the responsiveness of purchases of y (all other goods, or some other good, depending on the circumstances of the analysis) to changes in the price of x, and, as usual, both point and arc cross elasticity formulas can be written. In general, the cross elasticity of demand is the value of the rate of percentage change of purchases of y divided by the rate of percentage change in the price of x, and the point cross elasticity formula is

$$E_{y_{p_x}} = \frac{p_x}{y} \frac{\partial y}{\partial p_x}.$$ (4–10)

Assuming $\partial y/\partial p_x = .17142 > 0$ and $y = 60$, we have

$$E_{y_{p_x}} = \frac{p_x}{y} \frac{\Delta y}{\Delta p_x} = \frac{100}{60} (.17142) = .2857.$$ (4–11)

That is, purchases of y decrease by $.17142$ units for each one cent decrease in the price of x, and a 1 percent decrease in the price of x decreases purchases of y by $.2857$ of 1 percent. If the total percentage decrease in the price of x is equal to $- \Delta p_x/p_x = .28/1.00 = 28$ percent, we have the total percentage decrease in purchases of y as $(.2857)(.28) = .07996$, and the total decrease in units of y as $(60)(.07996) = 4.80$.

Note that the decrease in the price of x produces a *shift* in the demand curve of y *if* total expenditures on x change, because one of the assumptions subject to which the demand curve of y has been drawn (prices of all other goods remain constant) has been changed.

Such a situation is illustrated in Figure 4–11. In this diagram the marginal utilities of x and of y are assumed to be *dependent* on each other. That is, the marginal utility of y may change with that of x, and vice versa. The consumer is initially in equilibrium at A and Y' in Figures 4–11A and 4–11B, respectively. He spends $OPAX$, or $60,

Figure 4–11

ILLUSTRATION OF CROSS ELASTICITY OF DEMAND

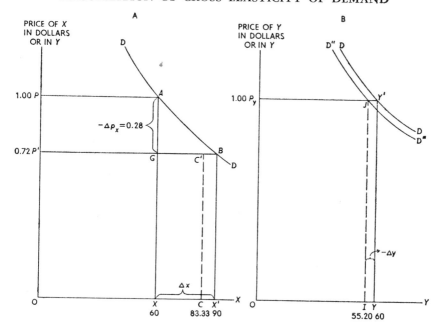

on x and $OP_yY'Y$, or \$60, on y in these initial equilibrium positions.

After the price of x declines by $\Delta p_x = -\$.28$, while the price of y remains constant, he attains the new equilibrium positions at B and J. Thus, after the price change, he consumes XX' more of x, and his total expenditures on x have increased by $CC'BX' = \Delta E = \$4.80$, while his total expenditures on y have decreased by $YY'JI = \Delta y p_y = -\$4.80$. In the final equilibrium positions he thus consumes 30 additional units of x, and IY, or 4.80, units less of y.

On the basis of our assumed data, purchases of y thus change in the *same* direction as the price of x changes, and the demand curve of y *shifts* to the left; but purchases of x change in the opposite direction from the price change, and there occurs a movement *along* (*no shift in*) the demand curve of x.

In Figure 4–11, we are not assuming that "other things remain equal" (or *ceteris paribus*) as the price of x changes, as we did in the case of Figure 4–9, and, thus, we are not employing the *partial* equilibrium analysis of Marshall. Instead, we are assuming that "other things change equally" (or *mutatis mutandis*) as the price of x changes, and we are employing the more general Walrasian type of analysis. For we have allowed y to change along with x and the price of x.

A Variable Marginal Utility of the Numeraire

It has just been noted that the explanation of Figure 4–11 abandons the assumption that all other things are equal and employs a more general analysis than Marshall undertook. Indeed, most of Marshall's propositions can be demonstrated in a more general way without assuming the marginal utility of the numeraire constant, and such an analysis is the subject of the next chapter.

However, instead of being able to demonstrate that the demand curve *must* have a negative slope *because* the marginal utility of the numeraire is assumed constant, *since* we will assume the marginal utility of the numeraire *variable,* we will merely be able to specify the *conditions* under which demand curves will have negative slopes. This matter is one of our concerns in the next chapter, which explains the contemporary "indifference" analysis of demand and also explains some statistical studies of demand. The contemporary analysis, we will see, rests on the foundations laid by Marshall.

SELECTED READINGS

ALLEN, R. G. D. *Mathematical Analysis for Economists,* pp. 108–16 and 254–57. London: Macmillan & Co., Ltd., 1950.

FRIEDMAN, MILTON. "The Marshallian Demand Curve," *Journal of Political Economy,* Vol. LVII (December, 1949), pp. 463–95. (A view different from that adopted in the text is presented on p. 491.)

LEFTWICH, RICHARD. *The Price System and Resource Allocation,* pp. 49–65. Rev. ed. New York: Holt, Rinehart & Winston, Inc., 1960.

MARSHALL, ALFRED. *Principles of Economics,* Book III, chaps. i–v and Mathematical Notes I–V. 8th ed. London: Macmillan & Co., Ltd., 1938.

SAMUELSON, PAUL A. "Constancy of the Marginal Utility of Income," *Studies in Mathematical Economics and Econometrics* (eds. O. LANGE, F. McINTYRE, AND T. O. YNTEMA). Chicago: University of Chicago Press, 1942. The reader whose mathematical training is limited will benefit most from reading pp. 75–76, 78, 80, and esp. p. 91. The reader with the necessary mathematical equipment will benefit from a close examination of the entire essay.

TINTNER, GERHARD. *Mathematics and Statistics for Economists,* pp. 41–42 and 119–20. New York: Rinehart & Co., Inc., 1954.

5 Indifference Curve Analysis

Introduction

An English economist, F. Y. Edgeworth, introduced the use of indifference curves in 1881,[1] but it was not until 1934 that two other English economists, J. R. Hicks and R. G. D. Allen, popularized the use of indifference curve techniques in economic analysis.[2] Edgeworth developed indifference curves in order to take account of the fact that the utility of a given commodity may be a function not only of its own quantity but of the quantity of other commodities possessed, and Hicks and Allen further developed the technique because of their desire to avoid the notion that utility is measurable. This chapter explains indifference analysis and concludes with a survey of some statistical studies of demand.

A. BASIC CONCEPTS

Definition of an Indifference Curve

Figure 5–1 depicts a family of indifference curves. Indifference curves may be defined as iso-utility curves, or as *constant total utility curves,* curves such that total utility remains constant *along them* as the quantities of commodities possessed by the consumer change. The family of indifference curves in Figure 5–1 is thus a family of contour lines such as those depicted in Figure 3–7 in Chapter 3. Higher indifference curves represent higher levels of equal total utility than do

---

[1] F. Y. Edgeworth, *Mathematical Psychics* (London: C. K. Paul & Co., 1881). See also Alfred Marshall, *Principles of Economics* (8th ed.; London: Macmillan & Co., Ltd., 1938), Mathematical Note XII, p. 844.

[2] J. R. Hicks and R. G. D. Allen, "A Reconsideration of the Theory of Value," *Economica,* New Series, Vol. I (February, 1934), pp. 52–76; and *Ibid.,* Vol. I (May, 1934), pp. 196–219. See also J. R. Hicks, *Value and Capital* (2d ed.; Oxford: Clarendon Press, 1946), Part I.

Figure 5-1

A FAMILY OF INDIFFERENCE CURVES

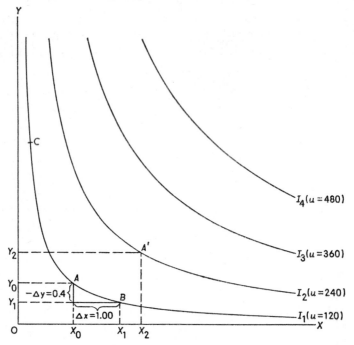

lower indifference curves, but along an indifference curve $\Delta u = 0$, or total utility does not change.

Mathematically, indifference curves are defined by the equation

$$\Delta u = u'_x \Delta x + u'_y \Delta y = 0 . \tag{5-1}$$

This equation, of course, is also already familiar to the student as Equation (3-4) in Chapter 3, and he may wish to refresh his memory by reviewing the discussion of it and of the diagrams in Chapter 3. Equation (5-1) states that the product of the marginal utility of x when y is assumed constant (or u'_x) multiplied by the change in the quantity of x (or by Δx) plus the product of the marginal utility of y when x is constant (or u'_y) multiplied by the change in the quantity of y (or Δy) must produce no change in total utility as these two quantities change.[3]

Since the marginal utilities of x and of y are both assumed to be positive (which means that the consumer is better off if he has more of

───────────

[3] For a more sophisticated mathematical treatment, see R. G. D. Allen, *Mathematical Analysis for Economists* (London: Macmillan & Co., Ltd., 1950), pp. 334–40 and p. 344.

either without a change in the quantity of the other commodity), it follows that *along* an indifference curve an increase in the quantity of one of the commodities must be accompanied by a decrease in the other. That is, Δy must be negative, or y must decrease in a movement to the right from A to B along indifference curve I_1 in Figure 5–1, or Equation (5–1) above would not be equal to zero, and, therefore, total utility would not be constant along I_1. A single indifference curve thus depicts different combinations (quantities of x and of y) which must yield equal total utility to the consumer, or among which he is indifferent, hence the name, "indifference curve."

Indifference curve theory, it is argued, eliminates the necessity of assuming that utility is measurable and avoids the use of the concept of "diminishing marginal utility." For if the tastes of the consumer are given, it is theoretically possible (but never has in fact been done) to derive his indifference curves merely from his expression of his preferences for given combinations of commodities x and y. That is to say, he need not specify by how much he prefers a given combination of x and of y to another combination. What he has to do is specify that he does or does not prefer one combination to another, or that he is indifferent among several combinations.

Consider now the "family" of indifference curves in Figure 5–1. Say that the total utility at point A in Figure 5–1 on indifference curve I_1 is equal to 120 units, and that it is derived from the consumption or possession of OX_0 units of x and OY_0 units of y. At point B the total utility of the combination at B is the same as that at A by definition, for A and B lie on the same indifference curve. But at B the quantity of x is OX_1 and the quantity of y is OY_1. Thus the quantity of y has decreased by Δy, while the quantity of x has increased by Δx. The total change in total utility between A and B must be zero by definition, for total utility is the same at A and at B (otherwise they would not lie on the same indifference curve). Our formula in Equation (5–1) states that the product of the marginal utility of x when y is constant (which is positive), multiplied by the change in x (which is also positive between A and B), must be just offset by the product of the marginal utility of y when x is constant (which is also positive), multiplied by the change in y (*which must therefore be negative*) between A and B. Otherwise total utility would not be the same at B as it is at A.

Greater total utility is shown by higher indifference curves in Figure 5–1. Thus the total utility of I_2 is 240, while that of I_3 is 360. More of y and also more of x would locate the consumer at, say, A' on I_2, and thus he would be on a higher indifference curve. All combinations on higher indifference curves are preferable to all combinations on lower indifference curves. Thus indifference analysis apparently concerns itself with comparisons of preferences rather than of utilities.

Characteristics of Indifference Curves

A system of indifference curves has three basic characteristics. *First*, indifference curves cannot intersect. To permit them to intersect would involve inconsistent definitions. In other words, if total utility is the same at all points on a given indifference curve and is defined as greater on a higher indifference curve, then if two indifference curves crossed, we would not only be saying that total utility was the same on the two different indifference curves but also that it was both greater and less on each curve than on the other (!), for one curve would lie above the other above the point of crossing and below the other below the point of the crossing. Thus we would be asserting that total utility is the same as, greater than, and less than a given amount on *both* indifference curves. This statement violates the definition of an indifference curve as a curve along which total utility remains constant.

Second, indifference curves are generally drawn to slope downward to the right, as in Figure 5–1. This means that if the consumer's total utility is to remain constant when he acquires an additional unit of x, he must give up some amount of y. If this were not so, for example, if the indifference curves were horizontal lines, this fact would mean that the consumer would acquire the same amount of total utility from more x and the same amount of y as he acquires from less x and the given amount of y. In such a case, the utility of the additional units of x would have to be zero so that they added nothing to total utility. Similarly, if the curves were vertical lines, this fact would mean that additional units of y added nothing to total utility.

Third, indifference curves are convex toward the origin of the indifference map. This is how they have been drawn in Figure 5–1. The condition that the indifference curves are convex to the origin does not rest upon an assumption that the marginal utility of income diminishes, but rests upon an assumption that the *marginal rate of substitution* (defined next) diminishes. (The term "marginal" is redundant but traditional.)

The Marginal Rate of Substitution as a Ratio of Quantities

The *marginal rate of substitution of y for x, or S_{yx}, is defined as the amount of y the consumer is just willing to give up to acquire one* *small additional unit of x at a point* (or between two points) *on an indifference curve.* Mathematically it is defined as

$$-\frac{\Delta y}{\Delta x} = S_{yx} , \qquad (5\text{-}2)$$

where Δx is one (small) unit. Thus if the consumer were just willing to give up .4 units of y for one additional unit of x at point A in Figure 5–1, we would have $-(\Delta y/\Delta x) = S_{yx_a} = -(-.4/1) = .4$. And if he were willing to give up 3 units of y for 1 unit of x to the left of A at C, then $S_{yx_c} = 3$. Between C and A the marginal rate of substitution has thus decreased. That is to say, the amount of y which the consumer is willing to give up for one additional unit of x at A, where he has less y, or $S_{yx_a} = .4$, is less than the amount of y which the consumer is willing to give up for a unit of x at C, where he has more y, or $S_{yx_c} = 3.00$. Thus x has become *relatively* more important in the consumer's budget at C, and y has become *relatively* less important. This characteristic imparts convexity to the indifference curves. A decreasing marginal rate of substitution thus means that the indifference curves are convex to the origin, but it does *not* mean that the marginal utility of income decreases, for, by definition, $S_{yx} = -(\Delta y/\Delta x)$ is not the same thing as $\Delta u/\Delta m$, the marginal utility of income.

Substitutes and Complements

If the commodities x and y are perfect substitutes for each other, the indifference curves will be a straight line as depicted in Figure 5–2A.

Figure 5–2

SUBSTITUTES AND COMPLEMENTS

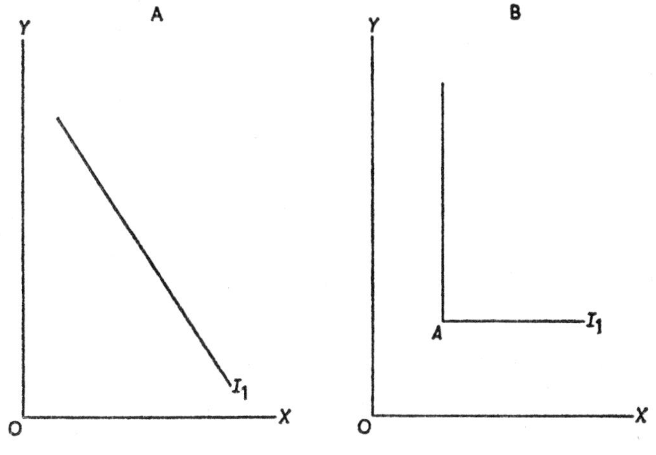

In such a case the consumer would be willing to substitute x for y or y for x at a constant rate irrespective of the amount of each that he has. (Banks are usually willing to exchange nickels for dimes at a constant 2 for 1 rate.)

On the other hand, if the commodities x and y are used together, for example, right and left shoes, they are called complements. In such a case the indifference curve will have a right angle as indicated in Figure 5–2B. The sharp break in the curve at A shows that one of the goods is useless without the other.

The Marginal Rate of Substitution as a Ratio of Marginal Utilities

The definition of the indifference curve stated by the previous equation can be used to derive the marginal rate of substitution. First, the equation which defines an indifference curve,

$$u'_x \Delta x + u'_y \Delta y = 0 , \qquad (5\text{–}1)$$

can be manipulated to produce

$$u'_x \Delta x = -u'_y \Delta y \qquad (5\text{–}3)$$

by subtracting $u'_y \Delta y$ from each side of it. Further, by dividing both sides of the result in Equation (5–3) by $u'_y \Delta x$, we have

$$\frac{u'_x}{u'_y} = -\frac{\Delta y}{\Delta x} = S_{yx} , \qquad (5\text{–}4)$$

the *marginal rate of substitution*.

Now consider the meaning of the term above, $S_{yx} = -(\Delta y/\Delta x)$. This term, the rate of substitution of y for x, has already been defined as the slope of indifference curve I_1 between A and B in Figure 5–1 when x is allowed to change by *one small unit*. Since the term on the left in Equation (5–4) is the *ratio* of the marginal utilities of x and of y, it follows that the slope of the indifference curve, or S_{yx}, the term on the right in Equation (5–4), represents this same ratio. Thus, S_{yx} is really the ratio of the marginal utilities of x and of y, and it is also equal to the reciprocal of the ratio of the marginal utilities of y and of x. Moreover, these ratios are measured by the ratio $-(\Delta y/\Delta x)$ to which they are equal.

The Budget Equation Once Again

The budget equation can be represented graphically as follows. First let us write the budget equation as

$$p_x x + p_y y = M , \qquad (3\text{–}1) = (5\text{–}5)$$

where M, of course, represents the given money income, as before. From this it follows that if the quantity of x consumed is equal to zero $(x = 0)$, the equation reduces to

$$0 + p_y y = M ,$$ (5-6)

and that the quantity of y is equal to

$$y = \frac{M}{p_y} .$$ (5-7)

Figure 5-3

EFFECT OF A PRICE CHANGE ON BUDGET EQUATION LINE

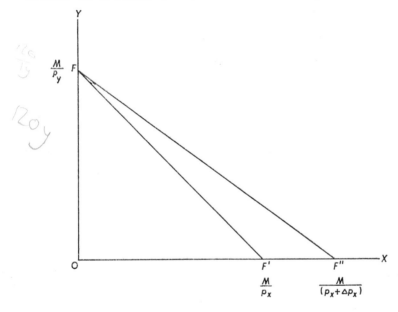

If we assume as before that the price of y is $1.00, the quantity of y is then the same as the number of units of purchasing power contained in M, and y is the *numeraire*. Let us assume that the original money income, M, of the consumer amounted to $120. Then the number of units of y which could be bought with that income, if none of it were spent on x, is equal to $120/$1.00 = 120y$.

Accordingly, let us locate a point F on the Y axis in Figure 5-3 such that the distance OF is equal to $120y$.

Similarly, if none of the consumer's money income is spent on y and all of it is spent on x so that $y = 0$, it follows that the quantity of x consumed is equal to

$$p_x x + 0 = M \; ; \tag{5-8}$$

$$x = \frac{M}{p_x} \cdot \tag{5-9}$$

If, now, the price of each unit of x is taken in y as equal to one unit of y (for they are equal in dollars in our example), it follows that the income equal to $120y$ of the consumer will also enable him to buy 120 units of x at most if he buys no y. Thus we can locate a point on the X axis in Figure 5–3 at F', and the distance OF' represents 120 units of x. The line FF' now represents the budget "constraint" or the budget equation and shows the *maximum* quantities of either y or x, or of both (at any point on the line), that the consumer could purchase with his given income at the given prices of x and of y.

Furthermore, the absolute (numerical) value of the slope of the line FF' in Figure 5–3 is equal to the ratio of OF/OF', and this is the same as $(M/p_y)/(M/p_x) = (M/p_y)(p_x/M) = p_x/p_y$. This magnitude, of course, is nothing other than the ratio of the prices of x and of y, or the price of a unit of x in terms of y. Since in our arithmetical example we have assumed $p_x = 1$ and $p_y = 1$, we have $p_x/p_y = 1$.

A decrease in the price of x with no change in the price of y means that *more* x can now be purchased with the same amount of money income when no y is purchased, while the maximum amount of y which can be purchased with that money income remains unchanged, for the price of y has not changed. Thus such a price decrease shifts the line FF' to the right to, say, FF'', indicating that more x can now be obtained for the same amount of y, while purchases of y remain unchanged. And so, if no y at all is bought, purchases of x can increase by $F'F''$ to OF'' or to $M/(p_x + \Delta p_x)$ units of x.

B. THE THEORY OF CONSUMER BEHAVIOR

The Equilibrium Condition Illustrated by an Indifference Diagram

Now recall that the equilibrium condition in Marshall's theory of consumer behavior (Chapter 4) requires that the *ratios of the marginal utilities of respective commodities to their prices must be equal in equilibrium, so that the utility of the marginal unit of income devoted to any one use is just exactly equal to the utility of the marginal unit of income devoted to any other use.* Mathematically, the condition is stated by the equation,

$$\frac{u'_x}{p_x} = \frac{u'_y}{p_y} \cdot \tag{5-10}$$

This equation can be rewritten (by multiplying both sides of it by p_x and dividing both sides by u'_y) as

$$\frac{u'_x}{u'_y} = \frac{p_x}{p_y} . \tag{5–11}$$

The reformulated equation states that, in equilibrium, the *ratio* of the marginal utilities of x and of y must be equal to the ratio of the prices of x and of y.

Figure 5–4

THE MARSHALLIAN EQUILIBRIUM CONDITION ILLUSTRATED BY INDIFFERENCE CURVES

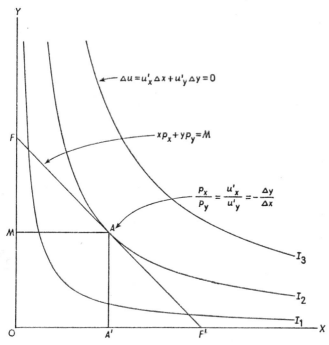

Now S_{yx} has already been defined in Equation (5–4) above as equal to the ratio of the marginal utilities of x and of y and also as equal to the slope of the indifference curve (at a point, or over a very small one unit range of x). Thus it follows that we can put together two diagrams like Figures 5–2 and 5–3 and provide a graphical representation in Figure 5–4 in terms of indifference curves of the Marshallian equilibrium condition.

In short, in Figure 5–4 the equilibrium condition, that the ratios of the marginal utilities of the commodities to their prices must be equal, takes the form of a point of tangency between a budget equation line,

FF', and an indifference curve, whose slopes are equal at point *A* (or over a very small range). At point *A* in Figure 5–4 we thus have a graphical depiction of Equation (5–11), for the consumer is there maximizing his total utility from a given money income, *M*, or from his given amount of purchasing power, *m*, at given prices. Thus, *in equilibrium* (at *A* in Figure 5–4), *according to the indifference curve analysis, the utility of the marginal unit of income must be the same in all the uses to which income is devoted, just as this condition must be fulfilled in Marshallian analysis.* [The reader may wish to review the discussion of Equation (4–5) in Chapter 4.]

The Equilibrium Position Analyzed

At *A*, in Figure 5–4, the consumer purchases *OM* of *y* and *OA'* of *x*. He cannot reach a higher level of total utility with the given price ratios by redistributing his expenditures in any other way. If he reduced his purchases of *x* and acquired more *y*, he would move along *FF'* toward *F* from *A*, but this action would put him on a lower indifference curve, for *FF'* cannot be *tangent* to a higher curve than I_2. Similarly, if he increased his purchases of *x* and reduced his holdings of *y*, he would again move to a lower indifference curve by moving along *FF'* from *A* to *F'*. A budget line can be tangent only to one convex indifference curve, and no higher indifference curve can be reached with the given income and the given prices than the one to which the budget line is tangent by definition. For the indifference curves are convex to the origin by assumption.

The equilibrium position depicted at the point of tangency at *A* in Figure 5–4 can be characterized as a picture of the assumption that the consumer is happiest when he is distributing his given money income most nearly in accordance with his preferences, and that with more income he would be even happier. Thus it involves the basic value judgment that consumers "should get what they want." The present analysis, however, says nothing at all about whether the consumer's "happiness" increases at an increasing, decreasing, or at a constant rate as he moves from a lower to a higher indifference curve and thus nothing at all about whether or not the marginal utility of income increases, decreases, or remains constant.

The Effect of a Price Change

Suppose now that the consumer is initially in equilibrium at *A* in Figure 5–5, and that, after a decrease in the price of *x*, he finds himself in a new equilibrium position at *B*. Since the price of *x* has decreased,

Figure 5–5

PRICE CONSUMPTION AND INCOME CONSUMPTION CURVES

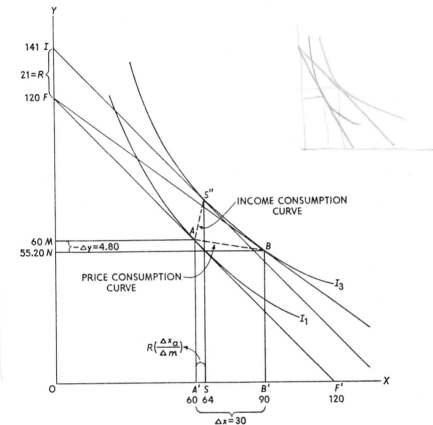

this means that the given income measured in y, OF, will now purchase a greater quantity of x than before. Accordingly, the new budget
equation line will shift from FAF' to FB in Figure 5–5. At B the new
budget line will by assumption (and definition) be tangent to a higher
indifference curve (I_3) than before, indicating that total utility has
increased as a result of the price decrease.

Let us now assume that the consumer purchased 60 units of x at A
in Figure 5–5 at a price of one y each, and that, after the price decreased to $.72y$, he increased his purchases of x to 90 units at B. Also
assume that the total money income of the consumer amounted to
$120, or $120y$, as before. Then in the initial position at A the con-
sumer purchased 60 units of y, or OM of y, in Figure 5–5 and 60
units of x, or OA' of x. Since the price of a unit of y is one y, the

amount of y and the amount *spent* on y can both be measured on the Y axis. After the price change, in the new position at B the consumer purchased 90 units of x, or OB' of x, and 55.20, or ON, units of y. The distance, $MN = \Delta y = -4.80y$, represents a *decrease* in y resulting from the increase in total expenditures on x as the price of x declines. Also, $NM = -\Delta y = 4.80y$ represents the *increase* in the total amount spent on x as its price has declined (i.e., $\Delta E > 0$). Thus, it is immediately clear that the demand for x in the assumed example is elastic, for total expenditures on x have increased while those on y have decreased, with money income constant. Also, we see that the change in total expenditures on x is the negative of the change in total expenditures on y, that is, $\Delta E = -\Delta y$ in units of y.

The Price Consumption Curve

The curve AB in Figure 5–5 is known as a price consumption curve. It connects successive positions of equilibrium produced by price changes. Some contemporary theorists have demonstrated that it is possible to derive demand curves from indifference curves because if we knew the indifference curves it would only be necessary to allow the price of the commodity to change in order to derive from such curves the quantities of it purchased at different prices. That is, *if* we knew that the consumer would purchase OB', or 90, units of x at B, when he has 55.20, or ON, units of y, and his total income is $120y$, we would also know that he would buy 90 units of x at a price of $.72y$ each. And so we could plot this point, along with the data for point A on a demand curve for x. Some rather refined graphical procedures have been developed to illustrate this point.[4]

Thus to know the quantities of x and of y which the consumer would purchase *from his indifference curves and his total income* is to know his demand curve. That is, if we know that he holds 55.20 units of y at B and purchases 90 units of x out of a total money income equal to 120 units of y, we also know that the 90 units of x must be costing him $120.00y - 55.20y = 64.80y$, and that the price of each unit of x in terms of y must thus be $64.80/90 = .72$.

This exercise is mainly useful because it demonstrates that the price consumption curve AB in Figure 5–5 is *not* a demand curve. The *slope* of the price consumption curve illustrates whether or not Δy is positive, negative, or zero, and, thus, whether or not the demand for x is inelastic, elastic, or has an elasticity equal to unity. If the curve AB

---

[4] See, for example, Tibor Scitovsky, *Welfare and Competition* (Homewood, Ill.: Richard D. Irwin, Inc., 1951), pp. 42–47.

slopes down and to the right as it does in Figure 5–5, the demand is elastic, for Δy is negative, that is $ON < OM$. If Δy is zero, the curve AB would be horizontal, that is, it would be parallel to the X axis in Figure 5–5, and the elasticity of demand would be unity or $ON = OM$. (This case is illustrated in Figure 5–6.) If Δy is positive so that $ON > OM$, the curve AB slopes up and to the right (so: $/$), and the demand will be inelastic (not depicted).

The Income Consumption Curve; "Normal," "Inferior," and "Neutral" Goods

In Figure 5–5, the curve AS'' is the *income consumption curve,* and the distance $A'S$ on the X axis represents the increase in purchases of x which would result from a subsidy equal to R (an increase in income equal to R) given to the consumer when prices are constant at their level at A.

The *income consumption curve* (to be distinguished from the price consumption curve) *shows how purchases of x and of y change as income changes when prices are constant.* It can be described in terms of the slope of the income demand curve, $\Delta x_a / \Delta m$. That is, if the rate of change of purchases of x as income changes is positive, $\Delta x_a / \Delta m > 0$, the quantity of x purchased will increase when income increases and prices are constant, and both curves will slope up and to the right. Thus total expenditures on x will likewise increase in this situation. (Compare the discussion of income demand curves in Chapter 4.) In such a case the commodity is classified as a *normal commodity, defined as one of which purchases increase as income increases with prices constant.*

Let us now use the subscript a to indicate that prices are constant at their level at A, where $p_x = \$1.00$, and the subscript b to indicate that prices are constant at their level at B, where $p_x = \$.72$. Then we have $A'S = (R)(\Delta x_a / \Delta m)$, or the total change in purchases of x is equal to the increase in income times the rate of change of purchases of x as income changes when prices are constant at A. Thus $A'S$ is the total change, while $\Delta x_a / \Delta m$ is the average rate of change. (The reader who has difficulty with these concepts may want to review the explanation of the difference between the marginal quantity and the total change in the total quantity which appears in Chapter 3.)

The magnitude, $A'S = (R)(\Delta x_a / \Delta m)$, is arithmetically equal to $(21.00)(.1905) = 4.00x$ in our diagram, for it has been assumed that $\Delta x_a / \Delta m = .1905$ and that $R = 21.00$ in Figure 5–5. The curve AS'' slopes up and to the right in Figure 5–5 *because* the quantity of x

purchased increases as income increases. *In the case of a normal commodity, the income consumption curve AS'' will always slope up and to the right.* This is the meaning of the condition, $\Delta x_a / \Delta m > 0$. That is, in such a case S must lie to the right of A' on the X axis, for purchases of x increase as income increases with prices constant.

However, if $\Delta x_a / \Delta m < 0$, the income consumption curve AS'' would slope up and to the left, and S would lie to the left of A' on the X axis. *In this case the commodity would be classified as inferior, for purchases decrease as income increases with prices constant.*

Finally if $\Delta x_a / \Delta m = 0$, the curve AS'' would be a vertical line, parallel to the Y axis as in Figure 5–6, and the quantity of x purchased would be the same after the increase in income as before. *Such a commodity can be defined as a neutral commodity because purchases do not change as income increases when prices are constant.* Thus in the case of a neutral commodity, $A' = S$ on the X axis in Figure 5–6. This special case will be further discussed later.

Graphically, S'' can be located in Figure 5–5 by drawing a new budget equation line, IS'', parallel to FAF', tangent to I_3 at S''. Thus IS'' has a slope equal to the (unchanged) price ratio, p_x/p_y. The new line is drawn at a level I, above the original point F, just equal to the increase in income (R), measured in units of y. In our case, in Figure 5–5, the distance FI has thus been made equal to R/p_y, and this distance represents an increase in y of 21.00 units, or $R = \$21/\$1.00 = 21y$.

Since the distance, OF, represents 120 units of y, the distance, OI, represents $120 + 21 = 141$ units of y. The reason why the new budget line IS'' is drawn parallel to the old line FAF' is to show that the price ratios have remained unchanged as income has increased by $R = FI$, the amount of the subsidy. Also, S'' represents the new equilibrium position of the consumer on the higher indifference curve, I_3. The slope of I_3 at S'' is, of course, the same as the slope of I_1 at A, for prices have not changed.

In the new position, the Marshallian equilibrium condition must be fulfilled at S'' just as it was at A. For, since the prices of x and of y have not changed as income has changed by FI, in the new position at S'' the marginal rate of substitution, S_{yx_s}, is the same as it is at A. However, this does not necessarily mean that the marginal utilities of x and of y have not changed. The condition that $S_{yx_s} = S_{yx_a}$, which refers to the *ratios* of these marginal utilities, could be fulfilled if the marginal utilities of x and of y remained constant, or if both were proportionately greater, or if both were proportionately less in the new position at S''

than in the old at A. If both were greater, the marginal utility of income would have increased; but if both were less (the most reasonable assumption), the marginal utility of income would have decreased. The marginal utility of income (u'_s) at S'' is *not* the same thing as the marginal rate of substitution (S_{yx_s}) at S'', nor do these two concepts refer to the same notion at A. (Note again that $u'_s = u'_{x_s}/p_x$, while $S_{yx_s} = u'_{x_s}/u'_{y_s}$, and these are different concepts.)

Vertically Parallel Indifference Curves

In Figure 5–6 the indifference curves have been drawn parallel in a vertical direction. That is, the slopes of all the different indifference curves are the same at all points which are intersected by vertical lines such as AS'' and QB. In this case the indifference curves are horn-

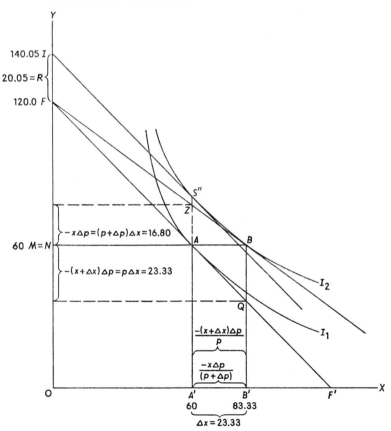

Figure 5–6

VERTICALLY PARALLEL INDIFFERENCE CURVES

shaped or widemouthed, and their slope at a given point depends only upon the marginal utility of x, for that of y is constant. (*Note A* at the end of this chapter contains a mathematical proof.) All additional units of y have the same value to the consumer.

In the case of Figure 5–6, the slope of indifference curve I_2 is exactly the same at S'' as that of I_1 at A, *but now also* the quantity of x purchased at A is exactly the same as at S''. In short, the rate of change of purchases of x as income changes is zero, or $\Delta x_a / \Delta m = 0$ also. Consumption of x does not change when income changes while prices remain constant. For, in Figure 5–6, the quantity of x consumed at S'' at the higher income of OI is precisely the same, OA', as it is at A at the lower level of income of OF. All of the increased income accumulates in the form of y, or $\Delta y_a / \Delta m = 1$, i.e., the rate of change of purchases of y as income changes is equal to unity or to 1.

The economic reason for this result is exactly the same in the case of Figure 5–6 as that which was given in the analysis of Figure 4–9 in Chapter 4 in Marshallian terms. Since the marginal utility of y is constant, the increase in income equal to R cannot disturb the equilibrium if it is received in the form of y, and thus there is no reason for consumption of x to change. If the increase in income were received in the form of x, the ratio of the marginal utility of x to its price would be lowered relative to the ratio of the marginal utility of y to its price (which remains constant), and the consumer, finding himself in disequilibrium, would divest himself of x until he had utilized all of the increased income to purchase y, thereby restoring at S'' the equality between the ratios which had previously existed at A.

C. THE EFFECT OF A PRICE CHANGE

Process of Readjustment: Variable Marginal Utility

In Figure 5–7 assume, as before, that the consumer was initially in equilibrium at A where I_1 is tangent to budget line FAF' and that after the price decreased, as indicated by FB, he found himself eventually in the new position at B. The *process* of his readjustment can be explained as follows.

As soon as the price of x declined, the consumer found himself in disequilibrium at Z, with increased purchasing power or income in the form of additional y equal to $-x\Delta p = AZ$, where he held OA' of x and $A'Z$ of y. Eventually he attained a new equilibrium position at B.

The total increase in purchases of x equal to $A'B'$ can be thought of as consisting of two parts. First, the consumer spent AZ of y for

$A'C$ of additional x at the price of $(p + \Delta p)$. Thus, $A'C = -x\Delta p / (p + \Delta p) = 23.33x$. Second, he also increased his total expenditures on x by AN' of y, increasing his consumption by an additional CB', at the price of $(p + \Delta p)$. Thus, $CB' = -\Delta y / (p + \Delta p) =$

Figure 5-7

THE PROCESS OF READJUSTMENT TO A PRICE CHANGE

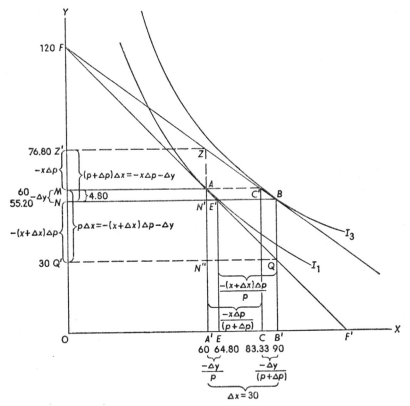

$6.67x$. His movement was *along* price line FZB, and $A'B' = A'C + CB' = 23.33x + 6.67x = 30.00x$. The total change in x is thus accounted for.

The Case of a Price Increase

The case can also be treated as one of a price increase, with the initial position at B, where the consumer purchased OB' of x and $B'B$ of y. In the following explanation we will use $(x + \Delta x) = 90$, $(y + \Delta y) = 55.20$, and $(p + \Delta p) = .72$ as the values in the initial position at B, and $x = 60$, $y = 60$, and $p = 1.00$ as the values at A, in order to be able to relate the explanation more explicitly to the diagrams. Thus, after the price increased from $(p + \Delta p)$ to p, or by $p - (p + \Delta p) = -\Delta p = .28$, and x and y changed by $-\Delta x$ and $-\Delta y$, the consumer found himself at A. The initial quantity of x now cost him $(x + \Delta x)(-\Delta p) = (90)(.28)$ more than before. Accordingly, he first reduced his purchases of x by $B'E$ by moving *along price line QAF*. But, since he was not yet in equilibrium at E', he next reduced his total purchases of x by EA', increasing his total expenditures on y by NM or $N'A$. The total *decrease* in purchases was $B'A'$, or $B'E + EA' = [(x + \Delta x)\Delta p]/p + \Delta y/p = (90)(-.28)/1.00 + (-4.80)/1.00 = -25.20x - 4.80x = -30x = -\Delta x$. Again the total change in x (a decrease) is accounted for.

Process of Readjustment: Constant Marginal Utility

If the marginal utility of the numeraire, y, is assumed constant, the indifference curves are vertically parallel and the rate of change of purchases of x as income changes is zero. Thus, in Figure 5–6, which depicts this case, as soon as the price of x declined, as indicated by budget equation line FZB, the consumer found himself in disequilibrium at Z as before. Again he readjusted by increasing his purchases of x and moving to B. However, once he had expended the increase in spending power or income equal to AZ, he had acquired $A'B'$, or $-x\Delta p/(p + \Delta p)$, of x; and, this amount *is* the total change in x. Total expenditures on x remained constant when the price of x declined. Thus, $\Delta y = 0$ and $\Delta x_a/\Delta m = 0$. The amount spent for the additional quantity of x, or $(p + \Delta p)\Delta x$, is now just exactly equal to the increase in income $(-x\Delta p)$, and the distance, AZ, in Figure 5–6 represents both magnitudes, for $\Delta y = 0$. The change in total expenditures on x, or ΔE, is merely the negative of the change in total expenditures on y, or $\Delta E = -\Delta y$. Therefore, if $\Delta y = 0$, although the price of y is not zero, $\Delta E = 0$. And so, since total expenditures on x remain constant, the elasticity of demand is unity in this case.[5]

When the case is treated as one of a price increase, with the initial position at B, we see that the consumer found himself after the price increase at Q, in Figure 5–6, where the original quantity of x, OB', now costs QB more in terms of y. Thus he readjusted by reducing his expenditures on x in terms of y by exactly QB, the change in cost of the quantity purchased at B, or by $-(x + \Delta x)\Delta p$, and again the total amount spent on x did not change. And so, in Figure 5–6, the

[5] The reader who is familiar with Slutsky's Equation No. 46 may be interested in the proof appearing in *Note A* at the end of this chapter.

total amount spent on x, *and, therefore, the quantity of y,* is the same both at A and at B, although the quantity of x purchased is greater in the initial position at B than at A, having *decreased* since $[(x + \Delta x) \Delta p]/p = B'A'$.

The Negatively Sloped Demand Curve: "Income" and "Substitution" Effects

In the preceding chapter, Marshall's argument that the demand curve must have a negative slope when the marginal utility of the *numeraire* is assumed constant has been explained. Contemporary indifference analysis dispenses with the assumption of constancy and defines the conditions under which, even though the marginal utility of the numeraire is variable, the demand curve will have a negative slope. There are various versions of this proof. In this section the basic proof, first invented by Eugen Slutsky,[6] which makes use of the cost-differences defined in Chapter 3, will be employed.

Slutsky's argument is essentially as follows. First, assume that in Figure 5–8 the consumer was initially in equilibrium at A and eventually attained a new equilibrium position at B after the price decrease. We know that he experienced an increase in income or spending power equal to $-x\Delta p$ as a result of the price decrease. But, it can be shown that if, either simultaneously with the price decrease or after he attains the new position at B at the new price of x (it makes no difference to the result what we assume in this regard), the consumer is taxed by an amount exactly equal to this increase in income, *he will, nevertheless, be purchasing more of x after the tax and the price decrease than he was purchasing at the old price in the position at A.* By taxing the consumer by an amount equal to the change in purchasing power resulting from the price decrease, *part of the change in purchases,* the so-called *income* or *indirect effect* on his purchases of the price change, is canceled out. But part of the total effect will remain. That part of the total effect on his purchases which is *not* canceled out was called by Slutsky by the name of *residual variation in demand,* and today it goes by the name of *substitution effect* or *direct effect* of the price change.

In Slutsky's analysis, the total effect on purchases of x of the price change is thus factored into two parts: (1) the *income* or *indirect* effect; and (2) the *substitution* or *direct* effect. Graphically, the effect

[6] Eugen Slutsky, "On the Theory of the Budget of the Consumer," reprinted in Kenneth Boulding and George Stigler (eds.), *Readings in Price Theory* (Homewood, Ill.: Richard D. Irwin, Inc., 1952), pp. 27–56, esp. pp. 41–42.

of such a tax is shown in Figure 5–8 by drawing a new budget equation line, *TALT'*, *through point A,* the initial equilibrium position,
parallel to the new price line, FC'BF''. The line is drawn *through*
point *A* to insure that after the tax, the consumer will be able to
purchase exactly the same quantities of *x* and of *y* as he did before the

Figure 5–8

INCOME AND SUBSTITUTION EFFECTS ILLUSTRATED

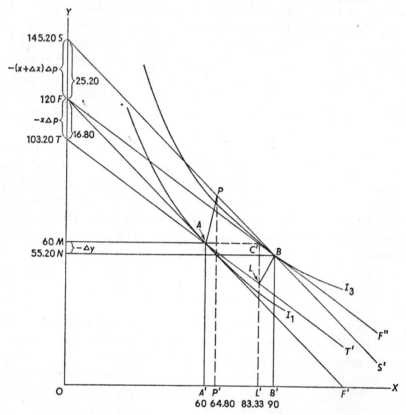

price change. This construction insures that the amount of the tax will
be *just* $-x\Delta p$. The line is drawn parallel to the new price line because the tax is levied at the new price of *x,* and the slope of the new
price or budget equation line reflects the new ratio of the prices of *x*
and of *y.* Thus, in Figure 5–8, the amount of the tax is $-x\Delta p$, or *TF,*
and it amounts to $16.80, or 16.80 units of *y.*

The next step in the argument is as follows. Since the budget equation or price line, *TALT',* which shows the effect of the tax, passes
through A, it follows that if after the tax the consumer merely pur-

chased the original quantities of x and of y, he would not be in equilibrium—for the line $TALT'$ *intersects* the indifference curve I_1. Consequently, *if the consumer were subjected to such a tax, he would nevertheless still increase his purchases of x beyond their level at A, because he can still increase his total utility by substituting x for y at the new price ratio even though all of the increase in spending power* $(-x\Delta p)$ *is taken away from him.*

Thus, after such a combined tax and price decrease, the consumer would not remain at A, but he would move to L in Figure 5–8. The distance $A'L'$ represents the *substitution* or *direct* effect. *At L he purchases more x than at A, but less than he would have purchased at B. This is the crux of the matter.* Alternatively, we can say that if the consumer were subjected to such a tax after he has attained B, he would reduce his purchases of x from B' to L'. This reduction in purchases is equal to the rate of change of purchases of x as income changes at the new price of x times the *decrease* in income resulting from the tax. Or, in Figure 5–8, the *income* or *indirect* effect on purchases amounts to $L'B'$, which is the same as $(-x\Delta p)(\Delta x_b/\Delta m)$. If we assume $\Delta x_b/\Delta m = .3968$, then, since $-x\Delta p = 16.80$, it follows that $(16.80)(.3968) = 6.67x = L'B'$ in Figure 5–8.

Now *the substitution effect on purchases must always have a sign which is just the opposite of that of the price change. Why?* Because the indifference curves are assumed to be convex to the origin. That is, if the consumer is taxed by an amount equal to the increase in spending power, the line $TALT'$ drawn through A will still intersect indifference curve I_1, making it profitable for him to change the commodity composition of his purchases because the price ratio has also changed. After the tax *and* the price change, the consumer would not be in equilibrium at A!

But the sign of the income effect can only be determined empirically because we can only determine empirically whether people will consume more, or less, or the same amount of any given commodity when their income increases while prices are unchanged.

The total effect on purchases is the sum of these two effects. In Figure 5–8, $A'B' = A'L' + L'B'$, and if $L'B' = 6.67x$ in our assumed case, then $A'L' + 6.67x = 30x$, the total change in x, or $A'L' = 30x - 6.67x = 23.33x$.

The argument, therefore, is that in any case in which the rate of change of purchases of x as income increases is positive, $\Delta x_b/\Delta m > 0$, so that purchases of x increase as income increases when prices are constant: (1) *since* a price decline increases income $(-x\Delta p > 0)$, the

indirect effect will be positive; and (2) *since* the direct effect is always positive when price declines, the total change in x must be positive $(\Delta x > 0)$ when price declines $(\Delta p < 0)$. Therefore, $\Delta x \Delta p <$
0, or the change in x and the change in price have opposite signs, and
the demand curve has a negative slope. (We use $\Delta x_b / \Delta m$ here because the consumer spends the increase in income at the lower price.)

It has already been noted in the preceding section that if purchases
of x increase as income increases when prices are constant, i.e., if
the rate of change of purchases as income changes is positive,
$\Delta x_a / \Delta m > 0$, the commodity is classified as *normal*. Thus we can summarize the argument in the preceding paragraph by saying that *the
demand curve will always have a negative slope if the commodity is
normal*, for then the income and substitution effects operate in the
same direction.

Can we similarly say that it will have a positive slope if the commodity is inferior? Unfortunately, for a neat conclusion, the answer
to this question is *not in every case, in fact, only in unusual cases*. For,
if the commodity is inferior, $\Delta x_b / \Delta m < 0$, the income effect will be
negative. In such a case, since the total effect is the sum of the income
and substitution effects, the commodity will still have a negatively
sloped demand curve when price declines, provided that the positive
substitution effect is *absolutely* greater (a greater number when the
signs of the two effects are ignored) than the negative income effect.

Only if the income effect is negative and absolutely greater than the
substitution effect will their sum be negative. Only in such a case is it
possible for the demand curve to have a positive slope, which means
merely that purchases decrease when price declines, or that $\Delta x \Delta p > 0$
so that Δp and Δx have the same sign.

The same results can be obtained by treating B as the initial position
and A as the final position in Figure 5–8. In such a case the consumer
is initially at B; and after the price rises, as indicated by the shift of
price line FBF'' to FAF', he finds himself at A. If, either simultaneously with the price rise or after it, he is given a subsidy absolutely equal to the reduction in income $[(x + \Delta x)\Delta p]$ which he
has suffered as a result of the price increase, he will be overcompensated. For such a subsidy is depicted graphically by drawing the
new budget equation or price line $SPBS'$ *through* point B, *parallel* to
the higher price ratio line, FAF'. Since the line passes through B, it
must *intersect* the original indifference curve, I_3. This fact means that
by substitution the consumer could attain a point like P on a higher
indifference curve than I_3 after such a price increase and subsidy. He

would not be in equilibrium at B after a price rise *and* a subsidy, so he would move to P.

In the price increase case, the *income* effect is the distance $P'A'$, which is simply the effect of the *decrease* in income times the rate of change of purchases of x as income increases at the higher price of x. The substitution, or direct, effect of the price change is the distance $B'P'$. Thus, as a result of the price increase, the consumer has experienced a *reduction* in purchasing power equal to $-(x + \Delta x)\Delta p =$ \$25.20, or 25.20y. If he were given a subsidy equal to this amount, the indirect or income effect of the price change would just be canceled out. Consequently, the reduction in consumption from B' to P', which would remain, must be the substitution effect. It is negative in this case because the price has increased. The total income effect is also negative in this case, since $(x + \Delta x)\Delta p < 0$, while $\Delta x_a/\Delta m > 0$. Thus purchases decrease by more than $B'P'$ when price rises. The income or indirect effect is $P'A'$, and the sum of $B'P' + P'A'$ is the total effect on purchases produced by the price change, or $B'A'$. Since $\Delta x_a/\Delta m > 0$, it is clear that x is a normal commodity in Figure 5–8. (We use $\Delta x_a/\Delta m$ here since the consumer reduces purchases after the price has risen.) And so, in this case, price rises, but purchases decrease, and the demand curve has a negative slope, $\Delta p \Delta x < 0$. Again, the direct and indirect effects operate in the same direction (that is, in the opposite direction from the price change).

D. A "WELFARE" APPLICATION; STATISTICAL STUDIES; ALTERNATIVE APPROACHES

The Edgeworth Box Diagram: The Gains from Trade

It is possible to show by means of indifference curve analysis that, assuming the distribution of income as given, an arbitrary fixed allocation of consumption goods to two individuals will not, except possibly by coincidence, produce as high a level of total satisfaction for the two *together* (the society as a whole) as would be attained if the individuals were left free to trade. In short, what follows is a graphical depiction of the proposition that when goods are distributed in accordance with people's preferences, these people will be "happier" than under any other scheme of distribution not in accordance with their preferences.

This demonstration was first developed by F. Y. Edgeworth, and hence its designation as the "Edgeworth Box Diagram." In Figure 5–9, assume that the total quantity of Y available to two individuals, designated A and B, is equal to O_AG, and that the total quantity of X is O_AH. A's indifference curves are convex to the origin O_A, and B's indifference curves are drawn convex to the origin O_B. Thus B's indifference diagram is rotated 180° from its usual position. The "box" O_AGO_BH represents the total amount of X and of Y available to *both* individuals.

Figure 5–9

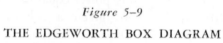

THE EDGEWORTH BOX DIAGRAM

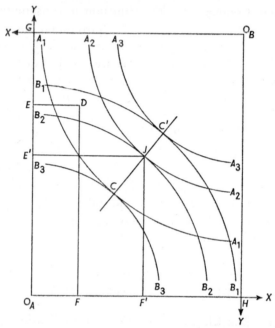

Assume now that the individuals are located at D. Then A will hold O_AE of Y and O_AF of X, while B will hold GE of Y and HF of X. Suppose now that the individuals are left free to trade. If A gives up $E'E$ of Y to B in exchange for FF' of X, A will attain position J on curve CJC'. Thus, in this exchange, A will have moved from point D *below* his own indifference curve A_2 to a point J on a higher indifference curve, A_2. B will similarly move from D, a point *below* his indifference curve B_2 to J on B_2. Thus both individuals have attained higher total utility surfaces as a result of the trade.

At J an indifference curve of A is just tangent to an indifference curve of B. (The box is full of undepicted indifference curves.) Thus, at J, the marginal rates of substitution of A and B for these two goods are the same, for the slopes of their indifference curves are the same.

The line CJC' represents different points of tangency between various indifference curves of A and B. Any point on CJC', *which is known as the contract curve,* can be shown by an argument similar to the preceding one to represent a higher level of total utility *for the two individuals together* than does any point not on the curve. However, movements *along* the contract curve involve a redistribution of income in favor of one or another of the parties, and so, although it is possible to improve A's position by moving him further along the contract curve toward C', or to improve B's position by moving him further along the contract curve toward C, the diagram does not provide any basis for determining which of *such* movements would be "best." Thus the Edgeworth Box Diagram shows the *gain from trade,* "assuming the distribution of income as given." Where on the contract curve the individuals will happen to be in a given case depends on their relative bargaining power, that is, on how much of the commodity which each prefers more he can obtain from the other for a given amount of the commodity he prefers less. Again we see that price theory concerns itself with *relative, not absolute,* maximum problems.

Henry Schultz's Classic Econometric Study of Demand

The death of Henry Schultz, a former professor of economics at the University of Chicago, in 1938 at a comparatively early age, cut short his brilliant work in the field of demand theory. Schultz's pioneer work, *The Theory and Measurement of Demand,*[7] contains a comprehensive survey of demand theory up to the date of publication of his book, as well as a complete description of the data and statistical methodology employed to derive sixteen agricultural commodity demand curves, thirteen for the United States and three for Canada. Some of Schultz's statistical methods have today been superseded, but his work stands as a major achievement in every respect and remains remarkably modern in comparison with recent work in this field.

One of the principal problems in the statistical determination of demand curves from market data may be stated in the form of a penetrating question asked by E. J. Working, "What do statistical demand curves show?"[8] That is, is it possible to determine statistically the theoretical demand curve from data which pertain only to the *points of in-*

---

[7] Henry Schultz, *The Theory and Measurement of Demand* (Chicago: University of Chicago Press, 1938).

[8] E. J. Working, "What Do Statistical 'Demand Curves' Show?" reprinted in Boulding and Stigler (eds.), *Readings in Price Theory,* pp. 97–115.

tersection of the theoretical unknown demand curve with a theoretical unknown supply curve at different points in time?

Schultz argued that he had taken account of this difficulty by restricting his study to agricultural commodities, for (1) their demand curves may be assumed to be reasonably stable; (2) their annual production is marketed within a certain period, making possible a more accurate determination of average prices than is true in the case of goods produced in a continuous flow; and (3) they were, at the time his book was written, produced under conditions approximating the theoretical conditions of perfect competition. Thus Schultz argued that the data relating to prices and quantities at given times were "essentially observations of the coordinates of points of intersection of a more or less fixed demand curve with a moving supply curve."[9]

Schultz's Sugar Demand Curve Equation

For an example of his work, let us examine Schultz's study of the demand for sugar. Schultz was somewhat troubled by whether to consider quantity the dependent variable or whether to consider price the dependent variable. Consequently, he derived equations to fit each case. Only his equations containing quantity as the dependent variable will be considered below. Schultz also determined logarithmic as well as linear equations, and derived equations based on total consumption and on money prices of sugar as well as equations based on per capita consumption and on "real" or deflated prices. Only the latter will be discussed below.

Schultz's basic assumption was that the quantity of sugar consumed depended both on prices and on time, or $x = f(p,t)$, during the period in question. He determined that the equation of the curve which most accurately described the data for sugar during the period 1875–95 was

$$x = 70.6200 \text{ lbs.} - 2.259p + .8371t .^{10} \qquad \text{(Sc. 3.2)}$$

This curve was fitted by the statistical method of "least squares," which involves minimizing the deviations of the actual observed values from a line of "best fit," drawn through the data, and, hence, defines the equation of the curve. The terms in the equation were given the following meaning: *x*, the per capita consumption of sugar in pounds at any given time during the period was equal to (1) a constant amount, 70.62 pounds; (2) less 2.26 pounds multiplied by the real price, *p*, in cents; and (3) plus .84 pounds multiplied by the number of years

---

[9] Schultz, *op. cit.*, p. 136.

[10] *Ibid.*, p. 187.

which had elapsed since July 1, 1885. The real price of sugar was determined by dividing the wholesale money price of sugar by a price index number. The date of origin, *t*, was taken as July 1, 1885. Thus one year after the date of origin, *t* was equal to *1*, two years later it was equal to *2*, and so on. During the period in question the deflated wholesale price varied from 2 cents to 16 cents, and per capita sugar consumption varied from 35 to 70 pounds.

The coefficients (the arithmetical values accompanying *p* and *t* in the equation) can be interpreted as follows. The term, $-2.259p$, shows that a change of 1 deflated cent in the price per pound of sugar was accompanied by a change of 2.26 pounds in the opposite direction in the per capita consumption of sugar. Thus the demand curve had a negative slope. Also, the value, $.8371t$, shows that during the period the demand curve kept shifting upward at a rate of .84 pounds per year.[11]

Schultz also employed a probability formula and demonstrated that the probability that the coefficient of *p* was zero during the period in question was very small. Thus, consumption depended on price. However, he also cautioned that the use of the probability formula as a basis for testing the goodness of fit of the curve, or for testing the reliability of his conclusions, was suspect. For sampling theory requires that the universe from which the sample is drawn can be defined, and in the case of a time series this is not possible.[12]

Richard Stone's Study of Consumer Expenditure and Behavior

A more recent study of consumer demand was published in 1954 by members of the Department of Applied Economics of Cambridge University.[13] This study includes estimates of income elasticities obtained by reducing expenditure elasticities obtained from budget data to 90 percent of their value. In addition, various "substitution" elasticities are estimated. These substitution elasticities are defined "as the contributions made to demand" or to purchases by substitution of other commodities for the commodity whose price has decreased when "real income" and other prices are held constant."[14] "Real income" in this context apparently means "total utility."

---

[11] *Ibid.*, pp. 187–89.

[12] *Ibid.*, pp. 211–15.

[13] Richard Stone (ed.), *The Measurement of Consumers' Expenditures and Behavior in the United Kingdom, 1920–1938* (Cambridge, England: Cambridge University Press, 1954), Vol. I.

[14] *Ibid.*, p. 262.

The statistical procedures employed in this study are far more sophisticated than those employed by Schultz. However, the statistical problems involved in all such studies are prodigious. There is room for much further work in this area. Indeed, one well-known econometrician, who provided a comprehensive review of both the Stone and the Schultz studies in 1955, remarked that "on the problem of assessing our results, we have probably not advanced at all" since the original Schultz study. This writer also noted that these studies involve "art" as much as they do science.[15] (The Schultz study is further considered in Appendix C to this book, and the theoretical basis of the Stone study, which rests upon the work of Professor J. R. Hicks, is also critically evaluated there.)

Marshallian versus Indifference Analysis; Alternative Approaches

Analysis of consumer behavior by means of indifference methods provides an alternative to the Marshallian analysis. To some extent the two methods supplement each other. However, the preceding pages make clear that indifference analysis rests upon restrictive assumptions just as does the Marshallian analysis. Both theories assume that commodities are divisible, that consumers are rational, and that they seek to maximize satisfaction. In short, both theories employ precisely the same equilibrium condition.

Indifference analysis substitutes the concept of a "marginal rate of substitution" for the concept of "marginal utility of income," and thus *apparently* concerns itself with a comparison of preferences rather than with the measurement of utility. But, in the final analysis, the use of taxes and subsidies, having a total utility either exactly or roughly equivalent to that change in total utility which the consumer experiences as a result of a price change, for purposes of isolating the income and substitution effects does, in fact, imply that *changes in utility* can be measured, quite as much as does Marshall's theory.

In recent years there have been applications of probability theory to utility analysis, but these analyses, though interesting, have not provided much further insight into the problem of actual consumer behavior.[16] Somewhat more fruitful have been some of the investigations

---

[15] Wm. C. Hood, "Empirical Studies of Demand," *Canadian Journal of Economics and Political Science,* Vol. XXI (August, 1955), pp. 309–27, esp. p. 327.

[16] See John Von Neumann and Oskar Morgenstern, *Theory of Games and Economic Behavior* (2d ed.; Princeton, N.J.: Princeton University Press, 1947), chap. i and Appendix; Milton Friedman and Leonard J. Savage, "The Utility Analysis of Choices Involving Risk," *Journal of Political Economy,* Vol. LVI (August, 1948), pp. 279–304, reprinted in Boulding and Stigler (eds.), *Readings in Price Theory,* pp. 57–96; C. E. Fer-

of consumer expectations[17] and investigations undertaken in conjunction with macroeconomic studies,[18] but these have not yet reached such a degree of reliability that they can serve as a basis for actual forecasts. Nor, as has been noted in Chapter 3, has the problem of measuring the effect on the consumer's surplus of a price change been solved. In this connection, it is instructive to consider briefly a recent study of the subject by a Congressional Committee.

Recommendations of the Price Statistics Review Committee (PSRC)

In 1961 the Subcommittee on Economic Statistics of the Joint Economic Committee of the Congress held hearings on a report on government price statistics prepared by a committee of economists under the Chairmanship of Professor George J. Stigler acting under a contract made by the Bureau of the Budget with the National Bureau of Economic Research.[19] In addition to the many technical questions involving problems of sampling and of the introduction of quality changes into contemporary government index numbers, the question of the theoretical basis of index numbers was also considered at some length during these hearings.

Of interest in terms of the subject matter of this chapter and the appendices to this book is one of the statements concerning the report of the PSRC made by the Commissioner of Labor Statistics, Mr. Ewan Clague. He said in part, in commenting on the recommendations of the Committee:

The committee expresses the opinion that a "constant-utility" or "welfare" index would be superior to a consumer price index for most purposes and should be developed to supersede the present index. In the Bureau's opinion, this is the most far reaching of the committee's recommendations. While the PSRC recognizes that full development of such an index may be a long-range problem, it favors any steps that will change the present CPI in this direction. The committee uses the terms "constant-utility" or "welfare" index in the sense of what theorists generally call a true cost-of-living index.

. . . It is important to note that the committee's strong preference for a wel-

---

guson, "An Essay on Cardinal Utility," *Southern Economic Journal,* Vol. XXV (July, 1958), pp. 11–23; and William J. Baumol, *Economic Theory and Operations Analysis* (New York: McGraw-Hill Book Co., Inc., 1961), pp. 331–46.

[17] George Katona, *The Powerful Consumer* (New York: McGraw-Hill Book Co., Inc., 1960).

[18] For a useful survey of work in this area, see Ruth P. Mack, "Economics of Consumption," in B. F. Haley (ed.), *A Survey of Contemporary Economics* (Homewood, Ill.: Richard D. Irwin, Inc., 1952), Vol. II, pp. 39–82.

[19] *Government Price Statistics* (*Report* of and *Hearings* before the Subcommittee on Economic Statistics, Joint Economic Committee, 87th Cong., 1st sess.) (Washington, D.C.: U.S. Government Printing Office, 1961).

fare index is the motivating force behind the various recommendations it makes. Thus, while some recommendations are pertinent to, and can be evaluated in terms of applicability to conventional fixed-weight indexes, other recommendations are acceptable only if one first accepts the committee's overriding preference for the welfare index approach.[20]

The Subcommittee, in its *Report* on the hearings, noted that

> Statistics users from industry, labor, and agriculture appearing or represented at the hearings were generally opposed to trying to go very far in the direction of an index which puts major emphasis on attempting to measure how much a given level of satisfaction, or welfare, costs in one period of time as against another. They based their opposition somewhat upon the concept of such an index but mostly upon the impossibility of finding proper measures for such satisfactions. The academic witnesses who appeared the last day of the hearings were more hopeful that something could be done in working toward a welfare index and that it would be worthwhile to devote research effort in that direction.[21]

In its recommendations and findings the Subcommittee accordingly stated:

> It is not clear to the subcommittee that the extended discussion in the hearings and the report of two kinds of indexes, one designed to price a level of *constant living* and the other designed to price a *constant level* of living, were sufficiently conclusive to enable us to formulate any recommendations in this area. A number of the comments and recommendations we have set forth are directed toward what seems to be a practical working conclusion at this time: namely, that the concept of a pure constant utility or welfare index is so elusive as to make it difficult even to discuss in the abstract, and at the same time a rigidly fixed market basket of goods would be unrelated to the fast-moving world we live in. In practice, we try to measure the change in prices of a package of goods and services which consumers indicate by their performance in the marketplace gives them equivalent satisfactions. Nonetheless, the concept of trying to approximate as closely as possible the cost of a constant level of living for the group of people whose purchases are represented by the index is worth additional work.
>
> This whole area of exploration is one in which our recommendation for continuing research has particular significance.[22]

The Appendices to This Book

The appendices to this book deal with a number of problems of the type mentioned in the quotations from the report of the Subcommittee given above. These appendices are intended primarily for reference and for use in a graduate course. The material in them is probably too

---

[20] *Ibid., Hearings,* Part II, p. 578.

[21] *Ibid., Report,* p. 5.

[22] *Ibid., Report,* pp. 12–13. (Italics in the original.)

time consuming and too difficult for use in an undergraduate course. Appendix A contains new graphical and arithmetical illustrations of the basic Slutsky equations, Appendix B contains a discussion of Marshall's consumer surplus analysis, Appendix C contains an explanation of Professor J. R. Hicks's method of isolating income effects[23] together with a further discussion of Henry Schultz's study of demand, and Appendix D deals with the question of index numbers.

NOTE A TO CHAPTER 5

This note is included primarily for the benefit of the reader who is already familiar with Slutsky's Equation No. 46.[24] If both sides of Slutsky's Equation No. 46 are multiplied by the total change in price (dp_i), the product is the total change in x_i, or dx_i.[25] If the equation is, in addition, multiplied by $(p_i + dp_i)$, the product is the amount spent for additional x_i, or

$$(p_i + dp_i)(dx_i) = \left[u' \frac{M_{ii}}{M} - x_i \frac{\partial x_i}{\partial s}\right][(dp_i)(p_i + dp_i)] . \quad \text{(S-46b)}$$

In the case in which the rate of change of purchases of x as income (s) changes is zero, or $\partial x_i/\partial s = 0$, the preceding equation reduces to

$$(p_i + dp_i)(dx_i) = \left[u' \frac{M_{ii}}{M}\right][(dp_i)(p_i + dp_i)] .$$

Note that the first term on the right in Slutsky's equation is the "substitution" term and can never be zero, but $\partial x_i/\partial s \gtreqless 0$.

Now our own Equation (4–4a.1) can be multiplied by -1 to read:

$$(p + \Delta p)\Delta x = -x\Delta p + \Delta E = -x\Delta p - \Delta y . \quad \text{(4–4a.2)}$$

In this equation, neither x nor Δp can ever be zero. However, $\Delta E = -\Delta y$ can be positive, negative, or zero. Thus, setting $\Delta E = 0$, we have

$$(p + \Delta p)\Delta x = -x\Delta p .$$

It follows, therefore, when ΔE and $\partial x_i/\partial s$ are both equal to zero that

$$(p + \Delta p)\Delta x = -x\Delta p = \left[u' \frac{M_{ii}}{M}\right][(dp_i)(p_i + dp_i)].$$

---

[23] See his *Value and Capital* (Oxford: Oxford University Press, 1946), and his *A Revision of Demand Theory* (Oxford: Oxford University Press, 1956).

[24] See Eugen Slutsky, "On the Theory of the Budget of the Consumer," reprinted in Boulding and Stigler (eds.), *Readings in Price Theory*, pp. 27–56, esp. p. 40.

[25] Compare Slutsky's own treatment of his Equation No. 51, *Ibid.*, p. 42.

That is, when the rate of change of purchases of x as income changes is zero, the indifference curves are vertically parallel, and the amount spent for the additional quantity of x is equal to the change in spending power, while $\Delta E = 0$, and $E_d = 1$.

The fact that constancy of the marginal utility of the numeraire is depicted by vertically parallel indifference curves is well known.[26] Professor Boulding has stated that vertically parallel indifference curves can also occur when the marginal utility of x changes proportionately with that of y. This proposition seems logical enough *when the simple case* of a change in income alone is considered, but the logic is less clear when a price change is considered. If the marginal utility of x changes proportionately with that of y, we have

$$\frac{\Delta u'_x}{u'_x} = \frac{\Delta u'_y}{u'_y} \, . \tag{i}$$

Now in the initial equilibrium position we must have

$$u'_x = (u'_y)(p) \, . \tag{ii}$$

And in the final equilibrium position we must have

$$(u'_x + \Delta u'_x) = (u'_y + \Delta u'_y)(p + \Delta p) \, . \tag{iii}$$

But from (i) we have

$$\Delta u'_x = \frac{\Delta u'_y}{u'_y} u'_x \, , \tag{ia}$$

and, substituting this into (iii), we have

$$u'_x + \frac{\Delta u'_y}{u'_y} u'_x = (u'_y + \Delta u'_y)(p + \Delta p) \, , \tag{iv}$$

or

$$\frac{(u'_x)(u'_y + \Delta u'_y)}{u'_y} = (u'_y + \Delta u'_y)(p + \Delta p) \, , \tag{iva}$$

or

$$u'_x = \frac{(u'_y + \Delta u'_y)(p + \Delta p)(u'_y)}{(u'_y + \Delta u'_y)} = (u'_y)(p + \Delta p) \, . \tag{ivb}$$

Equations (ivb) and (ii) are consistent only if $\Delta p = 0$! Apparently, in the case in question, the only price consistent with equilibrium is the price in the initial equilibrium position, and if the marginal utility

[26] See Hicks, *Value and Capital*, pp. 39–40; and Kenneth Boulding, *Economic Analysis* (3rd ed.; New York: Harper & Bros., 1955), pp. 815–16.

of x changes proportionately with that of y, no new equilibrium position will be attained when the price of x changes. Accordingly, if the indifference curves are vertically parallel and a new equilibrium position is attained when the price of x changes, the marginal utility of x cannot change proportionately with that of y.

SELECTED READINGS

ALLEN, R. G. D. *Mathematical Analysis for Economists,* pp. 339–40, 438–42, and 509–17. London: Macmillan & Co., Ltd., 1950.

BOBER, M. M. *Intermediate Price and Income Theory,* chap. iii. New York: W. W. Norton & Co., Inc., 1955.

BOULDING, KENNETH. *Economic Analysis,* chaps. xxxvi and xxxvii. 3rd ed. New York: Harper & Bros., 1955.

BUSHAW, D. W., AND CLOWER, R. W. *Introduction to Mathematical Economics,* pp. 102–42. Homewood, Ill.: Richard D. Irwin, Inc., 1957.

HENDERSON, JAMES M., AND QUANDT, RICHARD E. *Microeconomic Theory,* chap. ii. New York: McGraw-Hill Book Co., Inc., 1958.

HICKS, J. R. *Value and Capital,* Part I. 2d ed. Oxford: Clarendon Press, 1946.

KENEN, PETER B. "On the Geometry of Welfare Economics," *Quarterly Journal of Economics,* Vol. LXXI (August, 1957), pp. 426–47.

LEFTWICH, RICHARD H. *The Price System and Resource Allocation,* pp. 60–94. Rev. ed. New York: Holt, Rinehart & Winston, Inc., 1960.

MARSHALL, ALFRED. *Principles of Economics,* Mathematical Note XII. 8th ed. London: Macmillan & Co., Ltd., 1938.

SCHULTZ, HENRY. *The Theory and Measurement of Demand.* Chicago: University of Chicago Press, 1938.

STIGLER, GEORGE. *The Theory of Price,* chap. v, esp. pp. 79–80. Rev. ed. New York: The Macmillan Co., 1952.

STONE, RICHARD (ed.). *The Measurement of Consumers' Expenditures and Behavior in the United Kingdom, 1920–1938.* Cambridge, England: Cambridge University Press, 1954.

PART **|||**

PRODUCTION AND COSTS

The "Laws of Return"; The Theory of Production

Introduction

Logically the theory of the demand for products should be followed by a discussion of supply. In a very real sense, supply depends on costs, although the kinds of costs which are taken into account in a particular analysis depend on the time period which is under consideration. Thus the costs which are important in the short run are different from those which are important in the long run. The concept of cost, however, can be best understood in the light of the theory of production. For this reason we will first consider the theory of production and the relationships between product curves and cost curves and then turn our attention to the concept of supply.

The *laws of return* are statements of the principles according to which output is supposed to vary as inputs vary, or as a single input is varied, depending on the particular type of return which is under consideration. It is both necessary and important to distinguish between the case in which only one input varies so that the *proportion* among the inputs changes and the case in which all inputs are varied proportionately.

In general, the theory of production parallels the theory of demand, and anyone who understands the former should have no difficulty in comprehending the latter. Moreover, just as there is a Marshallian "utility" approach and a contemporary "indifference" approach to the theory of demand, so are there two different but related approaches to the theory of production, the "traditional" approach and the "isoquant" approach. Both will be explained, and the chapter will conclude with a summary of some statistical studies of production.

The Production Function

The production function is the economist's way of stating symbolically the assumption that the output of a firm depends on its inputs. It is generally written as $X = f(a, b, \ldots n)$, which means that the total product, X, depends on the amounts of the various inputs, a, b, $\ldots n$, used by the firm per unit of time. Now the total product, or total output X, can be varied, either by changing proportionately the quantities of all inputs simultaneously, or by changing the proportions in which given inputs are used.

If a proportionate change in all inputs produces a proportionate change in the product, for example, if doubling all inputs produces twice as much output, the production function is said to be *linearly homogeneous.* The assumption that the production function is of this nature is important in some econometric studies of the production function, and it is also made in the use of linear programming techniques which are explained in Part VII. Such an assumption may or may not be realistic in a given case. Moreover, we may note now that if production functions in the real world are in fact linearly homogeneous, and if prices of the inputs are assumed constant, the size of the most efficient unit of production, that is, of the most efficient plant, becomes indeterminate under perfect competition because then any one size unit is just as efficient as any other size unit. We will consider this question further in Chapter 9.

A simple example of a linearly homogeneous production function is one described by the relation

$$X = A\sqrt{ab} , \tag{6-1}$$

where A is a positive constant. Letting $A = 12$, we have for the value of X in the case of this function when $a = 1$ and $b = 1$:

$$X = 12\sqrt{(1)(1)} = 12 . \tag{6-1'}$$

Now if we double a and double b, we have

$$X = 12\sqrt{(2)(2)} = 24 , \tag{6-1''}$$

or twice as much output.

In the case of such a simple linearly homogeneous production function, as a is increased while b remains constant, or as b is increased while a remains constant, X increases at a constantly diminishing rate but never attains a maximum value. Also when either a or b is zero, nothing is produced.

A more complicated example of a linearly homogeneous production function is stated by the relation

$$X = \sqrt{2Cab - D(a^2) - E(b^2)} , \tag{6-2}$$

where C, D, and E are all positive constants and where $C^2 > (D)(E)$. This function will be arithmetically illustrated in the following discussion.

A. THE TRADITIONAL APPROACH

The Principle of Diminishing Average Returns

There are two different statements of the *Principle of Diminishing Returns to a Variable Input* which are concerned with the effect on output of variations in one input only, other things assumed constant.

Marshall and his predecessors stated the principle generally in *average* terms[1] by asserting that: other things equal, if the quantity of one input was increased by equal increments per unit of time, while the quantities of other inputs were held constant, and technology likewise remained unchanged, eventually total output would increase *less than proportionately*. This statement of the principle thus emphasizes the fact that after a certain quantity of the variable factor has been employed, *average output* begins to decline. This principle is depicted graphically in Figure 6–1, and the arithmetical values on which Figure 6–1 is based are contained in Table 6–1A.

The statement of the principle of diminishing *average* returns to the variable factor is often applied in welfare economics. That is, in the works of earlier economists and, indeed, in the works of some contemporary ones, the notion of maximum average product, the highest ratio of total output to population, is taken as a measure of economic well-being. Thus, assuming the distribution of income as given, a society with a high output per member is better off than one with a low average product. Moreover, the argument runs, if in a given society the average product could be increased by increasing the use of labor, welfare would be increased by policies aimed at increasing population. Conversely, in societies in which average product is low because of overpopulation, welfare could be increased by increasing output relative to population and by reducing population relative to output (presumably by birth control measures). Indeed, the principle of diminishing average returns originated in the discussions of economists like Thomas Malthus, David Ricardo, and Sir Edward West, who were concerned with the problem of the pressure of population on the means of subsistence. We will have occasion to consider this question again later in Chapter 14, when we consider the doctrine of economic rent.

---

[1] Alfred Marshall, *Principles of Economics* (8th ed.; London: Macmillan & Co., Ltd., 1938), pp. 150–56.

A Graphical and Arithmetical Illustration

Both Table 6–1A and Figure 6–1 show how the total product, X, changes when the quantity of the variable factor, a, is increased, technology and the quantity of the other factor, b, remaining constant, according to our assumed production function in Equation (6–2). A change in technology would involve shifting the entire total product curve in Figure 6–1 into a new position and change the values of X in Table 6–1A.

The arithmetical values contained in Table 6–1A are based on Equa-

Table 6–1A
DIMINISHING MARGINAL AND AVERAGE RETURNS

(1)	(2)	(3)	(4)	(5)	(6)	(7)	(8)	(9)	(10)	(11)
a	b	X	$\dfrac{X}{a}$	$\dfrac{\partial X}{\partial a}$	a	b	X	$\dfrac{X}{b}$	$\dfrac{\partial X}{\partial b}$	
0.78	10	1.00	1.28	368.00	1	12.80	1.28	0.10	−28.80	Stage I
1.00	10	12.65	12.65	28.46	1	10.00	12.65	1.27	− 1.58	for a,
1.50	10	22.58	15.05	15.05	1	6.67	15.05	2.26	0.00	III for b
			Point of Diminishing Average Returns to a							
			Point of Absolutely Diminishing Returns to b							
2	10	28.98	14.49	11.00	1	5.00	14.49	2.90	0.69	
3	10	37.95	12.65	7.38	1	3.34	12.65	3.79	1.58	
4	10	44.27	11.07	5.42	1	2.50	11.07	4.43	2.26	
5	10	48.99	9.80	4.08	1	2.00	9.80	4.90	2.85	Stage II
6	10	52.54	8.75	3.05	1	1.67	8.75	5.25	3.42	for both
7	10	55.14	7.88	2.18	1	1.43	7.88	5.51	3.98	a and b
8	10	56.94	7.12	1.40	1	1.25	7.12	5.70	4.57	
9	10	57.97	6.44	0.69	1	1.11	6.44	5.80	5.17	
10	10	58.31	5.83	0.00	1	1.00	5.83	5.83	5.83	
			Point of Absolutely Diminishing Returns to a							
			Point of Diminishing Average Returns to b							
11	10	57.97	5.27	−0.69	1	0.91	5.27	5.80	6.57	Stage III
12	10	56.94	4.75	−1.40	1	0.83	4.75	5.70	7.38	for a,
										I for b

Notes:

(I). $X = \sqrt{2Cab - D(a^2) - E(b^2)}$, $C = 40, D = 40, E = 6, b = 10.$

(II). $\dfrac{\partial X}{\partial a} = \dfrac{Cb - Da}{\sqrt{2Cab - D(a^2) - E(b^2)}} = \dfrac{Cb - Da}{X}$.

(III). $\dfrac{\partial X}{\partial b} = \dfrac{Ca - Eb}{\sqrt{2Cab - D(a^2) - E(b^2)}} = \dfrac{Ca - Eb}{X}$. Now when $a = 1.5$,

$\dfrac{\partial X}{\partial b} = \dfrac{(40)(1.5) - (6)(10)}{22.58} = 0$. Similarly, when $a = 10$,

$\dfrac{\partial X}{\partial a} = \dfrac{(40)(10) - (40)(10)}{58.31} = 0$.

(IV). Column (8) can be thought of as the total product when a is kept constant at 1 unit and b is varied. Thus Column (8) is the same as Column (4), which is the average product of a at different ratios of a and b. Column (9) can be computed either by dividing Column (3) by Column (2) or by dividing Column (8) by Column (7).

tion (6–2) in the case in which $C = 40$, $D = 40$, $E = 6$, and $b = 10$. The third column in Table 6–1A thus shows how total product varies in the case of these assumed values as a changes when b is held constant at ten units. In order to determine the value of X when $a = 1$ and

Figure 6–1

DIMINISHING MARGINAL AND AVERAGE RETURNS TO
A VARIABLE INPUT

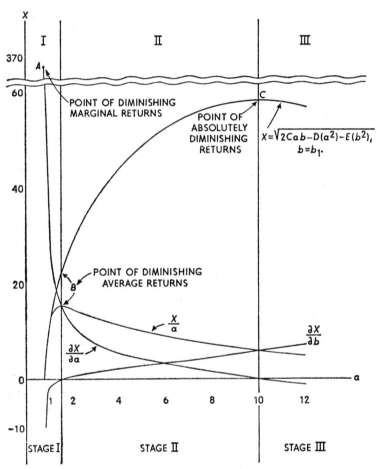

$b = 10$, we substitute the appropriate values into our Equation (6–2) as follows:

$$X_{1,10} = \sqrt{(2)(40)(1)(10) - (40)(1^2) - (6)(10^2)} = 12.65 . \quad (6\text{--}2')$$

And when a is increased by one unit while b is not changed, so that $a = 2$ and $b = 10$, we have, similarly,

$$X_{2,10} = \sqrt{(2)(40)(2)(10) - (40)(2^2) - (6)(10^2)} = 28.98 . \quad (6\text{--}2a')$$

But now note that in the case in which a and b are *both* doubled from their original values so that $a = 2$, $b = 20$, we have

$$X_{2,20} = \sqrt{(2)(40)(2)(20) - (40)(2^2) - (6)(20^2)}$$
$$= \sqrt{3,200 - 2,560} = \sqrt{640} = 25.298 . \qquad (6\text{-}2b')$$

This amount is exactly twice 12.649, the value of $X_{1,10}$, the output previously obtained from the use of half as much input of a and b. Thus our function is linearly homogeneous, as defined above. That is, when the inputs are increased proportionately, output also increases proportionately.

In Figure 6–1, the curve X/a is the average product curve, or the curve of the per unit amount of the product at different inputs of a. The arithmetical values of X/a appear in the fourth column of Table 6–1A. In Figure 6–1 this curve rises throughout the range of Stage I, which ends at 1.5 units of a. The average product curve, X/a, begins to decline at the Point of Diminishing Average Returns to the Variable Factor. This point is identified by the letter B and in words in Figure 6–1. The curve then declines throughout Stages II and III.

Stage of Increasing Average Returns: Stage I

Stage I is known as the *Stage of Increasing Average Returns to the Variable Factor.* Throughout this stage the average product curve, X/a, rises. In our diagram and in our table, the Stage of Increasing Average Returns *ends at point B, the Point of Diminishing Average Returns.* This point *is identified by the fact that it is the point at which the curve of the marginal product of a, $\partial X/\partial a$, crosses the average product curve, X/a.*

The curve of the marginal product of a in Table 6–1A is the curve of the *exact* rate of change of total product as input of a changes, or the curve of the partial derivative $\partial X/\partial a$. An illustration in terms of average rates of change is given later in Table 6–1B. The method of obtaining the derivative is not really an essential point in our explanation, and so we will merely assert that the formula for this exact rate of change in the case of our assumed production function is

$$\frac{\partial X}{\partial a} = \frac{Cb - Da}{\sqrt{2Cab - D(a^2) - E(b^2)}} = \frac{Cb - Da}{X} .$$

Similarly, the formula for the exact rate of change of X as b changes when a remains constant is equal to

$$\frac{\partial X}{\partial b} = \frac{Ca - Eb}{\sqrt{2Cab - D(a^2) - E(b^2)}} = \frac{Ca - Eb}{X} .$$

By substituting the given values of C, b, D, E, and X into these formulas and by allowing a to assume different values, the arithmetical values of $\partial X/\partial a$ and of $\partial X/\partial b$, the marginal products of a and of b, respectively, can be obtained and entered in our table in the relevant columns. [See notes (II) and (III) to Table 6–1A. Thus, in Table 6–1A and Figure 6–1, the indicated value of $\partial X/\partial b$ is the one which corresponds to the indicated value of $\partial X/\partial a$.]

Since our production function is linearly homogeneous, Equation (3–3) from Chapter 3 can be employed to explain the relationship among the various magnitudes given in Table 6–1A. The reader will recall that this equation states Euler's Theorem, namely that in the case of a homogeneous function,

$$X = \frac{\partial X}{\partial a}a + \frac{\partial X}{\partial b}b \ . \tag{3-3}$$

This theorem thus states that in the case of a homogeneous production function, the total product is equal to the sum of the respective marginal products of the inputs multiplied by the amounts of the relevant inputs used.[2] At the Point of Diminishing Average Returns to the Variable Factor (B in Figure 6–1), where $a = 1.5$, we have the arithmetical value for this equation as

$$X_{1.5,10} = (15.05)(1.5) + (0)(10) = 22.58 \ . \tag{3-3'}$$

Similarly, when two units of a are being used, we have the arithmetical result,

$$X_{2,10} = (11.0)(2) + (.69)(10) = 22.0 + 6.9 = 28.9 \ . \tag{3-3''}$$

As a matter of fact, we can generalize, for when $\partial X/\partial b = 0$, or when the marginal product of b is zero, Equation (3–3) reduces to

$$X = \frac{\partial X}{\partial a}a + (0)b = \frac{\partial X}{\partial a}a \ . \tag{3-3a}$$

From this it follows, by dividing both sides of the equation by a, that

$$\frac{X}{a} = \frac{\partial X}{\partial a} \ , \tag{3-3b}$$

when the marginal product of the fixed factor, b, is zero. In short, the marginal product of a is equal to the average product of a when the marginal product of the fixed factor is zero, and in our Table 6–1A, we see that this is, indeed, the case at B, when $a = 1.5$ units.

---

[2] See Sidney Weintraub, *An Approach to the Theory of Income Distribution* (Philadelphia: Chilton Co., 1958), pp. 10–11.

Similarly, when the marginal product of a is zero, $\partial X/\partial a = 0$, we see as before that

$$\frac{X}{b} = \frac{\partial X}{\partial b}, \qquad (3\text{-}3c)$$

or the average product of b is equal to the marginal product of b, and this result occurs at ten units of a in our table.[3]

It follows from Euler's Theorem and the fact that our production function is assumed to be linearly homogeneous that whenever the marginal product of a is greater than the average product of a, the marginal product of b *must* be negative. [See Equations (3–3) and (3–3′).] Thus the Stage of Increasing Average Returns to the Variable Factor, or Stage I in our diagram, is characterized by the facts that the marginal product of a is positive and greater than the average product of a, and the marginal product of b is negative.

Stage of Diminishing Average Returns: Stage II

The curve of the marginal product of a crosses the a axis and so becomes equal to zero at ten units of a in our diagram, and this point marks the *Point of Absolutely Diminishing Returns,* the point *at which total product is a maximum and begins to decrease absolutely.* It is identified by the letter C and in words in Figure 6–1. The range between point B and point C in our diagram is Stage II, the *Stage of Diminishing Average Returns to the Variable Factor.* It thus *lies between the Point of Diminishing Average Returns and the Point of Absolutely Diminishing Returns.* In Stage II, total product continues to increase, but less than proportionately. (See Table 6–1A and Figure 6–1.) That is, throughout Stage II the condition exists that the marginal product of a is less than the average product of a, and thus it also fol-

---

[3] The fact that the average product of a is the same numerically as the average and marginal products of b when ten units of a are being used in Figure 6–1 arises from the fact that we have assumed $b = 10$ in the arithmetical illustration, and $\partial X/\partial a = 0$ when $a = 10$. If we had assumed $b = 1$, the marginal and average products of b would be equal to the total product at the point at which the marginal product of a is zero. For by Euler's Theorem, it follows that when $b = 1$, and when $\partial X/\partial a = 0$, we have $X/b = (X/b)(b) = (\partial X/\partial b)(b) = X$. A number of writers have drawn diagrams in which the marginal product of b is equal to the total product when the marginal product of a is zero, but have failed to explain the reason for this special result. Many writers also draw the total product curve with a point of inflection and then "assume that the production function is linearly homogeneous." A thorough search of the literature has failed to reveal a single case in which a writer has *specified* a linearly homogeneous production function which produces such a total product curve! The procedure of drawing the curve in this way and then assuming it to be linearly homogeneous is confusing, and those who draw the curve in this way and make the assumption have the burden of stating the specific function they are employing. A nonlinearly homogeneous production function will be illustrated in Chapter 7.

lows, again from Euler's Theorem, that the marginal product of *b* in this stage must be positive. The average product of *a* decreases.

Stage of Absolutely Diminishing Returns: Stage III

Stage III is known as the *Stage of Absolutely Diminishing Returns to the Variable Factor*, and it *is characterized by the fact that total product declines absolutely*, that is, by a negative marginal product of *a* and a positive, but declining, average product of *a*. In this stage the marginal product of *b* is positive, while the marginal product of *a* is less than the average product of *a* and is negative.

The Marginal Product of *b*

The fact that the marginal product of *b* is negative in Stage I means that too much of *b* is being used with *a* in this stage, or, alternatively, that too little of *a* is being used with a given amount of *b*. Thus, beginning with the sixth column of Table 6–1A, we see the effect of decreasing the amount of *b* used with one unit of *a*. As the quantity of *b* used with *one* unit of *a* is diminished in the seventh column of the table, the marginal product of *b*, shown in the tenth column of Table 6–1A, increases from −28.8 to 0 in Stage I. This means that too much *b* is being used with the given quantity of *a* in Stage I. Also, in the first five columns of the table we see that as the quantity of *a* used with the given quantity of *b* in Stage I is increased, the average product of *a* rises. Thus too little *a* is being used with the given amount of *b*.

Note that the ratio between *a* and *b* in the first two columns of Table 6–1A is the same as the ratio between *a* and *b* in the sixth and seventh columns of the table. That is, for example, $10b/1.5a = 6.67b/1a$, and the ratios are equal. (See also Note IV to Table 6–1A.)

The Principle Is Reversible

The data relating to the marginal product of *b* can also be read from the bottom of the table to the top. By doing so, we see that by increasing the quantity of *b* employed with one unit of *a*, the average product of *b* can first be made to increase. Thus, the Stage of Absolutely Diminishing Returns to *a* is the Stage of Increasing Average Returns to *b*. Or, Stage III with regard to *a* corresponds to Stage I with regard to *b*. When we read the table from bottom to top, we also see that the Point of Absolutely Diminishing Returns to the variable factor *a* represents the Point of Diminishing Average Returns to the fixed factor *b*. Stage II is the same for both *a* and *b*, except that the marginal products are moving in opposite directions. In reading Table 6–1A from the bottom to the top, we are, in effect, moving from a point on the a axis toward the origin in Figure 6–1, thereby decreasing the amount of a used with the given amount of b.

The Point of Diminishing Average Returns to a thus represents the Point of Absolutely Diminishing Returns to b, and, finally, the Stage of Increasing Average Returns to a represents the Stage of Absolutely Diminishing Returns to b. Thus the principle of diminishing average returns is *symmetrical* with respect to a and b.

Effect of Assumption of Linearly Homogeneous Production Function

When the production function is linearly homogeneous, the marginal product and the average product are independent of the scale of production and depend only on the ratio between the inputs. The meaning of this condition can be illustrated by first writing Euler's Theorem as before:

$$X = \frac{\partial X}{\partial a}a + \frac{\partial X}{\partial b}b \ . \tag{3-3}$$

Now, since the production function is linearly homogeneous, a proportionate increase, k, in a and b produces a proportionate increase in output, or in X, and so

$$kX = \frac{\partial X}{\partial a}ka + \frac{\partial X}{\partial b}kb \ . \tag{3-3d}$$

In the case in which the marginal product of b is zero, we have already seen that the marginal product of a is equal to its average product, or

$$\frac{X}{a} = \frac{\partial X}{\partial a} \ , \tag{3-3b}$$

and, arithmetically, in the case of our assumed data we have produced

$$\frac{22.58}{1.5} = 15.05 \ . \tag{3-3b'}$$

Accordingly, at the point at which the marginal product of b is zero in the case of our new function in (3–3d) above, we also have this equality, or

$$\frac{kX}{ka} = \frac{X}{a} = \frac{\partial X}{\partial a} \ . \tag{3-3e = 3-3b}$$

For example, if $k = 2$, which means that we have doubled our inputs of a and of b and also doubled our output, the arithmetical values would be

$$\frac{2(22.58)}{2(1.5)} = \frac{45.16}{3.0} = 15.05 . \qquad (3\text{–}3e' = 3\text{–}3b')$$

Thus the marginal product of a and the average product of a are the same as before, but these values now occur at inputs of a and of b which are exactly twice as great as before. That is, the marginal product and the average product are independent of the scale of production.

We will see in the next chapter, that, in such a case, long-run marginal cost and long-run average cost are identical and are the same horizontal line, parallel to the X axis. In other words, long-run marginal and average costs are constant in such a case. However, if the production function shows either increasing or decreasing returns to scale, the preceding statement cannot be made.

Table 6–1B

DIMINISHING RETURNS IN TERMS OF AVERAGE RATES
OF CHANGE

(1)	(2)	(3)	(4)	(5)	(6)	(7)	(8)	(9)	(10)	(11)
a	b	X	$\dfrac{X}{a}$	$\dfrac{\Delta X_a}{\Delta a}$	a	b	X	$\dfrac{X}{b}$	$\dfrac{\Delta X_b}{\Delta b}$	Stage
0.78	10	1.00	1.28	53.00	1	12.80	1.28	0.10	−3.930	Stage I
1.00	10	12.65	12.65	19.86	1	10.00	12.65	1.26	0.677	for a and
1.50	10	22.58	15.05	15.05	1	6.67	15.05	2.26	0.000	III for b
			Point of Diminishing Average Returns to a							
			Point of Absolutely Diminishing Returns to b							
2	10	28.98	14.49	8.97	1	5.00	14.79	2.90	1.10	
3	10	37.95	12.65	6.32	1	3.34	12.65	3.79	1.90	
4	10	44.27	11.07	4.72	1	2.50	11.07	4.43	2.54	
5	10	48.99	9.80	3.55	1	2.00	9.80	4.90	3.12	Stage II
6	10	52.54	8.75	2.60	1	1.67	8.75	5.25	3.69	for both
7	10	55.14	7.88	1.80	1	1.43	7.88	5.51	4.25	a and b
8	10	56.94	7.12	1.03	1	1.25	7.12	5.70	4.77	
9	10	57.97	6.44	0.34	1	1.11	6.44	5.80	5.49	
10	10	58.31	5.83	0.00	1	1.00	5.83	5.83	5.83	
			Point of Absolutely Diminishing Returns to a							
			Point of Diminishing Average Returns to b							
11	10	57.94	5.27	−0.34	1	0.91	5.27	5.80	6.17	Stage III
12	10	56.94	4.75	−1.80	1	0.834	4.75	5.70	7.85	for a and I for b

The student should note that the exact rate of change, $\partial X/\partial a$, which has been used in Table 6–1A is not the same thing as the average rate of change, $\Delta X/\Delta a$, used in Table 6–1B above. He may wish to refer to Chapter 3 to refresh his memory concerning the difference between these two concepts.

In Table 6–1A the marginal product of a has been determined by the formula given earlier. In Table 6–1B, the marginal product of a is defined as equal to $\Delta X_a / \Delta a$, for the benefit of the student who is troubled by the use of the calculus formula in Table 6–1A. Thus, in Table 6–1B, when $a = 2$, we have $\Delta X_a / \Delta a = (37.95 - 28.98) / (3 - 2) = 8.97/1 = 8.97$. Similarly, when $a = 1$, we have $\Delta X_a / \Delta a = (22.58 - 12.65)/(1.5 - 1) = 9.93/.5 = 19.86$. Also, when $a = 1.5$, we know from the preceding discussion that the marginal product of b is zero, and so the marginal product of a must be equal to its average product at this point. Thus, when $a = 1.5$, we have $\Delta X_a / \Delta a = (22.58 - 0)/(1.5 - 0) = 15.05$. The marginal productivity of b is determined in Table 6–1B as a *residual*, by applying Euler's Theorem, although strictly speaking this theorem can only be used in the case of infinitesimal changes in the variables, as in the case in Table 6–1A. In any case, both our tables illustrate the same principles and relationships.

The Principle of Diminishing Marginal Returns

Many contemporary economists state the principle we have been discussing in *marginal* terms rather than in average terms, by asserting that, other things equal, if the quantity of one input is increased by equal increments per unit of time while the quantities of other inputs are held constant and technology likewise remains unchanged, eventually output increases at a *decreasing* rate.[4] Thus this statement emphasizes the Point of Diminishing *Marginal* Returns to the Variable Factor, a, which is also identified in words and by the letter A in Figure 6–1, and which occurs at .78 units of a in Table 6–1A and in Figure 6–1. In our case the marginal productivity of a diminishes as soon as a positive amount of product X is obtained. The average product, X/a, nevertheless continues to increase throughout Stage I because the marginal product of a is greater than the average product in this stage, or $\partial X / \partial a > X/a$. In our case the Point of Diminishing Marginal Returns to the Variable Factor lies within Stage I, the Stage of Increasing Average Returns to the Variable Factor.

The reason why contemporary economists prefer the statement of the Principle of Diminishing Returns to the Variable Input in marginal, rather than in average, terms will become clear in the next chapter, which contains an explanation of costs. Note now, however, that in terms of the variable input, a, the *cost* of the amount of product ob-

---

[4] George Stigler, *The Theory of Price* (rev. ed.; New York: The Macmillan Co., 1952), p. 111.

tained from the marginal unit of a is the reciprocal of the amount of product which can be obtained from using an additional small quantity of the variable input, a. Thus, if the marginal productivity of a is decreasing, the marginal cost of the product in terms of a (the amount of a needed to produce an additional unit of product) must be increasing.

An important function of the assumption of diminishing marginal productivity, we will learn later, is to place this restriction on the behavior of marginal cost. The theory of the way in which the firm determines how much to produce from existing capacity rests upon an assumption of an eventually increasing marginal cost, and ultimately, therefore, upon an assumption of an eventually diminishing marginal product of the variable input.

Preliminary Definitions of Short Run and Long Run

Full definition of the concepts of *time, short run,* and *long run,* must be postponed to the next chapter. However, for the purpose of making use of these concepts in the discussion which follows, we can define the *short-run period of time as a period during which the firm can change its output from existing capacity* but *cannot change its capacity.* Thus, in the short run, the firm can vary its variable inputs but cannot vary its fixed inputs. Short-run analysis thus is associated with the principles of diminishing marginal and average returns to variable inputs. *In the long run the firm can change its existing capacity.* Thus, in the long run, all inputs are variable, and there are no fixed inputs. That is, long-run analysis is related to the concept of returns to scale.

Short-Run Average Cost of Production: Special Cases

The principle of diminishing returns, whether stated in average terms or in marginal terms, relates to the *proportions* in which inputs are used, *not* to the quantities of all of them which are used. It is a short-run concept. If the cost of input b is zero, that is to say, if b is so plentiful that it is a free resource and has no price, the short-run average cost of production of X will be least at the point at which the average product of a is a maximum, the Point of Diminishing Average Returns to a. For by definition, if the average product of a is a maximum, the cost per unit of product in terms of a is then at a minimum at the same point. Thus the short-run average cost of production, if a is the only resource having a cost, must be least at the *beginning* of Stage II.

On the other hand, for the same reason, if a is a free resource and b has a price, the short-run average cost of production will be least at the point at which the average product of b is a maximum, or at the *end* of Stage II. Recall that in Table 6–1A, at the point at which the marginal product of a is zero (ten units of a), the average product of b is a maximum; and the average product of a is a maximum at the point (1.5 units of a) at which the marginal product of b is zero.

If neither a nor b is a free resource, the minimum short-run average cost of production lies somewhere *within* Stage II, where the marginal products of both factors are positive. The precise proportions in which the two factors will then be employed at the minimum short-run average cost depends both on their relative prices and productivities. We will consider the question further in the next chapter.

Marshall's "Principle of Substitution"

Just as in the theory of demand the consumer will be maximizing his total utility from a given income at the point at which the ratios of the marginal utilities of various commodities to their prices are equal, so in the theory of production is the total product which can be produced from *given expenditures* on inputs at a maximum at the point at which the ratios of the marginal productivities of the different inputs to their prices are equal. This condition can be stated symbolically as

$$\frac{f_a}{p_a} = \frac{f_b}{p_b} = \cdots \frac{f_n}{p_n} = d \, , \tag{6–3}$$

where f means marginal product, or $f_a = \partial X / \partial a$ and $f_b = \partial X / \partial b$, and p_a and p_b are the prices of the *variable* inputs, a and b, respectively. [The term $(\cdots f_n / p_n)$ means that the condition must hold for all inputs, irrespective of the number of them in the problem.] In the equation, d represents a dollar's worth of output.

The condition thus states that the amount of output obtained from an additional dollar's worth of expenditures on any one variable input (or d) must be just exactly equal to that obtained from an additional dollar spent on any other. Marshall called the condition *the principle of substitution,* for if it is not met, total output can be increased with *the given amount of total expenditures* by increasing expenditures on relatively more valuable inputs and reducing expenditures on relatively less valuable ones.

The condition is always met for *all* inputs at *some* (one) point on every short-run cost curve, even though expenditures on the fixed input cannot be changed, and *it must always be met for all variable inputs.* We will discuss the question of cost curves in detail in the next chapter. For the present, if we assume that the price of a unit of a is $10 and the price of a unit of b is $1.00, the condition will be met *in our case* of $b = 10$, when 31.80 units of X are being produced with 2.273 units of a. In this case we have for the equation,

$$\frac{f_a}{p_a} = \frac{9.72}{\$10} = \frac{f_b}{p_b} = \frac{.972}{\$1.00} = .972X = d \ . \tag{6-3'}$$

Thus the condition is met for both the fixed and the variable inputs at *one* point in the case of our function when $b = 10$. We will make much use of this principle in the next section as well as in later chapters of this book.

Returns to Scale

The concept of "returns to scale" relates to changes in the *quantities* of all factors employed, *not* to a change in *the proportion* in which given factors are employed. Thus it relates to the behavior of total output as *all* inputs are varied and is a long-run concept. As we have already seen, if total product or output (X) increases proportionately as all the inputs are increased proportionately, the case involves constant returns to scale, and the production function is linearly homogeneous. As we have also already seen, this type of production function is not inconsistent with the principles of increasing or diminishing marginal or average returns to the variable factor, for even though output increases proportionately as inputs are increased proportionately, this fact alone does *not* require or result in a situation in which output changes proportionately *when one factor only is changed* and others are held constant.

If total output increases more than proportionately as all inputs are increased proportionately, say that X triples while all inputs are doubled, the case involves increasing returns to scale and decreasing long-run average cost. If the total output increases less than proportionately, say that total output doubles when inputs are tripled, the case involves decreasing returns to scale and increasing long-run average cost. Note that variation of all inputs occurs in this case, and "returns to scale" are thus concerned with "long-run costs," while "diminishing returns to a variable input" relate to "short-run costs." We will discuss these questions further in the next chapter. Our next problem is to consider a "different" approach to the problem of production.

B. THE ISOQUANT APPROACH

Definition and Characteristics of Isoquants

An *isoquant*, or isoproduct curve, *is a contour line and represents the different combinations of two inputs with which a given amount of product can be produced.* Thus, product, like utility, is measured as an *elevation* in such a contour map.

In Figure 6–2 is depicted an isoquant. All along *Iq* 16.85, total

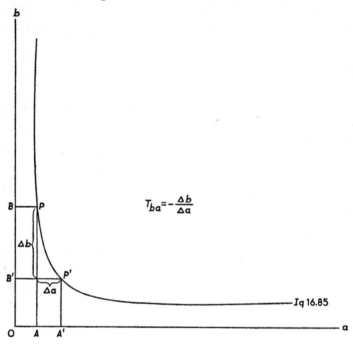

Figure 6–2

AN ISOQUANT OR ISOPRODUCT CURVE

product, *X,* is the same, just as along a given indifference curve, total utility is the same. At point *P,* the quantity of input *b* required to produce 16.85 units of *X* is *OB,* while the quantity of *a* required is *OA.* As one moves to the right along the isoquant, the quantity of *b* required to maintain output constant diminishes while the quantity of *a* needed increases. Thus at *P′* the quantity of *b* has decreased to *OB′,* while that of *a* has increased to *OA′.*

The equation of an isoquant is, of course, the same as that of any other contour line, or

$$\Delta X = f_a \Delta a + f_b \Delta b = 0 \,, \tag{6–4}$$

which is already familiar to the student both as a form of Equation (3–4) and because of its similarity to the formula for indifference curves contained in Equation (5–1). The symbols f_a and f_b represent the marginal products of *a* and of *b,* respectively. As usual, the equation requires that if X, the total product, is to remain constant, or $\Delta X = 0$, *since* the marginal products of a and of b are both assumed positive in the relevant range, as a increases, b must decrease along the isoquant. In general, therefore, isoquants will be convex to the origin within the relevant range and negatively sloping.

In Figure 6–3 is depicted a family of isoquants. The isoquants in this

Figure 6–3
ISOQUANTS AND RIDGE LINES

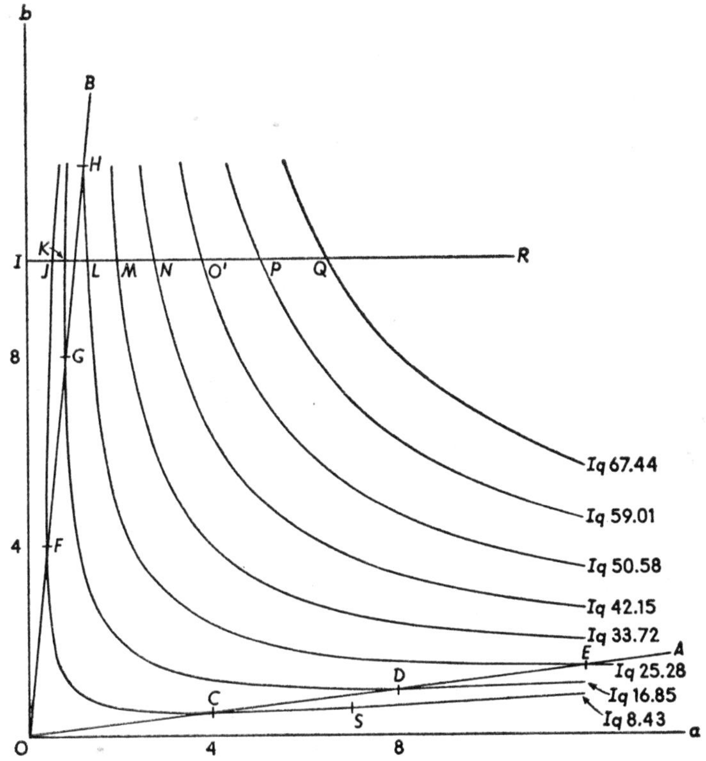

diagram have been drawn on the basis of our production function, $X = \sqrt{2Cab - D(a^2) - E(b^2)}$. To facilitate our graphical exposition, different values of the constants have been employed in the present analysis from those used in the preceding section. Thus we now use $C = 40$, $D = 5$, $E = 4$ as the values of these constants. Again our function is linearly homogeneous.

Table 6–2 contains the values used for the first four of the isoquants depicted in Figure 6–3 and illustrates again that the production function is linearly homogeneous. Thus one a and one b produce 8.43 units of X, and twice as much *a* and *b* produces twice as much X, or 2*a* and 2*b* produce 16.85 units of X (the slight discrepancy is due to

Table 6–2
PRODUCTION DATA

X = 8.43		X = 16.85		X = 25.28		X = 33.72	
a	b	a	b	a	b	a	b
1	1	. . .	. . .	. . .	. . .	. . .	. . .
2	0.58	2	2	. . .	. . .	. . .	. . .
3	0.49	3	1.4	3	3	. . .	. . .
4	0.48	4	1.16	4	2.32	4	4
5	0.49	5	1.04	5	1.95	5	3.27
6	0.53	6	0.98	6	1.74	6	2.80
7	0.57	7	0.96	7	1.60	7	2.50
8	0.61	8	0.95	8	1.51	8	2.32
9	0.66	9	0.96	9	1.47	9	2.18
10	0.72	10	0.98	10	1.46	10	2.08
11	0.78	11	1.05	11	1.45	11	2.02
12	0.84	12	1.06	12	1.44	12	1.96
0.56	2	. . .	. . .	. . .	. . .	. . .	. . .
0.46	3	1.37	3	. . .	. . .	. . .	. . .
0.42	4	1.12	4	2.28	4	. . .	. . .
0.44	5	0.95	5	1.89	5	3.23	5
0.45	6	0.92	6	1.68	6	2.79	6
0.47	7	0.86	7	1.51	7	2.44	7
0.51	8	0.84	8	1.42	8	2.24	8
0.55	9	0.86	9	1.38	9	2.07	9
0.59	10	0.88	10	1.32	10	1.95	10
0.65	11	0.89	11	1.29	11	1.90	11
0.73	12	0.90	12	1.26	12	1.84	12

rounding of numbers). Similarly, 2*a* and .58*b* will produce 8.43 units of X, and twice as much of *a* and *b*, or 4*a* and 1.16*b*, will also produce 16.85 units of X.

Note that the isoquants in Figure 6–3 do not cross, just as indifference curves do not cross; to permit them to do so would involve inconsistent definitions.

The Technical Rate of Substitution

The slope of the isoquant between P and P' in Figure 6–2 is equal to the ratio of the marginal products of *a* and *b*, f_a/f_b. That is, just as we manipulated the definition of indifference curves to derive the marginal rate of substitution, S_{yx}, in Chapter 5, so can we now manipulate the definition of an isoquant to derive what is called the *technical rate of substitution,* T_{ba}. All that is necessary is to subtract $f_b\Delta b$ from both sides of Equation (6–4) so that

$$f_a\Delta a = -f_b\Delta b ,\qquad\qquad (6\text{–}4a)$$

and to divide both sides by $f_b\Delta a$ to produce

$$\frac{f_a}{f_b} = -\frac{\Delta b}{\Delta a} = T_{ba}\qquad\qquad (6\text{–}5)$$

As before, this ratio represents the slope of the curve corresponding to a one (small) unit change in a, say between P and P' in Figure 6–2. Thus, in Figure 6–2, $T_{ba} = f_a/f_b = -(\Delta b/\Delta a) = B'B/AA'$ represents the technical rate of substitution, which, in turn, is equal to the ratios of the marginal products of a and b, f_a/f_b. Alternatively, T_{ba} represents the amount by which b must be reduced if output of X is to remain constant along an isoquant as the input of a increases by one small unit from A to A'.

Returns to Scale

Returns to scale are depicted in Figure 6–3 by lines from the origin such as OA and OB, which *intersect* different isoquants. Since our contour lines are based on a production function which is linearly homogeneous, distances along OB such as OF, FG, and GH, which represent segments along *any* straight diagonal line from the origin produced by the intersection of the diagonal with different contour lines, must be equal. Similarly, along OA, distances OC, CD, and DE are equal. Along any other straight diagonal line from the origin, similar distances similarly produced would also be equal.

Diminishing Returns

The line IR depicts the way in which output varies as the amount of a changes while that of b is held constant at the level OI, or ten units. Since $IJ > JK$, we see that initially output can be doubled with less than double the input of a along IR when b is held constant at the level OI. However, we also note that $KL > JK$, and that $LM > KL$, $MN > LM$, etc. In short, increasing quantities of a are required to produce *equal increases* in output beyond K. Thus beyond input JK, returns to the variable factor a diminish, while between J and K, returns to the variable factor a increase. For example, by substituting the appropriate arithmetical values into our function, we have $a = .59$ as the amount of a required to produce 8.43 units of X when $b = 10$; and so $IJ = .59a$. Thus, $IJ > JK$ but $JK < KL$, or $.59a > .29a$ but $.29a < .44a$.

Ridge Lines

Our lines OB and OA in Figure 6–3 have in fact been drawn to do double duty. They have been drawn through points such as F, G, H, and C, D, E, respectively, at which the isoproduct curves become momentarily parallel to the respective axes. Thus at C, Iq 8.43 is parallel to the a axis, and beyond C it slopes up and to the right. At C, for example, four units of a are being used with .48 units of b to produce 8.43 units of X. To the right of C, at S, seven units of a are being used with .57 units of b *to produce the same amount of* X, for C and S are on the same isoquant. Thus by moving to the left from S to C, the firm can actually maintain its output by reducing *both* the amount of a and of b employed.

The region between OB and OA is actually Stage II of our previous analysis, the Stage of Diminishing Returns to the Variable Input. Points between OA and the a axis, such as S, lie in the Stage of Absolutely Diminishing Returns to the Variable Input, a. The region to the left of OB, between OB and the b axis, represents the area of Increasing Returns to the Variable Input, a. The lines such as OA and OB, which join points at which the contour lines become parallel to the respective axes, are known as *ridge lines*. In the case of a linearly homogeneous production function such as ours, these ridge lines are straight lines through the origin. However, if the production function were not homogeneous and linear, the lines OA and OB would probably be convex to their respective axes.

A Cross-Section View

Figure 6–4 depicts two curves which show how total product varies as a varies at different levels of b. Thus when $b = 10$, or OI, in Figure 6–3, the cross-section curve, IR, which is an airplane pilot's view of the mountain, appears as it is depicted in Figure 6–4 to someone approaching the mountain from the plains. (Compare Figure 6–4 with Figures 3–6 and 3–7.) Again, when $b = .95$, in Figure 6–3, the cross-section curve is as it, too, appears in Figure 6–4. The curves in Figure 6–4 are, of course, similar to the curve which is depicted in Figure 6–1, for that curve is also a cross-section curve, and it could similarly be related to a contour map, although not to the one depicted in Figure 6–3, for it is based on values of the constants in our function different from those used in drawing Figure 6–3.

Note that point D on the lower curve in Figure 6–4, when $b = .95,$ corresponds to point D in Figure 6–3. At point D in Figure 6–4, total product is a maximum, and the marginal product of a is zero. Point D marks the Point of Absolutely Diminishing Returns to the Variable Input in Figure 6–4. So also, in Figure 6–3, beyond D, the isoquant slopes up and to the right, while at D it is parallel to the a axis, indicating that this is the point of zero marginal product of a, the Point of Absolutely Diminishing Returns to the Variable Input.

Figure 6–4
COMPARISON OF DIFFERENT CURVES OF RETURNS
TO VARIABLE INPUTS

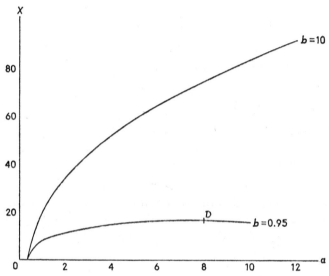

In the case of the upper curve ($b = 10$) in Figure 6–4, no maximum value of the total product is shown because the maximum falls to the right of the maximum amount of a measured on the a axis in the diagram. Similarly, none of the contour lines depicted in Figure 6–3 is shown as having a point of zero slope corresponding to the maximum value of the product at this level of b (OI), since in the case of this diagram, this value, too, occurs at a higher level of a than is there depicted.

Elasticity of Substitution

If a and b were perfectly substitutable, the isoquants would be straight lines. When no substitution at all is possible and the inputs must be used in fixed proportions, the isoquants are right-angled. The degree of curvature of the isoquants is thus taken as a measure of the degree of substitution possible between the two inputs. A high degree of curvature of the isoquants indicates that the inputs are not easily substitutable, and a low degree of curvature indicates a high degree of substitutability.

The measure of this substitutability is expressed in relative terms and called the *elasticity of substitution.*[5] It measures the relative rate of change of the proportion between the factors as the technical rate of substitution changes. The formula for this elasticity when the proportion is defined as b/a is

$$\frac{\dfrac{a}{b}\Delta\left(\dfrac{b}{a}\right)}{\dfrac{\Delta T_{ba}}{T_{ba}}} , \qquad (6\text{–}6)$$

which can be interpreted as

$$\frac{\text{Relative change in the proportion between the inputs } (b/a)}{\text{Relative change in the technical rate of substitution}} .$$

We will illustrate this concept arithmetically in Chapter 12.

The Isocost Line

The equivalent in the theory of production of the budget equation in the theory of demand is the isocost line, which represents the maximum amount of the different combinations of inputs which the firm can purchase at the given prices of the inputs and with a given cost or outlay, T. Thus we can write:

$$p_a a + p_b b = T , \qquad (6\text{–}7)$$

where T represents the total cost or outlay of the firm. Setting $p_a a$ equal to zero, we have

$$0 + p_b b = T , \qquad (6\text{–}8)$$

and

$$b = \frac{T}{p_b} , \qquad (6\text{–}9)$$

which provides us with the formula for the distance OF in Figure 6–5. Similarly, we have

---

[5] For a more precise definition, see R. G. D. Allen, *Mathematical Analysis for Economists* (London: Macmillan & Co., Ltd., 1950), pp. 340–43.

$$0 + p_{a}a = T,$$ (6-10)

and

$$a = \frac{T}{p_a} = OG \text{ in Figure 6-5.}$$ (6-11)

Assume now that the total outlay, T, amounts to $8.00 and that the price of b is $1.00 per unit of time. Then we have $OF = \$8.00/\$1.00 = 8$ in Figure 6-5. Similarly, if the price of a is $3.65

Figure 6-5

ISOQUANT ILLUSTRATION OF THE PRINCIPLE OF SUBSTITUTION

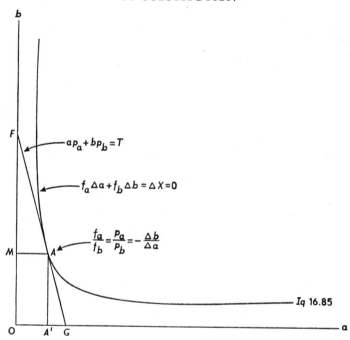

per unit of time, we have $OG = \$8.00/\$3.65 = 2.19$ in Figure 6-5. Thus the absolute value of the slope of the line FG is equal to $OF/OG = (T/p_b)/(T/p_a) = (T/p_b)(p_a/T) = p_a/p_b$, the ratio of the price of a to that of b. Arithmetically, $OF/OG = 8/2.19 = p_a/p_b = \$3.65/\$1.00 = 3.65$.

Determination of the Equilibrium Position Quantities

Again, just as in the case of indifference curve analysis we derived the equilibrium condition from a manipulation of the Marshallian equilibrium condition [see the discussion of Equation (5–10) in Chapter 5], so we can now derive the equilibrium condition of production from a simple manipulation of Equation (6–3). All that is necessary is for us to multiply both sides of Equation (6–3) by p_a and to divide both sides by f_b, to produce

$$\frac{f_a}{p_a}\frac{p_a}{f_b} = \frac{f_b}{p_b}\frac{p_a}{f_b} = \frac{f_a}{f_b} = \frac{p_a}{p_b} = -\frac{\Delta b}{\Delta a} = T_{ba} . \qquad (6\text{–}12)$$

The term T_{ba} has already been defined in Equation (6–5).

In short, tangency between an isocost line and an isoquant, as depicted at A in Figure 6–5, represents the equilibrium position in the theory of production, just as tangency between a budget line and an indifference curve represents the equilibrium position in the theory of demand. In the case of the theory of production, the equilibrium condition applies to all variable inputs in the short run and to all inputs in the long run and states that the output from an additional dollar's worth of expenditure on any one input must be the same as that obtained from an additional dollar's worth of expenditure on any other input. And so at A in Figure 6–5, $f_a/f_b = p_a/p_b = -(\Delta b/\Delta a) = T_{ba}$.

Effect of a Change in the Price of One Factor: Total Outlay Constant

The isoquants depicted in Figure 6–6 assume, as before, that the production function is linearly homogeneous. In the initial position at A, OM of b is used with OA' of a to produce 16.85 units of product at the given relative prices of b and a as indicated by tangency of isocost line FAG and Iq 16.85 at A. Assume now that the price of a decreases, as indicated by isocost line FBH, while that of b remains unchanged. As soon as the price of a declines, the equilibrium is disturbed. The firm accordingly increases its use of a, until, in the new position at B on Iq 25.28, it is using $A'B'$ more of a and also MN more of b, while output has increased (by one half), with no increase in the total outlay.

Points O, A, L, and I lie on the line which defines returns to scale when the firm uses the given proportions of factors employed at point A. Thus the slopes of Iq 16.85 and Iq 25.28 are the same at A and I. Since the new equilibrium position of the firm is at B, which lies on scale line OCB, rather than at I on scale line $OALI$, it is clear that the price change has produced both a change in the proportions in which factors are employed and a higher scale of operations without a change in total outlay. For the proportions in which factors are used are different by definition *along OALI* from what they are *along OCB*. Also, more of *each* input is being used at B than at A.

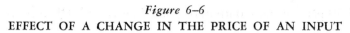

Figure 6–6

EFFECT OF A CHANGE IN THE PRICE OF AN INPUT

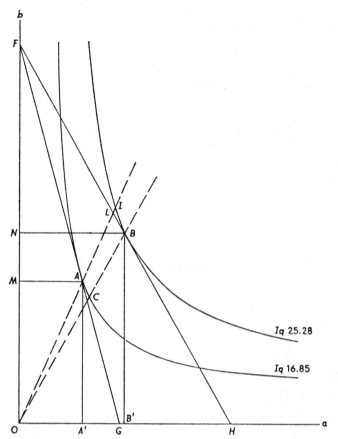

If the firm had continued its given level of total outlay, equal to *OF*, after the decrease in the price of *a*, without changing the proportions in which the factors were employed, it would have moved to *L* after the price change. At *L*, however, total output obtainable from the given outlay is less than at *B*, for *B* is a point of tangency between *FBH* and *Iq* 25.28; and *L* lies on a product contour line *below Iq* 25.28 and represents a smaller total product. At *L* the firm would not have been in equilibrium, and it would not have been maximizing the output from the given expenditure on factors, for it would have produced less than 25.28X which is obtainable at *B* with the given outlay.

In order to obtain the same level of output *at the old price ratio,* that is, before the price change, the firm would have had to increase the scale of its operations by 50 percent and thus to increase its outlay for factors in the same proportion, for this is the only way it could have attained 50 percent more output, or point I on Iq 25.28, before the price decrease.

Effect of a Change in Total Expenditures on Inputs

Now, in Figure 6–7, if the firm had increased its outlay on factors by 50 percent, that is, by FJ, where $2FJ = OF$, it could have increased its output by 50 percent and reached I on Iq 25.28 at the old price

Figure 6–7

ILLUSTRATION OF EFFECT OF PROPORTIONAL CHANGE IN INPUT
PRICES OR OF CHANGE IN TOTAL EXPENDITURES ON INPUTS

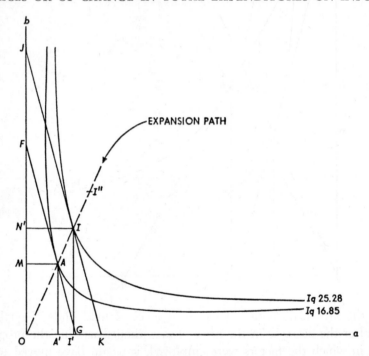

ratio. In this case since I and A lie on the same scale line, the proportion between the factors is the same at A and at I. A mere change in total outlay without a change in the price of an input does not change the proportions in which inputs are used in our case.

Effect of a Proportional Change in the Prices of All Factors

If the prices of a and of b decrease proportionally, the effect on the firm's production possibilities is the same as would be that of an equivalent increase in the outlay for inputs without a price change. For in such a case the ratio of the prices of the factors remains unchanged, and thus the slope of the new isocost line is the same after the proportionate price change as it was before. This case is also illustrated by Figure 6–7. If the prices of a and of b each fall by 50 percent so that $2FJ = OF$ and $2GK = OG$, the slope of the isocost line, JIK, is the same as that of the previous isocost line, FAG. Where the firm was previously in equilibrium at A, it can now attain the new equilibrium position of I, with a 50 percent higher output, by moving from A to I, or by an increase in scale alone. In our case of a linearly homogeneous production function, a proportional change in the prices of all inputs changes only the scale of operations and leaves the proportions among the inputs unchanged; but a change in the price of only one input changes both the level of output and the proportions among the inputs. We will consider the question of returns to outlay further in the next chapter.

The Expansion Path

Figure 6–7 also indicates that the *expansion path* of the firm is along the line $OAII''$ in the present case. *At given input prices, the firm would expand the scale of its operations along a line from the origin formed by the points of tangency of successive parallel isocost lines with isoquants.* In the present case, since the production function is linearly homogeneous, the expansion path is a straight line. This straight line expansion path corresponds to the situation depicted in the case of constant long-run average costs in Figure 7–5 in the following chapter, and reflects the fact that returns to scale are assumed to be constant in Figures 6–7 and in 7–5. If returns to scale were not constant, the expansion path would not be a straight line. An example of an expansion path, in the case in which the production function exhibits first increasing, then constant, and, finally, decreasing returns to scale, appears in Figure 7–8 in the next chapter.

Effect on Output of Price Changes Unpredictable

The effect on *output* of a firm of changes in the prices of inputs in the real world is not predictable. A firm operating under conditions of less than perfect competition may find it unprofitable or undesirable to increase output beyond a certain level. If it is maximizing profits and cannot increase its share of the market (or does not wish to for fear of adverse public opinion), it may, in fact, under such circumstances, decide to minimize the cost of the inputs required to produce the given output. However, logic still leads to the conclusion that there must, nevertheless, be some substitution of the relatively cheaper factor of production for the relatively more expensive one. Thus in Figure 6–8,

Figure 6–8

EFFECT ON THE EXPANSION PATH OF A NONPROPORTIONAL
INPUT PRICE CHANGE

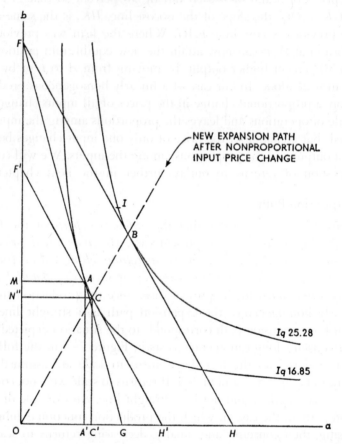

a firm, which was originally in equilibrium at *A,* might shift to *C* and continue to produce the *same output* at the lower price of *a* rather than to increase its output by moving to *B* after a decrease in the price of *a* as indicated by *FBH*. In such a case, use of *a* would increase by *A'C'* while that of *b* would decrease by *N"M,* for *a* has become relatively cheaper. At *C* the firm produces the same output as at *A* and has substituted the relatively cheaper factor for the relatively more expensive one. In short, a nonproportional change in input prices will *shift* the expansion path, but the effect on *output* cannot be determined without more facts.

Thus, just as it is impossible to prove deductively that demand curves do have negative slopes, or that returns to variable factors do diminish in a given case in the real world, so it is impossible to predict from the definitions and from the equilibrium conditions how firms will adjust their *output* in response to changes in the prices of the factors without making factual assumptions about the actual state of affairs in the real world. Again we see that economic theory is concerned not with predicting real world situations, but merely with the fashioning of definitions and analytical devices which may or may not aid us in the analysis of particular factual situations.

Isoquants and Linear Programming

But this is not to say that the concepts of isoquants and isocost lines are of no value to business administrators in solving their problems or to government agencies, such as the Department of Defense, once the basic goals of their given activities have been determined. Indeed, these concepts have been and are being employed to determine which of various given alternative methods of attaining given objectives is the "best." The name "linear programming" has been given to this selection process, and an elementary explanation of it will be presented in Part VII of this book.

C. EMPIRICAL STUDIES

Professor Cookenboo's Study of Crude Oil Pipelines

A classic study of a production function for the United States as a whole was made in 1934 by Professor Paul H. Douglas. His study can, however, best be examined in conjunction with the discussion of the marginal productivity theory of income distribution and will be covered in Chapter 12 of Part V later.[6] A different study of crude oil pipeline production functions was published by Professor Leslie Cookenboo, Jr., in 1955.[7] This study is interesting, among other reasons, because it contains a diagram showing contour lines or production isoquants based upon engineering assumptions and empirical data.[8] Professor Cookenboo has argued that crude oil pipelines are subject to increasing physical returns to scale because less friction is incurred per barrel of crude oil transported through the line in a large diameter pipe than in a small diameter pipe. Thus the amount of horsepower needed to send a given amount of oil through a pipeline depends upon the diameter of

---

[6] Paul H. Douglas, *The Theory of Wages* (New York: The Macmillan Co., 1934).
[7] Leslie Cookenboo, Jr., *Crude Oil Pipe Lines and Competition in the Oil Industry* (Cambridge: Harvard University Press, 1955).
[8] *Ibid.*, Chart 1, p. 15.

the pipe. A larger diameter pipe requires less horsepower for an equal volume of "throughput." The "throughput" or volume of crude oil transported is the output (our X), while the diameter of the pipe and the horsepower needed to force the oil through the pipe are the inputs. The production function derived by Cookenboo exhibits the same type of returns to scale at all levels of inputs, although it is not linearly homogeneous.[9] This study represents an attempt to derive the production function from engineering data and to base estimates of costs of production upon the derived function. Most empirical studies of costs rely on accounting data and do not look behind the accounting data to the production function. Some of these will be discussed in the last section of the next chapter, and the two procedures will be contrasted.

Studies of Aggregate Productivity by the National Bureau of Economic Research

Numerous studies of the productivity of labor and capital in the United States economy as a whole have been made under the auspices of the National Bureau of Economic Research.[10] One of these studies by Dr. Solomon Fabricant was discussed at length during one of the hearings on *Employment, Growth and Price Levels* before the Congressional Joint Economic Committee in April, 1959. This Committee, under the Chairmanship of Senator Paul H. Douglas, whose work as an economist on production functions has already been mentioned above, considered some of the difficulties involved in measuring *output* of an entire economy through time. Thus, Dr. Fabricant testified:

. . . One is the problem of measuring output, which involves combining into a meaningful aggregate a changing variety of old and new goods, and services as well as physical commodities. A special difficulty arises in putting a figure on the quantity of services produced by government to meet collective wants. This is a particularly troublesome type of service to measure in anything like real terms. This accounts for the greater confidence most statisticians have in the estimate of productivity for the private economy, exclusive of government.

A general deficiency of all measures of output—and thus of productivity—is their failure to take account of change in the quality of output. . . . This, it

---

[9] *Ibid.*, pp. 14–24.

[10] See, for example, John W. Kendrick, *Productivity Trends: Capital and Labor* (National Bureau of Economic Research, Occasional Paper 53) (New York, 1956); and Solomon Fabricant, *Basic Facts on Productivity Change* (National Bureau of Economic Research, Occasional Paper 63) (New York, 1958). See also Albert Rees, "Patterns of Wages, Prices and Productivity," *Wages, Prices, Profits and Productivity* (Columbia University: The American Assembly, 1959), pp. 11–36.

is likely, subjects them to a downward bias. And, to repeat, the indexes of output per unit of labor and tangible capital combined, though broader than any other indexes now available, fail to cover adequately the investment in education, science, technology, and social organization that serves to increase production. . . .

The technical questions raised above (which I have selected from a host), are, of course, matters primarily for the producer rather than the user of productivity statistics. But for the user it is important to be aware of the sharp differences made in the rate of growth of productivity by technical choices not always specified . . . namely, whether output or input is defined in one way or another, or weights or components of output and input are determined by this rather than that method, or the data are selected or estimated from one or another source.[11]

The preceding testimony brings into sharp relief the problems involved in attempting to estimate changes in productivity in an entire economic system through time. Fabricant's study argues that indexes of productivity based on a comparison of output with an input unit of *both* labor and tangible capital are better measures than are indexes based on comparisons of output with indexes of either input alone. Such a composite capital-labor index has been produced by Fabricant and other economists of the National Bureau of Economic Research by using a "dollar's worth of service" of inputs in the base period as a measure of a unit of input. Using this type of a combined input index, Fabricant estimated that between 1899 and 1953 output had increased at a rate of 1.7 percent annually. The index of output per unit of labor during this period was similarly estimated at 2.0 percent annually, while that of capital was estimated at 1.0 percent annually. The combined input index was thus interpreted as a weighted average of the other two.[12] Data of this type are of considerable importance in the study of problems of economic development.

It is interesting to note that in testifying further concerning his conclusion, Fabricant remarked that during the period in question, the United States had "moved along the production function and the production function itself has moved." The language of price theory has thus, quite clearly, penetrated into the Halls of Congress! The National Bureau studies are closely related to the earlier study by Senator Douglas, and we will consider this matter again in Part V. Our next

---

[11] *Employment, Growth and Price Levels* (Hearings before the Joint Economic Committee, Part 2, "Historical and Comparative Rates of Production, Productivity and Prices," 86th Cong., 1st sess.) (Washington, D.C.: U.S. Government Printing Office, 1959), pp. 352–53.

[12] *Ibid.,* pp. 293–99. Fabricant acknowledged his reliance upon a study by John W. Kendrick which has since been published under the name of *Productivity Trends in the United States* (Princeton: Princeton University Press, 1961).

problem, however, is that of learning the basic concepts of *costs* and how these are related to the concepts of production. This is the task of the following chapter.

SELECTED READINGS

ALLEN, R. G. D. *Mathematical Analysis for Economists,* pp. 284–89, 315–22, and 339–43. London: Macmillan & Co., Ltd., 1950.

BACHMURA, F. T. "Man-Land Equilization through Migration," *American Economic Review,* Vol. XLIX (December, 1959), pp. 1004–17.

BOULDING, KENNETH. *Economic Analysis,* pp. 585–90 and 733–44. 3rd ed. New York: Harper & Bros., 1955.

HENDERSON, JAMES M., AND QUANDT, RICHARD E. *Microeconomic Theory,* pp. 42–53 and 62–64. New York: McGraw-Hill Book Co., Inc., 1958.

LEFTWICH, RICHARD H. *The Price System and Resource Allocation,* pp. 107–35. New York: Holt, Rinehart & Winston, Inc., 1960.

MARSHALL, ALFRED. *Principles of Economics,* pp. 150–72. 8th ed. London: Macmillan & Co., Ltd., 1938.

STIGLER, GEORGE. *The Theory of Price,* pp. 96–121. Rev. ed. New York: The Macmillan Co., 1952.

7 Cost of Production

Introduction

In this chapter we will make use of the concepts developed in the preceding chapter and explain the way in which cost concepts are related to those of production. The arithmetical and graphical examples employed in this chapter are merely continuations of those employed in the preceding chapter. We will first consider the philosophical basis of costs, and then we will analyze the behavior of costs in the short run and in the long run. The chapter concludes with a survey of some statistical studies of costs in the short run and in the long run.

A. PHILOSOPHICAL CONCEPTS OF COST

Real Cost

The *real costs* of production were defined by Marshall and other neoclassical economists as the exertions (or disutilities) of all the kinds of labor and the "abstinences or rather the waitings required for saving the capital" needed to produce goods.[1] Thus, according to their view, the ultimate basis of cost was a set of psychological concepts based on a hedonistic philosophy. In the case of land, since neither the disutility of labor nor the abstinence from current consumption, which constitutes one definition of saving, accounted for either its existence or its quality, no real cost was thought to be present. In general, land was considered to be a "gift of nature."

Today few economists employ the "real cost" doctrine. Such a doctrine breaks down when confronted by the fact that the salaries and wages of persons in some unattractive occupations (garbage collec-

---

[1] Alfred Marshall, *Principles of Economics* (8th ed.; London: Macmillan & Co., Ltd., 1938), p. 339.

tion?), in which the disutility of working is presumably very high, are lower than those of persons employed in presumably more attractive positions. Other explanations such as lack of education or opportunity or ability may be more realistic. Moreover, notions of "disutility" have been rejected by many economists for the same reason that they have rejected the concept of "utility;" namely, that it is "too subjective" a concept to be treated "scientifically."

Opportunity Cost

The notion of *opportunity cost,* that is, that the cost of any particular course of action is the amount of gain which could have been obtained by pursuing the next most desirable alternative, originated in the work of various Austrian economists who wrote between 1871 and 1914 and is widely accepted today.[2] In its modern form, the opportunity cost doctrine generally appears as a statement that the cost to the society of producing a unit of any given product, X, is the amount of the next most desirable product, say Y, which could be produced with the given marginal amount of input. Marshall explicitly adopted the opportunity cost doctrine in his explanation of the consumer's surplus thesis in the *Principles*.[3]

Whenever choice is involved, the opportunity cost doctrine may be employed. Thus, it is argued, even a complete dictator is faced with choices, and, hence, the opportunity cost doctrine is applicable to his decisions. However, the choices which are compared must be real and not illusory if the doctrine is to have meaning. Where there is no real or close alternative, the opportunity cost doctrine is useless, or at least misleading. Such a situation may exist in the case of highly specialized inputs for which alternative uses are difficult to find.

From the social point of view, the opportunity (or alternative) cost of unemployed inputs is zero. Thus, the cost to a society of putting unemployed inputs to work (for example, the unemployed members of the labor force during a period of depression) is zero—for the total output of some commodity or service will be increased by such action without a reduction in the total output of any other. At the same time, a problem of choice and of opportunity cost may arise with respect to the question of where to employ such unemployed inputs. Accordingly, we have a situation in which money costs do not reflect social costs or correspond closely to them.

---

[2] For a summary, see Lewis Haney, *History of Economic Thought* (3rd ed.; New York: The Macmillan Co., 1936), pp. 607 ff.

[3] Marshall, *op. cit.,* p. 125.

The opportunity cost doctrine ultimately employs the utility concept in one form or another. It has been noted that the doctrine involves the notion that the cost of any one commodity is the amount of the next most valuable commodity which could have been produced with the marginal amount of the given input. Where the two commodities are close substitutes, direct physical comparison of them may be possible, but, in general, comparison of different outputs must be made in terms of their money value. Thus, at bottom, the notion that price is a measure of value (of utility) inevitably enters into present-day notions of opportunity cost, and our notions of the *marginal social cost* (*MSC*) of various activities and undertakings eventually come to rest on the concept of utility. They are at bottom quite as subjective as are the real cost concepts of the neoclassical economists. Criticisms of various public activities by economists on grounds that the "marginal social costs" are too high relative to the benefits expected really constitute value judgments concerning such undertakings despite the fact that these judgments are presented in "scientific" language. Such judgments may be the judgments of wise men based on a thorough study of the facts, and, as such, they are worthy of respect, but they acquire no greater validity from the language which is used to present them than they would otherwise have.

B. MONEY COSTS

Total Cost

Money costs represent the expenses of production of the firm or individual. However, the term *total cost* which has been designated by the symbol, T, in Chapter 6, *does not* have the same meaning in economics as it does to the accountant or businessman.

By *total cost* the economist *means a money figure comprised of the costs of all the inputs or services of the factors of production which are necessary to produce the given output.* Thus, all of the payments for factor services, such as wages, interest, rent, and a normal profit for the entrepreneur, are included within the concept of total cost of production, unless otherwise stated.

The inclusion of a "normal profit" (however it may be defined for the purpose at hand) by the economist means that his definition of total cost differs from that of the accountant. Profits greater than "normal" which may be made by the firm or entrepreneur are not functional in the comparative static economic sense. Professor Schumpeter's theory of economic development, we will see later, contains a rationalization of such profits on the grounds that they provide the basis for economic progress, but that is a matter of value judgments. In the case of static analysis, greater than normal profits made by a monopolistic enterprise are usually considered a functionless surplus (or an "economic rent") by economists, for such profits can be extracted from the firm without reducing its efficiency or its output by definition.

Implicit Cost

From the point of view of the economist, total cost must include the *implicit costs* of production, the costs *to the firm of using in the given way, rather than in some other, those inputs which it owns.* Thus, a firm which finances its own inventory or expansion programs, instead of investing its surplus in some asset external to the firm, is entitled to a return on the self-invested capital. Similarly, an owner who performs labor service in his own business is entitled to a wage for his effort in addition to whatever normal profits he makes as an entrepreneur. Segregation of the various payments of this kind is a difficult problem, and, in our national income statistics, it is avoided, for example, by including in a separate category the income from "unincorporated enterprises." Such income is not profit alone but includes elements of other factor incomes or payments as well.

Explicit Cost

Explicit costs are all those payments made by the firm to others for the services of factors or inputs not owned by the firm. In general, accounting data are used as a source of information for explicit costs, but difficulties arise in their use. Some of these difficulties will be considered further in a later section of this chapter.

When the term *money cost* is defined as referring to the actual outlays of the firm, it cannot be taken to mean the same thing as *total cost.* Where the term "money cost" is used interchangeably with the term "total cost" in economics, what is meant is the money equivalent, however determined for the purpose of the analysis at hand, of all the explicit and implicit costs of producing the commodity or service in question. In this book the term "money cost" will be employed in the second sense only.

C. THE DISTINCTION AMONG VARIOUS TIME PERIODS

Like so many of the other concepts which we have been considering, the distinction among various periods of time in economic analysis was first suggested by Marshall.[4] Thus, he noted that both the nature of the equilibrium conditions and the determinants of these conditions depend upon the length of the period of time which is assumed in the analysis. A brief discussion of each of the four time periods which he defined follows.

The Very Short-Run or Market Period

The *very short-run* or the *market period refers to a period of time during which a firm cannot change its output at all,* and the analysis of its activities is concerned principally with the effect of expectations and inventories on prices. The next chapter will deal with an analysis of the factors which are thought to be important in the determination of product prices in the very short run. The willingness of suppliers to sell in the short run is generally assumed to depend on considerations different from those which are important during longer periods of time.

The Short Run

The term *"short run" refers to a period of time sufficiently long to allow some, but not all, variables in the problem to change.* Thus, the principle of diminishing returns, which relates to the effect on total output of variations in one or more inputs, with all other inputs and all other conditions held unchanged, relates to a short-run time period. In the theory of the firm, *the short run is a period of time sufficiently long to allow the firm to change its output from existing capacity, but not sufficiently long to allow the firm to make changes in its capacity.* The effect of this definition is to allow an analysis according to which some costs are allowed to change, but plant size is kept unchanged. What constitutes a short-run period (or any other time period for that matter) in the case of a given industry depends on the conditions of production in that industry, and thus a short period in regard to one type of activity might constitute a long period of time in regard to another.

The Long Run

The term *"long run" refers to a period of time sufficiently long to allow all of the economic variables in the problem to change except those which are related to the economic growth of an industry or of a group of industries and not of a single firm.* In the case of the theory of the firm, for example, *in the long run, all costs are allowed to vary,*

---

[4] *Ibid.,* pp. 373–79, esp. pp. 378–79.

and thus there are no fixed costs. Consequently, the plant size is no longer considered fixed but becomes an additional variable in the problem. The principle of returns to scale, in which all inputs are allowed to vary, is an example of long-run analysis.

The Very Long Run—Secular Change

Very long run in economics means secular change. That is, this term refers to a period of time sufficiently long to permit the analysis to take into account the effect of the decline or the rise of entire industries. For example, an analysis which took account of the effect of the invention of the automobile and the development of the automobile manufacturing industry on the production of surreys with fringes on their tops would take into account still further variables beyond those considered in the case of "long-run" analysis. Problems of economic development, at least when they are studied from an historical point of view, involve this type of analysis.

D. COSTS IN THE SHORT RUN

An Alternative Definition of Total Cost: The Total Cost Curve

Total cost, or T, has been defined in a preceding section as a money figure comprised of all the costs of the inputs, or services of the factors of production, which are necessary to produce a given output. In short-run analysis, which assumes that the plant size is fixed and thus that the problem is one of explaining the cost of producing from existing capacity, an alternative definition of total cost can be usefully employed.

Thus, *the total cost of any given output in the short run can be defined as equal to the sum of all of the fixed and variable costs of the firm.* The *fixed costs, which were called supplementary costs* by Marshall, are defined as all those costs which do not vary as output varies, such as interest on the fixed investment, taxes, etc. The *variable costs,* which Marshall *identified as special, direct,* or *prime costs,*[5] are *all those costs which do vary as output varies,* such as the cost of labor, raw materials, etc.

We can define short-run total cost, or *T,* symbolically as

$$T = F + V = bp_b + ap_a , \qquad (7\text{-}1)$$

where *T* stands for total cost of any given amount of output; where $F = bp_b$ represents the total fixed cost, or the amount of the fixed factor used times the price of the service of a unit of the fixed factor;

---

[5] *Ibid.,* pp. 359–62.

and where $V = ap_a$ represents the variable cost, or the amount of the variable factor used times the price of its service.

In Figure 7–1 is depicted a total cost curve. The data on which Figure 7–1 is based appear in Table 7–1, which, in turn, is based on

Table 7–1

DATA RELATING TO SHORT-RUN TOTAL COSTS OF PRODUCTION*

	Units				Dollars		
(1)	(2)	(3)	(4)	(5)	(6)	(7)	(8)
X	a	b	p_a	$ap_a = V$	p_b	$bp_b = F$	$T = F + V$
1.00	0.780	10	10.00	7.80	1.00	10.00	17.80
5.00	0.820	10	10.00	8.20	1.00	10.00	18.20
8.00	0.870	10	10.00	8.70	1.00	10.00	18.70
12.65	1.000	10	10.00	10.00	1.00	10.00	20.00
22.58	1.500	10	10.00	15.00	1.00	10.00	25.00
28.98	2.000	10	10.00	20.00	1.00	10.00	30.00
31.80	2.273	10	10.00	22.73	1.00	10.00	32.73
37.95	3.000	10	10.00	30.00	1.00	10.00	40.00
44.27	4.000	10	10.00	40.00	1.00	10.00	50.00
48.99	5.000	10	10.00	50.00	1.00	10.00	60.00
52.54	6.000	10	10.00	60.00	1.00	10.00	70.00
55.14	7.000	10	10.00	70.00	1.00	10.00	80.00
56.94	8.000	10	10.00	80.00	1.00	10.00	90.00
57.97	9.000	10	10.00	90.00	1.00	10.00	100.00
58.31	10.000	10	10.00	100.00	1.00	10.00	110.00

* Output data based on Table 6–1A. Note that the data for the Stage of Absolutely Diminishing Returns has been omitted because it is irrelevant.

the data for the Stages of Increasing and Diminishing Returns to the Variable Input, *a*, obtained from our production function in Chapter 6 contained in Table 6–1A. The data for the Stage of Absolutely Diminishing Returns to *a* is irrelevant and has been omitted. Within this range, the total cost curve slopes up and to the left, for as total costs increase, output actually diminishes, and no rational firm would operate under such conditions. Although it is undesirable from a social point of view for firms to be operating in the Stage of Increasing Returns to Variable Inputs (for average costs can always be reduced within this stage), the data for it have been included because they will be useful in our later explanations and analysis.

Table 7–1 and Figure 7–1 thus contain a translation into terms of money costs of both of the principles of diminishing returns illustrated in Table 6–1A.

The Total Fixed Cost Curve

Total fixed costs, F, have been defined as all those costs which do not vary as output varies. Thus, in Table 7–1 when input *b* is held constant at ten units and the price of a unit of b is \$1.00, we have $F = bp_b = (10)(\$1.00) = \$10$ at all levels of output. (The price of b is assumed to include a certain fixed amount representing a "normal profit," however it may be defined.)

Figure 7–1

SHORT-RUN TOTAL COST CURVES

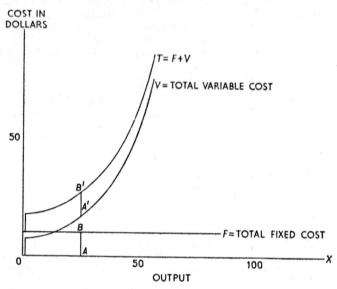

Since the total fixed costs do not vary as output varies, and since we assume that the price of b remains constant (which amounts to assuming that the firm purchases inputs in a perfectly competitive market and cannot affect the price by its own actions), the total fixed cost curve is a horizontal line parallel to the X or output axis in Figure 7–1. Total fixed costs are thus a constant amount equal to AB in Figure 7–1.

The Total Variable Cost Curve

Total variable costs, or V, have been defined as all those costs which do vary as output varies. Thus, in Table 7–1, when input a varies and the price of a unit of a or p_a is taken to be equal to \$10, the variable cost of production of 12.65 units of X is equal to \$10 because one unit of a costing ten dollars is required to produce this much output in a plant of the size $b = 10$. Assuming that the price of a remains constant, the total variable cost of all outputs can also be computed, as it has been in Table 7–1.

In Figure 7–1, the slope of the total cost curve is the same as that of the total variable cost curve, for the total cost is produced by adding a constant amount (the fixed cost) to the total variable cost. Thus, the graphical difference between the total cost curve and the total variable cost curve is merely that the former lies above the total variable cost curve at all levels of output by the distance $A'B' = AB$, which is the amount of the fixed cost, or $10 in our example.

Short-Run Average Cost Curves

Short-run *average* cost curves are depicted in Figure 7–2, which is based on Table 7–2. Both will be employed in explaining the various average, or per unit, cost curves.

Figure 7–2

SHORT-RUN AVERAGE COST CURVES

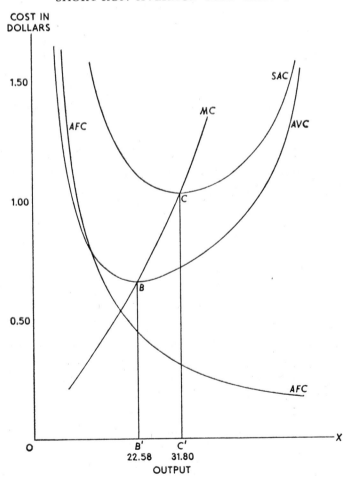

Table 7–2

SHORT-RUN AVERAGE COST DATA*

Units	Dollars					
(1)	(2)	(3)	(4)	(5)	(6)	(7)
X	$ap_a = V$	$\frac{V}{X} = AVC$	$bp_b = F$	$\frac{F}{X} = AFC$	T	$\frac{T}{X} = SAC$
1.00	7.80	7.80	10.00	10.00	17.80	17.80
5.00	8.20	1.64	10.00	2.00	18.20	3.64
8.00	8.70	1.09	10.00	1.25	18.70	2.34
12.65	10.00	0.79	10.00	0.79	20.00	1.58
22.58	15.00	0.66	10.00	0.45	25.00	1.11
28.98	20.00	0.69	10.00	0.35	30.00	1.04
31.80	22.73	0.72	10.00	0.31	32.73	1.03
37.95	30.00	0.79	10.00	0.26	40.00	1.05
44.27	40.00	0.90	10.00	0.23	50.00	1.13
48.99	50.00	1.02	10.00	0.20	60.00	1.22
52.54	60.00	1.14	10.00	0.19	70.00	1.33
55.14	70.00	1.27	10.00	0.18	80.00	1.45
56.94	80.00	1.40	10.00	0.17	90.00	1.58
57.97	90.00	1.55	10.00	0.17	100.00	1.72
58.31	100.00	1.72	10.00	0.17	110.00	1.89

* Based on Table 6–1A.

Since the definition of total cost has been written in Equation (7–1) as

$$T = F + V = bp_b + ap_a , \qquad (7\text{–}1)$$

the short-run average, or per unit, cost can be obtained merely by dividing both sides of this equation by X to produce

$$SAC = \frac{T}{X} = \frac{F}{X} + \frac{V}{X} = \frac{bp_b}{X} + \frac{ap_a}{X} . \qquad (7\text{–}2)$$

Now the term on the left, T/X, is the short-run average cost, commonly designated SAC, and is equal to the sum of the average fixed cost, $AFC = F/X$, and the average variable cost, $AVC = V/X$. Since the total fixed cost, F, remains constant as output, or X, increases, it is clear that the average fixed cost, F/X, must decline constantly (up to the point of absolutely diminishing returns)—for it consists of a fixed or constant numerator, F, and an increasing denominator, X. The average fixed cost curve is a rectangular hyperbola, and it has been so depicted in Figure 7–2.

The average variable cost and the average or per unit cost curves do *not* constantly decline. Reference to Figure 7–2 shows that they are U-shaped in that diagram. The reason why these two average cost curves are assumed to have this shape can be seen most clearly by reference to

Table 7–3, which shows the relationship between the average and the marginal cost and product curves. Table 7–3 appears on page 162.

The Relationship between Average Cost and Product Curves

Consider the algebraic definition of average variable cost given in Equation (7–2) above. We have written, $AVC = V/X = ap_a/X$. Now, $V = ap_a$ is the amount of the variable input multiplied by its price. And the formula for the average variable cost can be rewritten as $AVC = V/X = (a/X)(p_a)$. But the term a/X in the preceding formulation is the same thing as $1/(X/a)$; and X/a, the denominator in this reciprocal, has already been defined in Chapter 6 as the average product of the variable factor, a. Thus we see that the average variable cost is really equal to the reciprocal of the average product of the variable input, multiplied by the price of the variable input, or

$$AVC = \frac{1}{\dfrac{X}{a}}p_a = \frac{p_a}{AP}.$$

That is, the average variable cost is really the cost of each unit of X in terms of a, multiplied by the price of one unit of a. In Column (3) of Table 7–2, we see that the average variable cost can be determined directly from the total variable cost and the output data; and it can also be determined from the production data presented in Table 6–1 and the price of a as shown in Column (7) of Table 7–3.

Since the average variable cost is merely the reciprocal of the average variable product multiplied by the price of the variable input, it follows that if the average product curve (AP) has a *maximum* point, the average variable cost curve (AVC) must have a *minimum* point. The U shape of the average variable cost curve is thus derived directly from the assumption of the existence of the first two stages of *average* returns to the variable input.

The minimum average variable cost of $.66 in Table 7–3 occurs at point B in Figure 7–2, when 1.5 units of a are being used with 10 units of b and 22.58 units of X are being produced. At this same point, the average product of a is a maximum equal to 15.05 units in Column (5) of Table 7–3, which is based on Table 6–1A of the preceding chapter.

In Table 7–3, as in Table 6–1A, the average product (AP) of a is equal to the marginal product (MPP) of a when 1.5 units of a are used with 10 units of b to produce 22.58 units of X. At this same level of output, the marginal cost (MC) of X is equal to the average variable cost (AVC) of X. [Compare Columns (6) and (7) in Table 7–3.]

Table 7–3

SHORT-RUN AVERAGE AND MARGINAL COST AND PRODUCT DATA*

$(p_a = \$10)$

		Units				Dollars	
(1)	(2)	(3)	(4)	(5)	(6)	(7)	(8)
X	a	$MPP = \dfrac{\partial X}{\partial a}$	$\dfrac{1}{MPP}$	$AP = \dfrac{X}{a}$	$MC = \dfrac{p_a}{MPP}$	$AVC = \dfrac{p_a}{AP}$	$SAC = \dfrac{T}{X}$
1.00	0.78	368.80	0.003	1.28	0.03	7.80	17.80
5.00	0.82	73.40	0.013	6.09	0.13	1.64	3.64
8.00	0.87	45.60	0.022	9.19	0.22	1.09	2.34
12.65	1.00	28.50	0.035	12.65	0.35	0.79	1.58
22.58	1.50	15.05	0.066	15.05	0.66	0.66	1.11
28.98	2.00	11.00	0.090	14.49	0.90	0.69	1.04
31.80	2.27	9.72	0.103	13.99	1.03	0.72	1.03
37.95	3.00	7.38	0.135	12.65	1.35	0.79	1.05
44.27	4.00	5.42	0.185	11.07	1.85	0.90	1.13
48.99	5.00	4.08	0.245	9.80	2.45	1.02	1.22
52.54	6.00	3.05	0.328	8.75	3.28	1.14	1.33
55.14	7.00	2.18	0.459	7.88	4.59	1.27	1.45
56.94	8.00	1.40	0.714	7.12	7.14	1.40	1.58
57.97	9.00	0.69	1.449	6.44	14.49	1.55	1.73
58.31	10.00	0.00	....	5.83	....	1.72	1.88

* Output data based on Table 6–1A, where $X = \sqrt{2Cab - D(a^2) - D(b^2)}$, and $C = 40$, $D = 40$, $E = 6$, $b = 10$, and a has the values shown in Column (2) above. Also, $\partial X/\partial a = (Cb - Da)/X$, and $\partial X/\partial b = (Ca - Eb)/X$.

Thus the maximum point of the curve of the average variable *product* of *a* in Figure 6–1 occurs at the same level of output as does the minimum point on the curve of the average variable *cost* of *a*, or at *B* in Figure 7–2. However, this level of output is not that at which the short-run average cost of production (*SAC*) is a minimum, for the latter occurs when 31.80 units of *X* are being produced, or at *C* in Figure 7–2. The reason for these relationships will be explained further below.

Definition of the Marginal Cost

The definition of the marginal cost is completely parallel with that of marginal utility given in Chapter 3. The *marginal cost, MC, is the exact rate of change of total cost, T, as output, X, changes.* Symbolically we have $MC = \partial T/\partial X = t_x$. Alternatively, it is sometimes defined as equal to the average rate of change of total cost as output changes $(\Delta T/\Delta X)$, or as the change in total cost corresponding to a (one small) unit change in output.

By a process of reasoning similar to that employed in demonstrating the relationship between average variable cost and average product earlier, it can be shown that the marginal cost is equal to the reciprocal of the marginal product multiplied by the price of the variable input. That is, by defining the marginal cost as the average rate of change of total cost as output changes, we have

$$SMC = \frac{\Delta T}{\Delta X} = \frac{\Delta a}{\Delta X}p_a = \frac{1}{\frac{\Delta X}{\Delta a}}p_a = \frac{p_a}{\frac{\Delta X}{\Delta a}} = \frac{p_a}{MPP} \; .$$

Thus, "increasing marginal cost" is the result of the assumption of diminishing marginal productivity because the denominator in $SMC = p_a/MPP_a$ is the marginal product of a.

In Figure 7–2 the marginal cost curve depicts the exact rate of change. Column (6) of Table 7–3 contains the numerical values used in drawing this curve in Figure 7–2. In turn, Column (6) of Table 7–3 is based on the data for the marginal productivity of a which appears in Column (3) of Table 7–3 and also in Column (5) of Table 6–1A.

Marginal Cost Independent of Fixed Cost

Marginal cost is independent of fixed cost and can be defined alternatively as the rate of change of total variable cost as output changes. To understand this proposition, consider the following argument.

We have already defined total cost as

$$T = F + V = bp_b + ap_a \; . \tag{7-1}$$

Now the fixed costs have already been defined as those which do *not* change as output changes. It follows that the change in fixed cost as output changes must be zero, or $\Delta F = 0$. And since, from Equation (7–1), we know that any *given* change in total cost must be accounted for by the sum of the changes in those costs which define total cost, we have

$$\Delta T = 0 + \Delta V = 0 + \Delta a p_a \; . \tag{7-3}$$

Next, by dividing both sides of Equation (7–3) by ΔX to produce the data on a per unit basis, we have

$$\frac{\Delta T}{\Delta X} = 0 + \frac{\Delta V}{\Delta X} = 0 + \frac{\Delta a p_a}{\Delta X} = SMC \; , \tag{7-4}$$

or the short-run marginal cost. Thus the short-run marginal cost can be defined *either* as the rate of change of total cost as output changes *or* as the rate of change of variable cost as output changes. And so, the slope of the total cost curve, $\Delta T/\Delta X$, which is marginal cost, is equal to the slope of the total variable cost curve. We have thus shown in another way why the total cost curve and the total variable cost curve must be drawn with the same slope and have also shown that marginal cost is independent of the fixed cost.

The Least Cost Point: The Concept of Economic Capacity

The term *economic capacity* is a value concept. It is identified as the minimum point on an average cost curve. In other words, the point of economic capacity occurs at C in Figure 7–2, where 31.80 units of X are being produced with 2.273 units of a and 10 units of b at a cost of $32.73.

The concept, *economic capacity,* is not the same thing as the concept of the *physical capacity* of the plant, for total output can be increased at a higher average cost of production beyond 31.80 units of X in Figure 7–2 and in Table 7–3. Indeed, the point of short-run *physical* capacity occurs at the Point of Absolutely Diminishing Returns to a, for at that point additional units of the variable input add nothing to the total product, while costs continue to rise.

The *point of economic capacity can be identified as the least cost point,* the point at which the marginal cost curve cuts the average cost curve *from below.* This cost condition (known in mathematical economics as a "second-order condition") is merely a requirement that marginal cost be increasing at the point at which it is equal to the average cost of production, for otherwise the two might be equal at a maximum rather than at a minimum point on the average cost curve.

Note in Figure 7–2 that the minimum point (C) of the average cost curve occurs at a higher level of output (further to the right on the X axis) than that at which the minimum point (B) of the average variable cost curve occurs. The reason why this is so is that the average cost is the sum of the average variable cost and the average fixed cost. Since the average fixed cost declines continuously as long as output increases, the sum of these two magnitudes, or average cost, will also decline as long as the average variable cost declines. At B in Figure 7–2 the average variable cost begins to rise, while the average fixed cost continues to decline. However, the sum of these two magnitudes will begin to increase only when the increase in the average variable cost begins to exceed the decrease in the average fixed cost. Thus, the minimum point of the average cost curve must always occur at a higher level of output than does the minimum point of the average variable cost curve.

(In depicting the various cost curves graphically, it is good practice to draw the various average cost curves first and then to draw the marginal cost curve cutting the average variable and average cost curves at their respective minimum points.)

Joint Costs: Fixed Proportions

When two products can only be produced in fixed proportions, they are treated as a single product. Marshall noted that, for some purposes, mutton and wool could be treated as a single commodity, but that even in this case it is sometimes possible, through careful breeding practices, to change in the long run the proportions in which such joint products are produced.[6]

One method of dealing with commodities which can only be produced in fixed proportions is to define a unit of the composite commodity, say Q_x, as equal to the fixed proportion, say k, of one commodity, X_1, plus one unit of X_2, or symbolically to write $Q_x = kX_1 + 1X_2$. The price of Q_x can then be taken as equal to $kp_{x_1} + p_{x_2}$. The average cost of Q_x is then simply the total cost of production divided by the total number of units of the composite commodity produced, or $T/Q_x = AC_{q_x}$, and the marginal cost is $\partial T/\partial Q_x = t_{q_x}$.

Joint Costs: Variable Proportions; Product Transformation Curve

When the proportions in which joint commodities are produced can be varied, their separate marginal costs can be determined even though these costs are not independent. What is required is a determination of the way in which the total cost of production varies as the quantity of one of the joint products is changed while the amount of the other remains constant.

Such a case has already been explained in Chapter 3 (see Figure 3–6), and it is defined by movements along curves such as those exemplified by the equation, $u = f(x, y = y_0)$. It follows, therefore, that contour lines can also be used to depict such cases. In this case, the contour line is known as a *product transformation curve*.

In Figure 7–3, OX_1 measures the output of X_1, and OX_2 measures the output of X_2. Contour lines, such as T_1, T_2, and T_3, represent the different amounts of X_1 and X_2 which can be produced with given total outlays for inputs equal respectively to T_1, T_2, and T_3. With constant prices of inputs, higher contour lines thus represent greater quantities of inputs used. As usual, the definition of our contour line is given by the equation

$$\Delta T = \frac{\partial T}{\partial X_1}\Delta X_1 + \frac{\partial T}{\partial X_2}\Delta X_2 = t_{x_1}\Delta X_1 + t_{x_2}\Delta X_2 = 0 , \qquad (7\text{-}5)$$

---

[6] *Ibid.*, pp. 389–90.

Figure 7–3

ILLUSTRATION OF JOINT COST

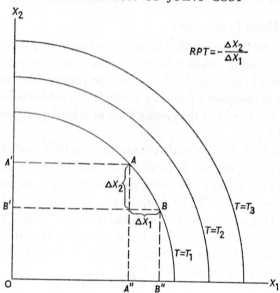

where $\partial T/\partial X_1 = t_{x_1}$ represents the marginal cost of X_1, and $\partial T/\partial X_2 = t_{x_2}$ represents the marginal cost of X_2. It is assumed that the marginal costs are positive and that additional units of either product can be produced only by using additional units of input, which are not free. Thus it follows from our by now familiar argument that if total cost is to remain constant, or $\Delta T = 0$, along a contour line, either ΔX_1 or ΔX_2 must be negative, while the other is positive.

Now, in the case of our indifference curve and isoquant diagrams, we assumed that the marginal utilities and marginal products respectively were positive, but diminishing, in the relevant range. Thus both our indifference curves and our isoquants were convex to the origin. However, our cost curves are reciprocals of the product curves, and although we assume the marginal costs positive, we assume that t_{x_1} increases, as X_1 is increased at the expense of X_2, and vice versa.

And by following our usual procedure and subtracting $t_{x_2}\Delta X_2$ from both sides of Equation (7–5), we have

$$t_{x_1}\Delta X_1 = -t_{x_2}\Delta X_2 .\tag{7–6}$$

Next, as usual, by dividing both sides of the preceding equation by $t_{x_2}\Delta X_1$, we produce

$$\frac{t_{x_1}}{t_{x_2}} = -\frac{\Delta X_2}{\Delta X_1} = RPT, \text{ the } \textit{rate of product transformation.} \tag{7–7}$$

This rate, which is the slope of the production possibility line in the range from A to B (which is taken to be infinitesimally small) in Figure 7–3, is equal to the ratio of the marginal costs of X_1 and X_2.

Product transformation curves are often employed in general welfare economics and have often been used in analyzing the welfare aspects of international trade.[7] In Chapter 17 we will explain a linear programming solution to a problem involving production of joint products from given inputs.

E. CONSTANT LONG-RUN COST

Definition of Long-Run Cost

The *long run has been defined as a period of time sufficiently long to allow changes in the existing capacity,* that is to say, in the existing size of the plant. Thus there are no fixed inputs in the long run because it is always possible for the firm to build a different size plant, thereby varying the amount of the factor, b, which has been held fixed in the short run. *In brief, in the long run, all inputs are variable.* The length of the time period assumed will vary from industry to industry, but this is a minor point and creates no difficulties.

The *long-run total cost of production* (T_L) *is the least possible cost of producing any given level of output when all inputs are variable.* Figure 7–4 contains the total cost curves for three different size plants (different values of b in our linearly homogeneous production function). The values of the constants assumed in our production function are $C = 40$, $D = 40$, and $E = 6$, as before. Thus curve T_1 in Figure 7–4 is the short-run total cost curve already depicted in Figure 7–1 when $b = 10$, while T_2 represents the total cost when $b = 20$, and T_3 represents the total cost when $b = 30$.

Now the short-run total cost of production of any given amount of output has already been defined in Equation (7–1) as equal to the sum of the total fixed cost and the total variable cost. The only difference between the total cost in the long run and in the short run is that in the former the fixed input, b, is also considered a variable. Consequently, the long-run total cost is defined by the equation

$$T_L = ap_a + bp_b, \text{ with all inputs variable.} \qquad (7\text{–}8)$$

Since the long-run total cost curve depicts the least possible cost of producing all possible outputs, it is a curve which is tangent to each

---

[7] See, for example, Wassily W. Leontief, "The Use of Indifference Curves in the Analysis of Foreign Trade," *Quarterly Journal of Economics,* Vol. XLVII (May, 1933), pp. 493–503.

short-run total cost curve at *one* point only. Tangency between the long-run total cost curve and the short-run curves, as at A', B', and C' in Figure 7–4, means that, at the given output levels, these respective total costs are equal.

In Figure 7–4 the long-run total cost curve is *linear,* that is, it is a straight line through the origin, because the production function is linearly homogeneous and the prices of the inputs are assumed to remain constant. (Figure 7–6 depicts a case in which the long-run total cost curve is not linear.) Thus Figure 7–4 represents a *special case,* in which the expansion path is a straight line.

The meaning of the proposition that the long-run total cost of pro-

Figure 7–4

**LONG-RUN TOTAL COST CURVE: LINEARLY HOMOGENEOUS
PRODUCTION FUNCTION**

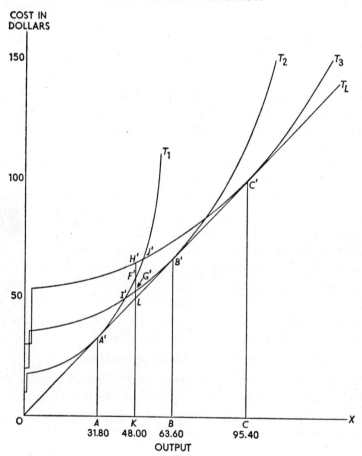

duction is the least possible cost of producing all possible outputs is depicted in Figure 7–4 also. Consider output OK. This output can be produced in Plant T_1 at a total cost of KF', for the perpendicular line KF' cuts T_1 at F'. However, this output can also be produced in Plant T_2 at a cost of KG', which is less than KF'. Moreover, the same output can be produced in Plant T_3 at a cost of KH', and this is the highest cost of all. Finally, the cost of KL, which is the long-run cost of production, is the smallest of all. If there were sufficient time to vary all inputs, the least cost of producing the given output would be found in a plant whose size is somewhere between that of Plants T_1 and T_2.

Constant Cost

It has been noted in Chapter 6 that if the production function is linearly homogeneous and prices of inputs remain constant, long-run average cost is constant and so is the long-run marginal cost. This situation is depicted in Figure 7–5, which contains the marginal cost (SMC) and the average cost curves (SAC) corresponding to the various short-run total cost curves in the special case depicted in Figure 7–4. An infinite number of such curves exists in the diagram, since b is assumed to be infinitely divisible, but only three are depicted. The reason why long-run average costs are constant in such a case is as follows. (Figure 7–5 appears on the next page.)

First, recall that when the production function is linearly homogeneous, both the marginal product and the average product are independent of the amount of inputs used. [See Equations (3–3) through (3–3e′) in Chapter 6.] From this fact it follows that the absolute (arithmetical) value of the *maximum* average variable *product* does not change when the scale of operations is changed, that is, when a larger plant is built and when proportionately more of both a and b are used and output also increases proportionately. For the ratio of a to b remains unchanged. Therefore the *minimum* average variable *cost* is not changed in such a case either. *Second,* if the amount spent on the fixed input is changed proportionately at constant prices while output changes proportionately, the average fixed cost, or the ratio between them, is also unchanged when the scale of operations is changed. From these two considerations it follows that the minimum average cost of production (the sum of the average variable and average fixed costs) is likewise unchanged when expenditures on inputs and output both change proportionately.

Therefore, the minimum short-run average cost of production is the same at all levels of output, and the long-run average cost of production is constant and equal to the minimum short-run average cost of production in each possible plant. For this reason, the long-run total cost curve, T_L, is drawn as a straight line through the origin in Figure 7–4, and the long-run marginal cost curve is identical with the long-run average cost curve in Figure 7–5.

Accordingly, in Figure 7–5, the long-run marginal cost curve (LMC) has been drawn as a horizontal line, equal to the long-run average cost (LAC) at the level $AA' = BB' = CC'$, also equal to the minimum short-run average cost of production, which is the same in all plants. In Figure 7–4, the tangency, or equality, between T_L and T_1, T_2, and T_3, respectively, at A', B', and C', thus corresponds to equality between LAC and SAC_1, SAC_2, and SAC_3 at these same points in Figure 7–5.

Figure 7–5

LONG-RUN AVERAGE COST CURVE: LINEARLY HOMOGENEOUS PRODUCTION FUNCTION

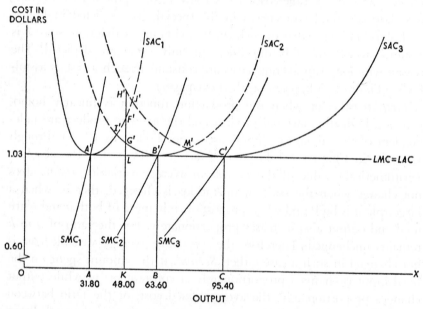

In Figure 7–5 we again see that output OK is produced most cheaply at a cost of KL, for there is an undepicted short-run average cost curve whose minimum point is tangent to LAC at L, and next most cheaply at a cost of KG' in Plant SAC_2, while the most expensive method of producing the given output is KH' in Plant SAC_3, as before, insofar as are concerned the plants whose costs of production are depicted. The minimum long-run average cost (KL) of output OK occurs in a plant whose size is between that of Plant SAC_1 and Plant SAC_2, a point which is seen much more clearly in Figure 7–5 than in Figure 7–4.

The Principle of Substitution and Costs

The Marshallian equilibrium condition, stated in Equation (6–3) which reads:

$$\frac{f_a}{p_a} = \frac{f_b}{p_b} \cdot \cdot \cdot = \frac{f_n}{p_n} = d , \qquad (6\text{--}3)$$

is met at all outputs (points) along the long-run average cost curve (*LAC*) in Figure 7–5 and at all points along the long-run total cost curve (T_L) in Figure 7–4. Recall that this condition states that the amount of output obtained from an additional dollar spent on any one *variable* input must be equal to that obtained from an additional dollar spent on any other *variable* input, when total expenditures are given.[8] The condition is necessarily met for all inputs both in the long run and in the short run at *any* point at which a short-run average cost curve is tangent to the long-run average cost curve, as at A', B', and C' in Figure 7–5. At such a point the short-run average cost and the long-run average cost are equal. In our *special* case, this tangency occurs at the minimum points of all the short-run cost curves. The statement that, when costs are constant, the optimum size of the plant is indeterminate thus means that all of the plants depicted in Figure 7–5 are equally efficient, since the minimum average cost of production is the same in each (or at all levels of output).

In other words, in our present case, movements along the long-run cost curve involve a proportionate change in inputs and in output, but *no* change in the proportions in which the inputs are used. That is, the expansion path is linear as in Figure 6–7. Some of the data used in drawing Figure 7–5 are contained in Table 7–4 and illustrate this fact. (See the column showing the ratio a/b.)

Table 7–4
SELECTED INPUT-OUTPUT DATA AT LEAST COST POINTS IN FIGURE 7–5

Least Cost Point	f_a	f_b	$\dfrac{f_a}{f_b}$	a	b	Ratio $\dfrac{a}{b}$	Output
A'	9.72	0.972	10.00	2.273	10	0.2273	31.80
B'	9.72	0.972	10.00	4.544	20	0.2273	63.60
C'	9.72	0.972	10.00	6.817	30	0.2273	95.40

[8] Marshall, *op. cit.*, p. 341.

F. RETURN TO OUTLAY

The Concept of Return to Outlay

The total cost of producing a given output can be thought of as the total *outlay* made by the firm. The term *"long-run return to outlay" refers to the way in which output behaves as outlay changes when all inputs are variable.* The term *"short-run return to outlay" refers to the case in which one input is held fixed.* Let us use the symbol T_L, which we have already used to mean long-run total cost, to mean long-run total outlay as well.

With constant prices, a proportionate change in inputs changes total cost, or outlay, proportionately also. That is, if the amounts of all inputs are doubled but their prices remain constant, total outlay is also doubled. Consequently in such a case, when the production function is linearly homogeneous, the terms *return to outlay* and *returns to scale* are often used interchangeably. For, in such a case, the proportions among the inputs do not change as outlay changes.

The term *returns to scale* has traditionally referred to proportionate changes in all inputs, which means that the proportions among the inputs are unchanged, while the term *return to outlay* is a more general concept and includes also cases in which the proportions among the inputs are changed. Thus a case in which *all* inputs are increased in different proportions, so that the ratios among them also change, must be explained in terms of the concept, *long-run return to outlay.*

The *long-run average return to outlay* at a given point *is the total output, when all inputs are variable, divided by the total outlay,* or X/T_L. The *long-run marginal return to outlay is the rate of change of total output as total outlay changes when all inputs are variable,* or the change in total output which results from an additional dollar spent on any one of the inputs, i.e., $\partial X/\partial T_L$.

The long-run marginal return to outlay is, in fact, the common *equilibrium* value of the ratios of the various marginal products to their respective prices in the Marshallian production equilibrium condition, just as the marginal utility of income, u'_0, is the common equilibrium value of the ratios of the various marginal utilities to their respective prices in the Marshallian consumer equilibrium condition stated in Equation (4–2) in Chapter 4.

We can prove this by letting d represent the marginal dollar's worth of product when the Marshallian principle of substitution is met, or by first writing Equation (6–3):

$$\frac{f_a}{p_a} = \frac{f_b}{p_b} = \cdots \frac{f_n}{p_n} = d . \qquad (6\text{-}3)$$

Now we have already defined the long-run total cost as

$$T_L = ap_a + bp_b \qquad (7\text{-}8)$$

when all inputs are variable. And we also know that any *given* change in total cost consists of the sum of the changes in the costs of the inputs, or

$$\Delta T_L = \Delta ap_a + \Delta bp_b , \text{ all inputs variable.} \qquad (7\text{-}9)$$

Further, we can break down Equation (6–3) into parts, or

$$\frac{f_a}{p_a} = d , \frac{f_b}{p_b} = d , \cdots \frac{f_n}{p_n} = d , \qquad (6\text{-}3a)$$

from which follows that

$$p_a = \frac{f_a}{d} , \ p_b = \frac{f_b}{d} , \cdots p_n = \frac{f_n}{d} . \qquad (6\text{-}3b)$$

(This formulation says that the marginal product of an input divided by the amount of product obtained from a marginal dollar's worth of *any* input is equal to the price of the input in the long run.)

And we can substitute this definition of the prices of the inputs for the nominal prices, p_a and p_b, in Equation (7–9), so that it will read

$$\Delta T_L = \frac{\Delta af_a}{d} + \frac{\Delta bf_b}{d} = \frac{f_a\Delta a + f_b\Delta b}{d} . \qquad (7\text{-}10)$$

Next, recall that in Chapter 3 we have explained Equation (3–2), which describes the movement from one contour line to another. Now, a movement from one contour line to another is a movement along the long-run cost curve, if the condition of the principle of substitution is met. That is, the movement is along the expansion path depicted in Figure 6–7. Equation (3–2) reads:

$$\Delta X = f_a\Delta a + f_b\Delta b ; (\Delta X \neq 0) . \qquad (3\text{-}2)$$

If, therefore, we now divide Equation (7–10) into Equation (3–2) [i.e., turn (7–10) upside down and multiply (3–2) by it], we will produce the long-run average rate of change of output as outlay changes, or the change in total output which results from an additional dollar spent on any of the inputs as we move along the expansion path in Figure 6–7. This, of course, is the definition of the long-run marginal return to outlay, and so we have

$$\frac{\Delta X}{\Delta T_L} = (f_a\Delta a + f_b\Delta b)\left(\frac{d}{f_a\Delta a + f_b\Delta b}\right) = d . \qquad (7\text{-}11)$$

In terms of the data provided in Table 7–4, we thus have

$$\frac{\Delta X}{\Delta T_L} = \frac{f_a}{p_a} = \frac{f_b}{p_b} = d = \frac{9.72}{\$10} = \frac{.972}{\$1.00} = .972X . \qquad (7\text{--}11')$$

At all points along the long-run outlay curve, in our special case, a dollar's worth of any of the inputs will produce .972 of one unit of product, for returns to scale and to outlay are constant. The reader may be reminded at this point that the statistical studies of productivity by the National Bureau of Economic Research—briefly described in the concluding section of the preceding chapter—make use of the concept of the productivity of "a dollar's worth of combined inputs."

Relationship between Returns to Outlay and Cost

Now consider the formula for the long-run marginal return to outlay, $\Delta X/\Delta T_L$. This formula is merely the formula for the *long-run marginal cost*, $\Delta T_L/\Delta X$, turned upside down. Or, $\Delta T_L/\Delta X = 1/(\Delta X/\Delta T_L)$. That is, since the long-run marginal return to outlay is equal to d (the common equilibrium value of the ratios of the various marginal products of the inputs to their respective prices), it follows that the long-run marginal cost is the reciprocal of this common equilibrium value, or $\Delta T_L/\Delta X = 1/d$. The economic sense of this should be clear enough: the common equilibrium value of the ratios specified in the Marshallian equilibrium condition, or the long-run marginal return to outlay, is the amount of output obtained from the marginal dollar spent on any of the inputs *when all inputs are variable*. And so, the long-run marginal cost is merely the cost in dollars of the marginal unit of output *when all inputs are variable*.

Moreover, in general, the long-run marginal cost will be equal to the short-run marginal cost at all points at which the long-run total cost curve is tangent to the various short-run cost curves (A', B', and C' in Figures 7–4 and 7–6) whether or not such points of tangency occur at the minimum points on the short-run curves, for such points lie on *both* curves.

The average return to outlay, X/T_L, is similarly the reciprocal of the long-run average cost, T_L/X. That this is the case seems obvious, and extended explanation seems unnecessary, since, clearly, $X/T_L = 1/(T_L/X)$.

G. LONG-RUN COST IN THE "NORMAL" CASE

The "Normal" Case: "Internal Economies and Diseconomies"

It is usually assumed that, in the "normal case," long-run average cost first declines, then remains constant, either momentarily or for some range of output, and finally increases. A long-run cost curve having these characteristics is depicted by T_L in Figure 7–6 and is explained by *"internal* economies and diseconomies."* The existence of these depends less upon empirical studies than on introspection. Thus Marshall defined the *internal* (to the firm) *economies* as those "dependent on the resources of the individual houses of business engaged in it [the industry], on their organization, and the efficiency of their management."[9] The division of labor or specialization, the power of a larger firm to use more complex and larger machines rather than more machines of the same kind, and the skills of management were thought by Marshall to be the principal sources of the internal economies, and present-day economists have not progressed very far beyond this catalogue.[10]

The *internal* (to the firm) *diseconomies* are generally based on a belief that eventually large bureaucratic organizations *must* become inefficient. This notion has recently been reformulated humorously as "Parkinson's law."[11] However, Marshall stated it seriously in a telling passage in the *Principles* when he said:

. . . the small employer has advantages of his own. The master's eye is everywhere; there is no shirking by his foremen or workmen, no divided responsibility, no sending half-understood messages backwards and forwards from one department to another. He saves much of the book-keeping, and nearly all of the cumbrous system of checks that are necessary in the business of a large firm; and the gain from this source is of very great importance in trades which use the more valuable metals and other expensive materials.[12]

Thus, not all of the economies of size operate in the same direction, nor are large plants necessarily the most efficient ones in the real world. Note that it is important to make a distinction between plants (producing units) and firms in this regard. A firm is an owning and controlling unit, and one firm may own or control many plants. To argue that multiplant firms are more efficient than single plant firms means that one must carry the burden of proving that economies in addition to those resulting from large-scale *operations* are found in large-scale *organizations.*[13]

[9] *Ibid.,* Book IV, chap. ix, esp. p. 266.

[10] Compare, for example, Richard Leftwich, *The Price System and Resource Allocation* (rev. ed.; New York: Holt, Rinehart & Winston, Inc., 1960), pp. 155–58; and George Stigler, *The Theory of Price* (rev. ed.; New York: The Macmillan Co., 1952), pp. 137–40.

[11] C. N. Parkinson, *Parkinson's Law and Other Studies in Administration* (Boston: Houghton Mifflin Co., 1957).

[12] Marshall, *op. cit.,* p. 284.

[13] See Arthur S. Dewing, "A Statistical Test of the Success of Consolidation," *Quarterly Journal of Economics,* Vol. XXXVI (1921), pp. 84 ff.

The "Normal" Case Illustrated

The "normal" case is most often described as one in which inputs are perfectly divisible and in which constant costs are assumed to be unlikely in the real world because of the existence of internal economies and diseconomies which operate to keep the production function from being linearly homogeneous. Some writers have argued that the reason why long-run costs are not constant is to be found in the existence of indivisibilities of some inputs, but their view seems today to be in the minority. The effect of indivisibilities will be analyzed later in this chapter. In our illustration we will assume that all inputs are perfectly divisible.

In order to analyze the "normal" case fully, let us amend our production function in such a way that average returns to scale will increase to some point, at which they will be momentarily constant, and that average returns to scale will decrease thereafter. Accordingly, let us write the production function as follows:

$$X = \sqrt{2Cab - D(a^2) - E(b^2)} + [F(kb - b^2) - Z], \qquad (7\text{-}12)$$

where F, k, and Z are additional constants greater than zero. The term in brackets represents the effect of internal economies and diseconomies associated with the "size" of the plant.

Let us further assume that $F = .1$, $k = 40$, and $Z = 40$. If these values are assigned to the indicated constants, in the special case in which $b = 20$, the arithmetical value of the term in brackets reduces to zero, or

$$[F(kb - b^2) - Z] = [(.1)(800 - 400) - 40] = 0 .$$

Thus, in the case in which $b = 20$, the short-run cost curve of the plant, SAC_{20}, will be identical with the short-run cost curve, SAC_2, in Figure 7–5.

However, in the case in which $a = 1$, $b = 10$, the situation will be different from the case of SAC_1, for then we will have

$$X_{1,10} = \sqrt{(2)(40)(1)(10) - 40(1^2) - 6(10^2)} + (-10) \qquad (7\text{-}12a')$$
$$= 2.65 .$$

We can compare this result with the case in which the inputs of a and b are *both* doubled, or

$$X_{2,20} = \sqrt{(2)(40)(2)(20) - 40(2^2) - 6(20^2)} + 0 \qquad (7\text{-}12b')$$
$$= 25.30 .$$

The last result shows that doubling of the inputs more than doubles the output, since 25.30 units of X are considerably more than twice 2.65 units. Output has increased *more than proportionately* with inputs.

Finally, consider the case in which three units of a are used with 30 units of b. In this case, our new production function produces

$$X_{3,30} = \sqrt{(2)(40)(3)(30) - 40(3^2) - 6(30^2)} - 10 \qquad (7\text{--}12c')$$
$$= 27.95 .$$

Output is now much less than 50 percent greater than when two units each of a and b are used, although the amounts of each of the inputs have been increased by 50 percent. Thus, output has now increased *less than proportionately* with inputs.

No further assumptions are necessary beyond addition to our production function of the term in brackets in Equation (7–12) which takes account of the existence of internal economies and diseconomies. Our short-run and long-run total cost functions are defined as they were in Equations (7–1) and (7–8) earlier, and all of the previous logic applies in the new situation. No new principles are involved, and, thus, the student who understands the case of constant cost should have no difficulty in understanding the present one.

The shapes of the short-run total cost curves, when $b = 12$, $b = 20$, and $b = 25$, are depicted by T_{12}, T_{20}, and T_{25}, respectively, in Figure 7–6. These short-run curves are characterized by a constantly increasing slope. That is, since in the short-run case the marginal product of the variable input in our production function begins diminishing as soon as a positive amount of output is obtained, the short-run marginal cost constantly rises.[14]

---

[14] The formula for the marginal product of a in the case of our new production function is exactly the same as it was before, or

$$f_a = \frac{Cb - Da}{\sqrt{2Cab - D(a^2) - E(b^2)}} ;$$

but the formula for the marginal product of b is now

$$f_b = \frac{Ca - Eb}{\sqrt{2Cab - D(a^2) - E(b^2)}} + [Fk - 2Fb] .$$

Because of the values which have been chosen for our constants, the *arithmetical* value of the marginal product of b in the case in which $b = 20$ is precisely the same at all levels of output as it is in our case of a linearly homogeneous production function. That is, in the case in which $b = 20$, we have

$$[Fk - 2Fb] = (.1)(40) - 2(.1)(20) = 0 ,$$

so that the arithmetical value of the term in brackets in the formula for f_b reduces to zero in this case. In short, when $b = 20$, there are neither external economies or diseconomies, and our production function produces *in this special case* the same arithmetical result as is produced by the linearly homogeneous production function assumed earlier.

Figure 7–6

LONG-RUN TOTAL COST IN THE "NORMAL" CASE

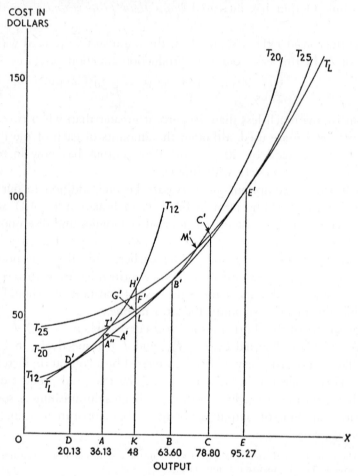

The long-run cost curve is labeled T_L in Figure 7–6, and it is seen now to be *not* a straight line. In the case of our particular production function, the long-run total cost curve, too, is characterized by a constantly increasing slope.

As before, we see in Figure 7–6 that the long-run total cost curve, T_L, is tangent to each of the short-run total cost curves at a single point. At each of these points, D', B', and E', respectively, the long-run and the short-run total costs for the particular output are equal. *However*, the points of tangency do *not* now have the interpretation which we placed on them in the case of our linearly homogeneous production function in Figure 7–4.

With the exception of B', the other points of tangency, such as D' and E' in Figure 7–6, *do not now mean that the long-run average cost and the minimum short-run average cost of production are equal at that point.* Nevertheless, it is still true that the long-run cost of production of any given output is the least cost of production of that output. Thus, in Figure 7–6, in the short run, the cost of producing output OK is KH' in Plant T_{12}, and less in Plant T_{20} where it is KG'; but it is least in the long run (KL) in a plant whose size lies somewhere between those of Plant T_{12} and Plant T_{20}.

This point can be seen more clearly by examining the average cost curves in Figure 7–7 which correspond to the total cost curves in

Figure 7–7

LONG-RUN AVERAGE COST IN THE "NORMAL" CASE

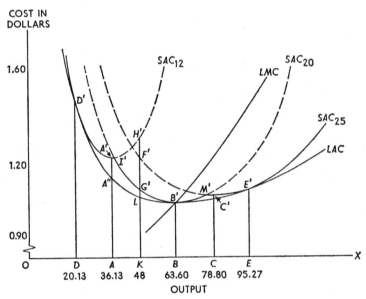

Figure 7–6. As before, the labeling of the two diagrams is parallel, and the output OK can be produced at the least average cost (KL) in the long run in a plant whose size lies between those of Plant SAC_{12} and Plant SAC_{20}. The highest average cost of production of output OK, equal to KH', occurs in Plant SAC_{12} in our diagram, and the lowest cost is KL.

The long-run average cost curve, LAC, depicted in Figure 7–7, is sometimes referred to as an *envelope curve,* since it is tangent to (touches at *one* point) each of the short-run average cost curves and intersects none of them. The term "envelope" curve may be an un-fortunate one. *For the long-run curve is not something apart from the short-run curves; it is defined in an economic sense by points on the short-run curves.* Indeed, *the long-run curve is simply a curve drawn tangent to the short-run curves at all those points at which the Marshallian equilibrium condition is fulfilled for all inputs, and this is the definition of the long-run curve.* As was noted in the preceding chapter, this condition is always fulfilled at *some* point on every short-run curve, although the point at which it is fulfilled does not also necessarily represent the minimum cost of production in the short run, since the firm is unable to vary its fixed inputs.

Since the points of tangency (D', B', and E') between the short-run and the long-run curves are located on both curves, only at such points are the output and the proportions and amounts in which the inputs are used the same both in the short run and in the long run. At the same time, the long-run average cost curve is tangent at *its* minimum point to the minimum point of only one short-run average cost curve. In Figure 7–7, this point is B' on SAC_{20}. At this point, the long-run and short-run average costs are equal and momentarily constant ($SAC_{20} = LAC$ at B').

At the output levels (or points) at which the long-run and short-run average costs are equal, the long-run and short-run *marginal* costs are also equal ($SMC_{20} = LMC$ at B'). The reason why this is so is that in the short run the marginal cost is equal to the reciprocal of the marginal product of the *variable* input times its price, while, in the long run, the marginal cost is equal to the reciprocal of the marginal product of *any* input times its price. The latter case thus includes the former, but the former does not include the latter.

Moreover, at B', *not only* are the long-run and the short-run total and average costs equal *but also* the long-run and the short-run marginal costs (in addition to being equal to each other) are equal to the long-run and short-run average costs. Thus, at B', we have $SAC_{20} = SMC_{20} = LAC = LMC$. For at B', in the short run, the ratios of the marginal products of all the inputs to their respective prices, *whether fixed or variable,* happen to be equal, just as the ratios of the marginal products of all the inputs to their respective prices are always equal in the long run. Finally, B' is also the point of maximum average return to outlay and the point at which the marginal and average returns to outlay are equal.

As a matter of fact, just as the long-run average cost first decreases, then reaches a minimum at B', and increases thereafter, so does the average return to outlay first increase, then reach a maximum at B', and decrease thereafter. For, as we have seen, these two concepts are reciprocals of each other. Table 7–5 shows the relationship of all these magnitudes to each other at the indicated points in Figures 7–6 and 7–7.

Table 7–5

LONG-RUN AVERAGE AND MARGINAL RETURNS TO OUTLAY AND COST

Point	Output X	Outlay or Cost T_L	Return to Outlay		Cost	
			$\dfrac{X}{T_L}$	$\dfrac{\partial X}{\partial T_L}$	$\dfrac{T_L}{X} = LAC$	$\dfrac{\partial T_L}{\partial X} = LMC$
D'	20.13	29.63	0.649	1.543	1.54	0.65
B'	63.60	65.45	0.972	0.972	1.03	1.03
E'	95.27	104.03	0.926	0.699	1.08	1.43

It may be useful to note that in Figure 7–7, any *output smaller than OB* will always be produced most cheaply by building a plant with a given least cost point and utilizing it to produce less than that given output, or at less than its minimum cost of production. Thus, for outputs less than *OB*, the long-run average cost curve will always be tangent to the *falling portion of a short-run average cost curve*. On the other hand, any *output greater than OB* will always be produced most cheaply by building a plant with a given least cost point and utilizing it to produce at more than its minimum cost of production, or more than its optimum output. And so, for outputs greater than *OB*, the long-run average cost curve will always be tangent to the *rising portion of a short-run average cost curve*.

Table 7–6 contains data applicable to the relevant points in Figures

Table 7–6

SELECTED INPUT-OUTPUT DATA FOR POINTS IN FIGURES 7–6 AND 7–7

Point	Output	Cost	f_a	f_b	d	$\dfrac{f_a}{f_b}$	a	b	$\dfrac{a}{b}$
Points of Tangency:									
D'	20.13	29.63	15.43	1.543	1.543	10.00	1.763	12	0.147
B'	63.60	65.45	9.72	0.972	0.972	10.00	4.544	20	0.227
E'	95.27	104.03	6.99	0.699	0.699	10.00	7.903	25	0.316
Minimum Points:									
A'	36.13	44.40	15.23	2.963	1.523	5.10	3.240	12	0.270
B'	63.60	65.40	9.72	0.972	0.972	10.00	4.544	20	0.227
C'	78.80	83.75	9.41	0.046	0.941	204.50	5.875	25	0.235

7–6 and 7–7 and illustrates the validity of an argument made by
Professor E. H. Chamberlin,[15] to the effect that the problem of long-
run costs involves questions *both* as to the amounts of inputs and as to
the proportions in which they are used.

Table 7–6 shows clearly that at the points of tangency, D', B', and
E', the *proportions* between the inputs (the ratios between a and b)
are different. Thus, movements along the long-run cost curve involve
changes *both* in the *amounts and* in the *proportions* in which the inputs are used, while movements along the short-run curves involve

Figure 7–8

THE EXPANSION PATH IN THE "NORMAL" CASE

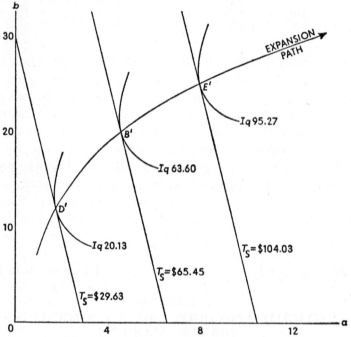

changes only in the proportions. The expansion path in the present
case is depicted in Figure 7–8; note that it is not linear.

Note also that at D', B', and E' in Table 7–6, all the ratios of the
respective marginal products (f_a/f_b) are respectively equal to the constant ratio (10) of the prices of a and b, but that at A' and C'—the

---

[15] Edward H. Chamberlin, "Proportionality, Divisibility and Economies of Scale,"
Quarterly Journal of Economics, Vol. LXII (February, 1948), pp. 229–62, esp. p. 257.
Note especially Figure 6 in the Appendix on p. 258. See also Harvey Leibenstein, "The
Proportionality Controversy and the Theory of Production," *Quarterly Journal of Econom-
ics*, Vol. LXIX (November, 1955), pp. 619–25.

minimum points on short-run average cost curves other than that of the optimum plant—this is not so. Also, note that in the case of the optimum size plant at B', the points of tangency and of short-run least cost coincide.

Recall that d is the amount of output obtained from a marginal dollar's worth of either input in our Equation (6–3) as we move along the expansion path in Figure 7–8. This value (d) in Table 7–6 is the same as the marginal product of b at the tangency points in our case, for the price of a unit of b is $1.00. It is also the same as one tenth of the marginal product of a at these points, for the price of a is $10. Finally, note that in Table 7–5 the marginal and average returns to outlay are equal to each other at B' (as well as to d in Table 7–6). And, as has been noted above, the long-run and the short-run marginal costs are also equal to each other and to the long-run and short-run average costs at this same point.

Effect of Indivisibilities

If the input b is infinitely divisible as we have assumed it to be, the long-run average cost curve is a smooth curve, as it has been depicted in Figure 7–7. If the input, b, were not finely divisible, the long-run average cost curve would consist of scallops (the solid portions of the SAC curves in Figure 7–7), such as $D'I'$, $I'B'M'$, and $M'E'$. In this case, the long-run average cost curve would consist of alternately falling and rising portions *accounted for by consecutive cases of diminishing average returns to the variable factor and not by internal economies and diseconomies.* In Figure 7–5, an assumption that b is indivisible would not affect the equality of $AA' = BB' = CC'$. It would mean that there are multiple points of equal minimum long-run average cost on the curve, $A'I'G'B'M'C'$. In the long run, various size plants are still equally efficient in this case.

The dashed portions of the short-run average cost curves are irrelevant in the long run, for these represent higher costs of production of given outputs than need be incurred in the long run, even if the input held fixed in the short run is not finely divisible. Indivisibility of inputs is probably a more realistic assumption than is that of their divisibility. The capacity of steel producers, for example, is not normally varied by infinitesimal amounts.

The Concept of Long-Run Economic Capacity

The point of tangency between T_L and T_{20} (or B'), which occurs at the minimum point of both the short-run and the long-run average cost curves in Figure 7–7, identifies the point of the *absolute minimum average cost of production,* or alternatively the point of *absolute maximum average return to outlay.* Thus the output, *OB,* to which is attached the average cost of production, *BB',* represents an output *both* at which the Marshallian equilibrium condition is fulfilled (for *B'* is on *LAC*), *and* at which inputs are being used in the "optimum" amounts (for *B'* is also the minimum point on a short-run average cost curve). Accordingly, *B'* represents the *point of long-run economic capacity,* and Plant T_{20} or SAC_{20} represents the *"optimum" scale of plant.* The *point of long-run economic capacity is* thus defined as the *point at which the "optimum" amounts of the inputs are being used in the "optimum" proportions.*

External Economies and Diseconomies

External economies were defined by Marshall as those which are external to the firm but internal to the industry, or as economies which depend on the "general development of the industry." Such economies, he argued, exist in the case of localized industries, which provide markets for special skills and opportunities for the growth of subsidiary and related industries producing by-products from what would otherwise be waste materials; and which, in general, operate in a climate of growth and enthusiasm.[16] The existence of external economies is thus dependent upon the existence of a growing market to absorb the output of the industry and related industries.

The effect of such external economies on the long-run total cost curve of the individual firm is to shift it downward, although not necessarily into a parallel position. Thus, in the long run, external economies reduce the minimum average cost of production. Since these economies are external to the firm but internal to the industry, their existence may result in a long-run industry supply curve which slopes down and to the right rather than up and to the right as it is usually drawn. This matter will be considered further in Chapter 9.

External diseconomies seem first to have been defined by Professor Jacob Viner as monetary or technological diseconomies resulting from the expansion of the industry as a whole.[17] Thus, the prices of some or

---

[16] Marshall, *op. cit.,* p. 266 and Book IV, chap. x.

[17] Jacob Viner, "Cost Curves and Supply Curves," *Zeitschrift für Nationalökonomie,* Vol. III (1932), pp. 23–46; reproduced in Richard V. Clemence (ed.), *Readings in Economic Analysis* (Cambridge: Addison-Wesley Press, 1950), Vol. II, pp. 8–35, esp. pp. 25–27. See also the Supplement by Professor Viner on p. 31.

of all inputs may rise as a result of increased demands for inputs on the part of all firms in an industry as they expand. This definition assumes that the supply of inputs is relatively inelastic. External diseconomies operate to shift the long-run average cost curve upward, and they result in an industry supply curve which slopes up and to the right in the usual way. We will consider the effect of such input price changes further in the next section of this chapter.

The Planning Curve

Some writers define the long-run cost curve as a "planning curve."[18] That is, they define the long-run average cost curve as an imaginary curve which *would* define the least average cost of all outputs *if* all inputs were variable. The difference between this definition and the one which has been used above is purely formal. The short-run average cost curves represent *alternative plants which could be built,* although in fact, of course, the given amount of output assumed for the purpose of the analysis will be produced in only one of the plants at a given moment of time. Alternatively, the various cost curves can be thought of as based on historical data. Econometric studies of costs use such data and will be considered later.

H. CHANGES IN INPUT PRICES

Costs depend not only on inputs and the length of time involved but also on input prices. In this section we will consider briefly the effect of the last of these three determinants of costs, and it will also be further considered in Chapter 12, which deals with the input market.

Short-Run Effect of Input Price Changes

In the short run, an increase in the price of a variable input will shift the average and marginal cost curves upward into a new position parallel to the old. Since variable costs will have changed, marginal cost changes in a similar way. The reason why these cost curves shift in a parallel way is that the numerators in the formulas for these costs change *proportionately* at all levels of output, while the denominators are unchanged.

An increase in the price of only a fixed input will not affect the cost of the variable inputs by assumption. In such a case, average cost will

---

[18] See Stephen Enke, *Intermediate Economic Theory* (New York: Prentice-Hall, Inc., 1950), pp. 276–78.

rise, but the new average cost curve will not be parallel to the old one. For then the numerator (F) in the formula for average fixed cost changes by a fixed amount, while the denominator (X) is not affected. At low levels of output, therefore, the average cost is increased more than at high levels of output, where the effect of the price change is spread out over more units.

Long-Run Effect of Input Price Changes

Since all inputs are variable in the long run, a proportional change in input prices will merely shift the LAC curve up or down in a parallel way as in Figure 7–9. But a nonproportional change in input prices

Figure 7–9

EFFECT ON LONG-RUN AVERAGE COST OF PROPORTIONAL CHANGE IN INPUT PRICES

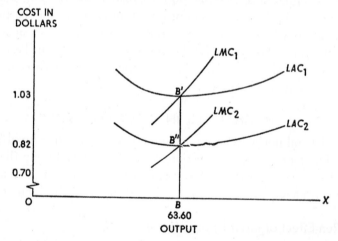

will result in substitution of the relatively cheaper input for the relatively more expensive one, whatever may be its effect on output. Thus, in the long run, the effect of a change in the price of either an input which has been held fixed in the short run, or of one which has been treated as variable in the short run, will be the same. The substitution process will operate to change the proportions among the inputs and to keep costs from rising as much as they would have in the short run if the price of a fixed input had increased. The new long-run average and marginal cost curves will not be parallel to the old, although they will lie above them because the proportions among the inputs will have changed. Such a case has already been discussed in terms of iso-cost lines and contour diagrams in Chapter 6, in conjunction with

Figure 6–6, and will be considered further in Chapter 12 when the input market is discussed.

I. ECONOMETRIC STUDIES OF COSTS

Studies of Short-Run Costs

Since the early 1940's, numerous statistical studies of short-run costs have been made, and a useful survey of most of them has been published by Professor Johnston.[19] Many of these studies seem to indicate that short-run marginal cost curves are linear (that is, that they are straight lines), at least throughout a portion of the range of output. Professor Joel Dean, for example, found in numerous studies that the decline in average cost was gradual and showed no tendency to increase as output increased.[20] And Professor Wilford Eiteman argued that it is likely that engineers design plants so that the variable factor is used most efficiently when the plant is operated close to the point of *physical* capacity, producing an average cost curve like that depicted in Figure 7–10.[21]

Figure 7–10

IDENTICAL POINTS OF ECONOMIC AND PHYSICAL CAPACITY

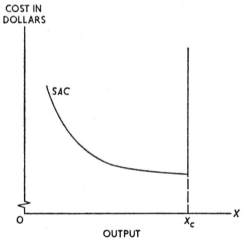

[19] John Johnston, *Statistical Cost Analysis* (New York: McGraw-Hill Book Co., Inc., 1960).

[20] Joel Dean, "Department Store Cost Functions," in O. Lange, F. McIntyre, and T. O. Yntema (eds.), *Studies in Mathematical Economics and Econometrics* (Chicago: University of Chicago Press, 1942), pp. 222–54. See also his *Managerial Economics* (New York: Prentice-Hall, Inc., 1951), chap. v.

[21] W. V. Eiteman, "Factors Determining the Location of the Least Cost Point," *American Economic Review,* Vol. XXXVII (December, 1947), pp. 910–18.

However, the results of such studies have not been conclusive, and, anyhow, if marginal cost rises eventually, the theory of the firm which we will discuss in the next part of this book is not much affected. The basic material for many of these statistical studies are accounting records of firms, and the cost data are then corrected to take account of changes in input prices. Two serious problems encountered are those of attempting to measure output when production is diversified and of eliminating the effects of technological change. Similarly vexing are problems relating to the influence of changes in the size of the firm. Finally, nearly all of the studies have used data relating to a range of output less than that of full physical capacity, and, of course, for this reason, they do not offer proof that average costs do not *eventually* rise, even in the cases studied.

One of the few studies (of department store operations) which definitely related to the entire range of output showed that marginal costs were constant under normal conditions, but showed also that they rose steeply during the seasonal Christmas peak. Thus, this study actually supports the traditional view. It may be, however, that average cost curves should be drawn relatively flat throughout some portion of their range and then allowed to rise fairly steeply, or to look like this: ⌣‿‿‿‿⌣. (In the case of our production function, such a curve would be produced if maximum [constant] average returns to outlay covered a range of from, say, $b = 20$ to $b = 30$, rather than being restricted to the point, $b = 20$.)

In this area of price theory, as in the others we have studied, there is room for much further work. For although the econometric studies of average costs do not disprove the assumptions made in orthodox theory, neither do they provide conclusive evidence that those assumptions are realistic or the only ones possible.

Professor George Stigler has, therefore, suggested that an alternative method of deriving cost curves from production functions should be used in place of the admittedly limited method of using basic accounting data and cost records.[22] However, this method involves the difficulty that economists are not production experts and really know very little about the facts of production in the real world! Such a method has, of course, been illustrated throughout this chapter and was employed in the study of crude oil pipelines by Professor Cookenboo discussed in the preceding chapter.

---

[22] "Round Table Conferences on Cost Functions and Their Relation to Imperfect Competition," *American Economic Review,* Proceedings, Supplement XXX (March, 1940), Part 2, pp. 400–402.

Studies of Long-Run Costs

The statistical problems involved in analyzing long-run costs are probably even more difficult than those which exist in the case of short-run costs. One study of economies of scale was made by Professor Joe S. Bain in 1954.[23] He submitted questionnaires to firms in each of twenty industries, including those producing durable, nondurable, and semidurable goods, and interviewed officials of these firms. His sample was admittedly biased in the direction of large industries.

On the basis of this study, it appeared that in nine of the twenty industries studied, an optimum size plant was one which accounted for less than 2½ percent of the total industry capacity, and, in five others, the fraction was greater than 7½ percent. Information concerning the shape of the long-run average cost curve was fragmentary, and no real conclusions concerning this point emerged from the study. Professor Bain did not provide a general conclusion regarding this point because of the diversity of the results he obtained.

Other studies (for example, a study of engineering and cost data which investigated the proposition that for many pieces of capital equipment cost varies directly with surface area, while capacity is related to volume) have also been made, but their results are also inconclusive.[24]

On the whole, specific knowledge concerning the behavior of long-run costs is today probably no greater than it was in 1922 when Professor Clapham, in a classic paper, "Of Empty Economic Boxes," called attention to the lack of it which then existed.[25]

Problems in the Measurement of Capacity

The problems of measurement of costs, especially in relation to the concept of economic capacity, have been emphasized by the Subcommittee on Economic Statistics of the Joint Economic Committee of the Congress in a report issued in July, 1962. Among other things, the Subcommittee commented on materials submitted at its hearings by saying:

---

[23] Joe S. Bain, "Economies of Scale, Concentration, and the Condition of Entry in Twenty Manufacturing Industries," *American Economic Review*, Vol. XLIV (March, 1954), pp. 15–39. See also his *Barriers to New Competition* (Cambridge: Harvard University Press, 1956).

[24] Frederick T. Moore, "Economies of Scale: Some Statistical Evidence," *Quarterly Journal of Economics*, Vol. LXXIII (May, 1959), pp. 232–45.

[25] J. H. Clapham, "Of Empty Economic Boxes," *Economic Journal*, Vol. XXXII (1922), pp. 305–14. This and related papers on the same subject may be found reprinted in Kenneth Boulding and George Stigler (eds.), *Readings in Price Theory* (Homewood, Ill.: Richard D. Irwin, Inc., 1952), pp. 119–233.

. . . the record reveals a lack of agreement on concepts and on generally accepted conventions for standardized measurements of capacity. This, of course, has had considerable consequences in producing a wide variety of capacity data which cannot be compared precisely with each other or with other economic data. But over and beyond this, the record revealed a number of additional inadequacies in existing capacity measures, including limited coverage, lack of detail, irregularity of reporting, and perhaps some difficulty of access to the information for some users. . . .

. . . it is apparent that there is much scattered material on capacity for various products and industries, for various time periods, but relatively few time series of consistent data. Even these time series must be characterized as being of inadequate quality, partly because of a lack of standardization of concepts, partly because of inadequate raw material for the computations, and partly because of still unsolved problems of measurement. The degree of ingenuity and skill utilized in developing the maximum of information from available raw materials is outstanding, but the results clearly indicate—as all witnesses appearing seemed to agree—that there is a substantial need for increased standardization and for an improved flow of basic information from which to construct measures of capacity.[26]

For these reasons the Subcommittee recommended that the Bureau of the Budget take the lead in "organizing a cooperative effort, involving both public and private agencies and individual experts," for the purpose of formulating acceptable standards and definitions in this area. A more dramatic illustration of the fact that the basic concepts and ideas of contemporary price theory are broad generalizations which cannot, except in unusual cases, be applied directly to specific policy problems could hardly be found.

This chapter completes our study of the factors lying behind various types of supply curves. In Part IV, which follows, we will consider, for the first time in this book, problems involving the interaction of supply and demand.

SELECTED READINGS

BAIN, JOE S. "Economies of Scale, Concentration, and the Condition of Entry into Twenty Manufacturing Industries," *American Economic Review,* Vol. XLIV (March, 1954), pp. 15–39.

BOBER, M. M. *Intermediate Price and Income Theory,* chap. v. New York: W. W. Norton, Inc., 1955.

---

[26] *Measures of Productive Capacity* (Report of the Subcommittee on Economic Statistics, Joint Economic Committee, 87th Cong., 2d sess.) (Washington, D.C.: U.S. Government Printing Office, 1962), pp. 7–8. Among the witnesses heard by the Subcommittee were Professor Lawrence R. Klein; Douglas Greenwald, manager, Economics Department, McGraw-Hill Publishing Co.; Daniel Creamer, director, Division of Economic Studies, National Industrial Conference Board; and Frank de Leeuw, economist, Division of Research and Statistics, Federal Reserve System.

CHAMBERLIN, EDWARD H. "Proportionality, Divisibility and Economies of Scale," *Quarterly Journal of Economics,* Vol. LXII (February, 1948), pp. 229–63.

CLARK, J. M. *Studies in the Economics of Overhead Costs.* Chicago: University of Chicago Press, 1923.

DEAN, JOEL. *Managerial Economics.* New York: Prentice-Hall, Inc., 1951. (Chapter 5 contains a summary of his statistical findings concerning cost functions.)

JOHNSTON, JOHN. *Statistical Cost Analysis.* New York: McGraw-Hill Book Co., Inc., 1960.

MARSHALL, ALFRED. *Principles of Economics,* Book IV. 8th ed. London: Macmillan & Co., Ltd., 1938.

NATIONAL BUREAU OF ECONOMIC RESEARCH. *Cost Behavior and Price Policy.* New York, 1943.

STIGLER, GEORGE. *The Theory of Price,* chaps. vii and viii. Rev. ed. New York: The Macmillan Co., 1952.

VINER, JACOB. "Cost Curves and Supply Curves," *Zeitschrift für Nationalökonomie,* Vol. III (1932), pp. 23–46. Reprinted in *Readings in Price Theory* (eds. KENNETH BOULDING AND GEORGE STIGLER), pp. 198–232. Homewood, Ill.: Richard D. Irwin, Inc., 1952.

PART IV

THE PRODUCT MARKET

8 Supply; The Determination of Market Price

Introduction

Part II of this book has been concerned with an explanation of the theory of demand. Part III has dealt with the relationship between theories of production and of costs. In the present Part IV these two threads of analysis are brought together in the theory of the firm.

In this chapter we will first consider the concept of *supply;* then we will examine the question of how prices are determined in the very short run. In Chapter 9, our concern will be the theory of the determination of prices and output and the definition of supply in the short run and in the long run in the limiting case of perfect competition. In Chapter 10, our problem will be that of analyzing the other limiting case of monopoly. Finally, in Chapter 11, we will consider cases involving situations in which some of the elements of perfect competition and some of the elements of monopoly are intermingled, and we will briefly examine some empirical studies of the behavior of firms.

A. BASIC CONCEPTS

The General Definition of Supply

The *supply of an individual seller is defined as the quantities of a given commodity which he stands ready to sell at all possible prices at a given moment of time.* Thus, the term *supply* refers to a *list* or a *schedule* of possible price-quantity combinations representing the attitude of one or more sellers, and it must be represented by a curve. Figure 8–1 depicts a family of supply "curves."

The assumptions on which a particular supply curve rests cannot be specified without also specifying the length of the time period which has been assumed in drawing the supply curve, and this question will

concern us further in the next chapter. In general, supply curves are
drawn sloping up and to the right, as in Figure 8–1, although there
are some exceptions to this rule which will also be considered in
greater detail later. This upward slope represents an assumption that, at
higher prices, sellers will offer more than they will at lower prices.

Figure 8–1

A FAMILY OF SUPPLY "CURVES"

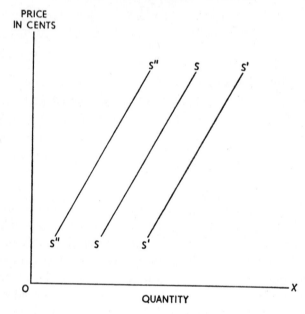

The total supply of a given commodity is, as in the case of the total
demand, merely the list of the sums of the quantities of the given
commodity which all sellers will offer at all possible prices at a given
moment of time. Thus if seller A will offer 5 apples at 10 cents each,
and if seller B will offer 7 apples at 10 cents each, and if these two
represent the total number of sellers in the problem, the total supply
at that price is 12 apples. At another price the total supply will
generally be different.

A Change in Supply

Just as in the case of a change in demand, a *change in supply involves shifting the entire supply curve.* An increase in supply means
that the supply curve has been shifted to the right, as indicated by the
new position of the curve *SS* in Figure 8–1. After the supply has increased, the new supply curve is *S'S'*. This fact means that the sellers

will now offer more of the commodity at all prices than before. A decrease in supply is depicted by a shift of the curve to the left to $S''S''$ and means that at all possible prices sellers will offer less.

Definition of "Quantity Supplied" or "Amount Sold"

A change in the *quantity supplied* results in a movement along the supply curve. And so, in Figure 8–2, if the price rises from OP to OP',

Figure 8–2

A CHANGE IN THE QUANTITY SUPPLIED

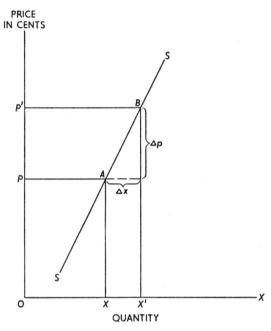

while the quantity supplied increases from OX to OX', the "amount supplied" has increased by XX'. Thus, *a change in the "quantity supplied" refers to a movement along the given supply curve.*

The Concept of Elasticity of Supply

Just as there is a concept of the elasticity of demand, so is there a parallel concept of the *elasticity of supply. The elasticity of supply is a measure of the responsiveness of sellers to price changes,* and, like the concept of elasticity of demand, it is stated in *relative* terms.

The *point* (at a point on the supply curve) elasticity of supply is defined as the absolute value of the rate of percentage change in sales divided by the rate of percentage change in price, and this definition results in the formula

$$E_s = \frac{p}{x} \frac{\partial x}{\partial p} .$$
(8-1)

In practice, *arc* elasticity formulas rather than point elasticity formulas are employed, since the former refer to small finite changes in prices and quantities. Also, as in the case of demand elasticity, unitary elasticity of supply is again taken as a convenient dividing line in the classification of commodities on the basis of their supply elasticity. Commodities whose elasticity of supply is *greater than unity* are said to *have* an *elastic supply*, while those whose elasticity of supply is *less than unity* are said to *have* an *inelastic supply*.

However, since the supply curve is positively sloping, while the demand curve is negatively sloping, the graphical depiction of unitary elasticity in the case of a supply curve is *not* the same as it is in the case of the demand curve. (Recall that unitary elasticity of demand has been depicted graphically in Figure 4-3 in Chapter 4 as a rectangular hyperbola.) Unitary elasticity of supply is depicted graphically by a straight line through the origin, as in Figure 8-3. We can prove this proposition as follows.

Since we are dealing with a finite change, let us define the arc (or average) elasticity of supply as

$$E_s = \frac{p}{x} \frac{\Delta x}{\Delta p} .$$
(8-2)

Now, in terms of Figure 8-3, we can write the preceding formula as

$$E_s = \frac{p}{x} \frac{\Delta x}{\Delta p} = \frac{AX}{OX} \times \frac{XX'}{BF} = \frac{AX}{OX} \times \frac{AF}{BF} ,$$

for $AF = XX'$. And since we are dealing with the similar right triangles, OXA and AFB, it follows that

$$\frac{AX}{OX} = \frac{BF}{AF} = \frac{1}{\dfrac{AF}{BF}} .$$

Next, by substituting this result for AX/OX in the earlier formulation, we have

$$\frac{AX}{OX} \times \frac{AF}{BF} = \frac{1}{\dfrac{AF}{BF}} \times \frac{AF}{BF} = \frac{BF}{AF} \times \frac{AF}{BF} = 1 .$$

Figure 8–3

UNITARY ELASTICITY OF SUPPLY

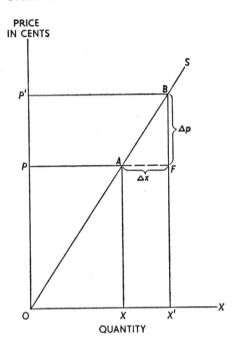

And so, in Figure 8–3, the elasticity of supply is unity along *OS*.

From this proposition it also follows that the elasticity of supply at a given point on any supply curve can be shown by the tangent to the curve at the point. Thus, in Figure 8–4, since the tangent (*OA*) to the supply curve, *SS*, passes through the *origin*, the elasticity of supply at *A* is unity. At *C*, the tangent (*ZC*) intercepts the *price* axis, and the elasticity of supply is greater than unity; while at *B* the tangent (*TB*) intercepts the *quantity* axis, and the elasticity of supply is less than unity. Thus the supply is elastic at *C* and inelastic at *B*.

At *A*, a very small change in the price will result in a proportionate increase in the amount supplied. At *C*, a small change in price will result in a more than proportionate increase in the amount supplied; and at *B*, a small increase in price will result in a less than proportionate increase in the amount supplied. Finally, if the tangent were perpendicular to the *X* axis (or parallel to the *Y* axis), the supply would be perfectly inelastic, and supply would be independent of price changes; but if it were parallel to the *X* axis (or perpendicular to the

Figure 8–4

GRAPHICAL DETERMINATION OF
ELASTICITY OF SUPPLY

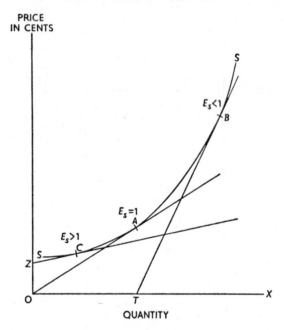

Y axis), the supply would be infinitely elastic, which would presumably
mean that sellers would offer their entire supply at the given price.

B. SUPPLY IN THE VERY SHORT RUN

The Definition of "Market" Supply

The *very short-run*, or the *market, period* has already been defined
in the preceding chapter as a period of time during which output
cannot be changed. Thus the term *market supply refers to total stocks
or inventories in the hands of sellers.* The market supply curve depicts
the attitudes of sellers towards their inventories during a period of time
in which inventories cannot be increased.

Shifts in the market supply curve result from changes in the attitudes
of sellers towards their inventories, and such shifts are often responses
to *changes in expectations* of the sellers. Market supply curves are
usually drawn with a positive slope. The positive slope of the curve,
which is merely the horizontal sum of the individual supply curves,
can be explained in terms of the relationship between the marginal

utility of purchasing power to sellers and the marginal utility to them of the inventory being depleted.

That is, as a seller sells more and more units of a given commodity, since his stocks of it are diminishing, the marginal utility of the commodity to him rises; while at the same time, since his stock of purchasing power increases with his sales, the marginal utility of his purchasing power decreases. And so, sellers are willing to part with additional quantities of the commodity only if ever higher prices are offered for such additional quantities; that is, if ever larger amounts of money are offered for additional units of the commodity. Therefore, the market supply curve usually has a positive slope.

The Backward-Sloping (or "Regressive") Supply Curve

However, just as Giffen's case constitutes an exception to the proposition that demand curves should be drawn with a negative slope, so does the *backward-sloping* (or "regressive") supply curve, depicted in Figure 8–5, constitute an exception to the general proposition that supply curves should be drawn with a positive slope.

It has been argued that the *backward-sloping* supply curve (which should not be confused with the *forward-falling* supply curve depicted later in Figure 9–12B) may apply in the short run to the case of some agricultural commodities,[1] and in some instances to the labor supply.

For example, it may be that, in the case of some agricultural commodities, if farmers are interested in a *given* cash income to meet their fixed charges and do not contemplate leaving their farms under unprofitable conditions when prices of the products they produce decline (and in the absence of governmental restrictions), they may actually increase their acreages in the hope of thereby increasing or maintaining their cash incomes constant by producing and selling more at the lower prices.

Thus, in Figure 8–5, when the price is OP_1, production will be P_1Q, but a *decline* in the price to OP_2 will *increase* production to P_2A. The supply curve is positively sloped in the normal way in the range from O to A. Thus up to price OP_2, production increases as price rises.

This type of supply curve has also sometimes been used to describe the labor supply in particular areas. One study of economic development problems in Africa concluded that in the particular area studied the amount of labor time available depended, to some extent, upon the

---

[1] See Kenneth Boulding, *Economic Analysis* (3rd ed.; New York: Harper & Bros., 1955), pp. 223–25.

"targets" set by the workers for themselves. For example, the study cited the case of natives who worked for several years to save enough to buy bicycles (targets desired both "for . . . usefulness and prestige"), and the bicycles thus became "the limit" of their horizon.[2]

Such a case can also be described graphically in terms of Figure 8–5, where the Y axis can be assumed to measure the wage rate. At a

Figure 8–5

A BACKWARD-SLOPING OR REGRESSIVE SUPPLY CURVE

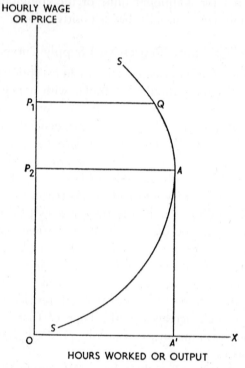

low hourly wage rate, a given number of hours of labor is forthcoming. As the wage rate is increased, the supply of labor increases up to point *A,* at which point the supply curve becomes parallel to the *Y* axis, and the labor supply is at a maximum. Thereafter, an increase in the hourly wage rate actually reduces the amount of labor which is available because it makes attainment of the "target" possible in a

---

[2] Elizabeth E. Hoyt, "The Impact of a Money Economy on Consumption Patterns," *Agrarian Societies in Transition* (Annals of the American Academy of Political and Social Science, Vol. CCCV) (May, 1956), pp. 12–22. But also see Elliot J. Berg, "Backward-Sloping Labor Supply Functions in Dual Economies: The Africa Case," *Quarterly Journal of Economics,* Vol. LXXV (August, 1961), pp. 468–92.

much shorter period of time. Thus, a decrease in the wage rate from OP_1 to OP_2 would produce more effort. The problem of wages is considered more fully in Chapter 13.

In general, the backward-sloping supply curve is thought to relate to very short-run or to short-run situations (which may be unstable), since farmers cannot forever go on producing at less than the cost of production, and the consumption habits of people who think in terms of targets can be changed, or new targets can be set before them.[3]

Supply in the Short Run and in the Long Run Considered in the Next Chapter

The definitions of supply in the short run and in the long run under perfect competition are based upon the equilibrium conditions of the firm. For this reason, the statement and explanation of these definitions can be most economically treated in the next chapter as part of the explanation of the theory of the firm under perfect competition. However, the definitions and concepts learned so far are sufficient to enable us to deal with the next logical problems, those of the meaning of the *equilibrium price* and of the determination of *market price,* or of *price in the very short run.*

C. THE DEFINITION OF THE "EQUILIBRIUM PRICE"

Marshall's Explanation of the Equilibrium Price

An equilibrium position has already been defined in Chapter 2 as one from which there is no tendency to move. In general, provided certain other conditions (to be explained later) are met, an equilibrium price will be established at the point at which supply equals demand. Marshall's explanation of this condition can be given with the help of Figure 8–6.

In Figure 8–6, the equilibrium price is OP_0 and the equilibrium quantity is OX_0. How do we know that this is the case?

Assume that the price in Figure 8–6 were OP_1. At this price, the amount offered by sellers would be $OX_1 = P_1A$, but the amount demanded by buyers would be only $OX_2 = P_1B$. Since sellers are willing to sell more at this higher price than buyers will purchase, competition among sellers must drive the price down until there is just exactly as much offered for sale as buyers will purchase. This condition is ful-

---

[3] In general, see William J. Baumol, *Economic Dynamics* (2d ed.; New York: The Macmillan Co., 1959), pp. 118–23.

filled at E, at the price OP_0, where the quantity exchanged is OX_0. At this price there is no further reason for sellers to compete, since sellers can find purchasers for all the goods they are willing to sell at this price.

Similarly, assume that the price were OP_2. At this lower price, sellers would be willing to sell only OX_4, although buyers would be willing to buy OX_3. In this case, since buyers want more goods than sellers are willing to offer at the lower price, competition by buyers will drive the price up to OP_0, where the quantity OX_0 is exchanged. At the price OP_0 there is no longer any reason for the remaining

Figure 8-6

DETERMINATION OF THE EQUILIBRIUM PRICE

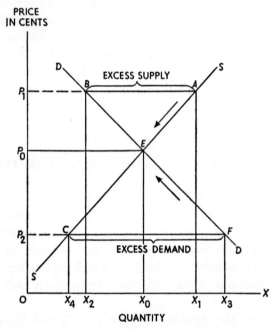

buyers to compete with each other, since they can buy exactly the amount they are willing and able to buy at that price.

Thus, since, at the price OP_0, there is no reason for either buyers to compete with other buyers or for sellers to compete with other sellers, there is no reason for the price to change. (Note that buyers do *not* compete with sellers.) Therefore, point E must be the equilibrium position; and since the supply and demand curves cross at this point, the supply and demand must be equal at the price OP_0.

The Walrasian Analysis

An alternative explanation of why E in Figure 8–6 must be the equilibrium position is due to the work of Leon Walras and involves the use of the concepts of *excess demand* and *excess supply*. Thus *excess demand* is defined as the amount by which the quantity which will be purchased at a given price exceeds the amount which will be supplied at that price, and *excess supply* is the negative of excess demand. In Figure 8–6, when the price is OP_2, the excess demand is $X_4X_3 = CF$, and when the price is OP_1, the excess supply is $X_2X_1 = BA$.

In equilibrium, at E, the excess demand is zero, and since excess supply is merely the negative of excess demand, it, too, is zero. Since both are zero, there are no forces tending to disturb the equilibrium. If excess demand is greater than zero, competition among buyers will force prices up; if excess demand is less than zero, or, alternatively, if excess supply is positive, competition among sellers forces prices down.

The idea that excess supply is the negative of excess demand introduces the consideration that buyers and sellers may be the same individuals. That is, people may stand ready to buy at certain prices, but they may also be ready to sell if prices rise to higher levels. We will not, however, pursue this line of analysis in this book.[4]

The Marshallian and Walrasian Analyses Compared

The Marshallian analysis rests upon an assumption that *quantity* adjusts as price changes, while the Walrasian analysis rests upon an assumption that *price* adjusts as quantity changes. Indeed, in his diagrams, Walras measured quantity on the Y axis and price on the X axis, which is just the reverse of the Marshallian graphical depiction.[5]

For most purposes, the difference in these two assumptions makes no difference to the result. Thus, for example, in Figure 8–7, E is the equilibrium position both according to the Marshallian and the Walrasian analyses; and after an increase in demand, E' is the new equilibrium position in both cases.

According to Marshall's assumption that quantity adjusts, the path of adjustment would be from E to M to E'. Thus in response to the increase in price, the quantity supplied would increase from OX_0 to

---

[4] For a detailed analysis of such questions, see Boulding, *op. cit.*, chap. v; and J. R. Hicks, *Value and Capital* (2d ed.; Oxford: Oxford University Press, 1946), chap. v.

[5] See Leon Walras, *Elements of Pure Economics*, trans. William Jaffé (Homewood, Ill.: Richard D. Irwin, Inc., 1954), esp. the diagrams in Lesson 6, and p. 106.

OX_1. In the new position, both the price and the quantity would be greater than before.

According to Walras' assumption, the path of adjustment would be a movement from E to W to E'; thus the price would have adjusted (risen) in response to an increase in demand. Since *both* price and

Figure 8–7

COMPARISON OF MARSHALLIAN AND WALRASIAN EXPLANATIONS OF EQUILIBRIUM PRICE

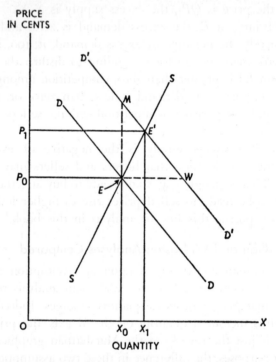

quantity have increased, it makes no difference in this case which of the two paths of adjustment is followed.

The Stability Conditions

However, as a number of writers have pointed out,[6] although equality of supply and demand is all that is needed for an equilibrium position to exist, an additional condition must be satisfied if the equilibrium is to be a *stable* one, that is, one to which there is a tendency

---

[6] Hicks, *op. cit.*, pp. 63–64; Baumol, *op. cit.*, pp. 118–22; Paul A. Samuelson, "The Stability of Equilibrium: Comparative Statics and Dynamics," *Econometrica*, Vol. IX (April, 1941), p. 103; Jacob Marschak, "Identity and Stability in Economics," *Econometrica*, Vol. X (January, 1942), pp. 70–74.

for the values of the variables to return after a small displacement has occurred.

According to Walras, in a diagram like Figure 8–8A, the equilibrium will be stable, if to the *left* of the point of equilibrium, say B in Figure 8–8A, the quantity supplied exceeds the quantity demanded; and if, to the *right* of the point of equilibrium, the quantity demanded is greater than the quantity supplied.[7] What this means is that, at prices higher than the equilibrium price, sellers will offer more

Figure 8–8

WALRASIAN AND MARSHALLIAN DEPICTIONS OF STABLE AND UNSTABLE EQUILIBRIUM POSITIONS

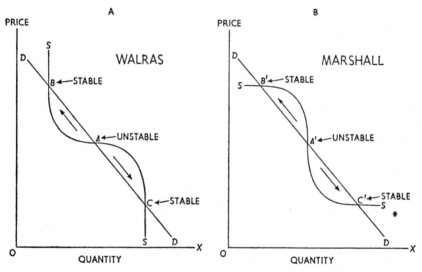

than buyers are willing to take, thus driving the price down to the equilibrium level; and, at prices lower than the equilibrium price, buyers are willing to take more than sellers are willing to offer, driving the price up to the equilibrium level.

In Figure 8–8A, the equilibrium is thus stable at B and C but unstable at A. A disturbance at A would result in a movement to a new stable equilibrium position either at B or at C.

In Appendix H of the *Principles*,[8] where he dealt with the problem of long-run supply, Marshall also discussed the problem of stability.

---

[7] Walras, *op. cit.*, p. 109. In Walras' own diagram, the price and quantity axes are the reverse of those in Figure 8–8A, and, therefore, in explaining his diagram, he reverses the use of words *left* and *right* from the way in which they are used in the text above.

[8] See Alfred Marshall, *Principles of Economics* (8th ed.; London: Macmillan & Co., Ltd., 1936), pp. 805 ff., esp. Fig. 38, n. 1, p. 806.

Although Marshall apparently discussed the problem in the context of increasing returns to scale, it is clear from his text that he assumed not only the existence of unexhausted internal economies but also the existence of external economies; and, as we know from our previous discussion of this concept, external economies result from the growth of the *industry* in response to changes in demand. In the next chapter we will see that his analysis involves *both movements along and shifts in* a firm's long-run average cost curve.

Figure 8–8B is similar to the diagram used by Marshall. According to Marshall, A' is an unstable equilibrium position, but B' and C' are stable positions. At first glance, there seems to be no difference between Figures 8–8A and 8–8B. However, in Figure 8–8A (Walras), at C the supply curve lies above the demand curve to the left of the point of stable equilibrium (the quantity supplied exceeds the quantity demanded at prices greater than the equilibrium price); and to the right of the point of equilibrium at $C,$ the demand curve lies above the supply curve (the quantity demanded exceeds the quantity supplied at prices lower than the equilibrium price).

In the case of Figure 8–8B (Marshall), however, the reverse is true. To the left of the equilibrium position at $C',$ the quantity demanded exceeds the quantity supplied at prices higher than the equilibrium price, and to the right of $C',$ the quantity supplied exceeds the quantity demanded at that price.

How can these two different conceptions of the problem be reconciled? In the literature generally, the Walrasian analysis is taken to refer to the short-run case, for example, to the case of the regressive or backward-sloping supply curve, while the Marshallian case is interpreted as one involving the long run. That is, according to Walrasian *short-run analysis,* an excess of demand will drive the price *up,* and, thus, a small disturbance at A may result in attainment of a new stable equilibrium at B in Figure 8–8A; while an excess of supply will drive the price *down* and produce a new stable equilibrium position at C in Figure 8–8A.

On the other hand, according to Marshall, *in the long run,* if there are unexhausted internal and external economies, an excess of demand over supply will increase output, reduce costs, and drive the price *down,* and, thus, a small disturbance at A' may result in attainment of a new stable equilibrium position at C' in Figure 8–8B; while an excess of supply at A' will increase costs, drive the price *up,* and produce a new stable equilibrium position at B' in Figure 8–8B, because of the reduction in various economies as output is reduced. (Neither Walras nor Marshall provides an example of the type of "disturbance" which causes the movement away from the position of unstable equilibrium. Marshall's case will be further considered in Chapter 9.)

The two explanations and statements of the stability conditions are thus reconciled.[9] The significance of this logical exercise is that it demonstrates that the assumptions which are made about the way in which the movement from one position of equilibrium to another occurs may affect the conclusions.[10] Professor Paul Samuelson has, therefore, argued that progress in economic analysis can only come about through the development of dynamic theories and that the alternative positions of equilibrium which are compared in static analysis are merely the limiting cases of a dynamic analysis.[11]

D. DETERMINATION OF MARKET PRICE (THE VERY SHORT RUN)

Effect of the Period of Time on Price; "Normal" Price

Marshall states the general principle that the shorter the period of time assumed in the analysis, the greater is the influence of demand on price, and the longer the period of time assumed, the greater is the influence of cost of production on price.[12]

Prior to the publication of his *Principles* in 1890, there had been considerable argument among economists as to whether demand *or* supply was the most important price-determining factor. A number of Austrian economists (Carl Menger, Friedrich Freiherrn von Wieser, and Eugen von Böhm-Bawerk),[13] who wrote between 1871 and 1914, sought to establish the proposition that utility was the most important determinant of economic value. Thus, in keeping with their argument, they took the position that demand (i.e., utility) was the most important price-determining factor.

Marshall dismissed this argument by remarking, in what has become a classic passage: "We might as well reasonably dispute whether it is the upper or the under blade of a pair of scissors that cuts a piece of paper, as whether value is governed by utility or cost of production."[14]

Thereupon, Marshall put both demand and supply into their proper

---

[9] An alternative explanation of the difference between them, involving the effect of a shift in demand upon the conclusions, can also be found in Baumol, *op. cit.,* pp. 118–22.

[10] For a further discussion of this point, see Melvin W. Reder, *Studies in the Theory of Welfare Economics* (New York: Columbia University Press, 1947), esp. Part II.

[11] Samuelson, *op. cit.,* pp. 97–120. See also his *Foundations of Economic Analysis* (Cambridge: Harvard University Press, 1947), pp. 1–20.

[12] Marshall, *op. cit.,* p. 349.

[13] For an account of their work, see Lewis H. Haney, *History of Economic Thought* (3rd ed.; New York: The Macmillan Co., 1947), chap. xxxi.

[14] Marshall, *op. cit.,* p. 348.

perspectives by noting that the period of time assumed in the analysis
is the crucial factor. Under perfect competition, in the very short-run
or market period, when stocks are assumed fixed or relatively fixed,
demand must necessarily exert a greater influence on prices. But when
enough time is assumed for output to increase, the short-run cost of
production (cost of production in a given plant) exerts some influence
also. And, in the long run, when existing facilities can be either
built up or withdrawn from production, price tends to approach its
"normal" level, that of cost of production, including a "normal" profit
for the entrepreneur. The first of these cases will be considered next,
but the last two cases will be considered in the following chapter
under the assumption of perfect competition, where "normal price"
and "normal profit" are also discussed.

Demand as the Principal Price-Determining Factor in the Very Short Run

The very short-run (or "market") case is illustrated in Figure 8–9.
Assume that E represents the initial equilibrium position. Since the

Figure 8–9

**EFFECT OF A CHANGE IN DEMAND IN
THE VERY SHORT RUN**

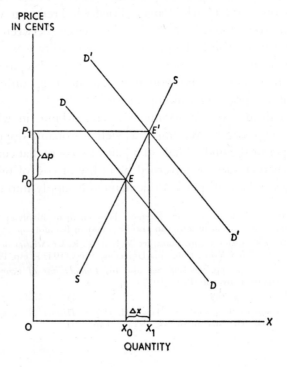

period of time assumed in the analysis limits the supply to the amount available from existing stocks, the supply curve is fairly steep, and the supply is rather inelastic. An increase in demand, *supply remaining unchanged,* must therefore produce an increase in price. Thus, price rises from OP_0 to OP_1 and quantity increases from OX_0 to OX_1 in the new equilibrium position at E'. Day-to-day dealings in the stock market, or in commodity exchanges, can be cited as examples of such markets. (Marshall used the illustration of dealings in a grain market in a country town.)[15]

It is to be noted that expectations with respect to the future may affect both the prices at which sellers are willing to sell and at which buyers are willing to buy, even when dealings are on a day-to-day basis involving goods of the type mentioned above. Thus, either the supply or the demand curve, or both together, may shift as a result of changes in buyers' or sellers' expectations, changes in their cash or liquid asset positions, or as a result of the influence of purchases made by competitors, friends and colleagues, and various other factors.

An Empirical Example

For example, shortly after the Korean emergency began in June, 1950, prices of many basic raw materials, as well as prices of many consumer goods, rose rapidly in response to consumers' and producers' expectations of shortages in the future. Table 8–1 shows the behavior of selected raw materials prices during this critical period.

Table 8–1 demonstrates clearly that many basic raw materials experienced sharp price increases between June, 1950 and February, 1951. These increases were largely attributable to the expectations of producers and consumers. (Note particularly the cases of rubber, tin, tungsten, and wool.) Raw materials producers were much influenced by their knowledge that United States stockpile objectives were, in general, far from being met in June, 1950, and their belief that United States government purchases would be greatly increased. By 1952, after a voluntary intergovernmental scheme for the distribution of raw materials among Free World countries had been in operation for some months, prices declined considerably, although not to their previous levels, largely because producers had come to realize that the governments in question did not intend to permit unbridled speculation in raw materials to continue. Some increases in supplies had also occurred.

Aside from expectations, a number of writers[16] have developed analy-

---

[15] *Ibid.,* Book V, chap. ii.

[16] See, for example, Kenneth Boulding, "A Liquidity Preference Theory of Market Prices," *Economica,* New Series, Vol. XI (1944), pp. 55–63, reproduced in Kenneth

Table 8–1

SELECTED INDIVIDUAL RAW MATERIALS PRICE RELATIVES
(1947–49 = 100)

Commodity	June, 1950	Feb., 1951	Average, 1951	Average, 1952
Aluminum	110.0	119.4	122.0	122.0
Copper:				
U.S.	105.8	116.4	116.4	116.4
Chile	97.8	. . .	123.4	155.5
Netherlands	83.7	246.5	. . .	228.5
Cotton:				
U.S.	110.9	125.0	138.2	114.0
Brazil	100.0	196.1	164.0	133.0
Jute	92.6	118.0	103.4	83.0
Pyrethrum	137.0	163.1	163.1	163.1
Rubber, natural	153.7	365.2	303.0	190.0
Tin	83.0	176.6	136.3	132.9
Tungsten:				
U.S.	97.7	228.3[a]	216.0[b]	216.0
Foreign	86.0	292.0	263.0	233.0
Wool, greasy:				
U.S.	123.9	259.5	198.8	113.8
Australia	133.1	258.7	263.4	130.3
Zinc:				
U.S.	125.3	147.4	152.1	138.4
U.K.	110.5	131.9	150.9	129.4

Sources: Based on Table II of my article, "The International Materials Conference in Retrospect," *Quarterly Journal of Economics*, Vol. LXXI (May, 1957), p. 270. The data serving as a basis for the price relatives are dollar prices quoted in the International Monetary Fund, *International Financial Statistics*; Bureau of Labor Statistics, *Prices and Price Relatives in the Revised Index*; and *Reports* of the Preparedness Subcommittee of the Senate Armed Services Committee, 81st and 82nd Congresses.
  a. Domestic ceiling.
  b. Domestic floor.

ses taking into account the effect of the existence of liquid assets on prices, and Professor A. C. Pigou argued that the total wealth position of buyers influences their expenditures.[17] His analysis was conducted in the context of macroeconomic problems. Indeed, as has been noted in Chapter 5, much of the contemporary statistical analysis of factors affecting demand, both in the short run and in the long run, has been conducted in the field of macroeconomics rather than in that of microeconomics, although the two are clearly interrelated.[18]

Boulding and George Stigler (eds.), *Readings in Price Theory* (Homewood, Ill.: Richard D. Irwin, Inc., 1952), pp. 311 ff; and his *A Reconstruction of Economics* (New York: John Wiley & Sons, Inc., 1950), esp. pp. 53 ff; and also see Helen Makower and Jacob Marschak, "Assets, Prices and Monetary Theory," *Economica,* New Series, Vol. V (1938), pp. 261–88, reproduced in Boulding and Stigler (eds.), *Readings in Price Theory,* pp. 283 ff.

[17] A. C. Pigou, *Employment and Equilibrium* (London: Macmillan & Co., Ltd., 1941), esp. pp. 96–130.

[18] For a discussion of macroeconomic theories and studies, see Gardner Ackley, *Macroeconomic Theory* (New York: The Macmillan Co., 1961), chaps. x, xi, xii.

E. ILLUSTRATIONS OF SUPPLY-DEMAND ANALYSIS

Effect of a Per Unit Tax

Assume that in Figure 8–10 the initial equilibrium position is A, where OX_0 units are sold at price OP_0. Next assume that a per unit tax (a given amount per unit of output) equal to $C'P_1 = CB$ is levied on the producers of the commodity. The effect of the tax will be to shift the supply curve up and to the left by an amount equal to $C'P_1 = CB$ at all levels of output, since, initially, the tax can be treated as an increase in the cost of production. The new supply curve, $S'S'$,

Figure 8–10

EFFECT OF A PER UNIT TAX OR OF A
PER UNIT SUBSIDY

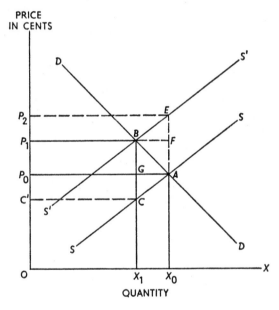

drawn parallel to the old, SS, will intersect the original demand curve (demand is assumed to remain unchanged) at B, where a new equilibrium position exists.

The effect of the tax will be to reduce the quantity purchased from OX_0 to OX_1 and to raise the price from OP_0 to OP_1. Now note: the price of X does not rise by the full amount of the tax, $C'P_1$ in our case. The price to consumers increases by P_0P_1, while the quantity purchased by them falls by X_1X_0, and the amount received by producers for each unit of X sold falls from OP_0 to OC', while the quantity sold by them likewise declines by X_1X_0. Thus, the entire burden of the tax is not shifted forward to the consumers, but part of it is absorbed by the producers.

Although consumers pay $CB = C'P_1$ more for the quantity OX_1 than they would have had to have paid for *this quantity* before the tax was levied, the actual increase in price to them amounts only to $P_0P_1 = GB$. Thus, those consumers *who remain in the market* after the tax pay only part of the tax. The remainder of the tax, $CG = C'P_0$, represents a loss to producers, who, being unable to sell the quantity OX_0 after the tax has been levied, reduce their sales to OX_1 and receive a return of $OC' = X_1C$ for each unit of output. Thus, producers receive $CG = C'P_0$ less per unit after the tax than before. Since $CG + GB = C'P_1$, the full amount of the tax is thus accounted for.

The extent to which such a tax may be shifted forward to consumers thus depends upon the elasticities of supply and demand. In the extreme case of a perfectly elastic supply and a perfectly inelastic demand, the full amount of the tax would be borne by the consumer. (The student should make a sketch here to test his understanding of the principle involved.) Forecasts concerning the ways in which specific taxes are shifted must thus rest upon knowledge of the underlying conditions of supply and demand in the industry. (The case of a lump sum tax will be considered in Chapter 14.)

Effect of a Per Unit Subsidy

The reverse of the case of a per unit tax is the case of a per unit subsidy granted to the producers. Assume in Figure 8–10 that the initial position is at B, where OX_1 units of the commodity are sold at a price of OP_1. Next, assume that a per unit subsidy equal to $C'P_1 = CB = AE$ is granted. The effect of the subsidy will be to shift the supply curve down and to the right from $S'S'$ to SS, and the new equilibrium position will be at A. Producers will receive a per unit amount of $X_0A + AE = X_0E$ for each unit of X sold. Consumers, however, will pay only X_0A for each unit they buy. The difference, AE, is the amount of the subsidy. In this case the price to consumers falls by $GB = AF$, and the quantity purchased increases by X_1X_0. Consumers will share in the subsidy along with the producers, since they are buying more at a lower price than before. Producers, on the other hand, will be selling more at a lower price than before; and because of the subsidy, their incomes will similarly have risen. Before the subsidy, they would have been willing to sell the amount OX_0 only if the price had risen by FE from X_1B to X_0E. But whether or not society as a whole is better off as a result of the subsidy cannot be determined without taking into account also the question of the *source* of the subsidy. Thus, forecasts concerning the ways in which subsidies will operate to benefit producers, consumers, and society as a whole must also rest upon an empirical knowledge of the conditions in the industry and of how the subsidy is raised.

Other Illustrations of Supply-Demand Analysis

Similar applications of supply-demand analysis to isolate some economic factors important in determining the effects of tariffs, to illustrate the operation of buffer stock schemes, and to explain the effects of black market operations, exist in the literature.[19] The student who is interested in pursuing these matters further may be referred to the reference cited in footnote 19. Our next task will be to examine supply-demand relationships in the short run and in the long run under perfect competition; this subject is treated in the following chapter.

SELECTED READINGS

BAUMOL, WILLIAM J. *Economic Dynamics,* chap. vii. 2d ed. New York: The Macmillan Co., 1959.

BERG, ELLIOT J. "Backward-Sloping Labor Supply Functions in Dual Economies: The Africa Case," *Quarterly Journal of Economics,* Vol. LXXV (August, 1961), pp. 468–92.

BOULDING, KENNETH. "A Liquidity Preference Theory of Market Prices," *Economica,* New Series, Vol. XI (1944), pp. 55–63. Reprinted in *Readings in Price Theory* (eds. KENNETH BOULDING AND GEORGE STIGLER), pp. 311–28. Homewood, Ill.: Richard D. Irwin, Inc., 1952.

————. *Economic Analysis,* chaps. iii, v, vi, viii, and xii. 3rd ed. New York: Harper & Bros., 1955.

EASTHAM, J. K. *Graphical Economics,* chap. v. Chicago: Quadrangle Books, Inc., 1960.

MARSHALL, ALFRED. *Principles of Economics,* Book V, chaps. i and ii, and Appendix H. 8th ed. London: Macmillan & Co., Ltd., 1938.

SAMUELSON, PAUL A. "The Stability of Equilibrium: Comparative Statics and Dynamics," *Econometrica* Vol. IX (April, 1941), pp. 97–100.

WALRAS, LEON. *Elements of Pure Economics,* Part II. Trans. WILLIAM JAFFÉ. Homewood, Ill.: Richard D. Irwin, Inc., 1954.

---

[19] See, particularly, Boulding, *Economic Analysis,* chaps. vi and viii.

9 The Firm and Industry Under Perfect Competition

Introduction

The central purpose of this chapter is to explain the theories of the firm in the short run and in the long run under perfect competition. In Chapters 6 and 7, the relationship between costs and production has been explored. In this chapter, the prices of the products produced by the firm are introduced into the analysis. We will see that these prices, which are assumed to be outside the control of the firm under perfect competition, interact with the costs of the firm to determine the level of the firm's output, both in the short run and in the long run, and also to determine the number of firms in the industry in the long run.

In the course of the explanation, the *general* short-run and long-run equilibrium and profit conditions of the firm will be developed, and it will be seen that the case of perfect competition is merely a special case falling within a more general one. Also, the definitions of *short-run supply* and *long-run supply* will be developed and explained.

Perfect Competition and Monopoly Contrasted

In model analysis, various degrees of competition may be conceived to exist. These shade imperceptibly from the limiting case of perfect competition, on the one hand, into the limiting case of monopoly on the other. Most of the cases in the real world lie between these two extreme or limiting cases.

Monopoly, which will be considered in the next chapter, is defined as the case of a single seller, enjoying the absence of competition of any kind, with complete control over the supply of the product, including control over entry into the industry. Some economists prefer to use the term "pure" monopoly to identify this case.

Perfect competition has already been defined in Chapter 2 as a state of affairs characterized by the following conditions: (1) there are a large number of buyers and sellers, none of whom thinks he can influence the price of the commodity through his own individual actions; (2) all sales involve perfectly homogeneous (interchangeable) commodities; (3) all buyers and sellers have perfect knowledge of the situation confronting them and of their alternatives; (4) all buyers and sellers behave rationally to maximize their own self interests (however defined) on the basis of that knowledge; and (5) freedom of entry into the market and perfect mobility of inputs exist.

As has been noted, between the two extreme cases there may exist others, for example, cases of large numbers of sellers dealing in differentiated or nonhomogeneous commodities, or cases of small numbers of sellers dealing in homogeneous commodities. Such cases, which involve the absence of one or more conditions of perfect competition, will be the subject of extended discussion in Chapter 11.

The two extreme cases of perfect competition and monopoly probably do not exist anywhere in the real world today. By developing the analyses and the theories of price and output determination in these two limiting cases first, however, we will be in a position better to understand how and why, in 1927, Professor E. H. Chamberlin eventually[1] came to the conclusion that by "blending" the relevant elements of these two cases, a more realistic analysis, one which, perhaps, describes more accurately the situation in the real world, could be developed. His work will be the basis of much of the analysis in Chapter 11, where we will also consider the related work of Professor Joan Robinson.[2]

Perhaps the principal difference between the analyses of perfect competition and monopoly arises out of the fact that in the case of perfect competition, it is assumed that the individual seller does not *think* he can, by his own actions, affect the price of the product which he sells. Thus, in making his decisions, he takes the market price as *given*. A monopolist, on the other hand, *knows* that he does affect the price by the amount he offers for sale. That is, since the demand curve of a monopolist is also *the* market demand curve, it is assumed that the monopolist does *not* take the market price as given in making his decisions. Of what significance for the problem at hand is this difference

---

[1] Edward H. Chamberlin, *The Theory of Monopolistic Competition* (7th ed.; Cambridge: Harvard University Press, 1956).

[2] Joan Robinson, *The Economics of Imperfect Competition* (London: Macmillan & Co., Ltd., 1934).

in assumed attitudes? It is the purpose of the next several chapters to answer this question, but, first, some new concepts must be defined.

A. REVENUE CONCEPTS

Total Revenue

Total revenue (R) may be defined generally as the revenue from sales obtained by a seller. It is equal to the number of units of the commodity sold, multiplied by the per unit selling price, or

$$R = PX, \tag{9-1}$$

where R is the total revenue from sales, P is the price of a unit of the commodity, and X is the quantity sold.

Figure 9–1

THE TOTAL REVENUE "CURVE" UNDER PERFECT COMPETITION

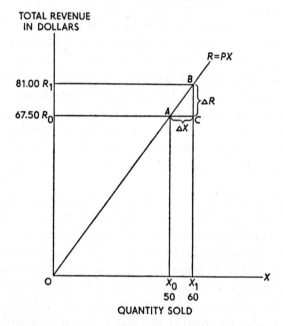

Under perfect competition, *since* the individual seller takes the market price as given, the total revenue curve is a straight line *(OR)* as in Figure 9–1. *The assumption that he takes the price as given means* (as has already been noted) *that he believes he will not affect the price no matter how much he offers for sale,* because his part of the total supply is insignificant in comparison with the total supply available in the market from all sellers together. From *his point of view,* the demand is perfectly elastic. However, the total revenue curve will not be a straight line if competition is not perfect, and in such a case the curve may look like the one in Figure 9–3B. Such cases will be examined in the two following chapters.

Marginal Revenue Defined

Marginal revenue (*MR*) is a concept analogous to the concepts of the marginal product and of marginal cost. That is, *marginal revenue is defined as the exact or average rate of change* (depending on the circumstances of the analysis) *of total revenue as sales change.* Thus, marginal revenue in Figure 9–1 is $\Delta R/\Delta X = CB/AC = 13.50/10 = 1.35$, the average slope of the total revenue curve between A and B.

We can define the total change in total revenue as the difference between the total revenue in a given new position, say at B in Figure 9–1, and a given original position, say at A in Figure 9–1. Then we have the total change as

$$\Delta R = (P + \Delta P)(X + \Delta X) - PX , \qquad (9\text{–}2)$$

where $(P + \Delta P)$ is the price in the new position at B, and $(X + \Delta X)$ is the new quantity sold at that price, while P is the price in the original position at A, and X is the quantity sold in that original position.

Thus, the total change in total revenue is

$$\Delta R = P\Delta X + X\Delta P + \Delta X\Delta P = (P + \Delta P)\Delta X + X\Delta P . \qquad (9\text{–}3)$$

The astute student will have noticed that the preceding formula is analogous to the formula for the change in the total amount spent on the price-changing commodity (ΔE) in the theory of consumer behavior. That is, the change in the total amount spent by all consumers for a price-changing commodity is also the change in total receipts of the firm as its sales increase.

The algebraic definition of marginal revenue can easily be obtained from the definition of the total change in total revenue by dividing Equation (9–3) by ΔX to put the data on a *per unit* basis, or

$$MR = \frac{\Delta R}{\Delta X} = (P + \Delta P)\frac{\Delta X}{\Delta X} + X\frac{\Delta P}{\Delta X} = (P + \Delta P) + X\frac{\Delta P}{\Delta X} . \qquad (9\text{–}4)$$

The definitions stated in Equations (9–3) and (9–4) are completely general. However, under perfect competition, since the individual seller takes the market price as given and does not think that he can affect the price by his own actions, price does not change as sales change, or $\Delta P = 0$. Consequently, in the *special* case of perfect competition, the formula for marginal revenue reduces to

$$MR = \frac{\Delta R}{\Delta X} = (P + 0) + X\frac{0}{\Delta X} = P. \qquad (9\text{-}4a)$$

Thus, *under perfect competition, marginal revenue is equal to the price of the product.* That is, each unit of output sold adds to the total revenue an amount just exactly equal to the previous price of the product, because the price remains constant. [If the seller reduces the price as sales increase $(\Delta X \Delta P < 0)$, the sale of an additional unit will add to total revenue an amount equal to the price $(P + \Delta P)$ of the product, but there will also be a reduction in total revenue resulting from the fact that those units which have previously commanded a higher price will now be selling at a lower price. The first term on the right in Equation (9–4), that is, the new price $(P + \Delta P)$, is known as the "sales gain," and the second as the "price loss." If competition is not perfect, the "price loss" causes marginal revenue to be less than price, as we will see in the next section and in the next chapter.]

The relationship between marginal revenue and the price under perfect competition is illustrated in Figure 9–2. Figure 9–2A depicts the situation of the *individual* seller. His marginal revenue curve is the

Figure 9–2

RELATIONSHIP BETWEEN INDIVIDUAL FIRM'S AVERAGE AND
MARGINAL REVENUE CURVES AND MARKET PRICE UNDER
PERFECT COMPETITION

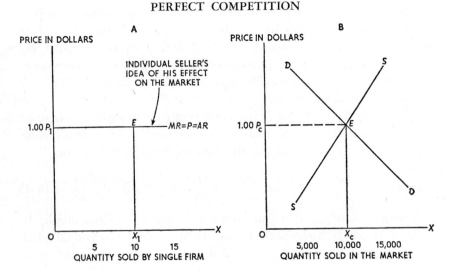

horizontal line $MR = P = AR$, parallel to the X axis, and is identical with the curve of the demand for his good, *as he sees it* (or with "the demand curve facing him"). The market demand curve, DD in Figure 9–2B, on the other hand, slopes down and to the right in the usual way. Thus, the *individual seller* thinks he can sell any amount *at the given market price, P_c,* without affecting that market price. Note that the scale along the X axis in Figure 9–2A shows that the individual seller sells ten units at the price $OP_1 = OP_c$, but that all sellers together sell ten thousand units in the market at that price (OP_c) in Figure 9–2B. Hence, this seller's belief in his own insignificance as a price leader or price setter is justified by the facts.

General Relationship between Marginal Revenue and Price

The *general* relationship between marginal revenue and the price can easily be explained by means of the elementary equations employed above. Note that in Equation (9–4) we have the *general* definition of marginal revenue as

$$MR = \frac{\Delta R}{\Delta X} = (P + \Delta P) + X\frac{\Delta P}{\Delta X}. \tag{9-4}$$

Now, the expression *on the right-hand side* in Equation (9–4) can be rewritten so that it reads:

$$(P + \Delta P) + X\frac{\Delta P}{\Delta X} = (P + \Delta P)\left(1 + \frac{X}{(P + \Delta P)}\frac{\Delta P}{\Delta X}\right). \tag{9-5}$$

Next, recall the definition of arc elasticity of demand given in Equation (4–4b) in Chapter 4, or

$$E_d = \left(-\frac{(P + \Delta P)}{X}\frac{\Delta X}{\Delta P}\right). \tag{4-4b}$$

Comparison of this definition with the term which is added to unity in the parentheses in Equation (9–5) above discloses that one is the negative reciprocal of the other:

$$\left(\frac{X}{(P + \Delta P)}\frac{\Delta P}{\Delta X}\right) = \left(-\frac{1}{E_d}\right).$$

Accordingly, by substitution, we can write the formula for the marginal revenue in Equation (9–4) in an alternative way as

$$MR = (P + \Delta P)\left(1 - \frac{1}{E_d}\right). \tag{9-6}$$

Thus, marginal revenue is equal to the new price multiplied by $1 - (1/E_d)$, irrespective of the degree of competition.[3]

Relationship between Marginal Revenue and Price Illustrated

Suppose that the elasticity of demand were infinitely great. In such a case the individual seller's demand curve would appear to him to be a horizontal line, parallel to the X axis as in Figure 9–2A. In our formula above, since $\Delta P = 0$ as sales change, while E_d is infinitely great, we have

$$MR = (P + 0)\left(1 - \frac{1}{\substack{\text{Infinitely} \\ \text{large} \\ \text{number}}}\right) = (P)(1 - 0) = (P)(1) = P \, .$$

Thus, again we see that, *under perfect competition, since the demand curve facing the individual seller is perfectly elastic, marginal revenue equals the price.* In Figure 9–2A, $MR = P$ at the level OP_1 at all points on the sales axis.

Next, consider the case in which the demand is inelastic. Suppose that $E_d = .2$. Then our formula would be:

$$MR = (P)\left(1 - \frac{1}{.2}\right) = (P)(1 - 5) = -4P \, .$$

Accordingly, *if the demand is inelastic, marginal revenue is negative and less than the price.* This case is illustrated in Figure 9–3. To the right of A in Figure 9–3B, the demand is inelastic; and to the right of A' in Figure 9–3A, marginal revenue is negative, i.e., the curve lies *below* the X axis.

Similarly, if the elasticity of demand is unity, or $E_d = 1$, our formula produces the result:

$$MR = (P)\left(1 - \frac{1}{1}\right) = (P)(1 - 1) = (P)(0) = 0 \, .$$

Thus, *when the elasticity of demand is unity,* as at A in Figure 9–3B, *marginal revenue is zero at A',* i.e., the curve *crosses* the X axis in Figure 9–3A. Note that at A, in Figure 9–3B, total revenue is at a maximum.

---

[3] The relation between marginal cost and average cost can similarly be shown to be
$$MC = AC(1 + 1/E_s) \, .$$
In general, see Robinson, *op. cit.,* chap. iii.

Figure 9–3

AVERAGE, MARGINAL, AND TOTAL REVENUE WHEN COMPETITION IS NOT PERFECT

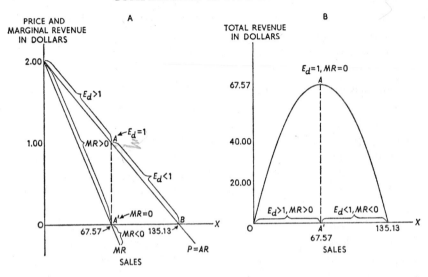

Finally, if the elasticity of demand is greater than unity, say $E_d = 5$, we have

$$MR = (P)\left(1 - \frac{1}{5}\right) = (P)(1 - .2) = .8P .$$

In this case, to the left of A in Figure 9–3B, we see that *when the demand is elastic, marginal revenue is positive.* It is also shown as positive but as *less than the price* in Figure 9–3A, i.e., the MR curve lies above the X axis.

Average Revenue

Average revenue is defined as total revenue divided by the number of units sold. Thus we have

$$AR = \frac{R}{X} = \frac{PX}{X} = P . \tag{9–7}$$

Average revenue is, thus, merely another term meaning "price of the product," and the "average revenue curve" is nothing more than the demand curve facing the individual seller, such as the horizontal line $MR = P$ in Figure 9–2A, or the sloping line $AR = P$ in Figure 9–3.

The *average revenue curve* must be distinguished from the total market demand curve depicted in Figure 9–2B. The former, as has been noted, is the individual seller's *opinion* of *his own* effect on the price;

the latter is the actual amount offered for sale at various prices by *all* the sellers in the market. It will be shown in the next chapter that, if the average revenue curve is a negatively sloping straight line, the marginal revenue curve declines at a rate which is exactly twice that of the former, and a method of deriving marginal revenue curves from average revenue curves will be explained.

B. SHORT-RUN EQUILIBRIUM CONDITION OF THE FIRM

Net Revenue Maximization as an Objective

It is generally assumed that a firm seeks to maximize its *net revenue* (*N*) or its pure profits from sales, or that it seeks to minimize its losses. *Losses can be defined merely as negative net revenue* ($N < 0$), *or as negative pure profits.* (Net revenue will be defined later.)

Whether or not the firm will be obtaining any net revenue or suffering any losses depends upon the relationship between the *price* of its product and the *average cost* of production of the given level of output. This relationship may be termed the *profit condition.* The same short-run equilibrium condition applies, however, whether the firm is maximizing profits or minimizing losses, and this condition, as it will be stated below, is also independent of the degree of competition in the market.

Definitions of Normal Profit and Normal Price

What is meant by the term *net revenue* (or *pure profits*) can best be understood by recalling that in Chapter 7 *total cost* has been defined to include a normal profit. Generally, a *normal profit is,* in turn, *defined as one which is "just large enough" to keep the "right amount"* of *entrepreneurship engaged in the activity in question in the long run.* What is a normal profit in a given industry thus depends on the facts in the case.

The inclusion by an economist in total cost of an amount equal to a normal profit means, of course, that the economist's definition of total cost differs from that employed by the accountant, or even from that employed by the businessman himself, and the practice implies that the economist has made a judgment that, on functional grounds, entrepreneurs are entitled to a "normal profit" in return for the services they render in organizing and controlling production.

A *normal price is similarly defined as a price which is just high enough to cover the full average cost of production of a unit of output in the long run;* that is, a normal price is a price sufficiently high to cover the proportionate part of the rent, wages, interest, and normal profit attributable as payments for the factor services employed in producing a unit of the product in the long run. These terms will be further explained in later chapters.

Net Revenue Defined

Net revenue, or *pure profit, is a return to entrepreneurs above and beyond a "normal profit."* It can be further defined as the difference between the total (gross) revenue from sales, R, as defined in the preceding section, and the total cost, including a normal profit, T, as defined in Chapter 7. Algebraically, we thus have

$$N = R - T = PX - (F + V) = PX - (bp_b + ap_a) , \qquad (9\text{--}8)$$

where N stands for *net* revenue, R is total or gross revenue from sales, and T is total cost or the sum of the total fixed ($F = bp_b$) and total variable ($V = ap_a$) costs. A *net* revenue curve, N, is depicted in Figure 9–4, which appears on page 226.

Marginal Net Revenue or Marginal "Pure" Profit Defined

The total change in *net* revenue, or in *pure profit,* as sales of the firm change is equal to the difference between the total change in total revenue as sales change (ΔR) and the total change in total cost (ΔT), or

$$\Delta N = \Delta R - \Delta T . \qquad (9\text{--}9)$$

The *marginal net revenue (MNR)*, or marginal *pure* profit, *is the average or exact rate of change* (depending on the circumstances of the analysis) *of net revenue as sales change.* Alternatively, it is the slope of the *net* revenue curve at a given point or over a given range in Figure 9–4. Thus, we have, dividing both sides of Equation (9–9) by ΔX to put the data on a per unit basis:

$$MNR = \frac{\Delta N}{\Delta X} = \frac{\Delta R}{\Delta X} - \frac{\Delta T}{\Delta X} = MR - MC . \qquad (9\text{--}10)$$

In words, the marginal *net* revenue or marginal pure profit (MNR) is equal to the difference between the *marginal* (gross) *revenue* or MR and the marginal cost or MC. Since the marginal cost, MC, is the slope of the total cost curve, while the *marginal revenue, MR,* is the slope of the total revenue curve, the marginal *net* revenue is nothing other than the difference between the slopes of these two curves, or alternatively, it is the slope of the total *net* revenue curve. In short, it

Figure 9–4

TOTAL COST AND REVENUE CURVES—FIRM EARNING
GREATER THAN NORMAL PROFIT

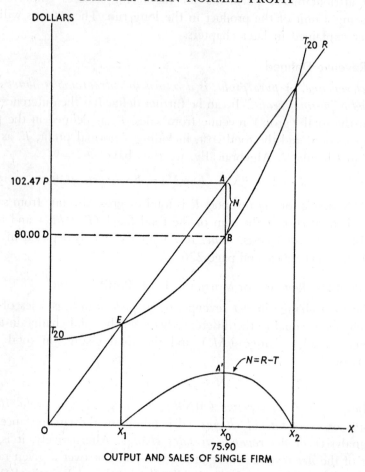

OUTPUT AND SALES OF SINGLE FIRM

is the addition to pure profit from selling an additional small amount of output.

With the preceding definitions firmly in mind, we are now in a position to write the general equilibrium condition of the firm in the short run and to explain why the case of perfect competition is merely a special case falling within a more general one.

The Equilibrium Condition of the Firm in the Short Run

Since it is assumed that the firm's objective is to maximize its *net* revenue or to minimize its losses (minimize its negative net revenue), irrespective of the degree of competition in the market, the following question arises: Under what condition will the objective be attained? The first answer is trivial: the objective will be attained in Figure 9–4 when output is at the level $OX_0 = 75.90$, for at A' the net revenue is at a maximum in that diagram. (Similarly, losses will be at a minimum in Figure 9–5 when the level of output OX_0 is produced.)

That is, the net revenue will be maximized in Figure 9–4 when N can no longer be increased. This condition will occur when marginal *net* revenue is zero, for marginal net revenue is the rate of change of total net revenue as sales change. To the right of A' in Figure 9–4, the net revenue begins to decline, for marginal net revenue is negative to the right of A'; and to the left of A', as sales and output are increased from 0, net revenue increases until A' is attained. (From 0 to X_1, marginal net revenue becomes *less* negative, hence it increases in this range also!) Net revenue is positive in the range of sales and output from X_1 to X_2, since the total cost curve (T_{20}) lies below the total (gross) revenue curve (R) in this range. (The cost curves used in this chapter are those derived in Chapter 7.)

It follows, therefore, that *the net revenue will be at a maximum,* so that there is no further incentive for the firm to increase its output or to reduce its output from the existing capacity (in the short run), at A', at the top of the N curve in Figure 9–4, for at that point the marginal net revenue is zero, or

$$MNR = \frac{\Delta N}{\Delta X} = 0 \ .$$

Since this is the case, we can set Equation (9–10), which defines marginal net revenue, equal to zero to find the relationship between MC and MR at that point, or

$$MNR = \frac{\Delta N}{\Delta X} = 0 = \frac{\Delta R}{\Delta X} - \frac{\Delta T}{\Delta X} , \qquad (9\text{–}11)$$

and by adding $\Delta T/\Delta X$ to both sides of this equation, we have

$$\frac{\Delta T}{\Delta X}\uparrow \ = \frac{\Delta R}{\Delta X} = MC\uparrow \ = MR \ . \qquad (9\text{–}12)$$

Thus, the firm will be maximizing its profits at that level of output and sales at which marginal cost is equal to marginal revenue, for at this point marginal net revenue is zero. (The reason for the arrow [↑] will appear below.)

At the point of maximum net revenue (A' in Figure 9–4), the slopes of the total cost and total revenue curves are equal. That is,

$MC\uparrow = MR$. The slope of the total revenue curve at A is equal to that of the total cost curve at B in Figure 9–4, and the distance $BA = X_0A' = \$22.47$ represents the net revenue from the level of output OX_0. For $BA = N = R - T$, and since marginal net revenue is zero at A' at the level of output OX_0 (i.e., net revenue is there at a maximum), profits are maximized at that level of output. Arithmetically, in Figure 9–4, we have the result:

$$N = R - T, \tag{9-8}$$
$$\$22.47 = \$102.47 - \$80 . \tag{9-8'}$$

Similarly, in the case of Figure 9–5, we have the result that losses are minimized at output $OX_0 = 57.96$, or

$$-\$7.84 = \$52.16 - \$60 . \tag{9-8''}$$

Figure 9–5

TOTAL COST AND REVENUE CURVES—FIRM OPERATING AT A LOSS

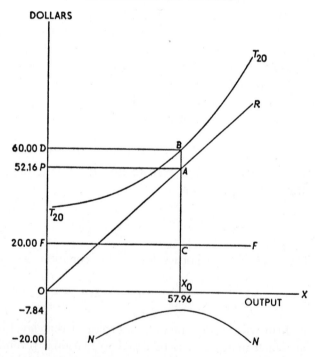

An Alternative Graphical Explanation

The same results can also be explained in terms of average and marginal cost and revenue curves. In Figure 9–6, since we are assuming perfect competition, the marginal revenue "curve" coincides with

Figure 9–6

AVERAGE AND MARGINAL REVENUE AND COST CURVES—FIRM EARNING GREATER THAN NORMAL PROFIT

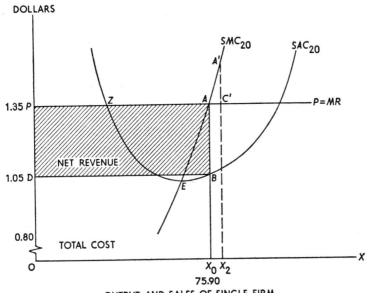

OUTPUT AND SALES OF SINGLE FIRM

the average revenue or price "curve," which is parallel to the X axis.

The firm is in equilibrium at A, since here the short-run marginal cost curve (SMC_{20}) cuts the marginal revenue curve ($P = MR$) from *below*. The condition that the marginal cost curve cut the marginal revenue curve from below (indicated by the arrow ↑) is a "second-order" condition imposed to insure that a maximum rather than a minimum position is attained. It applies *only* under perfect competition, as we will see in Chapter 10. What the condition guarantees is that at levels of output greater than the equilibrium level, additions to total cost (MC) are greater than additions to total revenue (MR), thus producing a negative marginal net revenue; while at levels of output less than the equilibrium level, additions to total revenue (MR) are greater than additions to total cost (MC), thus producing a positive marginal net revenue ($MNR > 0$). The symbol, MC ↑, means marginal cost is increasing.

The *general* equilibrium condition is $MC = MR$; but since under perfect competition $MR = P$, the equilibrium condition is sometimes written in this *special* case merely as MC ↑ $= P$.

Note also in Figure 9–6 that *since the price line $P = MR$ lies above the short-run average cost curve* (SAC_{20}), *a greater than normal profit is being made* ($N > 0$) at A. In the diagram, at output OX_0, the price or average revenue is $OP = \$1.35$, and the average cost (rounded to the nearest cent) is $OD = \$1.05$. The per unit (or average) profit is thus $DP = \$.30$. Total cost (T) is equal to average cost multipled by total output, or area $ODBX_0$, and total revenue (R) is average revenue multiplied by total sales, or area $OPAX_0$. (Sales and output are the same thing looked at from different points of view in this analysis.) Net revenue (N) is the difference between total revenue and total cost, or $OPAX_0 - ODBX_0 = DPAB$.

At A, marginal net revenue is zero, since marginal cost, X_0A, at that point is equal to the marginal revenue, X_0A. To the right of A, at say A', marginal cost is X_2A' and is greater than marginal revenue, which is X_2C' at the level of output OX_2. Thus, to the right of A, the marginal net revenue is negative, for $MC > MR$. To the left of A, marginal cost is less than marginal revenue $(MC < MR)$, and here marginal net revenue is positive. And so the equilibrium condition is fulfilled at A, and net revenue is maximized at output OX_0.

Similarly, in Figure 9–7 is depicted the case of the firm minimizing its losses. In this case, again $MC\uparrow = MR$ at A, but now the price lies *below* the short-run average cost curve and *above* the average variable cost curve. In Figure 9–7, $N < 0$, and the firm is minimizing losses. The same equilibrium condition applies:

$$\frac{\Delta T}{\Delta X}\uparrow = \frac{\Delta R}{\Delta X}, \text{ or } MC\uparrow = MR,$$

whether the firm is maximizing net revenue or minimizing its losses. However, *whether it is maximizing net revenue or minimizing losses can only be determined by considering the relationship between average cost and the price.* Moreover, the *loss* condition, that price will be less than average cost but must be greater than average variable cost, requires further explanation.

The Loss Condition: Variable Costs Must Be Covered

It has been noted that if the firm is to earn pure profit $(N > 0)$, the profit condition must be fulfilled that price is greater than average cost, or $P > AC$. However, if the firm is minimizing its losses, the condition $P < AC$ will exist and the condition $P > AVC$ *must* exist. What is the meaning of these last two conditions?

Consider Figures 9–7 and 9–5. In Figure 9–5, we have already seen that the firm is minimizing its losses, and that

$$N = R - T = -\$7.84 = \$52.16 - \$60 . \tag{9-8''}$$

Thus, the net revenue is negative, and the amount of the loss is $7.84.

Suppose the firm did not produce at all. In this case, it would lose all of its fixed costs amounting to $20, for these must be paid whether production occurs or not. Clearly, by producing output OX_0 in Figure 9–5, the firm loses less ($PD = \$7.84$) than if it did not produce at all and lost its fixed costs ($OF = \$20$).

Figure 9–7

AVERAGE AND MARGINAL REVENUE AND COST CURVES—FIRM
OPERATING AT A LOSS

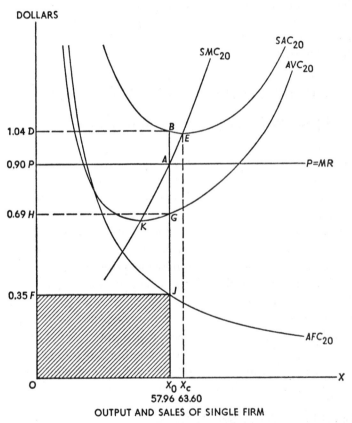

OUTPUT AND SALES OF SINGLE FIRM

The reason why the firm loses less by producing than by not producing can be seen clearly in Figure 9–7. Although the price of $OP = \$.90$ is less than the average cost of $OD = \$1.04$ (rounded to the nearest cent) when 57.96 units are being produced, the average variable cost is only $OH = \$.69$. Thus the average variable cost is less than the price by $\$.90 - \$.69 = \$.21$. This amount is available for reduction of the average fixed costs, which amount to $OF = \$.35$ per unit. On a per unit basis, therefore, the firm would lose ($\$.35$)(57.96) = $20 if it did not produce at all, but by producing the equilibrium level of output $OX_0 = 57.96$, it loses only $\$.35 - \$.21 = \$.14$ per unit, or $(\$.14)(57.96) = \$8.11$. (The difference between $\$7.84$ and $\$8.11$ arises out of the fact that the average cost has been taken as $\$1.04$ in Figure 9–7 when it is actually $\$1.035$.)

The total revenue in Figure 9–7 is area $OPAX_0$, while the total cost is area $ODBX_0$. The difference, area $PDBA$, represents the total negative net revenue or the total loss. Area $HPAG$ represents the excess of total revenue $(OPAX_0)$ above the total *variable* cost $(OHGX_0)$. Finally, area $OFJX_0$ represents what *would* be the loss from fixed charges alone *if* nothing were produced, and $OFJX_0 >$ $PDBA$ or $\$20 > \$8.11$. In fact, area $OFJX_0$ is equal to area $HDBG = HPAG + PDBA$.

C. THE DEFINITION OF SHORT-RUN SUPPLY

Curve of Short-Run Supply of the Individual Firm

Under perfect competition the short-run supply curve of the individual firm is defined as that part of the short-run marginal cost curve of the firm which lies above its average variable cost curve, or as that part of the marginal cost curve which begins at K in Figure 9–7 and rises thereafter.

The reason for this definition should be obvious. The short-run supply curve of the firm represents the amounts it would produce in the alternative possible short-run equilibrium positions in which it might find itself as the price of the product changes. Our definition rests upon the *usual* assumption that variable *input* prices do not change in the short run. If they do, the firm's short-run cost curves will shift upward in a parallel way and the firm's short-run supply curve will be a curve joining alternative possible short-run equilibrium positions on successively higher short-run marginal cost curves. Cases involving long-run changes in input prices are considered later.

The Short-Run Industry Supply Curve

The short-run industry supply curve under perfect competition is defined as the horizontal sum of the relevant ranges of the various marginal cost curves of the individual firms. Thus, in Figure 9–8B, the curve S_sS_s is merely the curve which is produced when curves such as $SMC_1 = S_1S_1$ and $SMC_2 = S_2S_2$ of Firms 1 and 2 in Figure 9–8A, *and of all other firms in the industry,* are summed horizontally. Note that the scale along the horizontal axis in Figure 9–8B is different from that in Figure 9–8A. The positive slope of the short-run industry

Figure 9–8
SHORT-RUN INDUSTRY SUPPLY CURVE

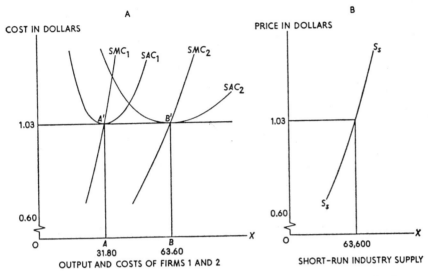

OUTPUT AND COSTS OF FIRMS 1 AND 2 | SHORT-RUN INDUSTRY SUPPLY

supply curve thus reflects the assumption of diminishing marginal productivity on which rests the assumption (or conclusion) of increasing marginal cost.

D. LONG-RUN EQUILIBRIUM CONDITION OF THE FIRM AND INDUSTRY

General Statement of the Long-Run Equilibrium Condition

In the long run there is sufficient time for the firm to change the size of its plant (to change its existing capacity), and with freedom of entry there is also sufficient time for new firms to enter the industry or for old firms to exit from it.

Under what condition will a firm have no incentive to build new capacity and will there be no incentive for additional firms either to enter or to exit from the industry? Obviously, when those firms remaining in the industry are making only normal profits (or, as we shall see below, alternatively, when the marginal firm is making only a normal profit, depending on one's point of view). Specifically, this means that net revenue will then be zero, or that

$$N = R - T = 0,$$

and this is the same thing as saying that total revenue is equal to total cost, or $R = T$. Moreover, $T = (AC)(X)$, or total cost is equal to average cost times the number of units produced. And, $R = PX$, or total revenue is equal to the number of units sold times the price per unit. Therefore, it follows that, in the long run, the normal price must prevail, or

$$\frac{PX}{X} = \frac{(LAC)(X)}{X} = P = LAC .$$

That is to say, the price of the product must be equal to the average cost of production in the long run.

However, the mere fact that the total cost is equal to total revenue, so that only a normal profit is being made and net revenue is equal to zero, does not guarantee that a firm will be in equilibrium. Thus, in the long run, for the firm and the industry *both* to be in equilibrium, so that neither exit from nor entry into the industry occurs, and so that no change in output from existing capacity (i.e., in output from existing plants) will be profitable, it is necessary that the short-run equilibrium condition and the zero net revenue condition be met simultaneously, or

$$SMC\uparrow = MR , \text{ and } P = LAC .$$

(Note marginal cost *increasing*.) In the special case of perfect competition, since marginal revenue and the price are equal, or $MR = P$, it follows that the long-run equilibrium position will be attained when

$$SMC\uparrow = MR = P = LAC .$$

Now, if it is true that this condition is met, then it will also be true that

$$MR = P = SMC\uparrow = SAC = LMC\uparrow = LAC ,$$

for $MR = P$ can be equal to *both* $SMC\uparrow$ and LAC only at the minimum point of the long-run average cost curve, as is the case at E, at output OX_0 and price OP_0, in Figure 9–9A.

When these conditions are met, firms will be operating in the long run under perfect competition in the "right" size plants, and the "right" number of firms will be producing in the industry. And so, the point of *long-run "economic efficiency,"* depicted as point B' in Figures 7–6 and 7–7 in Chapter 7, will be attained in the long run under perfect competition at E in Figure 9–9A.

Figure 9–9A will be utilized next to explain the reasons for the tendency towards the fulfillment of these long-run conditions under perfect competition.

The Tendency toward Long-Run Equilibrium (or "Normal Price") under Perfect Competition

In Figure 9–9A, the firm is initially in long-run equilibrium at E, where $OP_0 = \$1.03$ and $OX_0 = 63.60$, and where the condition is fulfilled:

$$P = LAC = LMC\uparrow \; = MR = SMC\uparrow \; = SAC.$$

In Figure 9–9B, the equilibrium position in the market is shown by the intersection of D_0D_0 and S_0S_0 at A_0, where the price is also $OP_0 = \$1.03$, but the quantity changing hands is 63,600 units or one thousand times the amount sold by the single firm. At E in Figure

Figure 9–9

LONG-RUN EQUILIBRIUM POSITION OF THE FIRM: LONG-RUN SUPPLY; CONSTANT COSTS: CASE I

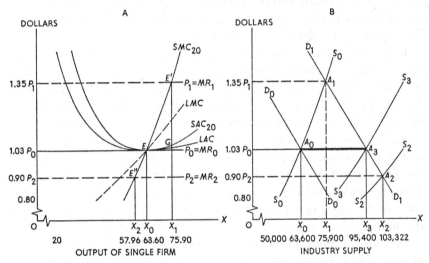

9–9A, net revenue or N is zero, since total cost ($T = OP_0EX_0$) is equal to total revenue ($R = OP_0EX_0$). That is, $R = T$, and $R - T = N = 0$.

Next, suppose that the demand increases as indicated by the shift to the right of D_0D_0 to D_1D_1 in Figure 9–9B. The price of X increases to $OP_1 = X_1A_1 = \$1.35$, and the quantity sold increases to $OX_1 = 75,900$ in Figure 9–9B. How is this increase in quantity brought about in the short run?

Obviously, each firm first increases its output from existing capacity beyond the optimum level. Thus, as price increases in the market to $\$1.35$ per unit of X in Figure 9–9B, the price received by the individual firm increases in Figure 9–9A from $OP_0 = \$1.03$ to $OP_1 = \$1.35$, while output of the individual firm likewise increases from $OX_0 = 63.60$ to $OX_1 = 75.90$ units. In the new short-run equilibrium position of the firm at E', $MC\uparrow = MR = P$ once more, but, at the same time, at the level of output $OX_1 = 75.90$, the price of $OP_1 = \$1.35$ is greater than the average cost of production of that output, $X_1G = \$1.05$. Thus, a situation has been created in which net revenue (or N) is now positive because $P = \$1.35 > AC = \$1.05$ or total revenue (R) exceeds total cost (T). Firms are making greater than normal profits at E', or $N > 0$.

What happens next? If there is freedom of entry, new firms will build plants and begin producing. Assuming that the inputs are freely available and that their supply is perfectly elastic, some new plants may be exactly like the old ones. (The case in which the supply of inputs is not perfectly elastic will be covered below.) The increase in the number of plants results in an increase in supply. Thus, in Figure 9–9B, the supply curve shifts down and to the right.

It may even shift as far as S_2S_2, in which case there have been mistakes in judgment, and output has increased too much. The industry has been temporarily overbuilt. Thus, after the entry of too many new firms or the excessive increase in the number of plants, the price falls to OP_2, and the new equilibrium position is A_2 in Figure 9–9B.

At this low price of $OP_2 = \$.90$ in Figure 9–9A, the full average cost of production will not be covered, $P < AC$, although the average variable cost of $\$.69$ (see Figure 9–7) will be covered, $P > AVC$. Thus, the individual firm reduces its output to the level $OX_2 = 57.96$ units of X, and a new equilibrium position exists at E'' in the case of the individual firm, for $MC\uparrow = MR$ once more at E''.

But, firms cannot go on forever producing at less than the full cost of production. Eventually, as fixed assets are depreciated and not replaced (for the full fixed cost is not covered at E''), some firms will leave the industry. How quickly this occurs will depend on many factors, including the questions of how specialized are the fixed assets, how easily can they be converted to other uses, and how old is the plant in question.

The ensuing exodus of some firms from the industry reduces the total supply available on the market. Thus, the supply curve in Figure 9–9B shifts next to the left from S_2S_2 to S_3S_3, and a new equilibrium position is established at the point A_3. In this position the price will once more be $OP_0 = \$1.03$, but the industry output will now be $OX_3 > OX_1$. Not all of the new firms will have left the industry, and not all of the additional plants will have been scrapped. For the original demand has increased, making it possible for more firms to remain in business making a normal profit at the old equilibrium price of $OP_0 = \$1.03$ and output of $OX_0 = 63.60$ in Figure 9–9A than before. Thus, although the output of the individual firm in the long-run equilibrium position (again at E) is once more the same as it was before the shift in demand occurred ($OX_0 = OX_0$), the total supply in the market has increased ($OX_3 > OX_0$) in Figure 9–9B because of the increase in the number of producing firms.

In the long run, therefore, there is a tendency under perfect competition (with freedom of entry) for firms to operate at the least cost point, E, in Figure 9–9A, and temporary displacements of the equilibrium result in an eventual return to the equilibrium position. In the process of our description, the long-run supply curves of the firm and of the industry have been defined implicitly. In the next and final major subdivision of this chapter, our task will be to define these curves explicitly under various assumptions concerning the existence of external economies and diseconomies or their absence. First, however, we must consider the question of whether or not all firms in an industry will operate at the same minimum long-run average cost of production.

Equality of Long-Run Minimum Average Costs of All Firms or Not?

Economists are not in agreement as to whether or not the minimum points of the long-run average cost curves of all plants in the industry lie at the same level. Nor are they in agreement as to precisely how this assumption, if it is correct, is to be rationalized. However, the long-run equilibrium position is a theoretical construction and not a position actually attained in fact. Thus, the controversy is of only limited significance. The long-run equilibrium position was defined by Marshall as one towards which there is a *tendency* to move; and, so, it represents a *limiting position* in the analysis.

The argument which is usually made for equality of the minimum long-run average costs of all plants in the industry runs in terms of opportunity costs. That is, even though some firms may be more favorably located with respect to inputs and some may have superior managements, in time, as other firms bid for these inputs or for the services of the superior agents of production, the firm in question finds that it must pay higher prices or salaries in order to retain such services. Thus, its cost curves shift upward until they are at the same level as those of all of the other firms in the industry.

An alternative approach is to conduct the analysis in terms of *the marginal firm.* The marginal firm is then defined as the one having the *highest* long-run minimum average total cost of all the firms remaining in the industry in the long run. All of the *infra-marginal firms,* that is, those whose minimum long-run average total costs are less than that of the marginal firm, enjoy the benefit of economic *rent,* a surplus. (Those whose minimum is greater cannot stay in business in the long run by definition!) This surplus arises from the fact that the price of the product must be sufficiently high in the long run to cover the full cost of the highest cost firm which remains in the industry, while these *infra-marginal* firms have a lower minimum average cost than the price at which the output is sold. Thus, for the marginal firm only, $P = AC$. (We will develop the concept of *rent* more fully later in Part V.)

Since the opportunity cost thesis is more often used in the literature than is the marginal firm thesis, the former will normally be used in the analysis in the following sections and chapters. It should also be noted that, under perfect competition, it is assumed that only single firm plants exist; hence the terms "plant" and "firm" are often used interchangeably in the literature in this special case.

When the conditions of perfect competition are not fulfilled, there is no tendency for firms to operate plants in the long run at the point of absolute minimum long-run cost of production, and the long-run supply curve can be specified only in particular cases by making additional assumptions about the nature and extent of the deviations from perfect competition. This matter will concern us further in Chapter 11.

E. SUPPLY IN THE LONG RUN

Long-Run Supply Defined

Under perfect competition, long-run supply is defined as the total supply which would be available from all plants operating at successive points of long-run economic capacity, as the industry expanded. In other words, the long-run supply in the case of Figure 9–9B is the horizontal line, A_0A_3, which connects the various points of long-run equilibrium *of the industry.*

At A_0 fewer firms are producing than at A_3. Since the line A_0A_3 is horizontal, or parallel to the X axis, it is clear that Figures 9–9A and 9–9B depict *the special case* of a long-run supply under conditions of *constant costs.* As we shall see shortly, the long-run supply curve need not be infinitely elastic; it may be positively sloping, if the case is one of increasing costs; or it may be negatively sloping, if the case is one of decreasing costs. There are, however, two different situations which may produce constant costs, and these must be examined before the other cases are discussed.

Long-Run Supply; Constant Costs: Case I

In the case of *constant long-run costs,* the prices of the inputs must be assumed to remain constant as larger quantities of them are used. There are two possibilities: (1) the production function is *not* linearly homogeneous; and (2) the production function *is* linearly homogeneous.

The *first* case has already been explained in the discussion of the tendency toward long-run equilibrium under perfect competition, depicted in Figure 9–9. The production function in Figure 9–9 has been assumed to be *not* linearly homogeneous, and we have seen that, even in such a case, the long-run supply curve may be a horizontal line parallel to the X axis, A_0A_3 in Figure 9–9B.

In the *second* case, if the production function *is* linearly homogeneous, the marginal product and the average product will be independent of the level of output. [See the discussion of Equation (3–3) in Chapter 6.] As we have seen in Chapter 7, in this case, the *long-run* marginal and average costs will be the same at all levels of output. In such a case, there will be *no minimum* long-run average cost of production, and the long-run supply will also be perfectly elastic. This case will be considered next.

Long-Run Supply; Constant Costs: Case II

In Figure 9–10A, the long-run marginal cost and long-run average cost curves have been drawn as a single straight line ($LAC = LMC = MR = AR = P$), and these curves are identical with the long-run supply curve of the individual firm. As a matter of fact, Figure 9–10A contains data from Figure 7–5 in Chapter 7, which, it will be recalled, rests upon the linearly homogeneous production function assumed in Chapter 6. Moreover, since the process of long-run adjustment in the case of Figure 9–10 is exactly the same as it is in the case of Figure 9–9, the various short-run variations in prices and supply are not depicted in Figure 9–10. Only the initial (A_0) and the final (A_3) long-run industry equilbrium positions are thus depicted in Figure 9–10B.

Now, Figure 9–10A contains the short-run average and marginal cost curves of *two alternative* or *different size plants* which could be built by *Firm 1*. These curves are of the normal U shape, as we have learned in Chapter 7. This firm would not, *in the long run,* produce the given output (OB) in the smaller Plant SAC_A, because the short-

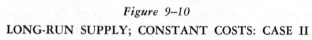

Figure 9–10

LONG-RUN SUPPLY; CONSTANT COSTS: CASE II

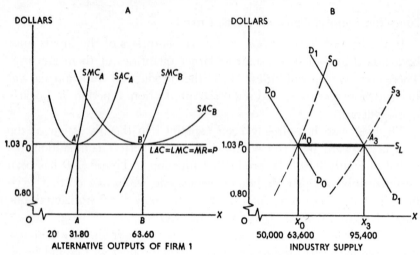

run marginal and the average costs of *the given output* (OB) are less (BB') in the larger plant (SAC_B) than they would be in Plant SAC_A. *Although the minimum long-run average cost of production and the long-run marginal cost are the same in all plants* (since $AA' = BB' = \$1.03$), *the level of output at which occurs the minimum short-run average cost is different in different size plants,* or $OA = 31.80 < OB = 63.60$.

Under the circumstances, if Firm 1 did not choose to increase its output to OB in the long run and were content, instead, to produce only OA, it could do so at the industry's minimum average cost without building a larger plant, for $AA' = BB'$. New firms entering the industry would, similarly, build that size plant in which, given the output which they intended to produce, the average and marginal costs were equal. All plants are equally efficient *by definition* when built for an *intended* level of output, if the production function is linearly homogeneous and input prices are constant.

Under these circumstances, it is apparent that, in the long run, the industry supply curve, $A_0 A_3$ in Figure 9–10B, must also be a horizontal line at the same level as the firm's long-run supply curve, $A'B'$, for it is merely the locus of points such as AA', BB', etc., at which the minimum long-run average costs of the different given levels of output are the same in all plants.

Thus, in the long run, when all inputs are assumed variable and costs are assumed constant, increases in output in response to increases in demand from D_0D_0 to D_1D_1 in Figure 9–10B can eventually be met equally efficiently through (1) the action of existing firms in building new plants of *any* size; or (2) by the entry of new firms which build additional plants of *any* size! In this case, the sizes of the plants, and thus the number of firms in the industry, must be determined by considerations other than those which have so far been taken into account by the analysis.

Moreover, in Figure 9–10A, not only are the long-run average and marginal cost curves an identical horizontal line parallel to the X axis, but also the average and marginal revenue, or price, lines are identical with the former! The problem cannot be solved. (In Figure 9–4, the long-run total cost curve would be identical with the total revenue curve.) [4] Thus, *when* perfect competition is assumed, a determinate solution depends on a rising marginal cost, although, as we will see in the next chapter, this condition does not exist under monopoly.

We can, therefore, summarize the preceding discussion by noting that the case of constant costs based on a linearly homogeneous production function, such as that in Figure 9–10B, implies that (1) there are no *internal* economies or diseconomies of production; and (2) there are no *external* economies or diseconomies of production. This second assumption is also made in Figure 9–9B, and there means, of course, that the long-run supply of inputs is infinitely elastic, or that increased use of inputs in the production of additional amounts of output does not result in higher prices of the inputs. Moreover, the increase in the industry supply can occur in the case of Figure 9–10, but not in Figure 9–9, either through the increase in the size of existing plants or as a result of the entry of new firms, because there is no one size plant which is more efficient than any other in Figure 9–10A.

However, the mere assumption of a linearly homogeneous production function will not produce the case of constant costs, unless the prices of the inputs are also assumed constant. In both cases, these assumptions are, of course, highly restrictive and rather unrealistic, and, thus, the assumption of constant costs can only be made in an analysis where such an assumption is not critical to the conclusions drawn. An example of the latter case would be an analysis which concerned itself only with problems of relative prices, such as David Ri-

---

[4] For a further discussion, see George Stigler, *Production and Distribution Theories* (New York: The Macmillan Co., 1941), p. 382, where he argues that this case leads to a continuous cycle of overproduction and underproduction in the industry in question.

cardo's illustration (1817) of the principle of comparative advantage in international trade.[5]

Long-Run Supply; Decreasing Costs: "Forward-Falling Supply Curve"

If the industry is one which experiences the benefits of external economies for the reasons given in Chapter 7, the long-run average cost curve of the individual plant will shift downward from LAC_A to LAC_B, as in Figure 9–11, as the output of the industry as a whole grows in response to the increased demand (from D_0D_0 to D_3D_3) for its products.

Figure 9–11

LONG-RUN SUPPLY; DECREASING COSTS: "FORWARD-FALLING" SUPPLY CURVE

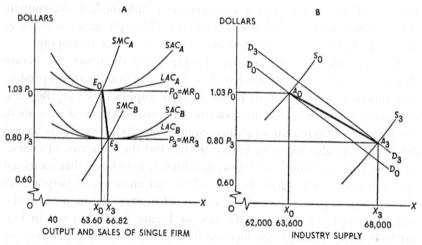

In Figure 9–11A, the curves SMC_A, SAC_A, and LAC_A represent the short-run marginal, the short-run average, and the long-run average cost curves of Firm 1 in equilibrium at E_0 *prior* to the growth of the industry. The curves SMC_B, SAC_B, and LAC_B represent these curves *after the industry has grown* as demand has increased from D_0D_0 to D_3D_3 *and the industry is once more in equilibrium* at A_3. The *process* by which it moves from the initial long-run equilibrium position to the new one is again essentially the same as that explained in conjunction with Figure 9–9 and occurs largely through the entry and exit of firms. However, in addition to the shift in the $P = MR$ curve in Figure 9–11A, as new firms enter, the cost curves also shift downward, and the size of existing plants may change.

---

[5] David Ricardo, *The Principles of Political Economy and Taxation* (Everyman's Library, New York: E. P. Dutton & Co., Inc., 1943), pp. 82–83.

The curve LAC_A is a reproduction of the curve LAC shown in Figure 7–7, in Chapter 7, which assumes that there exist *internal* economies and diseconomies and that the prices of the inputs are constant at the level: $p_a = \$1.00$, $p_b = \$1.00$. Thus, at all points along LAC_A, the Marshallian equilibrium condition, explained in Chapter 7, has been fulfilled, and as we have seen there, at E_0 in Figure 9–11A, we have

$$\frac{f_a}{f_b} = \frac{p_a}{p_b} = \frac{9.72}{.972} = \frac{\$10}{\$1.00} = 10 = T_{ba} \, . \qquad (6\text{-}3'')$$

The curve LAC_B incorporates the same assumptions concerning *internal economies and diseconomies* as does LAC_A *but has been drawn upon the additional assumption that, because of external economies, the prices of the fixed and variable inputs have both decreased to $p'_a = \$7.20$, $p'_b = \$.90$.* Thus at E_3, in Figure 9–11A, we have

$$\frac{f'_a}{f'_b} = \frac{p'_a}{p'_b} = \frac{9.0457}{1.1308} = 7.9999 = 8.0 = T_{ba} \, . \qquad (6\text{-}3''')$$

The rate of substitution, T_{ba}, has decreased since the price of b has decreased relatively less than has the price of a. Moreover, since the two prices have not decreased proportionately, the line E_0E_3 is not parallel to the Y axis in Figure 9–11A. The least cost point in the case of LAC_B occurs at a slightly higher level of output ($66.82X$) than it does in the case of LAC_A ($63.60X$). If the two prices had decreased proportionately, the curve LAC_B would have been vertically parallel to the curve LAC_A, as in Figure 7–9 in Chapter 7.

The line E_0E_3, formed by alternative points of long-run equilibrium, is the firm's long-run supply curve. The long-run industry supply curve is merely the sum of the individual firms' long-run supply curves, the line A_0A_3. The negative slope of this curve is explained in our analysis *solely* by external economies, since our analysis begins with the firm in a position of long-run equilibrium. Marshall's analysis of this case begins with a firm which possesses unexhausted *internal* as well as unexhausted external economies. There has been much argument in the literature as to what his analysis means.[6] Under perfect competition, a firm possessing unexhausted internal economies is operating on a falling portion of its long-run average cost curve and is not in long-run equilibrium. Marshall's analysis of the case is really a dynamic disequi-

---

[6] Alfred Marshall, *Principles of Economics* (8th ed.; London: Macmillan & Co., Ltd., 1938), p. 317 and Appendix H; and J. N. Wolfe, "The Representative Firm," *Economic Journal*, Vol. LXIV (June, 1954), pp. 337–49.

librium analysis involving *movements along and shifts in* the average cost curve.[7]

Long-Run Supply; Increasing Costs: The "Normal" Case

If a perfectly competitive industry is one which is subject to *external diseconomies* as defined in Chapter 7 earlier, the average and marginal cost curves of the individual firm will shift upward as the industry's output expands in response to increased demand for the product. The external diseconomies will generally be pecuniary in nature and will result in increased costs of inputs, for as additional firms enter the industry they will bid against existing firms for the given supply of inputs, thereby forcing the prices of the inputs to rise.[8] This case is considered by most economists to be the one most prevalent in the real world.

Figure 9–12

LONG-RUN SUPPLY; INCREASING COSTS: THE "NORMAL" CASE

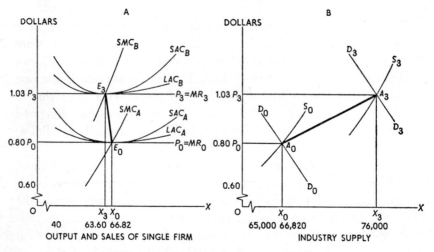

In Figure 9–12A, the firm is seen to be initially in long-run equilibrium at E_0, producing output OX_0 in Plant SAC_A at an average cost and price of OP_0. After expansion of the industry has occurred in response to an increase in demand from D_0D_0 to D_3D_3, the industry is once more in long-run equilibrium at A_3. At E_3, the prices of the inputs are assumed in our diagram to have increased in different pro-

---

[7] Marshall, *op. cit.*, p. 461.

[8] The definitive article on the question of external economies and diseconomies is Jacob Viner's "Cost Curves and Supply Curves," *Zeitschrift für Nationalökonomie*, Vol. III (1932), pp. 23–46, reprinted in Kenneth Boulding and George Stigler (eds.) *Readings in Price Theory* (Homewood, Ill.: Richard D. Irwin, Inc., 1952), pp. 198–232.

portions, while technology is assumed to remain constant. By a process of adjustment like that explained in conjunction with Figures 9–9 and 9–11, the firm again eventually finds itself in a new position of equilibrium at E_3, operating a slightly smaller plant, SAC_B, at a higher long-run average cost and price equal to OP_3.

The output of the firm has thus decreased in this case by X_3X_0. However, since the equilibrium was initially disturbed by an increase in demand, in the final equilibrium position the total supply of the industry must be greater than it was before the change in demand occurred, and a larger quantity will be sold by the industry as a whole at higher prices than before.

The decrease in the firm's output (or in the size of its optimum plant) has been the result of the disproportionate increase in the cost of inputs resulting from the increase in the number of plants in the industry. But, the number of firms is now greater than it was before the change in demand occurred, and the long-run industry supply curve has a positive slope as depicted by A_0A_3 in Figure 9–12B.

Thus, in Figure 9–12 has been depicted an interesting case in which the individual firm's long-run supply curve, E_0E_3, slopes up and to the *left*, but the industry supply curve, A_0A_3, slopes up and to the *right*. If the prices of all inputs had increased proportionately, the *individual firm's* long-run supply curve would have been a vertical line parallel to the Y axis (i.e., perfectly inelastic), and the size of the plant would have been exactly the same as it was before the increase in demand occurred. (See Figure 7–9.) However, the *industry* long-run supply curve would still have had a positive slope because the number of plants would have increased, and thus the total industry's output would have been greater than before the increase in demand.

Limitations of the Theory of Supply

The fact that supply curves rest upon cost curves, and, thus, ultimately upon the theory of production, in which it is assumed that technology remains constant, represents a serious limitation insofar as is concerned the accuracy of any predictions (forecasts) based upon them. Probably predictions based upon very short-run or short-run assumptions can be made with a much higher degree of accuracy than can those based upon long-run assumptions. The definitions of long-run supply, involving as they do the assumption of perfect competition, are thus much less useful as a basis for prediction or for purposes of policy making than are the former.

We have now covered one of the limiting cases, that of perfect competition. In the next chapter we will cover the other, that of monopoly.

SELECTED READINGS

ALLEN, R. G. D. *Mathematical Analysis for Economists,* pp. 152–57 and 196–200. London: Macmillan & Co., Ltd., 1950.

BAUMOL, WILLIAM J. *Economic Theory and Operations Analysis,* chap. x. Englewood Cliffs, N.J.: Prentice-Hall, Inc., 1961.

BODENHORN, DIRAN. *Intermediate Price Theory,* pp. 118–41. New York: McGraw-Hill Book Co., Inc., 1961.

CLARK, J. M. "Competition: Static Models and Dynamic Aspects," *American Economic Review,* Vol. XLV (Proceedings, 1955), pp. 450–62.

EASTHAM, J. K. *Graphical Economics,* chap. vii. Chicago: Quadrangle Books, Inc., 1960.

HENDERSON, JAMES M., AND QUANDT, RICHARD E. *Microeconomic Theory,* chap. iii. New York: McGraw-Hill Book Co., Inc., 1958.

ROBINSON, JOAN. "Rising Supply Price," *Economica,* New Series, Vol. VIII (1941), pp. 1–8. Reprinted in *Readings in Price Theory* (eds. KENNETH BOULDING AND GEORGE STIGLER), pp. 233–41. Homewood, Ill.: Richard D. Irwin, Inc., 1952.

STIGLER, GEORGE. *Production and Distribution Theories,* chap. xii. New York: The Macmillan Co., 1941.

VINER, JACOB. "Cost Curves and Supply Curves," *Zeitschrift für Nationalökonomie,* Vol. III (1932), pp. 23–46. Reprinted in *Readings in Price Theory* (eds. KENNETH BOULDING AND GEORGE STIGLER), pp. 198–232. Homewood, Ill.: Richard D. Irwin, Inc., 1952.

10 Monopoly; Monopsony; Bilateral Bargaining

Introduction

Like the term, *competition*, the term, *monopoly*, has different meanings in the works of different writers.[1] In this book the term *monopoly is defined to mean the case of a single seller, enjoying absence of competition of any kind, with complete control over the supply of the product, including control over entry into the industry.* Some writers call this case "pure" monopoly. So defined, monopoly does not exist in the real world and represents merely one limiting case in model analysis, just as the case of perfect competition, discussed in the preceding chapter, represents the opposite limiting case. Finally, the term *monopsony is defined, in a parallel way, to mean the case of a single buyer who is subject to no competition.*

In this chapter the traditional theory of the behavior of the firm which finds itself in a position of, or which acquires, monopoly power will first be explained. This theory is merely an application to the special case of monopoly of the general equilibrium conditions which have already been developed in detail in the preceding chapter. Next, the problem of price discrimination will be considered, and then the concept of monopsony and the problem of bilateral bargaining—the case in which a single seller faces a single buyer—will be examined. Cases involving the "intermingling" of conditions of monopoly and competition are treated in the next chapter.

A. MONOPOLY IN THE SHORT AND LONG RUN

Net Revenue Maximization as the Objective

Under monopoly, as under perfect competition, the firm is usually assumed to maximize its net revenue or to minimize its losses. Also,

---

[1] See Fritz Machlup, *The Economics of Seller's Competition* (Baltimore: The Johns Hopkins Press, 1952), p. 545, Notes 1–5, for a collection of such different meanings.

as in the case of perfect competition, the same short-run equilibrium condition applies, namely that $MC = MR$, whether the firm is maximizing its net revenue or minimizing its losses. Finally, as in the case of perfect competition, whether or not the firm will be maximizing its net revenue or minimizing its losses depends upon the relationship between the price of the product and the average cost of production of the given output.

What then is the difference between the two cases? The difference lies not in the equilibrium or profit conditions but in their welfare aspects. Analytically, the difference lies in the different degrees of control over prices held by the sellers in the two situations. In the case of monopoly, the individual seller is assumed to know that by his own actions he does affect the price because the demand curve facing him and the market demand curve are identical, and the market demand curve is not generally infinitely elastic. But in the case of perfect competition, as we have seen, the individual seller is assumed to think that he cannot by his own actions affect the price, and thus the demand curve facing him is depicted as a horizontal line parallel to the X axis and is *not* identical with the market demand curve.

The Monopolist's Demand Curve; Derivation of Marginal Revenue Curve

It has been noted in the preceding chapter that existence of monopoly conditions produces a negatively sloping firm's demand or average revenue curve and a marginal revenue curve which also slopes negatively and lies below the average revenue curve, as in Figure 9–3. As a matter of fact, when the average revenue curve is linear, the slope of the marginal revenue curve is exactly twice as great as that of the average revenue curve. This fact provides an easy way to derive the marginal curve from the average curve.

In Figure 10–1, the total revenue obtained from the sale of OA units at a price of OC is area $OCFA$. Now, if the marginal revenue is defined as the change in total revenue resulting from the sale of each additional unit of output, it follows that the sum of all the marginal revenues produced by the sale of OA units is also equal to total revenue. Therefore, the total revenue obtained from the sale of OA units is also equal to area $ODEA$, or $ODEA = OCFA$ in Figure 10–1. Thus we have $OCFA = OCB'EA + EB'F = ODEA = OCB'EA + CDB'$, and, therefore, the area of triangle CDB' is equal to that of triangle $EB'F$.

Now $DB'E$ has been drawn through the midpoint of CF (which is equal to OA). Thus $CB' = B'F$. Also, angles $DB'C$ and $EB'F$ are equal because they are vertical angles, and angles DCB' and $B'FE$ are both right angles. Thus, triangles CDB' and FEB' are also congruent. Corresponding sides and angles of the triangles are equal. Therefore CD and EF are also equal.

A simple method of drawing the marginal revenue curve, when the

Figure 10–1

RELATIONSHIP BETWEEN MARGINAL AND AVERAGE REVENUE CURVES

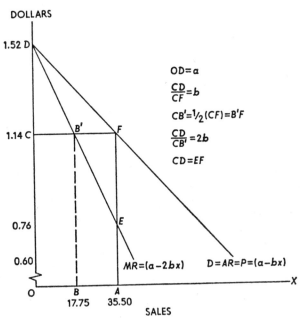

average revenue curve is linear and known, is thus to draw the marginal revenue "curve" from the origin of the average revenue curve, D, through the midpoint of *any* line dropped perpendicularly from the average revenue curve to the Y axis. Thus, if $D = AR = P$ is known, the marginal revenue curve can be drawn from D through the midpoint of CF at B'.

If the average revenue curve is not linear, the marginal revenue curve can still be determined graphically by a modification of the above procedure. However, since only linear average revenue curves are employed in this book, no space will be devoted to developing the method.[2]

That the marginal revenue curve will always lie below the average revenue curve can be seen easily by referring to Equation (9–6) which states the relationship between marginal revenue and price as:

$$MR = (P)\left(1 - \frac{1}{E_d}\right). \tag{9–6}$$

Only if the demand is infinitely elastic will the marginal revenue be equal to price, a point which has been demonstrated at length in the preceding chapter. Moreover, if the demand is inelastic, the marginal revenue will be negative. Although students sometimes seem to have the impression that a monopolist desires the demand for his product to be inelastic, it is clear that this impression is wrong. The misapprehension usually arises from a misapplication of the truth that, if the demand for his product is inelastic, a monopolist can increase his total revenue by raising his price, since in doing so he makes the marginal revenue *less negative* and may even make it positive. An example of a monopolist whose cost of production is zero at all levels of output may help to clarify this point.

Cournot's Case of the Costless Monopoly

Thus, in Figure 10–2 assume that a monopolist is selling a costless product, say water from a mineral spring, involving no cost of production. This example is due to Augustin Cournot (1838), a Frenchman, who was one of the earliest mathematical economists.[3]

The monopolist would be maximizing his total revenue when he was selling output OX at a price of OP, for, at this output, marginal revenue and marginal cost are both zero and hence equal. If he increased his sales further, say to OX', he would reduce his total revenue, for, at this higher level of sales, marginal revenue is negative (the curve lies below the X axis). And since at sales less than OX the marginal revenue is positive, he could increase his total revenue by increasing his sales. Thus $OX = 67.57$ is the equilibrium output, and $OP = \$1.00$ is the

---

[2] Both methods are developed in detail in Joan Robinson, *The Economics of Imperfect Competition* (London: Macmillan & Co., Ltd., 1934), Book V, chap. iv. The marginal revenue curves employed in this book are determined according to the formula $MR = a - 2bx$, while the average revenue curves have the formula $AR = a - bx$. The total revenue curve, from which the other two are derived, has the formula $R = ax - bx^2$. Thus $AR = ax/x - bx^2/x$, while $MR = \partial R/\partial x = a - 2bx$. The values assigned to the Y intercept (a) and to the slope (b) vary with the problem under discussion.

[3] Augustin Cournot, *Researches into the Mathematical Principles of Wealth*, trans. N. Bacon and Irving Fisher (New York: The Macmillan Co., 1897), chap. v.

equilibrium price. Since costs are zero, gross revenue (R) and net revenue (N) are equal, and since net revenue is maximized at output OX, area $OPAX$ is the largest rectangle which can be drawn under the demand curve. Also, since $MR = 0$ at output OX, it follows that $E_d = 1$ at A.

For purposes of comparison, it may be noted that under perfect competition, in the long run, output OX' would be *given away*. For in the

Figure 10–2

COURNOT'S CASE OF A COSTLESS MONOPOLY

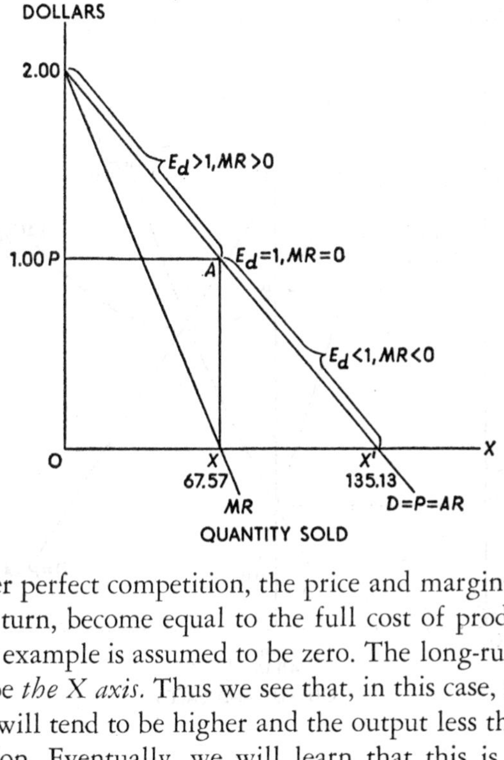

long run under perfect competition, the price and marginal revenue are equal and, in turn, become equal to the full cost of production, which in the present example is assumed to be zero. The long-run $(P = MR)$ curve would be *the X axis*. Thus we see that, in this case, under monopoly, the price will tend to be higher and the output less than under perfect competition. Eventually, we will learn that this is generally the case, a result which implies that, under monopoly, resources are misallocated.

Monopoly with Costs in Short-Run Equilibrium

Figure 10–3 depicts the equilibrium situation of a monopoly having a positive cost of production. The short-run cost curves in Figure 10–3 are identical to those drawn in Figure 9–6, which depicts a competitive firm making a greater than normal profit, and the student may wish to compare the two diagrams at this point.

In Figure 10–3 the monopolist finds himself in short-run equilibrium producing output OX_m (or 45.16 units) at a price of OP (or $1.33) and an average cost of X_mB (or $1.11), since the marginal cost and the marginal revenue are equal to each other ($.66) at E at that level of output and price. The total cost is area $OCBX_m = \$50.13$, and the total revenue is area $OPAX_m = \$60.06$. Area $CPAB = \$9.93$ repre-

Figure 10–3

MONOPOLY WITH COSTS IN SHORT-RUN EQUILIBRIUM POSITION

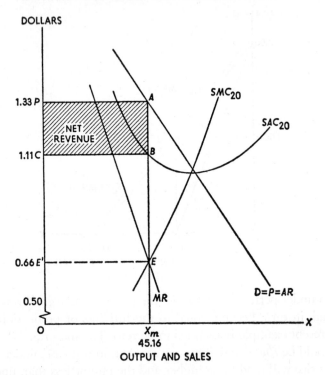

DOLLARS

1.33 P

NET REVENUE

1.11 C

SMC_{20}

SAC_{20}

A

B

0.66 E'

E

MR

0.50

$D=P=AR$

O

X_m
45.16

OUTPUT AND SALES

X

sents a greater than normal profit, or the amount of positive net revenue, $N = R - T = \$60.06 - \$50.13 = \$9.93$.

Under monopoly it is possible to make a greater than normal profit at an output greater than, equal to, or less than that of economic capacity, but under perfect competition it is possible to make a greater than normal profit *only* in the short run and at greater than capacity level outputs. This difference arises out of the fact that under perfect competition the $MR = P$ curve is a horizontal line parallel to the output axis, while under monopoly $MR < P$; and in the latter case both the MR and the $D = AR = P$ curves slope down and to the right.

That is, the general short-run equilibrium condition under monopoly is the same (except that the ↑ is omitted from MC) as it is under perfect competition, or

$$MC = MR \; ;$$

but, in the case of monopoly, since the demand curve facing the monopolist *is not infinitely elastic,* it is also true that the marginal revenue is less than the price, or

$$MR < P \; .$$

The profit condition, that is, the relation between the price and the average cost of the output (AC), determines the per unit amount of profit under monopoly, just as it does under perfect competition. In the short run, the monopolist will not produce if the *price* falls below the average *variable* cost. And he will minimize his losses if he produces when the *price* is greater than average *variable* cost, even if the price is less than average cost. Note, however, that this last statement does *not* say that the monopolist will not produce if the *marginal revenue* is less than the average variable cost. In the case of monopoly, $MR < P$, and it is to the relation between price (P) and average *variable* cost (AVC) that one must look to determine the answer. The definition of the short-run supply curve under perfect competition (as that portion of the short-run marginal cost curve beyond the point of its intersection with the average variable cost curve) is based on the fact that in that case $MR = P$. Thus, the same definition of short-run supply does not apply in the case of monopoly.

In the case of monopoly (and, indeed, in the case of any negatively sloped marginal revenue curve, including the cases of oligopoly and monopolistic competition discussed in the next chapter), it is possible for an equilibrium position to be attained even though the marginal cost curve is falling, provided only that the marginal cost is falling less rapidly than the marginal revenue is falling. That is to say, for an equilibrium position to be attained, it is necessary for the marginal cost to be greater than the marginal revenue at levels of output greater than the equilibrium level and for the marginal cost to be less than the marginal revenue at levels of output less than the equilibrium level. This condition insures that the marginal *net* revenue, or marginal pure profit, will be positive at outputs less than the equilibrium level and that it will be negative at outputs greater than the equilibrium level.

Such a case is illustrated in Figure 10–4. Since the marginal cost curve lies above the marginal revenue curve to the right of E and lies below the marginal revenue curve to the left of E, an equilibrium position exists at E, even though the marginal cost is falling at E.

Similarly, if the marginal cost were constant, since the marginal revenue curve would cut the marginal cost curve from above, it follows that a determinate equilibrium position exists in this case also. Thus, in the case of constant costs produced by a linearly homogeneous production function and constant input prices (see the discussion of Figure 9–10 in the preceding chapter), a determinate equilibrium

Figure 10–4

MONOPOLY IN EQUILIBRIUM WITH FALLING MARGINAL COST CURVE

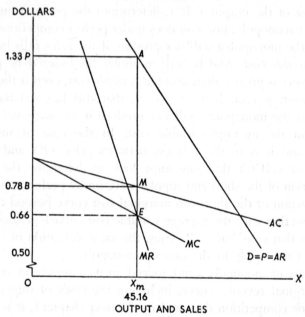

position exists under monopoly, while equilibrium is indeterminate under these cost conditions when competition is perfect.

Monopoly with Costs in Long-Run Equilibrium

In the long run a monopolist is able to change the size of his plant. In such a case, the monopolist would produce at the point at which the marginal revenue would be equal to *both* the short-run and the long-run marginal costs. Since the long-run marginal cost curve intersects each short-run marginal cost curve at one point, but not necessarily at the minimum point of the long-run average cost curve, a monopolist may produce in the long run an output less than that produced at the long-run least cost point and make a greater than normal profit in the process. (See Figure 10–6 for the normal profit case.) Precisely where the monopolist is located on the long-run average cost curve depends on the demand for the product, for the demand is not normally under the control of the monopolist. Indeed, he may even operate for a time at a loss.

Figure 10–5 depicts a special case of a monopolist in long-run equilibrium, producing the same level of output as would be produced in the long run under perfect competition. At B the marginal revenue

Figure 10–5

MONOPOLY PRODUCING AT LONG-RUN OPTIMUM POINT MAKING GREATER THAN NORMAL PROFIT

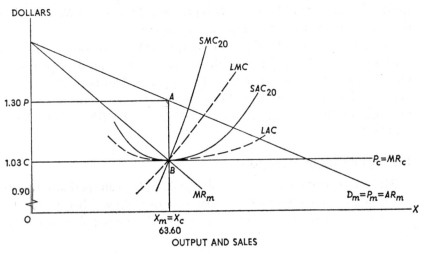

curve intersects both the short-run and the long-run marginal cost curves, which, in turn, intersect their respective short-run and long-run average cost curves at their minimum points. The short-run and long-run average cost curves are also tangent at their minimum points at B, indicating that output $OX_m = 63.60$ units is the optimum long-run output.

As a matter of fact, the cost curves in Figure 10–5 are identical to those which have been used to illustrate the case of the perfectly competitive industry in long-run equilibrium in the case of constant costs in Figure 9–9, although the long-run marginal cost curve has been omitted from the latter diagram. What is required for a monopoly to produce at the point of economic efficiency in the long run is that the demand curve, and therefore the marginal revenue curve, be located in such a way that the latter intersects the short-run and long-run marginal cost curves at the particular point where they intersect each other and at which they also intersect their respective average cost curves. There is, however, no particular reason why all these conditions should be met under monopoly.

Monopoly and Perfect Competition Contrasted

Figure 10–5 serves a double purpose, for it also allows us to contrast the cases of monopoly and perfect competition in long-run equilibrium. Assuming that the cost curves were the same in the two situations, Figure 10–5 discloses that under perfect competition the output $OX_e = 63.60$ units would be produced at a price of $OC = \$1.03$ and that this price would be equal to the average cost, so that only a normal profit would be made. For the line CB represents the curve $MR = P$ when the case is treated as one of perfect competition.

But under monopoly, the same output $OX_m = 63.60$ is sold at a price of $OP = \$1.30$, although the average cost of production is only $OC = \$1.03$. Thus, under monopoly, a greater than normal profit per unit equal to $CP = \$0.27$ is being made. The total net revenue of this monopolist is, of course, $(OPAX_m - OCBX_m = CPAB) = (\$82.68 - \$65.44 = \$17.24)$.

The Social Cost of Monopoly

The fact that monopoly is socially undesirable can, perhaps, best be illustrated by reference to Figure 10–6, which shows that, under monopoly, resources are wasted, even when the monopolist is making only normal profits.

In Figure 10–6, the marginal revenue is equal to both the short-run and the long-run marginal costs at E. Thus the monopolist is in long-run equilibrium, producing output $OX_m = 35.50$ at a price of $OP = \$1.14$. The total revenue is equal to area $OPF'X_m$, and the total cost is also equal to area $OPF'X_m$. Thus the net revenue is zero, and exactly a normal profit is being earned. The fact that a normal profit only is being earned can easily be seen from the fact that the demand curve is *tangent* to the average cost curve at F'. Point F' is also a point of tangency between the long-run average cost curve and the short-run average cost curve SAC_{15} (like point D' on SAC_{12} in Figure 7–7 in Chapter 7). Point B' is the point of economic efficiency, the minimum point on the long-run average cost curve, and lies to the right of F'.

Our diagram thus shows that even though the monopolist is in a position of long-run equilibrium making only a normal profit, output is less ($OX_m = 35.50$) than it would be in the long run under perfect competition (it would be $OB = 63.60$); and the average cost of production is greater ($OP = \$1.14$) under monopoly and the price higher ($OP = \$1.14$) than they would be under perfect competition (where both would be equal to $BB' = \$1.03$).

Figure 10–6

MONOPOLY IN LONG-RUN EQUILIBRIUM MAKING ONLY
NORMAL PROFIT

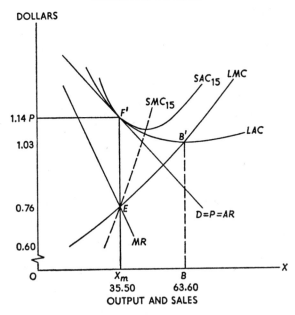

As a matter of fact, because the demand curve facing the monopolist slopes down and to the right, our diagram shows that when a monopolist is making only a normal profit, he must be producing in the stage of increasing *returns to scale* (although he may be producing in the stage of diminishing average or marginal returns to the variable inputs). That is, an increase in the amounts of *both* inputs *a* and *b* would increase output more than proportionately. Alternatively, the monopolist produces in this case under the conditions of increasing long-run and short-run return to outlay and, therefore, under conditions of decreasing long-run and short-run average cost; for an increase in the amount spent on the variable input would reduce average cost along SAC_{15}, while an increase in the amounts spent on *both* inputs would reduce average cost along *LAC*. Thus, according to static analysis, monopoly is socially undesirable. (The argument that monopoly profits are necessary for economic progress is examined in Chapter 18.)

B. PRICE DISCRIMINATION

Definition and Conditions of Price Discrimination

Price discrimination can be defined as the act of selling identical products to different buyers at different prices. In order for price discrimination to be effective, there must be some basis for classifying purchasers, commodities, markets, or sales. Moreover, it must not be possible for purchasers themselves to resell the products to other persons who would otherwise purchase from the original seller. For, if this action were possible, those purchasing at lower prices could resell at discounts to those who would normally be forced to purchase from the original seller at higher prices. Finally, it is clear that the ability to discriminate implies some degree of control over the market, either by a seller who voluntarily gives, or by a purchaser who coerces a seller into giving, a lower price.

A Method of Separating Markets

An interesting example of the importance of the condition that markets must be separate if price discrimination is to succeed has been provided by Professor Corwin Edwards in his study of international cartels for a United States Senate Subcommittee. According to the study, an international chemical cartel agreement existed in 1941 relative to acrylic products, including methyl methacrylate powders used in making dentures. Prices of the moulding powder in the United States were fixed by the cartel in the following way: methyl methacrylate powders were sold to commercial moulders at a basic price of eighty-five cents a pound, but a price of forty-five dollars a pound was charged for the same product when sold to dental laboratories and dentists.[4] Some of the purchasers of dental supplies, however, soon discovered that they could obtain the methyl methacrylate for dentures by purchasing it as a commercial moulding powder. The cartel thereupon undertook to consider the problem of preventing such "bootlegging purchases." An interesting method, although there is no evi-

---

[4] *Economic and Political Aspects of International Cartels* (A Study Made for the Subcommittee on War Mobilization of the Committee on Military Affairs of the United States Senate, Monograph No. 1, 78th. Cong., 2d. sess.) (Washington, D.C.: U.S. Government Printing Office, 1944), p. 13 and pp. 18–19. (Numerous other instances of impairment of quality are also cited in this study; see esp. pp. 15–19. The study was an analysis of materials in the files of the Antitrust Division of the Department of Justice.)

dence that it was ever actually put into operation, was proposed in a letter from one of the cartel members to another. The letter read in part as follows:

> Our discussion of the Pure Food and Drug Law and pulling acrylic dentures under it leads me to wonder if the manufacturers of the commercial moulding powders might not add an ingredient which would not affect the moulding properties, but which would disqualify it under the act. Naturally it would be omitted from the strictly denture powder. . . .
>
> Under the very finicky regulations of the above act, however, it may be the slightest trace of the right agent, too little to constitute harm to moulding (or health either as a matter of fact) would suffice to have bootleg products in bad.
>
> A millionth of one percent of arsenic or lead might cause them to confiscate every bootleg unit in the country. There ought to be a trace of something that would make them rear up.[5]

The reply, on the following day, from the cartel participant to whom the proposal was addressed, indicated that it was taken quite seriously:

> . . . We agree with you that if we could put some ingredient in our commercial moulding material which would disqualify it under the Pure Food and Drug Act, this would make a very fine method of controlling the bootleg situation. We shall take this matter up with our development department and advise you whether any such material could be used.[6]

The rationalization of monopoly profits as a source of funds for research and economic development minimizes, if indeed it does not ignore, this aspect of the matter.

Justifiable Discrimination: The Public Utility Case

In some situations, for example in cases of public utilities, *where large fixed facilities are already in existence and would otherwise go unemployed except for the practice of price discrimination,* a case can be made for this type of pricing policy. Railroad rates are an example. In the instance of railroad rates, it is usually argued that discrimination in favor of a low-rated commodity works no hardship and may be beneficial to the society as a whole, provided: (1) that the low-rated commodity will not move at a higher rate; (2) that the rate charged to the low-rated commodity is high enough to cover the variable costs and make some contribution toward covering the fixed charges; and (3) that the rate on the higher rated commodities is not increased as a result of the discrimination. This argument, of course, is analogous to the argument that a firm will minimize its losses even if $P < AC$ when

---

[5] *Ibid.*, pp. 18–19.
[6] *Ibid.*, p. 19.

$MC\uparrow = MR$, provided that the price is high enough to cover the average variable cost, a point which has already been discussed in detail in the preceding chapter. This question will be considered further in Chapter 16 later.

A Case of Two Market Price Discrimination

Assume that there is a monopolist producing a given output from a given total expenditure on inputs to be sold in two different markets which meet the conditions for price discrimination. In which market will the price be higher? The answer to this question can be found rather easily by making use of the equilibrium conditions and the equation stating the relationship between the marginal revenue and price, or Equation (9–6).

First, consider the fact that if the firm is to maximize profits or minimize losses, it must make the *marginal cost of the total output sold in both markets equal to the marginal revenue in each of the two markets.* That is, it is necessary that

$$MC = MR_1 = MR_2 , \tag{10-1}$$

where MR_1 is the marginal revenue in the first market, MR_2 is the marginal revenue in the second market, and MC is the marginal cost of the *total output* sold in both markets.

Next, by substituting the formula [Equation (9–6)] stating the relationship between the marginal revenue and price into Equation (10–1), we have

$$MC = MR_1 = (P_1)\left(1 - \frac{1}{E_{d_1}}\right) = MR_2 = (P_2)\left(1 - \frac{1}{E_{d_2}}\right). \tag{10-2}$$

From the preceding equation, *it follows that the price will be higher in the market having the less elastic demand.* To illustrate this point, assume that the elasticity of demand in the first market is 10, or $E_{d_1} = 10$, and that in the second market it is $E_{d_2} = 5$. Substituting these values into Equation (10–2) above, we have

$$MC = MR_1 = .9P_1 = MR_2 = .8P_2 . \tag{10-2a}$$

Since the marginal revenues in the two markets are equal to each other (as well as to the common marginal cost of the total output), it follows that the price is higher in the second market, where the demand is less elastic.[7] For, if the marginal revenue and the marginal

---

[7] For a graphical explanation of this case, see M. M. Bober, *Intermediate Price and Income Theory* (New York: W. W. Norton & Co., Inc., 1955), pp. 214–17.

cost were equal at, say, 9, we would have in the case of the first market $.9P_1 = 9$, $P_1 = 10$; and in the case of the second market we would have $.8P_2 = 9$, $P_2 = 11.25$. Thus the price is higher in the second market where the demand is less elastic. (*Note:* In neither case is the demand inelastic, for in such a case the marginal revenue would be negative!)

It is beyond the scope of this book to undertake an extended discussion of price discrimination. One of the earliest and perhaps still most instructive treatments of price discrimination appears in Alfred Marshall's *Industry and Trade.*[8] An extensive treatment of the topic of price discrimination can also be found in Joan Robinson's *The Economics of Imperfect Competition.*[9]

C. MONOPSONY

Monopsony Defined

Monopsony can be formally defined as the case of a single buyer who is not in competition with any other buyers for the output which he seeks to purchase, and as a situation in which entry into the market by other buyers is impossible. Often the discussion of monopsony is carried on in conjunction with the problem of factor pricing, and we will encounter the question of monopsony again in Part V of this book.

In general, the analysis of monopsony is analogous to the analysis of monopoly. That is, in the case of monopoly we recognize that the monopolist does know that he influences the price of the product by the amount he offers for sale; and in the case of monopsony, or of a single buyer, we recognize that the buyer influences the supply price of his purchases by the amount he buys. Also, the supply curve of the industry from which he buys is his average cost curve, and his marginal cost is greater than his average cost.

A Monopsonist Selling in a Perfectly Competitive Market

Thus, in Figure 10-7, the curve $AC_B = S_S$ represents the supply curve of the selling industry from which the monopsonist buys and is also his average cost curve. (The subscript B indicates the function of

---

[8] Alfred Marshall, *Industry and Trade* (London: Macmillan & Co., Ltd., 1919), esp. Book III. See also my article, "A Curious Case of Neglect: Marshall's *Industry and Trade,*" *The Canadian Journal of Economics and Political Science,* Vol. XXI (August, 1955), pp. 339–53, esp. pp. 343–48, where I have shown the extent to which Marshall's treatment anticipates that of Mrs. Robinson.

[9] Joan Robinson, *The Economics of Imperfect Competition* (London: Macmillan & Co., Ltd., 1934), Book V.

a buyer; the subscript S indicates the function of a seller.) Assume that the supplying industry is perfectly competitive. Then the industry supply curve is nothing other than the horizontal sum of the relevant portions of the marginal cost curves of the firms in a perfectly competitive industry as explained in the preceding chapter.

The curve MC_B in Figure 10–7 represents the cost of additional purchases to the monopsonist (buyer). For, since the industry supply curve slopes up and to the right, and since this curve *is* the monopsonist's average cost curve, it follows that the marginal cost to the

Figure 10–7

MONOPSONY IN BUYING; PERFECT
COMPETITION IN SELLING

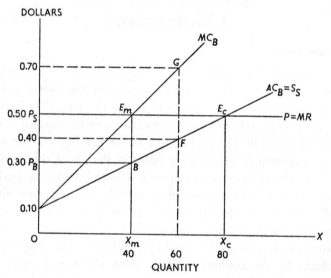

monopsonist must be greater than his average cost, according to the explanation of the average-marginal relationship given in Chapter 3. That is, the monopsonist must pay an ever higher price for additional units of the product. Thus, by increasing his purchases, since he pays the higher price for *each* of the units which he purchases, he increases his total cost *not merely* by the cost of each additional unit purchased, *but* by this cost *plus* the sum of the additions to the cost of each of the previous units purchased.

For example, in the case of Figure 10–7, the monopsonist may purchase 40 units at a price of $.30 each, and his total cost will be $12. But if he increases his purchases to 60 units, the price increases to $.40 per unit at F, and his total cost is $24. The increase in his total cost is thus $24 - 12 = 12$. When he is purchasing 60 units, the marginal cost is \$.70 at G. Thus the marginal cost is greater than the price to him or than his average cost of \$.40. The additional $60 - 40 = 20$ units purchased have a total cost of $(20)(\$.40) = \$8.00$, and this amount is less than the increase in total cost of \$12 by \$4.00. However, the previously purchased 40 units now each cost the monopsonist \$.10 more, or a total of \$4.00 more. And it is this increased cost of the previously purchased units which accounts for the difference between the marginal cost and the average cost. Thus, MC_B lies above AC_B.

Since we are assuming that the monopsonist sells in a perfectly competitive market $(P = MR)$, the usual analysis of a seller who sells in a perfectly competitive market already explained in the preceding chapter also applies here. Thus the monopsonist is in equilibrium, maximizing his profits at E_m where his marginal cost and his marginal revenue are equal. However, even though he is selling in a perfectly competitive market, he is making a greater than normal profit (or enjoying an economic surplus) equal to BE_m per unit, for he sells output $OX_m = 40$ at a price of $OP_S = \$.50$ but purchases his goods at a price of $OP_B = \$.30$. Accordingly, he enjoys a surplus equal to $BE_m = \$.20$ per unit. If there were perfect competition in buying, as there is in selling, in the long run the quantity $OX_c = 80$ units would be sold at the same price, and the economic rent or greater than normal profits would disappear. Since $OX_m < OX_c$, monopsony results in the underemployment of productive inputs in the industry from which the monopsonist purchases.

The Case of a Monopsonist Who Is Also a Monopolist

Figure 10–8 contains the same monopsony marginal and average cost curves as are depicted in Figure 10–7. However, in Figure 10–8, it is assumed that the monopsonist is also a monopolist in the resale of the product. Thus, the condition $P = MR$ no longer holds and, instead, we have $P > MR$. The curve $AR_S = P_B$ represents the demand curve facing the monopsonist-monopolist in the market in which he sells; thus it is his average revenue curve. The curve $D_B = MR_S$ represents the marginal revenue curve associated with the average revenue curve.

As usual, the equilibrium position is found by locating the intersection at E of the curve of the marginal cost to the monopsonist (MC_B) and the curve of his marginal revenue. When the same amount is sold by a monopsonist-monopolist as was sold by the monopsonist-competitor, the price is higher than before. Thus the quantity $OX_m = 40$ is now sold at a price of $OP_S = \$.60$, although its average cost is $OP_B = \$.30$ as before. The economic rent, or greater than normal profit, now amounts to $BE' = \$.30$ on a per unit basis. Of this amount, $BE = \$.20$ results from the monopsonist's activities in the purchase of his products, while the remainder, $EE' = \$.10$, is the result of his monopolistic position in the resale market.

Thus the monopsonist-monopolist finds that his profits are swelled, *both* (1) by virtue of his position as the single seller in the resale

Figure 10–8

MONOPOLY AND MONOPSONY COMBINED

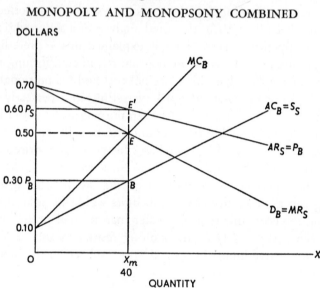

market *and* (2) by virtue of his position as the sole purchaser in the market of original sale. In Part V, we will consider cases involving monopsony in the market for factors of production.

D. BILATERAL BARGAINING

Definition of Bilateral Bargaining

Bilateral bargaining is the term applied to denote the case in which a monopolist in the sale of products faces a monopsonist in the purchase of products. That is, in this case, a single seller faces a single buyer. An understanding of the basic logical principles involved in this extreme case will be useful in the next chapter and in the section on income distribution later, where cases involving the "intermingling" of monopoly and competitive conditions are considered.

In Bilateral Bargaining the Outcome Is Indeterminate

In Figure 10–9, the curve $MC_S = AC_B$ represents the curve of the marginal cost of a selling monopolist, and thus it also represents the curve of average cost to a buying monopsonist, or the prices which must be paid by the buying monopsonist for the various amounts he can buy for resale from the selling monopolist.

Figure 10–9

ILLUSTRATION OF BILATERAL BARGAINING

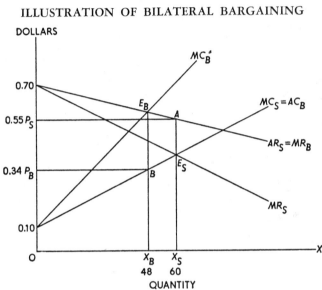

The curve $AR_S = MR_B$ represents the marginal revenue from resale curve of the buying monopsonist, and thus it also represents the demand curve facing the selling monopolist, or his average revenue curve. (The buying monopsonist does not *resell* under perfect competition.)

The curve MR_S represents the marginal revenue curve of the selling monopolist. Thus, at E_S, where the MC_S and the MR_S curves intersect, the selling monopolist would be maximizing his net revenue. Accordingly, he would have the objective of attempting to sell output OX_S at a price of $OP_S = X_SA$.

Finally, the curve MC_B represents the curve of the marginal cost of purchases to the buying monopsonist. Thus at E_B, where the MR_B and MC_B curves intersect, the buying monopsonist would be maximizing his net revenue from resale. Accordingly, he would have the objective of attempting to purchase the quantity OX_B at a price of $OP_B = X_B B$. Note that $OP_B < OP_S$. Thus the outcome is indeterminate because the buyer's price is below the seller's price.

A Real World Example of Bilateral Bargaining

An interesting and instructive example of bilateral bargaining between an oligopolistic supplier and oligopsonistic buyers (for resale) is found in the case of *Standard Oil Co.* v. *Federal Trade Commission*.[10] This case involved an action by the *FTC* under the price discrimination section of the Robinson-Patman Act. According to the Supreme Court, the *FTC* had made a finding of fact in this case that the oil company (petitioner) had

> . . . sold its Red Crown gasoline to its "jobber" customers at tank-car prices. Those prices have been $1\frac{1}{2}\not{c}$ per gallon less than its tank-wagon prices to service station customers for identical gasoline in the same area. In practice the service stations have resold the gasoline at the prevailing retail service station prices. Each of the petitioner's so-called "jobber" customers has been free to resell its gasoline at retail or wholesale. Each, at some time, has sold some of it at retail. One now sells it only at retail. The others now resell it largely at wholesale. As to resale prices, two of the "jobbers" have resold their gasoline only at the prevailing wholesale or retail prices. The other two, however, have reflected, in varying degrees, petitioner's reductions in the cost of the gasoline to them by reducing their retail prices of that gasoline below the prevailing rates. The effect of these reductions has thus reached competing retail service stations in part through retail stations operated by the "jobbers" and in part through retail stations which purchased gasoline from the "jobbers" at less than the prevailing tank-wagon prices.[11]

The defendant argued in this case that the price discriminations had been granted "to meet the equally low price of competitors" in the area and that, under the relevant section of the statute, such a defense was a complete defense, *irrespective of the effect on competition of the price discrimination.* The Supreme Court sustained this view, thereby validating oligopolistic price discriminations given under the indicated conditions as a method of doing business, as well as bilateral bargaining as a system of pricing. The "jobber" buyers in the case each possessed sufficient storage facilities to be able to take delivery of gasoline from the seller in amounts up to ten times those which could be handled by the regular service stations. The Court recognized the existence of possible cost savings to the seller resulting from this fact, but, in making its decision, proceeded "on the assumption" that such

---

[10] 340 U.S. 231, 71 S. Ct. 240.

[11] *Ibid.*

cost savings did "not entirely account" for the more favorable prices given to jobbers. The Court apparently failed to recognize the fact that the defendant could have met competition from other gasoline suppliers in the area by reducing prices equally to all of its purchasers, *without discriminating among them!*[12]

Meaning of Indeterminacy

The problem of what output will be sold at what price cannot be solved with the limited data assumed in Figure 10–9. That is, the solution to the problem is *indeterminate.* Many economists argue that what this word means is that either more assumptions or more data are needed before the problem can be solved, not that it cannot be solved if they can be obtained. However, if the economic entities whose behavior is being analyzed or explained by a given theory are so few in number that no regular behavior pattern can be assumed as a basis for additional assumptions, it is extremely difficult to develop a general theory to fit the case. A few writers have tried, and some have tried to avoid the implications of the term "indeterminacy" in this context, but none has really been successful.[13] In the absence of regular behavior patterns and in the absence of facts, as economic theorists, we are apparently forced to adopt a procedure of classification and description of all the hypothetical possibilities rather than one of explaining actual situations. The question of the extent to which this condition also exists in attempts to explain actions of the firm under conditions in which monopolistic and competitive elements are "intermingled" will be treated next in the following chapter.

SELECTED READINGS

HICKS, J. R. "Annual Survey of Economic Theory: The Theory of Monopoly," *Econometrica,* Vol. III (1935), pp. 1–20. Reprinted in *Readings in Price Theory* (eds. KENNETH BOULDING AND GEORGE STIGLER), pp. 361–83. Homewood, Ill.: Richard D. Irwin, Inc., 1952.

MACHLUP, FRITZ. *The Economics of Sellers' Competition.* Baltimore: The Johns Hopkins Press, 1952.

MARSHALL, ALFRED. *Industry and Trade.* London: Macmillan & Co., Ltd., 1919.

---

[12] For another interesting case involving the questions of oligopsony and bargaining, see *Automatic Canteen Co.* v. *Federal Trade Commission,* 346 U.S. 61, 73 S. Ct. 1017, especially the dissenting opinion of Justice William O. Douglas.

[13] See, for example, William J. Fellner, *Competition Among the Few* (New York: Alfred A. Knopf, Inc., 1949), p. 14; George J. Stigler, *The Theory of Price* (New York: The Macmillan Co., 1946), p. 266; and Joe S. Bain, *Price Theory* (New York: Henry Holt & Co., Inc., 1952), pp. 190–436.

ROBINSON, JOAN. *The Economics of Imperfect Competition,* Book V. London: Macmillan & Co., Ltd., 1934.

U.S. SENATE SUBCOMMITTEE ON MONOPOLY, COMMITTEE ON THE JUDICIARY. *Bigness and Concentration of Economic Power—A Case Study of General Motors Corporation.* Staff Report. Washington, D.C.: U.S. Government Printing Office, 1956.

WEISS, LEONARD W. *Economics and American Industry,* chap. v. New York: John Wiley & Sons, Inc., 1962.

WILCOX, C. *Competition and Monopoly in American Industry.* Temporary National Economic Committee Monograph No. 21. Washington, D.C.: U.S. Government Printing Office, 1941.

11 Conditions of Monopoly and Competition "Intermingled"

Introduction

It has been emphasized in the preceding chapters that the two limiting cases of perfect competition and "pure" monopoly do not describe real world situations. In between these two extreme cases lie the cases of the real world. Static analysis of the latter requires recognition of the fact that conditions of monopoly and competition are in fact "intermingled." In general, such an analysis usually involves relaxing one or another of the conditions of perfect competition or of pure monopoly (depending on which end of the spectrum is chosen for a point of departure) and introducing some of the conditions from the other extreme into the problem. Thus, by assuming that conditions of monopoly and competition are "intermingled" in the product market, that is, by assuming that the demand curves facing individual firms are less than infinitely elastic (for reasons to be given shortly), it is thought that a more realistic analysis of the firm can be made.

In this chapter we will consider problems involving such conditions and also the question of whether or not the simple profit maximization motive assumed in the preceding chapters is realistic. In addition, some empirical studies of the behavior of firms in the real world will be briefly summarized.

A. BASIC CONCEPTS AND HISTORICAL BACKGROUND

Definitions of "Product Differentiation" and "Selling Costs"

The term *"product differentiation" is defined as the existence of a preference, real or fancied, in the mind of the buyer for the product of a given seller.* Thus, by assuming that products are differentiated (e.g., that buyers may prefer one *brand* of toothpaste or one *make* of automobile over another at given prices or within given ranges of prices), the analyst abandons the assumption that products are homogeneous, one of the basic conditions of perfect competition.

Selling costs are defined as those costs which are incurred in order to sell the product and must be distinguished from the costs of production of the product. Any form of advertising, of which the sole purpose is to switch the buyer's taste from one brand to another rather than merely to inform him, is, of course, one type of selling cost. Premium and bonus stamp schemes are another.

Classification of the Conditions of Competition

It is conventional to categorize or classify firms according to the nature of the competitive conditions under which they operate. And, although different writers have suggested that various kinds of terminologies be employed in such classifications,[1] the one presented below is the one most generally used. Thus, firms are usually classified as being within one of the following categories:

    I. Monopoly—single seller.

    II. Duopoly—two sellers.

    III. Oligopoly—more than two sellers, but not a large number.

        A. Undifferentiated Oligopoly—a few sellers selling perfectly homogeneous commodities (e.g., raw material producers; products such as sulphur, crude oil, copper, and other minerals).

        B. Differentiated Oligopoly—a few sellers selling nonhomogeneous or differentiated products (e.g., the automobile industry).

    IV. Monopolistic Competition—this term originally meant "conditions under which competition and monopoly are intermingled." Today it has come to mean the case of numerous sellers selling nonhomogeneous or differentiated products (e.g., the case of gasoline service stations).

    V. Perfect Competition—see page 217.

The outline can be expanded by explicitly noting the existence or lack of freedom of entry in categories II–IV inclusive. Moreover, a similar outline can be made to cover the cases of the single buyer (monopsony), of two buyers (duopsony), and of several buyers (oligopsony).

The Concept of an Industry: Meaningful or Not?

When products are highly differentiated, it is no longer possible to speak unambiguously in every case of the "industry" or of the "supply

---

[1] See, for example, Robert Triffin, *Monopolistic Competition and General Equilibrium Theory* (Cambridge: Harvard University Press, 1940); and Fritz Machlup, *The Economics of Sellers' Competition* (Baltimore: The Johns Hopkins Press, 1952), esp. pp. 79–132.

of an industry." In such a case, as in the case of monopoly, the line of demarcation between the single firm and the industry becomes fuzzy.

In some contexts, for example, the term "supply of automobiles" may be inappropriate because the supply curves of Ford, Chevrolet, Plymouth, and Rambler automobiles cannot be summed horizontally for the purposes of the analysis at hand, since these products are differentiated. In other contexts, however, an aggregation of such quantities may be meaningful. Moreover, for some analytical purposes it may be convenient to treat the producers of a number of *related* differentiated products (which are substitutable only within certain price ranges) as belonging to a "group." This procedure has sometimes been followed in the literature, and an example of its use is given later.

Brief Historical Sketch of the Development of the Analysis

Augustin Cournot (1838), the French mathematical economist, was among the first economists to analyze the effect of changing the number of sellers assumed in the theory of the firm.[2] Cournot began with the case of a monopolist selling water from a mineral spring (which has already been explained in the preceding chapter) and then considered the case of duopoly and the effect of further increases in the number of sellers. His duopoly case will be explained below.

Some contemporary writers attribute the introduction of the additional variables of selling costs and product differentiation to the publication of Professor Chamberlin's *The Theory of Monopolistic Competition,* which grew out of his Ph.D. thesis at Harvard in 1927.[3] But these variables and the fact that, in the real world, neither conditions of perfect competition nor those of (pure) monopoly prevail had already been recognized by Marshall in 1919.[4]

What Marshall did not do, however, was to provide a neat logical or graphical presentation in which these additional variables were incorporated into the theory of the firm. It remained for Professor Chamberlin to do so, and the analysis which follows later rests heavily on his pioneering work in this field.

In England, largely as a result of arguments aired between 1922

---

[2] Augustin Cournot, *Researches into the Mathematical Principles of Wealth,* trans. N. Bacon and Irving Fisher (New York: The Macmillan Co., 1897), esp. chap. vii.

[3] Edward H. Chamberlin, *The Theory of Monopolistic Competition* (7th ed.; Cambridge: Harvard University Press, 1956). See also his "The Origin and Early Development of Monopolistic Competition Theory," *Quarterly Journal of Economics,* Vol. LXXV (November, 1961), pp. 515–43.

[4] For a detailed documented support of this statement, see my article, "Marshall's *Industry and Trade:* A Curious Case of Neglect," *Canadian Journal of Economics and Political Science,* Vol. XXI (August, 1955), pp. 339–53.

and 1930 in the *Economic Journal* (the official journal of the Royal Economic Society), an analysis which employs nearly the same dia-grammatical apparatus and quantitative concepts as does Professor Chamberlin's work was published in 1934 by Mrs. Joan Robinson.[5] She had been greatly assisted in her work by Mr. R. F. Kahn. The articles in the *Economic Journal* had been concerned with the problem of the establishment of competitive long-run equilibrium under condi-tions of increasing return. As early as 1926, Professor Piero Sraffa had published an article suggesting that the time had come "to abandon the path of free competition and turn in the opposite direction, namely, towards monopoly" in an attempt to provide a more realistic theory of the firm.[6] The English version of the theory of the firm when condi-tions of competition and monopoly are intermingled was thus de-veloped by former students of Marshall and their students, while the initial American version was the work of one man.

Chamberlin's treatment of the problem pays far more attention to the variables of product differentiation and selling costs than does Mrs. Robinson's treatment; and, indeed, since Marshall also became interested in the problem while examining the problems of pricing in the railway industry, Chamberlin's treatment is much closer both in origin and in spirit to that of Marshall than is that of Mrs. Robinson. Chamberlin has himself described his work as a "reorientation" of the theory of value, while British writers have, for the most part, thought of their work primarily as an extension of the neoclassical "kit of tools." There is, in fact, a philosophical difference between these two approaches.

Although the reformulation of the static theory of the firm in the manner indicated above was greeted in the 1930's as a revolution, to-day many writers are dissatisfied with the fact that little progress has been made in developing a dynamic theory of the firm, and others are dissatisfied with its failure to provide any really significant insights into the behavior of large firms or into their price policies. On the whole, the progress which has been made since the publication of Professor Chamberlin's and Mrs. Robinson's books has consisted largely of re-fining concepts, of further classifying situations, and of providing new names for the basic categories which Chamberlin identified. It is to

---

[5] Joan Robinson, *The Economics of Imperfect Competition* (London: Macmillan & Co., Ltd., 1934).

[6] Piero Sraffa, "The Laws of Returns," *Economic Journal,* Vol. XXXVI (December, 1926), pp. 535–45, at p. 542. See also Peter Newman, "The Erosion of Marshall's Theory of Value," *Quarterly Journal of Economics,* Vol. LXXIV (November, 1960), pp. 587–601.

analyses involving these categories that our attention will be turned next.

B. DUOPOLY

Cournot's Solution to the Problem

Duopoly has already been defined as the case of two sellers. Cournot dealt with the duopoly problem by assuming that each of the sellers sold a costless homogeneous commodity (water from a mineral spring)

Figure 11–1

COURNOT'S SOLUTION TO THE DUOPOLY PROBLEM

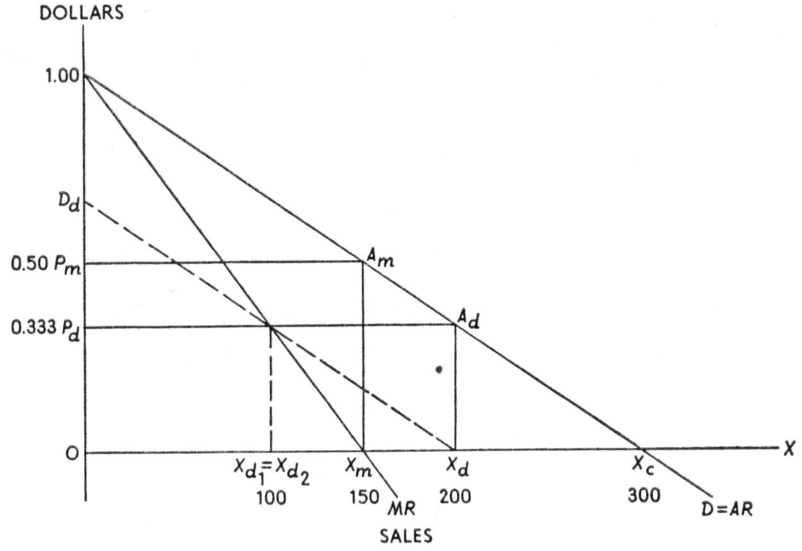

which was available to him in unlimited supply, and that each sought to maximize his net revenue according to an assumption that his rival would not change the *quantity* the latter was currently offering for sale. Thus, Cournot's model involved a *conjectural variation* set equal to zero. This term is used to designate the extent to which one seller takes into account the effects of his own actions upon his rival's actions.

Cournot's case is represented graphically in Figure 11–1, which, like Figure 10–2, can be used to analyze the case of a costless monopolist. In Figure 11–1 the monopoly price would be $OP_m = \$.50$, and the monopoly output would be $OX_m = 150$, since the marginal net revenue is zero at that output. (Recall that in this case $MNR = MR$.) Moreover, since there are no costs of production, in the long run the perfectly competitive price would be zero, and output $OX_c =$ 300 would be *given* away. Note also that in Figure 11–1, the rectangle, $OP_mA_mX_m$, is, as before, the largest rectangle which can be inscribed under the demand curve.

Cournot then assumed that a second seller entered into the market and that his sales encroached upon the sales of the first. The second seller maximized his net revenue according to an assumption that the first would continue to sell quantity OX_m.

But this assumption was wrong, for the first seller changed his sales to maximize his net revenue in the new situation by assuming that the second seller would continue his current sales unchanged. In turn, the second reacted to this new situation by again changing his sales and maximizing his net revenue, again assuming that the first seller would keep his sales unchanged at the new level, and so on.

The ultimate equilibrium position would be reached, according to Cournot, when the amount offered by both sellers was equal to $n/(n + 1)$ times the competitive output, where n is the number of sellers. This formula can be applied to the case of any number of sellers. In the case of two sellers, the amount offered for sale by them together in equilibrium would be $2/(2 + 1) = \frac{2}{3}$ of the competitive output, or $OX_d = (\frac{2}{3})(OX_c) = (\frac{2}{3})(300) = 200$; and the amount offered by each of the sellers individually would be half this amount $(OX_{d_1} = OX_{d_2} = OX_c/3 = 100)$, or one third of the competitive output. Thus the total supply in the final equilibrium position would be $OX_d = 200$ in Figure 11–1. The profit made by the two sellers together would be area $OP_dA_dX_d$, for the price would be OP_d. The duopolists' demand curves would be identical and parallel to the total demand curve in Figure 11–1. That is, *each* duopolist's demand curve would be the same as D_dX_d.

Cournot's formula, $n/(n + 1)$ times the competitive output, shows clearly that as the number of sellers increases (or as n increases), the competitive situation is approached, while as the number of sellers decreases, the monopolistic situation is approached. Thus, in the case of monopoly in Figure 11–1, we have the monopoly output as $[n/(n + 1)][OX_c] = OX_m = (\frac{1}{2})(300) = 150$, and Figure 10–2 can be similarly explained. The introduction of cost curves does not change the solution to the problem.[7]

---

[7] For a further discussion of this case, see Chamberlin, *The Theory of Monopolistic Competition*, chap. iii; for a numerical illustration, see Machlup, *op. cit.*, chap. xii; and for a different graphical depiction, see J. K. Eastham, *Graphical Economics* (Chicago: Quadrangle Books, Inc., 1960), chap. viii.

Bertrand and Edgeworth

In 1883 another Frenchman, Joseph Bertrand, believing that he was criticizing Cournot's model, actually produced a different model based on different assumptions.[8]

In Bertrand's model, the competitors were assumed each to believe that the other would maintain his *price* constant, irrespective of the action taken by his rival. Each was also assumed to have an unlimited output. Under these circumstances, Bertrand argued, the competitive price would be charged and the competitive output would be produced, for the rivals would simply engage in a price war until the competitive equilibrium position had been attained. That is, if one of the rivals cut his price, believing that the other would not follow this price cut, as soon as the second seller did cut his price the first would lose sales. Thus, the first would, in turn, undercut the second, and so on. Bertrand, too, assumed a zero conjectural variation.

F. Y. Edgeworth, the English mathematical economist,[9] changed Bertrand's assumption concerning the unlimited supply available to each seller and assumed that the output of each would be limited in such a way as to make it impossible for either seller to satisfy the entire demand at lower price levels. Thus, a lower limit was fixed below which the price would not fall. The result, according to Edgeworth's model, was a price fluctuating between the monopoly price and the lower limit. In this case also the conjectural variation is zero.

Criticisms of the Duopoly Models

The assumption of a zero conjectural variation has been criticized as unrealistic by many writers.[10] However, Professor William Baumol has taken the position that oligopolistic interdependence plays only a small role in "day-to-day decision-making."[11] His view was anticipated in a study dealing with bureaucracy in large corporations which was made for the Temporary National Economic Committee in 1941. The authors commented:

A second consequence of machine technology and corporate finance is the very complexity of giant organizations. The vaster they become, the more diffi-

---

[8] For a further discussion, see Machlup, *op. cit.*, chap. xii.

[9] F. Y. Edgeworth, *Papers Relating to Political Economy* (3 vols.; London: Macmillan & Co., Ltd., 1925), Vol. II.

[10] See, for example, Chamberlin, *The Theory of Monopolistic Competition*, chap. iii.

[11] William J. Baumol, *Business Behavior, Value and Growth* (New York: The Macmillan Co., 1959), chap. iv.

cult are the structural problems of organization, coordination, and control, and the human problems of incentive and leadership. Large corporations like other large human enterprises, are bureaucratic. They tend to live by fixed rules rather than acumen, by the meshing of many component parts rather than the quick decisions of an entrepreneur. Organization grows in importance as size increases and trusteeship gains ascendency. And like other large organisms, the larger the modern corporation becomes, the more it tends to move slowly, to adapt itself with increasing difficulty, be increasingly concerned with its inner rules and procedures. Hence, it stands in danger of losing that flexibility of price adjustment and resiliency of managerial outlook which is the most valuable social asset of free competition.[12]

According to this view, the assumption of a short-run zero conjectural variation would be quite realistic. Whatever may be the facts in the case, it is at least clear that the solutions of the duopoly problem vary, depending on what is assumed. Moreover, duopolists and oligopolists may lack the knowledge on which to base their responses to competitors' actions or be uncertain as to what the competitors' responses to actions will be.

C. OLIGOPOLY

Oligopolistic Indeterminacy; Military Strategy; Feedback

Oligopoly has already been defined as the case of a few sellers. How few is a matter decided by the individual model builder. The number must be small enough so that each seller understands that by his own actions he will influence the price at which he can sell and that he may stimulate his rivals to action also; but, in general, there must be more than two sellers. Thus, the study of oligopoly is merely an extension of the study of duopoly. Product differentiation and selling costs can be included in either analysis.

Indeed, models may be built in which there are oligopolists selling homogeneous products, or in which there are oligopolists operating in a cartel, or in which there are oligopolists selling differentiated products; and, moreover, freedom of entry may or may not be assumed. There are today no models of oligopoly behavior which are accepted as generally applicable, and the results which are derived from the models are as varied as the assumptions on which the models rest.

One analyst has gone so far as to suggest that a study of Clausewitz's

---

[12] Marshall E. Dimock and Howard K. Hyde, *Bureaucracy and Trusteeship in Large Corporations* (Temporary National Economic Committee, Monograph No. 11) (Washington, D.C.: U.S. Government Printing Office, 1940), pp. 3–4.

Principles of War would provide many "striking parallels between military and business strategy," as well as a general theory applicable to the oligopoly problem.[13] Another has argued that the "feedback principle" should be applied to oligopoly problems.[14] A feedback principle in this context is to be understood as a self-correcting control system in which the existence of a difference between the desired result and the actual existing state of affairs sets in motion forces to correct the discrepancy. Thus, changes in profits and in current prices of sellers are considered as variables, and a continuous process of computation and error correction, analogous to the process of self-correction of the course of a space missile in flight, is visualized. The model also incorporates a device for selecting the "conjecture function."

The Theory of Games

A different but related approach is to be found in the application of the theory of games to duopoly and oligopoly problems. Professors von Neumann and Morgenstern[15] have argued that since, in an oligopolistic situation, the individual seller does not control all of the variables, he acts similarly to the player of any other game. For example, he may act to secure that result which will be *least* harmful to himself, no matter what his opponent decides to do, including the possibility that his rival may react in the most unfavorable way from the player's point of view. An explanation of what is involved in their argument can be given with the help of Table 11–1.

Assume that there is a given demand for the output of a group of oligopolists and that profits are proportional to sales. Thus, if the oligopolist's sales increase, the sales of his competitors will decrease in an offsetting way to keep the group's total sales constant. The assumptions that the demand is constant and that profits are proportional to output means that the *total* profit is also constant. Assume also that the total maximum profit which can be earned by all the oligopolists together amounts to 200 units.

Table 11–1 shows the amount of profit the oligopolist believes he can make as a result of various alternative strategies which he may adopt if his competitors also adopt various strategies. Thus, the oligopolist's alternative policies are assumed to include: (1) raising

---

[13] K. W. Rothschild, "Price Theory and Oligopoly," *Economic Journal*, Vol. LVII (September, 1947), p. 307.

[14] Tun Thin, *Theory of Markets* (Cambridge: Harvard University Press, 1960).

[15] John von Neumann and Oskar Morgenstern, *Theory of Games and Economic Behavior* (2d ed.; Princeton: Princeton University Press, 1947). See also Martin Shubik, *Strategy and Market Structure* (New York: John Wiley & Sons, Inc., 1959).

prices; (2) keeping prices unchanged; (3) lowering prices; and
(4) increasing his advertising. The last-mentioned policy could be
further subdivided into the use of various forms and types of advertising (television, radio, handbills, newspapers, etc.), with each type
treated as a separate policy, or into combinations of these types, or
combinations of these types with strategies relative to prices. Product
differentiation could also be included in such a table as one possible
strategy.

Strictly speaking, Table 11–1 presents a duopoly situation, since the

Table 11–1
AN ILLUSTRATION OF GAME THEORY AND OLIGOPOLY BEHAVIOR

		Competitors' Alternative Strategies			
		Raise Prices	Prices Unchanged	Lower Prices	Increase Advertising
	Raise Prices	107	92	(88)	99
Oligopolist's Alternative Strategies	Prices Unchanged	110	106	(94)	97
	Lower Prices	116	108	(100)	102
	Increase Advertising	108	109	(96)	98

oligopolist's competitors are assumed to react as a group, all in precisely
the same way, to his own action. This assumption is made in order to
simplify our illustration, although it is not necessarily realistic. The
policies which are open to the oligopolist are also open to his single-
minded group of competitors, and Table 11–1 takes account of these
possible policies. The oligopolist's strategies are the *row* headings,
and his competitor's policies are the *column* headings. (Rows are read
horizontally; columns are read vertically.)

Thus, in Table 11–1, we see the oligopolist's belief that *if* he lowers
his prices and *if* his competitors do not change theirs, his profits will be
108—this number appears at the intersection of the row showing his
profits if he adopts a policy of lowering his prices and the column
which shows his profits if his competitors do not change their prices.
In this case his competitors will earn 92, since $200 - 108 = 92$,
and the gain of one party is a loss to the other. That is, our illustra-

tion involves what is known technically as a *zero-sum* game, because the total profit remains constant and the problem posed is concerned with how this constant total is to be shared by the two players (the oligopolist and his competitors). Thus, one participant's gain is the other's loss. (Strictly speaking, our example illustrates a *constant-sum* game, but it is common practice to use the term *zero-sum* game to identify this case.)

Table 11–1 shows that if the oligopolist keeps his price unchanged while his competitors raise their prices, his profits will be 110, while if he raises his price while they raise theirs, his profits will be 107. And, if he keeps his price unchanged while his competitors increase their advertising, his profits will be 97, which is more than the amount of profit he would make (94) if his opponents lowered their prices instead of increasing their advertising in response to his action (in this case, in response to his inaction). Given the knowledge of the various possibilities open to him, as well as those open to his competitors, and given the ability to quantify the effects of the combinations of these various policies in terms of profits (a very large order indeed!), the oligopolist must then decide which of the available policies to adopt.

One possibility, although by no means the only one, is to *"play it safe."* That is, he may assume that his opponents will always follow that strategy which produces the worst possible result from his own point of view. Thus, pessimistically, he may believe that if he decides to raise his price, his opponents will, in fact, lower theirs, and his profit from this course of action will be 88. If he is consistent in his pessimism, he will also believe that if he keeps his price unchanged, his opponents will lower their prices, and his profit will be 94; if he lowers his price, his opponents will lower theirs also, but his profits will be 100; and, finally, if he increases his advertising, his opponents will lower their prices, and his profits will be 96. All these numbers have been circled in Table 11–1.

Accordingly, the pessimistic oligopolist will thus adopt that course of action, from among those which provide him with various *minimum* gains, which will provide him with the *maximum* minimum gain. In the present case, therefore, he would believe that his best policy would be to lower price. For, in this case, his gain will be the greatest (100), according to his belief that the worst will happen. Thus his policy of "playing it safe" results in the adoption of that policy which produces the *maximum minimum* gain!

In Table 11–1 the difference between the total profit which can be earned by all the oligopolists together and the profit earned by the oligopolist in question represents the amount earned by his competitors. Thus, the numbers in Table 11–1 can also be thought of as representing losses to his competitors. Assume now that the competitors adopt the strategy of maximizing their own profits. In such a case they will seek to minimize the profits earned by the oligopolist, for these represent their "losses." Accordingly, they will respond to his policy of lowering price by lowering their own prices. For, if they respond by keeping their prices unchanged, their loss will be 108; if they respond by raising their prices, their loss will be 116; and if they respond by increasing advertising, their loss will be 102. But if they respond by lowering their own prices, their loss will be only 100. They are thus following the strategy of selecting the policy which will produce the *minimum maximum* loss.

The policies of the oligopolist and his competitors are mutually consistent in our example and result in the establishment of a stable equilibrium position, technically called a "saddle point," since the *maximum minimum* of the oligopolist (100) is equal to the *minimum maximum* (100) of his competitors. However, if these two magnitudes were not equal (and they need not be), a stable equilibrium would not be attained. Various methods have been developed to approximate the solution in such cases. One of these is to allow a player to adopt several different or "mixed" strategies in an attempt to take advantage of his opponents' mistakes or to keep them off balance and to permit the players to make use of the laws of probability in evaluating their own and their opponents' strategies; but a discussion of such refinements, as well as removal of the zero-sum and two-player constraints of our illustration, are beyond the scope of this book.

In the final analysis, the application of game theory in this area amounts to an assumption that businessmen do play a game of business according to a general theory of the way in which games are played, and that they are seeking to maximize profits in some rational way. In this respect, the behavior assumptions of game theory are not really very different from those made in the marginal analysis. So far, the great hopes which have been held for the application of game theory in this area of analysis have not been realized. Indeed, its principal value seems to lie in the fact that it provides a fertile field wherein the imagination may roam in analyzing oligopoly problems.[16]

Under the circumstances, any attempt to explain all the other models

---

[16] For an excellent discussion of the use of game theory in economic analysis, see William J. Baumol, *Economic Theory and Operations Analysis* (Englewood Cliffs, N.J.: Prentice-Hall, Inc., 1961), chap. xviii.

of oligopolistic behavior which exist in the literature would exhaust the writer and the reader as well.[17] No general theory will be developed. Instead, a few representative examples will be discussed. One, which is interesting because of its historical importance, is due to Professor Chamberlin, and we will consider it next, although our diagrams differ somewhat from the ones used by him.

Professor Chamberlin's Small Group Case

Professor Chamberlin's approach to the problem rests on the conception of a small *group* of oligopolists producing differentiated products, which are nevertheless close substitutes for each other.[18]

An understanding of his argument (which can also be applied to a

Figure 11–2

PROFESSOR CHAMBERLIN'S *DD* AND *dd* CURVES

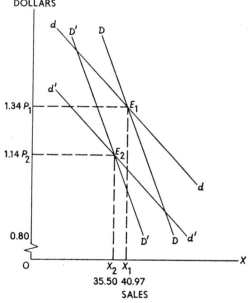

large "group" of firms producing slightly differentiated products) will be facilitated by reference to Figure 11–2, in which are depicted *dd* curves and *DD* curves. A *dd* curve is really nothing more than the $AR = P = D$ curve employed in our previous diagrams. It shows the firm's belief as to how much it can sell at all possible prices, provided

---

[17] See, for example, Joe S. Bain, *Price Theory* (New York: Henry Holt & Co., Inc., 1952), pp. 267–349.

[18] See Chamberlin, *The Theory of Monopolistic Competition*, pp. 71–116.

that *all other firms keep their prices fixed at a given level,* that is, provided that all other firms continue charging, say, OP_1. The DD curve
in Figure 11–2 shows the amount the firm can in fact sell at all possible prices *if all other firms always charge the same price as the dd
firm.* Thus, the DD curve represents the proportional part of the market (the actual market share) of the firm in question. If there were
only one firm, DD and dd would be identical. As the total number of

Figure 11–3

TWO RELATED GRAPHICAL ILLUSTRATIONS OF
OLIGOPOLY EQUILIBRIUM CONDITIONS

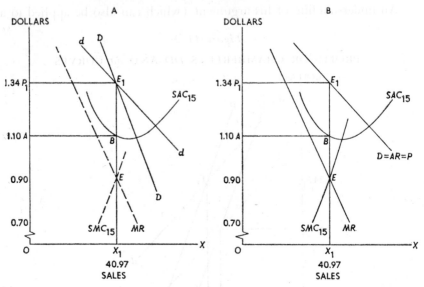

firms in the market increases and the share of the firm in question decreases, DD shifts to the left to $D'D'$. As the share of the firm in question increases, DD shifts to the right. Any given dd curve intersects a
given DD curve at only one point, and a given DD curve is made up of
points on a number of different dd curves. Thus DD is intersected by
both dd and $d'd'$ in Figure 11–2, and so is $D'D'$.

Figure 11–3A contains the dd and DD curves from Figure 11–2 and
short-run cost curves. At the price of OP_1, the firm is in short-run equilibrium, producing output OX_1. The equilibrium position is found by
locating the intersection at E_1 of the dd and DD curves. By dropping a
perpendicular from this point to the X axis, the *equilibrium output* is
determined. By drawing a horizontal line parallel to the X axis from
E_1 to the price axis, the *equilibrium price* is determined. In Figure

11–3A, the firm has a total cost of $OABX_1$, and its total revenue is $OP_1E_1X_1$. Thus, its *net* revenue is AP_1E_1B.

For purposes of comparison, Figure 11–3B shows the same situation in terms of the standard marginal and average revenue curves employed in the two preceding chapters. In the case of Figure 11–3B, the equilibrium point is located by determining the point of intersection between the marginal cost and marginal revenue curves at E. As in the case of Figure 11–3A, the net revenue is AP_1E_1B. Note that the MR and SMC curves have also been partially depicted in Figure 11–3A. Thus we see that addition of the DD curve in Figure 11–3A is the element distinguishing that diagram from Figure 11–3B.

According to Professor Chamberlin's analysis, *if* there is freedom of entry, *if* the market of each seller in the "group" is the same size, *if* the elasticity of demand in each market is the same, and *if* the cost conditions are the same, in the long run only normal profits will be made. This case is depicted in Figure 11–4. In this diagram *dd* has shifted

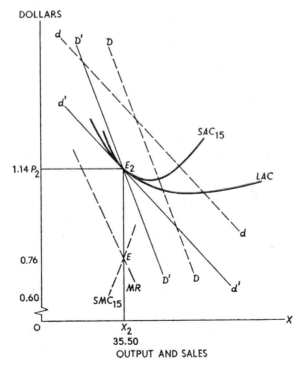

Figure 11–4

OLIGOPOLISTIC FIRM IN LONG-RUN EQUILIBRIUM
MAKING NORMAL PROFIT

downward from its original position to $d'd'$, where it is *tangent* to both
the short-run and the long-run average cost curves at E_2. In addition,
the DD curve has shifted to the left to $D'D'$, as a result of the entry of
new firms, and now *intersects* the short-run and long-run average cost
curves at the point at which they are tangent to each other and to $d'd'$.

Such a long-run position of equilibrium is, thus, one possibility, but
it is only one possibility. As Chamberlin notes, although the assumptions concerning freedom of entry and the identity of the demand and
cost conditions of all of the members of the group are useful for
analytical purposes, in the real world they are seldom, if ever, met.
Consequently, if freedom of entry does not exist, there is no reason why
the *tangency solution* depicted in Figure 11–4 should, in fact, exist.
Instead, all of the members of the group may make greater than normal
profits in the long run.

Unused Capacity as a Barrier to Entry

Figure 11–4 depicts an alternative way of showing the effect of
oligopoly power on the allocation of resources. At E_2, although only
normal profits are being made, the firm is in long-run equilibrium on a
downward-sloping portion of the long-run average cost curve. Thus
Figure 11–4 depicts in a slightly different way the same kind of economic "waste" (the existence of unused capacity) as was depicted in
Figure 10–6 in the preceding chapter, because, in the latter case, a
normal profit is also being made.

The existence of unused capacity may serve as a barrier to entry of
new firms or as a device for maintaining monopolistic or oligopolistic
control over a market. Thus, in *United States* v. *Aluminum Company of
America,* a case which seems to be more often cited for the *dictum* that
monopoly "thrust upon a defendant" would not constitute a violation
of the Sherman Act than for the actual holding of the Court, Judge
Hand said:

> It would completely misconstrue "Alcoa's" position in 1940 to hold that it was
> the passive beneficiary of a monopoly following upon an involuntary elimination
> of competitors by automatically operative economic forces. . . . This increase
> and this continued and undisturbed control did not fall undesigned into "Alcoa's"
> lap; obviously it could not have done so. It could only have resulted, as it did
> result, from a persistant determination to maintain the control, with which it
> found itself vested in 1912. There were at least two abortive attempts to enter
> the industry, but "Alcoa" effectively anticipated and forestalled all competition
> and succeeded in holding the field alone. . . . It was not inevitable that it
> should always anticipate increases in the demand for ingot and be prepared to
> supply them. Nothing compelled it to keep doubling and redoubling its capacity

before others entered the field. It insists that it never excluded competitors; but we can think of no more effective exclusion than progressively to embrace each new opportunity as it opened, and to face every newcomer with new capacity already geared into a great organization, having the advantage of experience, trade connections and the elite of personnel. . . .[19]

The Effects of Selling Costs and Product Differentiation

Selling costs can be introduced into the analysis by depicting them graphically as an addition to the cost of production. Thus, in Figure

Figure 11–5

ONE METHOD OF TREATING SELLING COSTS

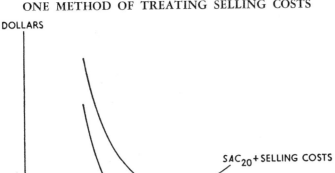

11–5, the selling costs are assumed to add an equal amount per unit of output to the cost of production. The object of selling costs (assume they are "combative advertising") is presumably to shift the firm's demand curve up and to the right, that is, to acquire for the firm a larger share of the market. What precisely will be the effect of such "combative" advertising depends on the assumptions one makes. If the firm does succeed in shifting its demand curve to the right, while at the same time its costs have risen because of advertising, it may or may not make greater profits than before, depending upon the extent to which each curve is shifted.

Similarly, product differentiation may result in shifting the average

19 *United States* v. *Aluminum Co. of America,* 148 Fed. (2d) 416 (1945), at pp. 430–31. (Alcoa was found guilty of "monopolizing" under the Sherman Act.)

cost curve upward in the same way as selling costs, since production of a fancier product increases the per unit cost and the object of product differentiation is also to increase the firm's share of the market. Again, the effect on the firm's profit position depends on the assumptions one makes.

If, as a result of increased advertising expenditures or product differentiation, the firm succeeds in shifting its demand curve to the right, its share of the market increases at the expense of other producers, while at the same time its costs are also rising. It may increase its profits for a while. However, if other firms retaliate, the demand curve may once more shift to the left and a tangency solution may be the end product.

Under the circumstances, it is conceivable that advertising by each of the firms may take the form of an attempt (perhaps by means of trade association activities) to make inroads on the markets of firms outside the group and be directed against products outside the group. Thus consumers may be invited to buy a boat instead of another car. In such a case, the relative positions of the firms within the group could remain unchanged, but all their demand curves could shift to the right at the expense of a shift to the left in the demand curves of the members of some other "group."

Advertising as a Barrier to Entry

Finally, firms may follow a policy of "live and let live" with respect to each other, but direct their advertising efforts mainly at keeping newcomers from entering the group. In such a case, monopolistic profits may be retained indefinitely by all of the members of the group, unless cost curves are shifted in such a way as to produce the tangency solution. Thus, in *American Tobacco Co.* v. *United States* in 1946, the Supreme Court remarked:

In each of the years 1937, 1938 and 1939, American, Liggett and Reynolds expended a total of over $40,000,000 a year for advertising. Such advertising is not here criticized as a business expense. Such advertising may benefit indirectly the entire industry, including the competitors of the advertisers. Such tremendous advertising, however, is also a widely published warning that these companies possess and know how to use a powerful offensive and defensive weapon against new competition. New competition dare not enter the field, unless it be well supported by comparable national advertising.[20]

---

[20] *American Tobacco Co.* v. *United States,* 328 U.S. 781 (1946), at p. 797. (The defendants were found guilty of having conspired to establish a monopoly.)

The Rise and Decline of Large Firms: Empirical Studies

The problem of the exit and entry of new firms into an established industry was raised by Marshall in a classic passage in the *Principles* which has since become known as the "trees of the forest" argument. In this passage, Marshall compared the process of displacement of established firms by newcomers with the way in which younger trees may displace older ones in a forest. However, he also noted in the Eighth Edition of the *Principles* that large corporations sometimes stagnated instead of being replaced by vigorous, new firms. And in *Industry and Trade,* which was first published in 1919, he was even more apprehensive.[21]

Many writers have referred to Marshall's parable of the "trees of the forest" without noting the qualifications which he himself attached to it in the *Principles.* Moreover, his *Industry and Trade* has today been almost lost from sight, probably partly because it has been considered an "institutional" rather than a "theoretical" work. A careful reading of this book is worth the effort involved. Clearly the question of the factors determining exit and entry must vary from case to case and cannot be solved by a reliance on deductive reasoning alone. Two recent empirical studies of the subject are worth noting briefly in this context.

The first of these studies, by Professor A. D. H. Kaplan in 1954, involved an examination of the extent to which positions of leadership had been maintained by the 100 largest industrial firms of the United States in five selected years between 1909 and 1948. Kaplan concluded that the challenge to entrenched leaders by competitors was significant during the period and that increases in the size of large-scale enterprises did not produce a decline in the intensity or scope of competition.[22]

However, a more recent study by Professors Norman R. Collins and Lee E. Preston in 1961, covering the 100 largest firms in the period from 1909 to 1958, provides conclusions which are diametrically opposed to those of Kaplan.[23] That is, they have concluded that firms currently at the top of the industrial pyramid are more likely to remain

---

[21] Alfred Marshall, *Principles of Economics* (8th ed.; London: Macmillan & Co., Ltd., 1938), pp. 315–16; and Marshall, *Industry and Trade* (London: Macmillan & Co., Ltd., 1919).

[22] A. D. H. Kaplan, *Big Enterprise in a Competitive System* (Washington, D.C.: The Brookings Institution, 1954), esp. pp. 235 ff.

[23] Norman R. Collins and Lee E. Preston, "The Size Structure of the Largest Industrial Firms, 1909–1958," *American Economic Review,* Vol. LI (December, 1961), pp. 986–1011.

there than were their predecessors, although they do not attempt to explain why this result is likely.

Different (but related) studies by Professor Joe S. Bain have shown that the average rate of return on owner's equity after tax has generally been higher in industries in which a small number of firms account for a large proportion of the total output than in other industries,[24] and Bain has also done much work on the problem of the nature of barriers to entry of new firms.[25]

The Oligopoly Kinky Demand Curve: Price Rigidity

Figure 11–6 illustrates the oligopoly kinky demand curve, so-called because the demand curve is thought to consist of the dark portions of the dd and DD curves which have a "kink" or a point of intersection at E_1. This demand curve was invented by Paul M. Sweezy in 1939[26]

Figure 11–6

THE KINKY DEMAND CURVE

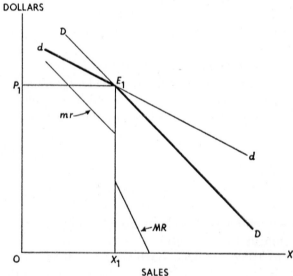

[24] See Joe S. Bain, "Relation of the Profit Rate to Industry Concentration: American Manufacturing, 1936–1940," *Quarterly Journal of Economics,* Vol. LXV (August, 1951), pp. 293–324.

[25] Joe S. Bain, *Industrial Organization* (New York: John Wiley & Sons, Inc., 1956); and Bain, *Barriers to New Competition* (Cambridge: Harvard University Press, 1956).

[26] Paul M. Sweezy, "Demand under Conditions of Oligopoly," *Journal of Political Economy,* Vol. XLVII (August, 1939), pp. 568–73, reprinted in Kenneth Boulding and George Stigler (eds.), *Readings in Price Theory* (Homewood, Ill.: Richard D. Irwin, Inc., 1952), pp. 404–9.

to explain why, *once an oligopoly price had been determined,* it would remain fixed in place, or rigid. After the price has been determined, the demand curve is said to consist of the dark line dE_1D in Figure 11–6. Note that in this case the marginal revenue curve is discontinuous and consists of mr and MR, or two parts, and that the marginal cost curve may be within the range of the discontinuity.

The oligopolist believes that if he increases his price, no rival will follow him upward, and, so, he believes that the demand curve facing him *at prices higher* than OP_1 is highly elastic and looks like curve dE_1. Further, he believes that if he lowers his price below OP_1, all of his rivals will likewise lower their prices and that, therefore, he will not increase his share of the market by this action. Thus, the demand curve facing him at prices below OP_1 is taken to be E_1D. Since the oligopolist cannot gain a larger share of the market by increasing his price and cannot gain by lowering his price, he leaves the price fixed at OP_1. And so do all the other members in the group. If E_1 lies above the average cost curve, greater than normal profits are made. Thus, rigid prices are explained according to this theory.

Empirical Studies of Price Rigidity

Professor George Stigler has made an empirical study of the oligopoly kinky demand curve and has rejected the idea that it exists. However, Stigler's statistical tests did not involve very many producers, and what might be shown by a larger sample is not altogether clear from his study.[27] Moreover, Stigler's study is not concerned with refuting the notion that rigid prices exist, but merely with testing the theory of the kinky demand curve.

Considerable evidence of price rigidity does exist,[28] as does evidence that prices are administered rather than being market-determined, and these matters have been the subject of extensive congressional investigation, most recently in 1957 and 1958.[29]

In addition, a study of selected manufacturing firms by Professor

---

[27] George Stigler, "The Kinky Oligopoly Demand Curve and Rigid Prices," *Journal of Political Economy*, Vol. LV (October, 1947), pp. 432–49.

[28] See, for example, Gardiner C. Means, *Administrative Inflation and Public Policy* (Washington, D.C.: Anderson Kramer Associates, 1959). (Dr. Means, together with A. A. Berle, did the first empirical work in this area in the 1930's.)

[29] See, for example, *Administered Prices, Automobiles* and *Administered Prices, Steel* (Reports of the Subcommittee on Antitrust and Monopoly, Senate Committee on the Judiciary, 85th Cong., 2d sess.) (Washington, D.C.: U.S. Government Printing Office, 1958); and *Administered Prices, Part I, "Opening Phase—Economists' Views"* (Hearings before Subcommittee on Antitrust and Monopoly, Senate Committee on the Judiciary, 85th Cong., 2d sess.) (Washington, D.C.: U.S. Government Printing Office, 1957).

Harold Levinson made in 1960 shows that in the period between 1947 and 1958, percentage changes in prices and percentage changes in output were *not* related in any important way, nor were such price changes related to changes in productivity per production worker man-hour. Instead, changes in prices were most clearly related to profit levels during most of the years since World War II, and, after 1951, a strong relationship was also found to exist between changes in gross hourly earnings and prices,[30] suggesting that wage increases have been passed on to consumers.

D. MONOPOLISTIC COMPETITION

The Short Run

Monopolistic competition has today come to mean a state of affairs in which there are a large number of firms selling slightly differentiated products and in which freedom of entry exists. Gasoline service stations are an example. In the short run a firm will, as usual, be maximizing its profits at the point at which the marginal cost and the marginal revenue are equal. Since there are numerous firms, the demand curve facing the individual firm will be relatively elastic (as in Figure 11–7). Except for this fact, however, the analysis is quite similar to the analyses which have already been presented. (See pages 281–83.)

In terms of Professor Chamberlin's *dd* and *DD* curves, the short-run situation will be similar to that depicted in Figure 11–3 earlier. In the short run, the firm may make greater than normal profits equal to AP_1E_1B in Figure 11–3. In terms of the marginal analysis, Figure 11–3B would depict the situation. Since the marginal cost and the marginal revenue are equal at E, output would be fixed at OX_1, and the price would be OP_1, with net revenue equal to AP_1E_1B.

The Long Run

In the long run, since there is freedom of entry, profits greater than normal cannot exist. Thus, the entry of new firms would push the *dd* curve to $d'd'$ as in Figure 11–4, where it is tangent to both the long-run and the short-run average cost curves, while the *DD* curve would shift to the left to $D'D'$ and intersect the two cost curves at the same point. Profits would be normal in this situation, since total cost and total revenue are both equal to $OP_2E_2X_2$. However, there is wasted capacity,

---

[30] *Postwar Movement of Prices and Wages in Manufacturing Industries* (Joint Committee on the Economic Report, Study Paper No. 21, 80th Cong., 2d sess.) (Washington, D.C.: U.S. Government Printing Office, 1960).

since the price is equal to the average cost at a level above the minimum long-run average cost.

The same analysis can be conducted in terms of the standard marginal revenue and cost curves, as in Figure 11–7. Thus, the firm will be in long-run equilibrium when the short-run and long-run marginal cost and the marginal revenue are equal at E. Output at this point would be OX_0, and the price would be equal to the long-run and short-run

Figure 11–7

FIRM IN LONG-RUN EQUILIBRIUM UNDER MONOPOLISTIC COMPETITION

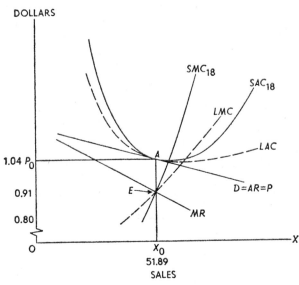

average costs which are equal at A. Thus, the total revenue and the total cost are both equal to OP_0AX_0, and net revenue is zero. Again the waste of economic capacity is indicated by the fact that the price is equal to the average cost at a point located on the downward-sloping portion of the long-run average cost curve, which means that, by increasing output, average costs would be further reduced.

Product Differentiation and Selling Costs under Monopolistic Competition

Differentiation of the product and selling costs can be introduced into the analysis as before, by shifting the cost curves upward to show the increased expenditures for these purposes and by shifting the demand curve to the right also to show the effect of a given seller's activities on his share of the market. If other firms retaliate in order to retain their shares of the market, consumers will pay higher prices for the products, since the average costs of all firms will increase.

An interesting study has been made by the Department of Agriculture of the effect of the use of trading stamps by retail establishments. The study was based on a survey of 199 trading stamp companies, and the authors of the study have remarked:

> Wide variations were found among stores with respect to the effect of stamps. The first stores to take on stamps in a particular area usually use stamps as a competitive device which they hope will increase sales and thereby decrease costs enough to offset the additional cost of stamps. Some stores adopt stamps as a defensive measure to meet competition of others who give stamps. Stores not using trading stamps as a competitive device may emphasize lower prices to hold present customers and attract new ones. In some instances, stamp competition is met by giving premiums in ways other than through stamps and by other promotional devices.
>
> Consumers are interested in trading stamps for reasons other than the effect on retail prices. . . .
>
> In stores adding stamps, the increase in the wholesale-retail price spread, on the average, was greater than in the nonstamp stores, but it apparently was substantially less than the increase in their costs resulting from the added cost of stamps, higher wage rates, and other factors.[31]

E. THE PROFIT MAXIMIZATION HYPOTHESIS

The Usual Assumption of Profit Maximization

The usual assumption concerning the motivation of the firm is that it seeks to maximize its short-run or its long-run profits. Whether or not these two objectives are necessarily consistent, and what is meant by such assumptions, is not often clearly specified in the analysis. If the term "profit maximization" is interpreted broadly to mean that the firm simply seeks to maximize all of its objectives, the very breadth of the interpretation eliminates any empirical content from the assumption. If, on the other hand, the term is interpreted narrowly to mean that the firm seeks to make the difference between its short-run or long-run total revenue and the appropriate total cost as great as possible, the assumption is probably too narrow.

Clearly, firms also have objectives other than maximizing the difference defined above. Some may seek to maintain their shares of the market constant; others may seek to increase their shares of the market;

---

[31] United States Department of Agriculture, *Trading Stamps,* Marketing Research Report No. 295 (Washington, D.C.: U.S. Government Printing Office, 1958), pp. 27–29.

still others may wish to earn a fixed return on their invested capital. The motivations may be as varied as the personalities of the individuals who constitute the controlling interests in the firms. In the next subdivision, we will consider the results of one empirical study concerned with an examination of the problem of motivation of the managers of the firm. At the moment, however, it will be worthwhile to consider an alternative hypothesis concerning this motivation.

Professor Baumol's Maximization Thesis

Professor William J. Baumol has put forth a hypothesis, different from the usual one of profit maximization, concerning the motivation of managers of large firms.[32] His thesis rests on the fact that many large firms in the United States today are not controlled by their stockholders but are, in fact, under the control of management. Although he does not cite the evidence, a study by the Securities and Exchange Commission for the Temporary National Economic Committee in 1940 showed that about 60 of the 200 largest nonfinancial corporations in the United States were "without a visible center of control. . . . In many of these corporations the chief officers, though owning but little stock, may well have been in a position of control, relying largely on the power of the proxy machinery."[33]

In addition, of the 140 corporations with definite centers of control, 60 were controlled by other corporations, and some of the *controlling* corporations were among those included in the group of 60 for which no definite center of control could be established. Finally, in only 42 of the companies did the majority of the voting stock exercise control. With this background information, we can return to a consideration of Baumol's thesis.

He has argued that the principal motive of the managers of present-day corporations is *not* the maximization of *net* revenue but, instead, the maximization of *sales* revenue, subject to a constraint that the stockholders must be kept from being "unhappy," because the salaries and fringe benefits received by managers are more closely correlated with the size of the firm, measured in terms of total sales revenue, than with profits.[34]

The implications of this thesis are interesting. If it is correct, the

---

[32] Baumol, *Business Behavior, Value and Growth.*

[33] Securities and Exchange Commission, *The Distribution of Ownership in the 200 Largest Non-Financial Corporations* (Washington, D.C.: U.S. Government Printing Office, 1940), pp. 103–4.

[34] Baumol, *Business Behavior, Value and Growth,* chaps. vi and vii.

thesis means that firms do not fix their output at the point where marginal cost and marginal revenue are equal. Instead, they may produce *beyond* the point at which the net revenue is a maximum, that is, to some point at which the marginal cost is greater than marginal revenue, since total sales revenue may be greater at such a point than at the point of maximum net revenue.

The difference between Professor Baumol's assumption, that the firm's managers seek to maximize sales revenue subject to a profit

Figure 11–8

COMPARISON OF PROFESSOR BAUMOL'S MAXIMIZATION THESIS WITH THE USUAL THESIS

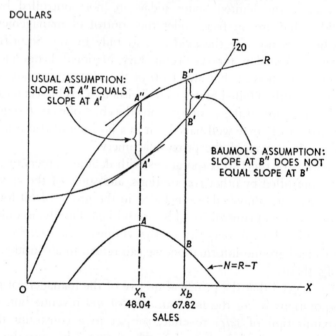

constraint in the form of some minimum dividend payment to stockholders, and the usual assumption, that the firm seeks to maximize net revenue, is illustrated in Figure 11–8. The usual assumption produces an equilibrium output of OX_n, since net revenue is at a maximum at A. That is, the slope of the total revenue curve at A'' is equal to that of the total cost curve at A'. Alternatively, marginal revenue and marginal cost are equal at output OX_n, and, hence, N is at a maximum at that output.

In Baumol's case, the output would be, say, OX_b, at a lower, but still positive, net revenue, and the slope of the total cost curve at B' would not be equal to that of the total revenue curve at B'' at this output. The difference between the net revenue at output OX_n and the net revenue at output OX_b, or $X_nA - X_bB$, is viewed by Professor Baumol as a "fund of sacrificable profits . . . devoted to increasing revenues as much as possible."[35] Professor Baumol has also incorporated the effects of selling costs and product differentiation into his analysis and has provided a number of interesting suggestions for further research; and he has also related his thesis to the problem of economic growth.

Empirical Evidence Relating to Baumol's Thesis

A number of other writers have dealt with similar hypotheses. Professor Harvey Leibenstein has examined the Baumol thesis from the point of view of organizational analysis, and a number of writers have made statistical studies of the motivation and compensation of corporation executives.[36] One such study, which, however, does not purport specifically to test the Baumol thesis (having been published before Baumol's work on the subject), has been made by Dean David R. Roberts. This study, which was based on data from the Securities and Exchange Commission, is full of interesting suggestions for further empirical work and indicates that compensation of executives is significantly related to corporate size as measured by sales but is *not* related to the profit *rate*. Roberts' study, however, is concerned with variations *among* companies rather than *within* companies.[37] In 1962, Professors McGuire, Chiu, and Elbing investigated correlations between executive incomes, sales, and profits for 45 of the 100 largest industrial corporations in the United States during the period from 1953 to 1959 inclusive and reported their conclusion that executive incomes are significantly related to sales (current and past), but their study does not rule out the possibility of a valid relationship between profits and incomes also.[38] This study was specifically designed to test Baumol's hypothesis.

---

[35] *Ibid.*, pp. 58–59.

[36] See Harvey Leibenstein, *Economic Theory and Organizational Analysis* (New York: Harper & Bros., 1960), Part IV; see also John C. Baker, *Executive Salaries and Bonus Plans* (New York: McGraw-Hill Book Co., Inc., 1940); and F. W. Taussig and W. S. Barker, "American Corporations and Their Executives: A Statistical Inquiry," *Quarterly Journal of Economics*, Vol. XL (November, 1925), pp. 1–51.

[37] David R. Roberts, *Executive Compensation* (Glencoe, Ill.: The Free Press, 1959), p. 64.

[38] Joseph W. McGuire, John S. Y. Chiu, and Alvar O. Elbing, "Executive Incomes, Sales and Profits," *American Economic Review*, Vol. LII (September, 1962), pp. 753–61.

F. MEASURES OF OLIGOPOLY POWER

Indexes of Concentration

Indexes of industrial concentration have been used in an attempt to measure the degree of oligopoly (or "monopoly") power in a number of studies.[39] Such indexes usually show the proportion of total industry output produced by each of the dominant firms.

A study made for the Subcommittee on Monopoly of the Senate Judiciary Committee, for example, shows that the share of total value added by manufacture in the United States accounted for by the 50 largest companies in 1954 had increased to 23 percent from the 16 percent share held by these same companies in 1947.[40] Such statistics are useful, but the measure employed assumes that the concepts of "firm" and "industry" or "group" are capable of precise definition. Moreover, these measures tell nothing about the strength of particular firms in particular markets. Nor do they take account of competition of substitute products. Thus, they are useful indicators but not absolute guides.

Profit Rate

Professor Joe S. Bain has examined the question of using the profit rate as a measure of monopoly power.[41] The difficulty in the case of this measure lies not only in the definition of the word "profit" but also in the fact that accounting data must be used in determining the rate. The objections raised against using accounting data as a basis for deriving cost curves in Chapter 7 apply with equal force against the use of the profit rate as a measure of monopoly power.

Elasticity Measures

Another measure which is interesting, but not very practical, has been suggested by Professor Abba Lerner, namely, that the degree of monopoly power be measured by the extent to which marginal cost diverges from the price,[42] or

---

[39] An extensive use of such indexes has been made by Leonard W. Weiss, *Economics and American Industry* (New York: John Wiley & Sons, Inc., 1961). Weiss makes use of *Concentration in American Industry* (Report of the Subcommittee on Antitrust and Monopoly, Senate Committee on the Judiciary, Committee Print, 85th Cong., 1st sess.) (Washington, D.C.: U.S. Government Printing Office, 1957).

[40] *Concentration in American Industry* (Report of the Subcommittee on Antitrust and Monopoly, Senate Committee on the Judiciary), Table 2, p. 11.

[41] Joe S. Bain, "The Profit Rate as a Measure of Monopoly Power," *Quarterly Journal of Economics,* Vol. LV (February, 1941), pp. 271–93.

[42] Abba P. Lerner, "The Concept of Monopoly and the Measurement of Monopoly Power," *Review of Economic Studies,* Vol. I (June, 1934), pp. 157–75.

$$Z_m = \frac{P - MC}{P}.$$

In any case in which perfect competition exists, since $P = MC$, $Z_m = 0$ in the above measure. However, the problem of how to measure the marginal cost in a practical sense is not faced by this formula, which actually reduces to the reciprocal of the price elasticity of demand.

Another elasticity measure has been suggested by Professor Robert Triffin, namely, that the reciprocal of the cross elasticity of demand be used,[43] since the Lerner measure does not take account of the existence of substitutes. However, the Triffin measure, too, suffers from a lack of being able to be determined in practice.

Various other measures have also been suggested, and the interested student may be referred to Professor Machlup's *The Political Economy of Monopoly* for a review of them.[44]

G. EMPIRICAL STUDIES OF THE BEHAVIOR OF FIRMS

Studies of the Use of Marginal Concepts by Businessmen

R. L. Hall and C. J. Hitch in 1939 used questionnaires directed toward some British businessmen in an attempt to determine whether they actually employed marginal concepts in making their decisions, and concluded that the marginal analysis was not descriptive of actual business behavior.[45] However, the Hall-Hitch sample was small, and their procedure has been criticized severely by a number of writers, including Professor Machlup,[46] who argued that written questionnaires are "hopelessly inadequate" to determine such questions; and, moreover, businessmen might be employing the marginal concepts without realizing that they were doing so. Professor Machlup cited his own business experience in support of his position.

In 1956 Professor James Earley investigated, again by means of questionnaires, the question of the extent to which 217 manufacturing companies, classified as "excellently managed" by the American Institute of Management, employed marginal concepts. He concluded that marginal concepts were used predominantly by the companies which responded (110 of them did) to the questionnaire and that these same

---

[43] Robert Triffin, *Monopolistic Competition and General Equilibrium Theory* (Cambridge: Harvard University Press, 1940), chap. iii.

[44] (Baltimore: The Johns Hopkins Press, 1952), chap. xii.

[45] R. L. Hall and C. J. Hitch, "Price Theory and Business Behavior," *Oxford Economic Papers*, No. 2 (May, 1939), pp. 12–45.

[46] See his *The Economics of Sellers' Competition*, chaps, i–iii.

firms took a short-term view of their problems and were extremely sensitive to innovations.[47]

Objectives of Large Firms

However, in 1958, Professor Robert Lanzillotti reported the results of a study of pricing objectives of large firms based upon interviews over a period of years with executives of a number of large companies. His study suggests, among other things, in contrast to the results of the Earley study, that large companies have "fairly well-defined" pricing goals based on long-term considerations.[48] Lanzillotti concluded that his study showed that no single hypothesis, like the profit maximization hypothesis, could explain the behavior of the large companies studied. Included among the twenty large companies studied were Alcoa, American Can Company, Standard Oil of New Jersey, and General Motors. The objectives of the managers of these companies, as reflected in their pricing goals, varied from maintenance of the company's given market share (American Can Company) to obtaining a fixed or "target" return (20% in the case of General Motors) on its investment. Lanzillotti also noted that more adequate empirical data were needed before many of the questions raised by his study could be answered, but his results clearly cast doubt on the maximization thesis.

More recently, Professor Martin Shubik has analyzed the problem theoretically and also surveyed the results of numerous controlled experiments relating to business games and attempts to test economic behavior; but he has noted that even if the intent of the players is known, unless there is an understanding of the environment in which the action takes place, prediction of behavior is not possible.[49]

The Challenge of the Present State of the Theory of the Firm

The fact that the theory of the firm is today admittedly in an unsatisfactory state (and that it may raise more questions than it answers) ought not to discourage the serious student from further investigations. Instead, it may be that this area of economic analysis represents one of our greatest challenges. The development of a satisfactory theory of in-

---

[47] James S. Earley, "Marginal Policies of 'Excellently Managed' Companies," *American Economic Review*, Vol. XLVI (March, 1956), pp. 44–70.

[48] Robert F. Lanzillotti, "Pricing Objectives in Large Companies," *American Economic Review*, Vol. XLVIII (December, 1958), pp. 921–40. See also A. D. H. Kaplan, J. B. Dirlam, and R. Lanzillotti, *Pricing in Big Business: A Case Approach* (Washington, D.C.: The Brookings Institution, 1958).

[49] Martin Shubik, "Objective Functions and Models of Corporate Optimization," *Quarterly Journal of Economics*, Vol. LXXV (August, 1961), pp. 345–75.

dustrial organization and business behavior is crucial to the development of policies for the further growth of the United States and all other industrialized countries and is also significant for the development of underdeveloped political and economic entities as well. These matters will be considered further in the last chapter of this book where Professor Schumpeter's theory of economic development is examined. However, before this problem can be dealt with, it is necessary to examine the theory of pricing in the factor or input markets, and such a study is undertaken next in Part V.

SELECTED READINGS

ADAMS, WALTER (ed.). *The Structure of American Industry.* 3rd ed. New York: The Macmillan Co., 1961.

BAUMOL, WILLIAM J. *Business Behavior, Value and Growth.* New York: The Macmillan Co., 1959.

CHAMBERLIN, EDWARD H. *The Theory of Monopolistic Competition.* 7th ed. Cambridge: Harvard University Press, 1956.

KAPLAN, A. D. H.; DIRLAM, J. B.; AND LANZILLOTTI, R. *Pricing in Big Business: A Case Approach.* Washington, D.C.: The Brookings Institution, 1958.

MACHLUP, FRITZ. *The Economics of Sellers' Competition.* Baltimore: The Johns Hopkins Press, 1952.

————. *The Political Economy of Monopoly.* Baltimore: The Johns Hopkins Press, 1952.

ROBINSON, JOAN. *The Economics of Imperfect Competition.* London: Macmillan & Co., Ltd., 1934.

SHUBIK, MARTIN. *Strategy and Market Structure.* New York: John Wiley & Sons, Inc., 1959.

WEISS, LEONARD W. *Economics and American Industry.* New York: John Wiley & Sons, Inc., 1961.

WILCOX, CLAIR. *Competition and Monopoly in American Industry.* Temporary National Economic Committee, Monograph No. 21. Washington, D.C.: U.S. Government Printing Office, 1940.

PART V

THE FACTOR MARKET

PART V

THE FACTOR MARKET

12 The Marginal Productivity Theory

Introduction

Many of the concepts and relationships which have been explained in the preceding chapters will be employed in the discussion of the factor market in the next four chapters. Indeed, the demand for inputs is called a *derived demand,* since it is derived from the demand for the product. That is, the demand of an individual firm and also of society for any input rests upon the value of the use of that input to the firm and to the society in the production of output.

In this chapter we will consider the factor market generally and provide an explanation of the *marginal productivity theory of income distribution,* the solution to the problem of the imputation or distribution of the value of the final product as payments for the services of the inputs which have been employed in producing it. The case of perfect competition in both markets will be fully treated.

Chapter 13 is concerned with the theory of wages and emphasizes cases in which the assumptions of perfect competition in factor and product markets are modified. Chapter 14 contains an explanation of economic rent, both according to the marginal productivity theory and as an economic surplus; and Chapter 15 explains various theories of interest and of profits. Thus, the present Part V of this book, consisting of the chapters mentioned above, is concerned with the problem of the "functional distribution of income."

Throughout Parts V and VI, we will use the symbols x and p_x, which were used in Parts I and II (rather than X and P, which were used in Parts III and IV), to identify the amount and price of the product respectively, since it will often be necessary to identify the *product* price with a subscript to avoid confusing it with an *input* price. The reader must be careful to note whether a *product* price (p_x) or an *input* price (p_a, p_b) is relevant in a particular discussion.

Historical Background

The origin of the marginal productivity theory of income distribution can be traced to the work of an early German writer, T. H. von Thunen, who wrote in 1826.[1] However, the marginal productivity theory did not achieve wide popularity or acceptance until it was independently rediscovered by a number of writers between 1870 and 1900. Among those who contributed to the development of the theory were the Austrian economists, Carl Menger, Fredreich von Wieser, and Eugen von Böhm-Bawerk; the French economist, Leon Walras; the English economists, Stanley Jevons, Philip Wicksteed, and Francis Y. Edgeworth; and the American economist, John Bates Clark.[2] The marginal productivity theory explained in this chapter is basically that developed by Professor John Bates Clark between 1890 and 1900, although the terminology employed in the explanation will be the contemporary terminology rather than that used by Clark.

This theory is not considered by contemporary economists to have any ethical significance. However, when he first presented it in 1890, Clark in fact argued and believed not only that he had discovered the fundamental principles according to which the final product would inevitably be shared in a static economy under conditions of perfect competition, but also that the resulting distribution was ethically or morally right.[3] The explanation in this chapter will ignore the ethical significance Clark sought to attach to the theory and deal with it only from an analytical point of view.

The extent to which the theory can be applied to real world problems and particularly to explain wages is a matter of dispute. Some attempts to test the theory statistically will be explained in a later section of this chapter.

A. BASIC CONCEPTS

Value of the Marginal Product Defined

The *value of the marginal product (VMP) is defined generally as the "value to the society" of the marginal unit of an input.*

---

[1] See, for example, Paul H. Douglas, *The Theory of Wages* (New York: The Macmillan Co., 1934), chaps. i and ii.

[2] *Ibid.* See also George J. Stigler, *Production and Distribution Theories* (New York: The Macmillan Co., 1941).

[3] See, for example, J. B. Clark, *The Distribution of Wealth* (New York: The Macmillan Co., 1900), pp. 6–7. Clark says in part: "Every day a definite amount is handed over by one class to another. Is this amount determined by a principle that humanity can approve and perpetuate? Does it treat men fairly? The issue is personal; but it is settled by a knowledge of purely functional distribution."

Marshall and other neoclassical economists conducted their analyses in terms of the *utility* of the marginal product. That is, they defined the marginal product of a given input as the rate of change of output as input changes ($\partial x / \partial a$) and spoke of the utility which could be obtained from the marginal unit of input.

Contemporary economists identify the *value of the marginal product* (*VMP*) *of an input as the marginal product of that input multiplied by the price of a unit of the output*, or as

$$VMP_a = \frac{\partial x}{\partial a} p_x = (MPP_a)(p_x) . \tag{12-1}$$

Note that the letters VMP_a are an *abbreviation* and *not a formula*.

Thus, the contemporary practice is to quantify the neoclassical measure by taking the price of a unit of the output as a measure of the value of a unit of that output at the margin, a procedure which is derived from Marshall's theory of consumer behavior. Ultimately, therefore, it is grounded upon a notion of utility.

Figure 12–1

VMP AND MRP CURVES OF INPUTS *a* AND *b*

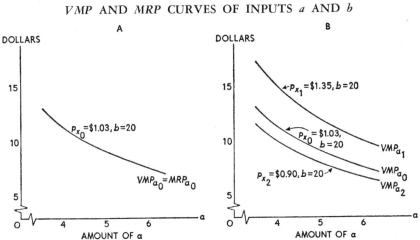

Figure 12–1A depicts the curve of the value of the marginal product of input *a* (or VMP_{a_0}) derived from the production function employed in the "normal" case in Chapter 6, when $b = 20$ and the price of a unit of *x* is assumed to be $1.03. A decrease in the price of the *product* to $p_{x_2} = \$.90$ shifts the curve to the left to VMP_{a_2}. Movements *along* the $VMP_a = MRP_a$ curve are produced by varying the amount of the input *a*, but a change in the amount of *b* also shifts the $VMP_a = MRP_a$ curve.

Under perfect competition in *product* markets, the VMP_a curve slopes down and to the right because of the principle of diminishing marginal returns to the variable input. Note that since the price of the product and the amount of b are held constant in Figure 12–1, the curve cannot slope downward to the right by reason of changes in the price of the product or in the amount of b.

Marginal Revenue Product

The marginal revenue product (MRP) is defined generally as the value to the firm of the marginal unit of an input. It is the rate of change of total revenue as the use of an *input* changes, or

$$MRP_a = \frac{\Delta R}{\Delta a}. \qquad (12\text{-}2)$$

Now the average rate of change of total revenue as *output* changes has already been defined in Equation (9–4) as the marginal revenue, or as $MR = \Delta R/\Delta x$; and the marginal productivity of an input, say a, has been defined in Chapter 6 as the rate of change of output as the input changes, or as $MPP_a = \Delta x/\Delta a$. By multiplying these two magnitudes together (see *Note A* at the end of this chapter), we produce an alternative definition of the marginal revenue product, or

$$MRP = (MR)(MPP_a) = \left(\frac{\Delta R}{\Delta x}\right)\left(\frac{\Delta x}{\Delta a}\right) = \frac{\Delta R}{\Delta a}. \qquad (12\text{-}3)$$

In the special case in which there is perfect competition in the sale of *products*, we also know from Equation (9–6) that the marginal revenue is equal to the price, since the *product* demand curve facing the individual seller is infinitely elastic. Accordingly, in such a case, since $MR = p_x$, it follows that

$$VMP_a = (MPP_a)(p_x) = MRP_a = (MPP_a)(MR). \qquad (12\text{-}4)$$

Thus, *in the special case of perfect competition in the sale of products,* the "value to the society" and the value to the firm derived from a marginal unit of *input* are the same because the price paid by consumers for the marginal unit of the product is equal to the addition to the firm's total revenue resulting from the sale of that marginal unit of product.

Alternatively, we can make use of Equation (9–6) and write

$$MRP_a = p_x\left(1 - \frac{1}{E_d}\right)(MPP_a), \qquad (12\text{-}3a)$$

which illustrates that if the elasticity of demand becomes infinitely great, this result is produced:

$$MRP_a = (p_x)(1)(MPP_a) = (p_x)(MPP_a) . \qquad (12\text{-}3b)$$

The last formula on the right is the same as that for VMP_a in Equation (12–1). Thus, in the *special* case of perfect competition in product markets, $VMP_a = MRP_a$; but *in the general case, VMP_a is not necessarily* equal to MRP_a. A graphical illustration of the latter situation appears in Figure 13–4 in Chapter 13.

Marginal Revenue Product as the Firm's Demand for Input

Since the curve of the marginal revenue product of a is the curve showing how the firm's total revenue changes as the amount of the input a employed changes when b and p_x are constant, it is the curve of the demand of the firm for that input *at a given price of the product when the amounts and prices of other inputs are given.*

Marginal and Average Cost of an Input; Input Supply Curve

We have already seen that the marginal cost of output is the rate of change of total cost as output changes. Similarly, *the marginal cost of any input is defined generally as the rate of change of total cost as the use of that input changes,* or as

$$MC_a = \frac{\Delta T}{\Delta a} . \qquad (12\text{-}5)$$

Average cost of any input is defined as the total cost of that input divided by the number of units purchased, or, in the case of input a, we have

$$AC_a = \frac{a p_a}{a} = p_a . \qquad (12\text{-}6)$$

The curve of the average cost of the input is thus the firm's input supply curve.

Relationship between Marginal and Average Costs of Inputs

The general formula employed to explain the relationship between marginal revenue and price of the *product* in Equation (9–6) can also be applied to the relationship between marginal cost and average cost (or price) of any *input*. Thus we have

$$MC_a = AC_a\left(1 + \frac{1}{E_{s_a}}\right) = p_a\left(1 + \frac{1}{E_{s_a}}\right), \qquad (12\text{-}7)$$

where E_{s_a} is the elasticity of supply of the input.

If there is perfect competition in the purchase of inputs, the individual firm will believe that it is so small a purchaser in relation to the total supply of inputs that it cannot affect the price of the input by the amount it buys. Thus, the supply curve facing the individual firm in the input market will be perfectly elastic as depicted in Figure 12–2.

Figure 12–2

INPUT SUPPLY CURVE FACING INDIVIDUAL FIRM UNDER
PERFECT COMPETITION IN THE FACTOR MARKET

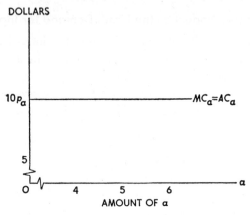

And if we substitute for E_{s_a} an infinitely large number in Equation (12–7), the result is

$$MC_a = AC_a \left(1 + \frac{1}{\text{Infinitely large number}} \right) = AC_a(1 + 0) = AC_a = p_a . \quad (12\text{--}7a)$$

Thus, in Figure 12–2, under perfect competition in the purchase of *inputs*, $MC_a = AC_a = p_a$. All three can then be depicted by a single horizontal line parallel to the X axis, just as the $MR = p_x$ equality is depicted by a similar line in the case of perfect competition in the *product* market. However, as we will see in Figure 13–6 in the next chapter, if conditions of competition and monopoly are intermingled in the factor market, we have $MC_a > AC_a = p_a$.

B. GENERAL EQUILIBRIUM CONDITIONS

Scope of This Section

The *general* short-run and long-run equilibrium conditions to be developed now apply both under conditions of perfect competition and under conditions in which competition is not perfect in either market, but they will be treated in this chapter with particular reference to the *special* case of perfect competition.

General Short-Run Input Equilibrium Condition: Marginal Productivity "Principle"

Consider the facts that (1) the short-run marginal cost *of an input* is the rate of change of total cost as the amount *of the input* changes $(\Delta T/\Delta a = MC_a)$; and (2) the marginal revenue product *of an input* is the rate of change of total revenue as the amount of the *input* changes $(\Delta R/\Delta a = MRP_a)$. For reasons which will be explained below, the general short-run equilibrium condition in the use of *variable* inputs is met when these two magnitudes are equal, or

$$MC_a = MRP_a, \ MC_b = MRP_b, \ MC_n = MRP_n, \qquad (12\text{-}8)$$

where all inputs $(a, b \ldots n)$ are variable. This equation can alternatively be written by making use of Equation (12–7), as

$$MC_a = p_a\left(1 + \frac{1}{E_{s_a}}\right) = p_x\left(1 - \frac{1}{E_d}\right)(MPP_a) = MRP_a. \qquad (12\text{-}8a)$$

Now Figure 12–1 depicts the case of perfect competition in the product market, and so $VMP_{a_0} = MRP_{a_0}$; and Figure 12–2 depicts the case of perfect competition in the factor market, and so $MC_a = p_a$. Thus, by combining the information from these two diagrams in Figure 12–3A, we have perfect competition in both markets.

Figure 12–3

**SHORT-RUN EQUILIBRIUM CONDITION FOR ALL VARIABLE INPUTS
AND LONG-RUN EQUILIBRIUM CONDITION FOR ALL
INPUTS UNDER PERFECT COMPETITION**

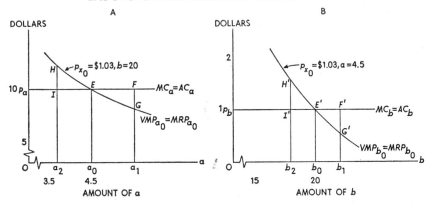

In Figure 12–3A, the firm is in equilibrium at E. For if it were to employ Oa_1 units of a, the MRP would be a_1G, but the marginal cost of a would be greater, or a_1F. Thus the firm would be adding more to its cost than to its revenue by employing additional units of a beyond Oa_0. Similarly, if it employed only Oa_2 units of a, the marginal cost would be a_2I, but the MRP would be greater, or a_2H. Thus, the firm could increase its profits by increasing the employment of a up to the point Oa_0, where the addition to total cost and the addition to total revenue are equal.

Similar diagrams can be drawn to explain the short-run equilibrium condition in the case of any other *variable* input. That is, if b were a variable and some other input, c, were held constant, the case of b would be described by Figure 12–3B. Thus, *for all variable inputs, in the short run,* the condition must be satisfied that the marginal cost of the input must be equal to its marginal revenue product, or $MC_a = MRP_a$. This condition is sometimes known as the *marginal productivity principle* or *doctrine*.

General Long-Run Input Equilibrium Condition

In the long run the firm will employ *all* of its inputs in such a way that the respective marginal revenue products of given inputs will be equal to their respective marginal costs. That is, *in the long run, the short-run equilibrium condition must be fulfilled for all inputs, including those which have been held fixed in the short run.* Assuming that b were held constant at 20 units in the short run, Figure 12–3A describes the situation with respect to input a, but since a and b are both variable in the long run and since $b = 20$ at the long-run optimum point, Figures 12–3A and 12–3B together depict the equilibrium positions with respect to a and b respectively in the long run.

Input and Output Equilibrium Conditions and the Principle of Substitution

Marshall's principle of substitution has already been employed many times in preceding chapters. This principle, it will be recalled, states that

$$\frac{MPP_a}{p_a} = \frac{MPP_b}{p_b} \cdots = \frac{MPP_n}{p_n} = d, \qquad (6\text{--}3)$$

or that, in equilibrium, inputs will be employed in such a way that the output obtained from an additional dollar's worth of any one *variable* input is just exactly equal to that obtained from an additional dollar's worth of any other *variable* input. The condition thus defines the point at which the inputs are being used in the most efficient *proportions* and must be met for all *variable* inputs in the short run and for *all* inputs in the long run.

How is this condition related to the present analysis? To answer this question, first *monetize* the principle by multiplying all of the *numerators* in the ratios in Equation (6–3) by the marginal revenue (MR) to produce

$$\frac{(MPP_a)(MR)}{p_a} = \frac{(MPP_b)(MR)}{p_b} \cdots = \frac{(MPP_n)(MR)}{p_n}$$

$$= (d)(MR) .$$

$$(12\text{–}9)$$

Equation (12–9) *is completely general insofar as product markets are concerned* and applies whether or not there is perfect competition in such markets, *but* it *assumes* that there is *perfect competition in factor markets.* That is, since it contains p_a, p_b, and p_n in the denominators of the ratios, it assumes perfect competition in input markets, or that the cost to the firm of an additional unit of a given input is equal to its price.

A completely general monetized formulation of the principle of substitution must take account of the facts that, if competition in the factor markets is not perfect, the marginal cost of the input will not be equal to the price, or average cost, of the input and that marginal cost is the relevant magnitude. (See the discussion of Figure 10–7 in Chapter 10.) Thus, a *completely general formulation* of this equation *would read* (where MC_a, MC_b, etc., are substituted for p_a, p_b, etc.):

$$\frac{(MPP_a)(MR)}{MC_a} = \frac{(MPP_b)(MR)}{MC_b} \cdots = \frac{(MPP_n)(MR)}{MC_n}$$

$$= (d)(MR) .$$

$$(12\text{–}10)$$

Now note that a completely general definition of the *marginal cost of output,* and one which is more general than the one used in Chapter 7 (which assumes input prices constant), is $MC_x = MC_a/MPP_a$. It follows that $MPP_a/MC_a = 1/MC_x$. Thus, assuming a, b, and n all represent *variable* inputs in the short run, since $d = 1/MC_x$, we have

$$\frac{(MPP_a)(MR)}{MC_a} = \frac{(MPP_b)(MR)}{MC_b} = \cdots = \frac{(MPP_n)(MR)}{MC_n}$$

$$= \frac{MR}{SMC_x} = 1 .$$

$$(12\text{–}10a)$$

That is, in general, *in any position of short-run equilibrium,* since $SMC_x = MR$, it follows that the *ratios of the marginal revenue products of all variable inputs* to their respective marginal costs are equal to unity.

And, in *any long-run equilibrium position, since all inputs are variable,* we have these *ratios* in the case of *all inputs* equal to unity:

$$\frac{(MPP_a)(MR)}{MC_a} = \frac{(MPP_b)(MR)}{MC_b} \cdots = \frac{(MPP_n)(MR)}{MC_n}$$

$$= \frac{MR}{SMC_x = LMC_x} = 1 \ . \tag{12-10b}$$

In this case we have, in addition, $SMC_x = LMC_x$. In both cases the ratios are also equal to $(d)(MR)$, since $d = 1/MC_x$.

Thus, *Marshall's principle of substitution stated in real terms* in Chapter 7 (where d is an amount of output) *defines the long-run return to outlay curve* assuming perfect competition in the factor market, while *the monetized principle* stated in Equations (12–10a and 12–10b) *defines the equilibrium position of the firm in the general case, either in the* • *short run or in the long run, depending on what is assumed,* but irrespective of the degree of competition in either market.

By making use of Equation (12–7), we can write Equation (12–10) in a useful way as

$$\frac{(MPP_a)\left[p_x\left(1 - \frac{1}{E_d}\right)\right]}{p_a\left(1 + \frac{1}{E_{s_a}}\right)} = \frac{(MPP_b)\left[p_x\left(1 - \frac{1}{E_d}\right)\right]}{p_b\left(1 + \frac{1}{E_{s_b}}\right)} \cdots$$

$$= \frac{(MPP_n)\left[p_x\left(1 - \frac{1}{E_d}\right)\right]}{p_n\left(1 + \frac{1}{E_{s_n}}\right)} \ . \tag{12-11}$$

In the special case of perfect competition in *both* markets, we have $E_d = E_{s_a} = \infty$, and thus $VMP_a = MRP_a$, etc.; and $p_a = MC_a$, etc.; and so, under perfect competition, we have

$$\frac{MRP_a = VMP_a}{MC_a = p_a} = \frac{MRP_b = VMP_b}{MC_b = p_b} \cdots = \frac{MRP_n = VMP_n}{MC_n = p_n} = 1 \ , \tag{12-12}$$

for all *variable* inputs in the short run and for *all* inputs in the long run.

Departures from perfect competition in the *product* market are reflected by the fact that the two terms in the *numerators* in Equation (12–12) are unequal. Departures from perfect competition in *factor* markets are indicated by the fact that the two terms in the *denominators* in this equation are unequal. These problems will be further considered in the next chapter.

The "Right" Amount of Inputs: Long-Run "Economic Efficiency"

Marshall's principle of substitution states the equilibrium condition relative to the *proportions* in which the inputs are being used but does *not* specify the equilibrium *amounts* of the inputs. That is, it is met at *one* point on every short-run cost curve and so it defines the long-run average cost curve, but it does not define the minimum point on that curve. However, in Chapter 9, we have seen that in the long run under perfect competition, there is a tendency for firms to operate at the least cost point as a result of the effects of the entry and exodus of new firms. (See the discussion of Figure 9–9 in Chapter 9.)

Equation (12–10b) shows that, in general, in *any long-run equilibrium position,* it must be true that the ratios of the MRP's/MC's are equal to unity and that the ratio of $MR/(SMC_x = LMC_x)$ is also equal to unity. Thus the ratio is merely another way of saying that $SMC_x = LMC_x = MR$ in the long-run equilibrium position. Now if there is perfect competition in both markets, we have in addition $MC_a = p_a$, etc., in the case of inputs, and $MRP_a = VMP_a$, etc., because $MR = p_x$ in the product market. And, finally, if the position is one of long-run equilibrium under perfect competition, we also have $SMC_x = LMC_x = MR = p_x = SAC_x = LAC_x$. Thus, it follows that in the long run, with all inputs variable, if there is perfect competition in both markets, our condition will read:

$$\frac{MRP_a = VMP_a}{MC_a = p_a} = \frac{MRP_b = VMP_b}{MC_b = p_b} \cdot \cdot \cdot = \frac{MRP_n = VMP_n}{MC_n = p_n} \tag{12-12a}$$

$$= \frac{MR = p_x}{SMC_x = LMC_x = SAC_x = LAC_x} = (d)(MR) = 1 .$$

In other words, in the long run under perfect competition, *all* inputs are used both in the "correct" proportions and in the "correct" amounts, and $N = 0$. Note, however, that Equation (12–12a) assumes perfect competition in both markets and is not as general as Equation (12–11). Equation (12–12a) is a basic equation of Welfare Economics, and we will consider it further in Chapter 16.

C. THE MARGINAL PRODUCTIVITY THEORY OF INCOME DISTRIBUTION

Statement of the Marginal Productivity Theory

The marginal productivity theory of income distribution originally stated that in the long run, under perfect competition, inputs would *tend* to receive a *real* rate of return which was just exactly equal to their marginal physical productivity in the production of outputs, or $p_a/p_x = MPP_a$. Moreover, according to the theory, the total return received by any one input (its share of the total product) could be computed by multiplying the rate of return by the amount of the input employed. Institutional arrangements determined the ownership of the inputs by individuals and were not dealt with by the theory because such arrangements were not matters of concern to economic theory. Finally, in the long run, under perfect competition, if each input received a return just equal to its "value to society," the total product would be just exactly exhausted, for the *normal* profits then being made by entrepreneurs would be just exactly equal to their marginal physical productivities also.

The theory can be applied to a firm, an industry, or an economy. However, some writers have noted that when the marginal productivity theory is applied to the firm, it is a theory of employment since the firm takes the price of the input as given under perfect competition, and that when the theory is applied to an economy as a whole, it is a theory of return to the input because, in such a case, the amount of the input is assumed to be given.[4] There is some basis for this distinction, but it is also accurate to define the theory as nothing more or less than a statement of the long-run equilibrium conditions of a firm, an industry, or an economy under perfect competition in both markets, depending upon the particular problem being considered.

A Graphical Illustration of the Marginal Productivity Theory

In the *Distribution of Wealth* in 1900, J. B. Clark utilized diagrams somewhat similar to the ones shown in Figure 12–4 to illustrate the marginal productivity theory.[5] However, he argued that in equilibrium under perfect competition in the long run, the marginal *physical* product (he used the term "final degree of productivity") of labor would be just equal to the *real* wage rate. Note that if $VMP_a = p_a = w_a$ in monetary terms, then $VMP_a/p_x = MPP_a = p_a/p_x = w_a/p_x$ in *real* terms, where w_a is the *money* wage rate and w_a/p_x represents the *money* wage divided by the price of the product, or the amount of the product which the money wage will purchase, *the real wage*. In the present context, the theory can be explained either in real or in monetary terms.

Clark asserted, but did not prove, that the total wage bill determined according to the marginal productivity theory in Figure 12–4A (rectan-

---

[4] Alan M. Cartter, *Theory of Wages and Employment* (Homewood, Ill.: Richard D. Irwin, Inc., 1959), esp. chap. ii.

[5] Clark, *op. cit.*, p. 201.

gle Ow_aEa_0) would be equal to wages determined as a residual in Figure 12–4B (triangle w_bHE'), and that interest determined according to the marginal productivity theory (rectangle $Ow_bE'b_0$ in Figure 12–4B) would be equal to interest as a residual (triangle w_aKE in Figure 12–4A). That is, he *merely asserted* that the total product would be just exactly exhausted if inputs were paid at a rate equal to their marginal productivities.

Clark argued that, in the long run, competition among employers would drive the wage rate ($w_a = p_a$) up to the point at which it was

Figure 12–4

ILLUSTRATION OF THE MARGINAL PRODUCTIVITY
THEORY OF INCOME DISTRIBUTION

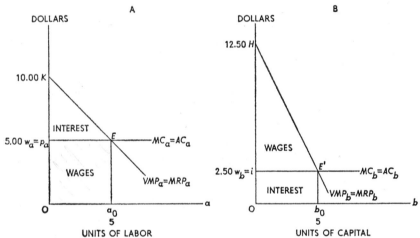

just exactly equal to the $VMP_a = MRP_a$ of the input. And competition among workers would keep the wage rate from rising above the point at which it was just equal to the $VMP_a = MRP_a$. Similarly, in the long run, competition among suppliers of capital would keep the price of capital (interest rate) from rising above the $VMP_b = MRP_b$ of capital, while competition among employers for the use of capital would insure that the interest rate was not less than $VMP_b = MRP_b$.

Clark summarized his theory by saying:

(1) Wages and interest are both determined by the law of final productivity.
(2) When, in an illustrative case, one of these incomes is so determined, the other appears to be a residuum.
(3) As a residuum, such an income would be left in the *entrepreneurs'* hands; but it is actually taken from them by a further action of the final productivity law.

(4) *Entrepreneurs'* profit and residual income are synonymous terms. The static conditions assumed in the present study preclude the existence of such *entrepreneurs'* gains.[6]

Note that Clark emphasized that the theory is static. It assumes that technology remains unchanged. The theory does *not* purport to explain the returns actually being received by any input in the real world *at any given moment of time.* Instead, it states that the *real* rate of return received by any input *tends in the long run under perfect competition* to be equal to the marginal product of that input.

It has been noted that Clark did not demonstrate that the total product would in fact be exactly exhausted if each input were paid at a rate equal to its marginal product. Yet this proof is critical insofar as the theory is concerned. A number of other writers subsequently devoted themselves to this task.[7] A demonstration can be given by use of Euler's Theorem.

Euler's Theorem and the Marginal Productivity Theory: The "Adding Up" Problem

Considerable use has already been made, in preceding chapters, of Euler's Theorem. This theorem, it will be recalled, is the basis of the statement that if the production function is linearly homogeneous, the total product will be just exactly equal to the sums of the respective marginal productivities of the inputs multiplied by the respective amounts of the inputs used, or

$$x = \frac{\partial x}{\partial a}a + \frac{\partial x}{\partial b}b + \cdots \frac{\partial x}{\partial n}n . \tag{3-3}$$

Now, the production function which is the basis of our present arithmetical and graphical illustrations is not linearly homogeneous, since we are currently using the function written to describe the "normal" case of the U-shaped long-run average cost curve used in Chapter 7.

However, this fact causes no great difficulty. Euler's Theorem also applies at the long-run least cost point, the point of long-run economic efficiency. For, at that point, returns to scale are momentarily constant. That this is the case can be illustrated by substituting into Equation (3-3) the values of the marginal products and the amounts of the inputs used when the long-run average cost is least at E in Figure 12–5B (which appears later). Thus we have

$$x_{4.544, 20} = (4.544)(9.72) + (.9719)(20) = 63.60 . \tag{3-3'}$$

---

[6] *Ibid.,* pp. 203–4. (Italics his. I have omitted a footnote reference used by Clark in this passage.)

[7] For the history of the proof, see Stigler, *op. cit.,* chap. xii.

In other words, if the *real* rate of return to input *a* in the long-run equilibrium position under perfect competition is 9.72 units of *x* while the *real* rate of return to *b* is .972 units when $p_a = \$10$ and $p_b = \$1.00$, the total product will be just exactly exhausted between them. The principle applies, of course, to any number of inputs. Moreover, since only normal profits are made in the long run under perfect competition, net revenue is zero, or $N = 0$, and no terms need to be included in the equation to take account of this fact.

Euler's Theorem can also be monetized by multiplying both sides of Equation (3–3) by p_x to produce

$$xp_x = \frac{\partial x}{\partial a}ap_x + \frac{\partial x}{\partial b}bp_x + \cdots \frac{\partial x}{\partial n}np_x. \qquad (12\text{–}13)$$

Arithmetically, at *E* in Figure 12–5B, we thus have

$$(63.60)(\$1.03) = (9.72)(4.544)(\$1.03) + (.9719)(20)(\$1.03)$$
$$= \$45.44 + \$20.00 = \$65.44. \qquad (12\text{–}13')$$

(There is a slight discrepancy due to rounding of numbers.)

In short, Equation (12–13) is a more complicated way of saying (Total Revenue = Total Cost) in equilibrium in the long run under perfect competition, but it also illustrates that, since, in that case, the prices of the inputs are equal to the money values of their respective marginal products, total revenue will be just exactly exhausted by total payments to the inputs. A graphical illustration of this equation appears in Figure 13–3 of the next chapter.

A More Generalized Factor Payment Equation

The monetized version of Euler's Theorem in Equation (12–13) applies only in equilibrium in the long run under perfect competition in both markets. A more generalized equation can be written to apply to the long-run equilibrium position irrespective of the degree of competition in the *product* market, *provided there is perfect competition in the factor market*. It is derived as follows.

First, if a firm is in long-run equilibrium, making only normal profits, total revenue will be equal to total cost ($R = T_L$). Now, in previous chapters, we have already written the following equations:

$$R = xp_x, \qquad (9\text{–}1)$$

$$T_L = ap_a + bp_b. \qquad (7\text{–}8)$$

Also, we have the definition of the marginal cost of output, when input prices are constant, in Chapter 7 as $MC = (1/MPP_a)(p_a)$. And we know from our discussion of the long-run average cost curve in Chapter 7 that the short-run and long-run marginal costs are equal at that level of output at which the long-run average cost curve is tangent to a given short-run average cost curve. And finally, we know that when a long-run equilibrium position is attained, these marginal costs must be equal to the marginal revenue. Thus, *in any position of long-run equilibrium (if input prices are constant), we have*

$$MR = MC_x = (1/MPP_a)(p_a); \text{ and } MR = MC_x = (1/MPP_b)(p_b), \text{ etc.}$$

Accordingly, it follows that

$$(MR)(MPP_a) = p_a, (MR)(MPP_b) = p_b, \text{ etc.}$$

We can substitute these values for the prices of the inputs into Equation (7–8) to produce the total cost *in such a long-run equilibrium position* as

$$T_L = a(MR)(MPP_a) + b(MR)(MPP_b) + \cdots n(MR)(MPP_n). \quad (7\text{–}8a)$$

Now, since the long-run equilibrium position in this case is assumed to be one in which net revenue is zero so that $T_L = R$, we can also write the following equation to define total revenue, $R = xp_x$, at the equilibrium point as

$$xp_x = a(MR)(MPP_a) + b(MR)(MPP_b) + \cdots n(MR)(MPP_n). \quad (12\text{–}14)$$

This equation shows that under the assumed conditions, if inputs are paid at a rate equal to their $MRP = (MPP)(MR)$, total revenue will be just accounted for by total costs. As written above, the equation applies only in the long run when $N = 0$. However, it can easily be amended, by adding N as a final term, to make it apply when greater than normal profits or losses are being made in the long run, or when $N \neq 0$. Thus, our final long-run equilibrium income distribution equation becomes

$$R = xp_x = a(MR)(MPP_a) + b(MR)(MPP_b) + \cdots n(MR)(MPP_n) + N. \quad (12\text{–}14a)$$

Under conditions of perfect competition in both markets, since $MR = p_x$ and $N = 0$, Equation (12–14a) produces precisely the same result as the monetized version of Euler's Theorem in Equation (12–13). However, Equation (12–14a) is more general than Equation (12–13), since the former applies irrespective of the degree of competition in the product market, although it assumes perfect competition in the factor market. An even more general equation which applies irrespective of the degree of competition in *either* market appears in the next chapter.

D. INTERRELATIONSHIP BETWEEN PRODUCT AND
FACTOR MARKET ILLUSTRATED

Constant Costs, Nonlinearly Homogeneous Production Function

Figure 12–5 illustrates constant costs. It brings together a diagram showing the equilibrium position of the firm with respect to the employment of inputs in the long run under perfect competition in the *factor* market with the corresponding diagram (Figure 9–9A from Chapter 9) showing the equilibrium position of the firm in the long run under perfect competition in the *product* market.

Figure 12–5

INTERRELATIONSHIP BETWEEN PRODUCT AND FACTOR
MARKETS IN THE CASE OF CONSTANT COSTS
AND PERFECT COMPETITION

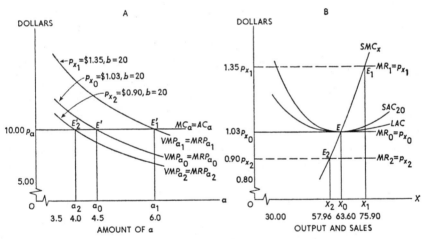

Thus, in Figure 12–5B, which is the same as Figure 9–9A, the firm is initially in long-run equilibrium in the *product* market at E producing output OX_0 at a price of Op_{x_0}; and in the *factor* market, it is in long-run equilibrium at E' employing Oa_0 units of a in an optimum size plant ($b = 20$). The total cost of input a is $Op_aE'a_0$. At E' the value of the marginal product of a is equal to the marginal cost of a in Figure 12–5A, and the long-run and short-run average and marginal costs of the output, OX_0, are equal to the marginal revenue and to the price at E in Figure 12–5B.

Assume now an increase in the demand for the product x. In the case of Figure 12–5B, this fact means that the firm will increase its output to OX_1 and attain a new short-run equilibrium position at E_1, where it will make greater than normal profits, since net revenue is now positive, $N > 0$. In order to increase its output in the short run in this way, the firm must increase its use of the variable input a to Oa_1 in Figure 12–5A. Thus the marginal productivity of a decreases, but the price of x increases in an offsetting way, so that the price of a remains unchanged. (The marginal productivity of b will also be different when a larger amount of a is used, but the firm cannot vary the amount of b in the short run.) At E' we have $MRP_{a_0} = (MPP_a)(p_{x_0}) = (9.72)(\$1.03) = \$10 = p_a$, and at E'_1 we have $MRP_{a_1} = (MPP_{a_1})(p_{x_1}) = (7.378)(\$1.35) = p_a = \$10$. The short-run marginal cost of x, however, has risen, for at output OX_0 we have $SMC_{x_0} = (1/MPP_a)(p_a) = (1/9.72)(\$10) = \$1.03$; and at output OX_1 we have $SMC_{x_1} = (1/7.378)(\$10) = \$1.35$. Greater than normal profits are made by the firm in the short run at E_1 in Figure 12–5B, because the price of x is greater than the average cost of that output, $p_{x_1} > SAC_{x_1}$.

Accordingly, in the long run new firms enter the industry while input prices remain constant, since the supply of them is assumed perfectly elastic. The total supply of the product thus increases, and the price of the product falls in Figure 12–5B to Op_{x_2}, while losses are incurred at output OX_2. The fall in product prices reduces the firm's use of input a to Oa_2 in Figure 12–5A, where it is on still another VMP curve. The marginal productivity of a rises as the amount of a used declines, but the price of x declines in an offsetting way so that the price of the input remains constant, as before.

Eventually, an exodus of firms gets under way, the supply of the product decreases, and the price of the product again rises. Thus, in Figure 12–5B, there is a tendency to return to the long-run equilibrium position at E in the case of the individual firm, and the total increase in market supply of the output (see Figure 9–9B) is attributed to the entry of new firms. The amounts of a and of b used by *all* firms (the industry as a whole) is greater than before because there are more firms in the industry than before. But in Figure 12–5B, as the firm regains its original zero net revenue long-run equilibrium position at E, the employment of input a by *this* firm is once more at its original long-run equilibrium level of Oa_0 in Figure 12–5A (and in Figure 12–3A), while that of b is also at its original level (Ob_0 in Figure 12–3B).

Increasing and Decreasing Costs

Figure 12–6 depicts a similar situation in the case of increasing costs. The original equilibrium position of the firm in Figure 12–6B, which is the same as Figure 9–12B in Chapter 9, is at E_0, and the original amount of input used is Oa_0 in Figure 12–6A. Assume again an increase in the demand for and in the price of the product. In the short run there will be greater than normal profits, and the amount of input *a* used will temporarily increase (not depicted).

Figure 12–6

INTERRELATIONSHIP BETWEEN PRODUCT AND FACTOR
MARKETS IN THE CASE OF INCREASING COSTS
AND PERFECT COMPETITION

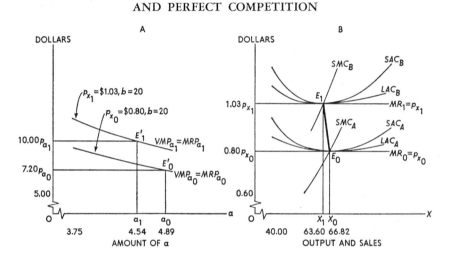

Figure 12–6B assumes that there are external diseconomies and that the prices of the inputs increase, although not in the same proportions, when the number of firms increases. (See the explanation of Figure 9–12 in Chapter 9.) Eventually, in the final new long-run equilibrium position at E_1, the price of the product will be greater than it was in the initial position (or $Op_{x_0} < Op_{x_1}$). Also, the price of input *a* is assumed to rise from $7.20 per unit to $10 per unit, while the price of input *b* is assumed to rise only from $.90 per unit to $1.00 per unit, and output will be slightly smaller in the new long-run equilibrium position at E_1 than it was at E_0. The firm's cost curves shift upward, but not in a parallel way, in Figure 12–6B.

This reduction in output *by the firm* is depicted in Figure 12–6A by the fact that a smaller amount of *a* is being employed in the new long-run position at E'_1 than was employed in the initial position at E'_0. For $Oa_1 < Oa_0$. In our diagram, the amount of *b* used remains the same. The curve of the VMP_b is not depicted, but, *in our case,* it would shift to the right as the price of *x* rose and the amount of *a* diminished. Increases in the price of x will always operate to shift the VMP_b curve to the right. In the case of our assumed production function, the marginal product of b decreases as the amount of a decreases. And, *with the chosen values in our example*, the *relative increase* in the price of x amounts to $\$.23/\$.80 = .287$, while the *relative decrease* in the marginal product of b amounts only to $.158/1.13 = .140$. Thus, the first of these influences is stronger in our case. (If the price of b had not also changed, the amount of b used would have changed.)

However, even though the amount of a decreases and the amount of b remains the same *in the case of the individual firm* in Figure 12–6, the total amount of both inputs used *by the industry* in the new long-run equilibrium position will be greater in our case than before the increase in demand. (See Figure 9–12B in Chapter 9.) For it was an initial increase in demand which caused the price of x to increase, and if each firm produces less after the increase in demand, the increase in the total amount in the market can only be accounted for by an increase in the number of firms. And, since the amount of x sold in the market has increased and the prices of both inputs have risen, the total use of both inputs has increased.

The case of decreasing costs, or of a forward-falling supply curve, can be analyzed in a similar way by treating E'_1 and E_1 as the initial long-run equilibrium positions and E'_0 and E_0 as the final positions in the diagram, as in Figure 9–11 in Chapter 9.

Thus the two markets depicted in Figure 2–1 in Chapter 2 and the relationship between them have finally been illustrated. Factor prices depend on the supply of the inputs and on the demand for inputs which is derived from the demand for products. If input prices remain constant when demand for output increases, output prices will also be constant in the long run; if input prices increase, costs will increase, and product prices will also rise in the long run; and if input prices decrease, costs will decrease, and product prices will fall in the long run.

Changes in Input Prices with Constant Product Prices

If input prices change while product prices do not, and the demand for the product remains unchanged, it is likely that other industries employing the given input have experienced increases in demand, thereby increasing the price of the input in question.

Figure 12–7 shows that an increase in the price of an input without an increase in the price of the product must result in a decrease in the amount of the input employed, *other things equal.* That is, if the price of the input rises from Op_{a_0} to Op_{a_2}, the employment of the factor will decline from Oa_0 to Oa_2. Similarly, a decrease in the price of the factor a to Op_{a_1} will, other things equal, increase the employment of the factor to Oa_1; but it will reduce the use of other inputs, since some of a will be substituted for them. The "other things equal" assumption, however, limits the analysis, and problems of this type are most easily analyzed by means of isoquant diagrams. One such case has already been discussed in conjunction with Figure 6–6 in Chapter 6.

Figure 12–7

EFFECT OF CHANGE IN INPUT PRICE WITH CONSTANT PRODUCT PRICE

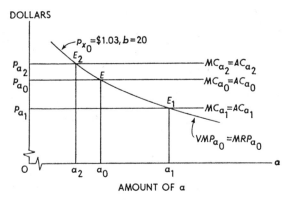

AMOUNT OF a

It should be noted also that an increase in the demand for output produced by *other* industries employing the given inputs will not necessarily result in a proportionate increase in the prices of the inputs. For inputs are not used in the same proportions in all industries, and an increase in the demand for a product of another industry may increase the demand for input b more than it increases the demand for input a. In such a case, if the price of b rises in a different proportion from that of a, the quantities of the inputs used will change, and the $VMP = MRP$ curves must shift. General, rather than partial, equilibrium analysis must thus be employed.

Arithmetical and Graphical Illustration of the Elasticity of Substitution

The elasticity of substitution is sometimes used in dealing with problems of the effect of changes in input prices. This measure, it will be recalled, has already been defined in Equation (6–6) in Chapter 6 as the relative change in the proportion between the two inputs divided by the relative change in the technical rate of substitution. If the elasticity of substitution is zero, inputs will be used in the same proportions, irrespective of what changes occur in their relative prices. On the other hand, if, as a result of a small increase in the price of *a*, the entire output were to be produced with *b* alone, the elasticity of substitution would be infinitely great. An arithmetical and graphical illustration of the use of this elasticity follows.

Figure 12–8A is based on Figure 6–8 and shows the firm initially in equilibrium at *A* on *Iq* 16.85. Assume that the price of *a* now declines from $3.65 to $1.75 per unit, while that of *b* remains constant at $1.00 per unit and that the firm continues to produce the same output as before. Since more of *a* is being used in the new position at *C* in Figure 12–8A, while less of *b* is being used, and since the price of *b* has not changed, it is clear that the total return to *b* has fallen below its previous level. As a matter of fact, in Figure 12–8A the total return to *a* has also declined from ($3.65) (1.37) = $5.00 to ($1.75) (1.52) = 2.66. *But what has happened to the relative return to a?*

One direct method of answering this question is to compare the return to *a* in terms of *b* before and after the price change. Thus, at *A*, we have the ratio between the earnings of the two inputs as

$$\frac{a_1 p_{a_1}}{b_1 p_{b_1}} = \frac{(1.37)(\$3.65)}{(3.00)(\$1.00)} = 1.66 \ .$$

After the price decrease, the ratio is

$$\frac{a_2 p_{a_2}}{b_2 p_{b_2}} = \frac{(1.52)(\$1.75)}{(2.66)(\$1.00)} = 1.00 \ .$$

The return to *a* has decreased *relative* to that of *b* as the price of *a* has declined and that of *b* has remained constant. Thus, in the case of our example, *a* and *b* are both earning less absolutely, but *a* is also earning less relatively than before.

Next let us compute the elasticity of substitution (a/b) in this case:

$$E_{ss} = \frac{\dfrac{b}{a}\Delta\left(\dfrac{a}{b}\right)}{\dfrac{-\Delta T_{ba}}{T_{ba}}} = \frac{(3/1.37)(.1148)}{1.90/3.65} = \frac{.2514}{.5205} = .4821 \ . \qquad (6\text{-}6')$$

The decline in the price of *a* has decreased the technical rate of substitution of *b* for *a* by 52.05 percent. At the same time, the ratio of the use of *a* to *b* has increased by only 25.14 percent. In other words, a 1 percent decrease in the technical rate of substitution of *b* for *a* produces an increase of less than one half of 1 percent (only .4821 of 1 percent, to be exact) in the ratio of the use of *a* to *b* in our example. (Since we are comparing the effect of the decrease in the technical rate of substitution of b for a with the change in the proportion of a to b, a minus sign has been placed before ΔT_{ba} in our formula.)

It follows, therefore, that the elasticity of substitution is less than unity and that total earnings of a have fallen relative to those of b. If the elasticity of substitution were equal to unity, the return to a would have remained unchanged relative to that of b, and if the elasticity of substitution had been greater than unity, the return to a would have increased relative to that of b. That is, the elasticity of substitution provides information similar to that provided by our simple comparison of the ratios of the earnings of the two inputs before and after the price change.

The relationship between the relative return to input a and the elasticity of substitution is illustrated in Figure 12–8B. In this diagram, the X axis measures the ratio between the inputs, a/b, and the Y axis

Figure 12–8

THE ELASTICITY OF SUBSTITUTION

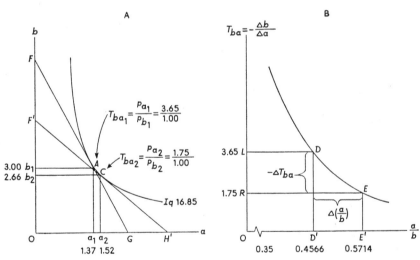

measures the technical rate of substitution of b for a, T_{ba}. The negative slope of the curve on which D and E are located shows that the technical rate of substitution of b for a diminishes as the proportion of a used with b increases. The elasticity of this curve is the elasticity of substitution.

Point D in Figure 12–8B represents the same equilibrium position as does point A in Figure 12–8A. After the price of a has declined, the new equilibrium position in Figure 12–8A represented by C appears as E in Figure 12–8B. Now recall that, in equilibrium, the Marshallian principle of substitution requires that the technical rate of substitution of b for a must be equal to the ratio of the prices of a and b, or, at A and at C in Figure 12–8A and at D and at E in Figure 12–8B, we must have

$$-\frac{\Delta b}{\Delta a} = \frac{p_a}{p_b}.$$

Next consider areas $OLDD'$ and $OREE'$ in Figure 12–8B. Since $OL = T_{ba_1} = p_{a_1}/p_{b_1}$ and $OD' = a_1/b_1$ in equilibrium at A and D, and since $OR = T_{ba_2} = p_{a_2}/p_{b_2}$ and $OE' = a_2/b_2$ in equilibrium at C and E in Figures 12–8A and 12–8B, it follows that area $OLDD' = (OL)(OD') = (p_{a_1}/p_{b_1})(a_1/b_1) = (3.65)(.4566) = 1.66$, the ratio between the earnings of the inputs *before* the price change. Similarly, area $OREE' = (OR)(OE') = (p_{a_2}/p_{b_2})(a_2/b_2) = (1.75)(.5714) = 1.00$, the ratio between the earnings *after* the price change. Again we see that, without output remaining constant, the relative position of a has worsened in terms of b, and both have suffered an absolute loss in earnings as a result of the decrease in the price of a.

In order for the *relative* return to a to have remained unchanged when the price of a decreased and the technical rate of substitution therefore also decreased, it would have been necessary for the ratio of a to b to have increased to .9486 in Figures 12–8A and 12–8B, and the isoquants would then have had to be very flat. That this is the case can be seen from the fact that in this case the ratio of the absolute returns at points C and E would then have had to have been 1.66, or

$$\frac{p_{a_2} a_2}{p_{b_2} b_2} = 1.75\left(\frac{a_2}{b_2}\right) = 1.66 ,$$

from which it follows that $a_2/b_2 = 1.66/1.75 = .9486$. The change in the ratio of a to b would then have been $.9486 - .4566 = .4920$. We can compute the *arc* elasticity of substitution between the points A and C or D and E, upon the assumption that the relative return to a did remain unchanged in this way as the price of a decreased, by using the technical rate of substitution in the *initial* position and the ratio between b and a in the *final* position in our formula. (This procedure is analogous to that which we employed in determining the arc elasticity of demand in Chapter 4, where we used the new position price and the initial position quantity, and it can be justified by an argument analogous to the one given there.) The ratio of b to a is merely the reciprocal of the ratio of a to b. Employing the indicated weights, we have the arc elasticity of substitution between A and C or between D and E according to these new assumptions as

$$E_{ss} = \frac{\frac{b_2}{a_2}\Delta\left(\frac{a}{b}\right)}{\frac{-\Delta T_{ba}}{T_{ba}}} = \frac{\left(\frac{1}{.9486}\right)\left(.4920\right)}{.5205} = \frac{.5186}{.5205} = .9963 .$$

Thus the arc elasticity of substitution is equal to .9963, or approximately to unity in this case, as it should be, since the relative return to a has been assumed to remain constant.

Some writers have employed the concept of elasticity of substitution to analyze the effects of factor price changes on the relative shares of the inputs, especially in cases of comparisons of returns to capital and labor. There are, however, many difficulties inherent in the use of this concept. Most especially, *it should be noted that this elasticity concept assumes that output remains constant when factor prices change,* since it is concerned with movement *along* an isoquant. This condition sharply limits the use which can be made of the concept in dealing with real world problems.[8]

E. EMPIRICAL STUDIES OF THE MARGINAL PRODUCTIVITY THEORY

Professor Paul Douglas' Study

It has been noted briefly in Chapter 6 that beginning in 1928, Senator Paul Douglas, who was then Professor of Economics at the University of Chicago, sought to derive production functions for a number of different regions and periods. His work in this field constituted a pioneering effort. In his major study, Douglas, together with Charles W. Cobb, attempted to determine the influence on production in the United States of capital and labor during the years 1899–1922. They measured capital (C) by an index number based on money additions to capital goods, and labor (L) by an index of the number employed in manufacturing in the given years. Product (P) was measured by an index of physical production, in which physical quantities of a variety of products

---

[8] For additional discussion and some criticisms of the concept, see R. G. D. Allen, *Mathematical Analysis for Economists* (London: Macmillan & Co., Ltd., 1950), pp. 340–43; Paul H. Douglas, *The Theory of Wages* (New York: The Macmillan Co., 1934), pp. 57–59; J. R. Hicks, *The Theory of Wages* (London: Macmillan & Co., Ltd., 1932), pp. 117–20; Abba P. Lerner, *The Economics of Control* (New York: The Macmillan Co., 1946), pp. 146–53; Joan Robinson, *The Economics of Imperfect Competition* (London: Macmillan & Co., Ltd., 1932), p. 256 and p. 230; and Sidney Weintraub, *An Approach to the Theory of Income Distribution* (Philadelphia: Chilton Co., 1958), pp. 138–39.

were reduced to index numbers and weighted by relative values added by manufacturing in given years.[9]

The method of least squares, which, as has been noted in Chapter 5, involves minimizing the deviations from the actual values of a line of "best fit," was then employed to derive the following production function for the United States:

$$P = 1.01L^{3/4}C^{1/4} = 1.01\sqrt[4]{L^3}\ \sqrt[4]{C}\ . \tag{D-1}$$

This production function is linearly homogeneous, and in the case in which either the input of C or of L is zero, P is also zero. The function thus involves diminishing returns to variable inputs and constant returns to scale.

The Cobb-Douglas production function states that a 1 percent increase in labor, with capital constant, will increase output by three fourths of 1 percent, while a 1 percent increase in capital, with labor constant, will increase output by one fourth of 1 percent. The fact that labor and capital are found to share in the total product in the proportion of 3 to 1 respectively is consistent with another widely held view that the total share of labor in the national product has constantly averaged about 75 percent in the United States.

However, aside from the fact that the statistical least-squares technique used is subject to criticism in the light of statistical theories developed since the study was made, a serious conceptual problem also exists in the case of the Douglas study. Precisely what is measured is not altogether clear because, although different grades of labor and capital do not pose a problem for the marginal productivity theory (each can be treated as a separate input), the Douglas study involves an attempt to measure the productivity of labor and capital in the "economy as a whole." In short, one of the unanswered questions is: What exactly are the labor and capital inputs of the economy as a whole?

For reasons such as this, the conclusions concerning the relative stability of labor's share of the national income, as well as the Douglas study and others based upon it, have not gone unchallenged. Professor Robert Solow, for example, has questioned the proposition that "the share of the national income accruing to labor is one of the great constants of nature, like the velocity of light or the incest taboo."[10] He has

---

[9] Douglas, *op. cit.* See also Douglas and Grace Gunn, "Further Measurements of Marginal Productivity," *Quarterly Journal of Economics,* Vol. LIV (May, 1940), pp. 339–428.

[10] Robert M. Solow, "A Skeptical Note on the Constancy of Relative Shares," *American Economic Review,* Vol. XLVIII (September, 1958), pp. 618–31.

pointed to the fact that the marginal productivity theory assumes technology constant, and he has also emphasized that the conception of aggregate distributive shares (the return to a factor multiplied by the number of units of it employed) for an economy as a whole is a nebulous one. He has defined "constancy" as the absence of fluctuations in the aggregate share of a factor as compared with its individual components and has argued that the belief that labor's aggregate share has not fluctuated, when it is defined in this way, is "probably" wrong.

Professor Irving B. Kravis has similarly rejected the notion that relative shares in the national income have been constant during the past half century in the United States.[11] Instead, he has found that there has been an increase in labor's share at the expense of the share of property owners, and he has suggested that this change may have occurred as a result of noneconomic factors, such as "our society's quest for social justice" in the form of governmental interferences with the regular market mechanism. However, if this reason is accepted, the marginal productivity theory is not refuted (although the Douglas conclusion would be), since the theory assumes an absence of such interferences. Indeed, such a reason might actually be used by some to support the theory, by arguing that, except for such interferences, the returns would have been determined in accordance with the theory!

Various related studies made under the auspices of the National Bureau of Economic Research have already been mentioned in the discussion of production functions in Chapter 6. As has been noted there, some of these emphasize the problems of measurement. On the whole, when the many problems involved are considered, the results of all these studies are far from conclusive,[12] but some progress in measurement has been made.

"Functional Distribution" in the National Income Statistics

Table 12–1 contains data concerning the shares of the total national income paid out as interest, rent, profits, and employee compensation as reported by the Department of Commerce. The table in which they appear is officially titled "National Income, by Distributive Shares." However, the student should realize that the classifications used in this ta-

---

[11] Irving B. Kravis, "Relative Income Shares in Fact and Theory," *American Economic Review*, Vol. XLIX (December, 1959), pp. 917–49.

[12] See, for example, John W. Kendrick, *Productivity Trends: Capital and Labor* (National Bureau of Economic Research Occasional Paper No. 53) (New York, 1956); and Solomon Fabricant, *Basic Facts on Productivity Change* (National Bureau of Economic Research Occasional Paper No. 63) (New York, 1959).

Table 12–1

NATIONAL INCOME, BY DISTRIBUTIVE SHARES, SELECTED YEARS

(In Billions of Dollars)

Item	1929	1933	1950	1958	1961
Compensation of employees	51.1	29.5	154.2	257.1	302.9
Proprietors' income	14.8	5.6	37.5	46.1	49.6
Rental income of persons	5.4	2.0	9.0	12.2	11.7
Corporate profits and inventory valuation adjustment	10.1	−2.0	35.7	37.2	46.2
Net interest	6.4	5.0	5.5	14.8	20.0
National income	87.8	40.2	241.9	367.4	430.2

Source: Federal Reserve Bulletin (Washington, D.C., March, 1962), p. 358. (Data collected by the Department of Commerce.)

ble are necessarily institutional rather than functional since the statistics are collected on an institutional rather than on a functional basis. In general, the data concerning compensation of employees and profits are reasonably reliable since they are collected from various government agencies having jurisdiction over social security and income taxes. However, the data concerning rental income of persons are quite unreliable, as are those relating to proprietors' income. The "rental income of persons" figure, for example, includes the imputed value of owner-occupied dwellings, and, as we will see in Chapter 14, it therefore includes more than merely the pure economic rent of land, while the "proprietors' income" figure contains elements of all of the types of functional returns. In short, although they are useful for many purposes, the national income statistics do *not* represent statistical compilations based upon the marginal productivity theory.

Alternative Macroeconomic Theories

In recent years there have been numerous attempts to develop macroeconomic theories of wages and of interest on grounds that such theories can be more directly related to the Keynesian national income approach than is true in the case of the marginal productivity theory and because of dissatisfaction with the marginal productivity theory. Some attention will be given in Chapter 15 to the macroeconomic interest theories, but consideration of the macroeconomic wage theories is beyond the scope of this book. However, the interested student may find the references to the latter indicated in the footnote below useful.[13]

---

[13] Kenneth Boulding, *A Reconstruction of Economics* (New York: John Wiley & Sons, Inc., 1950), chap. xiv; and Sidney Weintraub, *An Approach to the Theory of Income Distribution* (Philadelphia: Chilton Co., 1958).

Criticisms of the Marginal Productivity Theory

Numerous criticisms can be and have been made of the marginal productivity theory. Thus, the theory has been attacked on grounds that inputs are not homogeneous. Such an objection fails to recognize that the theory can be stated in terms of any number (n) of inputs. Lack of homogeneity does, however, create difficult problems for the statistician in this area. Other criticisms, such as the fact that the theory assumes technology constant, are more significant from a theoretical point of view. The facts that inputs are not mobile and that there are noncompeting groups of inputs, and that differences in ability exist among people, are considered in the following chapters where various theories of the returns to the broad traditional categories of the factors of production—land, labor, capital, and entrepreneurs—are examined.

NOTE A TO CHAPTER 12

In the text, the marginal revenue product (MRP) has been defined in Equation (12–3) as equal to

$$MRP_a = (MR)(MPP_a) = \left(\frac{\Delta R}{\Delta x}\right)\left(\frac{\Delta x}{\Delta a}\right) = \frac{\Delta R}{\Delta a}. \qquad (12\text{–}3)$$

Rewriting this equation by substituting into it the definition of marginal revenue provided in Equation (9–4), we have

$$MRP = \left((p_x + \Delta p_x) + x\frac{\Delta p_x}{\Delta x}\right)\left(\frac{\Delta x}{\Delta a}\right), \qquad (i)$$

or

$$MRP = (p_x + \Delta p_x)\frac{\Delta x}{\Delta a} + x\frac{\Delta p_x}{\Delta a}, \qquad (ii)$$

which is the same as the definition obtained by taking the derivative of the total revenue function, or

$$\frac{\partial(p_x x)}{\partial a} = p_x\frac{\partial x}{\partial a} + x\frac{\partial p_x}{\partial a}, \qquad (iia)$$

obtained by the standard rule for the differentiation of the product of two functions. An increase in sales will reduce price if the demand curve is negatively sloped. In such a case, $\Delta p_x/\Delta a$ is negative in the above equations. In the case in which price does not change as sales change (perfect competition in the sale of products), we have $\Delta p_x/\Delta a = 0$. The first term on the right in Equation (iia) is the increase in total revenue resulting from the additional output produced by the use of an additional unit of *input,* the "sales gain." The second term on the right (which is negative if price declines as sales increase with increases in the use of the input) is the reduction in total revenue resulting from the reduction in price of the previous quantity sold, the "price loss." The marginal revenue product is the algebraic sum of the two.

SELECTED READINGS

BOBER, M. M. *Intermediate Price and Income Theory,* chap. xiii. Rev. ed. New York: W. W. Norton & Co., Inc., 1962.

CARTTER, ALAN M. *Theory of Wages and Employment.* Homewood, Ill.: Richard D. Irwin, Inc., 1959.

CLARK, J. B. *The Distribution of Wealth.* New York: The Macmillan Co., 1938. (First published May, 1900.)

DOUGLAS, PAUL H. *The Theory of Wages.* New York: The Macmillan Co., 1934.

HICKS, J. R. *The Theory of Wages.* London: Macmillan & Co., Ltd., 1932.

MARSHALL, ALFRED. *Principles of Economics,* Book VI, chaps. i and ii. 8th ed. London: Macmillan & Co., Ltd., 1938.

SOLOW, ROBERT M. "A Skeptical Note on the Constancy of Relative Shares," *American Economic Review,* Vol. XLVIII (September, 1958), pp. 618–31.

STIGLER, GEORGE J. *Production and Distribution Theories.* New York: The Macmillan Co., 1941.

WEINTRAUB, SIDNEY. *An Approach to the Theory of Income Distribution.* Philadelphia: Chilton Co., 1958.

13 Wages

Introduction

The preceding chapter has contained an explanation of the marginal productivity theory of income distribution. Not all labor economists accept the marginal productivity theory as an explanation of wages. Some have developed new concepts, such as "job clusters," defined as a "stable group of job classifications," and "wage contours," defined as a "stable group of wage determining units," in an attempt to explain wages.[1] Others have examined such concepts and concluded that they are employed in such a way as to constitute merely a "disguised marginal productivity analysis."[2] Another group has argued that the entire marginal productivity analysis is unrealistic and inapplicable on grounds that businessmen do not make use of marginal concepts[3] and have heard a reply from an economic theorist that businessmen may make use of marginal concepts without knowing that they are doing so.[4] One labor economist has rather candidly summarized the current state of wage theory by remarking:

Despite almost two centuries of wage theorizing, modern wage theory still leaves much to be desired—especially with relation to short-run wage differentials and levels. Thus theorists are still at work trying to develop the perfect wage theory. Interdisciplinary approaches to the problem appear to offer the

[1] See John T. Dunlop, "The Task of Contemporary Wage Theory," in George W. Taylor and Frank C. Pierson (eds.), *New Concepts in Wage Determination* (New York: McGraw-Hill Book Co., Inc., 1957), pp. 117–39.

[2] See E. E. Liebhafsky, "A 'New' Concept in Wage Determination: Disguised Productivity Analysis," *Southern Economic Journal*, Vol. XXVI (October, 1959), pp. 141–46.

[3] See Richard A. Lester, "Shortcomings of Marginal Analysis for Wage-Employment Problems," *American Economic Review*, Vol. XXXVI (March, 1946), pp. 63–82; and Barbara Wooten, *The Social Foundations of Wage Policy* (New York: W. W. Norton & Co., Inc., 1955), chap. i.

[4] Fritz Machlup, *The Economics of Sellers' Competition* (Baltimore: The Johns Hopkins Press, 1952), chaps. ii and iii.

most hope for the future. In the meantime, the marginal productivity theory continues to be recognized as the most valid long-run explanation of the wage phenomenon; the bargaining theory offers most as a pragmatic explanation of the short-run wage setting mechanism in the mature economy.[5]

This chapter does not attempt to provide the "perfect" wage theory referred to in the preceding quotation. Instead, it will be concerned with a consideration of the problem of definition of the general wage level and with an examination of the way in which imperfections in the labor market are dealt with according to the marginal productivity principle under conditions in which competition and monopoly or monopsony are intermingled. The concluding section will briefly summarize some empirical studies of the question of how unions and minimum wage laws have affected wages.

A. BASIC CONCEPTS

Wages as the Price of the Services of Labor

Wages are the price of the services of labor. And just as one can talk about the general price level or about the price of a particular commodity, both in the short run and in the long run under various conditions of competition, so can a discussion of the wages of labor be concerned with the price of the services of labor under various such conditions. In this book the terms *wage and wage rate will be used interchangeably to mean the average money cost to the employer of one of a number of homogeneous units of labor service.* This cost to the employer may include not only the employee's money wage but also nonpecuniary employee benefits.

The Supply of Effort by an Individual

Marshall and the neoclassical economists argued that the individual worker's equilibrium position was the point at which the disutility of working was just equal to the wage received. The supply of effort offered by an individual was thus a function of the real wage rate and of the disutility of working.

Contemporary economists do not often make explicit use of the word "disutility" for the same reasons that they avoid the use of the term "utility." Instead, the supply of effort by an individual is generally made a function of the wage rate and of the desire for "leisure." Whether or not the difference between the "disutility" of working and the desire for "lei-

---

[5] Chester A. Morgan, *Labor Economics* (Homewood, Ill.: Dorsey Press, Inc., 1962), p. 83.

sure" is more than merely nominal is not altogether clear. The latter may merely be the negative of the former. At any rate, in the case of an individual, the relationship between the desire for income and the desire for leisure is often depicted by means of an indifference diagram, as in Figure 13–1. Total income is measured on the Y axis, while hours of

Figure 13–1

AN INDIVIDUAL'S INCOME-LEISURE INDIFFERENCE CURVE

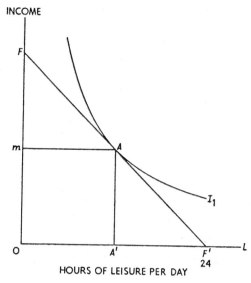

leisure time per day (L) are measured on the X axis, with 24 hours being taken as the maximum number of leisure hours in a day. The slope of the line FF' is the wage rate, the amount received for giving up an hour of leisure time. Thus by giving up $A'F'$ of leisure time, the individual acquires an income equal to $A'A$. At A, the individual is in equilibrium because the tangency condition explained at length in Chapter 5 is fulfilled. That is, the wage rate is equal to the marginal rate of substitution between income and leisure ($-\Delta m/\Delta L$) at A. The effects of changes in the wage rate can then be analyzed by ordinary indifference methods as explained in Chapter 5.[6] However, the problem is essentially one of motivation, and economists are dependent upon the researches of psychologists in this area. Moreover, the concept of *a wage* is complex, and

---

[6] See, for example, Kenneth Boulding, *Economic Analysis* (3rd ed.; New York: Harper & Bros., 1955), p. 798, for a derivation of the backward-sloping supply curve from such indifference curves.

where nonpecuniary elements are present, the difficulties of measurement are obvious. The statement that individuals will exert effort up to the point at which the income from additional effort equals the cost of exerting such effort in terms of leisure given up has no empirical content and cannot serve as a basis for policy. Indifference diagrams of the type depicted in Figure 13–1 are sometimes also used to illustrate how income taxes *may* affect the supply of effort or of saving, but these also have no empirical content.[7]

B. THE CONCEPT OF A GENERAL WAGE LEVEL

Short-Run Supply of Labor in an Economy

Just as the existence of product differentiation creates logical difficulties in attempts to define an industry product supply curve, so does the lack of homogeneity in the labor force cause difficulties in attempts to define "the supply of labor" available to a firm, an industry, or a society. The concept of the short-run or long-run supply of labor available to one of these economic entities is useful for some purposes but must be used with care since it cannot be defined with any high degree of precision.

The supply of labor available in an economy is usually taken to be dependent upon (1) the size of the population; (2) the sex composition of the population; (3) the age distribution within the population; and (4) the attitude of the population towards work. In the short run, the first three of these factors are held constant, while the last is assumed to be a function of the wage rate. That is, it is usually assumed that the attitude of the population towards work is such that it can be influenced in the short run by the wage rate, as explained in the discussion of Figure 13–1 in the preceding section. Changes in the size of the population, in its sex composition, or in its age distribution involve shifts in the labor supply curve.

The regressive or backward-sloping supply curve, which has already been explained in conjunction with Figure 8–5 in Chapter 8, can be interpreted as a depiction of one possible attitude toward work by a population and is based on the assumption that, after income has reached some given level, the desire for leisure overrides the desire for income so that, at very high levels of wages, less effort will be forthcoming than at lower levels. Marshall cited such a case (and may be the original source of the idea) but argued that it was an exception to the general rule

---

[7] See J. K. Eastham, *Graphical Economics* (Chicago: Quadrangle Books, Inc., 1960), pp. 243–52.

that an individual would work harder and longer the higher the *real* rate of pay received in exchange for his effort.[8] That is, Marshall believed that, in general, the curve of the short-run supply of labor (*SS*) available in the economy would slope up and to the right as in Figure 13–2.

Figure 13–2

THE GENERAL WAGE LEVEL

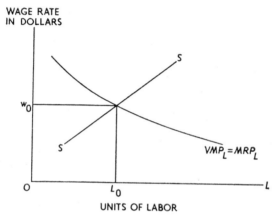

that an individual would work harder and longer the higher the *real*

The Market Demand for Labor Services

Problems arise in any attempt to define the market demand curve of labor *in an economy as a whole* as equal to the $VMP_L = MRP_L$ of a number of *homogeneous* units of labor. It would be necessary to multiply the marginal physical product of such homogeneous units by the average level of product prices to produce the curve so labeled in Figure 13–2, and the curve would shift up or down as the general price level changed, changing the level of employment (as illustrated in the case of a single firm in Figure 12–6 in the preceding chapter).

The neoclassical economists employed diagrams such as Figure 13–2 but defined the magnitudes in *real* terms. That is, the Y axis was identified as measuring the real wage (w/p_x), and the X axis measured the supply of homogeneous units of labor available in the economy. *The demand curve was interpreted as measuring the marginal physical product of the homogeneous* (or "standard") *labor supply of the economy.* Thus, they were able to argue that employment could always be increased by reducing the real wage rate (as illustrated in Figure 12–7 in the preceding chapter) and could assume full employment at all times.

---

[8] Alfred Marshall, *Principles of Economics* (8th ed.; London: Macmillan & Co., Ltd., 1938), pp. 528–29.

The Equilibrium Level of Wages; Validity of the Analysis

If the analysis is conducted in real terms, the same sort of conceptual validity attaches to the "equilibrium level real wage" (Ow_0 in Figure 13-2) as attaches to the concept of "the general price level." In this form, the analysis is widely employed in the field of macroeconomic analysis to explain neoclassical theories. But the entire apparatus, whether defined in real or in money terms, is subject to many qualifications.

Noncompeting Groups

For example, the analysis based on Figure 13-2 must assume that the supply of labor is homogeneous. Clearly, this assumption is unrealistic. Throughout the economy, there are workers who compete with each other within a group but not with members of other groups. Thus, doctors and truck drivers do not compete in the short run. Existence of such noncompeting groups means that a single diagram referring to the economy as a whole, such as Figure 13-2, cannot be used where precision is important. To meet this objection, a great many such diagrams would have to be drawn, one for each noncompeting group, to explain wage differentials which may arise from the lack of mobility among such groups. Of course, it is possible that the sons of truck drivers may become doctors so that a higher degree of homogeneity in the labor force exists in the long run than in the short run, but, in the long run, the curves may also shift.

Equalizing Differences

Even *within* noncompeting groups, there are differences in *money* wages. These are often explained by the existence of "equalizing differences," differences in "psychic income," or differences in the attractiveness of various jobs within such groups. An example often given is that of a teacher of law whose money income is less than that of his ex-classmate practitioner. The former, it is argued, has a real income which is just as high as that of the practicing attorney, and if it were possible to monetize the psychic income accruing to him from the pleasant surroundings in which he works, the real wages received by the two would be equal. But equalizing differences are not the sole explanation, and anyhow they cannot be measured. Moreover, age may keep older faculty members from changing jobs even after the psychic income has become negative, and pressures and tensions exist in academic life, just as they do elsewhere.

Differences in Ability and the Effect of Scarcity; Discrimination

Differences in ability may also produce differences in wages even within noncompeting groups. One baseball pitcher may win twenty games a year, and his salary for the next season will undoubtedly be greater than that of another who has won only six games. Twenty-game winning pitchers are scarce. And an effective press agent may increase the salary of an entertainer by creating a demand for the services of that individual. Discriminations based on age, sex, race, nepotism, communities of interest, and religion may also result in differences in wages within noncompeting groups. All these factors are usually treated as imperfections in the labor market by economic theorists, and, often, many of them are mentioned and then dismissed from further consideration on grounds that they are noneconomic factors. Wages, at any rate, are not uniform throughout the economy, and the tendency towards equalization is frustrated in many cases.

The Long-Run Supply of Labor

Marshall argued that in the long run the effect of increases in wages upon the birth rate and upon the death rate would determine the supply of labor. Moreover, he believed that although an increase in wages would be just as likely to lower as to raise the birth rate, it was almost certain to lower the death rate. For these reasons, Marshall argued that rising wages would be accompanied by an increase in the long-run supply of labor.[9]

His view is supported by a study made in 1961 by Professor Richard A. Easterlin under the sponsorship of the National Bureau of Economic Research. Easterlin studied the relationship between economic factors and the growth of population in the United States from 1855 to 1954 and concluded that the "baby boom" in the United States during and after World War II was not, in fact, as had been widely believed, a reversal of a downward trend in population. Instead, he argued that it represented the natural and consistent response of the urban native-born white population to economic factors. This group had become relatively more important as a determinant of population in the period of the boom. In past periods of economic expansion, the demand for additional labor had been met by increased immigration and increased entry into the labor market by young native-born workers, but neither of these two factors was present in the period following World War II. The birth

---

[9] *Ibid.*, p. 529.

rate of the foreign-born and the rural native-born white populations had been low in the late 1920's and early 1930's, a depression period, and immigration was restricted in the 1950's. As a result, an exceptional job market existed in this period for those in family-founding ages in the United States and led to the "baby boom." Easterlin's study thus emphasizes the fact that an analysis of the relationship between growth of population and economic factors must take account of the various components of the total population and the different influences to which they may be subject.[10]

Wages in the Long Run

Since increases in the supply of labor shift the labor supply curve to the right, does it follow that wages must decline in the long run? This, of course, was the position taken by T. R. Malthus (1798), who argued in his well-known work, *An Essay on Population*,[11] that the pressure of population on the supply of food would depress wages to the subsistence level (and even, temporarily, below that level). Malthus failed to foresee the impact of the industrial revolution. The rapid development of technology means that the MPP_L curve may shift up and to the right with the passage of time. Thus, attempts to forecast long-run wage levels must involve not only a forecast of the way in which population will change but also a forecast of the future progress of technology.

What determines wages and the level of employment in the case of individual firms? This is our next problem.

C. THE MARGINAL PRODUCTIVITY THEORY APPLIED TO WAGES

Average Gross Revenue Product Defined

The *average gross revenue product* (*AGRP*) *of any input is the total revenue* (*R*) *divided by the number of units of that input,* or

$$AGRP_L = \frac{R}{L}.$$ (13–1)

This concept will be helpful in relating diagrams describing the output situation of a firm to diagrams depicting the input situation.

An average gross revenue product curve is depicted in Figure 13–3A. Our curve rises, reaches a maximum, and then declines. Thus, in Figures

[10] R. A. Easterlin, "The American Baby Boom in Historical Perspective," *American Economic Review*, Vol. LI (December, 1961), pp. 869–911.

[11] T. R. Malthus, *An Essay on Population* (Everyman's Library No. 692; London: J. M. Dent & Sons, Ltd., 1914), p. 15.

13–3A and 13–3B, when the firm is using $OL_0 = 4.544$ units of labor and producing $OX_0 = 63.60$ units of output, while the price of the product is $p_{x_0} = \$1.03$, we have $AGRP_L = R/L = OP' = L_0A' = \$14.40$.

The average *net* revenue productivity ($ANRP$) of a given input can also be defined as equal to the total revenue productivity attributable to

Figure 13–3

WAGE DETERMINATION: CASE I, PERFECT COMPETITION IN BOTH MARKETS

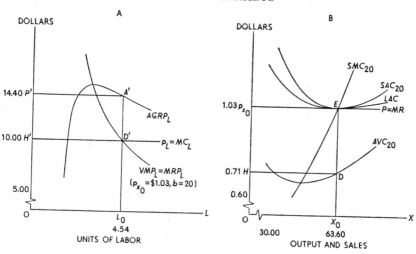

that input divided by the number of units of the input, and some writers employ the concept extensively;[12] but it is superfluous to our analysis, and we will not use it.

Case I: Perfect Competition in Both Markets

We have already seen in Chapter 12 that if perfect competition is assumed to exist in both factor and product markets, the firm will employ inputs up to the point at which the VMP's = MRP's are equal to the MC's = p's of the inputs, and it will be earning only normal profits. In Figure 13–3B, the firm is in long-run equilibrium under perfect competition in both product and factor markets, making only a normal profit. The situation with respect to labor (L) only is depicted in Figure 13–3A, but a similar diagram could be drawn to depict the case of input b. In Figure 13–3A we have $R = OP'A'L_0$, $(MRP_L)(L) = (L)(p_L) = OH'D'L_0$, and $(MRP_b)(b) = (b)(p_b) = H'P'A'D'$; and although

---

[12] See Alfred W. Stonier and Douglas C. Hague, *A Textbook of Economic Theory* (2d ed.; London: Longmans Green & Co., Ltd., 1957), esp. pp. 238–39.

the scales of the two diagrams are different so that in Figure 13–3B the geometrical areas are not equal to their respective counterparts in Figure 13–3A even though the numerical values are equal, we have $R = Op_{x_0}EX_0$, $(MRP_L)(L) = (L)(p_L) = OHDX_0$, and $(MRP_b)(b) = (b)(p_b) = Hp_{x_0}ED$. Thus, the correspondence between the input and the output diagrams is illustrated. Areas $OH'D'L_0$ and $OHDX_0$ represent the return to or cost of labor, the variable factor in the short run; and areas $H'P'A'D'$ and $Hp_{x_0}ED$ represent the return to b, the remaining input. Figure 13–3B represents a long-run equilibrium position of the firm in the product market, and Figure 13–3A represents a long-run equilibrium position in the factor market. Figure 13–3 is, therefore, a graphical illustration of our monetized version of Euler's Theorem, which has been arithmetically explained in Equation (12–13′) in the preceding chapter.

Case II: Perfect Competition in Factor but Not in Product Market

Figure 13–4 depicts the situation when there is perfect competition in the factor market but not in the product market. In such a case, since $MR < p_x$, we know from Equation (12–3a) that the marginal revenue product is less than the value of the marginal product, or

$$[MRP_L = (MPP_L)(MR)] < [VMP_L = (MPP_L)(p_x)] .$$

Thus, in Figure 13–4A, the MRP_L curve lies *below* the VMP_L curve. In Figures 13–4A and 13–4B, the scales of the two diagrams are again dif-

Figure 13–4

WAGE DETERMINATION: CASE II, MONOPOLY AND COMPETITION
INTERMINGLED—GREATER THAN NORMAL PROFIT

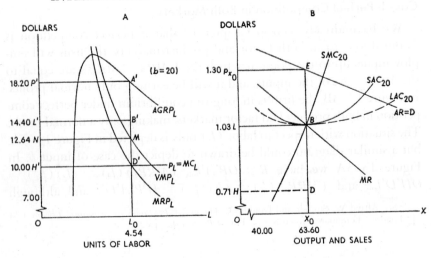

ferent so that the corresponding geometrical areas in the two diagrams are not equal, although their numerical values are the same. Thus in Figure 13–4A we have $R = OP'A'L_0$, $(MRP_L)(L) = (L)(p_L) = OH'D'L_0$, and $(MRP_b)(b) = (b)(p_b) = H'L'B'D'$, while in Figure 13–4B we have $R = Op_{x_0}EX_0$, $(MRP_L)(L) = (L)(p_L) = OHDX_0$, and $(MRP_b)(b) = (b)(p_b) = HLBD$. The firm is making a greater than normal profit equal to $Lp_{x_0}EB = \$17.24$ in Figure 13–4B, and this area corresponds to $L'P'A'B'$ in Figure 13–4A.

One other piece of information is also given in Figure 13–4A. The distance $D'M$ between the MRP_L and VMP_L curves at the equilibrium level of employment is the excess of the market value of the marginal unit of labor above its value to the firm. However, this case does *not* involve exploitation of labor, although some economists at one time thought so.[13] As Professor Chamberlin has noted, the existence of imperfections in the product market insures that the MRP curves of *all* inputs will lie below their respective VMP curves. Thus, it is improper to assert that any single input is being exploited in such a case. What the case illustrates is that production is inefficient when valued by the market price standard if competition is not perfect.[14] This point can be made more clear by reference to Figure 13–5, which depicts another case

Figure 13–5

WAGE DETERMINATION: CASE II, MONOPOLY AND COMPETITION
INTERMINGLED—NORMAL PROFIT CASE

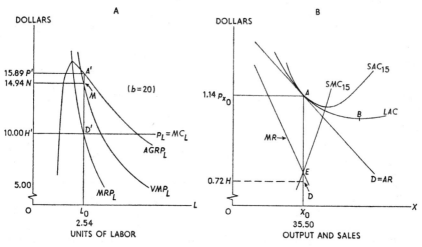

[13] See Joan Robinson, *The Economics of Imperfect Competition* (London: Macmillan & Co., Ltd., 1934), p. 282.

[14] Edward H. Chamberlin, *The Theory of Monopolistic Competition* (Cambridge: Harvard University Press, 1956), chap. viii.

of perfect competition in the factor market and monopoly and competition intermingled in the product market. In this case the firm is making
only a normal profit. In Figure 13–5A we have $(MRP_L)(L) = OH'D'L_0$ and $(MRP_b)(b) = H'P'A'D'$, and in Figure 13–5B these
magnitudes are represented by areas $OHDX_0$ and $Hp_{x_0}AD$, respectively.
The distance $D'M$ in Figure 13–5A cannot represent a greater than normal profit made at the expense of labor since the firm is not making a
greater than normal profit in Figure 13–5B! This distance represents
the fact that the "value to the society" of the marginal unit of labor is
greater than it is to the firm at the equilibrium level of employment
and, thus, that resources are being underemployed in this firm. The same
point is illustrated in Figure 13–5B by the fact that the firm is in
equilibrium on a downward-sloping portion of its long-run average cost
curve (at A), indicating underemployment of inputs.

Case III: Perfect Competition in Product Market; Monopsony in Labor Market

Figure 13–6 illustrates a case of perfect competition in the product
market, since $MR = AR = p_x$ in Figure 13–6B, and thus $VMP_L =$

Figure 13–6

**WAGE DETERMINATION: CASE III, PERFECT COMPETITION
IN PRODUCT MARKET PLUS MONOPSONY**

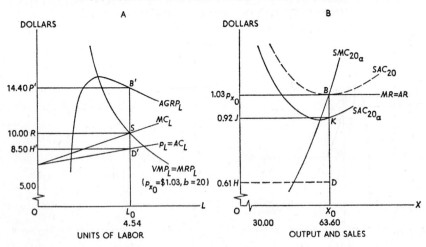

MRP_L in Figure 13–6A; but it also illustrates monopsony in the labor
market, since $MC_L > AC_L = p_L$ in Figure 13–6A. Perfect competition is
assumed to exist in the markets for other inputs.

The reason why the marginal cost of labor is greater than its average cost under monopsony in Figure 13–6A has already been discussed in detail in conjunction with Figure 10–7 in Chapter 10. Additional units of labor can only be purchased at higher prices, and, thus, in order to increase his employment of labor, the employer must pay a higher price for all the units of labor employed. That is, he must not only pay a higher rate to obtain an additional unit of labor but he must also increase the rate at which all previously employed units are paid.

Such a case involves true exploitation of labor. In Figure 13–6A, the amount of the input employed is $OL_0 = 4.544$, and the wage rate is $OH' = \$8.50$. The marginal cost of labor at this level of employment is $OR = \$10$ and is equal to the $VMP_L = MRP_L$ at S. The total wage bill is $OH'D'L_0$ in Figure 13–6A, and this area corresponds to area $OHDX_0$ in Figure 13–6B. The amount paid to input b is area $RP'B'S$ in Figure 13–6A and corresponds to area $HJKD$ in Figure 13–6B.

The firm is making a greater than normal profit equal to $JP_{x_0}BK$ in Figure 13–6B, and this area corresponds to area $H'RSD'$ in Figure 13–6A. Note that the firm is selling under perfect competition in the product market and producing that long-run equilibrium level of output which would normally be produced under perfect competition in both markets. *However,* the monopsonistic position of the firm in the labor market results in a *depression* of the average cost curve to a lower level (SAC_{20_a}) than if there were perfect competition in the factor market (SAC_{20}). Thus the average cost of $OX_0 = 63.60$ units of output in the monopsonistic case is only $OJ = \$.92$ in Figure 13–6B, while under perfect competition in both markets it would be $Op_{x_0} = \$1.03$. And so the firm makes a greater than normal profit in this case *at the expense of labor* equal to $(R = \$65.45) - (T = \$58.62) = (N = \$6.83)$, or to area $H'RSD'$ in Figure 13–6A, or area $Jp_{x_0}BK$ in Figure 13–6B. (The slight discrepancy is due to rounding of numbers.)

Case IV: Monopoly and Competition Intermingled Plus Monopsony

Figure 13–7 illustrates a case of monopoly and competition intermingled in the product market and of monopsony in the factor market. Figure 13–7 is nothing more than a combination of Figures 13–4 and 13–6. The abnormal profit arising from the absence of perfect competition in the product market in Figure 13–7A is $N_p = L'P'A'B'$, and this area corresponds to area $Lp_{x_0}AB = \$17.24$ in Figure 13–7B. The greater than normal profit arising from exploitation of labor as a result of the firm's monopsonistic position in the factor market in Figure 13–7A is $N_f = H'RSD' = \$6.82$, which corresponds to area $JLBK$ in Figure 13–6B. Thus, $N = N_p + N_f = \$17.24 + \$6.82 = \$24.06$.

Figure 13–7

WAGE DETERMINATION: CASE IV, MONOPOLY AND
COMPETITION INTERMINGLED PLUS MONOPSONY

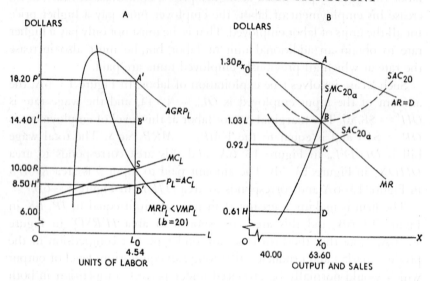

UNITS OF LABOR   OUTPUT AND SALES

We can apply our general income distribution equation from Chapter 12 to this case if we take account of the fact that in the case of monopsony in the factor market, the relevant input is paid at a rate equal to its price rather than at a rate equal to its MRP. Thus, substituting p_L for $(MR)(MPP_L)$ in Equation (12–14a), we have

$$R = xp_x = L(p_L) + b(MR)(MPP_b) + (N_p + N_f), \qquad (13\text{--}2)$$

or

$$R = \$82.68 = \$38.62 + \$20.00 + \$17.24 + \$6.82 . \qquad (13\text{--}2')$$

And so the total net revenue is

$$N = N_p + N_f = \$17.24 + \$6.82 = \$24.06 .$$

The Bargaining Area

Area $H'RSD'$ in either Figure 13–6A or 13–7A is sometimes called the *bargaining area*. Other things equal (i.e., assuming static conditions), adoption of a minimum wage law or action by a labor union can be effective within this area in raising wages without reducing employment and, depending on the extent to which wages are raised, may even increase employment. The effect of minimum wage laws and union actions on wages and employment, *assuming static conditions,* is the next topic.

D. EFFECTS OF UNIONS AND MINIMUM WAGE LAWS

Introduction

If a minimum wage law is adopted, all workers within the covered class receive at least the same minimum wage. This fact means that the marginal and average costs of labor service are the same to the employer, unless the minimum wage is set below the existing equilibrium wage level and, therefore, has no effect. In the case of a minimum wage law, the marginal and average costs of labor can be depicted by a single horizontal line, such as $w_1 U_w$ in Figure 13–8A. Action by a union with

Figure 13–8

EFFECT OF UNION ACTION ON WAGES: CASES I AND II

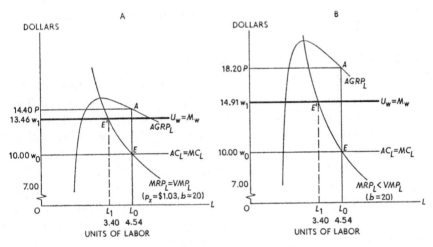

respect to wages also produces this identity between the marginal and average costs of labor, since all workers within a given class receive the same wage. Thus the two cases can be analyzed in precisely the same way. What follows is the customary analysis. This analysis is partial equilibrium analysis and, as such, assumes that other things remain unchanged as wages are increased. Obviously, such an assumption is quite unrealistic, and some of the limitations of this analysis will be noted after the first two standard cases have been explained.

Case I: Perfect Competition in Both Markets

Assuming perfect competition in both markets, partial equilibrium analysis leads to the conclusion that an increase in wages in Figure 13–8A, from Ow_0 to Ow_1, must produce unemployment. For, assuming other things equal, the minimum wage law or union action to increase wages will merely shift the $AC_L = MC_L$ line upward to $U_w = M_w$, and a new equilibrium position will be established at E', where the condition $MC_L = MRP_L$ is once more fulfilled. Employment falls to OL_1.

Case II: Perfect Competition in Factor but Not in Product Market

In this case also, partial equilibrium analysis leads to the conclusion that an increase in wages from Ow_0 to Ow_1 in Figure 13–8B must produce unemployment of the input for precisely the same reason as in the case of perfect competition in both markets. Action by a union or a minimum wage law merely shifts the $AC_L = MC_L$ curve upward to $U_w = M_w$ and a new point of intersection with the fixed MRP_L curve. Again employment falls to OL_1.

Limitations of the Preceding Analyses

The preceding analyses are both sharply limited by the fact that they assume that other things remain unchanged as wages are increased. That is, they employ the partial equilibrium method. If wages rise, the equilibrium condition will have been disturbed; and both the preceding analyses argue that in order to maintain output constant at its previous level, substitution of other inputs for the relatively more expensive input, labor, must occur while the price of the product rises. In such a case, the quantities of other inputs used will increase, and the marginal productivity of labor will change. The prices of other inputs must also change, unless it is assumed that their supply is perfectly elastic. However, the increase in the quantity of other inputs may *shift* the MRP_L curve, while the increased cost of all inputs will increase the price of the product, and this price change in turn will also operate to shift the MRP_L curve.

Accordingly, although the conclusions derived from the partial equilibrium analysis in these two cases are probably correct, and an increase in the wage rate will reduce employment of the factor under the given assumptions, it is extremely unlikely that the new equilibrium position will lie on the same MRP_L curve as that on which the initial position was located. Both these customary analyses are thus illustrations of the limitations of the partial equilibrium method of analysis. Sometimes it produces the correct answer for reasons which may be wrong or at least misleading.

Case III: Perfect Competition in Product Market; Monopsony in Labor Market

Figure 13–9A shows the effect of an increase in wages as a result of a minimum wage law or union action in the case in which monopsony exists in the labor market. Assume that the initial wage paid is L_0D' in Figure 13–9A and that this amount is less than the value to the firm of

Figure 13–9

EFFECT OF UNION ACTION ON WAGES: CASES III AND IV

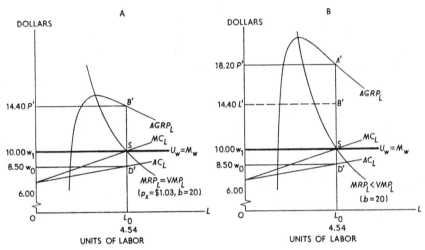

the marginal unit of input L_0S. Introduction of a uniform wage by law (or union action) substitutes the horizontal ($U_w = M_w$) marginal and average cost of labor curve at the level Ow_1 for the previously existing positively sloping MC_L and AC_L curves, *which must now be ignored.* Thus, the marginal and average costs of labor are the same to the employer at all levels of input after the law or the union action. The new marginal cost of labor is Ow_1, and it is equal to the marginal revenue product of labor, which is also Ow_1 at the level of employment OL_0, or at S. Hence no change in employment occurs. As long as the increase in wages is less than the previous difference ($D'S$) between the marginal and average costs of labor under monopsony, employment will increase. After wages reach the level of Ow_1, the situation becomes identical with Figure 13–8A. The reason why employment will increase at any wage level between Ow_0 and Ow_1 is that the horizontal $U_w = M_w$ line would then intersect the $MRP_L = VMP_L$ curve to the right of the perpendicular L_0B'. Area $w_1P'B'S$ represents the payment to input b, and area w_0w_1SD' represents the greater than normal profit made by the firm prior to the union action or the adoption of the minimum wage law.

What the diagram demonstrates then is that if an input is being paid less than it is worth to the firm, the firm can be forced to increase the rate of pay to just exactly the worth of the input without making any other changes. In short, a minimum wage law or action by a union can eliminate any real exploitation which exists, and the limitation on such action is the size of the bargaining area, w_0w_1SD'. The fact that other things are assumed unchanged in this analysis does not limit the conclusion *in our case,* since the amount of labor employed does not change in Figure 13–9A.

Case IV: Monopoly and Competition Intermingled Plus Monopsony

Figure 13–9B is related to Figure 13–7B and shows the effect of action by a union or a minimum wage law in a situation in which competition is not perfect in either market. In this case, as in the case of Figure 13–9A, wages can be increased by w_0w_1, the difference between the marginal and average costs of labor resulting from the monopsonistic position of the firm, without decreasing employment. At wages between Ow_0 and Ow_1, employment will increase as before; at wages above Ow_1, the case becomes identical with that depicted in Figure 13–8B. If they are raised by exactly w_0w_1, the firm's greater than normal profit is reduced from $w_0w_1SD' + L'P'A'B'$ to $L'P'A'B'$.

Empirical Studies

It has been noted that the preceding analysis is static and employs partial equilibrium analysis. Thus it assumes that the curves do not shift. In a dynamic economy, the curves do shift, not only as a result of readjustments in the amounts of the inputs used but also as a result of changes in demands for products and as a result of technological development. Thus, in given cases, it is quite possible for wages to increase as minimum wage laws are adopted or as unions act to increase wages, without a reduction in employment, even when there is perfect competition in the factor market, if productivity is also increasing and the wage increases are not greater than the increase in labor's productivity.

Statistical studies of the effects of labor unions on wages are inconclusive, probably inevitably so. Professor Clark Kerr has argued that trade unionism has not had an important effect on labor's share of the national income.[15] Professor Harold Levinson, on the other hand, concluded in 1954 that, given the government policy of maintaining low interest rates and rents (especially during World War II), labor unions have obtained for organized labor a greater share than would otherwise have been the case.[16]

Probably most of the economists testifying before the Joint Economic Committee in 1959 on (among other things) the subject of the effect of union practices on prices and employment agreed that unions had not been effective in increasing labor's share at the expense of other factors. For example, Professor George Hildebrand, a well-known labor economist, cited two reasons for the apparent negligible influence of collective bargaining. First, he thought that unions had little incentive to raise wages *at the expense of profits,* since wage increases could be obtained on other grounds, and he doubted that unions had the power to do so. And second, he also noted that management usually responded with laborsaving devices and new organization of work, which reduced costs, thereby permitting money wages to rise without a reduction of profits.[17]

In 1960, an exhaustive three-year study of the effects upon wages, prices, and employment of the $1.00 minimum wage set by law was completed by the Department of Labor. Professor Donald E. Cullen, in a survey of minimum wage laws, has commented on this study as follows:

. . . Confronted with this identical set of facts, Senator Goldwater claimed they supported his warnings against the dire effects of any increase in the present minimum. Secretary of Labor James Mitchell interpreted them as justifying no more than a 15-cent increase, and Senator Kennedy pointed to them as evidence that a 25-cent increase could easily be absorbed! Nor was this dispute limited to politicians or to labor and management circles, for professional economists also could not agree on what this mountain of statistics really proved about the impact of the minimum wage laws.[18]

One explanation of the inability to draw simple, neat generalizations concerning the impact of union action or of the minimum wage laws is

---

[15] Clark Kerr, "Labor's Income Share and the Labor Movement," in George W. Taylor and Frank C. Pierson (eds.), *New Concepts of Wage Determination* (New York: McGraw-Hill Book Co., Inc., 1957), p. 287.

[16] Harold Levinson, "Collective Bargaining and Income Distribution," *American Economic Review,* Vol. XLIV (May, 1954), pp. 308–16.

[17] "The Effect of Increases in Wages, Salaries and the Prices of Personal Services, Together with Union and Professional Practices, upon Prices, Profits, Production and Employment," *Employment, Growth, and Price Levels* (Hearings before the Joint Economic Committee, U.S. Congress, 86th Cong. 1st sess.) (Washington, D.C.: U.S. Government Printing Office, 1959), Part 8, p. 2529.

[18] Donald E. Cullen, *Minimum Wage Laws* (Bulletin 43, New York State School of Industrial and Labor Relations) (Ithaca, N.Y.: Cornell University Press, 1962), p. v.

that the conditions of competition under which they operate are different among different industries. Another is that the problem of wage theory is not independent of but, instead, is closely related to the theory of the firm, and, therefore, it seems unlikely that the problem of wage theory will be solved until a more adequate theory of the firm has been developed.

Fortunately, there is considerably more agreement and certainty among economists with respect to the theory of rent or economic surplus than there is with regard to wage theory. It is to this topic that we will turn next in the following chapter.

SELECTED READINGS

CARTTER, ALAN M. *Theory of Wages and Employment.* Homewood, Ill.: Richard D. Irwin, Inc., 1959.

CHAMBERLIN, EDWARD H. *The Theory of Monopolistic Competition,* chap. vii. 7th ed. Cambridge: Harvard University Press, 1956.

CULLEN, DONALD E. *Minimum Wage Laws.* Bulletin 43, New York State School of Industrial and Labor Relations. Ithaca, N.Y.: Cornell University Press, 1962.

LESTER, RICHARD A. "Shortcomings of Marginal Analysis for Wage-Employment Problems," *American Economic Review,* Vol. XXXVI (March, 1946), pp. 63–82.

LEVINSON, HAROLD. *Unionism, Wage Trends, and Income Distribution, 1914–1947.* Michigan Business Studies, Vol. X, No. 4. Ann Arbor, 1951.

LIEBHAFSKY, E. E. "A 'New' Concept in Wage Determination: Disguised Productivity Analysis," *Southern Economic Journal,* Vol. XXVI (October, 1959), pp. 141–46.

MARSHALL, ALFRED. *Principles of Economics,* Book VI, chaps. ii–v. 8th ed. London: Macmillan & Co., Ltd., 1938.

MORGAN, CHESTER A. *Labor Economics.* Homewood, Ill.: Dorsey Press, Inc., 1962.

ROBINSON, JOAN. *The Economics of Imperfect Competition,* chaps. xxiii–xxvi. London: Macmillan & Co., Ltd., 1934.

STONIER, ALFRED W., AND HAGUE, DOUGLAS C. *A Textbook of Economic Theory,* chap. xii. 2d ed. London: Longmans Green & Co., Ltd., 1957.

TAYLOR, GEORGE W., AND PIERSON, FRANK C. (eds.). *New Concepts in Wage Determination.* New York: McGraw-Hill Book Co., Inc., 1957.

14 Economic Rent

Introduction

This chapter provides an explanation of the concept of *economic rent,* a surplus above and beyond the full cost of production, which arises from the inelasticity of the supply of an input. There is probably fuller agreement among economists with respect to the nature and source of economic rent than exists with regard to any other income share. The theory of rent at the intensive and extensive margins of production developed by David Ricardo and others between 1813 and 1815 will be explained first. Then we will examine the Marshallian concept of quasi rent, the matters of urban rent, and "rent of ability," and, finally, we will consider the effect on production of a lump-sum tax equal to the economic rent, a problem first dealt with by Henry George in 1871.

A. THE RICARDIAN THEORY OF RENT

Economic Rent Defined

Economic rent must be distinguished from the concept of *contractual* rent. The latter is a periodic payment made for the services obtained from or for the use of an input or product, the latter term being defined broadly. Thus, one may "rent" an automobile, a house, a farm, or a factory. The amount of the periodic contractual payment is not, however, the same thing as what is meant by *economic* rent. For, as has been noted above, economic rent is a term applied to that part of the payment for the use of an input which arises because its supply is not perfectly elastic. Contractual rent paid for use of land, for example, will be much larger than the economic rent of the land, since the former will include a sum necessary to pay the interest on the landlord's investment in improvements of the land and may include a sum to cover depreciation of the buildings and sums to cover insurance, taxes, and other payments.

Development of the Ricardian Rent Doctrine

The doctrine of economic rent was first fully developed in the course of a debate between David Ricardo and Thomas R. Malthus on the English "Corn Laws" between 1813 and 1815. After the defeat of Napoleon at Waterloo, the Congress of Vienna, under the leadership of Prince Metternich, undertook to reconstruct Europe along royalist lines. In England, the Tory government, under the influence of Castlereagh and Wellington, favored the landed aristocracy and adopted legislation favorable to their interests. One such program of legislation was the "Corn Laws," which levied high duties on the importation of foodstuffs. Since population was also increasing, this action insured high prices. Malthus favored the laws. Ricardo, even though he was himself a landowner, argued that rent was a *price-determined* cost rather than a *cost-determined* price and opposed the laws.[1] What was the nature of Ricardo's argument? It is to this matter that we turn first.

Rent at the Intensive Margin of Production

Figure 14–1 illustrates the Ricardian rent doctrine as it applies to production at the *intensive* margin of use of an input. The intensive margin is reached as the result of diminishing returns to the variable input when one input must be held fixed because it is in short supply. Although Ricardo developed his argument in terms of the marginal product, the same argument can be made in terms of the marginal and average costs.

Assume in Figure 14–1A that the MC and AC curves represent the cost curves when varying quantities (sometimes called "doses") of a combined input, capital and labor, are applied to a given quantity of land, say 20 acres. Now we already know that the curve of the marginal cost of x is nothing more than the reciprocal of the curve of the marginal product of the combined unit of input, multiplied by the price of such a unit of input. Similarly, the average variable cost of x is nothing more than the reciprocal of the average product of such a combined unit of input multiplied by the price of that unit. Thus, if marginal returns to the combined input diminish, the marginal cost of x will rise; and if the curve of the average product of the combined unit of input is the shape of an inverted U, with a maximum point, the average

---

[1] See John Fred Bell, *A History of Economic Thought* (New York: Ronald Press Co., 1953), pp. 227–31.

cost curve will also be U-shaped, with a minimum point, as in Figure 14–1A.

Let us designate the combined input, capital and labor, by the symbol a and the fixed input, land, by the symbol b. Assume also that the return to the farmer is labor cost included in the price of a. Next assume that input b, or land, is a free good when OX'_0, or less, units of product are sold in the market place in Figure 14–1B. Under these circumstances, since a

Figure 14–1

ECONOMIC RENT AT THE INTENSIVE MARGIN OF PRODUCTION

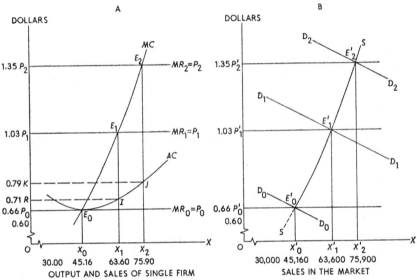

is a variable input while the fixed input, b, is a free input, we have already learned in Chapter 6, during the discussion of Figure 6–1, that production will occur at the point of diminishing average returns to the variable input, a. This point is represented by E_0 in Figure 14–1A, where the marginal and average costs are equal. Note that according to our assumption that land is a free good, so that $p_b = 0$, the average cost and the average variable cost are identical in Figure 14–1A. Thus the short-run supply curve actually begins at E'_0 in Figure 14–1B. As long as input b, or land, is a free good, and assuming that all plots of 20 acres are of equal grade and quality, farmers will not in the long run produce at levels greater than OX_0 on the given size plots of land. Instead, they will employ additional units of land up to the point of diminishing returns to the variable input on each additional unit, if necessary.

Next, however, assume that there is an increase in population which results in a shift of the market demand curve in Figure 14–1B to the right to D_1D_1. The increased demand results in a higher price of the product and in pressure on farmers to increase production. Assume also that although the supply of land was ample so that land was a free resource when the amount of product exchanging hands in the market was OX'_0, as soon as more than this amount is produced, no more land is available. Farmers are therefore forced to increase production by making fuller use of their existing capacity, since that capacity cannot now be increased.

Since the price of the product has risen from $\$.66$ per unit to $\$1.03$ per unit, the farmers will increase their input of the variable factor, a, with the given quantity of the fixed factor, b, up to the point at which the marginal cost of the output is exactly equal to the new higher price of the output. Thus, after the increase in demand, the equilibrium output will be $OX_1 = 63.60$, and the price will be $OP_1 = \$1.03$ in Figure 14–1A. Area RP_1E_1I now represents a surplus above the cost of the combined input, a, and all of it accrues to the fixed factor, b, whose supply cannot be increased as the demand for the output increases.

Since the supply of land, or input b, is limited, other farmers cannot undertake to produce the product without purchasing the land from the existing owners or without offering to pay them a sum for its use. Thus, the land, which was previously a free resource at the lower level of demand for the product, has now acquired an economic value. And so area RP_1E_1I represents economic rent. It is a surplus or "unearned increment" which has arisen as a result of the inelasticity of the supply of land, or input b.

As population increases further, again shifting the product demand curve to the right to D_2D_2 in Figure 14–1B, the price of the product again increases. In Figure 14–1A, this increase in demand is reflected by an even more intensive use of the land by the individual farmer, as output from the existing unit of land is increased to OX_2. After the second price increase, the economic rent is area KP_2E_2J. Thus, from the social point of view, economic rent is seen to be a price-determined cost, an economic surplus which arises out of the scarcity of a factor of production.

If the farmer does not own the land himself and has merely been making use of land owned by someone else, no rent can be extracted from him as long as land is a free good. But, as soon as the demand for the product increases sufficiently so that production occurs in the stage of diminishing returns to the variable input (at levels of output greater than OX_0 in

Figure 14–1A), a rent must be paid to the titleholder. For if the farmer does not do so, others, enticed by the prospect of the economic rent, will bid for the use of the land, offering the titleholder a part of the economic rent in exchange. A process of competitive bidding will then take place and continue until the entire sum equal to the economic rent is being paid to the titleholder, or until all the greater than normal profits have accrued to him. Thus, the titleholder has been able to obtain a return equal to the economic rent merely by virtue of his position as a titleholder as a result of the increase in population which has made his land valuable. In this case, the farmer's average cost curve would shift upward to, say, $AC + $ Tax in Figure 14–3A.

Rent as a Mechanism for Allocating Resources

A marginal productivity explanation of rent has also already been given in Chapter 12. Thus, once land becomes scarce, firms will use it up to the point at which the marginal value product of the land is just equal to its marginal cost. This point will occur at that level of output at which all the economic rent, equal to RP_1E_1I, is being received by the landlord. Most economists accordingly argue that rent, defined as the price of the use of land (natural resources), thus serves the economic function of allocating natural resources to their best uses. That is, only those bidders who are able to produce products enabling them to pay the highest rents will be able to obtain the services of the land. Hence, judged by the market standard (which takes no account of the interest of future generations, it may be noted), land will be allocated to its "best" uses in this way. This proposition is true, assuming that the prices of the products are a measure of the value of the use of the land; but as we will see in a later section, the entire economic rent can be extracted from the landlord by means of a lump-sum tax without affecting output, prices, or the cost of production, while a similar lump-sum tax equal to total wages paid to workers would drive wages below the subsistence level, with obvious effects. Thus, land rent and wages are not quite analogous.

What such an argument really seeks to establish is not that the scarcity of the resource, which gives rise to economic rent, is socially desirable but, rather, that economic rent may be a cost-determining price to a firm (if it does not itself own the scarce factor of production and must pay for its use) or to an industry, although from the standpoint of society, economic rent is a price-determined cost. Or, as Ricardo put it, "Corn is not high because a rent is paid, but a rent is paid because corn is high; and it has been justly observed that no reduction would take place in the price of corn although landlords should forego the whole of their rent."[2]

Rent at the Intensive and Extensive Margins of Production

Figure 14–2 illustrates the case of *differential* rent and involves consideration of both the intensive and extensive margins of production. Assume that there are three different 20-acre plots of land, with A the

Figure 14–2

ECONOMIC RENT AT THE INTENSIVE AND EXTENSIVE
MARGINS OF PRODUCTION

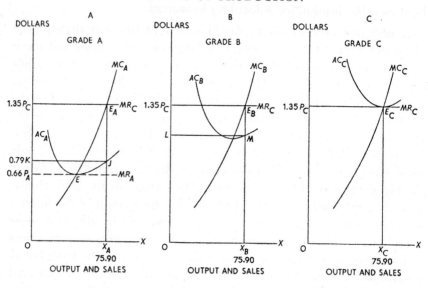

most fertile, B the next most fertile, and C the least fertile. In Figure 14–2A, as long as demand for the product is small, so that production will occur only at the point of diminishing returns on the best land (*E* in Figure 14–2A) and not at all on the inferior grades of land, no economic rent exists.

However, if the demand for the product increases as in Figure 14–1B so that the price eventually rises to $1.35 per unit of output, not only will it be profitable to increase production beyond the least cost point in Figure 14–2A thereby utilizing the Grade A land more intensively, but it

---

[2] David Ricardo, *The Principles of Political Economy and Taxation* (Everyman's Library No. 590; New York: E. P. Dutton & Co., Inc., London: J. M. Dent & Sons, Ltd., 1943), p. 38.

will also be profitable to bring into cultivation the less fertile grades of land, B and C, as in Figures 14–2B and 14–2C. Figure 14–2C illustrates the case of marginal land. The price, OP_c, is just equal to the average cost on Grade C land, and there is no economic rent. However, a price of OP_c will produce economic rent on land of Grades A and B, since this price is well above the average cost of production on these more fertile lands, and the rent is greater on A than on B because A is better grade land than B, or $KP_cE_AJ > LP_cE_BM$.

Thus, Figure 14–2 illustrates the proposition that production will be pushed *both intensively and extensively* up to the point at which the marginal cost of the output is equal to the marginal revenue or price. And so, as poorer grades of land are brought into production, and as better grades of land are used more intensively, economic rent arises as a surplus because of the fact that the supply of good land is limited. Again, it is clear that rent arises from scarcity of resources.

B. URBAN RENT; QUASI RENT; RENT OF ABILITY; LAND VALUATION

Urban Rent

Some of the same principles apply to rent of urban land as apply to agricultural land. In the case of urban land, it is the fact that not all locations are equally desirable or advantageous rather than the fact that not all grades of land are equally fertile (meaning good land is scarce) which gives rise to economic rent. Intensive use of urban land may involve building of skyscrapers. Additional doses of variable inputs may be applied to the fixed input in this situation, and taller buildings are more expensive to build. Thus, eventually, diminishing returns to variable inputs occur. But even if the site is not used intensively, a building in an advantageous location will produce more revenue than one in a poor location. An element of monopoly power is present.

The fact that a favorable location provides the firm with a degree of monopolistic power over its price and may give rise to greater than normal profits, as illustrated in Figure 10–5 in Chapter 10, emphasizes the fact that there is no conceptual difference between greater than normal profits made by a firm in the long run when freedom of entry is absent and the case of urban economic rent. For all practical purposes the two concepts can be treated as if they were identical.[3]

---

[3] For a treatment of urban rent as a monopoly income, see Edward H. Chamberlin, *The Theory of Monopolistic Competition* (7th ed.; Cambridge: Harvard University Press, 1956), Appendix D.

Quasi Rent

Marshall's concept of quasi rent is an extension of the Ricardian rent theory to inputs other than land. Quasi rents are payments to factors of production (e.g., capital goods) which arise from *short-run* inelasticities in their supplies. Thus, they are *short-run* price-determined costs or returns (depending upon one's point of view) and disappear in the long run under perfect competition, while Ricardian rent does *not* disappear in the long run. Quasi rents are sometimes defined as equal to the difference between total revenue and total *variable* costs, and thus, since all costs are variable in the long run, under perfect competition in the long run there are no quasi rents.[4]

Rent of Ability

Rent of ability is a term applied to that part of the income of an individual which is explained by the fact that he has special talents not possessed by mankind in general and which, therefore, are scarce. If such talents are valuable, the individual will receive an income because he possesses something which is wanted and of which the supply is limited. High incomes of gifted artists, athletes, and similar individuals are often explained in this way.

Land Valuation

The value of a piece of land is generally defined by the formula

$$V \text{ (in dollars)} = \frac{R \text{ (in dollars)}}{i}, \qquad (14\text{-}1)$$

where V represents the value of the land in dollars, R is the amount of the rent in dollars, and i represents an appropriate interest rate. This method of valuation rests upon the proposition that in the long run the rate of return on land and the rate of return on capital investments other than land will be equalized. Thus, if the rate of return on capital

---

[4] Some writers argue that in the long run the quasi rents will be equal to some "normal" sum (see Alfred W. Stonier and Douglas C. Hague, *A Textbook of Economic Theory* [2d ed.; London: Longmans, Green & Co., Ltd., 1957], p. 293), but this position only confuses the issue. Marshall's concept is a short-run concept, and normal profits are a long-run concept. Marshall (*Principles of Economics* [8th ed.; London: Macmillan & Co., Ltd., 1938], pp. 420–21) notes that quasi rents are not the same thing as "interest (or profits) on current investments," and he also specifically notes (note 1, p. 424) that quasi rents are "no part of cost under any conditions" and that "confident expectation of coming quasi-rents is a necessary condition for the investment of capital in machinery, and for the incurring of supplementary costs generally." Thus, quasi rents are nothing more than the difference between gross revenue and total *variable* costs. (See George J. Stigler, *The Theory of Price* [rev. ed.; New York: The Macmillan Co., 1952], pp. 191 ff., for a similar view.)

investments other than land is high, more funds will become available for such investments, driving down the rate of interest, while at the same time less funds are available for investment in land. If the return to land is above the return to capital, the reverse flow takes place. The same formula can also be applied to the valuation of *perpetual* fixed income securities (those without a due date), and we will employ Equation (14–1) in the discussion of interest theory in the next chapter.

C. THE EFFECT OF A LUMP-SUM TAX ON ECONOMIC RENT

Henry George and the Single Tax

In 1871 an American, Henry George, published a little book of 48 pages called *Our Land and Land Policy,* in which he advocated that there be levied a single tax on the value of land, irrespective of improvements. About six years later, having been forced to bear the main cost of making the book plates himself, he published *Progress and Poverty,* a book which outsold the most popular novels of the day and which was soon translated into many languages.[5]

In this book George dealt in a scholarly fashion with the existing theories of wages, of interest, and of rent, and argued that wages would be determined by the marginal product of labor.[6] He also developed the rudiments of a marginal productivity theory of interest[7] and accepted the Ricardian theory of rent, which he stated by saying: "The rent of land is determined by the excess of its produce over that which the same application can secure from the least productive land in use."[8]

Having thus defined economic rent as a functionless surplus arising from scarcity, George then argued that unequal distribution of wealth was the result of unequal ownership of land and that "we must make land common property." However, he did not feel it necessary to confiscate land in order to accomplish his objective; it was enough merely to confiscate the economic rent. Thus he advocated the adoption of a single tax upon economic rent of land in place of all other existing forms of taxation.[9] In terms of pure logic, George's argument has never been refuted, since a return which is by definition a functionless surplus cannot be justified on functional grounds! Replies to George's

[5] Henry George, *Progress and Poverty* (New York: Doubleday, Page & Co., 1905), p. x.

[6] *Ibid.,* p. 213. (J. B. Clark was considerably influenced by George in developing his own marginal productivity theory in 1890.)

[7] *Ibid.,* p. 187.

[8] *Ibid.,* p. 168.

[9] *Ibid.,* pp. 401–5.

argument have usually consisted of objections based upon the practical proposition that identification of the pure economic rent and its isolation from the other functionally justified factor returns included in contractual rent payments is impossible and of objections based upon the fact that although economic rent is a price-determined cost from the point of view of society, it is a price-determining cost from the point of view of the individual firm and the industry.

A Graphical Illustration of the Lump-Sum Tax Concept

Figure 14–3A shows that a lump-sum tax, equal to the economic rent, imposed on a firm which sells in a perfectly competitive market will have

Figure 14–3

EFFECT ON ECONOMIC RENT OF A LUMP-SUM TAX UNDER PERFECT COMPETITION AND UNDER CONDITIONS OF MONOPOLY AND COMPETITION INTERMINGLED

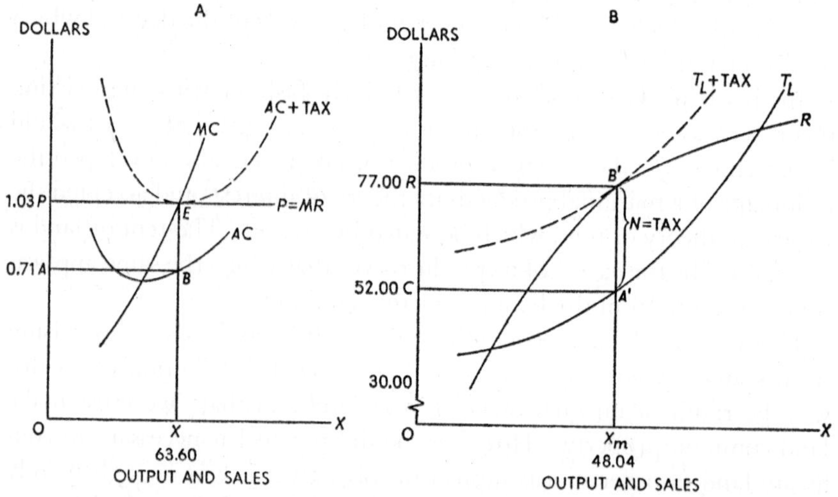

no effect on the price of the product or on the level of output. That is, in Figure 14–3A the firm is in equilibrium with $MC = MR = P$ at E, enjoying an economic rent equal to $APEB$ since its total cost is equal to $OABX$ while its total revenue is equal to $OPEX$. A lump-sum tax equal to $APEB$ will merely increase the firm's fixed costs, and thus the tax operates to shift the average cost curve upward to $AC +$ Tax. At E, the marginal cost will be equal to the minimum average cost, and these in turn will be equal to the price of the product and marginal revenue from sales, while output remains constant at OX. The lump-sum tax, equal to the greater than normal profits or rent enjoyed by the firm by virtue of its control over a scarce input, has thus been extracted with no effect on prices or output. If the scarce input were not owned by the firm, its average cost curve would be $AC + Tax$. In this case, the tax (equal to $APEB$) would be levied on the titleholder.

Henry George wrote *Progress and Poverty* largely as an attack on monopolistic control over land. However, there is no real difference between economic rent resulting from scarcity due to nature and greater than normal profits resulting from artificially created scarcities based upon control over entry into an industry. Thus, in Figure 14–3B, the firm is initially in equilibrium producing OX_m units of output, and its total revenue is equal to $OR = \$77$. Its total cost is equal to $OC = \$52$. The firm is enjoying an economic surplus (or a profit greater than normal as a result of its monopolistic position) equal to $A'B' = \$25$. That the firm is not operating under conditions of perfect competition is shown by the fact that the total revenue curve is nonlinear. That freedom of entry is absent from the market is indicated by the fact that it is making a greater than normal profit $(N > 0)$ in the long run.

The effect of a lump-sum tax, equal to the greater than normal profit or to the economic rent $(A'B')$, is shown by the upward shift of the total cost curve from T_L to $T_L + Tax$. The lump-sum tax again is treated as nothing more than an addition to the firm's total costs, since absence of freedom of entry artificially limits the use of inputs. The slopes of the total cost and total revenue curves are not affected, and, hence, the marginal cost and marginal revenue curves are not affected either.

Although the case of economic rent has been explained in Figure 14–3A by means of average and marginal cost curves, it could easily be explained in terms of total cost curves also. Similarly, the case of Figure 14–3B could as easily be explained in terms of average and marginal cost curves. Figure 14–3 thus illustrates that the result of the analysis of the effect of a lump-sum tax on economic rent is the same whether one uses marginal and average, or total, cost curves and further illustrates that the case of economic rent is identical with the case of greater than normal profits when there is an absence of freedom of entry. No economic justification in terms of static economic analysis can be given for accrual of the so-called "unearned increment" (the economic rent) to the firm. A dynamic rationalization of monopoly profits will be examined in Chapter 18 later.

Two factor returns, interest and profits, remain to be considered.

Both of these are treated in the following chapter which concludes our examination of the theories of income distribution.

SELECTED READINGS

BOULDING, KENNETH E. "The Concept of Economic Surplus," *American Economic Review,* Vol. XXXV (December, 1945), pp. 851–69.

GEORGE, HENRY. *Progress and Poverty.* New York: Doubleday, Page & Co., 1925.

MACHLUP, FRITZ. *The Economies of Sellers' Competition,* chap. viii. Baltimore: The Johns Hopkins Press, 1952.

MARSHALL, ALFRED. *Principles of Economics,* Book VI, chap. ix. 8th ed. London: Macmillan & Co., Ltd., 1938.

RICARDO, DAVID. *The Principles of Political Economy and Taxation.* New York: E. P. Dutton & Co., Inc., 1943.

WORCESTER, DEAN A. "A Reconsideration of the Theory of Rent," *American Economic Review,* Vol. XXXVI (June, 1946), pp. 258–77.

15 Interest and Profits

Introduction

Prior to the publication of *The General Theory of Employment, Interest and Money* by J. M. Keynes in 1936[1] and the impetus given to the study of macroeconomics by this classic work, many economists accepted, or at least paid lip service to, the neoclassical "real" or "time-preference" theory of interest. However, Knut Wicksell (1901) must be counted among the earliest exceptions to this rule, since his theory was a forerunner of the present-day "monetary" theories.[2] Modern interest theory involves the use of macroeconomic concepts as well as of those of microeconomics, but interest is, nevertheless, a "price." In this chapter, we will first briefly examine the real or time-preference theory and the contribution of Wicksell, and then we will consider three related contemporary theories of interest.

Economists also differ as to the various sources of profit and as to the importance of these sources. The concluding section of this chapter contains a brief survey of alternative theories of profits.

A. BASIC CONCEPTS

The Concept of "Pure Interest"

Just as the concept of economic rent must be distinguished from the concept of contractual rent, so does one find economists drawing a dis-

---

[1] J. M. Keynes, *The General Theory of Employment, Interest and Money* (New York: Harcourt, Brace & Co., 1936).

[2] Knut Wicksell, *Interest and Prices* (London: Macmillan & Co., Ltd., 1935); and Wicksell, *Lectures on Political Economy* (2 vols.; New York: The Macmillan Co., 1935). Joseph A. Schumpeter, *The Theory of Economic Development*, trans. Redvers Opie (Cambridge: Harvard University Press, 1934); J. M. Keynes, *A Treatise on Money* (New York: Harcourt, Brace & Co., 1930); and R. G. Hawtrey, *Currency and Credit* (London: Longmans Green & Co., Ltd., 1928) are among the later exceptions.

tinction between the "pure rate of interest" and various market rates. Among other reasons, market rates of interest differ because of differences in the maturity structures of loans, the element of risk, the nature of the loan, handling costs, tax features of various types of securities, and a host of legal, administrative, and operating procedures. Table 15–1 shows various long-term and short-term interest rates by type of borrower as of February 3, 1962.

Table 15–1

SHORT-TERM AND LONG-TERM INTEREST RATES, FEBRUARY 3, 1962

Type of Security	Per Cent Per Annum
Short Term:	
Prime commercial paper, 4 to 6 months	3.13
Finance company paper, 3 to 6 months	3.00
U.S. government, 3-month bills	2.705
U.S. government, 6-month bills	2.939
U.S. government, 9- to 12-month issues	3.26
U.S. government, 3- to 5-year issues	3.88
Long Term:	
Corporate bonds, Aaa	4.42
Corporate bonds, Baa	5.07
Industrial bonds	4.57
Railroad bonds	4.91
Public-utility bonds	4.61
State and local government bonds, Aaa	3.12
State and local government bonds, Baa	3.88
U.S. government bonds, 10 years or more	4.10

Source: *Federal Reserve Bulletin*, Vol. XLVIII, No. 2 (February, 1962), p. 196.

The "pure" rate of interest is defined in theoretical discussions as that rate which would be paid for a completely riskless loan, given the relevant time period. For practical purposes, the long-term United States government bond rate (4.10 percent in Table 15–1) is usually taken as the closest approximation to the long-term "pure" rate.

Consumption Loans versus Production Loans

Consumption loans, or loans made for purposes of consumption, are usually excluded from theoretical discussions of the interest rate in order to simplify the analysis. One method of dealing with consumer borrowing is to subtract this amount from gross saving and to include only the remaining saving in the analysis. Some theoretical formulations also omit consideration of government borrowing from first approximations. Production loans are those which are made for the purpose of putting inputs to work to produce output and are of primary importance in interest theory.

B. EARLIER THEORIES OF INTEREST

The Time-Preference or "Real" Interest Theory

The real or time-preference theory of interest is the neoclassical theory. In its simplest form, it argues that the reason why interest *can* be paid lies in the net marginal productivity of capital and that the reason why it *must* be paid is that people prefer current consumption to future consumption and will reduce their current consumption to make available saving for investment only if they receive a premium in the form of an interest payment.

The term *capital goods* is defined in different ways in the literature. It was originally coined by J. B. Clark, who distinguished between *capital*, which he identified as "a certain amount of 'money' permanently invested in a succession of perishable things," and *capital goods*, which he defined as "perishable things" in which the capital was invested.[3] For our present purposes it is enough to define capital goods as produced means of further production, and borderline cases need not detain us.

According to the time-preference theory, capital represents a distinct factor of production, the services of which can be paid for if the marginal (net) productivity of capital, as explained in Chapter 12, is positive. That is, it is argued that laborers are generally more productive when they use roundabout, or indirect, means of production (meaning when they make use of capital goods). It is the net productivity of capital embodied in capital goods which, thus, makes possible the payment of interest, although the net productivity of capital does not explain why interest *must* be paid.

However, since it is assumed that people prefer current consumption to future consumption and will only reduce their current consumption, thereby releasing resources for investment, if they are paid a premium in the form of interest, it follows that interest must be paid. What this assumption amounts to is an assumption that saving is a function of the rate of interest, and, of course, it is a basic assumption about the way in which people behave. It is further assumed that as the interest rate rises, since the premium paid for postponing consumption is thus increasing, the amount saved will increase. The development of the time-preference theory was largely due to the work of an Austrian economist,

---

[3] J. B. Clark, *The Distribution of Wealth* (New York: The Macmillan Co., 1938), chap. ix, esp. pp. 116–21.

Eugen von Böhm-Bawerk, who substituted it for earlier theories
adopted after 1836 by Nassau Senior and other English economists.[4]
(They had argued that interest was paid for "abstinence" from consumption.)

According to the time-preference theory, the supply of saving curve
was thus thought to have a positive slope (although writers differed in
their views as to its elasticity), while the curve of the demand for capital,
which was based upon the net marginal productivity of capital, was
believed to have a negative slope because of the principle of diminishing
marginal returns to capital (explained in Chapter 6). The demand for
capital is sometimes also known as an investment demand, and contemporary writers have employed the concept of *prospective* or *antici-*

Figure 15–1

THE EQUILIBRIUM RATE OF INTEREST—TIME-PREFERENCE
THEORY

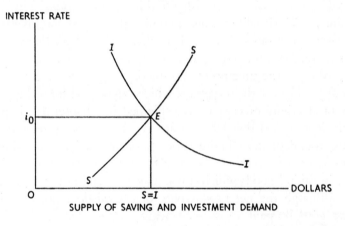

pated marginal net revenue productivity in defining it. This concept
sometimes also goes by the name of marginal efficiency of capital
(*MEC*) or marginal efficiency of investment (*MEI*).

Thus, in Figure 15–1, at the point at which the curve of the marginal
net productivity of capital crosses the saving curve, the *real* interest rate
is determined, and saving is equal to investment. In short, according to
the real or time-preference theory, the *real* interest rate in equilibrium
is equal to the net marginal productivity of capital at a given level of

---

[4] Eugen von Böhm-Bawerk, *The Positive Theory of Capital*, trans. Wm. Smart (New
York: The Macmillan Co., 1891).

use. All this, therefore, is a matter of simple supply-demand analysis.

The theory assumes that saving and the demand for capital are independent of each other and also assumes full employment, thereby making saving a function of the rate of interest. Many economists today believe that the saving schedule is interest inelastic. This is really a shorthand way of saying that the functional relationship between saving and the rate of interest is a very weak one, if it exists at all. Finally, in its simplest form, the time-preference theory ignores the fact that the speculative demand for and the supply of money exert an influence on the rate of interest and on the level of income. These matters will be considered later in this chapter.

Wicksell on the "Market" and the "Natural" Rates of Interest

In 1901 a Swedish economist, Knut Wicksell, introduced a relationship between the concepts of the "natural" or "normal" or real rate and the "market" rate into the analysis. In doing so, Wicksell sought to take account of the effect on the interest rate and on prices of changes in the supply of money.

Wicksell argued that the market and the normal or natural rates of interest would have to be equal for equilibrium to exist. In support of his argument, he noted that if for any reason banks made loans at rates materially lower than the natural rate, opportunities for profits by entrepreneurs would exist and investment would increase. Bankers, of course, would not know the natural rate since it is not defined as a measurable magnitude. Assuming full employment, with consumption constant, the increased investment would produce a rise in prices proportional to the increase in the money supply, and a spiral of increasing investment and rising prices would continue until the excess reserves of the banks were exhausted and the market rate of interest was raised to the level of the normal or natural rate.[5] Wicksell believed that only the continuous injection of additional money from outside the banking system (for example, "the incessant flow to them [banks] of new gold") would make it possible for banks to maintain the market rate permanently below the natural or normal rate. Thus, according to Wicksell, in equilibrium the natural or normal rate and the market rate are equal, but in disequilibrium they are unequal. Wicksell's theory is important because it emphasizes the effect of credit creation upon the interest rate, thereby introducing an additional variable into the analysis.

---

[5] Wicksell, *Lectures on Political Economy*, Vol. II, pp. 190–201, esp. pp. 198–201.

Contemporary interest theories all take account of the fact that the supply of and demand for money have something to do with the interest rate.

C. CONTEMPORARY THEORIES OF INTEREST

The Keynesian Liquidity Preference Theory

In 1936, in *The General Theory of Employment, Interest and Money*, J. M. Keynes stated the "liquidity preference" theory of interest. His theory does not in fact result in a determinate interest rate, but the concept of "liquidity preference" introduced by him has become a standard part of all contemporary interest theories in one form or another.[6] The Keynesian theory deals with *stocks* of money and *attitudes towards these stocks*.

Keynes argued that interest is a payment for the use of money and defined liquidity preference as a preference for holding wealth in the form of money rather than in the form of assets (securities). He distinguished among three different demands for money, namely, the transactions demand, the precautionary demand, and the speculative demand, and selected the speculative demand for particular emphasis in his theory.

Keynes first noted that there are various reasons why economic entities hold cash balances. In the first place, there is a *transactions* motive for holding money. That is, money is needed because receipts and expenditures are not synchronized. A certain proportion of the total money supply is needed to satisfy this demand, and this fact is usually stated by the relation $B_t = kY$, where B_t represents the amount needed for transactions, where k represents the transactions demand as a proportion of money income, and where Y represents money national income. The transactions demand for money depends upon the total value of business transactions and thus, in part, upon prices.[7] This demand for money is assumed to be independent of the interest rate at a given level of na-

---

[6] See especially chaps. xiii–xv.

[7] It can be shown that $B_t = kY$ is really another form of the Fisher Equation of Exchange ($MV = PT$) when the transactions demand is the only demand for money and when the velocity of circulation per period of time (V) is held constant, where P represents the general price level and where T represents physical transactions during the same period of time as V. The relation, $B_t = kY$, can also be shown to be merely another form of statement of the Quantity Theory of Money. See Gardner Ackley, *Macroeconomic Theory* (New York: The Macmillan Co., 1961), pp. 113–20, esp. p. 118; and Gerald Sirkin, *Introduction to Macroeconomic Theory* (Homewood, Ill.: Richard D. Irwin, Inc., 1961), pp. 128–29.

tional income and is assumed to remain constant in the short run, although it may change in the long run.

In addition to the transactions demand, it is assumed that there exist a *speculative* demand (B_s) and a *precautionary* demand (B_p) for holding money. The former, B_s, represents a demand for money to be used in "making money" by means of speculation in fixed income securities; the latter, B_p, represents a demand for money by an economic entity which feels that it may be confronted by unforeseen contingencies. For purposes of simplifying the analysis, we will assume that the precautionary demand is independent of the rate of interest and remains constant in the short run also. And so, in Figure 15–2, the precautionary and

Figure 15–2

THE LIQUIDITY PREFERENCE THEORY OF INTEREST

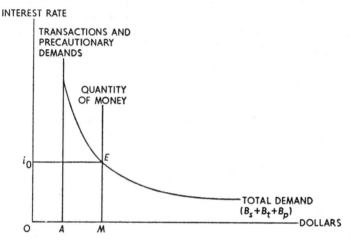

transactions demands for money can be summed and depicted as equal to the distance OA on the X axis at all interest rates, assuming a given level of income.

The speculative demand for money is the volatile element in the Keynesian analysis and must be further considered. The speculative demand can be added to the sum of the transactions and precautionary demands at a given level of national income to produce the total demand for money curve depicted in Figure 15–2. In Figure 15–2, at interest rate Oi_0 and the given level of income, the speculative demand is thus equal to AM, since the total demand at that interest rate is OM, and the sum of the transactions and precautionary demands is always equal to OA at the given income level. Depending upon expectations, an individual's liquidity preference will be different at different times, and it will also be different at different interest rates and levels of national income. Figure 15-2, it should be repeated, is drawn upon the assumption that national income is at a given level. In order to show the total demand for money at another level of national income, the curve of the total demand for money would have to be shifted. The fact that the liquidity preference is different at different interest rates when national income and expectations are given is reflected in the negative slope of the total demand for money curve; and this slope is, of course, necessarily the same as that of the speculative demand curve. Why has this curve been drawn with a negative slope?

Keynes answered this question by arguing that the speculative demand for money is particularly and inversely related to the interest rate, even if the other two demands are not. That is, at high rates of interest, speculators will prefer to hold bonds rather than money, both because such securities have a high rate of return and because of expectations that bond prices will rise or at least will not decline. Similarly, they prefer to hold money rather than bonds at low interest rates because the reverse is expected. This belief is based upon the valuation formula, given in Equation (14-1) of the preceding chapter, which relates the market price of a *perpetual fixed income security* (one without a due date) to its rate of return in the following way:

$$V = \frac{R}{i}. \qquad (14\text{-}1)$$

This formula was used in the preceding chapter as an explanation of land valuation, and it was noted there that the formula also applies to the case of perpetual fixed income securities. In the formula, R represents the return in dollars which is paid by contract on the perpetual fixed income security, while i is the market rate of interest, and V is the market value of the security. In the case of such a security, the return in dollars is equal to the stated rate of return times the face value of the security, or a 6 percent security with a face value of $1,000 produces a return of $60 per year. Since i in the formula represents the *market rate of interest,* it can vary. Now, if i is, say, 5 percent, we have

$$V = \frac{\$60}{.05} = \$1,200. \qquad (14\text{-}1')$$

Thus, the market value of a $1,000 perpetual security with a fixed return of 6 percent is $1,200 at a time when the market rate of interest is 5 percent. For, at the market rate of 5 percent, one would have to invest $1,200 in order to secure a return in dollars equivalent to that obtained from the given security. (See also *Note A* at the end of this chapter.)

If the fixed income security has a specified maturity date, the same inverse relationship between its price and the market rate exists. Thus, at a market rate of 5 percent, a ten-year bond bearing 5 percent interest compounded annually, with a maturity value of $1,000, would have a present value (V_p) of $613.91, or $V_p = $ Maturity Value$/(1 + i)^n = $ $1,000/(1.05)^{10}$. At the end of a year, if the market rate remained unchanged, the present value would be $644.61. If the market rate had risen to 6 percent, the present value would have been only $591.90, and a capital loss would have resulted. But a decline in the interest rate to 4 percent would have resulted in a present value of $702.59 and a capital gain. Thus, at high interest rates, the expectation of lower rates and of capital gains is great, and the speculative demand for money is low; and, at low interest rates, the expectation of higher rates and of capital losses is great, and the demand for money is strong. Therefore, the curve of the speculative demand for money has a negative slope, as depicted in Figure 15–2.

Keynes also assumed that the quantity of money (M) was interest inelastic, at least in the short run. The quantity of money is under the control of the central banking authorities, and, depending on what policies they adopt, the curve may or may not be as interest inelastic as it has been depicted in Figure 15–2. In the Keynesian formulation, interest is a payment for parting with liquidity, and Keynes argued that the interest rate would be determined by the intersection of the quantity of money curve with the total demand for money curve (at E in Figure 15–2). The equilibrium condition in the Keynesian liquidity preference theory is thus that the supply of money be equal to the amount demanded or desired in balances, or

$$M = B_s + B_t + B_p . \tag{15-1}$$

This condition, however, is the condition of *static monetary equilibrium only* and not the whole story. For the curve of the total demand for money will shift (the transactions demand will be different) as income changes, and the liquidity preference theory rests upon an assumed level of income and does not show how that income level is determined. That is, it is an incomplete theory. If we assume in Figure 15–2 that the *given* income level is the final equilibrium level and is consistent with the final monetary equilibrium, we have assumed away part of the problem.

According to the Keynesian theory, income will be in equilibrium only when planned saving and planned investment are equal, and the liquidity preference theory does not take this fact into account. In short, although his contribution was great and although he provided both the condition of monetary equilibrium and the condition of income equilibrium, Keynes failed to relate the two equilibrium conditions to one another in developing his liquidity preference interest theory and failed to emphasize the mutual interdependence of saving, investment, income, and the interest rate. Other contemporary theories, considered next, seek to overcome this deficiency.

The Supply of and the Demand for Loanable Funds

Introduction. The meaning and significance of the loanable funds theory and its relation to the liquidity preference theory have been the subject of considerable controversy in the literature.[8] Some writers follow the procedure of Keynes and assume income given at some level, thereby leaving themselves open to the criticism that their statements of the theory are wrong as well as indeterminate. Others argue that the loanable funds theory is a dynamic disequilibrium analysis.[9] In order to present both points of view in a reasonably compact treatment, our procedure will be as follows. First, the net supply of and the net demand for loanable funds will be defined, since there is general agreement as to the elements which make up these magnitudes and disagreement only as to what the analysis means. Then the so-called *static* loanable funds theory, which assumes the level of income as given, will be critically examined. In what follows, saving means planned saving, and investment means planned investment.

The Net Supply of Loanable Funds. The total supply of loanable funds comes from several sources. *One source is saving, defined as gross saving less consumption loans* $(S_g - L_c = S)$. Not all of saving becomes available as loanable funds, for reasons which will be given below. Moreover, saving does not depend closely upon the interest rate. Instead, saving is functionally related to income.

Consider personal saving. There are various reasons why people save. Some may save for a rainy day; some may save because they are forced to do so by means of social security tax payments and other institutional devices. Others may engage in semivoluntary saving in the

---

[8] See S. C. Tsiang, "Liquidity Preference and Loanable Funds Theories, Multiplier and Velocity Analysis: A Synthesis," *American Economic Review,* Vol. XLVI (September, 1956), pp. 539–64; and "Liquidity Preference and Loanable Funds Theories of Interest: Comment by Gardner Ackley" and "Reply by S. C. Tsiang," *American Economic Review,* Vol. XLVII (September, 1957), pp. 662–78; and Alvin H. Hansen, *A Guide to Keynes* (New York: McGraw-Hill Book Co., Inc., 1953), chaps. vi and vii.

[9] *Ibid.*

form of payments for various types of insurance policies; and people with high incomes may save automatically, since they have few purchasable desires which cannot be met with less than their full incomes. Under these circumstances, it is apparent that some personal saving would occur even if the interest rate were zero. Indeed, at very low interest rates, or at very low income levels, people may even be dissavers, meaning that they will borrow either for purposes of consumption or to improve their current cash positions.

In addition to the (personal) saving of individuals, a *second source* of loanable funds is the depreciation reserves and retained earnings set aside from current income by businesses. Both are probably more closely related to corporate policies and to the nature of the business enterprise in question (as well as to the expectations of its managers) than to the interest rate. In Figure 15–3 the curve, S, represents the sum of gross personal and business saving less consumption loans $(S_g - L_c = S)$ at various interest rates and a final equilibrium level of income. (Saving is *gross* when depreciation reserves are included.)

The S curve does *not*, however, represent the total amount of loanable funds. Aside from business and personal saving from current income, account must be taken of the fact that at any given time the amount of money which economic entities desire to hold as cash balances may not be equal to the total amount of money held. The difference between the amount of money which people want to hold in their balances and the amount they do hold may be defined as

$$H = (B_s + B_t + B_p) - M . \qquad (15\text{–}2)$$

Now H really represents the *difference between the amount desired in the speculative balance and the amount actually held in the speculative balance*, since, in the short run, both B_t and B_p are assumed to be independent of the rate of interest and to change slowly. If H is *positive*, the amount people want to hold is greater than the amount they do hold, and *hoarding* occurs. If H is *negative*, the amount held exceeds that which is desired in balances, and *dishoarding* occurs.

The difference between the amount desired in speculative balances and the amount actually held can be met either by offsetting changes in the supply of money (ΔM) or by offsetting changes in saving. Accordingly, in an economy in which there were no changes in the supply of money, the net supply of loanable funds would consist of the difference between saving from current income and hoarding (H), or

$$S - H = S_L , \qquad (15\text{–}3)$$

where S_L represents the total net supply of loanable funds.

At E in Figure 15–3, we see that H is zero and that the supply of loanable funds is equal to the supply of saving, since $S - H = S$; that is,
the $S - H$ and S curves cross. Above E, H is negative, and dishoarding
occurs; that is, $S - H > S$. Below E, H is positive, and hoarding occurs;

Figure 15–3

THE SUPPLY OF LOANABLE FUNDS

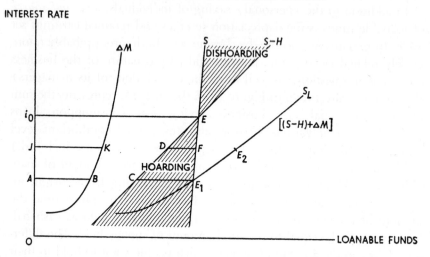

or $S - H < S$. Thus, hoarding $(H > 0)$ decreases the supply of loanable funds, and dishoarding $(H < 0)$ increases the supply of loanable
funds.

Finally, as Wicksell pointed out, in an economy containing credit-
creating institutions, the supply of new credit (ΔM) adds a third (or
fourth, if business saving is counted separately) source of loanable
funds. New bank credit is newly created money, since banks create new
deposit currency by making loans and investments. The limit on bank
loans is the amount of the banks' excess reserves. Excess reserves are
subject to the control of the central bank in the system. The ultimate
limit is governmental policy. When the banks' excess reserves are
low or declining, there is probably a correlation between the supply of
bank credit and the interest rate. However, when excess reserves are
very large, although there is probably a lower limit to the interest rate
fixed by the cost of handling loans, the correlation between the amount
of bank credit and the interest rate is less pronounced. Thus, above a
certain minimum interest rate, with large excess reserves in banks, the

supply of credit curve is probably fairly elastic; and in many diagrams, it is usually drawn nearly horizontal to, but at a certain minimum level above, the X axis for some range before it is permitted to rise. At very low interest rates (above the minimum level), the attitude of borrowers is a more important factor in determining the amount of credit than is the policy of the central bank. In Figure 15–3, the ΔM curve shows changes in the money supply at different interest rates.

And so the final equation defining the total net supply of loanable funds in a modern economy can be written as

$$S - H + \Delta M = S_L , \qquad\qquad (15\text{--}4)$$

where ΔM represents additions to the money supply, taken to mean increases in bank credit in most formulations of the theory. The S_L curve in Figure 15–3 thus represents the total net supply of loanable funds from all sources, at various interest rates. At E_1, since $(AB = \Delta M) = (CE_1 = H)$, we have $\Delta M - H = 0$, and the supply of loanable funds is equal to saving, since the S_L and S curves cross at that point, with $\Delta M > 0$ and $H > 0$.

Demand for Loanable Funds. Just as the total supply of loanable funds is the sum of various different supplies, so is the total demand for loanable funds similarly made up of different demands. *First,* there is the investment or business demand for funds (I), both the demand for long-term loans for purposes of investment in plant and equipment and the demand for investment in inventories. Basically, the business or investment demand for loanable funds rests upon the prospective marginal net revenue productivity of the investment or of capital. This concept has already been explained in this chapter and especially in Chapter 12. *Second,* there is the demand by governments (national, state, and local) for funds. The government demand (L_g) is motivated less by considerations related to the interest rate than by other considerations; thus the government demand for loanable funds is probably relatively inelastic. (Refunding operations by government agencies, however, are by definition functionally related to the interest rate.) The *third* demand for loanable funds is the demand of consumers (L_c) both for short-term and for long-term loans, a demand which ranges from the demand for funds for vacations to the demand for mortgage loans for housing. This demand has, however, already been taken into account in drawing the saving curve, since Gross Saving $- L_c = S$ in Figure 15–3. The *fourth* demand for loanable funds, the speculative demand, has also already been taken into account in drawing the $S - H$ curve.

The sum of the private investment demand (I) and the government demand for loans (L_g) thus produces the net demand for loanable funds, or

$$I + L_g = D_L . \tag{15-5}$$

The "Static" Loanable Funds Theory

The usual static loanable funds theory involves selecting a point at which the supply of loanable funds is equal to the demand for loanable funds and designating it as the equilibrium position at some given level of income. Now which of the positions, E, E_1, or E_2 in Figure 15–4, is to

Figure 15–4

THE EQUILIBRIUM RATE OF INTEREST—LOANABLE FUNDS THEORY

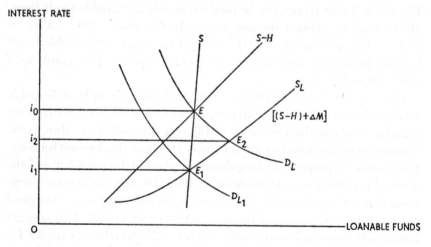

be selected as the equilibrium position? Different writers select different points.

Professor Gardner Ackley has argued that the orthodox loanable funds theory contains much confusion, since saving, investment, and income are all flow concepts, while hoarding and dishoarding refer to a difference between two stocks. These magnitudes cannot be defined without reference to some time period.[10] It is necessary, therefore, to specify a time period applicable to the analysis. Accordingly, he remarks that the loanable funds theory should be treated as a disequilibrium theory, concerned with a dynamic analysis, not as a static theory. Finally, his criticism concludes, when the loanable funds theory is interpreted as a statement of static equilibrium conditions, the theory

---

[10] Ackley, *op. cit.*, pp. 200–7.

contains few new insights. We will examine this argument in greater detail below.

First consider E_2 in Figure 15–4. *Selection of this point as the static equilibrium position represents a naïve approach.* At E_2 the supply of loanable funds is equal to the demand for loanable funds, and we have $S_L = D_L$, or

$$S - H + \Delta M = I + L_g . \qquad (15\text{-}6)$$

However, it can easily be shown that at E_2, income is not in equilibrium. Define income (Y) from the *expenditures* point of view as

$$Y = C + I + G , \qquad (15\text{-}7)$$

where C represents consumption expenditure, I represents gross private investment, and G represents government expenditure. Similarly define income (Y) from the *disposal* point of view as

$$Y = C + S + T , \qquad (15\text{-}8)$$

where T represents taxes, and C and S respectively represent consumption expenditure and gross saving less consumption loans. Then, setting these two equations equal to each other and eliminating C, which is common to the right-hand sides of both, we have the income equilibrium condition as

$$S + T = I + G . \qquad (15\text{-}9)$$

Next, define $G - T = L_g$, which says that government expenditures less taxes are equal to government borrowing. Then, rearranging our income equilibrium equation, we have

$$S = I + (G - T) = I + L_g . \qquad (15\text{-}10)$$

The last expression on the right in our equilibrium condition equation has, of course, already been defined in Equation (15–5) as the net demand for loanable funds.

Now, if we subtract our income equilibrium condition Equation (15–10) from Equation (15–6) which states that the supply of and the demand for loanable funds must be equal in equilibrium, we have

$$
\begin{array}{lll}
S - H + \Delta M = & I + L_g & (15\text{-}6) \\
-S & = -I - L_g & (15\text{-}10) \\
\hline
- H + \Delta M = 0 . & & (15\text{-}11)
\end{array}
$$

Thus, if income is to be in equilibrium simultaneously with the supply of loanable funds equal to the demand for loanable funds, the sum of dishoarding and the change in the money supply must be equal to zero, or

$-H + \Delta M = 0$. Alternatively, we can say $\Delta M - H = 0$, which means that the difference between the change in the money supply and hoarding must be equal to zero. Either statement is correct.

Now note, however, that reference to our earlier Figure 15–3 would show that at E_2 the amount of new money being created is greater than the amount of hoarding, or $(\Delta M = JK) > (H = DF)$. Accordingly, at E_2 in Figure 15–4, even though $S_L = D_L$, some of the private investment and government borrowing are being financed with new money, and income is *not* in equilibrium. Therefore, E_2 is not a full equilibrium position.

Next consider E. At E in Figure 15–4, the S curve crosses the $S - H$ curve. Thus, at E there is neither hoarding nor dishoarding. Now the $S - H$ curve and the S curve have been drawn *without taking into account the creation of new money.* Therefore, if ΔM *were* equal to zero, the relevant supply of loanable funds curve *would be* $S - H$. In this case, E would be the full equilibrium position. Let us see why.

Professor Ackley, using a different diagram, has argued that in the static equilibrium position both H and ΔM must be zero. It is not enough that their sum be zero in the case of the static analysis.[11] His argument can be explained in the following way. First, hoarding has already been defined as the difference between the amount of money people want to hold and the amount they do hold, or as

$$H = (B_s + B_t + B_p) - M . \tag{15-2}$$

Next, note that the condition of static monetary equilibrium has also already been stated to be

$$M = B_s + B_t + B_p , \tag{15-1}$$

which says that the amount of money held in balances must be equal to the amount economic entities desire to hold in their balances.

Then note that a comparison of Equations (15–2) and (15–1) leads to the conclusion that *in the static monetary equilibrium position, H must be equal to zero by definition.* That is, H has been defined as the difference between the amount of money desired and the amount held, and this difference *is* zero in the static equilibrium position.

Finally, since the condition $\Delta M - H = 0$ must be met if the static income and static monetary equilibrium conditions are to be met simultaneously, and since H must be zero for static *monetary* equilibrium to exist, it follows that ΔM must also be equal to zero when the two condi-

---

[11] *Ibid.;* see also his "Comment," *American Economic Review,* Vol. XLVII (September, 1957), esp. p. 664 and p. 668.

tions are met simultaneously. Thus, at E in Figure 15–4, where $H = \Delta M = 0$, both monetary equilibrium and income equilibrium are attained. We will see shortly that the Hicks-Hansen analysis explained below says the same thing in a different way.

Now consider E_1 in Figure 15–4, where the S and S_L curves intersect. At this point, saving and the supply of loanable funds are equal, and all the new money being created is being hoarded, since reference once more to our earlier Figure 15–3 will show that at E_1 we have ($\Delta M = AB$) = ($H = CE_1$), or $\Delta M - H = 0$. Thus, it may be possible for planned saving and planned investment plus government borrowing to be equal at E_1 and for some kind of monetary equilibrium to exist there, *but it is not possible for a static monetary equilibrium to exist at E_1, because H is not zero,* and therefore Equation (15–1) does not hold at E_1. And so, although many writers would apparently select E_1 in Figure 15–4 as the static equilibrium position, they seem to be explaining a dynamic disequilibrium situation.[12]

Many problems arise in an attempt to state the loanable funds theory as a dynamic theory. Such a theory falls outside the scope of this book, and the interested reader may be referred to the references cited in footnote 8 for a treatment of this matter.

The Hicks-Hansen Analysis

The Hicks-Hansen analysis, which dates from an article by Professor J. R. Hicks in 1937 and which was further developed by Professor Alvin Hansen in 1949, possesses an advantage over the static loanable funds theory (when E is selected as the point of equilibrium in Figure 15–4).[13] Both the monetary and the income equilibrium conditions can be depicted graphically in a single diagram, as in Figure 15–5, by means of this analysis, although some of our preceding diagrams are necessary to explain the derivation of Figure 15–5.

This analysis involves drawing a curve showing various combinations of income and interest rates at which the income equilibrium condition is met. (Note that the X axis now measures *income.*) Such a curve is

---

[12] See, for example, John F. Due and Robert W. Clower, *Intermediate Economic Analysis* (4th ed.; Homewood, Ill.: Richard D. Irwin, Inc., 1961), pp. 399–400; M. M. Bober, *Intermediate Price and Income Theory* (rev. ed.; New York: W. W. Norton & Co., Inc., 1962), pp. 385–93; and Walter W. Haines, *Money, Prices and Policy* (New York: McGraw-Hill Book Co., Inc., 1961), pp. 520–30. (Haines does not specify $\Delta M - H = 0$.)

[13] J. R. Hicks, "Mr. Keynes and the 'Classics'; a Suggested Interpretation," *Econometrica*, Vol. V (1937), pp. 147–59, reprinted in American Economic Association, *Readings in the Theory of Income Distribution* (Philadelphia: Blakiston Co., 1946); and Alvin Hansen, *Monetary Theory and Fiscal Policy* (New York: McGraw-Hill Book Co., Inc., 1949), chaps. iv–v.

depicted in Figure 15–5, where it has been labeled Saving = Investment + Government Borrowing, with the income equilibrium condition, $S = I + L_g$, written underneath the label to show that it is nothing more than a curve depicting the various alternative combinations of
interest rates and income levels at which the income equilibrium condition is met.[14] Point E in Figure 15–4 is *one* of the points on the $S =$
$I + L_g$ curve in Figure 15–5, since the S curve has been drawn in Fig-

Figure 15–5

THE HICKS-HANSEN ANALYSIS

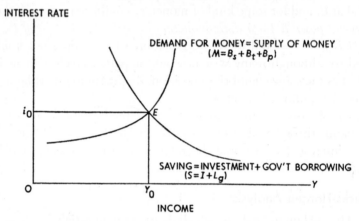

INTEREST RATE

DEMAND FOR MONEY= SUPPLY OF MONEY
$(M=B_s+B_t+B_p)$

i_0 E

SAVING = INVESTMENT+ GOV'T BORROWING
$(S=I+L_g)$

O Y_0 Y

INCOME

ure 15–4 on the assumption that income is at one given level. (The X
axis in Figure 15–4 does *not* measure income.) A higher level of income would shift the S curve to the right, and the new point of intersection of the shifted S curve and the D_L curve in Figure 15–4 would
provide a second point on the $S = I + L_g$ curve in Figure 15–5. In fact,
all the points on the $S = I + L_g$ curve can be derived by shifting the S
curve in Figure 15–4 in this way.

A second curve also appears in Figure 15–5. This curve shows the
various combinations of interest rates and income levels at which the
monetary equilibrium condition is met and has been labeled Supply of
Money = Demand for Money, with the monetary equilibrium condition
$(M = B_s + B_t + B_p)$ written underneath the label. Point E in
Figure 15–2 is *one* of the points on this curve in Figure 15–5, since the
Total Demand for Money Curve in Figure 15–2 has been drawn upon
the assumption that income is constant at one given level. (Again, the
X axis in Figure 15–2 does *not* measure income.) A higher level of income causes the Total Demand for Money Curve to shift up along the

---

[14] For the derivation of such a curve as well as of the one described below, see Alvin
Hansen, *A Guide to Keynes* (New York: McGraw-Hill Book Co., Inc., 1953), pp. 144–45.

Quantity of Money Curve in Figure 15–2 because the transactions demand would be greater even if the other demands remained constant. Such a new point of intersection of the Total Demand for Money Curve and the Supply of Money Curve in Figure 15–2 would provide a second point on the $M = B_s + B_t + B_p$ curve in Figure 15–5. Additional points on this curve can be determined by further shifting the Total Demand for Money Curve in Figure 15–2.

At E in Figure 15–5, where the $S = I + L_g$ and the $M = B_t + B_s + B_p$ curves intersect, the conditions of income equilibrium and of monetary equilibrium are met simultaneously, and income and the interest rate are mutually determined. Also at E in Figure 15–5, Wicksell's natural rate of interest is equal to the market rate. Now if the same income level is assumed in the liquidity preference theory depicted in Figure 15–2 and in the loanable funds theory in Figure 15–4, and if this level is equal to the income level OY_0 in Figure 15–5 at which the income and monetary equilibrium conditions are met simultaneously, and if the other data are the same in these diagrams, it follows that the same equilibrium position is depicted by E in all three diagrams. Figure 15–2 (the liquidity preference theory) merely depicts the fact that the monetary equilibrium condition has been met and *assumes* that the income equilibrium condition has been met. Figure 15–4 (the loanable funds theory) shows that the income equilibrium condition has been met and *implies* that the monetary equilibrium condition has been met (because E is located at the point of intersection of the S and $S - H$ curves when $\Delta M = 0$). Figure 15–5 (the Hicks-Hansen analysis), however, *shows explicitly* that the income and monetary equilibrium conditions must be met simultaneously and emphasizes more strongly than do the other two theories that the interest rate and income are mutually determined, given the four variables which are embodied in the two curves, or, alternatively, given the two equilibrium conditions and the necessary data. Interest theory, it is clear, has moved outside the traditional bounds of microeconomic theory and into the area of macroeconomic analysis, demonstrating again that the boundaries between the two branches of economics are not clear and sharp. Instead, they shade into one another throughout the spectrum of analysis. This fact is clearly illustrated by Figure 15–5.

D. THEORIES OF PROFIT

Introduction

Just as there are today different theories of interest, so are there today different theories of profits. Moreover, the term *profit* is defined differ-

ently by different writers. The purpose of this section will be to survey
briefly various theories of profits.

Profits as the Result of Uncertainty and Risk Taking

The idea that profit is a payment for the performance of the function of
assuming the *uninsurable* risks which face the producer has been given
great emphasis by Professor Frank Knight of the University of Chicago.[15]
According to him, the main sources of uncertainty facing the producer are
those relating to "the amount of supply to be expected from other producers and the consumers' wants and purchasing power."[16] Among the
uninsurable risks is the creation of credit by banks with its effect on price
levels and profit margins. Thus, opportunities are created for the making
of profits through exceptional foresight and good luck.[17] The possibilities of population changes, of discoveries of new sources of raw materials,
and of obsolescence as a result of technological change are additional
risks assumed by producers.[18] And so, Knight argues, since the uninsurable risk-bearing function must be performed in a dynamic economy
if output is to grow, profits are a necessary functional return paid for ac-
cepting the burden of uncertainty.

The idea that uncertainty has diminished in importance as a factor in
investment planning since the early 1930's has, however, recently been
advanced by William H. White in a paper prepared under the auspices
of the Brookings Institution for the Joint Economic Committee in
1962.[19] White has argued that large firms seldom gamble their entire
futures on a single new venture and that, therefore, it is not necessary
for them to invest so conservatively that they must be sure of success
from each new venture or else be compensated by a very high rate of
return which would result in a recovery of the initial investment over a
short period of time. Indeed, White has challenged the findings of a
statistical study by the economists of the McGraw-Hill publishing company which suggested the contrary. He has also argued that contemporary economists do not really understand how far and how significant
have been the advances made in scientific investment planning methods

---

[15] His views were first stated in a book, based upon his doctoral dissertation at Cornell
University, called *Risk, Uncertainty and Profit* (Boston: Houghton Mifflin Co., 1921).

[16] *Ibid.*, p. 318.

[17] *Ibid.*, p. 336.

[18] *Ibid.*, pp. 336–39.

[19] William H. White, "The Changing Criteria in Investment Planning," *Variability
of Private Investment in Plant and Equipment*, Part II (Joint Economic Committee, 87th
Cong., 2d sess.) (Washington, D.C.: U.S. Government Printing Office, 1962), pp. 1–23.

employed by firms in making their investment decisions.[20] Finally, White has also argued that the notion, discussed in Chapter 11, that the interests of managers do not correspond closely to the interests of stockholders in maximizing profits is wrong. Instead, he believes that "the merging of executives' economic interests with those of stockholders is particularly close under the incentive bonus system" so widespread today.[21]

Professor Lorie Tarshis has also recently pointed out that the questions of the effects of uncertainty of length of life of the proposed investment and of taxes on profits on the investment demand function "are matters which cannot be answered categorically by recourse to 'theory,'" and has suggested that if we wish to know the answer to such questions "we must dig out the facts."[22] In short, we have a good deal to learn in this area.

Profits as the Result of Monopolistic and Monopsonistic Positions

That profits can result from either a temporary or a permanent position of freedom from competition in a particular market has already been discussed in detail in Chapters 10 and 11 of this book. Little needs to be added to what has already been said there, except to repeat that the length of time during which such profits will be enjoyed depends upon the availability of substitutes and the extent to which the conditions of free entry into the market exist. Profits which result from the lack of competition differ, of course, from profits which are the result of uncertainty, since the amount of uncertainty is appreciably reduced, although it does not disappear altogether, if the firm is in a preferred position in a given market. Monopoly profits, as has been noted in the preceding chapter, are economic rent in a static analysis, although Professor Schumpeter, we will see, has argued that they are functional in a dynamic economy.

Profits as a Residual or Surplus

Various market conditions can give rise to windfall gains on the part of firms. But the surplus which arises in this way is usually temporary, that is, it is competed away or disappears when the circumstances giving rise to it have changed. Moreover, profits arising from windfall

[20] *Ibid.,* p. 18.

[21] *Ibid.,* pp. 22–23. The difference between the White and Baumol views (the latter is explained in Chapter 11) is a question of fact.

[22] Lorie Tarshis, "The Elasticity of the Marginal Efficiency Function," *American Economic Review,* Vol. LI (December, 1961), pp. 958–85.

gains, or from luck, are generally sporadic or casual occurrences; that is, they are not regularly earned by the same firms and are not earned by all firms in the economy.

Profits as a Result of Innovations

The Schumpeterian theory of economic development, which is discussed in some detail in the concluding chapter of this book, rests upon the notion that profits do not exist in a stationary economy but are payments accruing to entrepreneurs who have more intelligence and foresight in finding new and more valuable ways of using inputs than do other members of the society. Thus, it is argued, profits are a natural, inevitable, and beneficial incident of the normal growth process in a credit economy. Since this question will be considered in detail later, no further discussion of it is needed at this point.

The Present State of Distribution Theory

The various parts of the circular flow diagram, depicted in Figure 2–1, and their interrelationships have now been examined in detail. In the present Part V of this book, we have seen that distribution theory is not a closed issue, which can be learned by rote and parroted as answers to the questions it raises, any more than is any part of the rest of price theory. The current tendency to treat distribution problems within the framework of macroeconomic theory which is illustrated by the discussion of interest theory (and which also exists in the area of wage theory) is probably in the right direction, for it recognizes the interdependence of the various macroeconomic and microeconomic elements of the economic system much more fully than was probably the case prior to 1936.

Our next problem is to bring together into a unified whole the concepts and relationships developed so far. This task will be undertaken in the context of the treatment of static welfare economics which follows in Part VI.

NOTE A TO CHAPTER 15

The formula for valuation of a perpetual security stated in Equation (14–1) is the formula for finding the present value of an annuity (an income *stream*), when *n,* the number of periods, becomes infinitely great, or

$$V_p = [R]\left[\frac{1 - \dfrac{1}{(1 + i)^n}}{i}\right],$$ (14–1a)

where V_p represents the present value of the income stream, R represents the annual income *flow* (or rent) in dollars, and i is the interest rate. If n becomes infinitely great, the term $1/(1+i)^n$ reduces to zero, and the formula becomes

$$V_p = (R)\left(\frac{1}{i}\right) = \frac{R}{i}\,. \tag{14-1}$$

This formula must be distinguished from the formula for the present value of a *given* sum (a *stock*) due at the end of a specified period of time which bears compound interest to maturity, or

$$V_p = \frac{V_m}{(1+i)^n}\,, \tag{I}$$

where V_m represents the given sum (say, the face value of a bond bearing compound interest to maturity) and the other symbols have the meanings given above. In the case of a perpetual security, n becomes infinitely great as before, and the formula reduces to

$$V_p = \frac{V_m}{\text{Infinitely large number}} = 0\,. \tag{Ia}$$

That is, the present value of a sum which will never be paid is zero. The fact that i appears in the denominators in the formulas above means that these present values are related inversely to the interest rate. Both formulas are employed in Chapter 15.

SELECTED READINGS

ACKLEY, GARDNER. *Macroeconomic Theory*. New York: The Macmillan Co., 1961.

CONARD, J. W. *Introduction to the Theory of Interest*. Berkeley: University of California Press, 1959.

CULBERTSON, J. M. "The Term Structure of Interest Rates," *Quarterly Journal of Economics*, Vol. LXXI (November, 1957), pp. 485–517.

DUE, JOHN F., AND CLOWER, ROBERT W. *Intermediate Economic Analysis*, chaps, xvi and xvii. 4th ed. Homewood: Ill.: Richard D. Irwin, Inc., 1961.

HANSEN, ALVIN H. *A Guide to Keynes*. New York: McGraw-Hill Book Co., Inc., 1953.

KEYNES, J. M. *The General Theory of Employment, Interest and Money*. New York: Harcourt, Brace & Co., 1936.

KNIGHT, FRANK. *Risk, Uncertainty and Profit*. Series of Reprints of Scarce Tracts in Economics and Political Science No. 16. Aldwych, London: London School of Economics and Political Science, 1948.

PATINKIN, D. *Money, Interest and Prices*. 2d. ed. Evanston, Ill.: Row, Peterson, & Co., 1960.

SCHUMPETER, JOSEPH A. *The Theory of Economic Development*. Trans. REDVERS OPIE. Harvard Economic Studies, Vol. XLVI. Cambridge: Harvard University Press, 1951.

U.S. CONGRESS JOINT ECONOMIC COMMITTEE. *Variability of Private Investment in Plant and Equipment*, Parts I and II. Joint Committee Print, 87th Cong., 1st sess. Washington, D.C.: U.S. Government Printing Office, 1962.

PART **VI**

STATIC WELFARE ECONOMICS

16 Paretian Optimality and Neoclassical Welfare Analyses

Introduction

It has been pointed out in Chapter 1 that the conditions of economic welfare which are derived from the general microeconomic models of the economy are not *absolute* conditions. Instead, they are *static relative* conditions of "economic efficiency," or of maximization of total output from given inputs, provided that consumer's wants can be taken as data and provided that the distribution of income is assumed to be given.

It should not be supposed that these static conditions are the only possible welfare conditions, nor that the maximization approach of price theory is the only possible one. Indeed, the early classical economists, from Adam Smith to John Stuart Mill, were all concerned with welfare also, but their welfare analyses were centered more upon problems of capital accumulation and upon the dynamic process of economic expansion than upon the problem of allocation of given inputs to effective production of outputs.[1] In the works of these economists, quantities of satisfaction were taken to be proportional to quantities of goods, and the present-day conception that "more is better than less" finds its roots in this idea. From this point of view, welfare economics is as much or more concerned with problems of economic development as with problems of increasing output by making more effective use of inputs, and this question will be considered further in Chapter 18.

In this chapter, we will first critically examine the scarcity approach to the problem of welfare which was developed in the late 1930's and

---

[1] For an excellent discussion of this question, see Hla Myint, *Theories of Welfare Economics* (Cambridge: Harvard University Press, 1948).

1940's by the followers of an early Italian economist, Vilfredo Pareto,[2] and then we will examine some of the work of the neoclassical English economists, Alfred Marshall and A. C. Pigou.[3]

The static welfare conditions mentioned above are known in the literature as the conditions of the *Paretian optimum*. When the distinctions between marginal *social* costs and benefits and marginal *private* costs and benefits are ignored, these conditions are nothing more than a summary of the static general long-run equilibrium conditions of a perfectly competitive economy which have been stated separately at various places throughout this book. The first section of this chapter can, thus, be used to provide the reader with an introduction to contemporary static welfare analysis and, also, to provide a summary of the general long-run equilibrium conditions of the perfectly competitive economy. The distinction between *private* and *social* costs and benefits will be developed later, during the discussion of Pigou's contribution to welfare economics.

A. THE STATIC PARETIAN WELFARE CONDITIONS

1. The Static Condition of "Optimum Allocation of Products"

The first condition of "economic efficiency," or of welfare, is a statement that for all consumers in the economy the Marshallian consumer equilibrium condition must be met, assuming that the distribution of income and wants are given and that consumers should get what they want. Thus, it is argued, subject to these assumptions, goods will be optimally allocated when the marginal rates of substitution of any two consumers for any two goods selected at random are equal. That is, if these randomly selected consumers are on the contract curve in the Edgeworth Box Diagram depicted in Figure 5–9 in Chapter 5, goods are relatively optimally allocated. Since the diagram has already been explained in

---

[2] On this point, see Vilfredo Pareto, *Manuel d'Economie Politique* (2d ed.; Paris: Girard, 1927), pp. 617–18; J. R. Hicks, "The Foundations of Welfare Economics," *Economic Journal,* Vol. XLIX (December, 1939), pp. 696–712; Tibor Scitovsky, "A Note on Welfare Propositions in Economics," *Review of Economic Studies,* Vol. IX (November, 1941), pp. 77–88; Paul A. Samuelson, *The Foundations of Economic Analysis* (Cambridge: Harvard University Press, 1947), pp. 249–52; Nicholas Kaldor, "Welfare Propositions and Interpersonal Comparisons of Utility," *Economic Journal,* Vol. XLIX (1939), pp. 549–52; Abba P. Lerner, *The Economics of Control* (New York: The Macmillan Co., 1946); J. de V. Graaff, *Theoretical Welfare Economics* (Cambridge: Cambridge University Press, 1957); I. M. D. Little, *A Critique of Welfare Economics* (2d ed.; Oxford: Oxford University Press, 1957); Abram Bergson, "A Reformulation of Certain Aspects of Welfare Economics," *Quarterly Journal of Economics,* Vol. LII (February, 1938), pp. 310–34.

[3] Alfred Marshall, *Principles of Economics* (8th ed.; London: Macmillan & Co., Ltd., 1938), esp. Book V. chap. xiii; and A. C. Pigou, *The Economics of Welfare* (London: Macmillan & Co., Ltd., 1920).

detail in Chapter 5, no further explanation of it is needed at this point, except to note that the contract curve need not be a straight line (although it has been drawn as such for convenience in that diagram); nor need the indifference curves of the consumers be identical. In short, although the diagram has been drawn in the way in which it usually appears in the literature, this is a matter of convenience only and does not limit the conclusions.

In algebraic form, the static condition of a relatively optimum distribution of products, subject to the indicated assumptions, may thus be stated, where A and B are two consumers chosen at random and x and y are two commodities similarly chosen at random, as

$$\frac{MU_{x_A}}{p_x} = \frac{MU_{y_A}}{p_y} \quad \text{and} \quad \frac{MU_{x_B}}{p_x} = \frac{MU_{y_B}}{p_y}, \qquad (16\text{--}1)$$

or

$$\frac{MU_{x_A}}{MU_{y_A}} = \frac{MU_{x_B}}{MU_{y_B}}. \qquad (16\text{--}1a)$$

Note that neither the marginal utilities nor the quantities purchased by the two consumers need be the same. It is the *ratios* in the indicated equations which must be equal. This condition of welfare is met if consumers purchase under conditions of perfect competition, according to the assumptions made in the Marshallian and contemporary theories of consumer behavior. Acceptance of the orthodox theory of consumer behavior necessarily implies acceptance of the test for the optimum distribution of products given above.

2. The Static Optimum Product and Factor Market Condition

The static optimum product and factor market condition is that all firms in the economy must be producing and selling all products in the product market at the point of long-run economic efficiency (least average cost) under perfect competition. Although the condition is often stated in other language in the literature, in the final analysis, the preceding statement is what these different statements reduce to, provided that the distinctions between private and social benefits and costs are ignored. Note that the conditions of perfect competition can be met under decentralized state socialism and that private ownership of property is not one of the conditions of perfect competition as these have been stated in the opening paragraphs of Chapter 2. It has already been noted in Chapter 1 that this point was made by Professor Fred M. Taylor in his Presidential Address before the American Economic Association in 1928.[4] The conditions can be stated symbolically, where the symbols I and II represent firms chosen at random from the population of firms and x and y represent products, as

$$SMC_{x_I} = SAC_{x_I} = LMC_{x_I} = LAC_{x_I} = MR_x = p_x \, ,$$

$$SMC_{y_I} = SAC_{y_I} = LMC_{y_I} = LAC_{y_I} = MR_y = p_y \, ,$$

$$(16\text{-}2)$$

$$SMC_{x_{II}} = SAC_{x_{II}} = LMC_{x_{II}} = LAC_{x_{II}} = MR_x = p_x \, , \text{ and}$$

$$SMC_{y_{II}} = SAC_{y_{II}} = LMC_{y_{II}} = LAC_{y_{II}} = MR_y = p_y \, .$$

The condition must be met by all firms and all products produced in the economy, and a typical diagram for one firm and one product is that shown in Figure 12–5B in Chapter 12.

2a. The Static Optimum Product Transformation Condition

Most writers state a further condition relative to the product market, namely, that the ratio of the marginal costs of any two products produced by the same producer within the economy must be equal to the ratio of the prices of the products. However, if the condition $MC = P$ is met (as stated in Condition 2 above) for all firms and products in the economy, this further condition is also met. For, if the marginal cost of every product is equal to its price in the case of every firm, it follows that the ratio of the marginal costs of any two products will also be equal to the ratio of their prices. That is, if $MC_x = p_x$ and $MC_y = p_y$, it obviously follows by simple division that $MC_x/MC_y = p_x/p_y$.

2b. The Static Optimum Factor Market Condition

Many writers also state a static optimum factor market condition, according to which all firms must be purchasing all inputs under conditions of perfect competition in the *factor* market in the long-run equilibrium position. Symbolically, where a and b represent inputs, x and y represent outputs, and I and II represent firms, randomly chosen as before, we must then have

$$\frac{MRP_{a_{x_I}}}{p_a = MC_a} = \frac{MRP_{a_{y_I}}}{p_a = MC_a} = \frac{MRP_{b_{x_I}}}{p_b = MC_b} = \frac{MRP_{b_{y_I}}}{p_b = MC_b} =$$

$$(16\text{-}3)$$

$$\frac{MRP_{a_{x_{II}}}}{p_a = MC_a} = \frac{MRP_{a_{y_{II}}}}{p_a = MC_a} = \frac{MRP_{b_{x_{II}}}}{p_b = MC_b} = \frac{MRP_{b_{y_{II}}}}{p_b = MC_b} = 1 \, .$$

---

[4] Fred M. Taylor, "The Guidance of Production in a Socialist State," *American Economic Review*, Vol. XIX (March, 1929), pp. 1–8. See, also, Benjamin Ward, "The Firm in Illyria: Market Syndicalism," *American Economic Review*, Vol. XLVIII (September, 1958), pp. 566–89.

(In this equation, $MRP_{a_{x_I}}$ means marginal revenue product of a in the production of x by Firm I, $MRP_{b_{y_{II}}}$ means marginal revenue product of b used in the production of y by Firm II, etc.) This condition has already been illustrated in the case of one firm using two inputs to produce one product in Figure 12–3 in Chapter 12. Moreover, reference to Figure 12–5 and the accompanying discussion will show that, if Condition 2 is met, Condition 2b is also met. That is, since we know from our analysis in Chapters 7 and 12 that $SMC_x = p_a/MPP_a$, and since in any long-run equilibrium position $SMC_x = LMC_x = MR_x$, it follows that in such a position $MR_x = p_a/MPP_a$, or $MRP_a = (MR_x)(MPP_a) = p_a$. Thus, $MRP_a/p_a = 1$ as required by Equation (16–3). And since in Equation (16–2) we also have $SAC_x = SMC_x = LMC_x = LAC_x = MR_x = p_x$, it follows that in that equation we have $p_a = MC_a$ by assumption. In other words, if the marginal cost of the *output* is equal to both the average cost and price of the *output* and normal profits only are being made, the total revenue is exactly exhausted by the payments for the services of the factors at a rate equal to their prices, and no monopsonistic exploitation of the factors exists. Thus, there must be perfect competition in the factor market also, a point which is illustrated by Figures 12–3, 12–5, and 13–3 in Chapters 12 and 13, respectively.

2c. The Static Optimum Factor-Product Market Condition

Finally, some writers also state an additional condition, namely, that the marginal rate of transformation of any factor ($\Delta x/\Delta a$) into any product must be equal to the inverse ratio of their prices (p_a/p_x). Now the rate of transformation of a factor into a product is simply the marginal physical product of the input, or $MPP_a = \Delta x/\Delta a$. (See Figure 6–1 in Chapter 6.) Thus, this condition states that for any input and any product we must have $MPP_a = p_a/p_x$, or $(MPP_a)(p_x) = VMP_a = p_a$. And, of course, as we have already seen in Figure 12–5 in Chapter 12, this condition is met if there is perfect competition in both markets. Since Condition 2 assumes perfect competition in both markets, it encompasses Condition 2c also.

An Alternative Formulation of Condition 2

In Equation (12–12a) in Chapter 12, the optimum product and factor market conditions have been combined into a single equation in the case of a single product. The equation can be generalized to cover any number of products. Letting a and b represent any two inputs, x and y represent any two products, and I and II represent any two firms, all randomly chosen from the economy, we have

$$\frac{VMP_{a_{x_I}} = MRP_{a_{x_I}}}{p_a = MC_a} = \frac{VMP_{a_{y_I}} = MRP_{a_{y_I}}}{p_a = MC_a} = \frac{VMP_{b_{x_I}} = MRP_{b_{x_I}}}{p_b = MC_b} =$$

$$\frac{VMP_{b_{y_I}} = MRP_{b_{y_I}}}{p_b = MC_b} = \frac{VMP_{a_{x_{II}}} = MRP_{a_{x_{II}}}}{p_a = MC_a} = \frac{VMP_{a_{y_{II}}} = MRP_{a_{y_{II}}}}{p_a = MC_a} \qquad (16\text{--}4)$$

$$= \frac{VMP_{b_{x_{II}}} = MRP_{b_{x_{II}}}}{p_b = MC_b} = \frac{VMP_{b_{y_{II}}} = MRP_{b_{y_{II}}}}{p_b = MC_b} = 1 .$$

The equality of the VMP's and MRP's in the numerators [which is the one difference between Equations (16–3) and (16–4)] shows that there is perfect competition in the product market; the equality of the p's and MC's in the denominators shows perfect competition in the factor market. Since all the ratios are equal to unity, the firms are in equilibrium. Since the conditions are assumed to apply to all inputs, products, and firms, the equilibrium is general and long run, and no profits greater than normal are being earned.[5] Equation (16–4) says exactly the same thing as Equation (16–2). The former employs input prices explicitly and output prices implicitly, while the latter employs output prices explicitly and input prices implicitly. An illustration of Equation (16–4) in the case of one firm using two inputs to produce a single product has already been given in Figure 12–3 in Chapter 12.

Effect of Market Imperfections

As we have seen in Chapters 10, 11, and 13, market imperfections destroy the equalities in the numerators and denominators of Equation (16–4). Thus, existence of imperfections in either the product market or the factor market inhibits the attainment of "economic efficiency" as measured by the market price standard. Market imperfections are, of course, illustrated in Figures 10–3, 10–5, 13–6, and 13–7, as well as elsewhere in this book. However, it should be emphasized that according to the Schumpeterian view of the matter or to the view taken by J. M. Clark, cases of imperfections in the *product* market are not necessarily considered to be evidence of economic inefficiency. We will consider this question further in Chapter 18.

The Problem of Compensating Payments

In an attempt to avoid the problem of making value judgments with respect to movements along the contract curve in the Edgeworth Box Diagram (Figure 5–9), numerous economists sought in the period

---

[5] For a slightly different statement of the welfare conditions, see Lerner, *op. cit.,* chaps. vi and ix.

from 1935 to about 1950 to improve upon the criterion for judging economic reorganizations suggested by Pareto. His criterion was a simple one: namely, any change which improved the position of one individual (in his own opinion) without harming anyone else (in the latter's opinion) was an improvement which increased welfare. This criterion is a limited one because it avoids the case in which some are harmed and others are benefitted by a given policy proposal.

The criterion also rests on the basic value judgment that consumers should get what they want or, more broadly, that individuals are the best judges of their own welfare. (Do and should parents permit children to have as much candy as the children want all the time? That is, do experience, knowledge, and emotions affect one's judgment? And how far does an analogous question apply in relations among adults in a modern state?) None of the criteria suggested as improvements of the original Pareto criterion has successfully avoided the problem of value judgments, and none of these criteria seems actually to have been used in the solution of any public policy question. These criteria are not operationally feasible, and, we will see, they are probably not operationally meaningful either.

One of the first of the contemporary economists to suggest a new test for measuring improvements in total welfare was Nicholas Kaldor, who proposed that an improvement be defined in terms of whether or not those who gained from an economic reorganization placed a higher value figure on their benefits than did those who lost from that reorganization. This criterion, of course, assumes that individuals are the best judges of their own welfare, just as does Pareto's criterion. But there is also another difficulty, namely that in some situations an economic reorganization may produce a higher gain for the gainers than for the losers, while a reversal of the reorganization may produce a higher gain for the previous losers than for the previous gainers! Which of two such situations is preferable?

To meet this objection, Professor Tibor Scitovsky has argued that it is necessary to consider both the initial economic reorganization and its reverse; and only if the proposal meets both tests, can the redistribution be considered an improvement. Scitovsky's test obviously is a refinement of the Kaldor test, and, although it seeks to overcome one of the objections to the Kaldor test, it is nevertheless subject to the other objections which apply to that test.[6] It may be remarked, in passing, that all schemes for compensation of this type must also assume with Marshall

---

[6] See Kaldor, *op. cit.;* and Scitovsky, *op. cit.*

that the loser's income is above the subsistence level, since, if it is not, any loss of life would presumably be infinitely great, although this assumption has apparently never been mentioned explicitly by anyone except Marshall.[7] This assumption in itself involves some kind of value judgment.

And so the question arises as to whether or not compensation would actually have to be paid to the losers by the gainers. Most of the tests for compensation do not contemplate actual indemnification of the losers. Professor Melvin Reder has, however, pointed out that fear of uncompensated losses may be so great *before* a proposed economic reorganization takes place that, *viewed before it occurs,* the reorganization would not meet the tests proposed; while *after* a reorganization has taken place, the losses which the losers think they have suffered may not be as great as they had feared, and, thus, *viewed after the event,* the reorganization would pass the test!

It should also be pointed out that all these compensation measures seek to test the proposed economic reorganization against the *status quo.* That is, these measures rest on an assumption that the *status quo* is, in some sense or other, more desirable than alternative arrangements *other than those contemplated by the specific reorganization.* In short, they contain a built-in bias in favor of the existing state of affairs and put the burden of proof on the innovator.[8] How can we be certain that this procedure is valid?

Social Welfare Functions: The Bergson "Criterion"

It has been noted that none of the compensation tests has any practical significance because such tests are not operationally feasible and also because they are logically deficient. Many economists have therefore followed Professor Bergson and taken the position that a *Social Welfare Function* must be specified by methods other than those of economic analysis but that the maximization techniques of price theory can then be applied to this function as a basis for making meaningful objective statements about economic welfare. Such a position constitutes a recognition that, in the final analysis, value judgments must be made by someone.[9] Professor Bergson and others after him have formulated complicated mathematical demonstrations of the validity of this proposi-

---

[7] Marshall, *op. cit.,* p. 135 and Note VI, p. 841.

[8] This point has also been made by Paul Streeten in the Appendix to his translation of Gunnar Myrdal, *The Political Element in the Development of Economic Theory* (London: Routledge and Kegan Paul, Ltd., 1953), p. 216.

[9] See Bergson, *op. cit.*

tion,[10] but little purpose is served by developing them in this book.

The Bergson position, sometimes known as the Bergson Criterion, raises the question of whether decisions relative to the Social Welfare Function made by a majority vote can be taken as accurate representations of the values of a community. Professor Kenneth Arrow has investigated this problem and concluded that such a procedure may produce an irrational result.[11] His argument can be illustrated with the help of Table 16–1.

Table 16–1

POSSIBLE INDIVIDUAL PREFERENCES

| | Individual Preferences | | |
Alternatives	A	B	C
I	First	Third	Second
II	Second	First	Third
III	Third	Second	First

In Table 16–1, assume that three individuals, A, B, and C, prefer the mutually exclusive alternatives, I, II, and III, in the order indicated. According to the table, individuals A and C prefer Alternative I to Alternative II; individuals A and B prefer Alternative II to Alternative III; and individuals B and C prefer Alternative III to Alternative I. A majority thus prefers Alternative I to II, and II to III, but a majority also prefers Alternative III to I! Professor Arrow describes such a result as "irrational" and argues that it is not possible to pass from individual preferences to group decisions by the voting procedure suggested by Table 16–1.

Some writers have criticized Arrow's argument on the technical ground that his assumptions are not realistic.[12] Others have investigated similar questions and pointed out that the order in which votes are taken on mutually exclusive alternatives (taken one at a time) may affect the outcome. That is, in some cases, individuals may influence the outcome of an election of this kind by concealing their true prefer-

---

[10] The reader who requires such "proof" may be referred to the very elegant mathematical treatment in James M. Henderson and Richard E. Quandt, *Microeconomic Theory, A Mathematical Approach* (New York: McGraw-Hill Book Co., Inc., 1958), pp. 217–22.

[11] Kenneth J. Arrow, *Social Choice and Individual Values* (Cowles Commission Monograph No. 12) (New York: John Wiley & Sons, Inc., 1951), p. 11.

[12] See Clifford Hildreth, "Alternative Conditions for Social Orderings," *Econometrica*, Vol. XXI (January, 1953), pp. 81–91; and Leo A. Goodman and Harry Markowitz, "Social Welfare Functions Based on Individual Rankings," *American Journal of Sociology*, Vol. LVIII (November, 1952), pp. 257–62.

ences in votes on successive proposals so that the majority will may be defeated.[13]

The order in which the alternatives in Table 16–1 are voted upon may, in fact, affect the outcome, assuming that each individual casts either a positive or negative vote on each alternative proposal as it is put forward. If Alternative I is voted upon first, A would support it, since it is his first choice. On the other hand, B and C might both oppose it, if they took account of the fact that the proposals which they favored were also to be voted upon, and if B knew that A's second choice was proposal II. If proposal II were voted upon next, B would support it, since it is his first choice. At the same time, A would presumably also support II, since his first choice has been defeated and the alternative is III, his last choice. Thus II would prevail as the decision. Even if III were voted upon second, since it is A's third choice and B's second, both would presumably vote against it, if both were aware of the fact that, in doing so, they would insure the adoption of Alternative II.

On the other hand, if Alternative II were put forward first, only B would support it, and it would go down to defeat for reasons analogous to the reason why Alternative I would be defeated if it were the subject of the first vote. A and C would both vote against II on a first ballot because, by supporting it, they would be defeating their own first choices. In this case, Alternative III would be the eventual victor. And, finally, if Alternative III were the first to come forward for decision, Alternative I would be the group decision. Under these circumstances, it is not clear that any one of the alternatives can be truly considered the will of the majority.

Questions of this type have only recently begun to receive serious attention at the hands of a few economists. It is still a much more common procedure to adopt the Bergson "Criterion" of reference to an unspecified Social Welfare Function (either specifying that it is to be determined by majority vote or else leaving unanswered the questions of who is to determine it and how this is to be done) and then to argue that, given such a function, the techniques of price theory can be employed to determine the conditions necessary for maximizing social welfare. This approach, it is argued, insures the character of price theory as a "positive science." Actually, as has been noted in Chapter 1, this procedure also precludes an economist from making any public policy recommendations which are not consistent with the assumed and unspecified Social Welfare Function. More than this, as Gunnar

---

[13] In general, see Duncan Black, *The Theory of Committees and Elections* (Cambridge: Cambridge University Press, 1958).

Myrdal pointed out as early as 1932, this position also ignores the fact that there may be a process of interaction between the Social Welfare Function and the economic policies which are being implemented.[14] Indeed, Myrdal rejected the view that social policy can be judged from a "purely economic point of view" and described it as "thoroughly metaphysical."[15] Instead, he argued that the real problem was one of discovering conflicting social interests while "taking account of all the institutional changes which are feasible under political pressure."[16]

Myrdal's view anticipated a position taken recently by Professor Jerome Rothenberg. After a thorough survey of the most recent work in the field of static welfare economics, Rothenberg has argued that economists should turn to the concepts and recent work of social psychologists, anthropologists, and sociologists, who are seeking to determine empirically the "value consensus in any going society." According to Rothenberg's view of the matter, values do not exist independently of the institutional framework of a given society. Instead, "values are mutually engendering, mutually reinforcing, mutually sustaining."[17]

Probably one of the most articulate spokesmen for the point of view that economists do and should make value judgments is Professor Clarence E. Ayres, who has long argued that *instrumentalism, a process* of continuously testing actions against experience or a *process* of self-correcting value judgments, is the only valid form which the Social Welfare Function can take. Ayres believes that this principle applies to all cultures.[18] His conception of the Social Welfare Function which stems from the work of John Dewey and Thorstein Veblen, as that of actions being constantly corrected by accumulating experiences, is a *dynamic* one, not a static one of the type usually found in mathematical discussions of the subject. In fact, many policy makers in government (and in business!) do operate according to this technique and correct their wrong value judgments by changing or reversing policies where such action is called for (assuming they wish to retain their positions). Physical scientists are also constantly correcting previous mistakes and making new discoveries in this way.

A classic example is, of course, the discovery by Otto Hahn and Fritz

---

[14] Myrdal, *op. cit.*, chap. viii.

[15] *Ibid.*, p. 195.

[16] *Ibid.*, p. 199.

[17] Jerome Rothenberg, *The Measurement of Social Welfare* (Englewood Cliffs, N.J.: Prentice-Hall, Inc., 1961), chap. xiii, esp. p. 315.

[18] Clarence E. Ayres, *Toward a Reasonable Society* (Austin: University of Texas Press, 1961), esp. chap. vii.

Strassman that the uranium atom could be split, even though the "physicists wouldn't allow it."[19] At the time the discovery was made, it contradicted all the known laws of physics. Indeed, in 1934, five years before the Hahn-Strassman experiment, Enrico Fermi and others had split the uranium atom but had failed to understand what they had done, because none of the world's greatest physicists believed it to be possible.[20]

Some economists, however, who take the view that price theory is a "positive science," argue that hypotheses which have been "continuously-used and widely-accepted" for a great length of time, "without the development of any widely-accepted and internally consistent alternatives," derive a presumption of validity *from these facts alone.*[21] This view has been sharply challenged by Professor J. K. Galbraith, who has coined the term "conventional wisdom" to identify "ideas which are esteemed at any time for their acceptability."[22]

Galbraith's book, *The Affluent Society,* which has found both ardent admirers and severe critics, may be less important for the value judgments which he expresses in it than for his emphasis of the fact that an uncritical acceptance of the "conventional wisdom" precludes a researcher from looking for alternative and better solutions to problems. Thus, by attempting to devise measures of compensation in the case of economic reorganizations which will avoid value judgments and which utilize the *status quo* as *the* benchmark for judging the effects of a proposed reorganization, an estoppel may be created against the examination of alternative possibilities different from the one being contemplated. The neoclassical economists, it is to be noted, were not much troubled by the problem of how to avoid making such basic value judgments, and it is to a brief survey of the work of two of them that attention will next be given.

B. NEOCLASSICAL WELFARE ECONOMICS: MARSHALL AND PIGOU

Marshall and the Doctrine of Maximum Satisfaction

Marshall considered the equilibrium conditions of a perfectly competitive economy to represent conditions of *relative* economic efficiency. In addition to specifying the assumption that income must be above the

---

[19] The tale has often been told, and one of the most interesting versions appears in William L. Lawrence, *Men and Atoms* (New York: Simon & Schuster, Inc., 1959). Lawrence attributes the quoted statement to Professor Hahn, p. 27.

[20] *Ibid.* p. 12.

[21] See, for example, Milton Friedman, *Essays in Positive Economics* (Chicago: University of Chicago Press, 1953), p. 23.

[22] J. K. Galbraith, *The Affluent Society* (Boston: Houghton Mifflin Co., 1958), p. 9.

subsistence level, he also noted specifically that the distribution of income must be assumed to be given but argued that this assumption might properly be made in the early stages of an analysis, *provided that it was not forgotten altogether and was relaxed later.*[23] And, finally, Marshall argued that, in the case of commodities produced subject to decreasing long-run costs (increasing returns to scale) as a result of improvements in industrial organization, total welfare might be increased by subsidizing such industries by means of taxes levied on industries producing commodities subject to increasing long-run costs (decreasing returns to scale).[24] Thus, in Marshall's view, the argument that a position of long-run equilibrium of a perfectly competitive economy is also a position of maximum satisfaction was a limited one, subject to the conditions given above.

Marshall's argument concerning the increase in total welfare to be derived from subsidizing industries subject to decreasing long-run costs involves the use of his consumer's surplus concept, which is discussed in detail in Appendix B of this book. The consumer's surplus was defined by Marshall as the difference between the amount a consumer actually paid for a given commodity and the amount he was willing to pay for it. Individual consumers' surpluses are added together by assuming that all individuals' utility of income curves are identical. Thus, in Figure 16–1, the

Figure 16–1

SUBSIDIZATION OF A DECREASING COST INDUSTRY

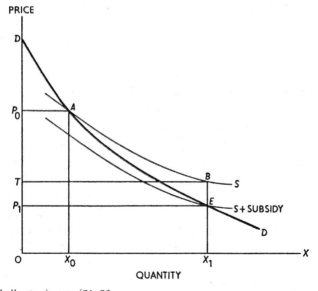

---

[23] Marshall, *op. cit.*, pp. 471–72.
[24] *Ibid.*, pp. 472–73.

aggregate consumers' surplus is the area P_0DA (under the demand curve) when the price is OP_0; and it is P_1DE when the price is OP_1. For the area $ODAX_0$ represents the value to consumers of the quantity OX_0 (see the discussion of Figure 3–2 in Chapter 3). This valuation rests on the theory that, when the price is OP_0 and purchases are OX_0, the value of the marginal unit is OP_0, while the value of the first unit consumed is greater than this amount, or OD. Thus, the total value is $ODAX_0$. The cost of this quantity (OX_0), however, is only area OP_0AX_0. The difference between $ODAX_0$ and OP_0AX_0 is the consumers' surplus, or P_0DA, on the quantity OX_0.

Some writers have made much of the fact that this definition involves an assumption that the demand curve intersects the price axis. This criticism misses the point. The assumption that the demand curve intersects the price axis is useful in explaining the definition of the consumers' surplus, but it is not necessary in analyses concerning the question of *changes* in the consumers' surplus resulting from price changes. The *change* in the consumers' surplus, as price declines from OP_0 to OP_1 in Figure 16–1, is area P_1P_0AE, and this is the critical area in Marshall's analysis.

According to Marshall, if the original supply curve in a decreasing cost industry is S in Figure 16–1, a subsidy equal to P_1T or EB will shift the supply curve down to $S + \text{Subsidy}$. The mechanics of this shift have already been explained in detail in conjunction with Figure 8–10 in Chapter 8, and the reader may wish to refer to the earlier discussion at this point. Marshall then measures the cost to the state of the subsidy as equal to area P_1TBE, or to a per unit amount of $P_1T = EB$ multiplied by the quantity sold ($OX_1 = P_1E = TB$). The gain to consumers resulting from the price decline to OP_1 will be area P_1P_0AE. If the latter is greater than the cost to the state (and in our diagram it has been drawn so that it *is* greater), the gain in the consumers' surplus is greater than the cost to the state, or $P_1P_0AE > P_1TBE$. However, a word of warning is necessary at this point.

The state must presumably obtain the tax money from some source or other in order to be able to pay the subsidy, and, therefore, a consideration of the loss of the consumers' surplus resulting from the collection of the tax is necessary. The "cost to the state" is a nebulous concept. The cost to the taxed individuals is really the relevant magnitude. Marshall was unable to prove that in *every* case the cost of the tax to the taxed individuals would be less than the "gain to the state" from spending the tax (or than the gain to the subsidized individuals, the really relevant magnitude, although these two magnitudes will not generally be the same). The slope of the supply curve in the increasing cost industry which is taxed determines this matter.[25] Thus, Marshall's analysis is useful as basis for identifying some of the issues involved but does not provide a policy to fit a specific case; and, like the other conclusions drawn from purely hypothetical reasoning in price theory, the argument must be cast in the subjunctive mood. It cannot be settled without the facts in a specific case.

Marginal Cost Pricing

Marshall's argument relative to subsidization of decreasing cost industries, as well as the demonstration that, under decentralized state socialism, the same static welfare conditions apply as apply under capitalism, gave rise in the late 1930's to various discussions of the desirability of pricing goods at their marginal costs, particularly in the public-utility sector. In this sector, plants are very large, and average costs fall for a considerable range of output[26] because of the high fixed costs.

The argument behind such proposals is as follows: if price is taken as a measure of the value of the service to the consumer, then pricing at marginal cost insures that output will be produced up to the point of its actual "worth" to consumers. Moreover, if such firms have been producing at less than capacity, an increase in output resulting from adoption of a marginal cost pricing policy will reduce the average cost of production. Unfortunately, however, if average cost is falling, we know from the explanation of the average-marginal relationship in Chapter 3 that marginal cost lies below the average cost of production. Thus, marginal cost pricing, in this case, leads to pricing at less than the full cost of production, and subsidization of the industry is necessary to make up the difference between the total revenue and the total cost. An alternative to marginal cost pricing is, of course, discriminatory pricing, and most public utility services in the United States do make prices on a discriminatory basis with the full blessing of regulatory commissions. The reader may be referred to the earlier discussion of this topic in Chapter 10.

---

[25] *Ibid.,* pp. 467–73.

[26] The two pioneers were R. H. Montgomery, "Government Ownership and Operation of the Railroads," *Annals of the American Academy of Political Science,* Vol. CCI (1939), pp. 137–45; and Harold Hotelling, "The General Welfare in Relation to the Problems of Taxation and of Railway and Utility Rate Regulation," *Econometrica,* Vol. VI (1938), pp. 242–69. Montgomery followed the Marshall-Pigou analysis; Hotelling was the forerunner of the modern theorists. In general, see Nancy Ruggles, "The Welfare Basis of Marginal Cost Pricing," *Review of Economic Studies,* Vol. XVII (1949–50), pp. 29–46; and Ruggles, "Further Developments in Marginal Cost Pricing," *Review of Economic Studies,* Vol. XVII (1949–50), pp. 107–26.

The criticisms which have already been applied to Marshall's subsidization proposal above also apply to the marginal cost pricing thesis (or to any other subsidization proposal). There is another problem which also arises. The use of the market price as a measure of the extent to which output should be increased rests upon the assumptions that the distribution of income is given, that consumers should get what they want, and all the rest of it. If these assumptions are not granted, then what?

Pigou and Marginal Social Costs and Benefits

The recognition of the existence of possible divergencies between marginal *social* costs and benefits and marginal *private* costs and benefits is largely due to the work of Professor A. C. Pigou,[27] a contemporary of Marshall in the latter's later years and also a great English neoclassical economist.

Pigou defined the marginal *social* benefit as the addition to national income from use of an additional unit of input and the marginal *private* benefit as the addition to the revenue of the firm resulting from the use of the additional unit of input. Thus, marginal private benefit is, in fact, what has already been defined as marginal revenue product, *MRP*. However, even under perfect competition, the marginal *social* benefit will not be the same thing as the value of the marginal product (*VMP*), unless the price of the product is a measure of its "social value."[28] A similar distinction may be drawn between marginal *social* cost and marginal *private* cost. The former is the opportunity cost to society of using a marginal amount of input in one way rather than in another. The latter is the cost to the firm of using a marginal amount of an input.

Divergencies between marginal social benefits and marginal private benefits may result from *external economies.* Divergencies between marginal social costs and marginal private costs may result from *external diseconomies.* Examples of *external economies* given by Pigou include the establishment of private parks by private firms to beautify a neighborhood (even though the public is not admitted to them and though no payment can be extracted from the public in the form of an addition to the price of the product produced by the firm) and the use by private firms of lighting devices which light streets in factory areas. Examples of *external diseconomies* are cases involving pollution of streams by waste materials from factories, pollution of the atmosphere

[27] Pigou, *op. cit.,* Part II, chap. vi.
[28] *Ibid.,* Part II, chaps. ii and vi.

by industrial dirt and smoke, and the need to sleep with eye shades in areas in which neon signs are prominent. In such cases, the firms do not charge a price sufficiently high to cover the full social cost of the product. That is, they make use of public facilities (streams and the atmosphere) without paying for them or charging consumers of the products the full social cost.

Pigou argued that to the extent that such divergencies can be measured by the "measuring rod of money," account must be taken of their existence in determining welfare. There are, however, many divergencies which cannot adequately be measured. Effects on health of smog, smoke, waste materials, and loss of sleep, aside from their effects on shrubbery, clothing, and houses, are extremely difficult to measure in terms of money, as are their effects on the fish populations of streams and on the loss in recreational facilities. In the same vein, Professor Valdemar Carlson has recently concluded, on the basis of a detailed and comprehensive study, that programs of economic security in the United States (unemployment compensation, old-age and survivor's insurance, medical care, and the like) involve an administrative allocation of the nation's income and are not determined by the price system, although the "values and ideology" of a free enterprise system serve as "a dominating and restrictive influence" upon such programs.[29] He has also remarked that traditional economic theory has no tools to deal with these problems.

A strong tendency thus exists in economic theory to measure marginal social cost merely by marginal private cost and marginal social benefit by the value of the marginal product (that is, by the marginal physical product multiplied by the price of the product), with the result that the insights gained from Pigou's analysis are lost in actual practice and effectively eliminated from consideration. This procedure is illustrated by the statement of the static welfare conditions in subdivision A of this chapter!

Tautological propositions, such as the statement that the state should engage in an activity only whenever the marginal social benefit derived from the expenditure exceeds its marginal social cost (as measured by market price and private cost of production respectively, that is, by the profitability of the activity to private firms), thus tend to take the place of analyses of existing problems and produce, probably, unintended justifications of the *status quo*. Reliance upon such propositions does not

---

[29] Valdemar Carlson, *Economic Security in the United States* (New York: McGraw-Hill Book Co., Inc., 1962), p. 206. Chapters ii, xiii, and xiv deal particularly with the problem of social costs.

offer a method of solving problems. On the contrary, it amounts to a flight into pseudo-scientific language as a means of conveniently avoiding the issues. Pigou's classification is useful only if one recognizes that it probably involves basic value judgments on the merits in the particular cases involved. In short, static welfare economics has not escaped the problem of value judgments.

C. THE FUNCTION OF THE STUDY OF STATIC WELFARE ECONOMICS; NEW TECHNIQUES

The study of static welfare economics, nevertheless, serves one useful function today: anyone who seriously and successfully engages in such a study will thereby acquire a fairly complete knowledge of the main body of the tools and language of price theory, as well as of their uses and their limitations. However, he will not thereby learn much about recent developments in the field nor about the extent to which new mathematical techniques are being employed in it.

The growing use of high-speed electronic computers and the growth in numbers of students of economics have resulted in many new developments, although it should be pointed out that not all of these are of lasting significance. It has already been noted in Chapter 11 that the application of the theory of games to oligopoly problems has not resulted in any significant advances in knowledge of how firms *actually* behave; similarly the use of probability theory in the field of consumer behavior has not produced any startling advances in this area. On the other hand, some of the developments are still too recent to be evaluated.

An example is the "simulation" of the actual working of economic models by means of high-speed electronic computers. Although simulation, understood as building a model and "making it work" by means of assumed data, is not a new idea, use of electronic computers has made possible the application of the technique in new areas. Thus models have been built and assumed data injected into them in the area of business cycle theory, in the field of management, in the theory of decision making, and particularly in the areas of oligopoly and of population estimation.[30] But very little practical use has so far been made of these models.

The application of probability theory to the decision-making process

---

[30] See "Simulation: A Symposium," *American Economic Review*, Vol. L (December, 1960), pp. 893–932, which contains articles by Guy H. Orcutt, Martin Shubik, and a joint article by G. P. E. Clarkson and H. A. Simon; and see also Guy H. Orcutt, Martin Greenberger, John Korbel, and Alice M. Rivlin, *Microanalysis of Socioeconomic Systems* (New York: Harper & Bros., 1961).

has also been undertaken, largely as an extension of the application of probability theory to consumer behavior, and the question of how the decision-making process is affected by the role in which the decision-maker sees himself is being studied.[31] What will come of this work remains to be seen.

Finally, the techniques of mathematical programming, of which linear programming is one example, are being applied to a variety of problems. Because of its widespread applicability to areas of management and government administration, and also because linear programming problems can be discussed in terms of the economic concepts explained in the preceding chapters of this book, this technique has been selected for detailed explanation in the next chapter. Its use is an example of the application of a recent mathematical development in the field of microeconomic theory.

SELECTED READINGS

ARROW, KENNETH J. *Social Choice and Individual Values.* Cowles Commission Monograph No. 12. New York: John Wiley & Sons, Inc., 1951.

AYRES, CLARENCE E. *Toward a Reasonable Society.* Austin: University of Texas Press, 1961.

GALBRAITH, J. K. *The Affluent Society.* Boston: Houghton Mifflin Co., 1958.

GRAAFF, J. DE V. *Theoretical Welfare Economics.* Cambridge: Cambridge University Press, 1957.

HICKS, J. R. "The Foundations of Welfare Economics," *Economic Journal,* Vol. XLIX (December, 1939), pp. 696–712.

LERNER, ABBA P. *The Economics of Control.* New York: The Macmillan Co., 1946.

LITTLE, I. M. D. *A Critique of Welfare Economics.* 2d ed. Oxford: Oxford University Press, 1957.

MARSHALL, ALFRED. *Principles of Economics,* Book V, chap. xiii. 8th ed. London: Macmillan & Co., Ltd., 1938.

MYINT, HLA. *Theories of Welfare Economics.* Cambridge: Harvard University Press, 1948.

PIGOU, A. C. *The Economics of Welfare.* London: Macmillan & Co., Ltd., 1920.

REDER, MELVIN W. *Studies in the Theory of Welfare Economics.* New York: Columbia University Press, 1947.

ROTHENBERG, JEROME. *The Measurement of Social Welfare.* Englewood Cliffs, N.J.: Prentice-Hall, Inc., 1961.

---

[31] See H. A. Simon, "Theories of Decision Making in Economics," *American Economic Review,* Vol. XLIX (June, 1959), pp. 253–83; and Harvey Leibenstein, *Economic Theory and Organizational Analysis* (New York: Harper & Bros., 1960).

SELECTED READINGS

PART **VII**

LINEAR PROGRAMMING

17 Basic Concepts of Linear Programming

Introduction

Linear programming is a mathematical technique for selecting the "best" method of attaining a given end or objective when the criteria of the "best" method are specified. It is not a technique for determining the criteria according to which the "best" method is defined. This technique has been formally defined as one of maximizing or minimizing a linear function of a number of variables subject to a number of restraints stated in the form of linear inequalities.[1]

The problem of maximization of the utility of the consumer's given money income has been treated in Chapters 4 and 5 as one of maximizing a nonlinear function of a number of variables subject to a restraint in the form of a single linear equality. In that case the utility functions are the nonlinear functions, and the linear restraint is the budget equation. Similarly, the theory of production explained in Chapter 6 also involves such a problem, and, in that case, the isocost line is a single linear restraint.

Linear programming techniques were first developed by mathematicians seeking to solve problems such as those of internal planning in the Air Force and other large organizations, and the fundamental work in this area was done by George B. Dantzig in 1947. Since that time, the technique of linear programming has been applied to a large number of managerial planning problems, and some economists have also sought to investigate the implications of this technique for economic theory in general.[2]

This chapter provides an explanation of the basic concepts of linear programming and then explains two methods of solving linear pro-

---

[1] In general, see Robert Dorfman, Paul A. Samuelson, and Robert M. Solow, *Linear Programming and Economic Analysis* (New York: McGraw-Hill Book Co., Inc., 1958).

[2] *Ibid.*, chap. xiv.

gramming problems. A *primal* maximization problem and its *dual* will be solved by the *complete description method,* and then the same maximization problem will be solved by the *simplex method.* First, however, some of the basic concepts of linear programming must be explained.

A. GENERAL CONCEPTS

The Concept of a Process

Figure 17–1 contains a number of scale lines[3] derived from the homogeneous linear production function employed in Chapter 6. The

Figure 17–1

SCALE LINES ILLUSTRATING DIFFERENT PROCESSES

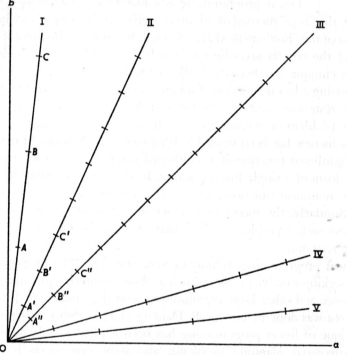

line *OI*, for example, shows the way in which total output changes as amounts of the inputs *a* and *b* are increased proportionately. Thus distance $OA = AB = BC$; and, at *A*, total product is equal to 8.425X; at *B*, it is equal to 16.85X; and, at *C*, it is equal to 25.28X. Also, at *B*,

---

[3] Diagrams like Figures 17–1, 17–2, and 17–3 were apparently first presented by Professor Robert Dorfman in " 'Mathematical' or 'Linear' Programming: A Non-Mathematical Exposition," *American Economic Review,* Vol. XLIII (December, 1953), pp. 797–825.

inputs of *a* and of *b* are exactly twice as great as at *A;* and, at *C,* they are three times as great as at *A.* Along the scale line *OI,* output increases proportionately as inputs are increased proportionately.

Similarly, along scale line *OII,* output increases proportionately as inputs are increased proportionately, and the same is true along the other scale lines, *OIII, OIV,* and *OV.* However, note that the output marks, such as *A, A′,* and *A″,* are not equidistant from the origin on all these scale lines. Output marks, such as *A, B, C,* and *A′, B′, C′,* are evenly spaced *along* any given scale line, but *OA > OA′, AB > A′B′,* etc.

Each scale line thus shows that total output changes proportionately when inputs are increased proportionately, but different scale lines depict the way in which total output changes when the inputs are used in different proportions. Now the different proportions in which the inputs are employed on different scale lines can be thought of as different *processes* according to which given quantities of output are produced. Thus scale line *OI* may be thought of as representing the amounts of output attainable from given quantities of inputs employed according to the given process, I, while scale line *OII* represents the various quantities of output obtainable from using different quantities of inputs according to another process, II, and so on.

The quantities of output obtainable from different inputs according

Table 17–1
PRODUCT OBTAINABLE FROM GIVEN INPUTS*

Process (or Scale Line)	Product (or Quantity of X)	Quantity of *a*	Quantity of *b*
I	8.425	0.420	4.00
	16.850	0.840	8.00
	25.275	1.260	12.00
II	8.425	0.685	1.50
	16.850	1.370	3.00
	25.275	2.055	4.50
III	8.425	1.000	1.00
	16.850	2.000	2.00
	25.275	3.000	3.00
IV	8.425	2.000	0.58
	16.850	4.000	1.16
	25.275	6.000	1.74
V	8.425	4.000	0.48
	16.850	8.000	0.96
	25.275	12.000	1.44

* Based on the function: $X = \sqrt{2Cab - D(a^2) - E(b^2)}$, where $C = 40$, $D = 5$, and $E = 4$, as in Chapter 6.

to the different processes which are the basic data of Figure 17–1 are contained in Table 17–1.

Each scale line thus represents a different process identified with a Roman numeral in Table 17–1, and, since output increases proportionately as inputs are increased proportionately *along* any given scale line, the production function is linearly homogeneous. How many such scale lines can be drawn in a given case depends on the number of processes available. If there are an infinite number of processes, this means that the factors *a* and *b* are infinitely divisible. Such an assumption has in fact been made in drawing the isoquants which have been depicted in Chapter 6.

Derivation of the Isoquants

Let us assume that there are five processes as indicated by the five scale lines in Figures 17–1 and 17–2. By joining with a straight line those points on the different scale lines which represent equal total amounts of output, we produce contour lines, or isoproduct curves such as $AA'A''$ and $BB'B''$ in Figure 17–2. The isoproduct curve $AA'A''$

Figure 17–2

LINEAR ISOQUANTS

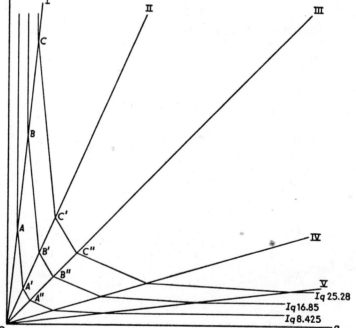

has been labeled Iq 8.425. This curve may be compared with its counterpart in Figure 6–3 in Chapter 6. In general, the two curves have the same shape, but the curve in Figure 17–2 assumes that substitution between any two processes occurs at a constant rate, while the curves in Figure 6–3 assume that the rate of substitution is not constant between any two such processes. Neither diagram assumes that the rate of substitution among *all* the processes is the same.

Thus, in linear programming, the isoquants are treated *as if* they were composed of straight line segments rather than as continuous curves, and, moreover, the isoquants are treated as having *corners* at points such as A, A', A'', etc.

Determination of Quantities of Inputs Employed

It is possible to combine isocost curves, such as those employed in Chapter 6, with isoquants of the type depicted in Figure 17–2 to explain the method of maximizing the total output which can be obtained from a given amount of expenditure on inputs with given prices of inputs, just as this procedure was explained in Chapter 6.

Thus, in Figure 17–3, the line FG represents the isocost line, just as it does in the case of Figure 6–5, when the price of input a is $3.65 per unit and the price of input b is $1.00 per unit. A firm with a total outlay of $8.00 for inputs would maximize its output from the given amount of expenditure on inputs at these given prices at B' (which is comparable to point A in Figure 6–5). At B', in Figure 17–3, the firm uses three units of b and 1.37 units of a to produce 16.85 units of product. The point of tangency between the isocost curve, $FG,$ and the isoquant in Figure 17–3 appears at the corner, B', indicating that Process II is the optimum process. (Figure 17–3 appears on page 418.)

Line $F'H'$ shows the firm attaining a higher level of output (25.28 units of X) with a smaller total outlay ($7.74) at different relative prices of a and b. The line $F'H'$ is tangent to Iq 25.28 *over the range* $C'C''$, which indicates that, at the new given relative prices of a and $b,$ both Process II and Process III are optimal and any combination of the two processes is also optimal. Along $F'H'$, the price of a is $1.58 per unit, and the price of b is $1.00 per unit. Thus, the optimum production program depends on the relative prices of the factors or inputs. In our diagram, the firm needs never to use more than a single process in order to produce the given output. At C', for example, the firm uses 4.5 units of b and 2.05 units of a, and at the given relative prices, we have $(\$1.00)(4.5) + (2.05)(\$1.58) = \$7.74$. And at C'' the firm uses three units of b and three units of a, and we have $(\$1.00)(3) + (3)(\$1.58) = \$7.74$. Thus the slope of the isoquant between C' and

Figure 17–3
ILLUSTRATION OF THE EQUILIBRIUM POSITION

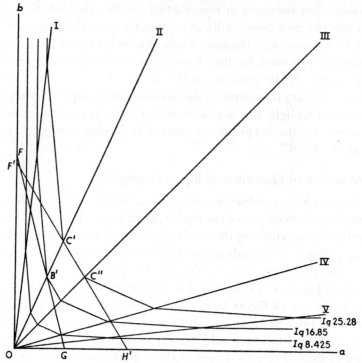

C'' is $(4.5 - 3)/(3 - 2.05) = (1.5)/(.95) = 1.58$, and this is equal to the ratio of the prices of a and b indicated by the slope of the isocost line $F'H'$.

The range $C'C''$ need not be that corresponding to a one-unit change in a, and we have thus abandoned the strict definition of the equilibrium condition of Chapter 6, which defines equilibrium only at a given point. Instead, we now accept *either* the criterion of tangency at a point between an isocost line and a contour line *or* tangency over a given range (not necessarily a one-unit change in a) of the isoquant as sufficient to satisfy the condition of output maximization.

B. THE COMPLETE DESCRIPTION METHOD: MAXIMIZATION PROBLEM

An Assumed Problem

The use of linear programming as a device for solving a maximization problem can be illustrated by assuming a concrete problem and solving it by this technique. Let us accordingly assume that a firm produces two products, X_1 and X_2, which can be sold in the market at given prices of \$20 and \$15, respectively. Thus $P_{X_1} = \$20$, and $P_{X_2} = \$15$. Assume also that the firm has available 60 units of input a, 24 units of input b, and 84 units of input c.

Let us also assume that one unit of X_1 requires five units of a, three units of b, and 12 units of c; and that one unit of X_2 requires 15 units of a, four units of b, and seven units of c. The problem facing the managers is, therefore, one of producing the maximum amount of revenue from the sale of products X_1 and X_2, consistent with the given prices of the products and within the limits or constraints imposed by the existing availabilities of inputs.

It is consistent with our constraints that the firm need *not* employ fully all units of the available resources. Also, we assume that the firm cannot produce negative amounts of the two products, X_1 or X_2, but that it need not produce any amount at all of one of them, or $X_1 \geq 0$, $X_2 \geq 0$.

The Objective Equation

The condition that the revenue obtainable from the quantity of products produced should be a maximum, subject to the given restraints, can be written in the form of an equation known as the *objective equation*, or as

$$P_{X_1}X_1 + P_{X_2}X_2 = \text{Total revenue (must be a maximum)}, \qquad (17\text{-}1)$$

or in terms of the prices we have assumed:

$$20X_1 + 15X_2 = \text{Total revenue (must be a maximum)}. \qquad (17\text{-}1a)$$

The Constraints

In order to understand fully the equations which can be written to state the condition that the quantities of inputs are limited and that different amounts of the respective inputs are required for the production of each of the two products, it is useful to summarize the input-output information as in Table 17–2, which appears on page 420.

We can now write equations which state the restrictions or constraints in terms of the individual inputs subject to which X_1 and X_2 must be produced. First, note in Table 17–2 that the maximum amount of input a which is available is 60 units; and that five units of a are required for the production of one unit of X_1, and 15 units of a are required for the production of one unit of X_2. Thus, the number of units of X_1 produced, multiplied by the amount of a required for each of them, plus the number of units of X_2 produced, multiplied by the

Table 17–2

INPUT-OUTPUT DATA

Input	Amount of Input Required for One Unit of Output		Total Amount of Input Available—
	X_1 Units	X_2 Units	Units
a	5	15	60
b	3	4	24
c	12	7	84

amount of *a* required to produce one unit of X_2, cannot be greater than but may be equal to or less than ($\leq$) 60 units of *a*. Algebraically, we thus can write:

$$5X_1 + 15X_2 \leq 60 . \qquad (17-2)$$

Similar equations can be written as the constraints imposed on production by the resource limitations in the cases of inputs *b* and *c;* or, reading across the data for *b* in Table 17–2, we have

$$3X_1 + 4X_2 \leq 24 ; \qquad (17-3)$$

and in the case of *c:*

$$12X_1 + 7X_2 \leq 84 . \qquad (17-4)$$

Now if we are willing to ignore the *less than* signs in our equations and to treat them as if they read *equal to* only, we can provide a graphical illustration of our problem and also indicate a method of solving it. Thus, if we rewrite Equation (17–2) as

$$5X_1 + 15X_2 = 60 , \qquad (17-2a)$$

by letting $X_1 = 0$, we can solve this equation for X_2, or

$$0 + 15X_2 = 60 ,$$

and so

$$X_2 = 4 .$$

And similarly, by letting $X_2 = 0$, we can produce:

$$X_1 = 12 .$$

Accordingly, in Figure 17–4, we can let distance $OA = X_1$ when $X_2 = 0$, and let distance $OB = X_2$ when $X_1 = 0$. Or $OA = 12X_1$, and $OB = 4X_2$. Thus, line AB in Figure 17–4 is a picture of data embodied in Equation (17–2a) above.

Similarly, we can solve Equations (17–3) and (17–4) and depict them graphically respectively by lines CD and EF in Figure 17–4. Thus $OE = 7X_1$, $OF = 12X_2$, $OC = 8X_1$, and $OD = 6X_2$.

The Feasible Region

Now consider points such as E, G, H, and B, in Figure 17–4. These points represent *corners*. At G, for example, line CD intersects line EF; and at H, line AB intersects CD. The area $OEGHB$, which has been

Figure 17–4
THE "FEASIBLE" REGION

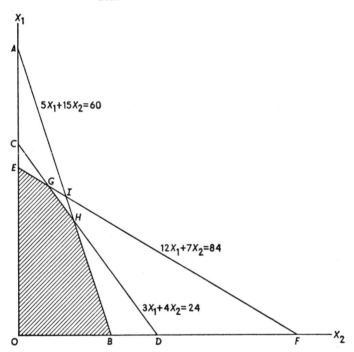

shaded, represents the common part of all the areas outlined by the various equations.

This area represents the so-called *feasible* region of production, and the optimal point of production always lies on the boundary of the feasible region. For, since linear programming analysis assumes constant returns to scale, it will always pay the firm to expand production up to the point at which the capacity limit for one or more of the inputs is reached.

The Optimum Solution

Now we already know the coordinates of points E and B, for we have determined from Equation (17–4) that $OE = 7X_1$ and from Equation

(17-2) that $OB = 4X_2$. In order to determine the coordinates of point H, we must treat Equations (17-2a) and (17-3a) as simultaneous equations and solve them for X_1 and X_2, or

$$5X_1 + 15X_2 = 60 , \qquad (17\text{-}2a)$$

and

$$3X_1 + 4X_2 = 24 . \qquad (17\text{-}3a)$$

Next, by multiplying Equation (17-3a) by 5 and Equation (17-2a) by 3 and subtracting the former from the latter, we have

$$
\begin{aligned}
15X_1 + 45X_2 &= 180 \\
-15X_1 - 20X_2 &= -120 \\
\hline
25X_2 &= 60 \\
X_2 &= 2.4 .
\end{aligned}
$$

And, by substitution of this result into Equation (17-2a), we have at H, $X_1 = 4.8$. Similarly, we can solve for the coordinates at G and have at G, $X_1 = 6.22$ and $X_2 = 1.33$.

Our final step now consists of substituting the values of X_1 and X_2 at the various corner positions into our objective equation and of determining which combinations of X_1 and X_2 at the given prices will produce the maximum revenue. Thus, for the output indicated at point E, we have $X_1 = 7$, $X_2 = 0$; and substituting these values into Equation (17-1a), we have

$$(\$20)(7) + (\$14)(0) = \$140 . \qquad (17\text{-}1a')$$

At G we have for the objective equation,

$$(\$20)(6.22) + (\$15)(1.33) = \$144.35 ; \qquad (17\text{-}1a'')$$

and at H we have

$$(\$20)(4.8) + (\$15)(2.4) = \$132 ; \qquad (17\text{-}1a''')$$

and, finally, at B we have

$$(\$20)(0) + (\$15)(4) = \$60 . \qquad (17\text{-}1a'''')$$

Thus, with the given amount of inputs, total revenue is maximized when X_1 and X_2 are produced in the proportions indicated by point G, with the given prices of these products. The total revenue at this point would be $144.35, and this amount is greater than that which can be obtained at any other point, subject to the given restraints.

On the other hand, if the price of X_1 were only $10 while that of X_2 were $15 as before, the point of maximum total revenue would be at H rather than at G. For at H, in such a case, our objective equation yields

$84 as the total revenue, while at the other points the equation yields results as follows: at E, $70; at G, $82.15; and at B, $60.

Determination of the Total Amount of Each Input Used

We have learned that on the basis of our assumed data the firm will maximize its total revenue when it produces 6.22 units of X_1 and 1.33 units of X_2. It is interesting to compute the total amount of each of the inputs which will be used in the final production plan. Thus, since one unit of X_1 requires $5a + 3b + 12c$, we learn that $6.22X_1$ are produced from $(6.22)(5)a + (6.22)(3)b + (6.22)(12)c = 31.10a + 18.66b + 74.64c$. Similarly, since one unit of X_2 requires the use of $15a + 4b + 7c$, the total amount of inputs used to produce $1.33X_2$ amounts to $(1.33)(15)a + (1.33)(4)b + (1.33)(7)c = 19.95a + 5.32b + 9.31c$. Adding these totals, we have the total amount of a used as $31.10a + 19.95a = 51.05a$ and the total amount of b used as $18.66b + 5.32b = 23.98b$. Or, when we take account of the fact that we have rounded our numbers, input b will be fully employed, for the total amount available is 24 units. Moreover, the total amount of c used is $74.64c + 9.31c = 83.95c$, and, again, noting that we have rounded our numbers, we see that input c will be fully employed. Resource a, on the other hand, is not fully employed, for only 51.05 units of a are used in the final plan, although 60 units of a are available. Thus, $60 - 51.05 = 8.95$ units of a are leftover or unutilized.

The Basic Theorem of Linear Programming Illustrated

Our solution illustrates *a basic theorem of linear programming: in the optimal solution, there will usually be exactly as many outputs produced as there are inputs used to capacity.* In the present case, two products, X_1 and X_2, are produced; and two of the inputs, b and c, are used to capacity, so that there are no unutilized or leftover amounts of these inputs at the optimal point, G, in Figure 17–4. We will later generalize and make further use of this proposition in explaining the *simplex method* of solving the problem.

C. COMPLETE DESCRIPTION METHOD: THE DUAL PROBLEM

"Shadow" or "Accounting" Prices

In general, every linear programming problem has a *dual*. The dual of the maximization problem just discussed is a counterpart of the maximization problem and raises the question: What is the value to the firm of additional units of inputs?

Consider input *a* which is not being fully employed in our problem of input allocation discussed above. What are additional units of input *a,* other things remaining unchanged, worth to the firm? Since additional units of *a* do not increase total output, in terms of their effect on total revenue additional units of *a* have a zero value to this firm. On the other hand, at the margin of production, additional units of *b* and *c* (which are fully employed) do have a positive value to the firm; for if the firm obtained additional units of these inputs, it could combine them with input *a* (which is not scarce insofar as are concerned the activities of this firm) to increase total product and hence total revenue.

The dual of the problem of resource allocation or of maximization of the total revenue obtainable from the production of X_1 and X_2 in our case is thus the problem of determining the values to the firm (or the imputed values) of the inputs employed at the margin. Such imputed values are sometimes referred to as "shadow prices" or as "accounting prices" of the inputs.

The Equations Rearranged

This problem can be solved readily by rearranging the data and the equations which have already been used in our maximization problem. In order to write these new equations, consider the fact that the value to the firm of all the inputs used to produce one unit of X_1 must be *at least equal to, and cannot be less than,* the amount of revenue obtained by the firm from the sale of one unit of X_1. Similarly, the value to the firm of all the inputs used to produce one unit of X_2 must be *at least equal to, and cannot be less than,* the amount of revenue obtained from the sale of one unit of X_2. Furthermore, the amount of revenue obtained from the sale of one unit of X_1 is equal to its price in dollars, and the amount of revenue obtained from the sale of one unit of X_2 is equal to its price in dollars. Thus, we can write the foregoing argument in the form of a series of equations which read:

$$5u_a + 3u_b + 12u_c \geq P_{X_1} = \$20, \qquad (17\text{-}5)$$

and

$$15u_a + 4u_b + 7u_c \geq P_{X_2} = \$15. \qquad (17\text{-}6)$$

In these equations, u_a, u_b, and u_c represent the "shadow prices" or the imputed values of the respective inputs (*a, b,* and *c*) employed. These "shadow prices" represent "the addition to total revenue of the firm resulting from the use of an additional unit of the given input at the margin of production." And we have already learned in Chapter 12 that this phrase constitutes a definition of the "marginal revenue product," or MRP, of the firm. Note that product prices P_{X_1} and P_{X_2} are assumed constant. Thus, $MRP = VMP$, and perfect competition in product markets is assumed.

Since inputs b and c are fully employed at the margin of production in our problem, it is clear that the values of these inputs at the margin are positive, or $u_b > 0$ and $u_c > 0$. On the other hand, input a is not fully employed at the margin, and the value to the firm of additional units of a is, therefore, zero, or $u_a = 0$. That is, use of additional units of a will not increase total product, and use of additional units of a will not increase total revenue when the firm is producing the quantities of X_1 and X_2 as indicated at G in Figure 17–4. Thus, the value of additional units of a to the firm at this point is zero.

Equations of the Primal and Dual Problems Compared

The student may be interested in comparing Equations (17–5) and (17–6) with Equations (17–2), (17–3), and (17–4). The number of inequalities in the dual problem (2) is equal to the number of variables (X_1 and X_2) in the original or *primal* maximization problem; and the number of variables (u_a, u_b, and u_c) in the dual problem is equal to the number of inequalities (3) in the primal problem. This relationship always holds in the case of a primal linear programming problem and its dual. Also note that the sense of the inequalities in the dual problem [Equations (17–5) and (17–6)] is the reverse of the sense of the inequalities in the original problem. Where we previously used the symbols of *less than* or *equal to* in the dual problem, we now use the symbols of *greater than* or *equal to*. Finally, the coefficients of X_1 and X_2 in the objective equation of the original problem, or P_{X_1} and P_{X_2} (the prices of X_1 and X_2 respectively), are the constants in the constraints in our dual problem. That is, P_{X_1} and P_{X_2} now appear on the right-hand sides of the inequalities in Equations (17–5) and (17–6), where previously they appeared on the left side in Equation (17–1).

The reason why the coefficients of X_1 and X_2 in the objective equation become the constants in the constraints of the dual problem is simply that, since the dual problem is concerned with an attempt to assign "imputed values" or "accounting" or "shadow" prices to the inputs, the sum of the values of the quantities of inputs used to produce a given product, say X_1, must be equal to or greater than the value (measured by its price in dollars) of the product which is produced. If the sum of the values of the quantities of inputs used to produce the final product were less than the value of the product produced, not all of the value of the final product would be "imputed" or accounted for.

The Objective Equation in the Dual Problem Explained

Let us now recall Euler's Theorem, stated in Equation (3–3) and discussed earlier in Chapters 3, 6, and 12. This theorem states that in the case of a linearly homogeneous production function, the total product is equal to the sum of the respective marginal products multiplied by the amounts of inputs used. Now, the total value of the product can be taken as equal to the amount of product multiplied by the price of the product, and, in the previous maximization problem, our object was to make this value, the total revenue from the sale of the product, as great as possible. In the present dual problem, we have written the condition in Equations (17–5) and (17–6) that the sum of the amounts of each of the inputs used multiplied by its imputed value must be equal to or greater than the price of a unit of product. It follows, therefore, that the sum of the imputed unit values of the inputs, each multiplied by the quantities of each of them which are available, or the total value of the resources employed, must be just equal to the maximum total revenue obtained from the sale of the product at the current prices.

Accordingly, our objective equation in the case of our dual problem can be written to read:

$$60u_a + 24u_b + 84u_c = P_{X_1}X_1 + P_{X_2}X_2 = \text{Total revenue.} \quad (17\text{–}7)$$

This formulation of the objective equation thus states that the respective imputed unit values (u) of the resources, multiplied by the amounts of each of them which are available, must be equal to the total revenue obtained from the sale of the products produced by means of the inputs. Generally, the objective equation is written as

$$au_a + bu_b + cu_c = W , \quad (17\text{–}8)$$

the minimum aggregate value of the resources employed, where a, b, and c represent the total amounts of the respective inputs used and u_a, u_b, and u_c represent the imputed unit values of the inputs, their marginal revenue products ($MRP = VMP$).

The Optimum Solution to the Dual Problem

Now, proceeding as we did in the maximization problem and recognizing the fact that the shadow price of resource a (which is not fully employed and is, therefore, in excess supply insofar as is concerned this firm) is equal to zero, or $u_a = 0$, we can write:

$$5(0) + 3u_b + 12u_c = \$20 , \quad (17\text{–}5a)$$

and

$$15(0) + 4u_b + 7u_c = \$15 .\qquad(17\text{-}6a)$$

As before, we can solve these two simultaneous equations (by multiplying the first of them by 4 and the second by 3 and subtracting) to produce the value of u_c, or

$$
\begin{array}{rl}
12u_b + 48u_c = & \$80 \\
-12u_b - 21u_c = & -\$45 \\
\hline
27u_c = & \$35 \\
u_c = & \$\ 1.299 .
\end{array}
\qquad(17\text{-}9)
$$

Now by substituting this value into Equation (17–5a) above, we have $u_b = \$1.466$. Thus, the imputed value of a unit of b at the margin is $\$1.466$ and that of a unit of c is $\$1.299$. Substituting these values into the original objective equation, or into Equation (17–7), we have

$$60(0) + 24(\$1.466) + 84(\$1.299) = (\$20)(6.22) + (\$15)(1.33) ,$$

$$\$35.18 + \$109.12 = \$124.40 + \$19.95 , \text{ or,}\qquad(17\text{-}7')$$

$$\$144.30 = \$144.35 .$$

The slight discrepancy is due to rounding of our numbers. Except for this fact, the total revenue has thus been imputed to the inputs according to their values at the margin of production. Presumably, in this situation, the firm would be unwilling to pay anything for an additional unit of a but would be willing to pay $\$1.299$ for an additional unit of c and $\$1.466$ for an additional unit of b, provided it could obtain an additional unit of each.

Graphical Comparison of the Primal and Dual Problems

For the purposes of comparison with the maximization problem, Equations (17–5a) and (17–6a) are plotted in Figure 17–5. We see in Figure 17–5 that the dual of the maximization problem produces an

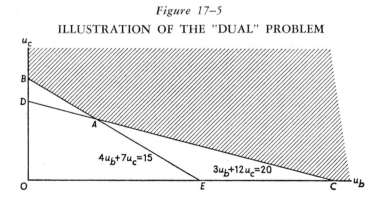

Figure 17–5

ILLUSTRATION OF THE "DUAL" PROBLEM

"unbounded area" (the shaded area BAC); and that, at A, the value of input c is $1.299, while the value of input b is $1.466. Thus, while the maximization problem produces a "bounded" area (the shaded area $OEGHB$ in Figure 17–4), the dual of the maximization problem, or the valuation solution, produces an "unbounded" area (the shaded area BAC in Figure 17–5). In each case, the solution to the problem appears at a corner.

The Basic Theorem Also Illustrated by the Dual Problem

The solution to the dual problem also illustrates the basic theorem of linear programming. We have two positive shadow prices, those of inputs b and c, and we have two inputs used to capacity, inputs b and c. Again we see that the number of variables in the optimum solution which take positive values is equal to the number of inputs or processes used to capacity.

D. THE SIMPLEX METHOD OF SOLUTION: MAXIMIZATION PROBLEM

General Description of the Method

In the preceding section, we have learned that the optimum solution to a linear programming problem must always lie at a "corner," as in Figure 17–4. The simplex method of solution makes use of this fact. Basically, this method is concerned with determining when the maximum total revenue from given inputs is being obtained by computing the *changes in total revenue* (ΔR) which would occur by moving in any direction from a given corner point, such as $O, E, G, H,$ or B in Figure 17–4. If the change in total revenue is positive ($\Delta R > 0$), thus signifying that total revenue can be increased by moving in a given direction (increasing the output of one of the products at the expense of another or changing the proportions in which the outputs are produced), the computation process is repeated, using the new corner position as a basis for further computations. Eventually when a corner position is reached, such that a movement from it *in any direction* would result in a negative change in total revenue ($\Delta R < 0$), the problem has been solved, and an optimal solution has been found. For, in this case, the total revenue obtainable from the given inputs must be at a maximum.

The Basic Theorem Reviewed

In the preceding section, we have also learned that in the optimum solution the production of the two products (X_1 and X_2) has involved the use of exactly two productive facilities (c and b) to capacity, while the third (a) has not been used to capacity. This solution, it has been noted, illustrates *the basic theorem of linear programming: namely, that in any optimal solution there will generally be exactly as many outputs produced as there are inputs or processes used to capacity.*

The Problem Reviewed

The student will recall that in Table 17–2 the input-product information assumed for our problem has been summarized; the *objective* equation has also been written as

$$P_{X_1}X_1 + P_{X_2}X_2 = R \text{ (must be a maximum).} \qquad (17\text{--}1)$$

We have also assumed that $P_{X_1} = \$20$ and $P_{X_2} = \$15$, and so

$$20X_1 + 15X_2 = R \text{ (must be a maximum).} \qquad (17\text{--}1a)$$

Making use of the assumed input-product information in Table 17–2, we have also written the following constraints:

$$5X_1 + 15X_2 \leq 60 \text{ units of } a, \qquad (17\text{--}2)$$
$$3X_1 + 4X_2 \leq 24 \text{ units of } b, \qquad (17\text{--}3)$$

and

$$12X_1 + 7X_2 \leq 84 \text{ units of } c, \qquad (17\text{--}4)$$

as the maximum amounts of the three inputs which are available and as the respective amounts of each input required for the production of the two products produced by the firm.

Introduction of Slack Variables

Now, in the complete description method, we have merely ignored the *less than* signs in the above equations and treated them as if they read *equal to;* and thereby we have produced Figure 17–4 and solved our problem. However, if there are many constraints in the problem, the complete description method may require much more effort than the *simplex* method now to be described. Thus, the complete description method is not much used in practice.

In the simplex method of computation, so-called *slack variables, representing any unused amounts of any of the inputs, are inserted into the inequalities above in order to turn them into equalities.* These slack variables may take a value of zero, or they may be greater than zero; but they can never be less than zero. Designating the slack variables generally by the symbol, L (meaning inputs leftover or unused), we can write Equations (17–2) to (17–4) as equalities in the following way:

$$5X_1 + 15X_2 + L_a = 60 , \qquad (17\text{--}10)$$
$$3X_1 + 4X_2 + L_b = 24 , \qquad (17\text{--}11)$$

and

$$12X_1 + 7X_2 + L_c = 84 , \qquad (17\text{--}12)$$

where L_a, L_b, and L_c represent the amounts of the inputs leftover when any given amounts of X_1 and X_2 are produced. In addition to these three equations, we have our objective equation:

$$20X_1 + 15X_2 = R \text{ (must be a maximum)}. \qquad (17\text{--}1a)$$

Characteristics of a Basic and Feasible Solution

Thus, at this stage of the proceedings, we have a total of four equations in six unknowns. However, we also have the basic theorem of linear programming which states that in any optimum solution, when total revenue is maximized so that $\Delta R = 0$, there will be exactly as many outputs produced as there are inputs or processes used to capacity. Moreover, *any* solution which satisfies this condition is known as a *basic solution,* whether total revenue is at a maximum or not.

Such a basic solution is satisfied in Figure 17–4 *at* any of the corners, $O, E, G, H,$ and $B,$ *and within* the feasible region, $OEGHB$. One possibility is that the firm produces zero (no) amounts of X_1 and X_2. In such a case we would be at the origin, $O,$ in Figure 17–4. Of course, in such a case, total revenue, $R,$ will also be zero (and thus the solution is by no means an optimum one), but it is, nevertheless, a starting point. And so, at O in Figure 17–4, nothing is produced, and no input is used to capacity. The basic theorem is satisfied.

The basic theorem of linear programming can now be restated generally to read that the total number of variables (both slack and basic) having a value different from zero must be no greater than the number of equations (as distinct from inequalities) which represent constraints in the linear programming problem. An explanation follows.

At O in Figure 17–4, we have $X_1 = X_2 = 0$ in our Equations (17–1a), (17–10), (17–11), and (17–12). Now *if* we set these two unknowns equal to zero in those equations, we will then have four equations in four unknowns! Thus, we can solve these equations for the remaining unknowns, L_a, L_b, L_c, and R.

That is, we can now rewrite our equations in the usual way to put the unknowns on the left-hand side as

$$R = 0 + 20X_1 + 15X_2 , \qquad (17\text{--}1a)$$
$$L_a = 60 - 5X_1 - 15X_2 , \qquad (17\text{--}10a)$$
$$L_b = 24 - 3X_1 - 4X_2 , \qquad (17\text{--}11a)$$

and

$$L_c = 84 - 12X_1 - 7X_2 . \qquad (17\text{-}12\text{a})$$

If $X_1 = X_2 = 0$, the solution to these equations is clearly: $R = 0$, $L_a = 60$, $L_b = 24$, and $L_c = 84$; and these are the values of the variables at the origin, O, in Figure 17–4. Our two basic variables (X_1 and X_2) have a value of zero; all of our *slack* variables (L_a, L_b, and L_c) have positive values (values different from zero), and total revenue (R) is zero. Thus, the number of basic and slack variables *together* having a value different from zero (3) is no greater than the number of equations (3) which represent constraints. Indeed, the numbers are equal. Moreover, we have a basic and feasible solution to the problem.

Now, when no output is being produced and when we are at the origin, O, in Figure 17–4, total revenue is zero, and no inputs are being utilized. In the context of our present problem, the use of negative amounts of inputs and a negative total revenue is nonsensical. Thus, *a second basic theorem of linear programming states that the basic solution is feasible only if the constant terms in our equations are all equal to or greater than zero.* This condition, of course, is satisfied at the origin, where $X_1 = X_2 = 0$, and also at all points in the feasible (shaded) region in Figure 17–4. Thus, when $X_1 = X_2 = 0$, our constants are $a = 60 > 0$, $b = 24 > 0$, and $c = 84 > 0$.

The Optimality Condition

Our problem, of course, is not yet solved, for it is that of finding the maximum total revenue which can be obtained from the given inputs at the given prices of the products. We now proceed to solve it by moving from the origin in Figure 17–4 to one of the other corner positions, say to E or to B, and, systematically, from that point to another corner position until, eventually, we reach a corner position such that by moving from it in either direction, the *change* in total revenue will be negative or zero ($\Delta R \leq 0$). At *this* corner position, the total revenue would be reduced by making further changes in the composition of our output; and, thus, total revenue will be at a maximum at this position. Basically, our method will be one of trial and error, although in the literature it has been given the fancy name of "successive iteration."

Now the addition to total revenue from producing an additional (first) unit of X_1 at a time when no units are being produced is simply equal to the price of a unit of X_1, or to \$20 in the present problem, and the addition to total revenue from producing an additional (first) unit of X_2 is the price of X_2, or \$15. These prices are the coefficients of X_1 and X_2, respectively, *in our objective equation*. If these coefficients are positive, this fact means that marginal revenue is positive, and, thus, total revenue can be further increased by increasing the output of the relevant product accordingly. Only if these coefficients were equal to zero would total revenue not be further increased by increasing the production of the relevant product. And, of course, if the coefficient in question were negative, obviously further production of the product would decrease the total revenue.

Thus, an *optimal solution* to our problem is one in which the coefficients of the variables in the objective equation are *not* positive. We can, therefore, state the optimality condition: *a basic solution is optimal, so that R is a maximum, when, and only when, none of the coefficients of the variables in the objective equation in the optimal solution is greater than zero.*

The Simplex Tableau and Computational Rules

At this point in the problem, various types of simplex tableaus (tables or matrices) of the coefficients and constants in the equations and their associated computational rules for solving simultaneous equations successively are brought into play by many writers on the subject.[4]

---

[4] An example of such a tableau is the following presentation of our equations:

Table 17–3

ILLUSTRATIVE SIMPLEX TABLEAU[a]
(Based on Equations Describing Origin in Figure 17–4)

Unknowns, or Positive Valued Variables	Solution Values or Constants	Coefficients of Zero Valued Variables		Line Number
		X_1	X_2	
R	0	20	15	(1)
L_a	60	-5	-15	(2)
L_b	24	-3	-4	(3)
L_c	84	-12^*	-7	(4)

[a] The use of tableaus somewhat similar to the one given above is illustrated in William J. Baumol, *Economic Theory and Operations Analysis* (Englewood Cliffs, N.J.: Prentice-Hall, Inc., 1961), esp. pp. 76–86; and in S. Vajda, *Readings in Linear Programming* (New York: Wiley & Sons, Inc., 1958), esp. chaps. xiii and xiv. The first simplex tableau was apparently presented by A. Charnes [in A. Charnes, W. W. Cooper, and A. Henderson, *An Introduction to Linear Programming* (New York: Wiley & Sons, Inc., 1953), p. 66], who stated that it was suggested to him by A. Orden and that the tableau was developed by Orden, Dantzig, and Hoffman. Tableaus similar to the one used by Charnes (but different from the one depicted above) are found in Robert W. Metzger, *Elementary Mathematical Programming* (New York: Wiley & Sons, Inc., 1953), esp. pp. 60–74; Kenneth E. Boulding and Allen W. Spivey (eds.), *Linear Programming and the Theory of the Firm* (New York: The Macmillan Co., 1960), esp. pp. 89–93; and Robert Dorfman, Paul A. Samuelson, and Robert M. Solow, *Linear Programming and Economic Analysis* (New York: McGraw-Hill Book Co., Inc., 1958), esp. pp. 85–92.

These tableaus and computational rules are not part of the *theory* of linear programming. They are, however, extremely useful short-cut methods devised to solve the various simultaneous equations successively, thereby reducing the clerical work involved. Also, such tableaus and computational rules can be taught to and used by persons who have no knowledge of the basic principles involved, and this fact makes it possible to use the technique more widely in business and government agencies than would otherwise be the case.

Since *this chapter is concerned with explaining the basic concepts* of linear programming *and the general simplex method* invented by Dantzig, and not with teaching a particular computational technique, only the elementary method of solving simultaneous equations by the process of substitution will be used in it to illustrate the method of finding an optimum solution to the problem. However, the equations applicable to the basic solutions obtained in this chapter will be collated, in the course of the analysis, with various computational rules by means of footnotes for the use of the student who wishes to study some of the simplex tableaus presented in references cited in the last footnote.

Analysis of Equations: The Corner at O (the Origin) in Figure 17–4

We now have the values of our variables at O in Figure 17–4 and know that $R = 0$. Our next problem is that of moving from O to either E or B in Figure 17–4. Since linear programming assumes that the production function is linearly homogeneous, there are constant returns to scale. Thus, if a small movement from O toward either E or B will increase total revenue, a movement all the way from O to E or B will also do so. This assumption of linear programming methods of solving problems is one which makes their solution possible, but it also represents the greatest limitation upon the use of these methods.

Let us write again the objective equation and analyze its meaning at O, the origin, in Figure 17–4. The equation reads:

$$R = 0 + 20X_1 + 15X_2 . \qquad (17\text{–}1a)$$

In this equation, at a time when total revenue is zero ($R = 0$), the addition to total revenue from production of an additional unit of X_1 is seen to be \$20, while the addition to total revenue from production of an additional unit of X_2 is less than this, or only \$15. *The numbers attached to X_1 and X_2 are their coefficients.* Since both coefficients are positive, we know that total revenue can be increased by increasing the production of either of these two outputs. Which output shall we choose to increase first?

The answer seems obvious. We will increase total revenue faster if we begin by increasing production of X_1, for a unit of X_1 has a higher price than a unit of X_2. Thus we will begin our computations by determining what will be the effect on total revenue from increasing production of X_1, rather than by beginning with a determination of what will be the effect of increasing production of X_2. And so, usually, *the variable having the greatest coefficient in the objective equation in the basic solution should be chosen as the first to be maximized.* Note that in terms of Figure 17–4, application of this rule means that we will first consider the effect of an increase in output of X_1 without changing the output of X_2.

Moving from O to E in Figure 17–4: The Basic Equations Analyzed

Since we wish to move from O to E and to maximize the total revenue while increasing the output of X_1 and at the same time to leave that of X_2 unchanged at zero, we must reduce the amounts of the inputs (employ the inputs) in such a way as to make the fullest possible use of them. Thus it follows that we must fully employ the entire availability of at least one of the inputs, even though we are unable to do so in the case of all inputs. When the unused or leftover amount of one of the inputs is equal to zero, that is to say, when one input has been completely utilized, we will be producing the maximum possible amount of X_1. And in the process of maximizing X_1 and of using up all of one input, we will be giving a positive value to one of our basic variables which has previously had a zero value (X_1) and giving a zero value to one of our slack variables which has previously had a positive value. Thus, we will be maintaining equality between the number of our equations and our unknowns and be able to solve these equations for the new values of the variables at E.[5]

Now what input constitutes the limiting factor of the output of X_1, when X_2 is equal to zero (at E) and, therefore, is not being produced at all? That is, which slack variable shall be set equal to zero in our equations in place of X_1?

In order to answer this question, let us write again the equations stating our constraints and analyze our problem. The equations are

$$L_a = 60 \begin{array}{|c} - 5X_1 \end{array} - 15X_2 \,, \qquad (17\text{–}10a)$$

$$L_b = 24 \begin{array}{|c} - 3X_1 \end{array} - 4X_2 \,, \qquad (17\text{–}11a)$$

$$L_c = 84 \begin{array}{|c} - 12X_1 \end{array} - 7X_2 \,. \qquad (17\text{–}12a)$$

---

[5] The process of solving the equations for the new values of the variables in a new basic solution is known in the literature as "shifting the basis." See Dorfman, Samuelson, and Solow, *op. cit.,* pp. 84–85.

Note that a box has been drawn around the X_1 values and their co-efficients (the numbers attached to X_1 in these equations) to emphasize the fact that X_1 *is the variable being maximized* at E. The coefficients of X_1 in these equations show the rates at which the respective inputs (a, b, and c) are reduced as production of X_1 is increased (this is the meaning of the minus sign in the equations), and the coefficients of X_2 have a similar meaning.

That is, when the signs are ignored, reference to Table 17–2 will show that these coefficients represent the amounts of each of the respective inputs needed to produce a unit of each of the respective outputs. And, since the linear programming technique assumes a linearly homogeneous production function, two units of X_1 require exactly twice as many units of all inputs as does a single unit, three units of X_1 require exactly three times as many units of all inputs as does a single unit, etc.

From the column of coefficients of X_1 shown in the box, we can deduce that if output of X_1 is increased by one unit, the quantity of input a unutilized or leftover (L_a) will be reduced by five units from 60 units to 55. The meaning of the positive numbers on the right-hand side of our equations is thus clear: these numbers represent the amounts of the inputs leftover or unused when no X_1 and no X_2 are being produced at O in Figure 17–4.

Consequently, if we divide the coefficients of X_1 (signs ignored) which represent the respective amounts of each of the inputs used up in the production of a single unit of X_1 into the positive numbers which represent the total unused or available amounts of the various inputs in our equations, we can determine the maximum number of units of X_1 which can be produced when no X_2 is produced and when one of the inputs is fully used up.

Thus, we have, ignoring the signs of the coefficients of X_1:

$$^{60}\!/_5 = 12 \text{ (which is point } A \text{ in Figure 17–4);}$$

$$^{24}\!/_3 = 8 \text{ (which is point } C \text{ in Figure 17–4); and}$$

$$\text{(smallest) } ^{84}\!/_{12} = 7 \text{ (which is point } E \text{ in Figure 17–4).}$$

And so we see that *seven* is the maximum number of units of X_1 which can be produced with the given inputs when $X_2 = 0$ and when one of the inputs is fully utilized. In short, input c, of which there are 84 units available when no units of X_1 or X_2 are being produced, is the input which limits the output of X_1 first. When seven units of X_1 are produced in this way, no amount of input c is leftover or unused; and so, at E in Figure 17–4, $L_c = 0$. Thus L_c must be set equal to zero in our new equations. At this level of output, there do, however, remain unused amounts of inputs a and b.

At point E in Figure 17–4, we will again have the values of two of our unknowns in our equations equal to zero. That is, at E, L_c and X_2 will be zero, but X_1 will be at a maximum; and L_a and L_b will have positive values, while R will also have a positive value.

We must, therefore, revise our equations in order to take account of these changes so that they will reflect the situation at E. How is this change to be accomplished?

The *first* step is to solve for the value of X_1 the equation [Equation (17–12a)] which contains as an unknown on its left-hand side that slack variable L_c, which is to be set equal to zero as a result of the maximization of X_1 (or which has a zero value at E in Figure 17–4). In the present case we must, therefore, solve Equation (17–12a) for X_1, because, at E, all units of input c will be utilized, and it follows that then no units of input c will be leftover or unutilized. Thus, L_c will be zero at E. Now Equation (17–12a) reads:[6]

$$L_c = 84 - 12X_1 - 7X_2 .\qquad(17\text{–}12a)$$

And so, by subtracting L_c from both sides and adding $12X_1$ to both sides, we have[7]

$$12X_1 = 84 - 7X_2 - L_c .\qquad(17\text{–}13)$$

Finally, by dividing both sides by the coefficient of the variable being maximized, or by 12, we have

$$X_1 = {}^{84}\!/_{12} - {}^{7}\!/_{12}X_2 - {}^{1}\!/_{12}L_c = 7 - {}^{7}\!/_{12}X_2 - {}^{1}\!/_{12}L_c$$
$$= 7 - ({}^{7}\!/_{12})(0) - ({}^{1}\!/_{12})(0) .\qquad(17\text{–}14)$$

Our *second* step is merely to substitute the value of X_1 found in Equation (17–14) above into Equations (17–1a), (17–10a), and (17–11a) to produce

$$R = 0 + 20({}^{84}\!/_{12} - {}^{1}\!/_{12}L_c - {}^{7}\!/_{12}X_2) + 15X_2$$
$$= 0 + 140 - {}^{20}\!/_{12}L_c + {}^{10}\!/_3 X_2 = 140 - ({}^{5}\!/_3)(0) + ({}^{10}\!/_3)(0) ,\qquad(17\text{–}15)$$

---

[6] In simplex tableaus, the coefficients of the variables in the equation, which contains as an unknown on its left-hand side the variable being set equal to zero in the basic solution, are the ones which appear in the "key," or "pivot," or "operator" row. This row is line (4) in Table 17–3 in footnote 4 of this chapter. The coefficient (−12) of the variable being maximized (X_1 in our case) is often identified with an *asterisk* as the "pivot" or "key" number (or as −12*) in the simplex tableau and is determined by dividing the constants by the coefficients of the variable being maximized, as explained in the text.

[7] This step corresponds to the procedure of interchanging the variable to be maximized and the variable to be set equal to zero. Thus, in Table 17–3 in footnote 4, the positions of X_1 and L_c would be interchanged as they have been in Table 17–4 in footnote 8.

$$L_a = 60 - 5(^{84}\!/_{12} - ^{1}\!/_{12}L_c - ^{7}\!/_{12}X_2) - 15X_2$$
$$= 25 + ^{5}\!/_{12}L_c - ^{145}\!/_{12}X_2 = 25 + (^{5}\!/_{12})(0) - (^{145}\!/_{12})(0) , \quad (17\text{–}16)$$

$$L_b = 24 - 3(^{84}\!/_{12} - ^{1}\!/_{12}L_c - ^{7}\!/_{12}X_2) - 4X_2$$
$$= 3 + ^{1}\!/_{4}L_c - ^{9}\!/_{4}X_2 = 3 + (^{1}\!/_{4})(0) - (^{9}\!/_{4})(0) . \quad (17\text{–}17)$$

And so, in Equations (17–14) through (17–17), since X_2 and L_c are *both equal to zero,* we again have four equations in four unknowns, and the values of our unknowns are:

$$X_1 = ^{84}\!/_{12} = 7 , \quad (17\text{–}14')$$

$$R = 140 , \quad (17\text{–}15')$$

$$L_a = 60 - 5(^{84}\!/_{12}) = 25 , \quad (17\text{–}16')$$

and

$$L_b = 24 - 3(^{84}\!/_{12}) = 3 . \quad (17\text{–}17')$$

Since R is now \$140, the situation at E is a definite improvement over that at O, although R is not yet at its optimum level. For the coefficient of X_2, or $^{10}\!/_3$, in our objective Equation (17–15) in this basic solution is still positive. Thus, a further iteration will be required. Before it is undertaken, a review of what has been done so far will be worthwhile.

The Simplex Procedure Summarized

The procedure used above can be briefly summarized as follows. *First, select as the variable to be maximized that variable in the objective equation of the basic solution* [Equation (17–1a)] *which has the greatest positive coefficient.* (In our case, since $P_{X_1}X_1 = 20X_1$ while $P_{X_2}X_2 = 15X_2$, we selected X_1 as the variable to be maximized, thereby undertaking to move from O to E in Figure 17–4.)

Second, find the variable which is to be set equal to zero in the new basic solution in place of the variable being maximized, so that the number of equations and the number of unknowns will remain equal. To do so, divide each of the coefficients of the variable being maximized (X_1 in our case) *into the constants* (the solution values of L_a, L_b, and L_c) *in the equations which represent constraints. Then select as the variable to be set equal to zero in the new basic solution that variable appearing on the left-hand side of these equations which is associated with the smallest quotient produced by the indicated division.* [In our case, the variable, L_c, on the left-hand side of Equation (17–12a) was selected.] This quotient represents the maximum amount of the variable being maximized which can be produced subject to *all* of the constraints.

Third, solve for the value of the variable being maximized (X_1 in our case) *that equation which contains on its left-hand side the variable which has been set equal to zero.* [In our case this is Equation (17–12a), since L_c is the variable taking a zero value in the new basic solution and appears on the left in that equation.]

Fourth, substitute the value found in step three above for the variable being maximized (X_1) *into the remaining constraints and into the objective equation and solve these equations for the new values of the unknowns in the new basic solution.* (Keep in mind that all of the variables on the right-hand side in these equations have zero values.)

Finally, fifth, although we have not yet covered this step, repeat the procedure just described as many times as necessary, moving from corner to corner of the feasible region until all of the coefficients of the variables in the objective equation applying to the given basic solution are either zero or negative, i.e., until the optimality condition has been met, and the problem is solved.

The Corner at E: Economic Meanings of the Coefficients

Our optimality condition requires that the coefficients of all the variables in the objective equation of the basic solution must be no greater than zero for the solution to be optimal. Is this condition fulfilled at E? Consider our new objective Equation (17–15) at E, which reads:

$$R = 0 + 140 - \tfrac{5}{3}L_c + \tfrac{10}{3}X_2 . \tag{17–15}$$

The condition is not fulfilled. Although the coefficient of L_c (or $-\tfrac{5}{3}$) is negative, the coefficient of X_2 is positive, or $\tfrac{10}{3} = 3.33$. Thus, the marginal revenue of X_2 at E is \$3.33, and total revenue can be further increased by increasing production of X_2, even though this action results in reduction of output of X_1. The procedure to be employed in increasing production of X_2 at the expense of X_1 is, as has been noted, simply a repetition of the procedure described in the preceding section. However, before we proceed to an optimum solution, it will be worthwhile examining the equations which have just been solved to see what *economic meanings* can be given to the various coefficients of the variables in them. These coefficients are the hearts of the various different computational tableaus and rules which have been invented (and modified) to solve linear programming problems mechanically.

Therefore, let us again write Equation (17–14), which defines the value of X_1 at E, and proceed to analyze it. The equation reads:

$$X_1 = \tfrac{84}{12} - \tfrac{1}{12}L_c - \tfrac{7}{12}X_2 . \tag{17–14}$$

The first term on the right in this equation ($\tfrac{84}{12} = 7$) has already been identified as the maximum amount of X_1 which can be produced when X_2 is zero and input c has been fully utilized at E. What are the meanings of the coefficients of L_c and X_2 in this equation?

The coefficient of L_c, or $-\frac{1}{12}$, represents the amount of X_1 which must be given up if an additional unit of c is to be left unutilized or left-over. For we know from Table 17–2 that 12 units of c are required to produce one unit of X_1. Thus the reciprocal of -12, or $-\frac{1}{12}$, represents the opportunity cost of using input c in some other way than in production of X_1 at E. That is, $\frac{1}{12}$ of a unit of X_1 must be given up to make available one unit of input c at E.

Similarly, the coefficient of X_2, or $-\frac{7}{12}$, represents the marginal cost of X_2 in terms of X_1. Reference to Table 17–2 will show that the amount of input c required to produce one unit of X_2 is seven units. And so, since one unit of input c costs $\frac{1}{12}$ of a unit of X_1, it follows that one unit of X_2 can be produced only if $(7)(\frac{1}{12}) = \frac{7}{12}$ of one unit of X_1 is given up at E, when input c is fully utilized.[8]

In the same way, an economic meaning can be given to the coefficients of the variables in the remaining equations which describe the new situation at E. In order to do so, it is helpful to enclose in brackets those numbers which enter into the computation of these coefficients. Note also, in the following equations, that X_2 has been factored out of the last term on the right in each of them, so that they read:

---

[8] The new values in the key or pivot row (or line) representing the new basic solution in a new simplex tableau are produced by dividing all of the old coefficients in that row other than the key or pivot number by the coefficient (or its negative as the case may be) of the variable being maximized, that is to say, by the key or pivot number. The new value which replaces the old key or pivot element is merely the reciprocal of the old key or pivot element. Equation (17–14) thus illustrates both these rules, since all of the new coefficients of the variables in that equation are merely the old coefficients from Equation (17–12a), divided by the negative of the pivot or key number. The result appears in line (4) of our new simplex tableau or matrix (Table 17–4), in which the positions of X_1 and L_c have been interchanged.

The result of the application of these two rules and of interchanging the positions of X_1 and L_c in Table 17–3 is illustrated by the new values appearing in our new tableau, Table 17–4, or

Table 17–4

A SECOND ILLUSTRATIVE SIMPLEX TABLEAU

Unknowns	Solution Values	Zero Valued Variables		Line Number
		L_c	X_2	
R		$-\frac{20}{12}$		(1)
L_a		$\frac{5}{12}$		(2)
L_b		$\frac{3}{12}$		(3)
X_1	$8\frac{4}{12}$	$-\frac{1}{12}$	$-\frac{7}{12}$	(4)

$$\text{(1)} \qquad\qquad \text{(2)} \qquad\qquad\qquad \text{(3)}$$

$$R = [\ 0 + (20)(^{84}\!/_{12})] - [(20)(\tfrac{1}{12})\ ]L_c + [\ \ 15 - (20)(^{7}\!/_{12})\ ]X_2\ ;$$
$$\text{(17--15a)}$$

$$L_a = [60 - (5)(^{84}\!/_{12})\ ] - [\ (5)(-\tfrac{1}{12})]L_c + [-15 - (5)(-^{7}\!/_{12})]X_2\ ;$$
$$\text{(17--16a)}$$

$$L_b = [24 - (3)(^{84}\!/_{12})\ ] - [\ (3)(-\tfrac{1}{12})]L_c + [\ -4 - (3)(-^{7}\!/_{12})]X_2\ .$$
$$\text{(17--17a)}$$

Consider now Column (1), or the first terms in brackets on the right in these equations. These terms are merely the new solution values of the variables in the position at E. They have been discussed in conjunction with Equations (17--14$'$) through (17--17$'$) earlier. $R, L_a,$ and L_b represent, respectively, the new total revenue at E, and the amounts of inputs a and b leftover or unutilized when X_1 is maximized.[9]

Next, examine the coefficients of L_c, the second group of terms in brackets on the right [Column(2)] of these equations. The coefficient of L_c in Equation (17--15a) shows the way in which total revenue declines as use of input c is decreased by one unit or as the unutilized or leftover amount of input c (or L_c) is increased by one unit. Thus,

$$\Delta R_1 = -(20)(\tfrac{1}{12}) = (20)(-\tfrac{1}{12}) = -\tfrac{5}{3}\ .$$

This coefficient is equal to the price of X_1, the coefficient of X_1 (or 20) in the original objective equation, multiplied by the amount of X_1 which can be produced ($\tfrac{1}{12}$) from the use of one unit of c. In short, *this coefficient is really the marginal revenue product of c in the production of X_1 or* $MRP_{c_{X_1}}$! The minus sign means that output of X_1 falls. See the L_c column in the table in footnote 8.

In the same way, the coefficient of L_c in Equation (17--16a) shows the reduction in the use of input a (or the increase in the amount of a leftover) which results from reducing output of X_1 (by $\tfrac{1}{12}$ of one unit) in order to reduce use of input c by one unit, thereby making the latter available for production of X_2. Thus,

$$\Delta L_{a_1} = -(5)(-\tfrac{1}{12}) = \tfrac{5}{12}\ .$$

[9] The first terms in brackets on the right [Column (1)] in these equations represent an illustration of the rule that the new value of each of the constants in our equations, except that of the constant in the equation containing the limiting constraint [Equation (17--13)], is equal to the old value of the constant in a given equation, *plus the product* of the old coefficient in that equation of the variable being maximized and the new value of the variable being maximized. The new value of L_a at E, Equation (17--16a) for example, is merely the old value of L_a at O in Figure 17--4, or 60, *plus the product* of the old coefficient (-5) of the variable being maximized (X_1) and the new value of that variable, or $84/12 = 7$. Thus, the new value is $L_a = 60 + (-5)\,(7) = 25$. For an illustration of a use of the rule, see Dorfman, Samuelson, and Solow, *op. cit.*, p. 91. However, this rule is not much used in simplex tableau computations, since the values in question can be determined also by a broader rule explained later in footnote 11.

And, also in the same way, the coefficient of L_c in Equation (17–17a) is produced by multiplying the reduction in the use of b, when output of X_1 falls by one unit (or 3), by the amount of X_1 which must be given up to reduce the use of input c by one unit.[10]

Now, finally, consider the coefficients of X_2 in Column (3) of these equations. In Equation (17–15a), the coefficient of X_2 is the marginal revenue of X_2 at E. That is, we can define the change in total revenue resulting from production of an additional unit of X_2 as equal to the amount of revenue obtained from sale of an additional unit of X_2 (or to the price of a unit of X_2 equal to 15 dollars), *less* the loss in total revenue resulting from the reduction in production of X_1 which must occur at E if an additional unit of X_2 is to be produced. And so, since the price of a unit of X_1 is 20 dollars, but only $\frac{7}{12}$ of a unit of X_1 must be sacrificed in order to produce one unit of X_2, we have the coefficient as

$$\Delta R_2 = 15 - (20)(\tfrac{7}{12}) = 15 - 11.67 = 3.33 = \tfrac{10}{3}.$$

Similarly, the coefficient of X_2 in Equation (17–16a) is the amount of input a which will be used up in the production of an additional unit of X_2 at E (or 15 units of a), less the amount of a used in the production of a unit of X_1 (or 5), multiplied by the amount of X_1 which must be sacrificed ($\frac{7}{12}$ of one unit) if an additional unit of X_2 is to be produced. Thus we have

$$\Delta L_{a_2} = -15 - (5)(-\tfrac{7}{12}) = -\tfrac{145}{12}.$$

And the coefficient of X_2 in Equation (17–17a) has a similar meaning in terms of input b.[11]

---

[10] The terms on the right in brackets in Column (2) of these equations are an illustration of the rule that the new coefficients of all the variables except that of the pivot or key variable in the column of the variable set equal to zero, generally identified as the *key* or *pivot* column, can be determined by dividing the old coefficients in that column by the key or pivot number and, if negative, depending on the way in which the table has been constructed. Since multiplication of such an old coefficient by the reciprocal of the pivot is the same thing as dividing the old coefficient by the pivot, this rule is illustrated by Column (2) above. In Table 17–4 in footnote 8, the values produced in this way, or, alternatively, the values in Column (2) of our equations, are entered into the L_c column, which then is the key or pivot column in the new basic solution. Some tableaus do not require the use of this rule. For an example of the use of the rule, see Vajda, *op. cit.*, chap. xiv, or Baumol, *op. cit.*, pp. 82–83.

[11] The method of computing the coefficients of the variables in brackets in Column (3) of our equations is an illustration of the general rule used in all simplex tableaus to provide the values of all the coefficients not determined by any of the other rules stated in previous footnotes. This rule, as we have seen from the explanation in the text of the way in which the new coefficients in Column (3) are determined, is not difficult to apply in practice, although the statement of it in words makes it sound forbidding. All the un-

One point of considerable importance has emerged from the preceding analysis of the meaning of the coefficients of the variables in our equations: the marginal revenue of X_2 is positive at E, and thus total revenue can be increased further by increasing production of X_2, even if this means reducing the production of X_1. Alternatively, since some of the coefficients of our variables are still greater than zero at E, a further iteration is indicated, for the optimal solution has not yet been found.

We could, of course, next reduce output of X_1 to zero and maximize production of X_2 in our equations, but such a procedure would mean jumping from point E in Figure 17–4 to point B, and we will generally find the optimum solution more quickly if we move systematically from corner to corner, that is, if we move along the boundary line from corner to corner consecutively. Moreover, if there are a great many corner positions in the problem, unless we move systematically from point to point, we may have difficulty in keeping our movements straight. (The various simplex computational devices which have been invented are most helpful in this respect, although in our simple illustration we are using the diagram in Figure 17–4 for this purpose.) Our next movement should, therefore, be from E to G in Figure 17–4.

The Move from E to G: A Second Iteration

We know from the preceding analysis that the coefficient (marginal revenue) of X_2 is still positive at E, and thus our next trial-and-error solution must involve an increase in production of X_2 and a decrease in production of X_1. But what variable should now be set equal to zero, as X_2 is increased from zero? Remember: if X_2 is to be made greater than zero, some other variable must become zero, or we will have more unknowns than equations.

We must repeat the procedure summarized earlier. That is, we must first write *the equations representing constraints* at E as follows:

---

determined coefficients in Table 17–4 can be obtained by means of this rule and entered into the blank row and column intersections in the table. The rule is:

| New value of an element or new coefficient | = | The corresponding old coefficient | − | Old coefficient from the same row in the key or pivot column | × | Old coefficient from the same column in the key or pivot row divided by the key number or the pivot. |

Thus, $\Delta L_{b_2} = (-4) - (3)(-\frac{7}{12}) = (-4) - (-3)\left(\frac{-7}{-12}\right)$. (See Table 17–3.)

This use of this rule is illustrated in all of the explanations of the use of the simplex tableau in the references cited in footnote 4. It also encompasses the rule stated in footnote 7. Thus, rules and a tableau together can be used to solve the problem.

$$X_1 = 7 - \tfrac{1}{12}L_c \boxed{- \tfrac{7}{12}X_2}, \qquad (17\text{-}14)$$
$$L_a = 25 + \tfrac{5}{12}L_c \boxed{- 145\tfrac{1}{12}X_2}, \qquad (17\text{-}16)$$

and

$$L_b = 3 + \tfrac{1}{4}L_c \boxed{- \tfrac{9}{4}X_2}. \qquad (17\text{-}17)$$

As before, a box has been drawn to enclose the column of X_2 values and their coefficients to emphasize the fact that X_2 is now the variable to be maximized. And, as before, we merely divide the coefficients into the total amount of X_1 being produced and into the amounts of the inputs (a and b) remaining unused at E (7, 25, and 3, respectively), ignoring signs, to learn which variable should next be set equal to zero. The smallest quotient obtained will identify the variable representing the most significant limitation of output of X_2 at E when X_1 is being maximized. Performing the operation, we have the quotient in the case of X_1 as $(7)(\tfrac{12}{7}) = 12$. Similarly, in the case of L_a we have the quotient as $2\tfrac{2}{29}$, and in the case of L_b we have the quotient as $1\tfrac{1}{3}$. The smallest value is $1\tfrac{1}{3}$, and, since it is associated with L_b, we see that L_b must next be set equal to zero in place of X_2. (Recall that L_c is already equal to zero.)

We must next solve Equation (17-17), which contains L_b on its left-hand side, for X_2, the variable to be maximized. And so, by adding $\tfrac{9}{4}X_2$ to both sides of Equation (17-17) and subtracting L_b from both sides, we have

$$\tfrac{9}{4}X_2 = 3 + \tfrac{1}{4}L_c - L_b. \qquad (17\text{-}18)$$

Further, by dividing both sides by $\tfrac{9}{4}$, we have the value of X_2 at G in Figure 17-4 as

$$X_2 = \frac{3}{\tfrac{9}{4}} + \frac{\tfrac{1}{4}}{\tfrac{9}{4}}L_c - \frac{1}{\tfrac{9}{4}}L_b \qquad (17\text{-}19)$$
$$= \tfrac{4}{3} + \tfrac{1}{9}L_c - \tfrac{4}{9}L_b = \tfrac{4}{3} + \tfrac{1}{9}(0) - \tfrac{4}{9}(0).$$

Next, substituting *this* value of X_2 into Equations (17-15) through (17-17), we have (the actual work will be omitted, and only the final simplified results are shown) the values of our other variables at G in Figure 17-4:

$$R = 144.44 - 35\tfrac{5}{27}L_c - 40\tfrac{5}{27}L_b = 144.44 - (35\tfrac{5}{27})(0) - (40\tfrac{5}{27})(0), \qquad (17\text{-}20)$$

$$L_a = 80\tfrac{5}{9} - 25\tfrac{5}{27}L_c + 145\tfrac{5}{27}L_b = 80\tfrac{5}{9} - (25\tfrac{5}{27})(0) + (145\tfrac{5}{27})(0), \qquad (17\text{-}21)$$

$$X_1 = 56\tfrac{5}{9} - 4\tfrac{5}{27}L_c + \tfrac{7}{27}L_b = 56\tfrac{5}{9} - (4\tfrac{5}{27})(0) + (\tfrac{7}{27})(0). \qquad (17\text{-}22)$$

In our new *objective* Equation (17–20) at G, the coefficients of the variables are all less than zero. Thus, the conditions of an optimum have been fulfilled, and G in Figure 17–4 represents an optimal solution.

The Corner at G: The Equations of the Optimal Solution Analyzed

Since L_b and L_c are both zero at G, there are exactly as many inputs being fully utilized (2) as there are outputs (X_1 and X_2) produced (2). Since the coefficients of L_b and L_c in the objective equation are less than zero, the optimality condition is satisfied. And so both the basic theorem of linear programming and the optimality condition are satisfied at G. Moreover, since L_b and L_c are both equal to zero, we can readily see from the first terms on the right in Equations (17–19) to 17–22) that

$$R = 144.44 \, ,$$

$$L_a = {}^{80}\!/_9 = 8\,{}^{8}\!/_9 \, ,$$

$$X_1 = {}^{56}\!/_9 = 6\,{}^{2}\!/_9 \, ,$$

and

$$X_2 = {}^{4}\!/_3 = 1\,{}^{1}\!/_3 \, .$$

The results are, of course, precisely the same as those which were obtained by the use of the complete description method earlier.

E. SIMPLEX METHOD: DUAL PROBLEM; SPECIAL PROBLEMS

The Dual Problem

One solution to the dual problem has already been given. The method of solving the dual problem independently by the simplex method is similar to the method of solving the primal problem. The simplex tableaus and computational rules explained in the references given in footnote 4 can also be employed. However, if the primal problem has been solved, so has the dual problem. Thus the shadow or accounting prices of the inputs c and b as determined in the solution to the dual problem are the coefficients of the variables taking a zero value in the optimal solution of the primal problem. That is, our Equation (17–20),

$$R = 144.44 - {}^{35}\!/_{27}\,L_c - {}^{40}\!/_{27}L_b \, , \tag{17–20}$$

shows that the marginal valuation of L_c at G in Figure 17–4 is ${}^{35}\!/_{27}$ and that of L_b at the same point is ${}^{40}\!/_{27}$.

Special Problems

Not all linear programming problems can be worked out as easily as the one solved in this chapter. However, a discussion of the methods of solution which are adopted when, for example, in deciding which variable to set equal to zero, division of the values in the constant column by the coefficients of the variable being maximized results in ties is beyond the scope of this book. So is the question of degeneracy, and so are questions of nonlinear programming and integer programming. These topics are covered in various works devoted exclusively or primarily to the subject of linear programming, and the interested student may be referred to the list of readings at the end of this chapter and to the references in footnote 4.

F. LINEAR PROGRAMMING AND WELFARE ECONOMICS

It has been demonstrated by some writers that the shadow prices and the allocation of resources which would be produced by a set of equations describing a linear program for the economy as a whole are precisely the same as those which would be produced automatically in a perfectly competitive economic system[12] or those which have already been explained in Chapter 16. Such a proof, however, does not result in a statement of the conditions of an absolute maximum, for it, like the other proofs of contemporary welfare economics mentioned in Chapters 1 and 16, rests upon the assumptions that the distribution of income can be taken as given and that the wants are ultimate data.

It seems unlikely that linear programming techniques have much to offer in this respect or that they provide the basis for a new welfare economics. Their principal usefulness seems to lie in the field of business administration and in the areas of governmental management in which they were first developed.[13] In the area of social policy, the use of such techniques poses many problems. For, in this area, the values of the coefficients in the objective equation must be determined by reference to noneconomic factors. What, for example, is the importance to society of increased expenditures on education or scientific research relative to the importance of increased expenditures on color television or mink coats, and how is it to be determined? As we have seen in the preceding chapter, this problem involves the specification of a Social Welfare Function, and neither linear programming nor price theory provides a method of determining such a function. Questions of this nature also arise in attempts to solve the problems of economic growth and development which will be briefly considered in the next chapter, the final one in this book.

---

[12] Dorfman, Samuelson, and Solow, *op. cit.,* chap. xiv.
[13] See Vajda, *op. cit.*

SELECTED READINGS

BAUMOL, WILLIAM J. "Activity Analysis in One Lesson," *American Economic Review,* Vol. XLVIII (December, 1958), pp. 837–73.

————. *Economic Theory and Operations Analysis.* Englewood Cliffs, N.J.: Prentice-Hall, Inc., 1961. (An excellent book for the reader without mathematical training.)

BOULDING, KENNETH E., AND SPIVEY, W. ALLEN (eds.). *Linear Programming and the Theory of the Firm.* New York: The Macmillan Co., 1960.

DORFMAN, ROBERT. "'Mathematical' or 'Linear' Programming: A Non-Mathematical Exposition," *American Economic Review,* Vol. XLIII (December, 1953), pp. 797–825.

————; SAMUELSON, PAUL A.; AND SOLOW, ROBERT M. *Linear Programming and Economic Analysis.* New York: McGraw-Hill Book Co., Inc., 1958. (This book is for mathematically trained readers. However, the general reader will benefit from reading pages 1–5, which contain an historical sketch of the technique.)

HENDERSON, JAMES M., AND QUANDT, RICHARD E. *Microeconomic Theory,* pp. 75–82. New York: McGraw-Hill Book Co., Inc., 1958.

VAJDA, S. *Readings in Linear Programming.* New York: John Wiley & Sons, Inc., 1958.

BEYOND STATIC PRICE THEORY

PART VIII

BEYOND STATIC PRICE THEORY

18 Profits and Progress: Defenses and Criticisms of Price Theory

Introduction

This is our concluding chapter. The time for a summing up and an evaluation is now at hand. In Chapters 2 through 16, we have been concerned with a careful and quite rigorous development of the elements of static price theory. Chapter 16, which dealt with an explanation of the static Paretian welfare conditions, marked the capstone of this structure. In Chapter 17, we studied linear programming as an example of a recent mathematical technique applied in the area of price theory, and we noted that Professors Dorfman, Samuelson, and Solow have demonstrated that, assuming wants as data and the distribution of income as given, one complicated linear program solved by an electronic computer for the economy as a whole would produce precisely the same allocation of resources as would be produced in the long run under conditions of perfect competition. In short, the computer would produce the conditions of the Paretian optimum as a solution to the problem. Thus, most of the problems first mentioned briefly in Chapter 1 have now been discussed in considerable detail.

One problem, however, remains: to what extent can the general model of price theory be employed in solving problems of economic growth and development? It is to this final question that we must now turn, and, in considering it, we will necessarily examine the rationalization of profit as a payment for entrepreneurship in a dynamic economy which was provided by Professor J. A. Schumpeter, as well as some general defenses and criticisms of price theory.[1]

---

[1] Parts of this chapter draw heavily on my article, "Institutions and Technology in Economic Progress," *American Journal of Economics and Sociology,* Vol. XIX (January, 1960), pp. 139–50.

Schumpeter's original thesis was that profits do not exist in a stable, stationary economy under conditions of perfect competition but are payments accruing to entrepreneurs in a *dynamic* system in return for their extraordinary intelligence and foresight in finding new and more valuable ways of using inputs.[2] His position concerning the absence of pure profits in a perfectly competitive economy in a long-run equilibrium position is identical to that of J. B. Clark (as explained in Chapter 12). Thus, Schumpeter's theory of economic development takes as its point of departure a model of a perfectly competitive economy similar to that described in Chapter 2 and seeks to carry the analysis beyond the limits of traditional static price theory by making profits the incentive for innovation.

At the same time, in its final form, the Schumpeterian theory rejects the static welfare conclusions drawn from the general model (such as those explained in Chapters 11 and 16) and argues that the "strategy" of large-scale establishments or units of control "which looks so restrictive when viewed in the individual case or from the individual point of time" has "come to be the most powerful engine" of economic progress and "in particular of the long run expansion of total output."[3] His theory has been identified as a description of the "capitalist process through historic time." A somewhat similar but not identical position has recently been taken by Professor J. M. Clark who, as we will see later, has suggested alternative but rather imprecise dynamic approaches to the problem. Clark emphasizes the *process* of competition as the source of economic progress.

Aside from the rather technical criticism of the general model of price theory on grounds that it is not dynamic (which appears in the work of the two writers mentioned above), other economists have different views about the extent to which the general model and the marginal analysis can be usefully employed in dealing with problems of steady economic growth, either in industrialized or in underdeveloped countries. Some have voiced broad criticisms to the effect that the model does not take account of enough variables, and others have argued that it does not take account of the right kind of variables. This group not only accepts the Schumpeterian and Clarksian criticisms but goes beyond them and argues that the general model is either irrelevant to the real world or else represents a special case.

---

[2] Joseph A. Schumpeter, *The Theory of Economic Development,* trans. Redvers Opie (Harvard Economic Studies, Vol. XLVI) (Cambridge: Harvard University Press, 1934); Schumpeter, Business Cycles (New York: McGraw-Hill Book Co., Inc., 1939); Schumpeter, *Capitalism, Socialism and Democracy* (New York: Harper & Bros., 1950).

[3] Schumpeter, *Capitalism, Socialism and Democracy,* p. 106.

Thus, it can be argued that the Schumpeterian theory, with its assumptions of the existence of a dynamic technology and of a particular set of permissive institutions, is a special case of a more general theory first published in 1944 by Professor Clarence E. Ayres.[4] The latter emphasizes the interrelationship between institutions and technology and is, therefore, not restricted to a consideration of the *particular* set of institutions assumed in the general model of price theory.

In this concluding chapter, we will first briefly examine the Schumpeterian explanation of profits, as well as Schumpeter's argument that monopoly profits are necessary to economic progress, in the light of the broader theory developed by Ayres. Then we will briefly consider the views (pro and con) of some other contemporary economists who have devoted much time and effort to the study of problems of economic progress and to the question of the extent to which the general model and the language and concepts of price theory may be useful in dealing with such problems. Finally, this book will conclude with a brief evaluation of these views and a statement by the author of his own position.

A. THE SCHUMPETERIAN THEORY OF ECONOMIC DEVELOPMENT

A Summary of Schumpeter's Thesis

Schumpeter's theory seeks to explain changes in "economic life" which arise from *within* the economic system but not changes which are "forced upon it from without."[5] His basic thesis is relatively simple. Assume an equilibrium circular flow of money and goods in which the volume of the flow remains constant, in which the services of all the factors of production are valued according to the marginal productivity theory of income distribution, in which total income is exhausted by factor payments, and in which consumer behavior is explained by the marginal utility theory. Assume also the existence of a free enterprise economic system, a dynamic technology, an absence of governmental favor or restriction, highly developed credit-creating institutions, and full employment of inputs. In short, assume the existence of a perfectly competitive economy in a position of stable, stationary equilibrium, but one in which technology is dynamic.

Economic development is then defined as a "spontaneous and discontinuous change in the channels of the flow," a change "which for-

---

[4] Clarence E. Ayres, *The Theory of Economic Progress* (Chapel Hill: University of North Carolina Press, 1944). This book has also been published in a paperback edition (New York: Schocken Books, Inc., 1962).

[5] Schumpeter, *The Theory of Economic Development*, p. 63.

ever alters and displaces the equilibrium state previously existing."[6] Once the given change has been incorporated into the system and the circular flow is again in equilibrium at a new higher level, the process of economic development is temporarily suspended until a further change occurs and the cycle is repeated. The precise process by which such a change is incorporated into the system is next described in detail.

Since "new possibilities" of employing differently the existing factors of production "are continuously being offered by the surrounding world, *in particular new discoveries . . . continuously . . . added to the existing store of knowledge,"*[7] while at the same time the broad mass of individuals in the given economic system prefer the relative security of habitual ways of doing things and living their daily lives, an opportunity exists for entrepreneurs, who "are a special type" and explanation of whose behavior presents a "special problem,"[8] to carry out new combinations of existing resources, thereby increasing the value of the output. (Note the assumption of a dynamic technology in the quotation.)

The theory begins with an assumption that the economy is in a position of stable, stationary equilibrium and assumes full employment. Schumpeter asserts that the necessary purchasing power required to enable entrepreneurs to bid resources away from their current uses, so that they may be put into new, commercially more valuable (it is hoped) uses, will be obtained by them from credit institutions. If the hope of profit is fulfilled, "the surplus realized is *ipso facto,* a net profit."[9] Once such a new combination has been established as a result of entrepreneurial activity, "the second act of the drama" is visualized as follows:

> . . . The spell is broken and new businesses are continually arising under the impulse of the alluring profit. A complete reorganization of the industry occurs, with its increases in production, its competitive struggle, its supersession of obsolete businesses, its possible dismissal of workers and so forth. . . . Only one thing interests us here: the final result must be a new equilibrium position, in which, with new data, the law of cost again rules, so that now the prices of the products are again equal to the wages and rents of the services of labor and land. . . .[10]

After the new equilibrium position has been attained, the stage is set for an eventual repetition of the first act. Alternate stages of prosperity and depression are thus normal incidents of economic growth.

---

[6] *Ibid.,* p. 64.

[7] *Ibid.,* p. 79. (Italics mine.)

[8] *Ibid.,* p. 81.

[9] *Ibid.,* p. 131. (Italics his.)

[10] *Ibid.*

This was the original "vision." Subsequently, Schumpeter argued that "perfect competition," which implies free entry into every industry, might make it "impossible to enter at all," since the hope of profits is an essential spur to progress. Therefore, he concluded that perfect competition with freedom of entry "is incompatible" with "the bulk of what we call economic progress."[11]

Evaluation of the Schumpeterian Thesis

Schumpeter himself was careful to distinguish between *innovation* and *invention* and remarked:

Economic leadership in particular must be distinguished from "invention." As long as they are not carried into practice, inventions are economically irrelevant. And to carry any improvement into effect is a task entirely different from the inventing of it, and a task, moreover, requiring entirely different kinds of aptitudes. Although entrepreneurs of course *may* be inventors just as they may be capitalists, they are inventors not by virtue of their function but by coincidence and vice versa. Besides, the innovations which it is the function of entrepreneurs to carry out, need not necessarily be inventions at all. It is, therefore, not advisable, and it may be downright misleading, to stress the element of invention as much as many writers do.[12]

Does this mean that a dynamic technology is unimportant for economic progress? To answer this question, let us consider the types of economic development Schumpeter listed. These include: (1) introduction of a new product or of a new quality of a product; (2) "introduction of a new method of production" (an example is a "new way of handling a product commercially"); (3) opening of a new market, "whether or not this market existed before"; (4) "conquest of a new source of supply," either a newly created or a previously existing one; and (5) reorganization of any industry, "like creation of a monopoly position (for example through trustification) or the breaking up of a monopoly position."[13]

These types clearly include cases involving increases in the commercial values of products or resources resulting from artificially created scarcities and from demand-creation. It seems impossible to assign any real meaning to a measure of "economic progress" computed on the basis of the money value of the output per head of population if that money value is partly determined by either of these two methods. For this measure has meaning only to the extent that it represents increases

---

[11] Schumpeter, *Capitalism, Socialism and Democracy,* p. 105.

[12] Schumpeter, *The Theory of Economic Development,* pp. 88–89. (Italics and quotation marks his.)

[13] *Ibid.* p. 66. (Parentheses his.)

in real output, if it has meaning at all. And so, at least insofar as is concerned that part of Schumpeter's theory which is an explanation of increases in the money value of output not due to artificial creation of scarcities or of demand, the theory does assume a dynamic technology. More than this: in the theory, the entrepreneur is treated as a *particular* type of technological device for introducing changes into a given type of economic system. Innovation and invention, we will see later, are both technological in nature. The Schumpeterian theory requires performance of the entrepreneurial function and a set of *permissive* social institutions, along with a dynamic technology.

Some writers have argued that the theory is inapplicable to underdeveloped countries because of its emphasis of private entrepreneurship.[14] But Schumpeter himself recognized that entrepreneurship may take different forms. The fact that, in underdeveloped countries, government officials may perform the entrepreneurial function is not really inconsistent with his basic thesis. The important element in his theory is the *function* of entrepreneurship, *not its form*.[15] Nevertheless, important though this element may be, it is *not enough alone* to explain economic progress. As Professor Benjamin Higgins has also pointed out, although it contains valuable insights, the Schumpeterian thesis does not state an operationally meaningful hypothesis. It assumes the existence of permissive institutions. That is, in a society in which development is occurring, the theory necessarily leads to the conclusion that the institutions are permissive, but it provides no way of identifying a set of permissive institutions.[16]

Empirical Studies

Professor Jacob Schmookler has recently sought to test the timing of the appearance of entrepreneurs as postulated by the Schumpeterian theory. By making a comparison of data relating to issuance of patents with indexes of economic activity, he has tentatively concluded that "invention and innovation are the responses of creative men to much the same stimuli which influence the economic behavior of other men," and he has found a "strong tendency for invention in a field to rise and

---

[14] See the summary of the critical literature and the defenses of Schumpeter on this point by Douglas Rimmer, "Schumpeter and the Underdeveloped Countries," *Quarterly Journal of Economics,* Vol. LXXV (August, 1961), pp. 422–50.

[15] All economists might not agree with this statement, however. On the question of forms of entrepreneurship, see Leo Silberman, "Evolution of Entrepreneurship in the Process of Economic Development," *Annals of the American Academy of Political and Social Science,* Vol. CCCV (May, 1956), p. 44.

[16] See Benjamin Higgins, *Economic Development* (New York: W. W. Norton & Co., Inc., 1959), pp. 141–42.

fall with the volume of sales in the field . . . to which the inventions relate."[17] In short, inventions increase as sales increase. On the other hand, Professor William H. Brown has studied the question of innovation in the machine tool industry and concluded that "innovation occurs when the demand for machine tools falls."[18]

What is interesting about these two studies is not that they contradict each other but that both refute Schumpeter's contention that entrepreneurs appear when the economy is "in equilibrium." Schumpeter's theory represents one possible explanation of how economic growth *may* occur, given the appropriate and necessary conditions, but it is *not the only* explanation. From the point of view of this book, his theory is an interesting example of an attempt to utilize the general model of price theory as a part of a dynamic analysis and an example of an attempt to rationalize monopolistic profits. But it can also be argued that his theory is merely a special case of a much broader theory, to be discussed next.

B. CLARENCE AYRES AND THE THEORY OF ECONOMIC PROGRESS

Professor Clarence Ayres has built upon foundations laid by Thorstein Veblen and John Dewey[19] and made a significant contribution of his own to the theory of economic progress. He has long argued that human behavior can be regarded as having two aspects, one *technological* and the other *institutional* or ceremonial, and that the progress of a culture through time can be analyzed in terms of the interaction between these two strategic variables, which are defined as functional categories for the purposes of his analysis; and he has undertaken to explain the relationship between the institutions and the dynamic technology which Schumpeter assumes.

Institutions as Variables

According to Ayres, since institutions and institutional behavior are considered a functional category, these terms refer to a certain type of social organization or to a particular aspect of social behavior which is

[17] Jacob Schmookler, "Invention, Innovation, and Business Cycles," *Variability of Private Investment in Plant and Equipment*, Part II (Joint Economic Committee, 87th Cong., 2d sess.) (Washington, D.C.: U.S. Government Printing Office, 1962), pp. 45–55, esp. p. 54; and see, also, National Bureau of Economic Research, *The Rate and Direction of Inventive Activity: Economic and Social Factors* (Special Conference Series, Vol. XIII) (Princeton: Princeton University Press, 1962).

[18] William H. Brown, "Innovation in the Machine Tool Industry," *Quarterly Journal of Economics*, Vol. LXXI (August, 1957), pp. 406–25.

[19] See Clarence E. Ayres, "The Co-ordinates of Institutionalism," *American Economic Review*, Papers and Proceedings, Vol. XLI (May, 1951), p. 50; and Ayres, *Toward a Reasonable Society* (Austin: University of Texas Press, 1961), pp. 27–32. (This section has been read by Professor Ayres and has benefited from his comments.)

qualitatively different from other aspects of social organization. Such behavior is not restricted to relations between persons and persons alone; it may involve relations between persons and things which are prescribed by habitual ways of thinking. Ayres argues that a number of special characteristics are common to all institutions and, indeed, that this fact is a basis for identifying institutional behavior. Among these characteristics are the following: institutions and ceremonial behavior are concerned with the determination of authority, with conferring rank and status on individuals; institutions involve behavior defined by mores (customs which have the force of moral law); myths are employed to explain the "rightness" of the mores and the validity of status; ceremonies are utilized to induce and publicize the status changes; and, finally, the institutions are supported and strengthened by the appeal they make to the emotions of the individuals who constitute the community in which the institutions exist.[20]

Ayres also notes that the institutions of any given community must be closely related in equilibrium and that a community is not in equilibrium unless its members share the same general beliefs, observe the same mores, respect the same authority, and participate in the same ceremonial observances. He then points out that the institutional behavior function is essentially static:

> For institutional behavior is peculiarly past-binding. The mores derive their authority from the past. The legends derive their authenticity from the past. The whole reference of every system of authority and status is to the past. To resist change is therefore the peculiar function of every such "establishment."[21]

In short, by its very nature, the institutional function sooner or later plays the part of a barrier to economic progress. Note that Schumpeter's theory also requires a stable society as its starting point. Schumpeter argues that the entrepreneur must conquer the resistance of tradition and the problems of uncertainty.[22] He must be the type of individual who will overcome the difficulty to be found in "the reaction of the social environment against one who wishes to do something new."[23]

But the resistance to change found in the institutional behavior pattern is not a *sufficient* condition in the Schumpeterian theory, even though it is a *necessary* condition. Similarly, the existence of the entre-

---

[20] For a further discussion, see Clarence E. Ayres, *The Industrial Economy* (Boston: Houghton Mifflin Co., 1952), pp. 43 ff; and Ayres, *Toward a Reasonable Society*, pp. 123–38.

[21] Ayres, *The Industrial Economy*, pp. 49–50. (Quotation marks his.)

[22] Schumpeter, *The Theory of Economic Development*, pp. 85–93.

[23] *Ibid.*, p. 86.

preneurs alone, without the dynamic technology, is a *necessary* but not a *sufficient* condition. It is *just* to the ability of the entrepreneur to overcome resistance to change and to introduce the fruits of the new technology into the economic system that Schumpeter attributes progress. The existence of a dynamic technology is, therefore, also a *necessary* condition in his theory, but he assumes its existence and does not explain it; and, so, his theory is incomplete.

Technology as a Variable

Since he describes institutional behavior as "past-binding" and identifies it as a barrier to economic progress, Ayres looks elsewhere and finds that *technology* is the dynamic element in economic progress. Technology is defined simply as the sum of all human tools and skills (skill being further defined as tool-behavior). The entrepreneur uses the tools of credit and calculation; he has a special skill in their use. Just as institutional behavior dominates some aspects of social organization, so does tool-behavior dominate others. Indeed, in any given activity, both functions may be present. Even the singing of a hymn during a religious service may require the use of a hymn book. Activities can be classified on the basis of which of the behavior patterns, institutional or technological, dominates; quibbling about borderline cases is fruitless.

But technology is not merely a human behavior function. It is a tool function as well, and the tools themselves play an important part in economic progress. For tools are capable of being combined and recombined with other tools to make different tools. New inventions and discoveries depend not only upon human ingenuity but also upon the previous existence of tools and devices. Ayres states that the "range of possible combinations is of course that of the natural universe."[24]

The technological process is cumulative. But, though technology is dynamic, economic progress must be recognized as a function of both variables. Unless the institutions are sufficiently permissive, technological progress may be extremely slow. *The theory does not state that technological progress must inevitably prevail.*

As a case in point, one may note that Russia, having placed men and tools in a particular relationship to each other in order to develop its man-in-space program, acquired a long lead over the United States for precisely the reason that the United States did not create a similar situation sufficiently early in point of time. The United States, on the other hand, has acquired a similar long lead in the production of mechanical

---

[24] Ayres, *Toward a Reasonable Society,* p. 113.

toothbrushes for analogous reasons. Invention, it should be pointed out, does not result from need, but, at a given point in time, need may affect the extent to which men and things are placed in a situation favorable to a particular kind of invention. So may the prospect of profit. Schmookler's finding—that patent issues and levels of economic activity are related—may be an example of this fact; so may it explain Brown's findings concerning innovation in the machine tool industry. If the conditions precedent are satisfied, technological progress will result. This is the common sense of the so-called "crash" program and its justification as a method of fostering technological change.

The dynamic and cumulative nature of technology is an underlying assumption of the Schumpeterian conclusion that monopoly profits are necessary as a method of financing research programs of private enterprise in a dynamic economy. But this underlying assumption does not validate that conclusion, for the assumption really amounts to some kind of value judgment about the way in which that research *should* be financed, rather than to a logical demonstration of how it *must* be financed, or, for that matter, rather than to a realistic assumption about how much of it currently *is* being financed in the United States and elsewhere today.

For example, in testimony given before the Joint Economic Committee in 1960, Mr. Allen Dulles, then Director of the Central Intelligence Agency, estimated that the annual average rate of growth of gross national product in the Soviet Union between 1950–58 was about 7 percent and concluded that "Soviet GNP has been growing twice as rapidly as that of the United States" during this period.[25] Mr. Dulles emphasized that technological progress may result from crash programs and concentration of effort in particular fields when he said:

> The Soviet Union is extremely proficient in certain areas, especially in the scientific and technological fields related to its military effort. In other areas which up to the present time the Soviets have considered secondary, their performance ranges from fair to mediocre. . . .
>
> . . . Some recent visitors to the Soviet Union remarked with surprise that they can send a lunik to the moon, but don't bother to make the plumbing work.[26]

Apparently, technological progress transcends institutional systems and various kinds of political arrangements, as Ayres contends. It can occur under a dictatorship with forced labor camps, as is true in the case

---

[25] *Comparisons of the United States and Soviet Economies* (Hearings before the Joint Economic Committee, 86th Cong., 1st sess.) (Washington, D.C.: U.S. Government Printing Office, 1960), p. 6.

[26] *Ibid.,* p. 2.

of the Soviet Union—provided that freedom of inquiry is permitted in the particular "nonpolitical" subject being investigated—as well as in a free society, if enough men and tools are brought into proximity with one another. Or, as Mr. Dulles also testified concerning the Soviet Union:

> Once they have determined upon a high priority project—and they have fewer echelons of decisions to surmount than we before the final go-ahead is given—they are able to divert to this project the needed complement of the ablest technicians in the U.S.S.R. which the particular task demands. They can also quickly allocate the necessary laboratory or factory space and manpower required. Today, although their overall resources are far less than ours, they can allocate whatever is necessary if the priority is high enough.[27]

How are research and development financed in the United States today? The Joint Economic Committee of the Congress reported in March, 1962:

> The Federal Government now supports about two-thirds of the research and developmental activities of the Nation. In the calendar year 1960, the latest period for which relatively complete data are available, expenditures in the United States for research and development totaled $14 billion, exclusive of capital expenditures. This figure represents all funds for research and development, whether spent in industry or otherwise (universities, research institutes, the Government itself, or other nonprofit organizations). . . . In calendar 1960, 58 percent of the total research and development in American *industry* was financed by the Federal Government.[28]

The Committee also noted that "it is not enough merely to discover new knowledge"; the knowledge must be put to use if economic progress is to result. But "present practices raise questions" because:

> Present research funds are concentrated in a few firms and industries, with the results largely "locked up" via patents or other barriers to wide use. The contrast between the picture in industry and that which has prevailed in agriculture is startling. For almost a century, research in agriculture has been sponsored and largely financed by the Federal Government through the Department of Agriculture and State experimental stations. The results of this research have been widely disseminated by the Government both in technical publications and in nontechnical instructions to operating farmers.[29]

The Committee then pointed out that output per man-hour in agriculture had grown at about double the rate in nonagricultural industries

---

[27] *Ibid.*, p. 3.

[28] *Annual Report* (Joint Economic Committee, 87th Cong., 2d sess.) (Washington, D.C.: U.S. Government Printing Office, 1962), p. 74. (Italics mine. I have omitted a footnote reference from the quotation.)

[29] *Ibid.*, p. 75.

during the past two decades. Moreover, the Committee added that only about 8 percent of the expenditure on research in 1960 had been spent for basic research, with the balance being spent on applied research and in engineering.

It also called attention to the fact that present governmental policies with respect to expenditures of research and development funds were concentrating research and developmental activities in a very small number of industries and large firms. The effect, according to former Attorney General Herbert Brownell in 1953, was that "in the future an increasing share of anticipated improved technologies and new product lines will be introduced by the industrial giants."[30] Thus, governmental policies and governmental expenditures, and not the Schumpeterian thesis, are the explanation of a great many of the research activities of oligopolistic firms in the United States today, just as governmental policies and expenditures are the explanation of the directions of research in the Soviet Union.

With respect to directions taken by some private research activities, some of the testimony concerning the drug industry given before the Subcommittee on Monopoly and Antitrust of the Senate Judiciary Committee by Dr. A. Dale Console, a former medical director of Squibb, is both interesting and instructive. He stated (and his position was supported by other witnesses with similar backgrounds) that:

> While the industry spokesmen would have us believe that all research is on wonder drugs or better medicinal products this is no more true than the euphemism of postgraduate medical education. They stress that there are many failures for each successful drug. This is true since it is the very essence of research. *The problem arises out of the fact that they market so many of their failures.* Between these failures which are presented as new drugs, and the useless modifications of old drugs, the addition of zinc to vitamins is a good example, most of the research results in a treadmill which moves at a rapid pace but goes nowhere. Since so much depends on novelty, drugs change like women's hemlines and rapid obsolescence is simply a sign of motion, not progress as the apologists would have us believe.[31]

In short, according to Dr. Console, some of the research is devoted to developing products for which a demand *can* be created, irrespective of whether or not the product serves any real or new function; and, even though the research may result in scientific failure, success may never-

---

[30] *Ibid.*, p. 74.

[31] *Administered Prices, Drugs* (Report of the Subcommittee on Antitrust and Monopoly, Committee on the Judiciary, Senate Report No. 448, 87th Cong., 1st sess.) (Washington, D.C.: U.S. Government Printing Office, 1961), p. 127. (Italics mine. I have inserted a comma after the word "novelty.")

theless be claimed for it and the result marketed. It has private economic value but no social economic value. Another witness testified that part of the purpose of research activity in the drug industry was "to modify the original drugs, the drugs based on real research as it were, mostly to modify the original drugs just enough to get a patentable derivative, but not to change it enough to lose the original effect."[32]

The Subcommittee has remarked that:

. . . If the drug industry subordinates basic research to minor modifications which hold greater assurance of commercial success, it is merely following the pattern of American industry generally. The difference, however, is that no other industry approaches drugs in stressing its research activity as the rationale for extraordinary profitmaking.[33]

But the Schumpeterian theory stresses this point in general terms, even though the Schumpeterian case for monopoly profits as a necessary condition of technological progress in a free society is far from being clear. This much, at least, seems obvious from our brief excursion into the real world of research and development. Ayres approaches the matter from a broader base; he examines the issues in terms of the interaction between the variables, institutions and technology.

Interaction between the Two Variables

In doing so, he employs the Veblenian concept of "the cultural incidence of the machine process"—an idea that the institutions themselves change in the course of and as a result of technological progress—to point out that new scientific knowledge may impinge upon the traditional ways of looking at things, causing the institutions themselves to change. However, he notes also that, where the rate of technological progress is slow, the institutions change slowly. Where Schumpeter says "capitalist rationality supplied the habits of mind that evolved the methods" used in modern hospitals,[34] Ayres says, "When everybody is born in a hospital, the childbirth death rate is lowered, and also the birthplace loses its ceremonial significance."[35] Schumpeter's statement loses sight of the fact that technology is the dynamic function, while Ayres' statement emphasizes it.

In short, Ayres' theory of economic progress casts the long-run problem in terms of two strategic variables: institutions and technology.

---

[32] *Ibid.*, p. 130. See the testimony of Dr. Frederick H. Meyers of the University of California.

[33] *Ibid.*, p. 131.

[34] Schumpeter, *Capitalism, Socialism and Democracy*, p. 125.

[35] Ayres, *The Industrial Economy*, p. 58.

It then argues that since the degree of economic development, which has occurred and which may occur in a given area, is a function both of the accumulated and imported technology (including that embodied in books as well as that embodied in capital goods) and of the permissiveness of the institutions, the policies and methods appropriate to one area may not be applicable to another. They must be tailored to fit the facts in specific cases. That is, the theory argues that what is needed is extensive research, on a case-by-case basis, into the institutional and technological aspects of economic progress and the formulation of policies which take into account the relationship which exists in a given case between the strategic variables identified by the theory.

The Schumpeterian theory takes the model of price theory as its point of departure and assumes the existence of permissive institutions or treats them as a parameter. Ayres' theory treats the institutions as a variable. Where Schumpeter's theory, in its final version, asserts the necessity of monopoly profits as a condition precedent to economic progress, Ayres' theory points to this question as a subject for study without ruling out the possibility that Schumpeter's conclusions may be validated by empirical investigation. Other contemporary economists interested in problems of economic development are also beginning more and more to emphasize the importance of institutional factors.

C. VIEWS OF REPRESENTATIVE CONTEMPORARY ECONOMISTS

We have already noted that contemporary economists differ in their views about the usefulness of the general model of price theory as a tool to be used in explaining or dealing with problems of steady economic growth. A brief survey of some representative views will be the final task of this book.

Full Acceptance of the Model: "Economic Positivism"

P. T. Bauer, who has devoted many years to the study of underdeveloped countries especially in Asia and Africa, has argued that those who dispute "the relevance of the propositions of economics to underdeveloped countries" have an "imperfect understanding of economics" and have not observed the situation in the underdeveloped countries closely enough.[36] He has also stated his own position quite bluntly:

I am now convinced of the very wide applicability to underdeveloped countries of the basic methods of approach of economics and of the more elementary conclusions stemming from these. I am thinking especially of the elements of

---

[36] P. T. Bauer, *Economic Analysis and Policy in Underdeveloped Countries* (Durham: Duke University Press; and London: Cambridge University Press, 1957), p. 15.

supply and demand analysis and its simpler conclusions, the tendency of people to seek activities and occupations which yield the highest net advantage within the opportunities open to them, the implications of the concept of complementary and competitive relationships between productive resources, and many others.[37]

Bauer thus goes further than merely asserting that all those things which are true by definition in economics are as true in underdeveloped countries as they are in industrial countries ("the elements of supply and demand analysis"), because he also argues that people in the underdeveloped countries behave in accordance with the assumptions made by economists. He rests this part of his case largely upon numerous instances in which his own personal experiences bear out his beliefs; but generalization from personal experience is always a dangerous procedure. His argument would be much more convincing if additional evidence were presented.

A counterpart, with respect to the industrialized countries, of the testament of faith of Bauer concerning the applicability of the model to underdeveloped countries, is the statement by Professor Milton Friedman of his "personal view" that:

> Existing relative price theory, which is designed to explain the allocation of resources among alternative ends and the division of the product among the co-operating resources which reached almost its present form in Marshall's *Principles of Economics,* seems to me both extremely fruitful and deserving of much confidence for the kind of economic system which characterizes Western nations.[38]

Both writers make a distinction between "positive economics" (the manufacture and manipulation of basic definitions which are independent of political considerations) and "normative economics" (the prescription of policies) and argue that these two functions are too often confused by economists.

Limited Acceptance and Outright Rejection: "Political Economy"

On the other hand, in an interesting study of the role of the economist as an official advisor, Professor W. A. Johr and Dr. H. W. Singer state that they have difficulty in seeing how "further refinement of the price theory as begun by Hicks in his work, *Value and Capital"* (for example, the four appendices to this book!) can make any contribution to the solution of pressing and immediate problems, although they recog-

---

[37] *Ibid.*

[38] Milton Friedman, *Essays in Positive Economics* (Chicago: University of Chicago Press, 1953), pp. 41–42.

nize that it would be a mistake to discourage a scholar from engaging in pure research merely because the usefulness of his possible results cannot be foreseen. They believe that "basic research should again devote more time to studying the ideological and political influences on the economy, as well as those exerted by private organizations and pressure groups, instead of putting its main effort into further refinement of pure theory, since practical problems cannot be solved without taking these influences into consideration."[39] And, finally, they also argue that it is not possible to distinguish between economic and noneconomic aims because all aims have a noneconomic aspect.[40]

Similarly, Professors Robert Dahl and Charles Lindblom argue that political matters cannot be separated from economic matters in the real world and point out that, given a value scheme broader than that posed by the market economy, "production deserves no general priority over better income distribution or many other social goals, especially intangibles, such as justice, fair play, and an equitable distribution of status, prestige, and control."[41] They suggest also that "preoccupation with choice-allocation theory" has permitted "economists to avoid some embarrassing problems." They note that, while one of the significant contributions "of the price system to economizing is that it makes possible manageable agendas," the mere simplification of the problems to be solved does not "necessarily result in a more vigorous pursuit of resource development and high resource output."[42] Finally, they point out that the price system is also a form of control and that "each form of control . . . has its characteristic frustrations."[43]

In contrast to the position of P. T. Bauer and his reliance upon his personal observations in underdeveloped countries as a basis for the conclusion that people in underdeveloped countries behave in accordance with the basic maximization behavior assumption made by economists, there is the position of Professor Walter C. Neale, who has devoted much time to the study of the Indian economy. He has argued that even though the Indian peasant farmer does not seek to make the marginal money cost of production equal to marginal revenue, he is not the less rational for all of that. Professor Neale believes that we need to devote funds to research designed for "developing a picture of the Indian

---

[39] W. A. Johr and H. W. Singer, *The Role of the Economist as Official Advisor*, trans. Jane Degras and Stephen Frowein (London: George Allen & Unwin, Ltd., 1955), p. 10.

[40] *Ibid.*, p. 111.

[41] Robert E. Dahl and Charles E. Lindblom, *Politics, Economics and Welfare* (New York: Harper & Bros., 1953), p. xxi and p. 133.

[42] *Ibid.*, p. 163 and p. 454.

[43] *Ibid.*, p. 471.

farmer" and for discovery of the factors "most relevant to peasant decisions: the importance of self-sufficiency, of family unity, of personal prestige, of family secrecy, of farmer-employee relations, of inter-caste relationships, of the availability and characteristics of the markets in which the peasant buys and sells," and a host of others.[44]

Similarly, Professor Benjamin Higgins, in a detailed and authoritative study of economic development, has concluded that the traditional tools of economic analysis are inadequate for the task of analyzing problems of economic growth.[45] He believes that new methods are needed and that the scope of developmental economics must be wider than that of price theory. Allocation of *given* inputs to their "best" uses is not enough. He has also stated his personal desire to see some of the elements of static welfare economics retained in development policy because "development is for people."[46] In keeping with this position, he has defined the overall goal of economic development as

. . . maximizing the rate of expansion of production, while giving due weight to people's wishes regarding the choice between goods and services or leisure, between more income now and more income later, and between a higher per capita income and larger families, as expressed in collective choices made by the smallest group whose decisions can be effective in promoting economic growth.[47]

Yet, as we have seen in Chapter 16, Professor Arrow has shown that it is not clear that collective choices produce rational decisions. On the other hand, collective choices based upon informed judgments are preferable from a personal point of view to judgments imposed by dictators according to whim or caprice as far as most of us are concerned, and it is difficult to see any alternative. It should be emphasized, however, that the *basis* of making the choice is as important as the *method* of making it.

Unlike Professor Higgins, who has devoted his attention primarily to underdeveloped countries in recent years, Professor J. M. Clark, one of the elder statesmen of the profession, has spent most of his life studying the problems of the economy of the United States. He has recently taken a position and an approach which are very close to those of Schumpeter in many respects. Clark also explicitly rejects the static welfare conclusions drawn from the general model of price theory and

---

[44] Walter C. Neale, "Economic Accounting and Family Farming in India," *Economic Development and Cultural Change,* Vol. VII (April, 1959), pp. 286–301, at p. 300.

[45] Higgins, *op. cit.,* p. 766.

[46] *Ibid.,* p. 438.

[47] *Ibid.,* p. 440.

emphasizes dynamic supply and demand functions. He argues that while such models may not produce determinate equilibrium positions, nevertheless, they come closer to describing the actual course of events in the economy than does the model.[48] Clark feels that contemporary price theory, especially the theory of the firm, involves "neglect of factors that are really important. Outstanding among these are the factor of time and differences between the demand and cost curves applying to different firms in the same industry." He thinks that neglect of these considerations involves "excluding precisely the factors that are necessary to effective competition under the conditions of modern industry and trade" in which oligopoly, differentiated and undifferentiated, is the usual state of affairs.[49] The problem for dynamic analysis, he continues, is to find "feasible and effective ways to take account of factors" such as "diversities between rival firms in their costs and their attitudes toward them, their time-perspectives, their size, and the elasticities of the demand schedules that different firms face or envision."[50]

Professor Clark's position, as indicated in the preceding paragraphs, has a great deal in common with the position of Schumpeter, described earlier. But it would be a mistake to think that Clark's views are identical to those of Schumpeter. Clark has never restricted himself to a consideration of "purely economic variables." He has rejected the notion that market valuations are the basis of social value, and almost forty years ago, in his *Studies in the Economics of Overhead Costs,* he was already emphasizing the idea that "narrow commercial efficiency" is not the same thing as "economic efficiency in the large," both because, in his view, prices are not a measure of social value and because prices ignore all those values which are not related to marketable objects and relationships.[51] Clark's view is essentially pragmatic and, therefore, flexible; he looks upon "competition as a dynamic process."[52]

D. SOME CONCLUDING REMARKS

Obviously the views of all the writers discussed in this chapter cannot be reconciled. This difference in views is merely evidence that there are many different interpretations of the real world and many unsolved problems to challenge the intelligence and ingenuity of econo-

---

[48] J. M. Clark, *Competition as a Dynamic Process* (Washington, D.C.: The Brookings Institution, 1961), p. x.

[49] *Ibid.,* p. 119.

[50] *Ibid.*

[51] J. M. Clark, *Studies in the Economics of Overhead Costs* (Chicago: University of Chicago Press, 1923), p. 466.

[52] This phrase is the title of his most recent book. See footnote 48.

mists and would-be economists. One may agree, for example, with P. T. Bauer that those things which are true by definition in economic theory are as true on the Gold Coast of Africa as they are in the United States or in other industrialized countries of the Western world and are also as true today as they were when Marshall first dealt with them in the *Principles*. But, in doing so, one need not agree with him that the *basic assumptions about human behavior* are also universally applicable, nor with Professor Friedman that they apply throughout the Western world. Questions of this kind are questions of "fact" and can only be settled by reference to the concrete situation under consideration.

Moreover, the problem of defining the word "fact" does not need to constitute an insurmountable difficulty. It is necessary only that there be sufficient agreement between ideas and their objects so that a basis for further action exists. What is essential is that there be a sufficient degree of flexibility in the method of analysis employed (or in the mind of the analyst or policy maker) so that readjustments can be made—in thought and in actions—if the actual result is different from that which has been anticipated or predicted. The essence of the scientific method does *not* lie in an abstention from making value judgments. On the contrary, it lies *just in the making of disinterested value judgments based upon the best data available* (defined as data whose accuracy are determined by the limits of tolerance of the problem itself) for the purpose of making further value judgments. It is important, for this reason, that value judgments be stated *explicitly*.

A position that the assumptions about behavior on which the general model of price theory rests are generally applicable to all cultures and at all times, like the Schumpeterian assumption that institutions are permissive and conducive to economic growth, precludes the analyst from investigating precisely these questions, even though they may be the ones which most need answering. A model which begins with an assumption begins with a limitation—the basic premise or assumption—and no more can be extracted from such a model than was contained in the original assumption. This is not to say that the use of deductive reasoning in economics is objectionable (indeed, it is essential), nor even that there is necessarily an objection to the building of general models dealing with hypothetical situations on the basis of assumptions, realistic or unrealistic, and to ascertainment of all of their implications. It is, however, necessary to recognize the limitations of this procedure. There is a real objection to an insistence by an analyst, who engages in such a procedure, that his results or his basic assumptions are universally and timelessly applicable and valid. Such a claim cannot be validated except by reference to factors external to the model he has built, while, at the same time, the conclusions which are drawn from such a model can never be proved or disproved since they are inherent in the assumptions which he has made. If these assumptions are about a hypothetical situation, it follows that the conclusions are applicable to that hypothetical situation, but it remains to be established that the hypothetical situation has relevance to the real world and, therefore, that the conclusions are similarly applicable to a real world situation.

It is for these reasons that this book has emphasized the explanation of the language of price theory and the use of that language as a means of communication and of organizing economic ideas and has not emphasized the use of price theory as a basis for "prediction" or as a basis for making "welfare" judgments. That is, despite the fact that they cannot be reconciled, all the views and approaches discussed in this chapter do have *one* thing in common: they all assume an understanding of the basic language and concepts of price theory on the part of the audience to which they are addressed. Economists may differ about how to solve problems and about what problems are important, but, as has been pointed out in the opening chapter of this book, they do have in common many basic concepts and a professional language which must be learned by anyone who wishes to join their number. Indeed, it is doubtful that anyone can understand their points of agreement, much less their points of disagreement, without understanding these concepts or that language. If the reader has acquired such an understanding with the help of this book, the book will have accomplished its principal purpose.

SELECTED READINGS

AYRES, CLARENCE E. *The Industrial Economy*. Boston: Houghton Mifflin Co., 1952.

———. *The Theory of Economic Progress*. Chapel Hill: University of North Carolina Press, 1944.

———. *Toward a Reasonable Society*. Austin: University of Texas Press, 1961.

BAUER, PETER T. *Economic Analysis and Policy in Underdeveloped Countries*. Durham: Duke University Press; and London: Cambridge University Press, 1957.

CLARK, J. M. *Competition as a Dynamic Process*. Washington, D.C.: The Brookings Institution, 1961.

DAHL, ROBERT A., AND LINDBLOM, CHARLES E. *Politics, Economics and Welfare*. New York: Harper & Bros., 1953.

FRIEDMAN, MILTON. *Essays in Positive Economics.* Chicago: University of Chicago Press, 1953.

HIGGINS, BENJAMIN. *Economic Development.* New York: W. W. Norton & Co., Inc., 1959.

JOHR, W. A., AND SINGER, H. W. *The Role of the Economist as Official Advisor.* Trans. JANE DEGRAS AND STEPHAN FROWEIN. London: George Allen & Unwin, Ltd., 1955.

SCHUMPETER, JOSEPH A. *Capitalism, Socialism and Democracy.* 2d ed. New York: Harper & Bros., 1950.

―――. *The Theory of Economic Development.* Trans. REDVERS OPIE. Harvard Economic Studies, Vol. XLVI. Cambridge: Harvard University Press, 1951.

ADVANCED DEMAND THEORY

An Arithmetical and Graphical Illustration of Slutsky's Basic Demand Equations

Introduction

Marshall's theory of demand and his demonstration that the demand curve will have a negative slope, when the marginal utility of the numeraire is assumed constant and the marginal utility of x is assumed to decrease, have been explained in Chapter 4.[1] An explanation of the Pareto-Slutsky theories of demand in terms of indifference analysis has been given in Chapter 5. This appendix shows that Slutsky's equations can also be illustrated in terms of ordinary demand curves. Appendix B provides a new interpretation of Marshall's consumer's surplus concept, while Appendix C shows the relationship of the analysis in these two appendices to the work of J. R. Hicks and further explains Henry Schultz's study of demand. Appendix D deals with some problems of index numbers.

1. BASIC CONCEPTS

The Total Effect on Purchases of a Price Change

Figure A–1 contains assumed data pertaining to a given commodity x and to a composite commodity y which again represents all the uses other than x to which the consumer can put his given money income, M.

---

[1] The material in this appendix is based substantially on my article, "Marshall and Slutsky on the Theory of Demand," *Canadian Journal of Economics and Political Science*, Vol. XXVII (May, 1961), pp. 176–91. (I have, however, changed some of the terminology, especially in Appendix B.)

As in Chapter 3, y represents dollars spent on all uses other than x, and the price of a unit of y is thus $1.00.

Assume now that we have data for only two points on the demand curve of x, the original position at A and the final equilibrium position at B. As before, let the original price of x at A be OP, or $p_x = \$1.00$;

Figure A–1

**A GRAPHICAL ILLUSTRATION OF THE EFFECT
OF A PRICE CHANGE**

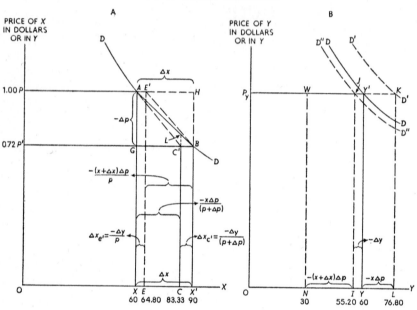

and let the original quantity of x be OX, or $x = 60$ units. After the price of x decreases to OP', let the new price of x be $\$.72$ and the new quantity of x, or OX', be 90 units. Thus $(p_x + \Delta p_x) = \$.72$ and $(x + \Delta x) = 90$. Also, $\Delta x = 90 - 60 = 30$. These values have been chosen primarily because they produce graphs which are easy to read and not because they describe a realistic situation. Note that $\Delta x = 30 > 0$ and $\Delta p_x = -\$.28 < 0$.

We know nothing about the size of the total money income of the consumer except that we may assume it to remain unchanged, and we do not know the amount which he is spending on all goods other than x in the initial position; that is, we do not know the value of y. Therefore, we are forced to rely on the data for the two market positions (which presumably are obtainable empirically) to make inferences about the unknown quantities.

First write again the budget equation, which states that all of the consumer's money income is accounted for by expenditures on x and on y, or

$$xp_x + yp_y = M .\qquad (3\text{–}1) = (A\text{–}1)$$

By designating y as the *numeraire* commodity, we can write our budget equation *in terms of y* as

$$\frac{p_x}{p_y}(x) + \frac{p_y}{p_y}(y) = px + y = \frac{M}{p_y},\qquad (A\text{–}2)$$

where $p = p_x/p_y$. From now on, all our equations will be written in terms of y in this form.

Money income, or M, remains constant by assumption, and only the price of x is allowed to change. Thus, eventually, after the price decrease, the consumer once more attains an equilibrium position by moving from A to B on the demand curve of x in Figure A–1A. His initial equilibrium position on the demand curve of y at Y' in Figure A–1B can also be indicated by marking off the distance OY as the quantity of y purchased in the initial position. What is his new position on the curve of y? How has his position changed?

A change in the price of x involves changing one of the assumptions subject to which the demand curve of y has been drawn and hence may involve a *shift* in that demand curve, but it involves merely a movement *along* the demand curve of x. Thus the new demand curve of y in Figure A–1B, after the price of x has declined and the consumer is at B in Figure A–1A, will usually be either to the right or to the left of the original demand curve of y. In the new position, the consumer will be either at a point like J or like K in Figure A–1B, *unless the total amount spent on x* and, therefore, also the total quantity of y consumed *remain constant* when the price of x declines. In short, unless the elasticity of the demand for x is equal to unity, the demand curve of y must shift when the price of x declines. (If the elasticity of the demand for x is unity, the demand curve of y will not shift, and the consumer will remain at Y' on DD.)

After the price decrease, the budget (constraint) equation in the new position at B will be

$$(p + \Delta p)(x + \Delta x) + (y + \Delta y) = \frac{M}{p_y}.\qquad (A\text{–}3)$$

Now with money income assumed constant, the change in the total amount spent on all other goods, or Δy, must be equal and opposite to the change in the total amount spent on x. We can thus set Equations

(A–2) and (A–3) equal to each other, for they are each equal to M/p_y, and produce an algebraic definition of Δy, *the change in the total amount spent on y, as follows:*

$$px + y = (p + \Delta p)(x + \Delta x) + (y + \Delta y) , \qquad (A\text{–}4)$$

or

$$y - (y + \Delta y) = (p + \Delta p)(x + \Delta x) - px , \qquad (A\text{–}5)$$

and so

$$\begin{aligned} \Delta y &= (px) - (p + \Delta p)(x + \Delta x) \\ &= -p\Delta x - x\Delta p - \Delta x\Delta p \ ; \end{aligned} \qquad (A\text{–}6)$$

and arithmetically:

$$\begin{aligned} \Delta y &= (1)(60) - (.72)(90) = -30 - (60)(-.28) - \\ &\quad (-.28)(30) = -30 + 16.80 + 8.40 = -4.80 \ . \end{aligned} \qquad (A\text{–}6')$$

From Equation (A–6), we see that the change in the total amount spent on y is the difference between the total amount spent on x at A (or px) and the total amount spent on x at B [or $(p + \Delta p) (x + \Delta x)$]. Thus $\Delta y = -\Delta E$ measured in units of y, where ΔE is the change in the total amount spent on x as defined in Equation (4–4) in Chapter 4.

From our arithmetical equivalents (or the data assumed) for points A and B, we see that in our case Δy is negative, for it amounts to $-4.80y$. Thus, total purchases of y have decreased by $4.80y$ as a result of the price decrease, while total expenditures on x have increased by $-\Delta y = -(-4.80y) = 4.80y$. At A the consumer was spending $60.00y$ for x, and at B he is spending $64.80y$ for x. The demand for x is therefore elastic, for $\Delta E = 4.80y > 0$.

By rewriting Equation (A–6) as follows, we can learn more from this definition:

$$(p + \Delta p)\Delta x = -x\Delta p - \Delta y \ . \qquad (A\text{–}7)$$

In order to rewrite Equation (A–6) in this way, we need, of course, only to subtract Δy from both sides of it and to add $(p + \Delta p)\Delta x = p\Delta x + \Delta x\Delta p$ to each side of it.

What our new Equation (A–7) states is that the *amount spent for the additional quantity of x* [or the product of the new price of x, $(p + \Delta p)$, multiplied by the change in the quantity of x (or by Δx)] *is equal to the difference between the increase in purchasing power* (or $-x\Delta p$) *and the amount of the change in total expenditures on all other uses* (or Δy). Thus arithmetically:

$$(.72)(30) = -(60)(-.28) - (-4.80) = 16.80 + 4.80 = 21.60 \ . \qquad (A\text{–}7')$$

Alternatively, we could write (A–7) as

$$(p + \Delta p)\Delta x = -x\Delta p + (-\Delta y) = -x\Delta p + \Delta E ,\qquad (A\text{-}8)$$

which says that the amount spent for the additional quantity of x is equal to the amount saved on all the original units of x purchased, or to the change in income, plus the change in the total amount spent on x, for $\Delta E = -\Delta y$.

In terms of Figure A–1A, we can see that area $P'PAG$ is equal to distance $P'P$ multiplied by $OX = P'G$, and this is the same as $-x\Delta p$ in our equations or $16.80y$ in our arithmetical example. This area thus again, as it did in Chapter 3, represents the *negative of the change in cost* of the original quantity, or *the increase in purchasing power* or in income resulting from the price decrease.

Also in terms of Figure A–1A, area $XGBX'$ is equal to the *amount spent for the additional quantity of x*, for it is equal to XX' multiplied by $OP' = X'B$, and this is the same as $(p + \Delta p)\Delta x$, or $21.60y$.

Thus, Equation (A–8) is an *ex post facto* quantifiable explanation of the total effect *on purchases* (but not on total utility) of the price change. It states that the reason why the consumer was able to purchase 30 additional units of x, or Δx, is that (1) he acquired additional purchasing power equal to the negative of the change in cost $(-x\Delta p)$, or $P'PAG = 16.80y$, and (2) he also reallocated his total expenditures, reducing his expenditures on y by $\Delta E = (-\Delta y)$, or by $4.80y = IJY'Y$, and increasing his expenditures on x by that same amount. That is how he paid for the additional amount (XX') of x consumed.

Clearly, $\Delta E = -\Delta y$ is included within area $XGBX' = (p + \Delta p)\Delta x$, for the latter is equal to the sum of an area equal to $-\Delta y$ plus $(-x\Delta p = P'PAG)$. Thus we can construct area $XGC'C = P'PAG$ within area $XGBX'$, and then the remainder, $XGBX' - XGC'C = CC'BX'$, must be equal to $-\Delta y$. Accordingly, area $CC'BX'$ represents the *change* in the total amount spent on x, or $\Delta E = -\Delta y$, and area $X'BC'C$ represents the *change* in the total amount spent on y, or Δy. And so, $X'BC'C$ in Figure A–1A is equal to area $YY'JI$ in Figure A–1B.

The Process of Readjustment to a Price Change: Price Decrease

In Figures A–1A and A–1B, as soon as the price of x declined to P', the consumer immediately found himself in disequilibrium at G and K, where his purchasing power had increased by $P'PAG$, or by $-x\Delta p = YY'KL$, and where he was consuming the original quantity of x equal to OX and a new quantity of y equal to OL. Since the ratio of the marginal utility of x to its price was there too low relative to the ratio of the marginal utility of y to its price, the consumer readjusted by increasing his purchases of x and reducing his purchases of y.

Our equations are based on assumed empirical data, and so we can be certain that in the position at G the ratio of the marginal utility of x to the new price of x was not equal to the ratio of the marginal utility of y to its price. Thus *even though* the marginal utilities of the two commodities are assumed to be *dependent,* it is still clear from the facts in the case that the consumer was not in equilibrium at G. For if he had been, he would not have increased his purchases of x beyond OX to OX' at B.

Consequently, the consumer was in disequilibrium at G and K, where the utility of his income had increased by an amount equal to that of $-x\Delta p = P'PAG$ units of y. The process by which he readjusted can be reconstructed as a matter of history. First he substituted all of the increased purchasing power equal to $P'PAG = XGC'C = YY'KL$ for XC of additional x and gained utility equal to $GALC'$ units of y in addition to the original increase in utility equal to $P'PAG$ units of y, thereby moving to C'. But he was not yet in equilibrium after this substitution, for his final position is not at C', but at B.

Thus, he further reduced his expenditures on y by $-\Delta y = IJY'Y$ in Figure A–1B and increased his expenditures on x by this same amount, or by $CC'BX'$ in Figure A–1A, acquiring an additional CX' of x as a result of this last substitution. In this process he gained utility equal to $C'LB$ units of y in addition to that which he had already acquired. The additional quantity of x, or CX', acquired from this last substitution was not acquired as a result of increased purchasing power produced by the price change. It was acquired as a result of a reallocation of the consumer's given income. Part only of the total gain in utility and part only of the total increase in purchases of x is accounted for *directly* by the increase in spending power. The remainder is accounted for by the change in total expenditures. The total amount spent for *additional x* is $XGBX' = IJKL$, and this is greater than $XGC'C$.

If the demand curve of x *were* a rectangular hyperbola, AC' in Figure A–1A, the gain in utility resulting from substitution *would* have amounted only to GAC', and the increase in purchases *would* have amounted only to XC. The area $C'AL$ represents *an additional gain* in utility *resulting from the substitution of the change in income alone* for additional x *because y also changed;* and the area $C'LB$ represents *a further gain* in utility *which resulted* from the fact that y changed, that is, that purchases of x were further increased by CX' *at the expense of y.* If we had the actual data for the two positions, A and B, we could in fact compute the gain in utility which resulted from this price change in units of purchasing power, or in units of y, and a method of doing so *approximately* will be explained in the next appendix.

Algebraically, the preceding explanation can be stated quantitatively by dividing our Equation (A–7) by $(p + \Delta p)$, the new price of x, or

$$\frac{(p + \Delta p)\Delta x}{(p + \Delta p)} = \frac{-x\Delta p}{(p + \Delta p)} - \frac{\Delta y}{(p + \Delta p)} = \Delta x . \qquad (A-9)$$

Arithmetically, we have

$$\frac{(.72)(30)}{.72} = \frac{16.80}{.72} - \frac{-4.80}{.72} = 23.33x + 6.67x = 30x . \qquad (A-9')$$

And, in Figure A–1A, $XC + CX' = XX'$.

The Case of a Price Increase

By treating the positions of the consumer at B in Figure A–1A and at J in Figure A–1B as if they were the original equilibrium positions, and by treating his positions at A and at Y' respectively as if they were his final positions, the reader can use these diagrams to explain the case of a price increase.

The quantitative algebraic expression, which explains the process of readjustment when the case is treated as if it were one of a price increase, can be obtained from our original definition of the change in the total amount spent on all other goods, Δy. All that is required is for us to write our original Equation (A–6):

$$\Delta y = -p\Delta x - x\Delta p - \Delta x\Delta p , \qquad (A-6)$$

to subtract Δy from both sides of it, and to add $p\Delta x$ to both sides of it, to produce

$$p\Delta x = -(x + \Delta x)\Delta p - \Delta y , \qquad (A-10)$$

or arithmetically,

$$(1.00)(30) = -(90)(-.28) - (-4.80) . \qquad (A-10')$$

Next, multiply both sides of this equation by -1 to reverse the movement to produce

$$-p\Delta x = (x + \Delta x)\Delta p + \Delta y , \qquad (A-11)$$

or

$$-30 = (90)(-.28) - 4.80 = -25.20 - 4.80 . \qquad (A-11')$$

Equation (A–11) thus states that the ultimate reduction of the consumer's expenditures on x (or $-p\Delta x$), which is area $X'HAX$ in Figure

A–1A, is equal to the sum of the increased cost of the original quantity of x at B, or to area $BHPP' = X'HE'E = NWJI$, and the reduction of the total amount spent on x at A, or $EE'AX = IJY'Y$.

In order to determine the precise amount of the reduction in purchases which is attributable respectively to the *loss* of purchasing power when price rises and to the change in the total amount spent on x, or to $-\Delta y$, we need only to divide Equation (A–11) by p, to produce

$$\frac{-p\Delta x}{p} = \frac{(x + \Delta x)\Delta p}{p} + \frac{\Delta y}{p} = -\Delta x \ . \qquad \text{(A–12)}$$

Arithmetically,

$$\frac{-30.00}{1.00} = \frac{-25.20}{1.00} + \frac{-4.80}{1.00} = -25.20x - 4.80x = -30x \ . \quad \text{(A–12')}$$

And in Figure A–1A, we have $X'E + EX = X'X$.

The acute reader may have wondered why we do not merely take Equations (A–7) and (A–9) and substitute new values of $x = 90$, $p = .72y$, etc., into them when we are treating B as the initial position and A as the final position in the price increase case. Such a procedure is, in fact, much simpler, but it makes identification of the two different situations more difficult when a single graph such as Figure A–1 is employed. Thus, for analytical and pedagogical reasons only, specific equations have been written to describe the price increase case in this section.

The Assumed Data

Throughout the remainder of this appendix however, we will use the single set of equations exemplified by Equation (A–7), for it is com-

Table A–1

ASSUMED DATA FOR ARITHMETICAL
ILLUSTRATION OF DEMAND EQUATIONS

	Price Decrease Case	Price Increase Case
Initial position	A	B
Final position	B	A
x	60.00	90.00
$(x + \Delta x)$	90.00	60.00
Δx	30.00	−30.00
p	1.00	.72
$(p + \Delta p)$	.72	1.00
Δp	−.28	.28
y	60.00	55.20
Δy	−4.80	4.80
M	120.00	120.00

pletely general, and we will make use of the preceding arithmetical values in all four of these appendices in illustrating the equations in the cases indicated in Table A–1.

The initial and final position values in the price increase case are thus the final and initial position values respectively in the price decrease case, and the signs of Δp, Δx, and Δy are reversed in the two cases.

2. THE BASIC SLUTSKY EQUATIONS

The Direct and Indirect Effects of a Price Change

Contemporary demand theory, we have seen in Chapter 5, distinguishes between so-called "income" and "substitution" effects *on purchases* of a price change. The *income* effect is formally defined as an effect on purchases produced or "caused" by a change in income, or the numeraire, *with prices constant*. The *substitution* effect is formally defined as the effect produced by the price change, *income remaining constant*. In Chapter 5, we have also used the term *direct effect on purchases* to convey the notion identified (poorly) in contemporary theory as a "substitution" effect, and the term *indirect effect* to convey the notion of the so-called "income" effect. The terms *direct effect* and *indirect effect* were first suggested by Henry Schultz.[2]

In our example, it will be seen shortly, the *direct* effect on purchases is the effect of the price decrease *if* expenditures on y remained constant (i.e., if $\Delta y = 0$) or $-x\Delta p/(p + \Delta p) = 16.80/.72 = 23.33x$, or XC in Figure A–1A. And the *indirect* effect is the effect of the average rate of change of purchases as income changes, $\Delta x_b/\Delta m$, multiplied by the total change in income (or in purchasing power) produced by the price change, or $(\Delta x_b/\Delta m)(-x\Delta p)$. The preceding definition serves also as an explanation of the reason why the term "income" effect has been given to this *part* of the total change in purchases of x produced by the price change. *It is the part "produced" by the combined action of the change in income and the rate of change of purchases of x as income changes when the price of x is constant at its new level.* That is, the *indirect* effect is

$$(\Delta x_b/\Delta m)(-x\Delta p) = \Delta x_{c'} = (-\Delta y)/(p + \Delta p) = 4.80/.72 = 6.67x ,$$

or CX' in Figure A–1A. It is that part of the total change in x which occurs *because* Δy is *not* equal to zero, or which occurs because y does change when the price of x changes.

---

[2] Henry Schultz, *The Theory and Measurement of Demand* (Chicago: University of Chicago Press, 1938), pp. 42–43.

When the case is treated as one of a price increase, with the initial equilibrium position at B and the final position at A in Figure A–1A, the direct effect is, of course, $X'E$, and the indirect effect is EX in the same diagram.

That this is the case can probably be most clearly explained by showing the relationship between the equations written in this appendix and the basic Slutsky Equation No. 46 on which the contemporary indifference analysis of demand rests.

An Equivalent of Slutsky's Equation No. 46

The contemporary indifference analysis is based on an article by Eugen Slutsky, which appeared in an Italian journal in 1915 and was then ignored. His equations were rediscovered independently in 1934 by Professors J. R. Hicks and R. G. D. Allen, and one of these equations has since been identified as "Slutsky's Equation," or as the "Fundamental Equation of Value Theory."[3] This equation has also been called "the cornerstone" of contemporary demand theory and will be reproduced below. The reader who does not understand its terms or the mathematical terminology in the following paragraph need not, however, throw up his hands in horror, for there is a simple equivalent of Slutsky's equation which can be derived from our definition of Δy and which will be set forth immediately thereafter.

Slutsky's equation really does nothing more than to state the effect on purchases of a price change in terms of exact rates of change and reads:[4]

$$\frac{\partial x_i}{\partial p_i} = u'\frac{M_{ii}}{M} - x_i\frac{\partial x_i}{\partial s} . \tag{S–46}$$

This equation states the per unit rate of change of purchases of commodity x_i when its price changes, while *money* income is assumed to remain constant. It is the *first term on the right* in Equation (S–46) which has been identified as the *per unit* "substitution" effect and the *second* on the right which has been identified as the *per unit* "income" effect by Professor Hicks and others. These terms can also be called by the names *per unit direct* effect and *per unit indirect* effect on purchases of

---

[3] Eugen Slutsky, "On the Theory of the Budget of the Consumer," reprinted in Kenneth Boulding and George Stigler (eds.), *Readings in Price Theory* (Homewood, Ill.: Richard D. Irwin, Inc., 1952), pp. 27–56, esp. pp. 39–43; and J. R. Hicks and R. G. D. Allen, "A Reconsideration of the Theory of Value," *Economica*, New Series, Vol. I (February, 1934), pp. 52–76; and *Economica*, Vol. I (May, 1934), pp. 196–219.

[4] Slutsky, "On the Theory of the Budget of the Consumer," *Readings in Price Theory*, Equation 46, p. 40.

the price change, following Henry Schultz's better terminology. The magnitude u' is identified in this equation as the marginal utility of "money," defined as the numeraire. The denominator of the ratio M_{ii}/M, or M, is identified as the "determinant of the first and second partial derivatives of the utility function," and the numerator, M_{ii}, is identified as the "cofactor" of elements in the determinant; while x_i is the original equilibrium position quantity and $\partial x_i/\partial s$ is the rate of change of purchases of x_i as income changes *when prices are constant.*

A simple equivalent of the Slutsky equation can be produced by dividing our Equation (A–9) by Δp [where the symbol, $(M = k)$, means *money* income is assumed constant]:

$$\frac{\Delta x}{\Delta p}, (M = k) = \frac{-x}{(p + \Delta p)} - \frac{\Delta y}{(p + \Delta p)\Delta p} . \qquad (A\text{–}13)$$

Equation (A–13) can be reconciled with Slutsky's Equation No. 46 by multiplying both sides of the latter by dp_i to produce the total change in x_i as

$$\left[dx_i = \frac{\partial x_i}{\partial p_i} dp_i \right] = \left[u' \frac{M_{ii}}{M} - x_i \frac{\partial x_i}{\partial s} \right][dp_i] . \qquad (S\text{–}46a)$$

Next, multiply both sides of this equation by $(p_i + dp_i)$ to produce the total amount spent for the additional quantity of x_i:

$$[(p_i + dp_i)dx_i] = \left[u' \frac{M_{ii}}{M} - x_i \frac{\partial x_i}{\partial s} \right][dp_i(p_i + dp_i)] . \qquad (S\text{–}46b)$$

Now in the case in which $\partial x_i/\partial s = 0$ and the indifference curves are vertically parallel as in Figure 5–6, the equation reduces to

$$[(p_i + dp_i)dx_i] = \left[u' \frac{M_{ii}}{M} \right][dp_i(p_i + dp_i)] . \qquad (S\text{–}46c)$$

Recall next that Equation (A–7) reads:

$$(p + \Delta p)\Delta x = -x\Delta p - \Delta y . \qquad (A\text{–}7)$$

In this equation, neither x nor Δp can ever be zero. However, Δy can be either positive, negative, or zero. Setting Δy equal to zero, we have $E_d = 1$ and

$$(p + \Delta p)\Delta x = -x\Delta p . \qquad (A\text{–}7a)$$

We can now set Equations (A–7a) and (S–46c) equal to each other, for they are both equal to $(p + \Delta p)\Delta x$. And so,

$$(p + \Delta p)\Delta x = -x\Delta p = \left[u' \frac{M_{ii}}{M} \right][dp_i(p_i + dp_i)] . \qquad (A\text{–}7b)$$

It follows also that

$$\Delta y = \left[x_i \frac{\partial x_i}{\partial s} \right] [dp_i(p_i + dp_i)] \,. \tag{A-7c}$$

Equation (A–13) is produced by dividing both sides of Equation (A–9) by Δp. Thus, Equations (S–46) and (A–13) are reconciled.

When our case is treated as one of a price increase, using the appropriate values from Table A–1, we have

$$\frac{\Delta x}{\Delta p}, (M = k) = \frac{-90}{1.00} - \frac{4.80}{(1.00)(.28)} = -90.0 - 17.142 = -107.142 \,. \tag{A-13'}$$

Thus, purchases of x *decrease* by 1.07142 units when price *rises* by *one cent*, i.e., $(.01)(-107.142) = -1.07142$, and the *direct* effect is seen to be equal to $-.90$ of one unit of x, while the *indirect* effect is equal to $-.17142$ of one unit of x. Since the average rate of change is negative, $\Delta x \Delta p < 0$, the demand curve has a negative slope. (Note that one cent is the same as $.01y$.)

And so the equation factors the effect of the price change *on a per unit basis* into two parts. The rules for determining when the demand curve will have a negative slope can be spelled out in terms of this equation, and this is the form in which they are often presented in the literature. However, when the rules are stated in terms of the basic Slutsky equation, the explanation is extremely difficult and sometimes confusing. The explanation in terms of indifference diagrams given in Chapter 5 utilizes the *total* direct and indirect effects on purchases and is based on Slutsky's Equation No. 51, which is explained in Appendix C.

An explanation of these rules in terms of simple demand curve diagrams can also be given by converting the Slutsky equation into an expenditures equation as explained below. This explanation yields some surprising conclusions and is probably more meaningful for a reader who is not mathematically trained than is the standard explanation. (The latter has been employed in Chapter 5 rather than the former primarily because the former represents a new approach.) Before presenting this explanation, however, it will be useful to review the definitions of *normal* and *inferior* goods given in Chapter 5 and to consider the ways in which the total expenditures behave when income increases if the commodity is normal, on the one hand, and if it is inferior, on the other.

Normal and Inferior Goods and Changes in Total Expenditures

A normal commodity has been defined in Chapter 5 *as one of which purchases increase as income increases when prices are constant.* Thus, in the case of a normal commodity we have $\Delta x_a / \Delta m > 0$; or the average rate of change of purchases of x, when income changes and prices are constant, is positive. This means that more of x will be purchased if income increases by, say, Δm_1 when prices are constant, for the total change in x is then equal to $(\Delta x_a / \Delta m)(\Delta m_1) > 0$. *An inferior good has* also *been defined as one of which purchases decrease as income increases when prices are constant.* Thus, in the case of an inferior good, $\Delta x_a / \Delta m < 0$. That is, the average rate of change of purchases of x, when prices are constant and income increases, is negative. This means that less of the commodity will be bought if income increases. Finally, *a neutral commodity is one of which purchases do not change as income changes.* Since, in this case, purchases of x do not change as income changes when prices are constant, we have $\Delta x_a / \Delta m = 0$.

With the foregoing definitions in mind, consider now the effect on total expenditures on a normal commodity $(\Delta x_a / \Delta m > 0)$ of an increase in income when prices are unchanged. Obviously if the quantity purchased increases, with constant prices, the total amount spent on the commodity must increase, and $\Delta E > 0$. But if the commodity is inferior $(\Delta x_a / \Delta m < 0)$ in the same situation, total expenditures on the commodity will decrease, for then purchases decrease as income increases while prices remain constant, and $\Delta E < 0$. And finally, if the good is neutral $(\Delta x_a / \Delta m = 0)$, total expenditures on the commodity will remain constant, for then $(\Delta x_a / \Delta m)(\Delta m_1) = (0)(\Delta m_1) = 0$, and $\Delta E = 0$. These results are employed in the following discussion.

The General Conditions of Negatively Sloping Demand Curves

One simple way to define the general conditions of negatively sloping demand curves is to write once more the expenditure Equation (A–7) and recall its meaning:

$$(p + \Delta p)\Delta x = -x\Delta p - \Delta y = -x\Delta p + \Delta E . \tag{A–7}$$

This equation states that the amount spent for the *additional* quantity of x (the product of the new price times the change in quantity) is equal to the difference between the change in income and the change in the total amount spent on all other goods when price declines.

From Equation (A–7) we see that *in the case of a price decrease,* the term on the left, the amount spent for the *additional* quantity of x, or $(p + \Delta p)\Delta x$, will be a positive quantity if the total amount spent on all other goods decreases, or if Δy is negative in the equation above. For then, since $-x\Delta p > 0$, the entire expression on the right-hand side of the equation will be positive. And the amount spent for the additional quantity of x will also be a positive quantity, even if the amount spent for all other goods increases $(\Delta y > 0)$, so long as it increases by less than the amount of the change in income (or if Δy is positive, but less than $-x\Delta p$ which represents an *increase* in purchasing power *when price declines* and hence is positive).

Now if the total amount spent on x increases when price falls, i.e., if Δy *is* negative and thus $\Delta E > 0$, the demand for x is elastic. In such a case, the entire expression on the right-hand side in Equation (A–7) must be positive. And since, on the left-hand side, the new price $(p + \Delta p)$ is *always* positive, Δx is also positive.

Thus, the demand curve must have a negative slope because the quantity has increased as price has declined, or $\Delta x\Delta p < 0$. Also, since Δy *is* negative, the indirect effect on purchases of x is positive, for purchases of x have increased as income has increased by $-x\Delta p$, with prices constant. And, since the income effect is positive, the commodity is normal, $\Delta x_b/\Delta m > 0$. *In fact, normal commodities are merely those whose price elasticity is greater than unity.* That is, $(-x\Delta p)(\Delta x_b/\Delta m) = -\Delta y/(p + \Delta p) = CX' > 0$ in Figure A–1, or $E_d > 1$, $\Delta y < 0$, and $\Delta E > 0$, whenever $\Delta x_b/\Delta m > 0$.

In the case of Figure A–1A, we have $(p + \Delta p)\Delta x = XGBX' = -x\Delta p - \Delta y = XGC'C + CC'BX' = 16.80y - (-4.80y) = 21.66y$. Since $\Delta y = -4.80y$, therefore $-\Delta y = 4.80y = \Delta E = CC'BX'$ is the change in the total amount spent on x. In Figure A–1A the *price elasticity* of demand is greater than unity, the demand curve slopes down and to the right, and the commodity is normal because $\Delta x_b/\Delta m > 0$. This is a surprising conclusion.

However, if the total amount spent on all other goods increases, but by less than the change in income when price declines (or if Δy is positive but less than $-x\Delta p$, total expenditures on x decrease $(\Delta E < 0)$, and the good is inferior. Then the demand for x is inelastic, but the demand curve is still negatively sloped. For $(p + \Delta p)\Delta x$ is still positive, even though in this case the indirect effect on purchases is negative, since Δy is positive. Thus the commodity is inferior $(\Delta x_b/\Delta m < 0)$, and $\Delta x\Delta p < 0$, $\Delta E < 0$, and $\Delta y > 0$.

And so, in the case of the new diagram in Figure A–2, we see that $(p + \Delta p)\Delta x = XGBX' = -x\Delta p - \Delta y = 16.80y - 2.40y = 14.80y$.

Now in this case $\Delta y = (2.40y > 0) = X'BC'C$, while $-x\Delta p = XGC'C$. In this case, therefore, the amount spent for the additional quantity of x, or $XGBX'$, is less than the change in income, $XGC'C$, and total expenditures on x have decreased. For the total amount spent on x at A is $OPAX = 60y$, but the total amount spent on x at B is $OP'BX' = (.72)(80) = 57.60y$. Thus the demand for x is inelastic,

Figure A–2

AN INFERIOR GOOD

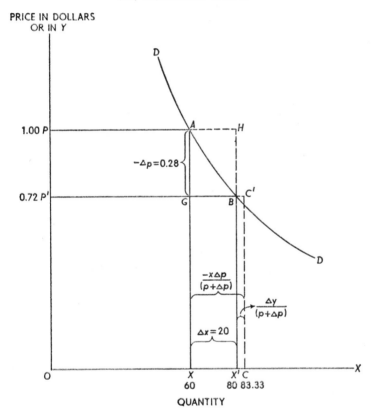

$\Delta E = -2.40y < 0$, but the demand curve nevertheless slopes down and to the right, and the commodity is inferior.

Finally, if the amount spent for all other goods increases by more than the amount of the change in income, obviously again the total amount spent on x must decrease. In this case, the indirect effect on purchases is again negative, for Δy is positive and $\Delta E < 0$. But, since Δy is greater than $-x\Delta p$, the indirect effect *overcomes* the direct effect of the price change in Equation (A–7), and $(p + \Delta p)\Delta x$ is negative.

This means that Δx is negative, for $(p + \Delta p)$, the new price, is always positive. Thus, this case also involves an inferior good $(\Delta x_b / \Delta m < 0)$, but one which has an upward-sloping demand curve $(\Delta p \Delta x > 0)$, or an abnormal commodity, for quantity and price decline together.

In the *Principles,* Marshall noted that such a case was once cited by a man named Giffen, who noted that a rise in the price of bread made so large a drain on the very limited resources (income) of poorer

Figure A–3

AN ILLUSTRATION OF GIFFEN'S CASE

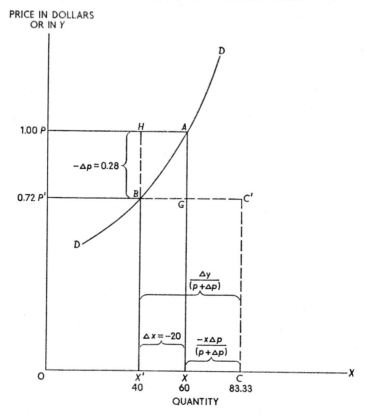

laboring families in the England of his day that they were forced to consume more, not less, of it when its price increased. Therefore this case is called, "Giffen's case." The elasticity of demand is negative if the commodity is inferior and abnormal.

Such a case is illustrated in Figure A–3. In this diagram, we have $(p + \Delta p) \Delta x = XGBX'$, for purchases of x have *decreased* from 60 units to 40 units as the price of x has decreased from 1.00 to .72 per unit. Our formula still applies, for it is still true that $(p + \Delta p)\Delta x = XGBX' = -x\Delta p - \Delta y = 16.80y - 31.20y = -14.40y$. However, Δy is now not only positive but it is also greater than the change in income, $-x\Delta p$. For $\Delta y = X'BC'C$ and $-x\Delta p = XGC'C$. (Arithmetically, $\Delta y = 31.20y > 0$ and $-x\Delta p = 16.80y$ as before.) The amount spent for the additional quantity of x is negative because purchases of x have decreased absolutely when the price of x has declined. Thus the demand curve slopes up and to the right in Figure A–3, and we have a depiction of Giffen's case.

In summary, note that the change in purchasing power, $-x\Delta p$, is always in the opposite direction from that in the price. Thus, *the direct effect of the price change*, the so-called "substitution" effect, *must always operate on purchases in a direction opposite from that of the price change. The indirect effect*, $(-x\Delta p)(\Delta x_b/\Delta m)$, however, *may operate on purchases in the same direction as, or in the opposite direction from, the price change, or it may be zero, or* $\Delta x_b/\Delta m \gtreqless 0$. *How it does is a question of fact in a given case. The total effect on purchases is the sum of these two effects.* Finally, the analysis can be carried on as easily in terms of expenditures as in terms of purchases.[5]

The Income Term in Slutsky's Equation No. 46

Now, the second term on the right in Slutsky's Equation No. 46, or $(x_i)(\partial x_i/\partial s)$, is the rate of change of purchases of x_i as income changes with prices constant, multiplied by the quantity of x_i consumed in the initial position. When this term is multiplied by the total change in price (dp_i), the product $[(x_i)(\partial x_i/\partial s)(dp_i)]$ is that part of the change in x which results from the change in income with prices constant. Thus, this term states the total *indirect* effect on purchases, and it is approximately equal to our own term, $\Delta y/(p + \Delta p)$, in Equation (A–9).

Accordingly, we can write:

$$x\Delta p \frac{\Delta x_a}{\Delta m} = \frac{\Delta y}{(p + \Delta p)}, \qquad (\text{A–14})$$

and solve this equation for $\Delta x_a/\Delta m$ to produce the average rate of change of purchases of x as income changes, prices constant. Thus, dividing both sides of Equation (A–14) by $x\Delta p$, we have

$$\frac{\Delta x_a}{\Delta m} = \frac{\Delta y}{(p + \Delta p)x\Delta p}. \qquad (\text{A–15})$$

[5] For a somewhat similar approach, see J. K. Eastham, *Graphical Economics* (Chicago: Quadrangle Books, Inc., 1960), pp. 65–66.

Recall that in our arithmetical example the subscript a attached to a symbol indicates that the price of x is constant at its higher level of one y in Table A–1, and the subscript b shows that the price is constant at its lower level of .72. Then we have the arithmetical equivalents of Equation (A–15) as

$$\frac{\Delta x_a}{\Delta m} = \frac{4.80}{(1.00)(90)(.28)} = \frac{4.80}{25.20} = .1905 \qquad (A\text{–}15')$$

and

$$\frac{\Delta x_b}{\Delta m} = \frac{-4.80}{(.72)(60)(-.28)} = \frac{-4.80}{-12.096} = .3968 . \qquad (A\text{–}15'')$$

And so, when the price of x is constant at its higher level ($p = 1$), a unit change in income changes purchases of x by .1905 of one unit; while a unit change in income, when the price of x is constant at its lower level, ($p = .72$), increases purchases of x by .3968 of one unit. These values have been employed in the diagrams in Chapter 5.

We can now also rewrite Equation (A–13) by substituting $(x\Delta p)(\Delta x_a/\Delta m)$ for $\Delta y/(p + \Delta p)$, to read

$$\frac{\Delta x}{\Delta p,(M = k)} = \frac{-x}{(p + \Delta p)} - x\Delta p \frac{\Delta x_a}{\Delta m} \frac{1}{\Delta p} ; \qquad (A\text{–}13b)$$

and this is the same as

$$\frac{\Delta x}{\Delta p,(M = k)} = \frac{-x}{(p + \Delta p)} - x\frac{\Delta x_a}{\Delta m} . \qquad (A\text{–}13b)$$

Equation (A–13b) is another equivalent of Slutsky's Equation No. 46, and the reader should compare the two equations at this point.

The Income Elasticity Determined from Price-Quantity Data

The income elasticity of the demand for a commodity has been defined in Chapter 4 as a measure of responsiveness of purchases to price changes, or as the absolute value of the percentage rate of change of purchases of the commodity divided by the percentage rate of change of income. It can be formulated as

$$E_{i_x} = \frac{m}{x} \frac{\partial x}{\partial m} . \qquad (A\text{–}16)$$

Computation of this elasticity requires that the given income, m, of the consumer be known, and *it can only be computed at given prices of x.* Let us therefore assume that the consumer's income was equal to $120m$ and that he also purchased $60y$ at A in Figure A–1. The term,

$\partial x/\partial m$, in Equation (A–16), is the exact rate of change, and for it we will have to substitute our average rates of change from Equations (A–15′) and (A–15″) to provide an arithmetical illustration of this elasticity.

First, in the case in which the consumer is at A and he experiences an increase in income without a price change, we have

$$E_{i_{x_a}} = \frac{m}{x} \frac{\Delta x_a}{\Delta m} = \frac{120}{60}(.1905) = .3810 \ . \tag{A-16′}$$

Thus, a 1 percent increase in the consumer's income when he is at A, while prices remain unchanged, would produce an increase in purchases of x equal to .3810 of 1 percent. We can further illustrate this income elasticity by assuming that the consumer received an increase in income equal to $\Delta m_1 = 16.80$ at A without a price change. Then we would have the following result as the effect of the income change on his purchases of x:

$$\Delta x' = x\frac{\Delta m_1}{m} \frac{m}{x} \frac{\Delta x_a}{\Delta m} = (60)(.14)(.3810) = 3.20x \ .$$

This result must be contrasted with the result in the case in which the consumer experiences an increase in spending power equal to $-x\Delta p = 16.80$ *as a result of a price decrease* while he is in the position at A in Figure A–1A. In this case it is necessary to use the rate of change of purchases of x as income changes at the new lower price of x (for after the price has decreased, the consumer substitutes at the lower price) in the income elasticity formula. Accordingly, in this case the income elasticity is

$$E_{i_{x_b}} = \frac{m}{x} \frac{\Delta x_b}{\Delta m} = \frac{120}{60}(.3968) = .7936 \ . \tag{A-16″}$$

As before, we have

$$\Delta x_c = x\frac{-x\Delta p}{m} \frac{m}{x} \frac{\Delta x_b}{\Delta m} = (60)(.14)(.7936) = 6.67x = CX'$$

as the change in purchases of x resulting from the indirect effect of the price change. (Note that $\Delta m_1 = -x\Delta p$, as in Chapter 3.)

It is clear, therefore, that in computing the income elasticity we must use that rate of change of purchases which takes account of the correct price in applying our income elasticity formulas. Also, the preceding illustration shows that it is possible to estimate income elasticities from price-quantity data, provided that the total income of the consumer is known. In a later section, we will see that it is also possible to estimate price elasticities if the rate of change of purchases of x as income changes is known.

The Arc Price Elasticity of Demand for the Price-Changing Commodity

The concept of price elasticity of demand has already been discussed in detail in Chapter 4. It has been defined as the responsiveness of buyers to price changes, or as the relative change in purchases of the commodity divided by the relative change in the price of the commodity; and the point elasticity of demand is defined by the formula, $E_d = (-p/x)(\partial p/\partial x)$.

If we multiply the statement of the Slutsky equation contained in our Equation (A–13) by the negative of the ratio $(p + \Delta p)/(x)$, we produce the *arc* price elasticity of demand formula which has already been written as Equation (4–4b) in Chapter 4. Thus:

$$E_d = \left[-\frac{(p + \Delta p)}{x}\frac{\Delta x}{\Delta p}\right] = \left[-\frac{(p + \Delta p)}{x}\frac{-x}{(p + \Delta p)}\right] - \left[-\frac{(p + \Delta p)}{x}\frac{\Delta y}{(p + \Delta p)\Delta p}\right] = 1 + \frac{\Delta y}{x\Delta p}, \qquad (A\text{–}17)$$

and this is the same as the result in Equation (4–4b), since $-\Delta E = \Delta y$.

When we use the data for the price increase from Table A–1, we have

$$E_{d_a} = 1 + \frac{4.80}{(90)(.28)} = 1 + .1905 = 1.1905 . \qquad (A\text{–}17')$$

Now we have already seen in Chapter 4 that *if* the total amount spent on x remains constant when the price of x changes, so that $\Delta y = 0$ in Equation (A–17) above, the second term on the right in that formula, $\Delta y/x\Delta p = -\Delta E/x\Delta p$, reduces to zero. Therefore, this price arc elasticity formula produces the same result ($E_d = 1$) as does the calculus point elasticity formula in such a case.

We have also already seen in Chapters 4 and 5 (in conjunction with the discussion of Figures 4–9 and 5–6) that in a case in which the rate of change of purchases of x as income changes is zero, or when $\Delta x_a/\Delta m = 0$, the marginal utility of the numeraire is constant. And we have again seen in the explanation of Equation (A–15) in this appendix that, when $\Delta x_a/\Delta m = 0$, it is also true that total expenditures on the commodity do *not* change when income changes with prices constant, or $\Delta y = 0$.

From these considerations, it follows that in any case in which $\Delta y = 0$, and the elasticity of demand is therefore equal to unity [in Equation (A–17)], and the marginal utility of the numeraire is constant, *all of any increase in spending power* ($-x\Delta p$) *resulting from the price change is spent on the price-changing commodity.* In short, *total* expenditures on x and on y remain constant in such a case, although all of the increase in income ($-x\Delta p$) is spent on the price-changing good. (A more formal proof will also be given later in this appendix, after certain additional definitions have been provided.)

It follows also from the foregoing proposition that the first term on the right in Equation (A–17), which is unity or 1, states the elasticity of demand *if* the marginal utility of the numeraire *were* constant; and the second term on the right, or $\Delta y / x\Delta p$, states the amount by which the elasticity of demand differs from unity *because* the marginal utility of the numeraire is *not* constant.

The meaning of the price arc elasticity formula can be further illustrated by interpreting the result provided in the case of a price increase in Equation (A–17). Since this equation produces the result, $E_{d_a} = 1.1905$, it states that, in our example, purchases of x will decrease by 1.1905 percent for each 1 percent increase in the price of x. (Recall that we have defined the price elasticity so that it will be positive in the case in which price and quantity change in opposite directions; hence a positive price elasticity in the case of either a price increase or a price decrease means that quantity changes in the opposite direction.)

Now the total percentage increase in the price of x when the initial position is taken to be B in Figure A–1 and Table A–1 is $\Delta p / p = .28/1.00 = .28$. Thus, the total percentage change in x is equal to $(.28)(1.1905) = .3334$. If we multiply this figure by the original quantity of x, we have $(.3334)(90) = 30 = XX'$ as the number of units by which purchases of x decrease when its price rises by .28, assuming that the consumer was initially at B in Figure A–1A.

Moreover, *if* the marginal utility of the numeraire had been constant, and so the elasticity of demand had been unity, purchases of x would have decreased by only $(.28)(1)(90) = 25.20$ units, or by the amount EX' in Figure A–1A. Thus, the distance XE represents the additional amount by which purchases of x decreased *because* the marginal utility of the numeraire was *not* constant.

Professor Paul Samuelson has also demonstrated in a different way that in a case in which *the utilities are dependent and the marginal utility of the numeraire is constant,* or when $\Delta x_a / \Delta m = 0$, "all of the increased income is spent on a single commodity." The preceding explanation provides an economic meaning for his result.[6]

Determination of Price Elasticity from Income-Quantity Data

In an earlier section, it has been shown that income elasticities can be determined from price-quantity data if total income is known. Conversely, price elasticities can be determined from income-quantity data by assuming various values for Δp. That is, we already know from our previous analysis that

$$x\Delta p \frac{\Delta x_a}{\Delta m} = \frac{\Delta y}{(p + \Delta p)} . \tag{A-14}$$

Thus, it follows that, by multiplying both sides of the preceding equation by $(p + \Delta p)$ and dividing both sides by $x\Delta p$, we have

$$(p + \Delta p)\frac{\Delta x_a}{\Delta m} = \frac{\Delta y}{x\Delta p} . \tag{A-14a}$$

Now this result shows that the second term on the right in our price elasticity formula [Equation (A–17)] is really nothing more than the rate of change of purchases as income changes multiplied by the new price of x. Thus, if we know this rate of change of purchases and assume various values for Δp, we can estimate arc price elasticities from income-quantity data. Our arc price elasticity formula would be

$$E_d = 1 + (p + \Delta p)\frac{\Delta x_a}{\Delta m} . \tag{A-17a}$$

In our price increase case, for example, this produces

$$E_d = 1 + (1.0)(.1905) = 1.1905 , \tag{A-17a'}$$

as in Equation (A–17′) before. [Equation (A–17a) is produced by substituting Equation (A–14a) into Equation (A–17).]

Slutsky's Equation No. 36

The concept of the rate of change of purchases of all other goods (or of y) as income changes when everything else is assumed constant $(\Delta y_a/\Delta m)$ is analogous to the concept of the rate of change of purchases of x as income changes when all other things are assumed constant, and it is employed in defining the income elasticity of y.

---

[6] Paul A. Samuelson, "Constancy of the Marginal Utility of Income," in O. Lange, F. McIntyre, and T. O. Yntema (eds.), *Studies in Mathematical Economics and Econometrics* (Chicago: University of Chicago Press, 1942), p. 85. (Samuelson also proves on p. 86 that when the utilities are *independent* the elasticity of demand cannot be unity, but that is *not* our case.)

In order to understand fully the concept of this rate of change, consider the following argument. First recall that we have assumed that total income is accounted for in equilibrium by expenditures on x and on y. Consequently, it follows that any *change* in income between any two positions must also be accounted for by the *change* in expenditures on x and on y.

Now we have already computed [in Equation $(A-15'')$] the rate of change of purchases of x as income changes when the price of x is constant at B, or at its lower level of $(p + \Delta p) = .72$ in our arithmetical example, as

$$\frac{\Delta x_b}{\Delta m} = \frac{\Delta y}{(x\Delta p)(p + \Delta p)} = .3968 . \qquad (A-15'')$$

It follows that the change in purchases of x resulting from an increase in income, say $\Delta m_1 = 20y$, *without a price change*, when the consumer is at B and the price of x is $.72 = (p + \Delta p)$, is equal to $(\Delta m_1)(\Delta x_b/\Delta m) = (20)(.3968) = 7.94x$ in Figure A–4A. Or, $(\Delta m_1)(\Delta x_b/\Delta m) = X'X''$ in Figure A–4A.

Figure A–4

THE EFFECT OF AN INCREASE IN INCOME, PRICES CONSTANT

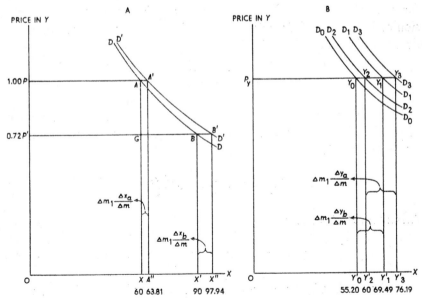

It also follows that the *amount of purchasing power spent for such an additional quantity* of x equal to $X'X''$ would be

$(p + \Delta p)(\Delta m_1)(\Delta x_b / \Delta m)$. Note that $(p + \Delta p) = .72$ is the current price. In Figure A–4A this magnitude (the amount spent for the additional quantity of x equal to $X'X''$) is depicted by area $X'BB'X''$, and also, arithmetically, $(p + \Delta p)(\Delta m_1)(\Delta x_b / \Delta m) = (.72)(20)$ $(.3968) = (7.94)(.72) = 5.71y$.

Consequently, the difference between the total change in income and the amount spent for the additional quantity of x with constant prices must be the resulting change in y, for y is our numeraire. Or, $\Delta m_1 - (p + \Delta p)(\Delta x_b / \Delta m)(\Delta m_1) = \Delta y_1$. Arithmetically, $20y - 5.71y = 14.29y$. Furthermore, the amount spent for the additional quantity of y must be equal to $(\Delta m_1)(\Delta y_b / \Delta m)$. This formula is another way of saying that the amount spent for additional y (of any change in income equal to Δm_1) is equal to the product of the rate of change of purchases of y as income changes with prices constant, multiplied by the change in income (for y is the numeraire, and hence *the amount of y and the amount spent for y are the same number*).

From these considerations, we have the basic proposition:

$$\Delta m_1 (p + \Delta p)\frac{\Delta x_b}{\Delta m} + \Delta m_1 \frac{\Delta y_b}{\Delta m} = \Delta m_1 , \qquad (A–18)$$

or, in words, *the total of any change in income must all be accounted for by additional expenditures on x and on y.* It also follows, by a division of both sides of Equation (A–18) by Δm_1, that we can thus produce Slutsky's Equation No. 36, or

$$(p + \Delta p)\frac{\Delta x_b}{\Delta m} + \frac{\Delta y_b}{\Delta m} = 1 . \qquad (A–19)$$

From this proposition, we have the definition of the rate of change of purchases of y as income changes, with the price of x constant at $(p + \Delta p) = .72$, as

$$\frac{\Delta y_b}{\Delta m} = 1 - (p + \Delta p)\frac{\Delta x_b}{\Delta m} . \qquad (A–20)$$

Arithmetically, we have

$$\frac{\Delta y_b}{\Delta m} = 1 - (.72)(.3968) = 1 - .2857 = .7143 . \qquad (A–20')$$

In Figure A–4B, the increase in the quantity of y is $Y'_0 Y'_1$, and the increase in expenditures on y at the lower price of x amounts to $Y'_0 Y_0 Y_1 Y'_1 = (\Delta m_1)(\Delta y_b / \Delta m) = (20)(.7143) = 14.29y$. The increased expenditures on x have already been computed as equal to

$5.71y = X'BB'X''$ in Figure A–4A. The sum of these two areas is equal to $14.29y + 5.71y = 20y = \Delta m_1$.

Note that a change in *money* income equal to $20y$ *without a price change* produces a *shift* in the demand curve of x *and a shift* in the demand curve of y. For, a change in money income without a price change amounts to a change in one of the assumptions subject to which *both* these demand curves in Figure A–4 have been drawn.

Thus, the case of *a change in money income without a price change is different from* that depicted in Figure A–1, which shows *the effect of a price change without a change in money income.* The latter case involves changing one of the assumptions subject to which the demand curve of y has been drawn (prices of other goods are assumed constant), but it does not involve a change in any of the assumptions subject to which the demand curve of x has been drawn. In Figure A–1, we have a *movement along* the demand curve of x and a *shift in* the demand curve of y. But, in Figure A–4, we have a *shift in both* demand curves.

Now when the price of x is $(p + \Delta p) =$ one y in Table A–1 and Figure A–4, we have for the rate of change of purchases of y as income changes with constant prices:

$$\frac{\Delta y_a}{\Delta m} = 1 - (p + \Delta p)\frac{\Delta x_a}{\Delta m} . \tag{A-21}$$

Arithmetically, in this case:

$$\frac{\Delta y_a}{\Delta m} = 1 - (1)(.1905) = .8095 . \tag{A-21'}$$

If the consumer were to receive the same increase in *money* income equal to $\Delta m_1 = 20y$ when he is in equilibrium at A and at Y_2 in Figure A–4 when the price of x is one y, the magnitudes of the changes in purchases of x and of y would be different from what they are in the previous case, for the rates of change of purchases of x and of y are different at A from what they are at B.

In this case, purchases of x would increase by $(20)(.1905) = 3.81x = XA''$ in Figure A–4A. Moreover, A' is on the same demand curve as B'. The *amount spent on* x would increase by $3.81y$, for p is equal to one y in our assumed example, and this increase in expenditures on x is depicted by area $XAA'A''$. In Figure A–4B, purchases of y would increase by $Y'_2Y'_3$. Note that Y_3 is on a *different* demand curve from the ones on which lie Y_0, Y_2, or Y_1. The increase in total expenditures on y resulting from this income change amounts to

$(20y)(.8095) = 16.19y = Y'_2Y_2Y_3Y'_3$ in Figure A–4B. Again we see that the changes in expenditures on x and on y account for the total change in income, or $3.81y + 16.19y = 20y = \Delta m_1$.

The Income Elasticity of the Demand for All Goods Other than x

The income elasticity of y is a measure of the responsiveness of purchases of "all goods other than x" to changes in income and is equal to the absolute value of the percentage rate of change of purchases of y divided by the percentage rate of change of income. It can be stated as

$$E_{i_y} = \frac{m}{y}\frac{\partial y}{\partial m} .\qquad\qquad (A\text{–}22)$$

As in the case of the income elasticity of x, this elasticity must be computed with given prices of x and y. Thus, in the case in which in Table A–1 we have $(p + \Delta p) =$ one y, we can compute this income elasticity in our example as

$$E_{i_{y_a}} = \frac{m}{y}\frac{\Delta y_a}{\Delta m} = \frac{120}{60}(.8095) = 1.6190 .\qquad (A\text{–}22')$$

Our income elasticity formula thus provides us with the conclusion that, in our case, if income alone changes by one percent when the consumer is at A and prices are unchanged, his purchases of y will increase by 1.619 percent. Thus a change in income equal to $20y$ will produce a change in purchases of y equal to

$$(y)(\Delta m/m)(\Delta y_a/\Delta m) = (60)(.1667)(1.619) = 16.19y = Y'_2Y'_3 .$$

The Cross Effect: Slutsky's Equation No. 47

Another of Slutsky's well-known equations (his Equation No. 47) states the rate of change of purchases of y as the price of x changes. It is sometimes known as the "cross-effect" equation and is used in defining the cross elasticity of demand. This equation can be obtained by writing the definition, explained above, of the rate of change of y as income changes with the price of x constant, or

$$\frac{\Delta y_a}{\Delta m} = 1 - (p + \Delta p)\frac{\Delta x_a}{\Delta m} ,\qquad\qquad (A\text{–}21)$$

and by substituting into it the value of Equation (A–15), or

$$\frac{\Delta x_a}{\Delta m} = \frac{\Delta y}{(p + \Delta p)x\Delta p} ,\qquad\qquad (A\text{–}15)$$

to produce

$$\frac{\Delta y_a}{\Delta m} = 1 - \frac{\Delta y}{x\Delta p} . \tag{A-23}$$

Next, by subtracting $\Delta y_a/\Delta m$ from both sides and by adding $\Delta y/x\Delta p$ to both sides, we have

$$\frac{\Delta y}{x\Delta p} = 1 - \frac{\Delta y_a}{\Delta m} . \tag{A-24}$$

Finally, by multiplying both sides by x, we produce the rate of change of purchases of y as the price of x changes when money income is assumed constant, or our equivalent of Slutsky's Equation No. 47:

$$\frac{\Delta y}{\Delta p},(M = k) = x - x\frac{\Delta y_a}{\Delta m} . \tag{A-25}$$

Arithmetically, in the price increase case in Table A–1 and Figure A–1, we have

$$\frac{\Delta y}{\Delta p},(M = k) = (90) - (90)(.8095) = 17.145 . \tag{A-25'}$$

The equation states the effect on purchases of y of an increase in the price of x (on a per unit [dollar] basis) when the consumer is at B in Figure A–1. Thus, if the price of x rises by one *cent* (or $.01y$) while the consumer is at B, purchases of y will increase by $.17145$ of one unit of y. That is, $(.01)(17.145) = .17145$. Or, a total increase of $.28y$ in the price of x produces a total change in purchases of y of $(.28)(17.145) = 4.80y = IY$ in Figure A–1B.

Thus we see that, in our case, *purchases of y* and the *price of x* change in the *same* direction, $\Delta y \Delta p_x > 0$. Therefore, the demand curve of y *shifts* to the right as the price of x rises, for one of the assumptions subject to which the demand curve of y has been drawn (prices of all other goods remain constant) has been changed. In order to provide a correct interpretation of our arithmetical result in the price decrease case, we must recognize the meaning of $\Delta y \Delta p_x > 0$ in our case of Figure A–1A.

Cross Elasticity of Demand

The cross elasticity of demand measures the responsiveness of purchases of y to the change in the price of x. It is defined as the absolute value of the percentage rate of change of purchases of y divided by the percentage rate of change of the price of x, and can be stated as

$$E_{y_{p_x}} = \frac{p_x}{y}\frac{\partial y}{\partial p_x}. \tag{A-26}$$

In our case, we have for this formula in the price increase case of Table A–1 and Figure A–1:

$$E_{y_{p_{x_a}}} = \frac{.72}{55.20}(17.142) = .2236. \tag{A-26'}$$

The result can be interpreted as showing the effect of a 1 percent change in the price of the given commodity, x, on purchases of all other goods, or y. Thus, an increase of 1 percent in the price of x when the consumer is at B produces an increase in purchases of y equal to .2236 of 1 percent. And so an increase of $(.28/.72)(100) = 33.88$ percent in the price of x when the consumer is at B produces an increase in purchases of y equal to $(.3888)(.2236)(55.20) = 4.80y = IY$ in Figure A–1B, and the demand curve of y shifts to the right when the price of x rises.

Constancy of the Marginal Utility of the Numeraire

The equations we have just written provide a simple and neat algebraic explanation of the case of constancy of the marginal utility of the numeraire. In such a case, purchases of x do not change as income changes when prices are constant. That is, as we have already noted in Chapters 4 and 5, in such a case, $\Delta x_a/\Delta m = 0$. If now we set $\Delta x_a/\Delta m = 0$ in Equation (A–21), we have

$$\frac{\Delta y_a}{\Delta m} = 1 - (p + \Delta p)(0) = 1. \tag{A-21a}$$

Since we now have $\Delta y_a/\Delta m = 1$, all of any increase in income *without a price change* will be spent on y. Moreover, if we set $\Delta y_a/\Delta m = 1$ in Equation (A–25), we see that it reduces to zero, or

$$\frac{\Delta y}{\Delta p, (M = k)} = x - x(1) = 0. \tag{A-25a}$$

This means that purchases of y do not change *when the price of x changes*. The demand curve of y does not shift in this case. Thus, all of the increased purchasing power resulting from a price decrease must be spent on x, and $\Delta y = 0$.

Finally, since $\Delta y = 0$ in such a case, Equation (A–17), which states the arc elasticity of the demand for x, reduces to unity,

$$E_d = \frac{(p + \Delta p)}{x}\frac{\Delta x}{\Delta p} = 1 - 0 = 1, \tag{A-17a}$$

and the cross elasticity of demand is zero. Thus the case of constancy of the marginal utility of the numeraire involves unitary elasticity of demand. (The reader may wish to compare this explanation with the analysis in Chapter 4 of Marshall's demonstration that the demand curve must have a negative slope when the marginal utility of the numeraire is constant.)

Substitutes and Complements

Substitutes and complements can thus be defined in terms of the "cross-effect" equation [Equation $(A-26)$] or, more simply, in terms of the effect on total expenditures on x and on y of the change in the price of x. If total expenditures on x increase when the price of x declines (the demand is elastic) while those on y decrease, the commodities x and y are substitutes. Thus, $\Delta y < 0$ or $\Delta x_a / \Delta m > 0$ or $\Delta E > 0$ each mean that the commodities are substitutes.

If total expenditures on x decrease when the price of x declines while those on y increase, the demand is inelastic or $\Delta y > 0$ or $\Delta E < 0$ or $\Delta x_a / \Delta m < 0$, and the commodities x and y are complements (for purchases of both increase absolutely), provided that $\Delta y < x \Delta p$. If $\Delta y > x \Delta p$, the case involves an abnormal commodity and a perverse result, since total expenditures on x decrease more than the change in income while those on y increase by more than this amount. Thus purchases of x decrease absolutely while those of y increase absolutely. The demand curve then has a positive slope.

If total expenditures on x and on y remain constant when the price of x declines (the elasticity of the demand for x is equal to unity), the commodities are not related. In such a case $\Delta E = 0$, $\Delta y = 0$, and $\Delta x_a / \Delta m = 0$.

In summary: (1) if the demand for x is elastic, the commodities are substitutes; (2) if the demand for x is inelastic, the commodities are complements, provided that total expenditures on x do not change by more than the change in income; and (3) if the elasticity of the demand for x is unity, the commodities are not related. Finally, (4) *if total expenditures on x change in the same direction as the price change by more than the change in income,* the demand curve has a positive slope which cannot be explained by the existing assumptions, and more assumptions (or facts) are needed.

The Neutrality of the Preceding Analysis

The breakdown or factoring and the analysis of the price change into two parts which is performed by our equivalent of the Slutsky equation is independent of the assumption that utility is measurable. Determination of the *effect on total utility* of the price change is a different problem from the one which has been the concern of this appendix, for the former is intimately concerned with the theoretical problem of formulation of an "ideal index number." The problem of the measurement of such a change in total utility, or the change in the "consumer's surplus," is the subject of Appendix B.

B

The Consumer's Surplus

Introduction: Marshall's Definition of the Surplus

It has been noted in Chapter 16 that Marshall defined the consumer's surplus as the difference between the amount a consumer would be willing to pay for a good rather than to go without it and the amount which he actually does pay.[1] The surplus on all units of a commodity consumed in a given position thus becomes the area under the demand curve above a horizontal line drawn to the Y axis at the level of the equilibrium price, provided that the demand curve intersects the Y axis. In Figure B–1, the surplus on OX units of x when the price of x is OP would thus be area DAP.

Defined in this way, the surplus cannot be computed because there is no assurance that the demand curve will intersect the Y axis. But this is not to say that *changes* in the surplus cannot be estimated, and this is precisely what Marshall's consumer's surplus analysis is all about. A new interpretation of Marshall's analysis and a solution to the problem of how to value the change in the consumer's surplus resulting from a price change (which was raised in Chapter 3) are offered in this appendix.

1. THE MEASUREMENT OF CHANGES IN THE SURPLUS

The Value of the Change in x Alone (V)

Suppose in Figure B–1 that the demand curve is taken as a straight line between the two points A and B only.[2] The arithmetical values

---

[1] Alfred Marshall, *Principles of Economics* (8th ed.; London: Macmillan & Co., Ltd., 1938), pp. 124–37. This appendix is based on my article, "Marshall and Slutsky on the Theory of Demand," *Canadian Journal of Economics and Political Science*, Vol. XXVII (May, 1961), pp. 176–92 and esp. pp. 185 ff, although the terminology has been substantially changed herein.

[2] Strictly speaking, this assumption limits the analysis to cases involving very small changes in the variables, but so does the use of calculus in economic analysis generally.

which have so far been assumed in Table A–1 in Appendix A to apply
to these two points will be taken to apply also in this chapter. If the demand curve is taken as a straight line between these two points *only,* it
follows that the *value of the change in x alone* to this consumer is
the area $XABX'$, designated by the symbol V.

Figure B–1

THE CHANGE IN THE CONSUMER'S SURPLUS

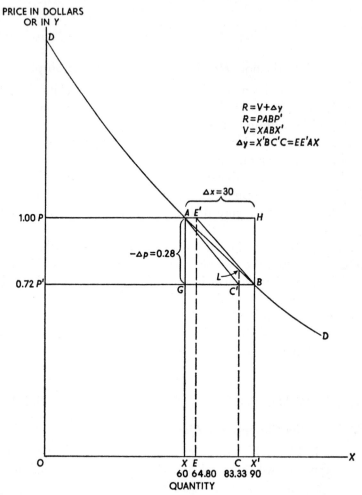

Or, the value to the consumer of the marginal unit of x when he is
at A is the value of XA of purchasing power devoted to all other uses,
an opportunity cost concept. Thus the value of the marginal unit of x
at A is equal to that of XA of y. Also, the value of the marginal unit of

x when the consumer is in the new position at B is equal to the value of $X'B$ spent on all other uses. Thus, if AB is taken as a straight line, the value of the change in x alone, measured in units of y, is equal to the area $XABX'$. And so, we can write:

$$V = \frac{XAHX' + XGBX'}{2} = XABX'$$
$$= \frac{p\Delta x + (p + \Delta p)\Delta x}{2} = p\Delta x + \frac{1}{2}\Delta p\Delta x .$$
(B-1)

Arithmetically, we have

$$V = \frac{(1)(30) + (.72)(30)}{2} = 25.80y .$$
(B-1')

Now the area $AHBG$ is equal to $-\Delta p\Delta x$ in our equations or to $-(-.28)(30) = 8.40$, and $-\frac{1}{2}\Delta p\Delta x$ is equal to either area AGB or area AHB, which are each arithmetically equal to $8.40/2 = 4.20$. By *assuming that the demand curve is a straight line between the two points A and B only, we are thus able to approximate in units of y the value of the additional units of x alone,* purchased as a result of the price change, as equal to $XGBX' + AGB$.

A Measure of the Change in the Surplus (R)

The *value of the change in x alone* (V) is, however, not the actual *change in the consumer's surplus* (R) produced by the price change. For y may also change as a result of the price change. If y also changes, R will be different from V by the amount of the change in y. Thus, we must write:

$$R = V + \Delta y .$$
(B-2)

This is our *basic* equation. It defines the change in the surplus, R, in units of y.

The magnitude R is a concept of comparative statics and approximates that change in the consumer's surplus between A and B produced by the price change when the quantities of x and of y are *both* assumed to be variable. Note that in Figure A–1 *all other things change equally.* Thus R measures in units of y the *difference* between two equilibrium positions. That is, if the consumer were subjected to a tax equal to R measured in units of y after he had attained the position at B after the price decrease and were then permitted to readjust, the total utility of his income after this readjustment would be approximately the same to him as it was before the price decrease. And, on the other hand, if he were given a subsidy equal to R, instead of experiencing

the price decrease while he is at *A*, and then permitted to readjust, he
would thereby attain approximately the same level of total utility which
he does attain as a result of the price decrease.[3]

In Figure B–2, if the consumer were to receive a subsidy equal to

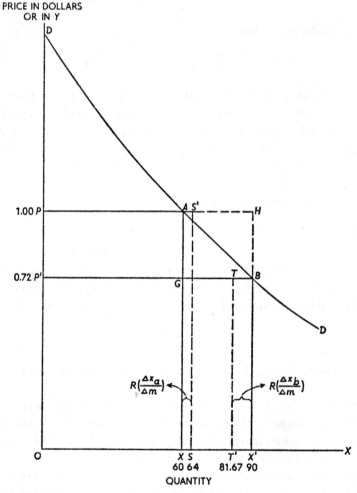

Figure B–2

EFFECT OF A SUBSIDY OR A TAX ON PURCHASES

R when he is at *A* and the price of *x* remained constant at the level of
p, presumably, if his behavior pattern is stable, he would increase his
consumption of *x* by *XS*. For this amount is equal to the change in

---

[3] See Fritz Machlup, "Professor Hicks' *Revision of Demand Theory,*" *American
Economic Review,* Vol. XLVII (March, 1957), pp. 122–35.

purchasing power equal to R multiplied by the rate of change of purchases of x as income changes, when the price of x is p, or $R(\Delta x_a/\Delta m) = XS$. Also, he would increase his consumption of y by $R - R(\Delta x_a/\Delta m)(p) = R(\Delta y_a/\Delta m)$, for the total change in income equal to R must be accounted for by expenditures on x and on y. At S' the total utility of his income would be the same to him as it is at B. [See Equations (A–18) and (A–20).]

Similarly, if the consumer were subjected to a tax equal to R after the price decrease when he is at B in Figure B–2, he would reduce his consumption of x by $T'X'$, for this is equal to $-R(\Delta x_b/\Delta m)$, and he would reduce his consumption of y by $-R(\Delta y_b/\Delta m)$. Thus the total decrease in income would be accounted for by expenditures on x and on y. [See Equation (A–20).] At T the total utility of his income would be the same to him as it is at A. Note that at B the price of x is $(p + \Delta p)$, where $\Delta p < 0$, and that the total utility of his income is less at A and T than it is at B and S'. Thus A and T lie on the same indifference curve, while B and S' lie on a higher indifference curve. (A and T in Figure B–2 correspond to A and T'' on I_1 in Figure C–5; B and S' correspond to B and S'' on I_3. See page 530.)

The meaning of R, the change in the consumer's surplus, can be further clarified as follows. The magnitude $p\Delta x$, or $XAHX'$ in Figure B–2, seeks to measure the *value of the change in x alone* in units of y according to an assumption that the value of each unit of x in the quantity Δx, or XX', is constant and equal to the utility of XA of y, the price of x in the original position at A.

Similarly, the magnitude $(p + \Delta p)\Delta x$ is *not only* the amount spent for the additional quantity of x. It is *also* a measure of the value of the change in x alone according to an assumption that the value of the additional units of x accumulates at a rate equal to the price at B.

The arithmetic average of these two measurements, or V, produces the value of the change in x alone according to an assumption that this value accumulates at a rate equal to the average of the two prices. The magnitude V is thus, in fact, the value of the change in x alone according to an assumption that the value of the additional units of x accumulates at a constantly decreasing rate between the two positions, as the quantities of x and y *both* change.

Clearly, under the linearity assumptions, if the marginal utility of income *devoted to x* decreases, the measure $p\Delta x$, or $XAHX'$, will overstate, and the measure $(p + \Delta p)\Delta x$, or $XGBX'$, will understate *the value of the change in x alone by precisely the same amount.*

Consequently, the measure V neither overstates nor understates the value of this change, and the difference between $p\Delta x$ and $(p + \Delta p)\Delta x$ is exactly equal to twice the amount of the overstatement and thus to twice the amount of the understatement, for our linearity assumption makes the understatement equal to the overstatement. However, the entire value of the change in x alone is not a net gain to the consumer, if consumption of y has been decreased in order to increase the consumption of x. Thus it is necessary to take account of the change in the quantity of y consumed in order to determine the value in units of y of the net gain resulting from the price change. (That is, $R = V$ only if $\Delta y = 0$.)

And so by substituting the definitions of V and of Δy from Equations (B–1) and (A–6) into Equation (B–2), we have the value of R in y as

$$R = p\Delta x + \tfrac{1}{2}\Delta p\Delta x + (-p\Delta x - x\Delta p - \Delta x\Delta p)$$
$$= -x\Delta p - \tfrac{1}{2}\Delta x\Delta p = -(x + \Delta x)\Delta p + \tfrac{1}{2}\Delta x\Delta p \ . \tag{B–3}$$

Arithmetically, in our case we have

$$R = (1)(30) + \tfrac{1}{2}(-.28)(30) - (1)(30) - (60)(-.28) - \tag{B–3$'$}$$
$$(30)(-.28) = 16.80 + 4.20 = 21.00y \ .$$

Substituting similar values into Equation (B–2) itself, we have

$$R = V + \Delta y \ , \tag{B–2}$$

and

$$R = 25.80y + (-4.80y) = 21.00y \ . \tag{B–2$'$}$$

(In order to compute the dollar value of R, it is, of course, only necessary to multiply R by \$1.00, since $p_y = \$1.00$.)

In terms of our diagram in Figure B–1, we have learned that R is equal to area $P'PAB$, which, in turn, is equal to $XABX' - CC'BX'$, for $XABX' = V$ and $CC'BX' = -\Delta y$. Thus, since $P'PAB = P'PAG + AGB$, it follows that $R = P'PAB = XGC'C + AGB$. In the diagram, R may be seen to be equal to the sum of: (1) the original increase in purchasing power equal to the negative of the change in cost, or $P'PAG = XGC'C$; plus (2) the gain from substitution of that change in income $(-x\Delta p)$ for an additional XC of x, or $ALC'G$; plus (3) the gain from substitution of $-\Delta y$ of y for an additional CX' of x, or $LC'B$.

The *total change in the surplus* resulting from the price change is thus measured in y by the amount of the change in income $(-x\Delta p)$ plus the gain from substitution $(-\tfrac{1}{2}\Delta x\Delta p)$. And so we have finally arrived at one solution to the problem of valuation of the change in the surplus which was raised in Chapter 3.

Now the solution to Equation (B–2) reads:

$$R = -x\Delta p - \tfrac{1}{2}\Delta x\Delta p = -(x + \Delta x)\Delta p + \tfrac{1}{2}\Delta p\Delta x \,. \qquad \text{(B–3)}$$

What this equation means is this: the magnitude $-x\Delta p$, the change in purchasing power, is a measure of the change in the surplus computed according to an assumption that there is no gain from substitution, and thus it measures the lower limit of the gain. For this reason, $-x\Delta p$ must be *increased* by the gain from substitution, or by $-\tfrac{1}{2}\Delta x\Delta p$ in our case in Figure (B–1), to produce the actual change in the surplus. Similarly, $-(x + \Delta x)\Delta p$ must be *decreased* by $-\tfrac{1}{2}\Delta p\Delta x$ to produce R, for $-(x + \Delta x)\Delta p$ assumes that the value of Δx accumulates at a constant rate equal to the price of x in the initial position, where it is greater than at B.

We see, therefore, that $-x\Delta p$ and $(p + \Delta p)\Delta x$ make the same assumption, namely, that the gain from substitution is equal to zero; and that $-(x + \Delta x)\Delta p$ and $p\Delta x$ make the same assumption also, namely, that the gain from substitution is a constant amount equal to $-\Delta p$ per unit of *additional* x. However, the price of x will be greater at A than at B in Figure B–1, whether price rises or falls, because the demand curve has a negative slope. Thus, if $\Delta p\Delta x < 0$, there will always be a gain from substitution, even when price rises; otherwise, there would be no explanation of why substitution occurs.

And so, in Figure B–1, when the case is treated as one of a price increase, with the initial position at B and the final position at A, the *loss* to the consumer resulting from a price increase will be *reduced* by the gain from substitution and will be $BHPP' - ABH$. This is the same as $R = -x\Delta p - \tfrac{1}{2}\Delta x\Delta p = -(90)(.28) - \tfrac{1}{2}(-30)(.28) = -21$ when we use the values for the price increase case from Table A–1.

2. MARSHALL'S ANALYSIS

Marshall's Measurement of the Change in the Consumer's Surplus

In the *Principles*, Marshall provides an arithmetical illustration of changes in the consumer's surplus. Marshall first assumes that the consumer buys 1 pound of tea when its price is equal to 20 shillings and increases his purchases to 2 pounds when the price declines to 14 shillings. Then Marshall asserts that the gain must be equal to *at least* 6 shillings, for the consumer now obtains for 28 shillings what is worth to him *at least* 20 shillings plus 14 shillings, or a total of 34 shillings.

In his illustration, Marshall neglects the gain from substitution because he sets $-\frac{1}{2}\Delta p\Delta x = 0$ *in measuring the gain,* although, at the same time, throughout his extended example he sets $\Delta y \neq 0$ *in measuring the change in purchases.* Thus Marshall's arithmetical example does not count the gain from substitution, and he explicitly notes this fact.[4] Alternatively, in measuring the *gain,* Marshall treats the demand as if it were *perfectly inelastic,* but in measuring the change in *purchases,* he *sometimes* assumes the demand *elastic* and *sometimes* assumes it *inelastic.* Thus, in his arithmetical example, since he computes the total gain as equal to $-x\Delta p$, Marshall does not include the gain from substitution and *understates* the total gain, *recognizing explicitly* that he has done so. In fact, Marshall's unstated formula is similar to our own, but he uses $R' = V' + \Delta y$, where $V' = (p + \Delta p)\Delta x$.

In Marshall's example, he assumes that: $x = 1$; $\Delta x = 1$; $(x + \Delta x) = 2$; $p = 20s.$; $(-\Delta p) = 6s.$; and $(p + \Delta p) = 14s.$ Applying the formulation developed in the preceding section, we have

$$R = V + \Delta y = \frac{20s. + 14s.}{2} + (20s. - 28s.) \tag{i}$$

$$= 17s. - 8s.$$
$$= 9s.; \text{ and also,}$$

$$R = -x\Delta p - \tfrac{1}{2}\Delta x\Delta p = -(1)(-6s.) - \tfrac{1}{2}(1)(-6s.) \tag{ii}$$
$$= 9s.,$$

a result different from Marshall's *because* it assumes that there *is* a gain from substitution equal to $-\frac{1}{2}\Delta p\Delta x$.

Since Marshall assumes that *the value of each unit of x in the quantity of x equal to Δx is constant and equal to the price in the new position,* we must set $\frac{1}{2}\Delta p\Delta x = 0$ in our Equation (B–3) [or in (ii)] to produce his result. And so

$$R = -x\Delta p + 0 = 6s. + 0 = 6s., \tag{iia}$$

and this *is* the result produced by Marshall.

Now Marshall takes the value of the first pound of tea which the consumer purchases as equal to $px = (20s)(1)$, and he also takes the value of the change in x alone as equal to $(p + \Delta p)\Delta x =$

---

[4] Compare Paul A. Samuelson, "Constancy of the Marginal Utility of Income," in O. Lange, F. McIntyre, and T. O. Yntema (eds.), *Studies in Mathematical Economics and Econometrics* (Chicago: University of Chicago Press, 1942), pp. 75–91, esp. p. 80 and p. 91. See, also, Marshall, *op. cit.,* pp. 124–27.

(14s.) (1) $= 14$s. Next, Marshall argues that, since the consumer obtains for 28s. what is worth to him 20s. $+ 14$s. $= 34$s., his gain must be equal to *at least* 34s. $- 28$s. $= 6$s. Thus, *in effect,* Marshall writes:

$$px + (p + \Delta p)\Delta x - (p + \Delta p)(x + \Delta x) = -x\Delta p , \qquad \text{(iii)}$$

and this can be rewritten as

$$-x\Delta p = (p + \Delta p)\Delta x + [px - (p + \Delta p)(x + \Delta x)] . \qquad \text{(iv)}$$

But the term in brackets is nothing other than the definition of Δy in our Equation (A–6). And so, we merely need to rewrite Marshall's proposition as

$$
\begin{aligned}
-x\Delta p = R' &= (p + \Delta p)\Delta x + \Delta y = V' + \Delta y \qquad \text{(v)} \\
&= (14\text{s.})(1) + [(20\text{s.})(1) - (14\text{s.})(2)] \\
&= 14\text{s.} - 8\text{s.} = 6\text{s.}
\end{aligned}
$$

The Two Measurements Compared

In his extended example in the *Principles,* Marshall computes the gain resulting from the change in cost of each unit *individually,* according to the formula $R' = V' + \Delta y$, and sums the total. He computes the total gain in this way as equal to 45s. If R is computed individually for each of Marshall's price-quantity changes by means of our own formula in Equation (B–2), the total gain is equal to 54s., and this result differs from Marshall's by exactly the *sum* of all the gains from substitution or by 9s. The results of the two sets of computations are set forth in Table B–1.

Table B–1

COMPARISON OF TWO METHODS OF MEASURING CHANGES IN THE CONSUMER'S SURPLUS

x	p	V'	V	Δy	$-x\Delta p$	Cumulated	R	$-\tfrac{1}{2}\Delta x\Delta p$
					\multicolumn{2}{c}{Marshall's Result}		
1	20.0	20.0	. . .	. . .	. . .	. . .	. . .	. . .
2	14.0	14.0	17.0	−8.0	6.0	6.0	9.0	3.0
3	10.0	10.0	12.0	−2.0	8.0	14.0	10.0	2.0
4	6.0	6.0	8.0	6.0	12.0	26.0	14.0	2.0
5	4.0	4.0	5.0	4.0	8.0	34.0	9.0	1.0
6	3.0	3.0	3.5	2.0	5.0	39.0	5.5	.5
7	2.0	2.0	2.5	4.0	6.0	45.0	6.5	.5
Totals	. . .	59.0	48.0	6.0	45.0	. . .	54.0	9.0

In Table B–1, the first two columns contain the data relating to the demand schedule of x assumed by Marshall in his explanation of the measurement of changes in the consumer's surplus. The third column in Table B–1 has been labeled V' and is really equal to $(p + \Delta p)\Delta x$, or Marshall's measure of the value of the change in x alone. Since in the first column of the table, x is assumed to change by one unit amounts, V' is really the price of x. The fourth column, V, is the arithmetic average of the two preceding prices, and the fifth column shows the change in the total amount spent on y as the price of x changes. Note that the change in y is positive in some cases and negative in others. Thus Marshall's example assumes that the demand is elastic at high prices and inelastic at low prices.

Marshall thus argues that the ultimate sum of the values of the entire 7 pounds of tea is 59s. (total V') and that since the consumer pays 14s. for 7 pounds at the lowest price of 2s. per pound, his total *gain* amounts to 59s. − 14s. = 45s.

However, in terms of Equation (B–2) and the values in Table B–1, our conclusion must be that in Marshall's example the value of the *additional* tea purchased amounts to 48s. (total V) and that an *additional* 6s. worth of y are purchased, making the *total gain* (total R) to the consumer equal to 54s. This differs from Marshall's result by exactly the sum of the gains from substitution, or 9s. in Table B–1.

Marshall's arithmetical example thus neglects *more* than merely the gain from substitution of additional x for the change in y *alone*. Marshall *also* neglects the effect of the substitution of additional x for the change in income $(-x\Delta p)$. Thus, he neglects the *entire gain from substitution*, not merely that part which results from the change in y alone. He states explicitly that he is assuming the "marginal utility of money constant." But, whatever this may mean, it does not mean that the marginal utility of the numeraire is constant.[5]

The Rate of the Gain from Substitution

The magnitude $-\frac{1}{2}\Delta p\Delta x$ represents an amount of purchasing power measured in y, which has been taken as approximately equal to the total gain from substitution. Let $\partial u'/\partial p$ be the *rate* of the gain from substitution. In order to determine the average rate of the gain, multiply Equation (A–9) by $-\frac{1}{2}$, which is the same as multiplying it by $-\Delta p/2\Delta p$, to produce $-\Delta p\Delta x/2\Delta p = -\Delta x/2$ or

$$\frac{\Delta u'}{\Delta p},(M = k) = \frac{-\Delta x}{2} = \frac{\Delta y}{2(p + \Delta p)} - \frac{-x\Delta p}{2(p + \Delta p)}. \tag{B-4}$$

[5] The preceding analysis agrees with the conclusion of Samuelson in *Ibid.*, pp. 81–91, which, however, differs from the view of J. R. Hicks, *Value and Capital* (2d ed.; Oxford: Clarendon Press, 1946), pp. 38–41. Hicks merely *asserts* (but does not prove) that Marshall assumed the marginal utility of the *numeraire*, or our y, constant.

This equation defines the rate of the gain from substitution when the price of x rises, while money income is constant.

Using the values from Table A–1 in the price increase case, we have

$$\frac{\Delta u'}{\Delta p,(M = k)} = \frac{4.80}{2(1.00)} - \frac{-25.20}{2(1.00)} = 2.40 + 12.60 = 15.0 . \quad (\text{B-4}')$$

Thus, in our case, the rate of this gain is positive as price rises. Substitution reduces the loss. Note that it will conversely be negative when price rises only *if* $\Delta y < 0$ and Δy is absolutely greater than $-x\Delta p;$ and thus $\Delta x \Delta p > 0$, that is, if the demand curve has a positive slope.

The preceding equation is our counterpart of one written by Henry Schultz, which reads:[6]

$$\frac{\partial u}{\partial p} = -u\frac{\partial x}{\partial m} - x\frac{\partial u}{\partial m} . \quad (\text{Sc. 3.15})$$

The first term on the right in Equations (B–4) and (Sc. 3.15) states the *per unit change* in the variable which results from the fact that the marginal utility of the numeraire is *not* constant. Note that, in Schultz's equation, this term contains the rate of change of purchases of x as income changes, when prices are constant; and, in our Equation (B–4), we have Δy in this term. And, as we know from the discussion of Equation (A–13), if $\Delta x_a/\Delta m = 0$, then it is also true that $\Delta y = 0$. Thus, the second term on the right in these equations states that change in the variable which would take place *if* the marginal utility of the numeraire y *were* constant, i.e., *if* $\Delta y = 0$.

The Total Gain from Substitution

Multiplication of both sides of Equation (B–4) by Δp produces the total gain from substitution ($\Delta u'$), measured in y, which results from the *price change*. Thus, we have

$$\Delta u' = \left[\frac{\Delta u'}{\Delta p,(M = k)}\right][\Delta p] = \frac{(-\Delta x)(\Delta p)}{2} = \frac{-\Delta x \Delta p}{2}$$

$$= \frac{\Delta y \Delta p}{2(p + \Delta p)} - \frac{(-x\Delta p)(\Delta p)}{2(p + \Delta p)} \quad (\text{B-5})$$

$$= \frac{\Delta y \Delta p}{2(p + \Delta p)} - \frac{-(x)(\Delta p^2)}{2(p + \Delta p)} .$$

---

[6] Henry Schultz, *The Theory and Measurement of Demand* (Chicago: University of Chicago Press, 1938), pp. 40–43. See also my article, "Marshall and Slutsky on the Theory of Demand," *Canadian Journal of Economics and Political Science*, Vol. XXVII (May, 1961), pp. 176–92, esp. pp. 185 ff.

In our price increase case in Table A–1, we have

$$\Delta u' = \frac{(4.80)(.28)}{2(1.00)} - \frac{(-90)(.784)}{2(1.00)} \tag{B-5'}$$
$$= .67 + 3.53 = 4.20 = BAE' + BE'H \text{ in Figure B-1.}$$

And, using the data for the price decrease case, we have

$$\Delta u' = \frac{(-4.80)(-.28)}{2(.72)} - \frac{(-60)(.784)}{2(.72)} = .93 + 3.27 \tag{B-5''}$$
$$= 4.20 = AC'B + AGC' = AGB \text{ in Figure B-1.}$$

A General Formula for the Change in the Surplus

We can now finally substitute the value of $\Delta u' = -\Delta p \Delta x / 2$ into Equation (B–3) to provide two different ways of computing the change in the consumer's surplus or R:

$$R = -x\Delta p + \frac{\Delta y \Delta p}{2(p + \Delta p)} - \frac{(-x)(\Delta p^2)}{2(p + \Delta p)}$$
$$= -(x + \Delta x)\Delta p - \frac{\Delta y \Delta p}{2p} + \frac{-(x + \Delta x)(\Delta p^2)}{2p} . \tag{B-6}$$

This formulation is analogous to one provided by Professor Hicks and will be discussed further in Appendix C.[7]

Using the values from Table A–1 in the case of a price increase, we have

$$R = -25.20 + .67 + 3.53 = -16.80 - .93 - 3.27 = -21.00 . \tag{B-6'}$$

Equation (B–6) above makes clear that the measure, R, takes account both of that change in purchases of x (and hence in the surplus) which *would* result *if* the marginal utility of y *were* constant *and* of that additional change which results because the marginal utility of y is *not* constant. Thus, R measures the total change in units of y because it assumes *both* $\Delta p \Delta x \neq 0$ *and* $\Delta y \neq 0$.

---

[7] Hicks, *op. cit.*, pp. 330–33.

Alternative Explanations and Econometric Studies

There exist in the literature four different (but related) explanations of the "income" and "substitution" effects on purchases of a price change in the case of an individual consumer, all of them derived from the basic Slutsky equations.[1] All these explanations make use of some kind of measure of the "change in the consumer's surplus." Both the different explanations and Henry Schultz's statistical study of demand, which employs one of them, will be considered below.

1. THE "COST DIFFERENCE" ANALYSIS

Slutsky's Equation No. 51

Two of the four pairs of income and substitution effects employed in contemporary analysis (the two explained in Chapter 5) grow out of a literal interpretation of Slutsky's Equation No. 51, which was used by him to isolate the so-called *residual variation* or the "substitution effect."[2] This equation can be written to show the effect on purchases of x and of y of a subsidy equal to the loss in purchasing power ($-x\Delta p$) given to the consumer after he has suffered a price increase. In our terms,

---

[1] Fritz Machlup, "Professor Hicks' *Revision of Demand Theory*," *American Economic Review*, Vol. XLVII (March, 1957), esp. pp. 124 ff, deals with three of them, but in the text I show that there are actually four. Discussion of the revealed preference approach, which is interesting primarily to mathematical economists, has been intentionally omitted from this book. The interested reader may be referred to H. S. Houthakker, "Revealed Preference and the Utility Function," *Economica*, Vol. XVII (May, 1950), pp. 159–74.

[2] See Jacob Mosak, "On the Interpretation of the Fundamental Equation of Value Theory," in O. Lange, F. McIntyre, and T. O. Yntema (eds.), *Studies in Mathematical Economics and Econometrics* (Chicago: University of Chicago Press, 1942), pp. 69–74; Paul A. Samuelson, "Consumption Theorems in Terms of Over-Compensation Rather than Indifference Comparisons," *Economica*, New Series, Vol. XX (February, 1953), pp. 1–9; and Eugen Slutsky, "On the Theory of the Budget of the Consumer," reprinted in Kenneth Boulding and George Stigler (eds.), *Readings in Price Theory* (Homewood, Ill.: Richard D. Irwin, Inc., 1952), pp. 41–42.

making use of Equations (A–13), (A–9a), and (A–25), we have Slutsky's Equation No. 51 as

$$\Delta x_c = \left[\left(\frac{\Delta x}{\Delta p},_{(M\,=\,k)}\right)(\Delta p)\right] + \left[\frac{\Delta x_a}{\Delta m}\Delta m_1\right]$$

$$= \left[\frac{-x}{(p+\Delta p)} - \frac{\Delta y}{(p+\Delta p)\Delta p}\right][\Delta p] + \left[\frac{\Delta x_a}{\Delta m}x\Delta p\right]$$

$$= \left[\frac{-x}{(p+\Delta p)} - x\frac{\Delta x_a}{\Delta m}\right][\Delta p] + \left[\frac{\Delta x_a}{\Delta m}x\Delta p\right]$$

$$= \frac{-x\Delta p}{(p+\Delta p)}\ ; \qquad\qquad\qquad\qquad\qquad \text{(S-51a)}$$

$$\Delta y_c = \left[\left(\frac{\Delta y}{\Delta p},_{(M\,=\,k)}\right)(\Delta p)\right] + \left[\frac{\Delta y_a}{\Delta m}\Delta m_1\right]$$

$$= \left[x - x\frac{\Delta y_a}{\Delta m}\right][\Delta p] + \left[\frac{\Delta y_a}{\Delta m}x\Delta p\right] = x\Delta p\ . \qquad \text{(S-51b)}$$

Arithmetically, using the data from Table A–1 in the case of a price increase, we have $\Delta x_c = -25.20$ and $\Delta y_c = 25.20$; and in the case of a price decrease we would have $\Delta x_c = 23.33$ and $\Delta y_c = -16.80$.

The first term on the right in Equation (S–51a) states the total effect on purchases of x of the change in the price of x, and similarly the first term on the right in (S–51b) shows the total effect on purchases of y of this price change. The terms, $(\Delta x_a/\Delta m)(\Delta m_1) = (\Delta x_a/\Delta m)(x\Delta p)$ and $(\Delta y_a/\Delta m)(\Delta m_1) = (\Delta y_a/\Delta m)(x\Delta p)$, show the effect of the relevant tax or subsidy.

From Equation (51) we see that, after the consumer has been subsidized by an amount absolutely equal to the decrease in income $(x\Delta p)$ when price has increased $(\Delta p > 0)$, what remains is the residual variation in x, or $(-x\Delta p)/(p+\Delta p)$, and the residual variation in y, or $x\Delta p$. This equation was Slutsky's method of isolating the "residual variation," or the so-called "substitution effect."

Similarly, if the consumer were taxed by an amount equal to the increase in income $(-x\Delta p)$ after the price decreased $(\Delta p < 0)$, he would, nevertheless, increase his purchases of x by $(-x\Delta p)/(p+\Delta p)$ and reduce his purchases of y by $x\Delta p$.

The result of such a tax equal to $-x\Delta p$, the increase in spending power or in income, imposed upon the consumer at B after he has experienced a price decrease when he was initially at A, is shown in Figure C–1 by point L. (Figure C–1 is a duplicate of Figure 5–8 and is reproduced here for convenience.)

Thus, assume in Figure C–1, as before, that the consumer eventually attained a new equilibrium position at B after a price decrease, as indicated by the shift of FAF′ to FB. Assume also that after the consumer

attained B (or simultaneously with the price change, it makes no difference to the end result), he was subjected to a tax equal to the change
in income $(-x\Delta p)$, or to $TF = 16.80y$ in Figure C–1. The tax is, as
has been explained in Chapter 5, measured graphically by drawing a
line TAL, parallel to the new price line, FB, *through* point A, the
initial equilibrium position. Thus, the tax reduces the consumer's income by an amount just large enough to enable him to purchase the

Figure C–1

A GRAPHICAL ILLUSTRATION OF SLUTSKY'S EQUATION NO. 51

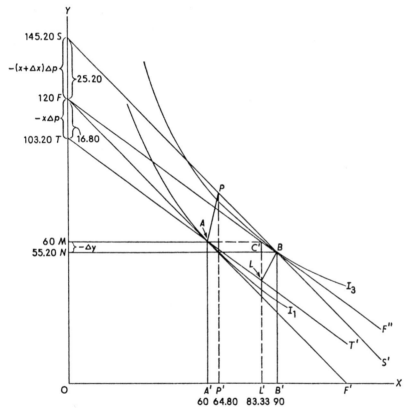

exact previous quantities of x and y at the new prices. However, the
diagram also makes clear that, if he can command A after the tax, he
can also command L, which represents a higher level of total utility
than that represented by A. For L is tangent to a higher indifference
curve than that (I_1) on which lies A, since TAL *intersects* I_1.

Clearly, the tax is too small. (We know from previous analysis in
Appendix B that it understates the actual change in the surplus be-

cause it assumes that the rate of the gain from substitution is zero and so fails to take account of the gain from substitution.) The move from A to L is identified as the *substitution* effect, and it always operates in a direction opposite to the price change. The movement from L to B is the *income* effect, and it is shown as positive in our case because LB, the income consumption curve, slopes up and to the right.

This analysis suffers from several defects. First, it is indirect. Second, it does not accurately measure the change in the consumer's surplus, for it ignores the entire gain from substitution. (Recall that $R = -x\Delta p - \frac{1}{2}\Delta x\Delta p$, and so, in general, $R \neq x\Delta p$.) Third, it does not explain the process of adjustment and consists merely of an unexplained factoring of the effect of the price change on purchases into two parts. Fourth, it does not show how to measure these parts. *In our terms* we can see that the distance $A'L'$ is, in fact, equal to $(-x\Delta p)/(p + \Delta p) = 16.80/.72 = 23.33x$; and the distance $L'B'$ is equal to $(-\Delta y)/(p + \Delta p) = (-x\Delta p)(\Delta x_b/\Delta m) = (16.80)(.3968) = 6.67x$. The former is the *substitution effect* and the latter the *income effect*.

Alternatively, let us again treat the quantity of x consumed at B in Figure C–1 as equal to $(x + \Delta x) = 90$ and the price at B as equal to $(p + \Delta p) = .72$, so that $\Delta x = 30 > 0$ and $\Delta p = -.28 < 0$. Suppose now that the consumer were given a subsidy equal to $-(x + \Delta x)\Delta p$ at the old price of x at A as an alternative to the price decrease. Or, in the case of a price increase, suppose he were subsidized by this amount after the price had risen when he was initially at B and he then once more attained the equilibrium position at A. (It makes no difference what we assume in this respect, the result is again the same in either case.)

Now $-(x + \Delta x)\Delta p$ is the increased cost of the old quantity at B when the case is treated as one of a price increase. The relevant subsidy required as compensation for this increased cost is determined graphically by drawing a line, SPB, parallel to the price line FAF', *through* point B. Thus, at the higher price of $p =$ one y at A, the consumer is able to purchase *exactly* the same amount of x and of y as at B at the lower price $(p + \Delta p) = .72$, if he is given a subsidy equal to $-(x + \Delta x)\Delta p$ when he is at A. But, if he can command B, then he can also command P, which is on a higher indifference curve than B, for the line SPB *intersects* the indifference curve (I_3) on which lies B. Hence, the consumer has been "overcompensated" in this case.

Applying Equation (51), we see that the distance $A'P'$ on the X axis is equal to $[-(x + \Delta x)\Delta p](\Delta x_a/\Delta m) = (-\Delta y)/p = (25.20)$

$(.1905) = 4.80x$ and is the *income* effect; while the distance $P'B'$ is equal to $[-(x + \Delta x)\Delta p]/p = 25.20x$ and is the *substitution* effect. Again, this method of analysis fails accurately to measure the change in the surplus and, in fact, overstates R by the gain from substitution. (See Appendix B.) And, again, this method fails to explain satisfactorily the process of substitution and consists merely of an unexplained factoring of the price change into two parts. Our formulation of Slutsky's Equation No. 51 permits us actually to measure these parts.

Appendices A and B show, and failure to emphasize this point is a shortcoming of all the alternative methods of analysis discussed in this appendix, that *the total change in x* produced by the price change *results from substitution, partly* from the substitution of the change in income $(-x\Delta p)$ *alone* for additional x, and *partly* from the substitution of Δy for additional x *because* the marginal utility of y is not constant.

The cost difference method of estimating changes in the surplus is employed in many current index number formulas, including Irving Fisher's "Ideal Index." In Appendix D, a new formula for an "ideal index" will be presented, and the existing index number theory will be shown to be a logical extension of Marshallian demand theory. At the moment, however, let us consider an econometric study which makes indirect use of the cost difference analysis of the problem. This study is the work of Henry Schultz.

Henry Schultz's Study of Demand

Henry Schultz's classic study of demand, published in 1938, has already been discussed in Chapter 5. The reader will recall that Schultz determined that the demand for sugar during the period 1875–95 was described by the equation[3]

$$x = 70.62 \text{ lbs.} - 2.259p + .8371t . \qquad \text{(Sc. 3.2)}$$

Schultz's Conclusions Amplified

The coefficient of p, or -2.26, in Schultz's equation is in fact the rate of change of purchases of sugar as its "real" price changes by one unit. Consequently, if we wish to consider the effect on purchases of a one-cent increase in the "real" price of sugar in terms of our own Equation (A–13) from Appendix A, we must write:

$$\frac{\Delta x}{\Delta p, (M = k)} = \frac{-x}{(p + \Delta p)} - \frac{\Delta y}{(p + \Delta p)\Delta p} = -2.26 \text{ pounds.} \qquad \text{(A–13)}$$

---

[3] See Henry Schultz, *The Theory and Measurement of Demand* (Chicago: University of Chicago Press, 1938), p. 187.

Schultz also found that the average (mean) "real" price of sugar during the period was 8.313 cents, and that the mean per capita consumption was 51.8 pounds,[4] and employed these values in computing the elasticity of demand during the period.[5] Let us therefore use these values and set $p = 8.313$ "real" cents and $x = 51.8$ pounds in our Equation (A-13). We also have from Schultz's Equation (Sc. 3.2), when $\Delta p = (1.0 > 0)$ "real" cent, $\Delta x = -2.26$ pounds in the opposite direction. Thus we also have $(p + \Delta p) = (8.313 + 1.0) = 9.313$ "real" cents and $(x + \Delta x) = (51.8 - 2.26) = 49.54$ pounds. And we also have from our Equation (A-6) the definition of Δy, or

$$\Delta y = (px) - (p + \Delta p)(x + \Delta x), \tag{A-6}$$

and

$$\begin{aligned} \Delta y &= (8.313)(51.8) - (9.313)(49.54) \\ &= (430.613 - 461.366) = -30.75 \text{ "real" cents.} \end{aligned} \tag{A-6''}$$

We now have sufficient arithmetical values, all derived from Schultz's basic equation of the demand curve, to substitute into the basic Equation (A-13) from Appendix A, or

$$\begin{aligned} \frac{\Delta x}{\Delta p}, (M = k) &= \frac{-51.8}{9.313} - \frac{-30.75}{(9.313)(1.0)} = -5.562 + 3.302 \\ &= -2.26 \text{ pounds.} \end{aligned} \tag{A-13''}$$

Note that the *direct* (-5.562) and *indirect* (3.302) effects have opposite signs and that purchases of sugar *increase* as income *decreases,* with prices constant.

The arc price elasticity of demand can now be computed by means of Equation (A-17) from Appendix A as

$$\begin{aligned} E_d &= \left[-\frac{(p + \Delta p)}{x} \frac{\Delta x}{\Delta p} \right] = \left[-\frac{(p + \Delta p)}{x} \frac{-x}{(p + \Delta p)} \right] - \\ &\quad \left[-\frac{(p + \Delta p)}{x} \frac{\Delta y}{(p + \Delta p)\Delta p} \right] = 1 + \frac{\Delta y}{x \Delta p}. \end{aligned} \tag{A-17}$$

Arithmetically, we have

$$\begin{aligned} E_d &= -\frac{9.313}{51.8}(-2.26) = 1 + \frac{-30.75}{(51.8)(1.00)} \\ &= 1 - .594 = .406 \text{ of 1 percent.} \end{aligned} \tag{A-17''}$$

The preceding value may be compared with Schultz's own result of

[4] *Ibid.,* Table 5, p. 180.

[5] *Ibid.,* Table 7, pp. 196–97 and pp. 215–16.

.36 of 1 percent in his linear equation and .38 of 1 percent in his logarithmic equation.[6] Of course, if we had used the *base* period prices and quantities in the elasticity formula as Schultz did, i.e., p/x, we would have produced exactly his result. However, his formula, $(-p/x)(\Delta x/\Delta p)$, does not produce the same result as the calculus formula when total expenditures on x remain constant. Use of the ratio $-p/x$ in the formula results in the following equation [by multiplication of both sides of Equation (A–13) by $-p/x$], which is the same as Schultz's formula in the case of price increase:

$$E_d = \left[-\frac{p\Delta x}{x\Delta p}\right] = \left[-\frac{p}{x}\frac{-x}{(p + \Delta p)}\right] - \left[-\frac{p}{x}\frac{\Delta y}{(p + \Delta p)\Delta p}\right]$$
$$= \left[\frac{p}{(p + \Delta p)} + \frac{p}{(p + \Delta p)}\frac{\Delta y}{x\Delta p}\right] . \tag{C-1}$$

$$E_d = \left[-\frac{p}{x}\frac{\Delta x}{\Delta p}\right] = \frac{(8.313)(-51.8)}{(51.8)(9.313)} - \frac{(8.313)(-30.753)}{(51.8)(9.313)(1.0)}$$
$$= \frac{430.61}{482.41} - \frac{255.65}{482.41} = .892 - .529 = .363 . \tag{C-1'}$$

This *is* the same result as that which Schultz obtained.

It is interesting, on the basis of Schultz's data, to determine what would be the effect of a subsidy absolutely equal to the change in income on consumption of sugar, other things equal, at the new price. Since we have already determined in Appendix A that this effect is given by the formula $(x\Delta p)(\Delta x_b/\Delta m)$, we need only to substitute the proper values into it to produce $(51.8)(1.0)(-.06374) = -3.30$ pounds. This result is obtainable from Equation (A–13″) also and shows that purchases *decrease* as income *increases*. Thus, sugar was an inferior commodity according to Schultz's data, and, *other things equal,* a per capita increase in spending power of 51.8 cents would have produced a *decrease* in sugar consumption of -3.30 pounds per capita annually during the period in question!

But other things never are equal, and so a word of caution is now in order. Some writers have implied that results like those obtained above are an adequate basis for economic policy. This proposition by no means follows, for the assumption that other things remain equal is not warranted, even if our statistical techniques were foolproof, which they are not. Indeed, to paraphrase Schultz: we must supplement our purely statistical results with all the theoretical and factual knowledge at our disposal in making policy.

---

[6] *Ibid.,* Table 7, pp. 196–97.

2. THE HICKSIAN "INDIFFERENCE" ANALYSIS

The Equivalent Variation

In the Mathematical Appendix to *Value and Capital,* Professor
J. R. Hicks has employed precisely the same equations as did Schultz
and Slutsky in stating the direct and the indirect effects of a price
change.[7] However, in his literal exposition and in his graphical explanation of these equations, Hicks has adopted a different interpretation from
that provided by Schultz.

Hicks's graphical analysis and his exposition both in *Value and Capi-*

Figure C–2

INDIFFERENCE CURVE ILLUSTRATION OF
EQUIVALENT AND COMPENSATING VARIATIONS

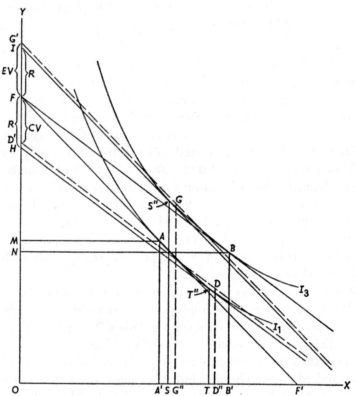

[7] J. R. Hicks, *Value and Capital* (2d ed.; Oxford: Oxford University Press, 1946),
pp. 307–309; and J. R. Hicks, *A Revision of Demand Theory* (Oxford: Oxford University Press, 1956).

tal and in a more recent book, *A Revision of Demand Theory*,[8] can be illustrated by means of Figures C–2 and C–3 (on page 524).

In terms of Figure C–2, Hicks has argued in *Value and Capital* that if the consumer were given a subsidy at the original price of *x* at *A* sufficiently great to enable him to attain *the same indifference curve* which he would otherwise attain as a result of a price decrease, the resulting change in purchases would measure the "income" effect, or the movement from *A'* to *S* in Figure C–2; and the remaining movement from *S* to *B'* on the *X* axis, or *S''B along the higher indifference curve, I₃*, can then be identified as the "substitution" effect.

Note that Hicks's argument involves a change in income which will enable a consumer to attain *a given level of total utility*, while the cost difference method involves a change in income which will enable the consumer to consume *exactly the previous quantities* of *x* and of *y*. Thus, in the cost difference analysis, the relevant new price lines indicating the levy of a tax or the granting of a subsidy, *TAL* and *SPB*, respectively, are drawn *through* the initial equilibrium positions *A* and *B*, respectively, in Figure C–1. But, if the object is to leave the consumer merely with the original amount of utility, such lines (*IS''* and *D'T''*) must be drawn *tangent* to the indifference curves in Figure C–2.

Thus, the Hicksian analysis also consists of a factoring of the price change into two parts and *apparently* (but, as we will see below, *only apparently*) involves a movement in Figure C–2 from *A to S'' between* two indifference curves and a movement *along* an indifference curve from *S''* to *B* in the subsidy case. However, in the indifference method, the magnitudes of the two effects of the price change are different from the magnitudes isolated by the cost difference method. The cost difference ($x\Delta p$), as we know from Appendix B, assumes $\Delta x \Delta p = 0$. What does Hicks assume? He assumes $\Delta y = 0$!

Hicks has designated the income change, which he thinks will produce the situation depicted by *S''* in Figure C–2, by the name of *Equivalent Variation*, (*EV*), *and he has defined EV in words in Value and Capital as that change in income which will make the marginal utility of "money" as numeraire* (our *y*) *constant*.[9] He has also identified it graphically in a later work[10] as equal to area *PE'BP'* in Figure C–3. Now these definitions of *EV* show that it measures merely that change

[8] Hicks, *Value and Capital*, pp. 29–33; Hicks, *A Revision of Demand Theory*, pp. 76 and 100.

[9] Hicks, *Value and Capital*, p. 33, pp. 38–41, and pp. 330–31; Hicks, *A Revision of Demand Theory*, p. 15.

[10] Hicks, *A Revision of Demand Theory*, p. 78 and pp. 95–100.

in total utility which *would* result *if the marginal utility of the numeraire were constant* and ignores that part of the gain from substitution which arises because $\Delta y \neq 0$ and the marginal utility of the numeraire is not constant! Thus, *EV* measures more than the cost difference $(x\Delta p)$ but does not measure the entire change in the surplus either.

Figure C–3

DEMAND CURVE ILLUSTRATION OF
EQUIVALENT AND COMPENSATING VARIATIONS

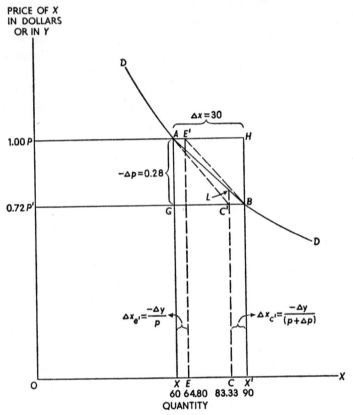

In Figure C–2, we see that R is in fact the correct measure of the change in the surplus and that R represents that amount of the numeraire which, *if* it *were* given to the consumer as an alternative to the price decrease, *would* enable him to reach *the same* indifference curve which he does in fact attain as a result of the price decrease. In Figure C–2, R is represented by the distance FI, while *EV* is represented by the distance FG' and is greater than R by IG'. That is, *EV* measures too great a subsidy because it ignores the gain from substitution of x for Δy.

In *Value and Capital,* Hicks has depicted the problem correctly;[11] but, in attempting to solve it by defining *EV* in words and, later, in *A Revision of Demand Theory,*[12] by depicting *EV* graphically, he has erred in thinking that what is required is the isolation of that change in income which measures the change in the surplus when the marginal utility of the *numeraire* is constant (at its level at *B*). He fails to note that the correct measure of the change in the surplus *must also take account* of the change in the marginal utility of the *numeraire.* Our measure, *R,* defined in Appendix B, does precisely that. Hicks's measure *EV* produces point *G* in Figure C–2, while *R* produces point *S''*.

In fact, Hicks's *EV* is quantifiable as $EV = -(x + \Delta x)\Delta p - [(x + \Delta x)\Delta p^2]/2p$, for this is the algebraic formula in Figure C–3 of the area *PE'BP'*. In Figure C–3, the measure *R,* defined in Appendix B earlier, is equal to area *PABP'*. This is less than *PE'BP'* by *ABE'* which is precisely the amount of the change in the surplus resulting from the facts that $\Delta y \neq 0$ and that the marginal utility of the *numeraire* is not constant. The measure *R,* therefore, takes account of the entire gain from substitution, while Hicks's measure does not. Thus, in Figure C–2 also, $EV = FG' > FI = R$ and $G \neq S''$. The reason why *R* is *less* than *EV* in these diagrams is that, in the case of a price increase, *the consumer substitutes in order to make a gain which will operate to reduce the loss he would otherwise experience* as a result of the price rise. Thus, the actual decrease in the surplus is less than the amount of the change in cost alone, and it is also less than merely the amount which the consumer would lose if he did not change his total expenditures on the price-changing commodity, unless the elasticity of demand happens to be unity. This statement is another way of saying, "unless the marginal utility of the *numeraire* is constant." (In such a case $EV = R$, we will see later.)

Thus, analytically, area *PE'BP'* in Figure C–3 represents the *reduction* in the surplus which the consumer would suffer *if* the price of *x* rose when he was at *B and if he did not change the total amount of his expenditures on x, thereby reducing his loss by substitution* of *XAE'E* of *y* for *XE* of *x*. And so Hicks's measure *EV,* in fact, rests upon an assumption that the marginal utility of the *numeraire* (our *y*) is constant at its level in the new position at *B* (or that the total amount spent on *x* remains constant when price changes). Thus, *EV* assumes $\Delta x_a/\Delta m = 0$ and $\Delta y = 0$. Accordingly, *EV* is greater than *R* and *does*

---

[11] Hicks, *Value and Capital,* p. 61; see also Alfred Stonier and Douglas Hague, *A Textbook of Economic Theory* (2d ed.; London: Longmans Green & Co., Ltd., 1957), p. 61, for a restatement of the Hicksian error.

[12] Hicks, *A Revision of Demand Theory,* pp. 99–100.

not measure the actual change in the surplus. Arithmetically, if $\Delta x_e = [-(x + \Delta x)\Delta p]/p = EX'$ in Figure C–3, then $(-\frac{1}{2}\Delta p \Delta x_e)$ $= -\frac{1}{2}(-.28)(25.20) = 3.53y$. Note: $\Delta x_e > 0$ and $\Delta p < 0$. Thus $EV = -(x + \Delta x)\Delta p + \frac{1}{2}\Delta p \Delta x_e = 25.20y - 3.53y = 21.67y = FG'$ in Figure C–2, while $R = FI = 21y$ and $IG' = .67y$.

Hicks's *EV* assumes that the rate of change of purchases of x as income changes is *zero* and that total expenditures on x are constant at their level at B. Therefore, *if* the consumer were given a subsidy equal to *EV* at A in Figure C–2, he would move to G, which is on a higher indifference curve than I_3. Thus G in Figure C–2 is not the same as S''. Also, the quantity of x purchased after such a greater subsidy would be $A'G''$ which is greater than $A'S$, or $(R)(\Delta x_a/\Delta m) < (EV)$ $(\Delta x_a/\Delta m)$ because $R < EV$.

And so the difference between Hicks's *EV* and our *R* is equal to that part of the change in the surplus which results from the fact that the marginal utility of y is not constant (i.e., that $\Delta y \neq 0$). This difference is equal to area ABE' in Figure C–3. Or, $EV - R = ABE'$ and, arithmetically, $21.67 - 21.00 = .67 = ABE'$ in Figure C–3; and also $.67 = IG'$ in Figure C–2.

The Compensating Variation

Hicks has also provided a further alternative explanation which makes use of the concept of the *Compensating Variation, CV,* in income.[13] *According to this explanation,* if the consumer were taxed by a sum equal to *CV* after the price decrease when he is at B in Figure C–2, the distance TB' would measure the "income" effect and the distance $A'T$ would measure the "substitution" effect of the price decrease. Hicks, in this case, interprets the "substitution" effect as *a movement along the initial indifference curve* from A to T'' and the "income" effect as the movement from T'' to B *between* two indifference curves. But he has also again further defined *CV* as equal to area $PAC'P'$ in Figure C–3 or as the change in the surplus computed with the marginal utility of "money" (interpreted as the *numeraire* or y) constant (at its level at A in this case).

Graphically, his analysis which employs *CV* is thus the reverse of his explanation in the case of the Equivalent Variation. Again, his measure *CV* fails to measure the entire change in the surplus. Thus, in terms of Figure C–2, if the consumer were taxed by $CV = D'F$ when he is at B, tangency would result between $D'D$ and an indifference curve *higher* than I_1. Thus, $D \neq T''$ in Figure C–2. This result is again clearly indi-

---

[13] Hicks, *A Revision of Demand Theory,* p. 76, pp. 95–100.

cated in Figure C-3, for $CV = PAC'P'$, but $R = PABP'$; and, thus, $R > CV$ in this case. Recall that the substitution always operates to increase the gain or to reduce the loss produced by the price change.

Again Hicks's measure CV, equal to $PAC'P'$ in Figure C-3, rests on an assumption that the consumer's total expenditures remain constant, *this time at their level at A*, or that $\Delta y = 0$. This point can be seen clearly in Figure C-3, where $CV = PAC'P'$ understates R, or $PABP'$, by the amount of the change in the surplus which results from the change in y, or by $AC'B$. Letting $\Delta x_c = XC = (-x\Delta p)/(p + \Delta p)$, we can compute Hicks's CV as equal to $-x\Delta p - \frac{1}{2}\Delta p\Delta x_c = PAGP' + AGC'$ in Figure C-3, while $R = PABP'$. Arithmetically, we have $CV = 16.80y - \frac{1}{2}(-.28y)(23.33) = 16.80y + 3.27y = 20.07y$, while $R = 21y$. If the consumer were taxed by CV or FD' in Figure C-2, *too little tax* would be taken from him, and he would reduce his consumption of x by less than TB' after the tax, for $(CV)(\Delta x_b/\Delta m) < (R)(\Delta x_b/\Delta m)$ because $CV < R$. (Or, $TB' > D''B'$ in Figure C-2.) Again the difference between CV and R is the change in the surplus which results from the change in the marginal utility of y between the two positions, or $21y - 20.07y = .93y = AC'L$ in Figure C-3, and $.93y = HD'$ in Figure C-2.

Only in the case in which the marginal utility of y is in fact constant (so that $\Delta y = 0$, and total expenditures on x are the same at both A and B) will $EV = CV$, as a number of writers have pointed out.[14] In this case, moreover, $EV = CV = R$, for $\Delta x_b/\Delta m$ is then zero. An illustration appears in Figure C-4 on the next page.

A Reconciliation of R, CV, and EV

Hicks's income variations can be reconciled with our measure R by making use of Equation (B-6), which appears in Appendix B and which reads:

$$R = -x\Delta p + \frac{(\Delta y)(\Delta p)}{2(p + \Delta p)} - \frac{(-x)(\Delta p^2)}{2(p + \Delta p)} \tag{B-6}$$

$$= -(x + \Delta x)\Delta p - \frac{(\Delta y)(\Delta p)}{2p} + \frac{-(x + \Delta x)(\Delta p^2)}{2p}$$

$$= FI = HF \text{ in Figures C-5 and C-2.}$$

Since Hicks's measure CV assumes $\Delta y = 0$ in the initial equilibrium position and his EV assumes $\Delta y = 0$ in the final position, we have

---

[14] See, for example, Kenneth E. Boulding, *Economic Analysis* (3rd ed.; New York: Harper & Bros., 1955), pp. 814-21, esp. pp. 814-16.

Figure C–4

CV, EV, AND R WHEN THE MARGINAL UTILITY OF THE NUMERAIRE IS CONSTANT

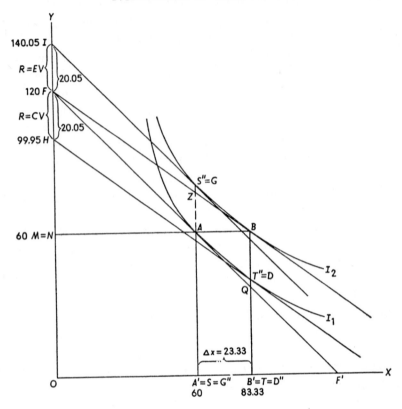

$$CV = -x\Delta p - \frac{(-x)(\Delta p^2)}{2(p + \Delta p)}; \text{ and } EV = -(x + \Delta x)\Delta p + \frac{-(x + \Delta x)(\Delta p^2)}{2p}.$$

Making use of the values employed in the case of a price decrease in Table A–1 in Appendix A, we have

$$R = 16.80 + .93 + 3.27 = 25.20 - .67 - 3.53 \qquad \text{(B–6')}$$
$$= 21y = FI = HF \text{ in Figure C–2;}$$

$$CV = 16.80 + 3.27 = 20.07y = D'F \text{ in Figure C–2; and}$$

$$EV = 25.20 - 3.53 = 21.67y = FG' \text{ in Figure C–2.}$$

Comparison of these formulations makes clear that *CV*, *EV*, and *R* make exactly the same assumptions save in one important respect. The measure *R* takes account of the additional gain from substitution which results from the fact that the numeraire is not constant ($\Delta y \gtrless 0$); while *EV* and *CV* assume $\Delta y = 0$ at different levels and so do not take changes in the numeraire into account, for Δy does not appear in their definitions.[15]

Moreover, Equation (B–6) shows clearly that the measure $-x\Delta p$ assumes that the gain from substitution is zero, while the measure $-(x + \Delta x)\Delta p$ assumes that the gain from substitution is equal to $-\Delta x\Delta p$; and Equation (B–6) also shows that CV and EV are merely *special cases* of R. Depending on the degree of curvature of the demand curve, $-x\Delta p$, $-(x + \Delta x)\Delta p$, or R may be the best measure in a given case. It is, however, clear that R will always be a closer measure than *one of the two measures*, $-x\Delta p$ or $-(x + \Delta x)\Delta p$, in any given case, and that R will always be a better measure than either of these in any case in which the total gain (loss) from substitution is greater than $-\frac{1}{4}\Delta x\Delta p$ and less than $-\frac{3}{4}\Delta x\Delta p$.

Thus, as is illustrated in Figure C–5, R is in fact the measure Hicks has tried to define. (See next page.)

Hicks's failure to do so arises out of his peculiar interpretation of Marshall's consumer's surplus analysis as one which rests on an assumption that the marginal utility of the *numeraire* commodity, y, is constant.[16] But, as we have seen in Appendix B, Marshall's consumer's surplus analysis does *not* make this assumption.

Moreover, the argument made by Hicks that the "substitution" effect along an indifference curve can be isolated by subjecting the consumer to that change in "real income" which will cause the *income term* "to disappear" *from Slutsky's Equation* No. 51 must be rejected, for *the* income change which causes *this term* to "disappear" in *that* equation is the negative of the change in cost, or the change in income produced by the price change, and this sum $(-x\Delta p)$ does *not* measure the whole change in the surplus. Instead, it ignores the gain from substitution! Hicks's position, of course, stems directly from a failure to distinguish

---

[15] See Hicks, *Value and Capital*, Additional Note A, pp. 329–33, for a formulation similar to that which is produced above as Equation (B–6). Hicks's complicated formulas can be reconciled with the one given above in Equation (B–6) if his:

$$\frac{\Sigma x_{rs} d_{pr} d_{ps}}{2} = \frac{x(\Delta p^2)}{2(p + \Delta p)} = \frac{(x + \Delta x)(\Delta p^2)}{2p},$$

which means that $\Delta y = 0$. For an explanation of this proposition in terms of the discussion in Hicks's *A Revision of Demand Theory*, pp. 81–82, see my article, "Marshall and Slutsky on the Theory of Demand," *op. cit.*, pp. 176–91, esp. pp. 188–90.

[16] Hicks, *Value and Capital*, p. 33, contains a clear statement by Hicks that *to him* "money" or "purchasing power in general" means consumption goods *other* than the price-changing commodity (our y). See also *ibid.*, pp. 38–41; and Paul A. Samuelson, "Constancy of the Marginal Utility of Income," in O. Lange, F. McIntyre, and T. O. Yntema (eds.), *Studies in Mathematical Economics and Econometrics* (Chicago: University of Chicago Press, 1942), esp. p. 80, p. 84, and n. 8. Samuelson also interprets Hicks as I have.

between the different assumptions made by Marshall in his various analyses. In this appendix, this difference, which, as has been noted earlier, seems first to have been drawn clearly by Professor Samuelson,[17] has been consistently employed.

Figure C–5

THE EFFECT OF A TAX OR SUBSIDY EQUAL TO R ON PURCHASES of x AND y WHEN PRICES ARE ASSUMED CONSTANT

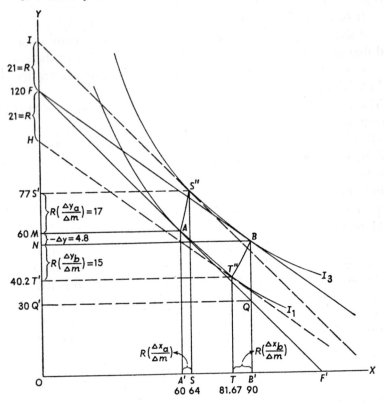

CV, EV, and R When the Linearity Assumption Is Abandoned

When the linearity assumption is abandoned, CV, EV, and R can be determined precisely only if the equation of the demand curve is known. In Figure C–3, if AB were a curve and not linear, we would have

$$R = V + \Delta y = (XGBX' + GAC' + C'AB) - CC'BX',$$

or

$$R = P'PAG + (GAC' + C'AB) = P'PHB - (BE'H + BAE')'.$$

---

[17] Samuelson, "Constancy of the Marginal Utility of Income," in Lange, McIntyre, and Yntema (eds.), *Studies in Mathematical Economics*, pp. 75–91, esp. pp. 78–80.

The last formulation comes close to being a graphical identification of the magnitudes Hicks has defined mathematically in Additional Note A to *Value and Capital* (p. 332), *but* Hicks there treats areas GAC' and $BE'H$ as equal, which means that $\Delta y = 0$ and thus $C'AB = BAE' = 0!$ In such a case $(-x\Delta p)/(p + \Delta p) = [-(x + \Delta x)\Delta p]/p$ and $EX' = XC$, so that $XE = CX' = 0$. In *A Revision of Demand Theory*, Hicks depicts CV and EV as $CV = P'PAG + GAC'$ and $EV = P'PHB - BE'H$, as in Figure C–3, and so again he sets $\Delta y = 0!$ Thus, CV ignores area $C'AB$, while EV ignores area BAE'. Area $C'AB$ is the gain from substitution because Δy is not zero in the price decrease case; and area BAE' is the gain from substitution because Δy is not zero in the price increase case. Thus, Hicks's measures assume the marginal utility of the numeraire constant even when the linearity assumption is abandoned. Hicks has himself made the assumption which he has mistakenly attributed to Marshall.

A General Conclusion concerning the Present Status of Demand Theory

It seems clear that contemporary demand theory has not progressed very far beyond the initial formulation of it contained in Book III of Marshall's *Principles*. It is a hedonistic theory, based on highly restrictive assumptions; and, despite all of the refinement to which it has been subjected, very little that is really important has been added to Marshall's original theory. Hicks's CV and EV are merely special cases of R, and R is a refinement of Marshall's measure. This fact alone should be enough to challenge the attention of the serious student of economics.

D | Index Numbers and Demand Theory

Introduction

Price and quantity index numbers are attempts to measure the welfare effects of price and quantity changes. They are logical extensions of the concepts of demand theory. Attempts to define "ideal index" numbers have generally consisted of a process of averaging indexes with known biases in opposite directions but have not involved the making of economic analyses of the reasons for such biases.[1] In this appendix, the *economic* reasons for such biases and the concept of an "ideal" index are analyzed.

1. THE ECONOMIC THEORY OF INDEX NUMBERS

Assumptions Made and Theories Employed by the Laspeyres and Paasche Indexes

One method of estimating the effect on the consumer's surplus of a price change, such as that depicted in Figure B-1 in Appendix B, is to employ the Laspeyres quantity index, or

$$L_q = \frac{\Sigma p_o q_n}{\Sigma p_o q_o}.$$ (D-1)

This index employs base period prices as weights in an attempt to measure the welfare effect of a change in the quantity of a commodity whose price has changed as a ratio of the *"value"* of the new quantity to the *"value"* of the original quantity. Whether we like to admit it or not, the index seeks to measure a change in total utility.

---

[1] In general, see Irving Fisher, *The Making of Index Numbers* (Boston: Houghton Mifflin Co., 1922); Bruce D. Mudgett, *Index Numbers* (New York: John Wiley & Sons, Inc., 1951); and Frederick C. Mills, *Introduction to Statistics* (New York: Henry Holt & Co., Inc., 1956), pp. 383–463.

In the terms of the symbols employed in previous chapters, this index can be rewritten as

$$L_q = \frac{\Sigma p_o q_n}{\Sigma p_o q_o} = \frac{p(x + \Delta x) + (y + \Delta y)}{px + y},$$ (D-2)

where y represents the amount spent on all goods other than x, as before.

The preceding definition can be rewritten by substituting into it the definition of Δy from Equation (A-6) from Appendix A which reads:

$$\Delta y = -p\Delta x - x\Delta p - \Delta x\Delta p,$$ (A-6)

and simplifying to produce

$$L_q = \frac{px + y - (x + \Delta x)\Delta p}{px + y}.$$ (D-3)

Now in any case of a price decrease, $\Delta p < 0$ where $\Delta x > 0$, such as that depicted in Figures B-1 or C-1, the term, $(x + \Delta x)\Delta p$, which is used in the numerator above, must be negative. Thus, in such a case, the numerator of L_q will exceed its denominator by $-(x + \Delta x)\Delta p$, for a negative quantity is being subtracted from $px + y$ in the numerator. (All possible combinations of Δp and Δx are presented in Table D-1 later.) And so it is clear that when $\Delta p < 0$ and $\Delta x > 0$, L_q seeks to measure the change in the consumer's surplus resulting from the price change according to a theory that "there exists a sum, taken by the index as equal to the negative of the change in cost of the new position quantity, or to $-(x + \Delta x)\Delta p$, such that if it were given to the consumer (added to his income) as an alternative to the price decrease in the initial position at A in Figures B-1 or C-1, he would be able to attain the same level of total utility as that which he does attain as a result of the price decrease." In short, in the given case, this index adopts what will hereafter be called the *subsidy* theory.

Conversely, in the case of a price increase, $\Delta p > 0$ where $\Delta x < 0$, the term $(x + \Delta x)\Delta p$ in Equation (D-3) will be positive, and the numerator of the index will then be smaller than its denominator by $(x + \Delta x)\Delta p$, for a positive quantity is then being subtracted. In such a case, the index adopts a *tax* theory. That is, it then seeks to measure the change in the surplus resulting from the price increase according to a theory that "there exists a sum, taken by the index to be equal to $(x + \Delta x)\Delta p$, such that if it were taken from the consumer as an alternative to subjecting him to the price increase, he would be reduced to the same level of total utility as that to which he is reduced by the price rise."

Thus, in the case in which $\Delta p \Delta x < 0$, the index adopts different theories of measurement, depending on whether the price of x rises or falls. There is *no* logical basis for a choice between these two different theories of measurement, although one may state a preference for the subsidy theory in the case of a price decrease on grounds that a decrease in price increases the surplus and for the tax theory in the case of a price increase on grounds that a price rise reduces the surplus. Therefore, it follows that any errors made by L_q relative to the measurement of the change in the surplus do *not* lie in the fact that different theories of measurement are employed. Rather, such errors must lie in the assumption that $-(x + \Delta x)\Delta p = P'PHB$ in Figure B–1 is the correct measure of the subsidy when $\Delta p < 0$ and $\Delta x > 0$ and that $(x + \Delta x)\Delta p$ is the correct measure of the tax when $\Delta p > 0$ and $\Delta x < 0$.

Analysis of Particular Indexes

We know from our previous analysis in Appendix B that the magnitude $-(x + \Delta x)\Delta p$ assumes that the value of Δx accumulates at a rate equal to the price in the *initial* equilibrium position at A in Figures B–1 and C–1. And it has also been shown that in the case of the Laspeyres quantity index,

$$L_q = \frac{px + y - (x + \Delta x)\Delta p}{px + y}, \qquad (D\text{–}3)$$

a subsidy theory is employed when $\Delta x > 0$ and $\Delta p < 0$. Clearly, in such a case, the index must always *overstate* the "true value index computed according to the subsidy theory" because L_q employs the subsidy in its numerator and $-(x + \Delta x)\Delta p$ overstates the actual change in the surplus by assuming that the gain from substitution is a constant amount equal to $-\Delta p$. If the demand curve is assumed to be linear and $\Delta x \Delta p < 0$, then $-(x + \Delta x)\Delta p$ overstates the change in the surplus by exactly the gain from substitution. *Thus, too great a subsidy is given, and the numerator is overstated.*

It has also been shown that in the case of a price increase, where $\Delta p > 0$ and $\Delta x < 0$, L_q employs a tax theory. In such a case, L_q will also *overstate* the "true value index computed according to the tax theory" *because it deducts too small a tax and again overstates its numerator.* If the demand curve is linear and $\Delta p \Delta x < 0$, since $-(x + \Delta x)\Delta p$ assumes that the value of x declines at a rate equal to the price in the initial position (which is now taken as B in Figure B–1 or C–1, where it is less than at A), this measure now understates the change in the surplus by exactly the amount of the gain from substitution. Thus, *the index levies too small a tax in its numerator.*

On the other hand, in the case of a price decline and a positively sloped demand curve ($\Delta p < 0$, $\Delta x < 0$), L_q will *understate* the "true value index computed according to the *subsidy* theory." For, in this perverse case of a positively sloped demand curve, substitution reduces the gain! And $-(x + \Delta x)\Delta p$ assumes that the loss from substitution is a constant amount equal to $-\Delta p$ per unit of additional x. Thus $-(x + \Delta x)\Delta p$ measures too small a subsidy. Note that $-(x + \Delta x)\Delta p < (-x\Delta p)$ here. *Since the subsidy is added in the numerator, the index understates the true value subsidy theory index.*

Finally, in the case of a price rise and a positively sloped demand curve ($\Delta p > 0$, $\Delta x > 0$), L_q will also *understate* the "true value index computed according to the *tax* theory." In such a case, substitution operates to increase the loss. Again $-(x + \Delta x)\Delta p$ assumes the loss from substitution to be a constant amount equal to Δp per unit of x. And so it measures too large a tax. Thus, L_q deducts *too large a tax in its numerator,* with the result that the index again *understates* the true value *tax* theory index.

We can similarly analyze the Paasche quantity index and the Laspeyres and Paasche price indexes, which can be written, by making use of the definition of Δy in Equation (A–6), as follows:

$$P_q = \frac{\Sigma p_n q_n}{\Sigma p_n q_o} = \frac{(p + \Delta p)(x + \Delta x) + (y + \Delta y)}{(p + \Delta p)x + y}$$
$$= \frac{px + y}{px + y + x\Delta p} ; \tag{D–4}$$

$$L_p = \frac{\Sigma p_n q_o}{\Sigma p_o q_o} = \frac{(p + \Delta p)x + y}{px + y}$$
$$= \frac{px + y + x\Delta p}{px + y} ; \tag{D–5}$$

and

$$P_p = \frac{\Sigma p_n q_n}{\Sigma p_o q_n} = \frac{(p + \Delta p)(x + \Delta x) + (y + \Delta y)}{p(x + \Delta x) + (y + \Delta y)}$$
$$= \frac{px + y}{px + y - (x + \Delta x)\Delta p} . \tag{D–6}$$

There are four possible price-quantity combinations which may result when the price and quantity of a commodity are both allowed to change. In addition, we have seen that there are two types of indexes and two basic theories. Thus, there are sixteen possible combinations. These are presented in Table D–1, which shows what result may be expected (and why) from each of these indexes in each case.

Table D–1

THE ASSUMPTIONS MADE AND THEORIES EMPLOYED BY THE PAASCHE AND LASPEYRES INDEXES

Type of Index	Amount of Subsidy	Amount of Tax	Where Levied or Granted	Over-states	Under-states
Case I: $\Delta p < 0, \Delta x > 0$					
L_q	$-(x+\Delta x)\Delta p$		Numerator	√	
P_q		$-x\Delta p$	Denominator		√
L_p		$-x\Delta p$	Numerator	√	
P_p	$-(x+\Delta x)\Delta p$		Denominator		√
Case II: $\Delta p > 0, \Delta x < 0, -\Delta x < x^*$					
L_q		$(x+\Delta x)\Delta p$	Numerator	√	
P_q	$x\Delta p$		Denominator		√
L_p	$x\Delta p$		Numerator	√	
P_p		$(x+\Delta x)\Delta p$	Denominator		√
Case III: $\Delta p < 0, \Delta x < 0, -\Delta x < x^*$					
L_q	$-(x+\Delta x)\Delta p$		Numerator		√
P_q		$-x\Delta p$	Denominator	√	
L_p		$-x\Delta p$	Numerator		√
P_p	$-(x+\Delta x)\Delta p$		Denominator	√	
Case IV: $\Delta p > 0, \Delta x > 0$					
L_q		$(x+\Delta x)\Delta p$	Numerator		√
P_q	$x\Delta p$		Denominator	√	
L_p	$x\Delta p$		Numerator		√
P_p		$(x+\Delta x)\Delta p$	Denominator	√	

* If $-\Delta x = x$, the consumer purchases no x after the price declines; if $-\Delta x > x$, he must be selling short. Neither case is significant in the context of the present analysis.

A summary will be useful of the generalizations which have been and can be derived from the previous analysis in conjunction with Table D–1. *First,* there are two basic theories of measurement, the *tax* theory and the *subsidy* theory. *Second,* the income change which makes use of the *new* position quantity assumes that the gain (loss) from substitution is equal to $-\Delta p\Delta x$, while the income change which makes use of the *initial* position quantity assumes that there is no gain from substitution. *Third,* in the case of negatively sloped demand curves ($\Delta p\Delta x < 0$), substitution operates to increase the surplus or reduce the loss ($-\frac{1}{2}\Delta p\Delta x > 0$); but in the case of positively sloped demand curves ($\Delta p\Delta x > 0$), substitution operates to increase the loss or reduce the gain ($-\frac{1}{2}\Delta p\Delta x < 0$)!

Fourth, in the case of $\Delta p\Delta x < 0$, even though they adopt different theories of measurement in a given case, both Laspeyres indexes consistently *overstate* their own relevant true value indexes *because* they make different assumptions about the gain from substitution, while the Paasche indexes behave in the reverse way. In the case of $\Delta p\Delta x > 0$, both Laspeyres indexes consistently *understate* their own relevant true value indexes for the same reasons, while the Paasche indexes again behave in the reverse way. Whether or not a given index will overstate or understate *its* own relevant true value index depends upon the slope of the demand curve and not upon the direction of the price change alone.

Fifth, L_q and P_p are reciprocals, and so are P_q and L_p; hence L_q and P_p make the same substitution-gain (-loss) assumption and employ the same theory in a given case, while P_q and L_p employ the same substitution-gain (-loss) assumption and the same theory in a given case. However, L_q and L_p make different assumptions and employ different theories in the given case, and P_q and P_p differ in this way also. Finally, *sixth,* Laspeyres indexes employ the relevant tax or subsidy in their numerators, while Paasche indexes employ it in their denominators.

The preceding generalizations suggest some principles which should be employed in the formulation of an "ideal" index. Consideration of the meaning of such an index is our next problem.

2. THE CONCEPT OF AN "IDEAL" INDEX

Irving Fisher's Ideal Index

In 1922, an American economist and statistician, Irving Fisher, developed the "Ideal Index," the geometric mean of the Laspeyres and Paasche indexes, by a process of trial and error. His procedure involved selecting a formula which would meet both the "time reversal" and the "factor reversal" tests and produce the "true value ratio."[2]

The time reversal test is merely a test to determine whether or not the given index will work both ways in time. That is, by taking the formula,

$$\frac{\Sigma p_n q_o}{\Sigma p_o q_o} = L_p\,,$$

and interchanging the time subscripts (substituting *o*'s for *n*'s, and vice versa), we produce

$$\frac{\Sigma p_o q_n}{\Sigma p_n q_n} = \frac{1}{P_p}\,.$$

---

[2] Fisher, *op. cit.,* esp. pp. 118–35.

According to the test, if we now multiply these two formulas together, or

$$L_p \times \frac{1}{P_p} = \frac{\Sigma p_n q_o}{\Sigma p_o q_o} \times \frac{\Sigma p_o q_n}{\Sigma p_n q_n} \,,$$

their product should be unity. However, in the case of $L_p \times \dfrac{1}{P_p}$ we have

$$\frac{\Sigma p_n q_o}{\Sigma p_o q_o} \times \frac{\Sigma p_o q_n}{\Sigma p_n q_n} = \frac{\Sigma p_n q_o}{\Sigma p_o q_o} \times \frac{\Sigma p_o q_n}{\Sigma p_o q_o} \neq 1 \,,$$

and the test is not met. (Note that in our case $\Sigma p_o q_o = \Sigma p_n q_n$.)

It has been noted that Irving Fisher, who invented this purely mathematical test, also invented the Ideal Index. This index is the geometric mean of the relevant Laspeyres and Paasche indexes and, in the case of the price indexes, has the formula

$$I_{o_p} = \sqrt{\frac{\Sigma p_n q_o}{\Sigma p_o q_o} \times \frac{\Sigma p_n q_n}{\Sigma p_o q_n}} = \sqrt{L_p \times P_p} \,, \qquad \text{(F-1)}$$

which does meet this test; for the new index is

$$\sqrt{\frac{\Sigma p_o q_n}{\Sigma p_n q_n} \times \frac{\Sigma p_o q_o}{\Sigma p_n q_o}} = \sqrt{\frac{1}{P_p} \times \frac{1}{L_p}} \,, \qquad \text{(F-2)}$$

and it is clear that

$$\sqrt{L_p \times P_p} \times \sqrt{\frac{1}{P_p} \times \frac{1}{L_p}} = 1 \,. \qquad \text{(F-3)}$$

What is involved in the test, therefore, is that

$$(I_{o_p})(1/I_{o_p}) = I_{o_p} \times I_{n_p} = 1 \,,$$

and if this is so, the test is met.

However, we now also see that the "time reversal" test is really equivalent to another of Fisher's suggested mandatory tests for an "ideal index," namely the so-called mathematical "factor reversal" test.

The factor reversal test involves interchanging the p and q factors of the index to produce a new index, and the product of the latter and of the former must be equal to the "true value" ratio, or to $\Sigma p_n q_n / \Sigma p_o q_o$, which, under our present assumptions, is also equal to unity. That is, the terms in the Ideal Price Index,

$$\sqrt{\frac{\Sigma p_n q_n}{\Sigma p_o q_n} \times \frac{\Sigma p_n q_o}{\Sigma p_o q_o}} = \sqrt{P_p \times L_p} = I_{o_p} \,,$$

are transformed into the Ideal Quantity Index,

$$\sqrt{\frac{\Sigma p_n q_n}{\Sigma p_n q_o} \times \frac{\Sigma p_o q_n}{\Sigma p_o q_o}} = \sqrt{P_q \times L_q} = I_{o_q} , \qquad \text{(F-4)}$$

by substituting the subscripts attached to the q's for those attached to the p's, and vice versa.

When the original and the transformed indexes are multiplied together, it is clear that

$$\sqrt{\frac{\Sigma p_n q_n}{\Sigma p_o q_n} \times \frac{\Sigma p_n q_o}{\Sigma p_o q_o}} \times \sqrt{\frac{\Sigma p_n q_n}{\Sigma p_n q_o} \times \frac{\Sigma p_o q_n}{\Sigma p_o q_o}} =$$

$$\sqrt{\left(\frac{\Sigma p_n q_n}{\Sigma p_o q_o}\right)^2} = \frac{\Sigma p_n q_n}{\Sigma p_o q_o} , \text{ the true value ratio.} \qquad \text{(F-5)}$$

Thus, cross multiplication of the Ideal Price and Ideal Quantity Indexes produces the true value ratio, or unity in our present case.

Our present analysis shows that neither the Laspeyres nor the Paasche indexes can meet this test, for

$$L_p = \frac{\Sigma p_n q_o}{\Sigma p_o q_o} \text{ transforms into } \frac{\Sigma p_o q_n}{\Sigma p_o q_o} = L_q ,$$

while

$$P_p = \frac{\Sigma p_n q_n}{\Sigma p_o q_n} \text{ transforms into } \frac{\Sigma p_n q_n}{\Sigma p_n q_o} = P_q .$$

Thus, neither $L_p \times L_q$ nor $P_p \times P_q$ can be unity. Our analysis reveals that the relevant Paasche and Laspeyres price and quantity indexes multiplied together in these tests make different substitution-gain (-loss) assumptions and adopt different theories of measurement. It follows, therefore, that in the case of Fisher's Ideal Index, which does meet these tests, what is employed is the *geometric average of the tax and subsidy theories!*

Alternative Formulas

We have seen that the indexes which are used to produce the Ideal Index adopt different theories of measurement. An even greater problem is the fact that they do not necessarily differ from their own true value indexes by equal amounts in opposite directions. Thus, the Ideal Index merely produces the geometric mean of two indexes, each of which errs in the opposite direction from its own true value index. In other words, Ideal does *not* result in the cancellation of opposing "biases." It is the geometric mean of two indexes which err in opposite directions from different standards, generally by different amounts!

Consequently, even though Ideal meets the purely mechanical factor reversal and time reversal tests, neither I_{o_q} nor I_{o_p} is a true measure of the actual change in the surplus or of prices. The indexes utilized by Ideal are in error before they are used to produce Ideal, and the errors made by them are not corrected by Ideal. Finally, no justification of Ideal can be given in terms of economic theory. This index cannot be rationalized; it can merely be asserted or defined.

Indeed, there is no such thing as *one* true value index; there are as many such indexes as there are theories of measurement. And there is no such thing as *one* ideal index; there are also as many as one can define. Some useful ones can be defined in terms of Marshallian analysis, and these will be stated next.

Suppose that the purpose of the index is to answer the question: how much has the surplus changed as a result of the given price change? An appropriate index to measure this change could be defined by making use of the measure R explained in Appendix B. Then we might have

$$I_{r_s} = \frac{\Sigma p_o q_o + R}{\Sigma p_o q_o} = \frac{OF + FI}{OF} \text{ in Figure C-2.} \qquad (D\text{-}7)$$

This index would assume the gain (loss) from substitution to be $-\frac{1}{2}\Delta x \Delta p$, as explained in detail in Appendix B. Since R is positive in the case of price decreases and negative in the case of price increases, the index would automatically adopt the subsidy theory in the case of a price decrease (when income increases) and the tax theory in the case of a price increase (when income decreases). It measures always from the base year and is even easier to calculate than Fisher's Ideal Index, for R can be determined from the data if we make the linearity assumption, although it cannot, of course, be determined precisely unless we do. Finally, the index uses all the data and only the data. It will be further evaluated in the concluding section of this appendix.

If, on the other hand, we want to answer the question of how the cost of living has been affected by the price change, we need merely to take the reciprocal of I_{r_s} and write:

$$I_{p_s} = \frac{\Sigma p_o q_o}{\Sigma p_o q_o + R} = \frac{OF}{OF + FI} \text{ in Figure C-2.} \qquad (D\text{-}8)$$

Thus, we would measure the price change by making the same substitution-gain (-loss) assumption and using the same theory as is used by I_{r_s} in a given case. Obviously $I_{r_s} \times I_{p_s} = 1$, and Fisher's tests are met. *Since changes in the consumer's surplus are additive, any number of commodities and opposing price changes can be handled by this index.*

Suppose, however, that the purpose of the inquiry is to answer the question: what has been the *value of the change in x alone?* Then we must write:

$$I_{v_s} = \frac{\Sigma p_o q_o + V}{\Sigma p_o q_o} = \frac{OF + NM + FI}{OF} \text{ in Figure C-2.} \qquad (D\text{-}9)$$

And, if the object of the inquiry is to determine what has been the effect of the *change in x alone* on the cost of living, we merely take the reciprocal of I_{v_s}, or

$$I_{p_{v_s}} = \frac{\Sigma p_o q_o}{\Sigma p_o q_o + V} = \frac{OF}{OF + NM + FI} \text{ in Figure C-2.} \qquad (D\text{-}10)$$

Although these indexes have been written above according to the subsidy theory, they can also be written to incorporate the tax theory as follows:

$$I_{r_t} = \frac{\Sigma p_n q_n}{\Sigma p_n q_n - R} ; \qquad (D\text{-}11) \qquad\qquad I_{p_t} = \frac{\Sigma p_n q_n - R}{\Sigma p_n q_n} ; \qquad (D\text{-}12)$$

$$I_{v_t} = \frac{\Sigma p_n q_n}{\Sigma p_n q_n - V} ; \qquad (D\text{-}13) \qquad\qquad I_{p_{v_t}} = \frac{\Sigma p_n q_n - V}{\Sigma p_n q_n} . \qquad (D\text{-}14)$$

The indexes presented in Equations (D–7) through (D–14) are based on a concept of an "ideal" index different from that generally prevailing in the literature. In the literature, *one* "ideal" index has generally been sought as the product of some sort of process of averaging indexes "which err in opposite directions," but the precise nature of the errors has never been isolated. The indexes presented above rest upon a concept of *ideal indexes* as indexes which, while not perfect, can at least be explained in terms of the existing demand theory and which also meet all of Fisher's tests. Moreover, since "income" and "substitution" effects are additive, these indexes can be generalized, or

$$\sum_{i=1}^{n} R_i = \sum_{i=1}^{n} V_i + \sum_{i=1}^{n} P_i X_i - \sum_{i=1}^{n} (P_i + \Delta P_i)(X_i + \Delta X_i) .$$

3. EVALUATION OF THE PROPOSED INDEX

This appendix shows that contemporary index numbers are closely related to, and can be explained in terms of, Marshallian utility of income analysis as explained in Appendix B. Moreover, by assuming that the demand curve is linear within the relevant range, it is possible to define operational "ideal" index numbers which meet all of the prescribed (Fisher) tests and which are just as easy to compute as Fisher's Ideal Index. In addition, the suggested indexes can be fully explained in terms of their economic meanings.

It may be objected, of course, that the linearity assumption limits the analysis to the case of small price changes at a given moment of time. Although this argument is true, if, by making such an assumption, we can further our understanding of the nature, limitations, and the theoretical implications of our existing index numbers and of demand theory in general, the objection is not well taken. As will be further noted below, such an objection can also be taken to the use of the Laspeyres and Paasche indexes and to the use of calculus generally in economic theory. It may be that this is a sound position to take, but few economists take it.

It can also be argued that a biased estimator with a small variance may be preferable to an unbiased estimator with a large variance. It is true that the size of the variance of the proposed estimator is hard to determine and depends on the curvature of the demand curve, the size of the price change, and the amount of the change in x. But the amount of the bias in current indexes is not known, and it, too, depends upon the curvature of the demand curve, the extent of the price change, etc. Table D–1 makes clear that in the case of the Laspeyres and Paasche indexes, not only does the *direction* of the bias depend upon the slope of the demand curve but also the *amount* of the bias depends upon the degree to which, in a given case, the demand curve departs from being either a vertical line (like AG in Figure B–1, which implies a perfectly inelastic demand) or a horizontal line (like AH in Figure B–1, which implies a perfectly elastic demand).

In any given case, therefore, the variance of *one* of these two indexes must always be greater than that of its counterpart measure suggested earlier in Equations (D–7) to (D–14). As a matter of fact, in any case in which the actual gain (loss) from substitution lies between $-\frac{1}{4}\Delta x\Delta p$ and $-\frac{3}{4}\Delta x\Delta p$, the measures mentioned above will produce more accurate results than will either the Paasche or Laspeyres indexes. For, in such a case, an index which uses $-x\Delta p$ as a measure of the change in the surplus will be using a magnitude which contains an error of *at least* $-\frac{1}{4}\Delta x\Delta p$, while an index which uses $-(x + \Delta x)\Delta p$ will similarly use a magnitude which errs by *at least* $-\frac{1}{4}\Delta x\Delta p$. But the measure, $R = -x\Delta p - \frac{1}{2}\Delta x\Delta p$, errs by less than $-\frac{1}{4}\Delta x\Delta p$ in such a case. Doubtless other situations giving rise to various probabilities will occur to the reader.

It should not be inferred, however, from the treatment of index numbers in this appendix that the author thinks that the problem of index numbers has been solved. Instead, since this appendix demonstrates the close relationship which exists between index numbers and demand theory, a more appropriate conclusion would be that the solution of the problem of defining index numbers of the type suggested by the Price Statistics Review Committee in its *Report*[3] is contingent upon the further development of demand theory, and it seems unlikely that any such development will come from within the framework of the existing theory.

---

[3] See the concluding section of Chapter 5 where the work of the Committee is described.

INDEX

Index